# THE
# ECONOMIC BACKGROUND
# TO INVESTMENT

This volume forms part of a series of text books published under the authority of the Institute of Actuaries and the Faculty of Actuaries and is designed to meet the needs of students preparing for the actuarial examinations.

# THE
# ECONOMIC BACKGROUND
# TO INVESTMENT

BY

## H. B. ROSE

*Professor of Finance at the*
*London Graduate School of Business Studies*

CAMBRIDGE

*Published for the Institute of Actuaries and the*
*Faculty of Actuaries*

AT THE UNIVERSITY PRESS

1966

PUBLISHED BY
THE SYNDICS OF THE CAMBRIDGE UNIVERSITY PRESS
Bentley House, 200 Euston Road, London, N.W.1
American Branch: 32 East 57th Street, New York N.Y., 10022
West African Office: P.O. Box 33, Ibadan, Nigeria

First printed 1960
Reprinted      1963
              1966

*First printed in Great Britain by Spottiswoode, Ballantyne & Co. Ltd.,*
*London and Colchester*

*Reprinted by offset-lithography at The Gresham Press,*
*Unwin Brothers Limited, Old Woking, Surrey*

# CONTENTS

PART VII

# INTERNATIONAL TRADE AND PAYMENTS

PART VIII

# GOVERNMENT POLICY AND ECONOMIC STABILITY

# PREFACE

I was asked by the Institute of Actuaries and the Faculty of Actuaries to write this book, which is intended to meet two needs. Its prime object is to serve as one of the text-books used for the financial and investment sections of the examination syllabus, its main role in this field being to deal with principles and general questions rather than with the detail of investment technique. Secondly, the book aims at making a broad survey of the economic background, from which the activities of the actuary can rarely be isolated. Whatever the specialized work on which he may be engaged, the actuary has had to familiarize himself in increasing measure with economic problems in general and those of government policy in particular. This is especially true, of course, of the actuary who finds himself directly concerned with the investment of life-assurance or pension funds, and it is by reference to this particular aspect of his task that I have selected from the many subjects that could be included in a book on applied economics. I have naturally confined my illustration of these matters to the United Kingdom.

This book lays no claim to originality, and there is no shortage of experts who have written with far greater authority than I possess both on the general principles of economic analysis and on particular aspects of finance. But year by year the potential reading list of the actuarial student in these fields has grown longer and longer, and it has become correspondingly more difficult for him, within the limited time at his disposal, to digest the balance of material that he requires. What this book lacks in originality and authority, therefore, I hope will be compensated for by its convenience to all who might wish to see the subject of investment presented within its economic framework and associated with certain matters, such as company accounts and national income statistics, that are usually treated in detail sufficient for the actuarial student only in specialized works.

In some respects this book is the reverse of the standard economics text-book. The latter usually deals with matters of general economic analysis and policy fairly extensively but with finance and investment only in very brief measure. I have treated financial questions at some length but have sketched in the economic background with what was intended to be a light hand, indicating broad perspectives rather than detail of fact or analysis. In order to help the interested reader to make good the many deficiencies resulting from this scheme of things, as well as those due to my own technical limitations, suggestions for further reading have been added.

The plan I have followed is indicated by the list of parts into which the book is divided. The basic problems of the market economy are introduced briefly, and some of their practical applications are discussed with reference to the behaviour of both producers and consumers, but especially of businesses. Part II is built round questions of business finance, presented within the general framework of the capital market, in which the main characteristics of various financial institutions are set out. An introduction to public finance follows in Part III because Budget and national debt operations bear closely on the workings of the banking system and on matters of monetary policy, and I wished to present these latter topics (in Part IV) directly in advance of the subject of interest rates, which, together with the determination of security prices and yields in general, is treated in Part V. In Part VI the behaviour of the national income is introduced by a discussion of national income statistics, which, partly because of their value as an instrument for economic diagnosis, proceeds in some detail. In this Part the analysis concentrates, for the sake of simplicity, on the domestic economy, and the omission of questions of international trade is made good in Part VII. Here, too, will be found a broad survey of some economic problems of the United Kingdom since the First World War; it is perhaps a pardonable simplification to consider these as aspects of international trade and payments. In the final chapters of the book I have dealt with matters that are best treated as an epilogue.

The book has been designed on the assumption that the reader has no technical knowledge of the subject, and I have aimed at introducing what might be difficult topics without plunging too rapidly into complexity; I have tried to avoid jargon throughout. Certain matters are treated in some, perhaps unexpected, degree of detail, either because of the requirements of the examination syllabus (as in the case of national income statistics) or because ten years of discussion—and argument—with actuaries in the field of investment have shown that these are topics on which detail would be welcomed. I am not an actuary, but in my work as head of the Economic Intelligence Department of a large assurance company between 1948 and 1958 I was in daily contact with actuaries concerned with investment policy. As a result I soon became aware of their interest in, for example, the details of monetary policy.

I am happy to say that I have been encouraged to include controversial matters; here I have tried to present a fair balance of views and where necessary have disclosed my own inclinations. Additions to the text made after receiving the proofs have been placed at the end of the book.

The weaknesses of the book are my own responsibility alone, but I am especially grateful to Mr. J. B. H. Pegler, F.I.A., Mr. F. M. Redington, F.I.A., Mr. H. Tetley, F.I.A., and Mr. H. W. Haycocks, F.I.A., for the provision of both advice and encouragement, and to Miss V. M. Pink, who undertook the labour of typing. Acknowledgment is due to the Controller of H.M. Stationery Office for permission to quote statistics from official publications. I should also like to record my apologies to my wife and children for having neglected them for so long during the book's preparation.

H. B. R.

PART I

# THE COMPETITIVE MARKET
# ECONOMY

*The superior figures refer to notes added during printing, which are gathered on pp. 647–8.*

# CHAPTER I

# INTRODUCTION TO ECONOMIC PROBLEMS

Investment and finance are part of the economic process, of the way in which society uses its material resources to satisfy its wants. Few aspects of economics can be satisfactorily studied in isolation, and the aim of this book is to present questions of investment and finance in their broad economic framework, first setting the scene of economic problems in an advanced industrial country like that of the United Kingdom before calling on to the stage our leading players.

Four questions underlie the economic problems of any community. They are: How much to produce? Of what? How? And, for whom?

## HOW MUCH TO PRODUCE?

The ultimate object of economic activity is to provide the goods and services that we desire as private individuals—food, shelter, clothing, household goods, travel, entertainment, and so on. The consumption of these constitutes our standard of living, and as the ultimate beneficiaries of economic activity we are all consumers. The provision of these goods and services is the process of *production*, up to the point at which they come into our possession as consumers, if they are goods, and at which they are used by us, if they are services.

The answer to the question 'How much to produce?' is not simply 'As much as possible from all the natural and man-made resources available.' The community does not necessarily benefit by attempting to use all of its resources; agricultural land and mineral deposits, for example, differ widely in richness, so that more may be produced by concentrating only on part and leaving the remainder unused. How much can be produced from a country's natural resources depends less on physical effort than on its equipment, its knowledge and its skill; a community that does not marshal its latent ingenuity to the full handicaps itself economically.

The most economical use of the community's human resources does not demand that these be worked to the bone, not only because child labour and long hours may be cruel or may dissipate human energies, but because leisure is one of the wants that it is the aim of economic activity to satisfy. Each of us can in some degree decide between more or less work and more or less leisure. Most of us, it is true, can choose only within the limits set by convention, statute, or formal agreement; but these change, as the fall in the length of the standard working week as the community has grown richer confirms.

For centuries the desire for an adequate standard of living has been accompanied by the desire for some degree of stability of incomes, employment and prices. In the last fifty years it has come to be accepted that it is on governments that the responsibility for maintaining overall economic stability must fall; and since the war, at least, governments have claimed an increasing measure of influence in many countries over the pace of economic growth. At the foundation of these policies is the desire of the community for what has become known as *full employment*, the desire to ensure the opportunity of useful work to all who seek it. Some unemployment there must be, for it takes time to change jobs, so that full employment is more easily if less exactly defined as a situation without 'excessive' unemployment, without the cruelty and the waste that widespread and prolonged unemployment entails. By preventing the destruction of economic confidence that prolonged unemployment and business losses can cause, the maintenance of full employment is thrice blessed: it can facilitate the initiative and experiment on which economic growth depends.

The government aims at maintaining full employment by ensuring whenever necessary that the flow of money expenditure on goods and services by the community as a whole is sufficient to call forth a level of production that will provide jobs for all who want them. When the flow of expenditure is deficient and widespread unemployment results, the situation is described as one of *deflation*. But the level of expenditure by the community is capable of being excessive in relation to the capacity of the economy to provide, at unchanged prices, all the goods and services for which people are willing and able to pay. In the colloquial phrase, there may be 'too much money chasing too few goods'. Shortages or rising prices will result, and this undesirable state of affairs is known as *inflation*. It is the object of government policy to avoid both extremes, so that the question of 'How much to produce?', in an economy in which goods are exchanged for money, cannot be dissociated from that of 'How much to spend?'

## OF WHAT?

The question 'How much?' is obviously meaningless except in relation to 'Of what?' The community becomes no richer by producing more and more of something that is not wanted at all; unless it valued work for its own sake it would be merely wasting its time. It would be losing the opportunity of having more leisure or of producing some alternative article that *was* wanted. In practice waste seldom occurs in this absolute sense—even the junk-heap has some value as scrap. Waste more frequently occurs when the combination of goods and services produced is regarded as less desirable than some other combination that the community's resources could yield. If its resources are being fully utilized, the community can have more of one good, or of leisure, only by giving up something else; but just what is the 'right' pattern of production is a complex and controversial question. Into the balance of alternatives must go the preferences of the community's members in their capacity as consumers for different goods and services and their preferences as producers for different kinds of work. A complex economy must have some means of recording the cost, in alternative production possibilities forgone, of the output of one good rather than another and of allowing its members to compare these costs with their preferences.

In a primitive economy alternatives might be few. How many cattle were raised, how much corn grown, might depend largely on custom, the bounty of nature and the needs of the individual family, which in the remote areas of Africa and Asia is still a self-sufficient economic unit. Throughout the centuries, in all but these few inaccessible places, the development of trade has widened the area of choice. Goods were first bartered for one another and then exchanged for some widely acceptable commodity, such as gold or silver, from which has developed the use of money as we know it today, so that in the course of time the self-sufficient family, tribal or village economy has been transformed into the 'market' or 'exchange' economy of the modern world, in which a coalminer in South Wales uses his money wage to buy shoes made in Northampton or cotton goods in Lancashire, while the coal he has produced is burned in London and Copenhagen.

In the modern economy the vast array of goods and services that can be produced brings to the problem of economic balance a complexity beyond the reach of any single mind or organizing body; and although we may be only too conscious of the imperfections of the economy, that it works at all successfully in such conditions is something not far short of miraculous. For the practicability of this gigantic sorting-out process we have to thank the use of money and the operation of prices. The use of money has enabled us to escape the cumbersome restrictions of barter, which would oblige a man wishing to exchange a sack of coal for a pair of size 9 brown shoes to find another willing to give up size 9 brown shoes for a sack of coal; and the operation of prices provides the community with a means of measuring the cost of one commodity in terms of others at the expense of which it is produced and of enabling the community's members to balance their preferences against this cost by allowing each of them to decide which prices are worth paying.

Another aspect of the problem of economic balance is the necessity for weighing the wants of today against those of tomorrow, for the goods that are used up now will not be available for use in the future. This is not just a question of conserving natural resources to meet future needs, by soil and forest care. Many goods that are produced are durable and so render or merely stand to make available when required a service over a period of time. By increasing its production of goods that will endure at the expense of those which are used up during the year the community is able to provide for the wants of future years.

The provision for future wants involves three types of goods. First, there are durable goods in the hands of consumers. Many goods possessed by consumers endure, but when economists refer to *consumer durable goods* they have in mind articles such as motor-cars, radio and television sets, refrigerators and washing machines; clothing is a borderline case. Secondly, there are the stocks of consumer goods awaiting sale, together with the foodstuffs, fuel, raw materials, semi-manufactured products and work in progress of all kinds held by producers. These are described as *stocks and work in progress*, or more simply as *stocks* or, in the American term, as *inventories*; an adequate level of stocks is essential to a smooth flow of production. Thirdly, there is the community's *fixed capital*. This includes producer durable or capital goods, such as factories, offices and shops, plant, equipment and vehicles, together with public buildings and equipment and also houses. Land and other natural resources, such as mineral deposits, are sometimes placed in the separate category of 'land', but it is convenient to include them in fixed capital.

Economists are usually interested in the part different goods play in production, so that the community's physical or 'real' capital is usually defined so as to exclude goods held by consumers, other than houses, for it is difficult to trace their use once they are purchased by consumers. Houses and flats, on the other hand, are included in the community's real capital mainly because the service they perform—the provision of accommodation—is so often purchased by the final consumer in return for a money payment, a rent, or can be so regarded for many purposes of economic analysis even in the case of owner-occupied houses. Thus the Inland Revenue authorities include in an owner-occupier's taxable income the 'imputed' rent of his own house.

By using part of its production to add to its physical capital the community is able to provide for the future in two ways. First, stocks act as a reserve which can be drawn on to meet needs greater than current production can satisfy. Secondly, and this is the outstanding characteristic of fixed capital goods, the *production* of the future can be increased by the construction of factories and equipment today, for the use of capital goods enhances the productivity of the community. If its resources are already fully employed, however, the community's future production of consumer goods and services can only be increased in this way if the members of the community are willing to refrain from consumption in the present, or if they are obliged to do so, for materials and labour that are used up to make machines to produce motor-cars in the future cannot make motor-cars today.

In financial matters the purchase of an asset is described as an act of *investment*, and the asset is part of the holder's financial capital. In economics additions to the stock of physical assets are also known as investment. Confusion can be avoided where the context does not make it clear which reference is intended by describing acquisitions of physical or real capital as *real investment* or by resorting to an alternative term in frequent use—*capital formation*. The relationship between financial and real investment is one of the themes to be discussed more fully in later chapters, but at this stage all that need be said is that finance is the provision of money for some purpose or other and that one of the most important purposes is the acquisition of physical assets. Just as there must be some means of deciding what part of the community's production shall be devoted to meeting future wants through the medium of real investment, so must there be some means of enabling finance to be supplied to businesses or government departments who can put it to good use in this way. This is one of the functions of the capital market, which consists of the banks and many other institutions.

Two further aspects of real investment are worth noting here. Each year, unless the future productive power of the stock of fixed assets is to be allowed to run down, the economy must make good the wearing out of its fixed capital assets, that is it must make some provision for what is known in economic analysis as the *depreciation* of its buildings, machines, tools and other fixed capital. The fact that part of the year's output of capital goods is bespoken to cover depreciation enables the distinction to be drawn between *gross* and *net* fixed investment, the latter being the value of the net addition to the community's stock of fixed capital after allowance for depreciation. As the stock of fixed capital grows year by year, depreciation will also increase, so that it is by looking at the level of net rather than gross investment that we can discern what provision the community is making for future consumption.

Secondly, because new capital goods may require a considerable period of time for their construction, and because, once built, their productive life may extend for many years, the necessity for looking ahead on the part of those who control the use of capital is vital if resources are not to be wasted on the use of capital assets for purposes which are not justified. However, at any moment the range of factors that may be relevant to the success of an investment project can rarely be distinguished in full, and the existence of change in economic affairs makes the accurate prediction of the course of those variable factors that can be identified as relevant a matter of great difficulty. As a result *risk* is involved in the use of capital and renders inescapable the existence of risk-bearers, whether capital is owned by the State or by private persons.

Risk may be transferred to those who are willing to bear it, but it cannot be avoided altogether. It may be borne by the business-man who owns his own factory, by the shareholders in a corporate concern, the members of a co-operative retail society or by the public in whose name a nationalized industry is operated. The risk attached to the use of capital is by no means the only form of uncertainty facing the economy's members; the risk of unemploy-ment caused by forces beyond his control is one that the wage- or salary-earner cannot escape, with consequences possibly of the greatest hardship. The justification for focusing attention in economic analysis on the risk incurred in the use of capital, however, lies in the special importance of the role of capital in the process by which the responsibility for allocating the community's resources is carried.

## HOW ?

All economies must have some means of deciding which are the most economical methods of producing the goods and services its members desire. In primitive economies the choice of method is restricted, but the replacement of barter by the many-sided possibilities of exchange through the medium of money has greatly extended the range of choice, and with the advance of scientific knowledge the range of techniques known to be feasible expands almost continuously. But the most economical method is not necessarily the latest to be evolved, nor always that which uses the most powerful machines. The input of different combinations of raw materials, labour and physical capital must somehow be compared with the output to be secured by each, if the most economical method is to be identified. This, too, is one of the functions of the price-mechanism in the market economy, since it enables the cost of different methods to be compared in money terms.

The question 'How?' transcends national boundaries, for the economy can obtain goods and services through international trade, importing them from abroad and paying for them out of the proceeds of other goods and services which it exports to the outside world. The ultimate responsibility for ensuring that the country maintains a satisfactory balance of international payments falls on the government.

## FOR WHOM ?

This is the question that looms so large in our political life—
how should incomes and wealth be distributed throughout the
community ? In the most primitive and isolated forms of economy,
in which no exchange of goods took place, the answer to the
question 'For whom?' may have been largely independent of
what types of goods were actually produced. Fixed proportions
may have been allocated, for example, to the priesthood and other
groups. With the development of production for exchange,
culminating in the use of money, the answers to the questions
'Of what ?' and 'For whom ?' have become interconnected.

In the market economy, in which the pattern of production is
influenced by the preferences of its individual members, if
supported by their ability to pay for what they desire, the composition of output will be affected by the distribution of incomes as
between rich and poor, men and women, town and country, for
our preferences as consumers reflect our social environment. It is
also true that the distribution of incomes is affected by the pattern
of production, for the incomes received by individual members of
the community are for the most part payments for their contribution to production, and the size of the reward for different types
of productive service will depend partly on the intensity of market
demand for the goods and services to whose output they are
directed. But an important object of the government's taxation
policy may be to modify the distribution of spendable incomes
created by market forces, according to its political lights.

### THE UNDERLYING ECONOMIC PROBLEM

Thus the four questions, 'How much to produce ?'; 'Of what ?';
'How ?' and 'For whom ?' are closely linked with one another,
and it is this interdependence that is responsible for much of the
complexity of economic analysis. They are, nevertheless, merely
four aspects of one basic economic question, the problem of
*scarcity*. Rich though a prosperous economy may be, its resources
are still scarce in relation to the wants that its members would
express if they could satisfy them without cost. None of the four
decisions would have to be taken if the resources of the community were sufficient to satisfy all our wants without restraint;
in this state of infinite abundance 'waste' would be meaningless

and 'economy', the practice of making the most of what is available, would be unnecessary.

In the real world we cannot have as much as we would like of all the goods and services which we would consume if they were free, and we have to economize by striking a balance between them. To be more precise, we have to strike a balance between the *satisfaction* that we derive from different goods and services, giving up the satisfaction that we would enjoy in having, say, more clothes rather than more food, and so on. The motives that influence the way in which men choose their occupation, organize their working life, spend their income or use their leisure are not confined to the material; and whereas the study of these motives is the subject of sociology, psychology and political analysis, it is their effect on the production and use of different goods and services that falls within the province of economics, which is not concerned with the moral or aesthetic values they may imply.

Although scarcity is always with us as individuals, it may not always apply to the economy as a whole. When unemployment is widespread it is not the case that the production of, say, houses can be increased only at the expense of the production of some other good. If sufficient labour and equipment are involuntarily unemployed, an increase in the output of houses can be obtained without the sacrifice of some existing satisfaction by the community as a whole. When there is extensive unemployment, what is a 'cost' to the individual—the sacrifice of something else in return for acquiring a house—is not so to society, for the resources from which the house has been constructed would otherwise have remained unused. It is only when the economy is in a state of full employment that the apparent scarcity of resources available to the individual members of the community reflects the real scarcity that rules the community as a whole.

Of course, even if there is full employment an increase in the output of houses may not necessitate a reduction in that of some other good, as long as the improvement in the state of productive techniques makes possible an increase in total output over a sufficiently wide area of the economy. The increase in productivity is the means by which we can have more of everything, but it does not abolish the problem of scarcity. In the past two hundred years our scientific knowledge has grown beyond measure, and in the Western world the standard of living of even the humblest has been raised far beyond the dreams of our ancestors; but economics is still with us even though the poor, in the eighteenth- and nineteenth-century sense of the word, are not. It is no accidental paradox that economic problems seem to have kept pace with our material possessions. For wants may multiply with the ability to satisfy them; the example of those who are richer than ourselves, the force of advertising and the appeal of new products may cause our appetites to grow by what they feed on. Indeed, in the modern world this is part of the mainspring of economic growth itself.

## ECONOMIC GROWTH

The pace of economic growth in the Western world over the past century, that is of production per man-hour worked, has advanced at a rate more rapid than that experienced in the previous history of mankind. Some historians have ventured the estimate that the improvement in living standards of the mass of the British people over the past hundred years has been comparable with that achieved over the previous five hundred, an observation that cannot easily set on a historical scale the great variety of goods and services available today, a variety that is quite without precedent. As far as any measurement can be made at all, the increase in the volume of production per man-hour over the past hundred years has been equivalent to a rate of growth of $1\frac{1}{2}$ per cent per annum, an advance that many expect to be surpassed in the future, on the ground that the pace of fruitful technical change is accelerating.

For this there is considerable evidence. The West moved from the mainly agricultural and commercial economy of the first half of the eighteenth century, still using largely natural power, through the hundred years and more of rapidly developing industry based on steam and iron, to the age of steel and electricity that was only in its sturdy infancy at the opening of the twentieth. Since then new products and techniques have changed our daily life at an almost bewildering rate. Oil, the combustion engine, wireless and synthetic materials transformed the face of the economy between the wars; now the promise of atomic energy, the gas turbine and the advance of electronics and chemical research seem to many to justify the description of yet a new industrial era. In agriculture progress has been less spectacular but no less vital.

Forms of organization, too, have continued to change. The growth of large-scale business organization can be traced to the extension of the joint-stock principle in the middle of the nineteenth century. In manufacturing, the development of large-scale production has utilized the economies of standardization, the productive power of modern machinery and the continued improvement in techniques of control and administration. There is no sign that this advance has been checked; new developments in the control of quality and of the flow of complex operations continue to bring a widening circle of industries within the range of mass-production methods. In retail distribution the closing years of the nineteenth century saw the development of the department store; the inter-war years brought the expansion of the 'multiple', and in more recent times the development of the self-service shop, the 'supermarket' of American terminology, appears to have introduced yet a new phase of retailing technique. In the field of finance the development of building societies and of hire purchase has extended the ownership of houses and of goods that were once rare luxuries. The development of insurance, through both private and State agencies, represents the pooling of risks that once had to be borne individually and so has brought a measure of security and certainty where previously protection against the hazards of business and personal life had been costly and even impossible.

Just what causes the pace of economic development to vary from age to age and from country to country is a complex question. Economic growth has been the product of progress in the state of knowledge in many fields and of the willingness and ability of the community to devote a substantial part of its resources to real investment. The contrast between the more prosperous and more rapidly growing economies of the world and their poorer neighbours is therefore not only a matter of natural resources and technical knowledge; the richer countries can generally be found to devote a larger proportion of their annual production to capital investment. Of course it is also true to say that the richer countries are in a better position to do so just *because* of their wealth—the production of poor countries is hardly enough to feed and clothe the population, let alone provide a surplus for the accumulation of capital assets. The richer countries, like the U.S.A., the United Kingdom or Western Germany, are able to devote between

15 and 25 per cent of their annual production to gross capital formation; countries like India, Ecuador or the Philippines find it difficult to put aside even 10 per cent of their very much lower output for this purpose.

Taking the necessary provision for the depreciation of existing assets into account, *net* capital formation in the underdeveloped countries may represent no more than 4 or 5 per cent of net national output, compared with the 10–15 per cent achieved by the more wealthy industrial countries. At these lower levels the contribution to production made by the growth of a poor country's physical assets is in many cases little more than enough to keep pace with the growth in population.

The low rate of net investment year by year of the poorer countries means that the value of the physical assets that they have built up is relatively small in relation to their production and their population. Even within the group of rich countries the disparity is considerable. In both the U.S.A. and the United Kingdom, for example, the stock of capital in existence represents roughly 2½ times the annual value of production, but the value of equipment per head in the U.S.A. is approximately twice that of the United Kingdom, which accounts for a large part of the difference in productivity between the two countries. The American worker can be thought of as having roughly twice the horsepower of his British counterpart at his elbow.

Important though capital investment is to economic growth, the relationship between the two is neither simple nor constant. Some forms of capital assets, such as roads and railway tracks, have a long life and are able to provide for an expansion of output with the aid of comparatively modest extra expenditure year by year, once they are built. Improvements in technique may lead to a more economic utilization of capital, and certain forms of equipment may be 'capital-saving', in that they enable the same level of production to be achieved with less capital than before— improvements in methods of communication are often of this nature. Industries differ in the volume of capital they employ, so that the total weight of capital required will vary with the composition of the nation's demand for different goods and services.

Economic growth is the product of men as well as machines, and the factors that lead men to consider economic growth desirable, and spur them on to make the kind of effort without which this advance could not have been achieved, reach beyond the boundaries of economics to sociology and even religion. The obvious, however, is worth stressing. Whatever factors may be operative at any particular place and time, economic growth involves change; and the seemingly perpetual advance in technology and economic organization that has continued for the past two hundred years in this country could not have occurred without experimentation, the eagerness to innovate and the willingness to accept its consequences. Change, of course, brings problems of its own, so that not all would equate economic growth, that is the rise in productivity, or production per head, with progress in the wider sense. The frictions caused by change are lessened by the opportunities presented by economic expansion, but the process of economic growth has involved more than changes in the equipment we use or the goods we produce. Economic growth has been based on specialization and the spread of trade, and it has been through the medium of trade that the difficulties caused by change have been diffused.

### SPECIALIZATION AND TRADE

Specialization increases productivity. It enables individuals—and whole communities—to concentrate on exploiting their natural or acquired skills and aptitudes and so to obtain the mutual gains afforded by the principle of comparative advantages. This principle states that it is to the material benefit of a group of producers if each concentrates on that line of production in which his comparative advantage is greatest. The engineer may be a better driver than the man who drives a taxi-cab, but because the knowledge of the former makes him a much better engineer than the latter and because engineering is more highly valued by the community than driving a taxi, it is to the benefit of them both that the division of labour is made in this way. Specialization allows complicated operations to be broken into simple steps and enables productive skill to be increased to the full by using different workers for each stage, without the loss of time that would arise if each had to pass from one stage to another; the control of a large number of employees is facilitated if their individual work is standardized. Without specialization the vast majority of goods that we use today could not be produced at all, for there would have been little replacement of manual by mechanical methods and no replacement of simple by complex machines.

Specialization is limited by the extent of the market, so that neither the division of labour nor mechanization could proceed far without the extension of trade. When the output of the individual producer is raised beyond his needs his surplus must be sold, and modern productive methods will not be undertaken unless justified by the market. Important advances in economic development, therefore, have often been associated with the spread of trade, both internal and international, whether this has been the result of better communications, of political harmony or of some improvement in the mechanism of the market itself, such as the use of money and the provision of credit.

Trade, however, brings economic interdependence. The subsistence family economy, producing only enough to meet its own needs, was self-contained, unaffected by events in a neighbouring community, let alone across the sea. Trade, on the other hand, has created new links between communities and between their individual members within them. The livelihood of cotton-spinners in Lancashire has become dependent on markets from London to Sydney; a dock strike in London can cause unemployment in the Midlands; and technical changes in the motor industry can alter the fortunes of steel-workers in South Wales. It is perhaps in the sphere of international trade that interdependence has become of critical importance, in creating two sorts of problems.

In the first place, we now tend to sink or swim together in the world economy, for economic disturbances in the more powerful countries are radiated to those with whom they trade. Secondly, countries that rely on the sale of particular products or services, or those tied to special sources of supply, may be forced to make painful adjustments while their neighbours remain comparatively undisturbed; thus Lancashire's cotton mills may be idle at a time of general prosperity owing to Japanese competition, or Denmark may suffer as a result of Britain's inability to supply her with sufficient coal. In these cases hardship may be eased by the contraction of the depressed industry and by the expansion instead of more prosperous trades, or by the replacement of scarce materials by substitutes. But when, as in the decade before the war, trade depression is general, the mobility of resources is only of limited assistance; switching from one market to another, for example, may result in gains only at the expense of other producers already operating with little margin to spare.

Whilst trade brings its benefits, enlarging markets and spreading prosperity as well as depression, the problem of economic interdependence has been intensified by the bewildering rapidity of change itself, so that prosperity has been achieved only at a price, the need to make frequent and perhaps difficult adjustments as a result of events outside our control. Interdependence and change have become the dominant characteristics of the whole world economy, and the desire to mitigate the problems they bring has been an important cause of the growth of State intervention in economic affairs. Social security measures, employment policy, and the protection of vulnerable industries from overseas competition can all be viewed, at least partly, in this light. Since the last war, in particular, a better understanding of the facts of interdependence in international trade has brought governments to act more in harmony, or at least to reduce conflict, in this field. Within most countries there has been a tendency to recognize our dependence on one another in a form that is not without its moral aspects.

Action to soften the impact of interdependence and change has not been confined to government policy, however; collective agreements by employers to stabilize prices and production, and trade-union practices designed to check dismissals caused by redundancy, for example, have nearly all been derived from the desire to limit the economic insecurity associated with interdependence and change. But as change is an essential ingredient of growth, the extent to which policies intended to moderate the effects of change can be pursued without limiting the pace of growth is, like many of the fundamental questions of economics, still open to controversy.

c

# CHAPTER 2

# A MIXED COMPETITIVE MARKET ECONOMY

## THE BRITISH ECONOMY TODAY

A country's economy can be looked at from several points of view. One useful perspective is that of its *national income*. This is a concept that is used frequently in economics and is considered in some detail in Chapter 33. The national income is a measure of the money value of the goods and services becoming available to the nation from its economic activity in any period. It approximates to the value of the goods and services it produces and so can also be defined as the *national product*.

The total value placed by the official statisticians on the national product in 1957 was approximately £19,000 million. In itself this is a formidable but not especially illuminating figure. The idea of the national income and product tells us more about the British economy, however, when we learn that in 1957 about two-thirds of the national product was used for personal consumption and that about one-fifth took the form of goods and services used by the central and local governments for purposes such as administration, defence and education. The nation devoted nearly one-fifth of its production to gross fixed investment. About one-quarter of the goods and services we used were imported from abroad, and so a similar quantity had to be exported to pay for them. For the country's chief resources are its skills, and even the one mineral in which it is rich, coal, is no longer sufficient to provide all of its fuel. Britain imports a wide range of raw materials and processed goods, and although its climate is benevolent and the land fertile, the economies of specialization have favoured the concentration of our efforts on industry and services, so that Britain imports about one-half of its food, the financial assistance given to agriculture by the government having helped to reduce this proportion from over two-thirds before the war.

This national product represents a standard of living throughout the country as a whole that is among the highest in the world.

Differences in the price-levels and consumption patterns of different countries make accurate comparison difficult, but the average Briton consumes a somewhat greater volume of goods and services each year than his counterpart in most European countries. Whereas his standard of living is between one-half and two-thirds of that of the average American or Canadian, it is something of the order of twelve times as high as that of the average Indian.

Behind these statistics are the people who produce the goods and services they represent. Since the first census in 1801 the population of the United Kingdom has risen from 16 to 51 million, the curve of growth having gradually levelled out following the decline in the birth-rate which began in the last quarter of the nineteenth century. At present the population is almost stationary in size and becoming older in composition. About 24 million people over the age of fifteen formed its working population in mid-1958, that is were gainfully employed or registered as seeking work, a figure that excludes the indispensable but unpaid services of the housewife. Of these 24 million, almost 8 million were women, nearly two-fifths of the female population over the age of fifteen.

Throughout the whole period since the 1801 census the main changes in the pattern of employment and production have been the fall in the share of agriculture and the striking growth in the relative importance of industry (manufacturing, building, fuel and power) and of services (transport, distribution, the professions, finance and administration). In 1958, less than one in twenty of those in civil employment was engaged in agriculture, forestry or fishing, and less than one in twenty-five in mining and quarrying. On the other hand, manufacturing provided work for just two-fifths and the metal-using trades alone for about one-fifth of those in employment, and building, gas, electricity and water engaged a further 8 per cent. Services employed a number almost as large as the whole of industry itself.

Forms of economic organization are varied. Apart from the 600,000 in the armed forces in 1958, about 5 million were engaged in public administration, State hospitals, etc., and in the nationalized industries. In all, about 6 million were employed by the State and by State-owned enterprises. Of the remaining 18 million there were, according to the National Insurance statistics, at least 2¼ million self-employed persons. Many of these were engaged in running the 400,000 separate farms, the 550,000 retail shops (of which about 70 per cent are single-shop firms) and the 160,000 small 'service shops' (garages, hairdressers, shoe-repairers, etc.). There are in addition large numbers of one-man firms or partnerships in the professions and in road transport.

### A 'MIXED COMPETITIVE MARKET ECONOMY'

No single expression can describe precisely the variety of forms of organization of which the British economy is composed and the range of behaviour they exhibit. But two aspects are worth emphasizing. First, we live in what is, by the test of ownership, a *mixed* economy; part of its resources are owned by the State, while the remainder are operated by private businesses. In terms of numbers employed, about one-quarter of the working population is engaged directly by the State and nationalized concerns. In terms of the ownership of fixed capital the role of the State is even more important, for it can be estimated that, including local authority houses, nearly one-half of the country's fixed capital is owned by the State—by the government and by the nationalized industries. Apart from the question of ownership, the government intervenes in our economic life over a wide field by one means or another. The production of many goods and services, therefore, such as those needed for defence, public administration and the social services, is undertaken directly as a result of government policy. But for the most part the questions of what shall be produced and how are resolved by the operation of market forces.

The mechanism of the market operates through some degree of *competition* between buyers and between sellers for the most part without direct co-ordination by the State; nationalized concerns as well as private producers take part in this process. The varying extent and nature of competition is a matter into which we shall have to go more closely, but by contrast with a primitive subsistence economy on the one hand and the centrally co-ordinated economy of State monopolies that appears to be the ideal of Communist society on the other, the description of the British economy as a mixed competitive market economy, if not the whole truth, is a reasonably accurate one.

There are in this country 14 million households, each of which can be regarded as competing for its share of consumer goods according to its ability and readiness to buy different articles at the prices at which they are offered. The changing pattern of their expenditure in turn influences the direction of production through the operation of what is usually if sometimes misleadingly called the 'profit motive'. In this context the word profit, which has of course a narrower technical accounting connotation, embraces the incomes of all producers whose activities are influenced largely by a comparison of the return to be obtained from the output of different goods and services.

Pecuniary self-interest is an alternative description of the mainspring of this mechanism; but this is an over-simplification, for few of us would admit to being dominated by the love of money. But profit, or income in its widest sense, is more than a personal motive for taking one job rather than another, or for undertaking the output of one article rather than another, or for adopting one method of production rather than another. Many productive enterprises, including the nationalized corporations, are guided by the 'profit motive' not so much, or not only, to gratify the desire for greater pecuniary gain on the part of those who manage or own them, but because the profit earned is looked on as a criterion of success and efficiency.

In this process businessmen occupy a strategic position, because their control over the use of physical capital places in their hands the decision as to what shall be produced. Businessmen, including in this vague term the managers of nationalized trading concerns, attempt to earn a satisfactorily high level of profits by comparing the sales of their goods, in terms of the prices that buyers as a whole are willing to pay for different quantities, with the costs of their production. Businessmen increase or decrease output according to the pressure of sales on the one hand and that of costs on the other. Competition, it is generally held, leads businesses to seek methods of producing at lower cost. The prospect of the high profits that may result from being first in the field stimulates businessmen to take the risk of introducing new goods or methods of production and to anticipate future demand; the fear or experience of losses causes businessmen to contract the production of goods that are unprofitable and to reject methods that are uneconomic. The process of adjustment to economic change is diffused throughout the whole economy, and the rewards for success and the penalties for failure are part of the process of adjustment itself; a competitive market economy creates its own economic incentives and its own economic sanctions for all types of producer, so that the movement of resources does not depend on political coercion. Freedom of occupation ranks high in our political ideals.

## FACTORS OF PRODUCTION

The profitability of different lines of production influences what different businessmen are prepared to pay for the resources they use. These consist of a multitude of goods and services, different kinds of labour, materials and equipment; but for many years economists have used the term *factors of production* to describe them in a single phrase. The point of this is that a tool, a machine, or a coalmine, for example, is already the embodiment of labour and of other natural resources such as iron ore, coal and timber, and also the product of other machines which in turn are the embodiment of other resources. It was once usual to classify factors of production into three or four types. 'Labour' was defined to include all forms of human effort. 'Land' denoted what have been described as the 'indestructible properties of the soil' and other gifts of nature, its uniqueness as a factor of production being sought in the proposition that its supply has been fixed for all times by 'nature'. 'Capital' was defined either as the embodiment of 'land' and 'labour' in some productive asset, or, on a more abstract plane, as the willingness and ability to abstain from current consumption that, in conditions of full employment, is essential to the production of capital goods. Some economists added a fourth factor of production, which they called 'risk-bearing' or 'enterprise', so that the man who undertook the risks of production became known as the 'entrepreneur'.

Economists now emphasize the convenience rather than the logic of expressing the multiplicity of different resources as if they are merely the embodiment of 'land', 'labour' and 'capital' in forms that can be regarded as homogeneous. In the first place, the distinction between 'land', defined as given by nature, and 'capital', reproduced by man, obviously cannot be a precise one. The land that is tilled today would not have its present productivity but for centuries of human effort applied to crop rotation, drainage, etc., and but for the use of capital in the form of fertilizers, irrigation works, canals and so on. The problem of soil erosion is a reminder that the properties of the soil are by no means 'indestructible'. The idea of a single factor of production called 'labour' obscures the fact that it is part of the task of economics to explain the contribution to production of different *types* of labour and the different levels of wages earned by each; as we are not all bricklayers, our 'labour' cannot be measured in some standard unit of physical production, in this case the number of bricks per hour we can lay. Thirdly, that risk-bearing and enterprise are essential in the changing economy is indisputable, but it is difficult to conceive of the supply of 'risk-bearing' or 'enterprise' in the abstract in a form that is capable of being measured with any practical success.

Whereas the owners of capital can be readily identified, it is difficult to single out the 'entrepreneur' in the real world. In the last resort the ordinary shareholders of a company bear the risk of its failure, but they may exercise little control over its operation; they may also be remote from the 'enterprise' that leads to its success. The seat of 'enterprise' may be found in its board of directors, whose salaries may be larger than their dividends, and in its salaried managers, who need not be shareholders at all. For this reason the admittedly no less vague but more common term 'businessman' has been retained in this book in place of the 'entrepreneur'.

The term 'factors of production' is therefore adopted here merely as a form of shorthand for the complex array of individual goods and services used in production, and as a reminder that the economic mechanism must decide not only how existing tools are to be used but also how natural resources should be employed to produce others.

Because the profitability of producing different goods and services influences the prices businessmen are prepared to pay for different factors of production, the latter tend to be attracted into those industries where demand by business is most intense. This demand is a 'derived' demand, reflecting the demand exerted or expected to be exerted by final consumers, so that the movement of resources into the intermediate stages of production is influenced by the pattern of demand for the goods and services at the end of the production process.

The demand by businesses on the one hand and the level of supply of different factors or production on the other determine the prices of different factors of production. In this way businessmen are provided with a yardstick for measuring costs, and the prices of factors of production in a fully employed economy tend to reflect their relative scarcity.

The operation of the market economy is by and large the operation of the 'price mechanism'; costs are only a form of price, and the relationship between prices provides both a yardstick for economic measurement and a signal for economic activity. But a yardstick is not always accurate, and a signal may fail; and this summary of the allocation of resources leaves many important questions untouched. The chapters that follow sketch in greater detail the behaviour of consumers and businesses and introduce some of the problems raised by the operation of competition and the price mechanism in practice.

# CHAPTER 3

# CONSUMERS AND PRICES

As individuals we have to decide what proportion of our income to spend, and on what. It is with the second question that we are at present concerned. Everyday experience shows our choice of consumer goods and services to be subject to a wide range of factors. Our level of income is obviously an important influence. So are the direction in which it is changing or is expected to change and the length of time we have had to adjust our habits to a new level of income. Occupation, age, marital status, size of family, the way income is pooled within the family—the many factors that we can class as part of a household's 'social environment'—are others about which useful generalizations can often be made. Within this framework can sometimes be discerned patterns that change periodically, like the fluctuations of expenditure due to the timing of replacement of clothing and durable goods. Advertising is another potent force. Some goods and services are *complementary*, that is they provide most satisfaction if used in conjunction with each other, like motor-cars and petrol. Others are close *substitutes*, like soap and synthetic detergents. Thus purchases of many goods and services are related to decisions made about others.

For simplicity of expression, this multitude of factors can be expressed as two elements—the consumer's total income and the collection of tastes, environmental influences and habits that we can call his 'preferences'. Given his income, then if his preferences remain constant the amounts that any individual purchases of different goods and services will depend on the relative prices of the articles of which he is aware. Because of this it is necessary to use the term 'preferences' to denote the consumer's attitude to different goods and services at *given* prices. A distinction must be drawn between changes in purchases caused by changes in preferences at *given* prices and those resulting from variations in prices themselves.

The consumer obtains the maximum satisfaction possible from his expenditure when no additional satisfaction can be obtained by shifting, say, a shillingsworth of outlay in a given period from one good and increasing the purchase of another by a shilling instead. In the language of economics the word 'utility' has come to be used instead of the everyday 'satisfaction', but the words are interchangeable. They are also neutral, implying no judgement as to the wisdom of a man's choice. The difference in total utility derived from a small change in outlay on any article is the utility obtained from the marginal unit of expenditure on it.

To put the matter another way, the consumer maximizes his utility or satisfaction when the utility he derives from his marginal unit of expenditure—say one shillingsworth—is the same for all goods purchased. This statement is a tautology, but it helps to explain the behaviour of consumers if considered in conjunction with the principle of *diminishing marginal utility*. By this is meant the proposition that, if a man's preferences remain constant the satisfaction that he derives from the consumption of the marginal unit of any good—the change in total utility due to consuming one unit more than before—decreases as the number of units consumed in a given period rises. This principle may be operative only after a certain point—the consumption of some goods may initially whet our appetite for more—but sooner or later the satisfaction derived from successive units of any good consumed tends to fall as the desire for it is gradually appeased.

### THE EFFECTS OF PRICE CHANGES

This principle and the proposition that the consumer maximizes his utility by equalizing the utility obtained from the marginal unit of expenditure on different goods and services help to explain why the amount that a consumer is willing to buy of a particular article often varies inversely with its price, if the state of his preferences, as defined above, does not change. To each consumer the price of any article represents the amount of other goods that have to be forgone if it is purchased. If the price of, say, cigarettes were to fall, this would mean that the marginal shilling spent on cigarettes would now buy a larger number of cigarettes than before. This marginal shilling would now provide a greater utility than, say, the marginal shilling per week spent by our consumer on beer. He would now increase his total utility if he spent more on cigarettes and less on beer. By shifting his expenditure in this direction the marginal utility to him of a shillingsworth of cigarettes would fall and that of beer rise until a new balance was reached. In this situation his outlay on beer would fall despite the fact that in absolute money terms its price had not increased, exemplifying how the essence of any price lies in its relation to other prices, especially to those goods for which it is a close competitor for the consumer's money.

### The Substitution Effect of Price Changes

This effect of a reduction in the price of an article in increasing its consumption is often described in economics as the 'substitution effect' of a change in prices, and its strength will thus depend on whether the article concerned has close substitutes to which the consumer is ready to transfer his favour. We should thus expect a fall in the price of salt, for example, to have little effect on the quantity of salt purchased, for there are no obvious substitutes for salt. A fall in the price of, say, chocolate in terms of that of sweets, on the other hand, might cause a marked diversion of spending from sweets to chocolate. Of course, the force of this substitution effect depends partly on the inertia of consumers' habits and on what may be called their price-consciousness. But for movements in relative prices to act in this way on the market as a whole does not require the reaction of *all* consumers.

### The Income Effect of Price Changes

There is another reason why a change in relative prices may affect the consumer's purchases that is usually described as the 'income effect'. If the price of one of the goods usually bought by a consumer falls while all others remain unchanged, the result is to increase his total real income, for it enables him to buy more of some goods and no less of others for the same total money outlay. Even a small rise in a consumer's real income will lead him to increase his purchases of at least some goods and services, and the strength of the income effect will depend on the nature of the good in question and on the proportion of his income that the consumer spends on it. Using the example of salt again, the fact that it is not a commodity which we are eager to consume in greater quantities as our real income rises means that the income effect due to a fall in the price of salt would not lead to a rise in the purchase of salt so much as to a rise in expenditure on other goods and services, and as we spend relatively little on salt the income effect overall would be small. But a similar percentage fall in the price of, say, refrigerators, purchases of which are greatly influenced by the level of real income, would be a different matter.

### DEMAND AND PRICES

The amount that people will buy of an article at a given price is their *demand* for it at that price, given the pattern of relative prices and the state of their preferences. To the observation that demand will expand if the price of an article is reduced and contract if it is raised there are several exceptions. The demand for the article concerned may be entirely unaffected if there are no close substitutes and if the income effect is transferred to other goods. In some cases demand may even rise when the price is raised and fall when it is lowered. There are three main examples of this seemingly perverse behaviour.

1. *Expectations of higher prices.* If a rise in price is thought to be only the first of a series, consumers may decide to make extra purchases before the next expected increase. This is less practicable, of course, in the case of perishable goods or others which cannot be held in consumers' stocks.

2. '*Inferior goods.*' These are goods of which we buy less as our real income rises; the income effect, in other words, is negative. Examples include: potatoes, bread and the cheaper sort of confectionery, which poor families buy in relatively large quantities; margarine that is replaced by butter when more can be spent on food; and ready-made clothes that give way to tailor-made suits. Changes in price may have the same effect as a change in total real income if the articles concerned form a sufficiently important part of a person's budget. Because of this condition these exceptions to the proposition that demand is stimulated by a fall in price are not common. The negative income effect is not as a rule strong enough to offset the substitution effect in favour of the article whose price has fallen.

3. *Quality judged by price.* The force of advertising and lack of knowledge or discrimination on the part of the consumer may lead him to associate quality with price, so that more of certain goods may be sold at a high price than at a low one. In many cases, however, advertising matter, sales service, or display and packaging

material may also vary with price, so that the same basic article may create quite a different impression on the consumer if sold in a different sales context.

Some goods may be bought chiefly to impress other people, and for this purpose a high price may be as impressive as the high quality it may also be thought to denote. Within certain limits, therefore, more fur coats and jewellery may be sold at higher than at lower prices.

## ELASTICITY OF DEMAND

### Price Elasticity

Given the level of total real incomes and the state of preferences, the demand for some articles will be considerably stimulated by a relatively small fall in price or curtailed by a small rise, whereas the demand for other goods will be very much less sensitive. The sensitivity of demand in response to a change in price when total income and preferences remain constant has come to be known as the elasticity of demand for the article concerned or, more precisely, to distinguish it from the sensitivity of demand in response to a change in income, as its price-elasticity of demand.

Price-elasticity of demand can be expressed as the percentage increase (decrease) in the quantity demanded resulting from a given percentage fall (rise) in price. Thus, if a 1 per cent fall in price leads to a 1 per cent increase in the quantity purchased, other things remaining equal, the price-elasticity of demand is unity. If the quantity purchased rises by more than 1 per cent when the price falls by 1 per cent, the price-elasticity of demand is greater than unity—if the quantity purchased rises by $1\frac{1}{2}$ per cent the price-elasticity of demand would be 1·5, and so on. If a 1 per cent decrease in price results in less than a 1 per cent rise in the quantity of purchases the price-elasticity of demand is obviously less than unity. Generally speaking, demand where elasticity is greater than unity is said to be *elastic*; where elasticity is less than unity, demand is said to be *inelastic*.

There are two extremes of elasticity of demand. When existing buyers are unwilling to alter the quantity they purchase irrespective of the price charged and no new buyers are attracted into the market as a result of a change in price, demand has zero elasticity, or is 'perfectly inelastic'. If, on the other hand, buyers will take any amount of an article, but only at one price, demand has infinite elasticity, or is 'perfectly elastic'. In the latter case a slight rise in price destroys demand completely.

Both extremes of price-elasticity are rare, but commodities may be sold in conditions of perfectly inelastic demand over a limited range of prices; in some cases the demand for an article may be so intense as to be quite unimpaired by a small rise in prices. More generally, commodities can be found—like matches or mustard—on which the consumer spends such a small proportion of his budget that quite a substantial proportionate increase in price may pass unnoticed or be received with indifference. For any article, however, the reaction of buyers, both actual and potential, to a large change in price will usually be more powerful than their reaction to a small one. The reaction of the whole potential range of buyers to a small change in price, moreover, will depend on the existing price itself; demand may be elastic within one range of prices and inelastic within another.

The most important factor affecting elasticity of demand is the possibility of substitution between different articles. Thus the possibility of substitution between butter and margarine, or between cotton and rayon textiles, will give each relatively high price-elasticities of demand. Another influence already indicated is the share that a particular commodity occupies in the consumer's total expenditure.

The demand for any good will be more elastic the greater the variability of the number of purchasers, even if the expenditure of those who were buyers at the original price does not change significantly. Goods that are purchased out of habit or through convention or compulsion will generally possess a relatively small degree of price-elasticity. The distinction between 'necessities' and 'luxuries' that is tempting in comparisons of elasticity is of small value, if only because of the difficulty of precise definition of these terms in a world where individual preferences show marked differences. Moreover, any individual article within a roughly similar class of goods may possess a higher price-elasticity of demand than that class of goods as a whole, because of the possibility of substitution. Thus 'bread' may be regarded as a 'necessity', but if the price of one type of bread, for whatever reason, were to change in relation to others, it might be found to possess a relatively high elasticity as compared with 'bread' as a whole. (Demand for the bread of an individual baker changing his prices in isolation from others could also be expected to be relatively elastic if shoppers could turn to or from other bakers; but this aspect of demand is the subject of a subsequent chapter.)

Estimates of the actual degree of price-elasticity of demand for different goods cannot be made with confidence. Price-elasticity as a measure of a *single* factor—reaction to price—can only be defined with the proviso that 'other things' remain equal, which in real life they rarely do. The reaction of consumers to a change in the price of bread, for example, may be complicated by a simultaneous change in the prices of other goods, possibly substitutes like biscuits, by contemporary changes in incomes or even in the number of bakers, all of which may affect the demand for bread. In real life, moreover, price-elasticity of demand cannot be considered apart from the time factor; it takes time for consumers to become aware of price changes and to depart from their customary behaviour.

Elasticity of demand can be considered in terms of the money *value* of purchases as well as the quantity bought. When price-elasticity of demand is unity, so that a 1 per cent fall in price is followed by a 1 per cent increase in the quantity purchased, the result is that the value of purchases remains approximately the same as before the change in price. This proposition is not exactly true. If 100 articles were first bought at £100 each, at a total value of £10,000, and the price then fell to £99, resulting in sales of 101 articles, the total value of purchases would then become £9,999. The explanation is that the proposition is valid only for infinitesimal changes in price; but for practical purposes the approximation can be accepted if the change in price is small.

If demand were inelastic, so that the quantity purchased did not rise proportionately as much as a fall in price, a reduction in price would cause a decline in the total value of sales. With inelastic demand a rise in price would result in a rise in sales proceeds. In the opposite case, where price-elasticity is greater than unity, a fall in price would raise the total value of purchases but an increase in price would reduce it.

The concept of price-elasticity of demand is useful in examining a number of problems. The price policy of a business concern or a nationalized enterprise will have to be drawn up in the light of what is thought to be the degree of elasticity for the product to be sold—the hope of greatly expanding sales by reducing prices was an important stimulus, for example, to the enterprise of pioneers of mass production like Henry Ford and Lord Nuffield. Comparisons of elasticity are also relevant to taxation policy. Other things being equal, if the object of a tax imposed on the purchase of a particular article is to provide the government with a high level of revenue the article must be one with a relatively inelastic demand (unless all possible substitutes are to be taxed as well). The imposition of a tax on a commodity the demand for which is very price-elastic, on the other hand, will tend to contract demand more severely.

### Income-elasticity of Demand

Elasticity is merely a measure of the sensitivity with which one factor responds to another, and on the side of demand there is another variable which has already been referred to, namely income. Income-elasticity of demand measures the response of demand to changes in consumers' incomes if prices remain constant. It can be defined in a manner analogous to price-elasticity, namely the proportionate change in the quantity of a particular article purchased that results from a small proportionate change in income. With income-elasticity equal to unity, a 1 per cent increase in income would lead to a 1 per cent rise in the quantity purchased. For goods possessing income-elasticity of less than unity purchases would not rise proportionately as fast as income, so that the proportion of income spent on these would fall. In the case of what have already been described as 'inferior goods', income-elasticity of demand is actually negative, for here the quantity purchased falls absolutely as income rises.

By and large the demand for 'luxuries' will be income-elastic, expenditure on these goods generally increasing more rapidly than income. The idea of a 'luxury' good is perhaps more easily justified in relation to income than to price-elasticity. Even in this context the term 'luxury', however, has no precise meaning. Like price-elasticity of demand, income-elasticity varies between different consumers and especially between consumers with different levels of income. The very poor are unlikely to take advantage of a modest increase in income to purchase a motor-car; at this level 'luxury' goods possess a low income-elasticity of demand and some 'necessities', like clothing, a relatively high one.

At higher levels of income the comparison of elasticities is likely to be reversed.

Those goods with a high income-elasticity of demand will be in rapidly rising demand as the country's standard of living increases. But because the demand for these goods is particularly sensitive to changes in income, the industries concerned also tend to suffer relatively severely in times of falling incomes, as in periods of trade depression, when unemployment spreads and business profits decline. The sensitivity of these industries to the economic climate is particularly marked in the case of those goods with a highly income-elastic demand that are also durable goods, expenditure on which can be so easily advanced when income is rising or postponed when it is not.

D

# CHAPTER 4

# BUSINESS COSTS AND OUTPUT

In the course of any period a business makes a variety of payments. It will pay wages and salaries, perhaps rent for its premises and interest on its bank overdraft or other outstanding debts; it will purchase materials of one sort or another and perhaps some form of capital equipment. Accountants differ on matters of detail, but in principle the normal rule is that the only payments which should be reckoned as the costs of a particular period's operations are those logically attributable to the activity of the business during that period. It might be misleading, for example, to count the full purchase price of a piece of equipment expected to last for ten years as part of the costs of the year in which it was bought. The cost of capital assets is usually spread over the major part of their expected working life by debiting to each year's operations only an allowance for the depreciation of the asset for that year.

To calculate the profits of any period, therefore, it is usual to include in a firm's costs only what are known as 'current' payments. The most common of these are: wages and salaries; cost of materials; rent of premises; interest on debts; depreciation of capital equipment. The profit earned in any period is the difference between the value of sales in that period and current costs, and it is usual to include in both sales and costs items for which no cash payment has yet been made, as long as they can be properly considered as belonging to the operations of the period.

The distinction is usually drawn between *gross* and *net* profits. The former represent sales proceeds minus all current costs properly chargeable to the period concerned, with the exception of depreciation; net profits are gross profits less depreciation. It is the residual item of net profits that is relevant to the assessment of a firm's profitability, for depreciation is a cost, and it is from net profits that taxes and dividends or other payments to the concern's owners are paid.

## UNRECORDED COSTS

Part of these payments out of net profits as conventionally calculated may really be a form of cost. Where the businessman running his own concern draws no salary for the purely managerial and administrative services he provides, some allowance is made for this in economic analysis if not in accounting practice. If a businessman will not be willing to run a concern indefinitely if it does not provide him with a return at least equal to what he could earn elsewhere in a managerial capacity, then an amount equal to this alternative 'opportunity cost' of his services is really part of the cost of production of the goods made by his concern; for if it is not recovered production will eventually cease. Similarly, the rate of interest paid on borrowed money is an accounting cost, but in economic analysis it is usual to go further and regard as a cost a nominal figure for interest in the case of those businesses that do not borrow but provide their own funds from retained profits and in the case of those businessmen who finance their concern from their own private resources free of interest. The case for considering this 'imputed' interest as a cost is that the proprietors of a privately-owned business will not provide it with finance indefinitely if they do not obtain a yield on their funds at least equal to what they could earn by lending them to borrowers with no risk of default, for example to the government. In the same way investors will not take up variable-dividend shares issued by companies unless they expect to earn a rate of interest higher than that provided by fixed-interest government securities.

These two costs, which will not appear as such in the accounts of a business the manager-owner of which does not draw a salary and which does not raise money on fixed-interest terms, represent the cost of unpaid managerial services and the cost of capital employed in the business. Thirdly, since the businessman risks losing the funds he has sunk into his concern he will not generally remain indefinitely in a line of business that does not yield some compensation for this risk over and above the rate of interest already mentioned. In the case of a company the capital of which is provided by shareholders who take no direct part in its operations the word 'businessman' is too vague; it is the shareholders who look to some minimum compensation for bearing risk. In practice some estimate can be made of unpaid managerial services and the opportunity cost of capital, but it is not easy to place a figure on the cost represented by the minimum return for risk-bearing that must be paid for funds to be retained in a particular line of business indefinitely or for new funds to be obtained to finance expansion. However, the necessity for such a minimum return for risk-bearing, sometimes described as a long-run 'normal' rate of profit, means that in a private-enterprise system new firms will not enter a line of business unless it is earned, and eventually existing firms in the industry will leave it.

These three 'unrecorded costs' must be covered by the prices of a firm's products in the long run if its owners seek the maximum return for their services and their funds. Some businesses which appear to yield a satisfactory return to their owners may therefore be regarded as unprofitable by the economist. It is not uncommon, for example, to find retail shops and other small concerns which yield no more than a return equal to the market value of the managerial services of their owner, providing no return on capital and no reimbursement for risk. These firms continue in existence either because of sheer inertia, the lack of knowledge on the part of their owners, or because the latter obtain sufficient satisfaction from business life itself.

State-owned corporations are not operated as a rule so as to earn a return for risk. They are usually enjoined by statute to cover their costs, including recorded interest charges, but beyond this the prices of the goods and services they produce need not be calculated so as to provide any compensation for the risk that the use of their resources in the industry concerned may prove to be uneconomic, and even the question of interest on the retained profits used inside the corporation may be disregarded.

## INTEREST, PROFIT AND INVESTMENT

Interest is the payment for the use of borrowed money. In the simplest case a loan of £100 in perpetuity on which the borrower has to pay £5 every year yields a rate of interest of 5 per cent per annum. The profit earned on the funds employed in a business —indeed the income from any form of property—can also be expressed as an annual percentage rate of return. Suppose a business purchases a machine for £1,000 and uses it for 10 years, after which its scrap value is negligible. If the use of the machine recovers its capital cost and adds £100 to the firm's net profits every year, after taking into account all other related costs incurred in using the machine, then the funds used to purchase the machine will have earned a rate of profit of 10 per cent per annum. If in addition the scrap value of the machine at the end of 10 years were, say, £100, this will have represented a further return equal to approximately 1 per cent per annum.

This is a highly simplified example of the concept of the rate of return. Most investment projects involve a stream of outlays lasting several years and yield a stream of receipts over a period. Neither expenditure nor receipts are likely to occur evenly over time. Businesses may therefore have their own methods of calculating a rate of return expected from an investment project in order to deal with these complications. The only method that takes into account all such problems, especially that of the shape of the time-stream of outlays and receipts, is that of 'discounting', that is finding by means of compound-interest calculations the 'present value' of a future stream of payments or receipts. The rate of return on a project is that rate of interest which, if used to discount its future receipts, leads to a present value equal to the present value of the future stream of the costs of the project. This principle will be familiar to those readers acquainted with compound interest, and it is not intended to enlarge on the question here. It must be observed, however, that in practice the great majority of businesses use much cruder methods of calculation.

A business that seeks to earn a profit will not raise money for capital investment projects that are not expected to yield a net return sufficient to meet the interest charge on the funds concerned, and its owners will generally seek a rate of return higher than this by some margin sufficient to compensate them for the risk of loss. Even if adequate funds are available in the business from past profits it is to the advantage of its owners if to the use of these funds is attached a nominal rate of interest—one of our three unrecorded costs—that is set at least equal to the rate obtainable on loans to risk-free borrowers. However, the rate of interest payable by different concerns on funds raised in the capital market will reflect not only the general level of interest rates, of which that obtainable on default-free government bonds is the most important constituent, but also their own credit status as assessed by investors. A more rigorous test, therefore, is to set this unrecorded cost at a level equal to the rate of interest that would be obtained by lending retained business earnings to concerns of a similar credit status.

In the private-enterprise sector of the economy, which capital projects are undertaken will depend on the relevant cost of finance or rate of interest on the one hand and expected rates of profit on the other. The higher the rate of profit expected, the higher will be the rate of interest that a business will be prepared to pay for finance, so that in a competitive capital market there will be a tendency for finance to be attracted towards those projects that promise the highest rates of return. The total volume of capital formation will also be affected, for given the rate of interest, the higher are the rates of profit expected over the whole range of possible projects the greater will be the volume of capital investment ranged beyond the marginal project, that is the one that is just worth undertaking.

The force of business expectations regarding the profitability of different capital investment projects works in two directions. The higher the expected rate of profit, the higher is the cost of finance that is worth bearing. Secondly, the more eager are businessmen to purchase individual items of equipment, the more ready will they be to bid up their price, so that in a competitive economy capital goods as well as finance are directed into those uses in which their productivity is expected by businessmen to be highest. If the demand for machine tools by, say, the vehicle trades becomes so intense as to cause a rise in their price, the result is to reduce the rate of profit obtainable from their purchase by other industries, for the cost of capital equipment, in the form of depreciation, is one to be deducted in calculating profit.

## FIXED AND VARIABLE COSTS

'Fixed' or 'overhead' costs are those which do not vary with a change in a firm's output. Interest on long-term debt, the rent of premises essential to the survival of a business, depreciation on buildings and plant owned by a firm will remain constant in the short-run whether output is raised or lowered, and so may the salaries of essential administrative, clerical and maintenance staff, particularly the salaries of the firm's management. Fixed costs reflect the concept of *indivisibility*; namely, that in most production processes some factors of production have to be present in certain minimum quantities for production to be possible at all but do not have to be increased in quantity for certain ranges of output. Fixed costs reflect the presence of a 'fixed' factor of production.

In the long run, of course, capital equipment wears out and need not be replaced if the output of the firm is forced to contract, so that which costs are 'fixed' depends on the length of time under review. The 'short run', in regard to business production problems, is usually defined as that period which is not long enough for major increases in capacity to be undertaken. In the short run, then, certain costs are fixed whether output rises or falls.

'Variable', 'prime' or 'direct' costs are those that vary with the size of the firm's output in the short run. Purchases of raw materials and components, the wages of operatives, fuel and transport charges usually come within this category. It is true that even in the short run the distinction between fixed and variable costs is not always clear-cut, for some costs may not be altered for a 2 per cent change in output but would be varied if output were to rise or fall by 10 per cent. Some items of equipment will wear out more quickly if worked harder, whereas other parts of the same equipment may endure for much longer. Nevertheless, the division of costs intò variable and fixed elements is a useful one for many purposes.

On the relative importance of fixed and variable costs will depend the effect on total profits of fluctuations in sales and output. Should sales decline, a firm whose costs are largely variable will be able to reduce its current outlay by more than a firm with a larger weight of fixed costs; it will therefore experience a smaller reduction in profits. On the other hand, should sales increase, the firm with the larger proportion of fixed costs will experience the greater expansion in profits. Differences in the 'gearing' of costs to output help to explain why some industries and firms suffer from relatively violent variations in profits even though the degree of fluctuation in their sales and output may be no greater than average. Industries which have a relatively large proportion of fixed costs in the short run, generally in the form of heavy capital charges, include shipping, railway transport, flour-milling, electricity generation and supply, and branches of the steel and chemical trades. But within all industries firms may possess different degrees of flexibility. A firm that uses subcontractors, for example, reduces the burden of overheads and passes to them some of the losses and gains of fluctuations in sales, at the expense of some loss of control; and a manufacturing firm may be relieved of the fixed costs of marketing by the use of wholesalers. A plant that is highly mechanized usually has a heavier burden of fixed charges than one that uses less capital and more labour; but in some industries, such as building and the boot and shoe trade, machinery can be hired. A firm which has several plants can close down the least efficient if sales fall and so may have smaller fixed costs than another of the same size operating with one gigantic plant.

The level of output at which fixed and variable costs together are just covered is a plant's 'break-even' point; below this, assuming the firm's prices do not change, losses will be incurred, but profits increase as output exceeds this level. A highly mechanized plant may be capable of producing at a low cost per unit at the level of output for which it was designed, but unless the normal level of output foreseen by businessmen through good years and bad is expected to exceed the break-even point by a sufficient margin it will not be worth installing. Thus the expected size of a firm's sales will help to determine whether methods of production involving high fixed charges are worth adopting.

### OUTPUT AND AVERAGE COST IN THE SHORT RUN

Given that a firm has a certain level of plant and equipment and a certain state of technical knowledge, what is likely to be the reaction of average cost per unit of production to changes in its output, if the prices it pays for the factors of production it employs remain unchanged? From zero output up to a certain point average costs are likely to fall as output increases, owing to the phenomenon of indivisibility; if certain costs remain fixed in total then fixed costs *per unit of output* must decline as output is increased. This is sufficient to cause a fall in average cost, including variable costs, until that level of output at which variable costs per unit of output rise sufficiently to offset the fall in fixed costs per unit of output.

Variable costs per unit of output, with a given plant and technical 'know-how', rise sooner or later as a result of the operation of *diminishing returns*. This principle states that if the *proportion* of any factor of production used in combination with other factors is increased beyond a certain stage the addition to total output resulting from the input of further units of the variable factor will eventually decline. The principle holds good if two conditions are satisfied: namely, that during the process there is no improvement in the state of technical knowledge and skills and that there are no 'economies of scale'. The second of these provisos is the subject of a subsequent section, but the former is easy to appreciate. The introduction of improved methods and the development of operative skill can lead to an increase in the output obtainable from an unchanged quantity of resources, so that the rate of increase in output need not fall off as the quantity of variable factors of production used rises in relation to the fixed factors.

The principle of diminishing returns is of general application and is not confined to business concerns. If the number of identically equipped men working an acre of agricultural land, for example, is increased, eventually their total output will not rise as fast as the number of men per acre. That is to say the average product per man will decline when the area worked by each man falls beyond a certain size. That agriculture affords a simple illustration of the possible application of the principle led economists like John Stuart Mill and Malthus over a century ago to expect the rapid increase in population then under way to cause a fall in the output of food per man to the point of near-starvation. Their gloomy prognosis helped to earn economics the title of 'dismal science', but it proved to be incorrect because it failed to foresee the increase in the use of capital per man in agriculture as in industry, in the form of harvesting equipment, tractors, and drainage, for example, as well as the improvement in agricultural skills and the opening up of overseas sources of supply by new forms of transport. In several countries of Asia and Africa, on the other hand, the operation of diminishing returns in agriculture is more evident, for the growth of population still threatens to outrun the supply of capital and the improvement in techniques.

To return to our firm with its given level of plant and equipment used in relation with variable quantities of other factors of production, it is possible to identify several causes of diminishing returns and the consequent rise in average cost beyond a certain level of output.

Hours of work cannot be extended without eventually causing fatigue, and an increase in the number of employees beyond a certain point will crowd the factory or shop floor, make supervision and control more difficult, and lead to waste. Maintenance costs rise if machines are used beyond a certain intensity. At just what level of output average costs will tend to rise will depend entirely on the individual characteristics of the firm. Some businesses may be able to defer this stage by multi-shift working and by more flexible control; others may be so geared to a particular level of output that a comparatively small increase throws them off balance.

Enquiries into the behaviour of costs in manufacturing show that in some industries average cost per unit, with a given plant and level of knowledge, will first fall and then remain more or less constant over a fairly wide range of output until the operation of diminishing returns becomes evident and average cost rises. Reliable evidence as to the exact behaviour of costs is not plentiful, but many economists believe that a flat-bottomed U-shaped curve will be followed by average cost as output increases with a given plant. Eventually average cost rises sharply as the capacity of the plant is strained to its limit, but the 'normal' level of operation of many plants is believed to be in the area of constant costs per unit.

Variable and thus average cost may rise with output for reasons other than the operation of diminishing returns, as strictly defined. The *quality* of the factors of production used may deteriorate as output increases. It may be necessary to recruit labour that in normal times would be rejected as unsuitable and to dispense with a full period of training in order to meet a sudden increase in orders. Most firms have several plants or items of equipment differing in efficiency, and the least efficient will generally be those unused at low levels of output, so that the commissioning of inferior equipment to meet peak demand will add to cost per unit of output.

Another possible cause of a rise in cost is an increase in the *prices* of the factors of production used: wages, material costs, interest charges, etc. This may be the result of the rise in the demand for them by the firms that are increasing their output. An increase in the demand for factors of production by any one firm in isolation will not, of course, have any appreciable effect on the prices of the factors it uses unless it is large in relation to the size of the total market for them, but an increase in demand by a whole industry that is expanding its output will naturally have a more marked effect. The actual course followed by the costs of any one firm will therefore be influenced by the actions of others.

### COSTS AND OUTPUT IN THE LONG RUN

In the long run, in which existing plant and organization can be replaced or enlarged, a firm's cost structure is likely to alter even if factor prices and the state of its technical knowledge remain constant. A firm will usually be able to replace its plant at some point of time by another perhaps of a similar capacity but capable of producing at a lower average cost per unit at a normal level of output. At any moment of time the plant in use by different firms in an industry may differ in efficiency; some concerns will be using old or inferior equipment while others will possess modern plant that enables them to produce at lower unit cost and so earns them a larger margin of profit per unit of output.

Whether it is worth replacing an existing machine by another of similar capacity but capable of producing at lower unit cost depends on the net return expected from each course of action. Early replacement will not be worth while if the interest and capital charges for depreciation and obsolescence on the net price of the new equipment (that is after deducting the second-hand or scrap value of the old) when added to the average variable cost per unit of output expected to be incurred in using the new plant are not sufficiently less than the average variable cost per unit alone incurred in the use of the old to justify the allocation of scarce funds to replacement. In this comparison the fixed costs incurred in the use of the old plant are accounted for by deducting from the price of the new equipment the second-hand or scrap value of the old, for it is the interest on this that is forgone by continuing to use the old plant; past capital charges are irrelevant. As existing plant grows older it eventually becomes worth replacing if only because variable costs usually rise through higher maintenance charges.

Thus in the long run average cost can be reduced by the replacement of existing plant by more efficient equipment, retaining the same overall scale of output. But average cost may be reduced by virtue of expansion of the size of the firm itself, through the operation of economies of scale and other factors.

## ECONOMIES OF SCALE

Economies of scale are said to result when average cost per unit falls as output is raised by means of an increase in the input of all the factors of production used, the proportion of one factor to another remaining unchanged. Large plants and large firms are usually those using a higher ratio of capital to labour than smaller ones, so that in practice the term is broadened to include economies obtainable when the size of plant or firm is increased, whether or not this involves a change in the composition of the resources used.

It is useful to distinguish between the possible economies of scale of the large *plant* and those of the large *firm*, which usually has several plants, none of which may be larger than those operated by its smaller rivals. A large plant may be able to produce a given article, or a given combination of articles, at relatively low cost because of the physical properties of equipment. A simple example, which applies to storage tanks, boilers, furnaces and ships, is the relation between cubic capacity and surface dimensions. Double the dimensions of a box and its cubic capacity is increased to eight times the original, but the materials required for its construction amount to only four times as much. The friction experienced by a ship is related to its surface area, whereas its payload is closely linked to its overall cubic capacity. The loss of heat suffered by a boiler is proportionate to the square of its dimensions, whereas its volume varies with their cube.

A second advantage of large-scale operations may be obtained through the principle of multiples, which is based on the fact that different units of equipment to be used together may have different optimum sizes, that is may operate at lowest average cost at levels of output which differ from one another. If two machines are used in sequence, one handling 20 units an hour and the other 10, two of the latter will have to be installed if the former is to be run to capacity. The most efficient scale, it will be seen, is represented by the lowest common multiple of the individual capacities used in combination. If the two machines were to possess capacities of 20 and 8 units an hour respectively, the lowest multiple that would keep all fully occupied would be two of the former (handling 40 units an hour) and five of the latter type (also handling 40 units an hour).

Thirdly, the larger the plant the more economical is it to employ full-time specialists. This is one aspect of the principle of indivisibility. Machines are examples of the specialized use of resources and cannot as a rule be constructed for economical use below a certain minimum size, and in a similar fashion many forms of specialist labour cannot be obtained on a part-time basis. It is economical to employ highly-skilled and highly-paid specialist technicians only if the scale of output justifies the expense.

Fourthly, economies can often be secured by standardization of processes and products, but standardization itself tends to warrant a larger plant by increasing the most economical size of individual departments, machines or assembly lines, for standardization reduces the problems of supervision and control.

If the multi-plant firm rather than the single-plant is considered, the principles of multiples and of specialization may be found to be equally applicable. Economies may be secured for the firm as a whole by operating a number of manufacturing plants, for example, if the optimum size of marketing, buying or administrative organization is relatively large. It is only the large firm that can profitably employ a full battery of specialists, especially those engaged in research, that modern technology requires in many industries. But some industries may be able to provide research facilities, at any rate, for its individual members through the medium of a common research organization financed by all.

The large firm, and to some extent the large plant, can also use its size to exploit the economies of pooled reserves, whether they are reserves of materials, labour or finance. These economies are derived from the probability that the greater the number of items subject to random fluctuations from a 'normal' magnitude the more likely are the deviations to cancel out, to leave the average value for them all nearer to the normal or expected value. Thus the ratio of reserve to total usage falls as the scale of operations increases, so that the cost of reserve per unit of output falls.

### DISECONOMIES OF SCALE

Economies of scale derived from increasing size of plant may not extend indefinitely. Technical factors may limit the size of equipment—the size of a machine may be restricted by inadequate foundations and that of a ship by dock or canal facilities. Material stresses may be more difficult to deal with, and breakdowns and other interruptions relatively costly. But in practice it is extremely difficult to discover from statistical research whether economies of scale give way to diseconomies when a plant reaches a certain size, if only because the large firms on which such studies must be based usually operate several plants rather than one large one. For this there are two main reasons. One is that transport and other distributive costs per unit of sales will be higher if a geographically dispersed market is served by one giant plant rather than a number of similarly dispersed plants, so that transport costs may offset the saving in manufacturing costs possible from the large plant. The other reason is that large firms usually take advantage of their size to produce a variety of products, which usually requires a number of plants.

Economists have therefore tended to place more emphasis on the eventual development of diseconomies of scale in relation to the growth of the firm as a whole, diseconomies arising ultimately from the difficulty of administration and control. The running of a large concern may necessitate the devotion of too great a part of its management's time to supervision of administrative detail rather than to the formulation of policy. The function of decision-taking is not one that is easily shared; ultimately the responsibility for reaching decisions in case of disagreement has to be borne by one person, and the area of activity which any one person can control satisfactorily is limited.

It does not necessarily follow, however, that, as between two firms in the same industry, the larger will always tend to experience greater difficulties of administration and control. The large firm can employ specialists to take some of the weight of supervision, research, preliminary appreciation and even co-ordination from the shoulders of its senior management. If a firm is below a certain size the members of its management may have to carry individually too many tasks that in a large concern can be delegated to specialists. The large firm may be able to reduce its administrative problems, even to the extent of gaining over the small one in this respect, by the use of computing and other equipment that speeds up the collection and assimilation of information on which successful administration may depend. Improvements in the techniques of administration and industrial relations tend continually to raise the level of operations at which administrative diseconomies of scale become significant enough to offset the operating advantages of large-scale output. The industries where large-scale operations are easily handled are those producing a small range of standardized products or involving standard processes, or in which administration takes the form of framing rules the application of which can be left to junior officers. Industries in which size brings difficult problems of control are those in which changes in market conditions, due for example to changes in fashion, are frequent and call for decisions at the highest level of management. Where personal contact with the customer is important, or where high-quality goods are made to the specification of customers, conditions also favour the small firm. However, a number of different activities may be brought together by means of the operation of separately administered companies subject only in regard to broad policy to the decision of a controlling company. Some of the advantages of scale, such as pooled reserves and the services of specialists, may thus be obtained without the diseconomies of complex administration.

In all industries, the large concern may be able to recruit management of a higher quality, not so much because of the glamour generated by successful advertising and public relations, but because the large firm necessarily offers a wider range of opportunities and usually provides better training facilities; it may also be less prone to nepotism. But this is not to deny that small concerns often possess a unique spirit based on the inspiration and pride of those who lead them.

## EXTERNAL ECONOMIES OF SCALE

A distinction can be drawn between 'internal' and 'external' economies of scale. The former are those derived by a firm from an increase in the scale of its own operations. External economies are those enjoyed by a firm as a result of an increase in the scale of output of *other* firms. External economies arise from the possibility of economies of scale in the operation of some service or industry common to a number of firms. The growth of an industry may render economical the development of specialized producers to replace at lower cost operations previously performed on a smaller scale by each firm. Thus the growth of the motor industry made it possible for components to be manufactured in bulk by specialist firms, and similar developments can be seen in other trades. Economies of scale may even be external to any single industry—the development of a number of industries in a particular area may lower the cost per unit of indivisible public services, fuel and power or transport facilities to them all, and may reduce labour training costs by creating a pool of skilled labour on which all can draw.

The important distinction between internal and external economies is that the former come within the range of influence of any one concern whereas the latter do not, except in the case of the concern whose activity is on a scale sufficient to affect the economic organization of the area in which it operates. A firm's capital investment programme will have regard to its internal economies, but not, as a rule, to possible external economies, because external economies accruing to any individual concern by virtue of its own operations alone are not generally likely to be significant. That external economies may be secured by a whole industry or a whole area through the expansion of a sufficient number of concerns is one of the factors that may justify government action taken to accelerate industrial development or to concentrate it geographically. Industry-wide action taken through the medium of trade associations and other bodies may secure similar benefits.

### DIVERSIFICATION AND INTEGRATION

Despite the advantages, by way of low unit costs of production, to be derived from specialization and standardization, many firms produce a variety of goods that may even transcend any one industrial classification. In most cases the narrowness of the market for any one article is the cause, but in others part of the economy of specialization is deliberately sacrificed for other gains. One important cause of diversification in general is the desire to reduce the risk of a severe collapse in profits that specialization may involve. In an industry where market demand is subject to rapid technical obsolescence or to changes in fashion, or to a wide variety of tastes, stimulated perhaps by competitive advertising, the risks attached to specialization may be great, especially if at the same time the proportion of fixed costs is high. A reduction in the degree of risk is not only desirable for its own sake but may also go some way as far as costs are concerned to offset the sacrifice of economy, for the lower the risk the lower will be the cost of obtaining finance and, perhaps, skilled labour and management.

The forms taken by diversification, which appears to have become more common in the past twenty years, may be influenced by the conditions of marketing or of supply or by the technical processes of industry. Some forms of diversification are described as 'integration', which may be horizontal or vertical. Horizontal integration refers to the production of different articles at the same stage of production; vertical integration occurs when a concern performs consecutive processes.

Horizontal integration may occur because of the existence of complementary or joint demand, such as record-players and records, or because of other marketing factors that render it advantageous for a supplier to offer his customers a 'full line'. Other forms of horizontal integration may be based on the importance of common resources, a common material, including the case of by-products, or common services, as in the case of research facilities. The exploitation of an established reputation or trade-mark to extend the range of output also falls in this category. Diversification of output may be the only method of reaping the economies of scale attached to any one stage of operation, to large-scale buying, selling or research, if markets for the individual goods or services produced are narrow. Diversification may enable a firm to offset seasonal fluctuations.

Some degree of vertical integration is present in most concerns. A firm may generate its own power, make its own tools and components, and may sell to final consumers by acting as its own 'middleman'. But most firms can choose the degree of vertical integration involved. In some industries technical factors make it advantageous to house consecutive processes in one plant, as in the steel industry, where the metal can be passed from one finishing stage to another without reheating. In others, such as cotton and wool textiles, the advantages of vertical integration are thought to lie in closer control over quality and in certainty of supply. Occasionally vertical integration occurs because a businessman believes that he can produce some component at a lower cost than the price at which he can buy it from elsewhere, because his supplier occupies a monopolistic position that is

E

reflected in an unduly high price; but the converse has also been true, in that firms may seek control over sources of supply in order to establish or consolidate their monopoly of the finished product.

What has been said here does not imply that integration is always advantageous; ambition may lead businessmen to give up too readily the benefits of specialization and to encumber themselves with activities which are difficult to assimilate within a single span of control, and examples are not lacking in which companies have finally relinquished what proved to be costly attempts at diversification. Some forms of vertical integration may actually increase risk by saddling a company with heavy fixed charges that rivals may be content to leave to their suppliers.

### SMALL AND LARGE FIRMS—A SUMMARY

At any moment of time some firms are growing and others contracting; the pattern of relative size does not remain constant in a competitive industry. In some industries large firms have an advantage because of the economies of scale attached to the large plant; but in those where economies of scale are unimportant once a certain size of plant is passed, the medium-sized firm is able to compete effectively with its larger rival, which is larger by virtue of its possession of a number of plants. Where pooled reserves are important, or where buying and selling organizations provide economies of scale, or where expensive research is necessary, the very large firm is better placed. Inquiries into a number of American industries show that the medium-sized concern often has costs as low as or even lower than the very largest firms; but the latter may offset the disadvantages incurred in controlling a very large and diversified concern by sheer bargaining power or by their ability to spend enough on advertising or on buying up sales outlets so as to hold their share of the market. Most industries consist of firms of varying size, the smallest concerns often being specialist producers of high-quality articles or the satellite suppliers of components to the large producers or assemblers. Small firms thrive in a geographically dispersed market for products whose transport costs are high and in markets subject to great variety and frequent changes of demand. Small firms also benefit in some industries by external economies of scale; the roads used by road-hauliers do not have to be owned by them, whereas the cost of the railway track is borne by the railways. In some industries marketing is provided on an industry-wide basis by large specialist concerns, so that even very small firms have access to a wide market.

Quality of management may work in either direction. Skilled management may enable the small firm to make up for the absence of economies of scale, especially in those industries where quality of design or flexibility of planning is important; on the other hand, a management that is especially skilled in large-scale administration may surmount the obstacles to growth that large-scale organization may otherwise present. Conversely, unskilled management may destroy the economies of large-scale output in any firm.

Detailed information on the composition of British industry is provided by the returns of the Census of Production. Those published for the post-war period, however, relate chiefly to 'establishments' or plants, and for the pattern of employment and production classified by firms we have still to rely on the Census for 1935. In the industries covered by the 1935 Census, mainly the manufacturing trades, building and contracting, mining, quarrying and public utilities, the range of size of firm was as shown in Table 1.

TABLE 1. *1935 Census of Production—Size of Firms*

| Number of employees per firm | Number of firms | Total number of employees | Percentage of total employment in industries covered |
|---|---|---|---|
| 1–10 | 204,151 | 826,700 | 10·3 |
| 11–49 | 31,756 | 795,809 | 9·9 |
| 50–99 | 9,459 | 656,237 | 8·2 |
| 100–499 | 9,722 | 1,993,241 | 24·8 |
| 500–999 | 1,270 | 878,764 | 11·0 |
| 1000–4999 | 909 | 1,759,928 | 21·9 |
| 5000 and over | 101 | 1,119,078 | 13·9 |
| Total | 257,368 | 8,029,757 | 100·0 |

The size of firms varies remarkably in all industries. But whereas very small firms abound in number, they provide a relatively small share of total output and employment. In 1935 the 1,000 or so firms with more than 1,000 employees, on the other hand, represented only 4 per cent of the total number of firms but included 36 per cent of all employees in the trades covered by the Census.

Information for the post-war period is fragmentary, but the same broad picture emerges. The Census for 1951 shows that, in the industries examined, firms with no more than ten employees numbered 144,124 but accounted for less than 6 per cent of total employment. We do know that at the end of 1956 there were 270,000 companies with a share capital but that the handful of giant companies earned a relatively large share of total profits. The hundred largest companies in manufacturing and distribution, for example, appear to earn rather more than one-third of the total income received by all companies in this sector, judging by estimates made by the National Institute of Economic and Social Research for 1954–5.* Many of these large companies operate in several industries, but those in which they predominate include chemicals, steel, motors and aircraft, heavy electrical engineering, tobacco, paper, shipping, and synthetic fibres. Industries where the representative size of firm is relatively small, on the other hand, include clothing, building and contracting, printing, and baking. In banking and insurance, the advantages of pooled reserves and the ease of large-scale administration make for large concerns; in distribution the large multiple store benefits from the economies of standardization, large-scale production and purchasing, while the department store trades on the advantage of offering a 'full-line' to its customers. The cost of transport that would have to be borne by shoppers if there were fewer shops helps to explain the survival of the small retailer.

The general degree of concentration is greater than would appear from the size distribution of firms, owing to the fact that most large companies have subsidiaries or interests in other concerns, perhaps in several industries. A wide variation is to be found in the size of establishment or plant in industry. Table 2 records the results of the 1951 Census of Production as far as manufacturing industry is concerned.

The mean size of plant in 1951 employed 126 persons, but one-half of the total number employed in manufacturing worked in plants employing roughly 350 persons or more. The mean size

* 'A Classified List of Large Companies Engaged in British Industry.' The National Institute of Economic and Social Research. London, 1955.

of plant employing more than 10 persons varied from 261 in metal manufacturing and 215 in vehicles and aircraft to 56 in clothing; there is obviously a connexion between the size of the average plant and that of the average firm in each industry. But because large firms own several plants the variation in size of plant, although wide, is not as great as that in size of firm.

TABLE 2. *Size of Establishments in Manufacturing, 1951*

| Number employed per establishment | Number of establishments | Total number employed | Percentage of total employment in manufacturing |
|---|---|---|---|
| 1–10 | 65,890* | 317,431 | 4·2 |
| 11–24 | 16,671 | 291,064 | 3·8 |
| 25–49 | 15,457 | 541,409 | 7·2 |
| 50–99 | 10,792 | 757,386 | 10·0 |
| 100–499 | 11,781 | 2,462,055 | 32·4 |
| 500–999 | 1,447 | 988,121 | 13·0 |
| 1000–4999 | 924 | 1,702,801 | 22·4 |
| 5000 and over | 60 | 535,251 | 7·0 |
| Total | 123,022 | 7,595,518 | 100·0 |

\* Number of firms.

This chapter has been concerned with the relationship between business output and costs. But the extent of the market and the degree of business competition may be even more potent forces determining the scale of output of different firms. The nature of markets and of competition, however, are closely related matters that influence many aspects of business operations and so call for further consideration in the following chapter.

# CHAPTER 5

# COMPETITION AND BUSINESS BEHAVIOUR

The term 'market' embraces the complex of relationships between buyers and sellers, perhaps the most important of which is the nature of the competition operative on each side. The effect of competition on market behaviour depends on the impact of a number of factors, which apply with different degrees of strength to different markets. In this chapter they are introduced so as to throw light on business operations, prices and profits, but the analysis can be adapted without difficulty to markets in factors of production.

## SUBSTITUTION BETWEEN PRODUCTS

The possibility of substitution by other products determines the extent to which the term 'industry' has any precise economic significance beyond referring to the fact that groups of firms are engaged in the production of similar goods or services, or use similar materials, or employ similar processes. What is more important in considering the market for any product is the extent to which it can be invaded by other goods that buyers regard as satisfactory substitutes at certain levels of relative prices. If substitution between the products of one industry and another is possible, the ability of firms in either to raise prices above the point at which the substitute becomes more acceptable to buyers is correspondingly restricted. Examples of the innumerable cases where, at certain relative prices and for certain uses, inter-product competition may be keen include: synthetic and natural fibres; copper and aluminium cable; cement, steel and timber as building materials; road and rail transport; natural and synthetic rubber; butter and margarine; carpets and other floor coverings.

## UNIFORMITY OF PRODUCT WITHIN AN INDUSTRY

Within any single industry the nature of the competition between the firms of which it is composed will depend to a considerable extent on whether their products are sufficiently uniform to render buyers indifferent as between the product of one firm and another if the prices charged are identical. In the case of certain goods, like copper and wheat, grading is possible, so that within each grade the product of one concern is indistinguishable from that of another. In this case freedom of buyers to deal with whom they please in a market in which all prices are known must tend to produce a situation in which all producers of the same grade will receive the same price, transport costs apart. If any one seller attempts to charge more than the ruling price his sales fall to nothing if buyers can turn to other sellers offering an identical product.

Many raw materials and agricultural products are to be found within this category. But several intermediate processed materials, most forms of capital equipment, and the majority of consumer goods do not. The products of different firms within most industries differ in design, style or quality in a way that makes objective grading difficult, so that the attitude of buyers to the goods of individual firms within the same industry must depend to some extent on subjective factors. This so-called 'product differentiation' may consist of basic differences in design arising from the conviction on the part of individual producers that their goods are superior, or from the operation of patent law, or it may arise from the desire of the businessman to carve out a secure market for his own product by creating in the mind of buyers the idea that his own goods are in some important fashion different from, and naturally superior to, those of his competitors.

Product differentiation in this last sense is most common in the case of consumer goods, especially those above the level of staple necessities. Whereas the makers of uniform products do not find it profitable to advertise except on an industry-wide basis, product differentiation is usually accompanied by competitive advertising and other forms of sales pressure aimed at capturing the enduring support of buyers. The subjective nature of this differentiation must be stressed in many cases, for the more obvious are the differences in the qualities possessed by the products of rival concerns the less need is there on the part of any of them to sharpen their indentity by advertising. Paradoxically, it is in the case of those goods which, if not uniform, have qualities whose virtues are not easily compared with those produced by other firms that competitive advertising is often most intense, supported by brand names and all the other paraphernalia aimed at securing the flanks of the individual concern's market. In other cases, individual firms may enjoy the goodwill of certain buyers merely because of the personality of their owners or employees, as in the case of retail shops, or because the services they have rendered in the past have in some way or other been highly appreciated by their customers.

Whatever the basis of differentiation, it presents a contrast with the industry in which buyers do not distinguish between the product of one concern and another, in that the prices charged by one firm can differ from those obtained by rival firms and may do so even though costs of production may be the same. Alternatively, prices, production costs and sales expenses per unit may all be different; and the individual concern that succeeds in 'capturing' its buyers can within limits raise its prices in isolation without suffering a complete collapse of sales.

## THE NUMBER OF FIRMS AND THE EXTENT OF COLLUSION

Given the degree of uniformity of product, the number of firms within an industry is particularly important in three respects. In the first place, where the number of firms is sufficiently large for each to be small in relation to the size of the total market, the action of any one will not affect the ruling price appreciably in the case of an industry selling a uniform product. If one farmer alone increases his output of wheat the market price of wheat is unlikely to fall as a result. Therefore the ruling price of wheat at any moment of time can be taken as given by every farmer, for no individual farmer can depress the market price by offering a larger quantity for sale or raise it by contracting his supply. If the number of producers of a uniform product is small, as in the case of primary aluminium, for example, each has to take into account the effect of his own action on the ruling market price, which is therefore to some extent under his control.

Where product differentiation exists, the effect of the action of any one firm in the industry on the constellation of prices will depend on just how distinct is the degree of differentiation in the minds of buyers and therefore on the extent to which buyers are prepared to substitute one producer's article for another. If differentiation is weak and the number of firms large the situation approaches that of a uniform product. If differentiation is marked, the individual firm has correspondingly more control over the price at which it can offer its goods.

Secondly, the number of firms in an industry determines the extent to which the action of any one is felt by its competitors. If one of a large number of firms in a particular industry increases its share of the market the corresponding loss is borne by many concerns, none of which may be affected seriously. The expanding firm does not have to consider the possibility that its advance will lead to powerful retaliation.

In an industry consisting of a small number of sellers, on the other hand, the policy of any one may have to be framed with the possibility of effective retaliation well in mind, so that price-cutting, for example, may seem a double-edged weapon. Of course, this begs the question of defining the industry and the market. There may be a large number of firms producing not dissimilar articles within a so-called industry, but two or three may be in very much closer competition than the others because of the pattern of product differentiation. On the other hand, competition between different producers of a uniform article may be broken up geographically by transport costs, the effect of distance being to create virtually separate markets each with its own price-level but within each of which exists a handful of mutually-sensitive concerns.

The third respect in which the number of firms within an industry may influence business behaviour concerns the practical possibility of collusion between them. The smaller the number of firms the easier is it for them to reach lasting agreement over such matters as the level of prices, the geographical division of markets, the terms on which materials are bought or goods supplied and the measures to be taken to keep out new competitors. When the number of firms is large the variety of business temperaments involved and the range of production costs at which different concerns can work profitably make agreement more difficult to reach, and collusion has to be formal; defection by the individual firm is harder to detect and also more tempting for being relatively slight in its effect on the rest of the industry and therefore less likely to bring retribution.

The situation in which the number of sellers is small is usually described in the technical language of economics as being one of *oligopoly*; that in which there is only one seller is that of *monopoly*.

The monopolist, by definition, has no rival sellers to contend with and can set whatever level of prices is most profitable, bearing in mind the elasticity of demand for his goods. But there are few cases of so-called monopoly where the threat of substitution by another product does not limit the extent to which this power can be exercised. Both types of market are the subject of further consideration.

### THE NUMBER OF BUYERS AND THE EXTENT OF COLLUSION

The effect on market behaviour of the number of buyers is the counterpart to that of the number of sellers. Where buyers are many and each small in relation to the market no individual buyer can influence the market price. Where buyers are few and individually large in relation to the total supply the action of each has a correspondingly greater effect on the ruling price. The situation in which there is only one buyer is that of *monopsony*; this is a rare case and usually implies that the buyer has a monopoly of his own product. A nationalized industry, however, may be a case in point; the British Transport Commission is almost the sole buyer of locomotives and rolling-stock in this country and therefore has some measure of control over the prices received by the suppliers of railway equipment, depending on the extent to which the latter can turn to overseas markets or to the production of other goods if the Transport Commission uses its bargaining power to depress profit margins unduly.

The number of buyers will also help to determine the extent to which they can agree on a common policy aimed at using their joint power to force sellers to accept lower prices than would prevail in the absence of collusion. In some industries dealers have been known to agree, for example, on the maximum prices they will offer on second-hand articles, especially those tendered in part exchange for new models, a device intended to prevent concealed price-cutting in the sale of new models. In other industries leading employers may reach some agreement on the terms to be offered to key personnel.

### FREEDOM OF DEALING

The degree of freedom of individual buyers and sellers to deal with whom they please may influence market behaviour in a number of ways. Individual buyers may be restricted in their ability to offer a high price for goods they urgently need or to take advantage of low prices offered by certain sellers; individual sellers may be prevented from offering low prices in order to expand their own sales. Restrictions on freedom of dealing may be intended to maintain quality by keeping out unqualified or inferior producers, as in the case of the professions, or may have the object simply of limiting competition in order to maintain prices and incomes.

### THE AWARENESS OF PRICES CHARGED

In some markets, such as the organized markets in certain commodities, the prices of most transactions are made known to all buyers and sellers; and the manufacturers of many widely-sold branded products attempt to enforce a publicly-known price for their goods. Awareness of the prices at which transactions occur is necessary if freedom of dealing is to lead to the development of a single market price for each type of good. In certain types of market, such as those in antique furniture, prices may be formed by secretly-conducted bargaining matches between individual buyers and sellers; no buyer or seller may be certain as to the most favourable price that can be obtained, and the same type of article may fetch different prices in different parts of the market.

Competition may also be blunted by the lack of complete awareness of comparative prices in another sense. Some goods and services are sold on complex terms, or may promise benefits that are complicated or uncertain, so that a comparison of prices is not easily made. Certain forms of life-assurance policy, for example, come within this category, which is partly a matter of product differentiation.

Paradoxically, however, secrecy of prices in the ordinary sense may be the means whereby agreements between buyers or sellers to limit competition, or statutory restrictions on prices, are broken. Even in the absence of complete secrecy, restrictions on competition may be evaded by disguised price-cutting, in the form of generous discounts on the purchase of large quantities or on cash settlement, or of 'trade-in' allowances and after-sales service. Conversely, buyers may succeed in obtaining larger quantities or ready delivery of scarce goods by offering to buy at fancy prices auxiliary equipment, fittings, spares or other associated goods.

## AIMING AT MAXIMUM PROFITS

In economics theoretical models of market behaviour are often constructed to examine the working of certain assumptions regarding market processes, assumptions that are chosen because of their apparent validity in practice or because they present a limiting case of the complexity experienced in the real world. One of the assumptions long used in economic theory is that businessmen employ the resources of their business so as to maximize their profits.

In the real world the formation of business policy is more complex, and not just by virtue of the fact that businessmen are human and may be as lazy as the rest of us or disinclined to pursue pecuniary gain to the limit at the expense of leisure and habit or some conception of the wider social interest. What is of particular interest in the study of business operations is that in certain market conditions the pursuit of maximum profits is not easily interpreted and that the development of corporate industry has itself led to the elevation of other motives in the determination of policy.

Contrast, for example, the industry making a uniform product and composed of a large number of firms with one in which there are only few firms and in which each values the goodwill of its customers. In the former the fact that customers do not distinguish between one firm and another means that no firm has anything to lose, through the sacrifice of goodwill, by charging the maximum price the market will bear in the short run. Secondly, no individual firm would gain by charging less than this price for fear that the spectacle of high profits might attract new firms into the industry at the expense of its profits in the more distant future, because its own action can have no appreciable effect on the ruling market price. Thirdly, no individual firm need consider the effect of its own actions on the policy of its rivals.

In the oligopolistic industry, in which the long-term goodwill of a firm's customers is important, on the other hand, experience suggests that businessmen will often charge prices below those that would maximize their profits in the short run. They will usually be more concerned with the fortunes of their concern in the long run and will be ready to sacrifice immediate profits for the sake of the loyalty of their customers. Goodwill may be important in industries consisting of a large number of firms, but it is likely to be a most potent consideration where there is only a handful of rival concerns. The goodwill of the government, which may threaten to impose price control in times of scarcity or to nationalize industries regarded as 'exploiting' their customers, is a similar consideration.

Secondly, in both oligopolistic industries and those dominated by monopoly, price policy may be conducted with one eye on the temptation presented by high prices and profits to other firms capable of invading the industry, so that prices may be pitched at a level at which entry into the industry by other powerful concerns is deterred.

Thirdly, and this is the aspect of market behaviour that is most difficult to express in clear theoretical terms, the policy of the individual firm in an oligopolistic industry has to take into account the reaction of its rivals, so that business strategy may take on some of the characteristics of opposing forces in games or in warfare, in which the aim of maximizing gains is no simple guide. Just as the use of thermonuclear weapons may cause the utter destruction of one side in a total war, so may total warfare between a handful of concerns threaten the complete destruction of the losers and, indeed, cause grievous damage even to the victor in the process, especially if, for the sake of ultimate victory, prices are driven down to very low levels in an industry in which fixed costs are heavy. The alternative of the cold war has its business analogy, in which there is no overt price competition, except in times of great stress, competition being relegated instead to the sphere of quality of product and of sales pressure.

Finally, the development of the joint-stock company, whose management are rarely large shareholders, has given prominence to motives other than maximum profits. Size of firm may be an even more influential standard of success than the level of profits, for the prestige of management and the range of power they exercise may reflect the scale of a firm's operations rather than its profitability; and there is some evidence to suggest that executive salaries are more closely linked to size of concern than to profits. As a result, firms may grow beyond the size most profitable to its owners. Because, beyond a certain point, the expansion of a firm *within* a particular industry may lead rival concerns to defend themselves by more vigorous competition or may result in the development of a monopoly position that is vulnerable to government action, 'empire-building' is more likely to extend the range of a firm's products than to enlarge its output of any one.

## THEORETICAL MODELS OF COMPETITION

The single term 'competition' is obviously an inadequate description of market relationships, in view of the differences in both the nature and the intensity of economic rivalry. In order to simplify the task of analysing the complexity of business life theoretical models of different types of market situation have been developed in economics, based on different postulates regarding the aspects of competition introduced above. It is not the object of this book, however, to explore the theories that have been constructed in this field. The remainder of this chapter merely introduces briefly some of the chief constructions used and their application to the complexity of business life. The main theoretical situations are:

Perfect or pure competition.
Imperfect or impure competition between many firms.
Oligopoly (and its counterpart on the side of buyers).
Monopoly (and its counterpart on the side of buyers).

## PERFECT COMPETITION

The postulates of perfect competition are: a uniform product; many sellers and buyers; no collusion between buyers or sellers; complete freedom of dealing and awareness of prices; sellers acting to maximize profits. Perfect competition is obviously a limiting case that is unusual in the real world; although approximations are to be found in the case of several raw materials—natural rubber and wool, for example—and primary foodstuffs, the organized commodity and currency markets, and in tramp shipping.

The essence of the model of perfect competition is the impersonal nature of the market. Buyers and sellers can individually take the ruling market price, of which there is only one, as given at any moment of time. For by hypothesis buyers are indifferent as between different sellers at a uniform price, and no single buyer or seller can influence the market price. The latter, at any moment of time, will be such as to equate supply with demand. That is, the ruling price will be such that the amount that buyers are prepared to take at that price will equal the amount sellers are willing to offer. This is the 'equilibrium' price; and the market is always in equilibrium, because, should the pressure of demand tend to exceed that of supply at any price, the latter will increase, stimulating supply and checking demand.

In the theory of perfect competition the market price moves according to changes in the pressures of demand and supply caused by alterations in tastes, in incomes, in the prices of competing products, in productive techniques and in the prices of the factors of production used. Corresponding to the concept of elasticity of demand is the elasticity of supply, that is the extent to which supply responds to a given change in price. If the pressure of demand increases, the degree to which prices and profit margins rise will be influenced by the elasticity of supply. If supply is elastic—if sellers are holding large stocks or if equipment is being used at below full capacity, for example—the tendency for prices to rise will bring forth a correspondingly large increase in supply, and so the rise in prices will be relatively smaller than in the case of inelastic supply. In the extreme case, in which supply is completely inelastic, the whole burden of adjustment is thrown on demand. If the latter increases, owing to a rise in buyers' incomes, for example, prices will rise by an amount sufficient to induce marginal buyers to curtail their purchases and so hold the value of total purchases in line with total supply.

In the same way the effect of a change in supply, due for example to a rise in costs, will depend on the elasticity of demand. If there are no substitutes and if the product occupies only a small part of the total expenditure of buyers, demand will be very inelastic, and the greater part of the rise in costs may be passed on in the form of higher prices with little change in total output and profits. If demand is elastic, on the other hand, less of a rise in costs can be passed on, so that output and supply will be decreased, at the expense of profits.

The distinction is usually made between short-run and long-run effects of changes in demand and supply. In the short run the number of firms in the industry and their capacity are fixed; if output is increased, with a given state of technique and with given factor prices, average costs per unit will rise unless there is a wide range of output over which costs per unit remain constant. In the longer run, firms can expand their capacity and economies of scale may be obtained, so that the rise in prices caused by an increase in demand may ultimately be retraced. If there are no obstacles to the entry into the industry of new firms attracted by high profits, a rise in profit margins due to an increase in demand will eventually stimulate supply by leading to an increase in the number of firms as well, thus destroying part of the rise in the profits of existing firms. Similarly, in the long run a fall in prices and profits due to a reduction in demand will be cushioned as marginal firms leave the industry. As long as the ruling price, which to the individual firm appears to be fixed by impersonal forces, is above average cost per unit of output, the firm will be making profits; the more efficient firms, with lower costs, will be earning larger profit margins and will have relatively large outputs.

This analysis gives a tolerably accurate picture of certain industries, if relatively few in number. But even in these cases reality may differ fundamentally from the model in the existence of one very large buyer or seller, usually a government agency acting to influence prices. Apart from this, some of the features of this analysis are apparent, particularly in the way in which frequent and sharp movements in prices and profits are characteristic of these industries. Demand is in some cases rather inelastic; in others, such as in agriculture, output may be inelastic in the short run. The size of stocks is therefore often the crucial factor. Price movements may be exaggerated or reduced by the effect of speculation. Longer-term fluctuations are often the result of the fact that each producer knows that his own action has no effect on the ruling price and so disregards the possibility that other producers may take similar steps to expand output in response to a high price. As a result a high price may cause such a large increase in production after the time needed to bring new capacity to fruition that a fall in price of unexpected magnitude eventually occurs, perhaps leading producers to curtail output unduly, and so on.

## IMPERFECT COMPETITION BETWEEN MANY FIRMS

Theories of market behaviour constructed to deal with the situation in which there are many buyers and sellers but in which there is no uniform product are much less clear-cut. In these conditions sellers have some control over their own prices, for the existence of product differentiation means that sellers may receive prices for their own goods that differ from those of competitors. The operation of advertising and other forms of sales pressure introduces another complication, for it implies that the demand for any one producer's wares is not independent of his total costs. In this situation the individual seller can raise his prices within some limits without losing the whole of his sales; similarly, if he lowers his prices a little he will gain custom, but he will not, as in the model of perfect competition, tempt all buyers to desert his rivals completely if their prices remain unchanged. Thus, with a given level of sales expenditure, the individual seller faces a situation in which, if other producers do not change their own prices, rather more can be sold at a lower price than a higher one. In the theory of perfect competition the choice, to put it crudely, is that between all or nothing.

Theoretical constructions still retain the idea of a market equilibrium between supply and demand, but it is not, unlike the theory of perfect competition, maintained through the regulating action of prices alone. Instead equilibrium is reached through the combined variation of product design and sales expenditure as well as of prices. The postulate that producers act so as to maximize their profits leads to the tautology that this aim will be achieved by means of an optimum combination of price, product design and sales expenditure, a combination that will vary for individual producers.

In the real world there are many industries in which a large number of firms sell a differentiated product, but market behaviour varies widely. Where differentiation is weak, similarities are to be found with the theory of perfect competition; where differentiation is sharp, the so-called industry is more akin to a number of industries each characterized by oligopoly or monopoly. Even in the former case, however, there are often a number of significant differences from the behaviour postulated in economic theory. The main difference is that prices tend to be much more rigid than theory would imply. One reason is that the individual seller may not be in a position to judge just what increase in the volume of sales he would achieve by lowering his price. Another is that he may regard price stability as necessary for maintaining the goodwill of his customers.

The individual seller may not, therefore, adjust his price to just what he thinks the market may bear, given his sales expenditure,

F

but may instead add some standard profit margin to his full average unit cost, or some mark-up to average variable cost designed to cover fixed costs and provide a profit. This margin may reflect what the seller regards as a 'fair' profit or may have been conventional in the industry as a whole for some time. Some economists believe this system of arriving at prices to be widespread, but we still have to ask three questions. For what level of output is average cost calculated? What determines the representative profit margin added to unit cost? What is the range of profit margins within the industry?

The answer often given to the first of these questions is that unit cost is calculated with reference to a 'normal' level of output. Whether this reply is as vague as it sounds depends on whether average cost is constant over a wide range of output, in which case it may not matter which level of output is regarded as 'normal' as long as it is within that range. The answers to the other two questions that have been elicited by investigations made into actual price-fixing methods suggest that 'average-cost-plus' pricing is not so rigid a practice as might appear; in the world of change, profit margins are in many industries adjusted under the stresses of changes in demand and in the force of competition. Profit margins may vary within the multi-firm industry below the ceiling set by demand conditions, and individual firms earn different profit margins on different lines of output. They will generally expect to earn a higher margin of profit on those goods in which they are innovators and those for which demand is inelastic, and steady profit margins on those which they regard as their 'bread-and-butter' lines.

In practice, it is true, small changes in the overall demand for this type of industry's products often leave prices unchanged, so that profits are increased as a result of higher output alone. Large and sustained increases, on the other hand, are correspondingly more likely to raise profit margins and prices as well as output, and may eventually, as in the case of perfect competition, cause an expansion of the capacity of producers and an increase in their number, bringing prices and profit margins in the long run back nearer to the initial level, if the prices of the factors of production needed to provide the increase in output do not rise. Changes on the side of supply, as in the case of a rise in costs, will have consequences that depend on how rigid is the practice of 'cost-plus' pricing; if demand is elastic for the goods of the industry as a whole, exact adherence to a 'normal' profit margin would mean a correspondingly greater reduction in output than if the rise in costs were absorbed partly at the expense of profit margins per unit of output.

The effect of product differentiation may be to keep the number of firms larger than it would be in its absence and so, by making the average firm smaller than it would otherwise be, prevent the full exploitation of economies of scale. The observation has often been made that the apparently greater reluctance of the British consumer to accept standardization than his American counterpart has hindered the development of low-cost mass-production methods in this country. But against this advantage of standardization must be set the desire on the part of consumers to express their individual tastes and the possible stimulus to technical progress that may arise from the existence of a variety of designs.

Some effects of the restriction of competition by collusion are discussed at a later stage. Here it may be noted that whether agreements to limit price competition succeed in raising profits depends on a number of factors, of which the most important are the possibility that new firms may enter the industry under the umbrella of high profit margins, and so keep down profits per firm, and the extent to which competition is diverted to costly sales expenditure or the provision of lavish 'services' to buyers.

## INDUSTRIES WITH FEW SELLERS

The number of firms in an industry may be small for a variety of reasons. The most common is that economies of scale are sufficiently important to cause the most efficient size of firm to be large in relation to the extent of the market. In industries like steel, motor vehicles, rayon and chemicals the large firm has a distinct advantage in the manufacture of the more standardized product. New entrants to this type of industry are rare, being deterred by the risk attached to committing the very large sums of money that would be needed to construct plants of the size required. Even if the would-be entrant has sufficient finance and technical skill, the possibility must be faced that a large proportion of buyers may through habit or some form of agreement be reluctant to divert their custom from existing firms. The cost of securing a foothold may be considerably increased by the necessity for embarking on a vigorous advertising programme and for setting up an expensive selling organization.

The barrier facing new firms is particularly formidable when established concerns have effective control over sales outlets or over the supply of some scarce but essential raw material. In other cases the advantage possessed by existing firms may lie in technical knowledge; it may be based on secret formulae relating to design or production technique, on the control of patents, or on special devices intended to defeat new competitors. An industry may be dominated by a few firms from its inception, or the number of firms may in time be reduced by mergers or by the acquisition of unsuccessful firms by the more prosperous concerns. The tendency towards oligopoly has in several industries been hastened by government action intended to reduce surplus capacity or to strengthen trades against foreign competition.

In this field economic theory has a difficult task, for market behaviour depends on the objectives sought by the dominating concerns and their reaction to each other's policy. On both scores there are several possible courses open to oligopolistic business, and generalization may be dangerous. What follows indicates the variety encountered in practice.

The gains to be derived from forcing existing competitors out of business may be very great; the successful firm may thus secure a monopoly in the industry or, by expanding its sales, reap the full benefits of large-scale production methods without achieving an outright monopoly position. In the past, competition to this end has not been merely a matter of charging prices as low as can be reconciled with reasonable profits. A firm with large financial reserves might be content to operate at very low profit or even at a loss for a limited period, if the result of selling at unduly low prices was to drive its rivals out of the industry. Alternatively, it might be prepared to spend sufficient amounts on advertising and other forms of sales pressure. These forms of destructive competition have been aptly described as 'cut-throat' competition.*

### Stable Price Policy

However, firms in an oligopolistic industry have often been reluctant to embark on vigorous competition, whether designed

---

* In practice, however, this term is often only too readily used to describe any price-competition that makes life uncomfortable for relatively inefficient producers.

to destroy another firm or merely to secure a larger share of the market. The ambitious business may have no way of knowing in advance how effective the reaction of its possibly more powerful competitors is likely to be and thus how costly may be the struggle for supremacy.

As a result industries dominated by a small number of large firms may operate along lines that are acceptable to all, especially to the dominating firm, whether or not agreement is formal. The practice of following the price-leadership of the larger firm has sometimes been accepted after a costly struggle; in return for the advantage of being able to take the initiative as to price policy, the larger firm may refrain from pressing its cost advantage to the full. The predominant firm may merely set itself the objective of maintaining a certain share of the total market. Prices may be formed on the basis of some 'fair' profit margin added to the average cost of the dominating concern or to that of what is considered to be a firm of 'average' efficiency; or the general level of profit margins may be set just below that at which outside firms are tempted to invade the industry.

Agreement or the logic of relative costs may confine smaller firms to the manufacture of non-standardized varieties of the industry's product, leaving the field of goods suitable for large-scale production to their more powerful competitors. This, indeed, is the pattern commonly to be found in oligopolistic industries; competition between large and small firms is moderated by their concentration on different types of product.

The fact that in this type of industry competition in price may be restrained does not mean that other forms of competition are necessarily absent. Quality and design become focal points of competition, and the gains from innovation may be great. Advertising costs may be kept up at high levels, and firms may vie with one another to establish a dominant sales organization. Competition is usually vigorous in the services offered to consumers; these may take the form, for example, of free delivery or maintenance, or the provision of spare parts at reduced prices. Economists are often critical of competition in selling expenses or in service when it results from the reluctance of firms to compete in price. Consumers may be given little opportunity to choose the level of services that they would prefer; many consumers might prefer to be provided with considerably less service in return for paying lower prices. Where price competition is restrained the diversion of competitive effort, to heavy advertising expenditure or to the maintenance of elaborate sales organizations that each firm finds necessary mainly because other firms in the industry so equip themselves, has been regarded by many economists as socially wasteful. Rivalry in selling costs in one form or another may prevent the potential economies of large-scale production from being passed on to consumers as lower prices and may levy a heavy charge on business profits. The absence or restraint of price competition has been subject to strong criticism when it has been thought to maintain the existence of inefficient producers whose survival is secured by preventing the more efficient concerns from operating at a level of output at which average cost is low.

The pattern of behaviour in oligopolistic industries has often proved unstable, and much depends on the sheer temperament of the businessmen involved. Periods of price warfare, caused by low demand or changes in technique, often follow quiescent times. But by and large prices tend to be relatively stable in the absence of a general change in costs; each concern, for example, may be reluctant to reduce prices for fear that its competitors will react in a similar fashion and equally reluctant to raise prices for fear they will not. An increase in demand is unlikely to cause prices to be raised unless it is large and sustained. When production is well below capacity a rise in demand may result in a fall in unit cost as fixed costs are spread over a larger output; it is thus even possible for prices to be reduced.

When demand exceeds the capacity of the industry long order-books are often preferred to high prices. Possible motives behind this restraint have already been indicated. Whatever the reason, prices may be held below the level at which supply and demand are in equilibrium, so that shortages develop and firms have to ration their customers. Voluntary price control is open to some of the objections that economists—and businessmen—often level at the control of prices by the government. It may prevent the supply of goods from moving to those customers who, as indicated by their willingness to pay higher prices, are in greatest need of them. Prices that are low in relation to demand encourage hoarding and the duplication of orders; the inducement to economize in the scarce commodity is blunted. Unofficial rationing may be out of alignment with customers' needs, suppliers paying undue attention to the bargaining power of large and established customers. Shortages result in lower efficiency and industrial rigidity.

Above all, the reluctance to take advantage of the opportunity of high profits may mean that the capacity of the industry concerned is expanded too slowly, either because without high profits the financial resources of existing firms are inadequate to finance rapid expansion or because outside concerns are not attracted into the industry. Thus what may appear to be the commendable and often public-spirited restraint by business in times of high demand is not without its possible social disadvantages. Prices that are low in relation to demand may be most easily justified, however, when the rise in demand is thought to be temporary and when, high prices or not, supply cannot be quickly expanded.

Finally, firms in an oligopolistic industry may be slow to expand capacity in response to an increase in demand. Oligopolistic industries are often those where the number of firms is small because expensive capital equipment is required for efficient operation, and high fixed costs expose a firm to substantial losses if demand falls. The managers of oligopolistic concerns are likely to weigh carefully the expansion plans of their competitors and so may be highly conscious of the danger of excessive growth. In the past these considerations have applied to some of the capital-goods trades—machine tools and shipbuilding, for example—and to the related steel industry, where severe fluctuations in demand were experienced in the inter-war years.

# CHAPTER 6

# THE RESTRICTION OF COMPETITION

## MONOPOLY

The word 'monopoly' is sometimes used loosely and in a pejorative sense, but it is intended to be applied here merely as a neutral and technical description of a situation in which a single commodity of a seller or service is faced with no important competition from sellers of the same product or near-substitute. Whether a monopoly is desirable or undesirable in the public interest is a question to be considered later in this chapter. Absolute business monopolies are rare, but important characteristics of monopoly may exist even where a single seller provides less than the whole supply, as long as his share of the market is large enough to give him undisputed control over the industry concerned. The term monopoly can also for convenience be extended to include the institution of the *cartel*, through which a number of sellers agree to fix prices and production quotas.

A business may be a monopoly because of its exclusive control over the supply of some raw material, or it may establish a monopoly position by virtue of the fact that production can be carried on efficiently only by plants of a very large size, which deters new entrants into an industry. There are, however, few instances where private concerns have been monopolies from their inception; monopolies or near-monopolies have usually been based on some type of combination between the few dominant concerns. Mergers have generally occurred in periods when the existence of excess capacity at a time when trade was slack led to the emergence of acute competition.

## STATUTORY MONOPOLIES

A monopoly may be conferred on a producer by Parliament. From the reign of Edward III, if not earlier, the privilege of sole manufacture, or of sole importation, or of sole dealing in some commodity, has from time to time been granted by the State. Originally these privileges were usually conferred in order to encourage the development of some new trade or the introduction into the country of some industry practised abroad and may be compared with the grant of patents and copyright. The institution of the patent is not in itself the cause of monopoly, since the patented design may have to face the competition of others, and in the absence of patents designs and formulae would merely be kept secret. In certain cases, however, the control of a group of related patents, like the possession of secret formulae, may be the basis of monopoly, especially if alternative designs can be 'blocked' by patenting all known modifications.

The reasons that have prompted Parliament to grant monopolies have been varied. In the case of the Bank of England, for example, the privilege of monopoly was conferred in return for services rendered to the State. A statutory monopoly may be created as a by-product of the State's desire to secure some objective entirely divorced from economic matters, as, for example, in the case of the British Broadcasting Corporation. The State has created monopolies for some industries, like railways, gas, electricity and water supply, that require such large amounts of fixed capital equipment that competition between different producers in the same area would involve a wasteful duplication of plant.

Until the inter-war years, examples such as these almost completely exhausted the field in which monopolies were created by Parliament. In 1922, however, appeared the first instance of a cartel agreement approved by Parliament in order to secure a different type of objective. This was the Stevenson Rubber Scheme, which, following the post-war slump, was intended to raise the price of rubber to a profitable level by prescribing maximum production quotas for plantations in Malaya and Ceylon. In 1930 the Coal Mines Act was passed to achieve similar results in the coal industry. Under the Agricultural Marketing Act of 1933 the prices of hops, milk, potatoes and various other products were regulated by Marketing Boards intended to be representative of the industries concerned. In 1936 an Act was passed to provide for the amalgamation of the fifteen companies comprising the country's beet-sugar industry into the British Sugar Corporation Ltd., in order to strengthen the position of the industry against the competition of imported cane-sugar. In most of these cases the creation of monopolistic or semi-monopolistic positions reflected the belief that, by raising the rate of profit in industries severely affected by the slump of the time, business activity would be revived and social distress eased.

Since the war, of course, certain important industries have been nationalized by the Labour governments of 1945–51. Underlying the Labour Party's policy of nationalization has been the thesis that State ownership of certain so-called 'basic' industries, e.g. steel and transport, is necessary to give the government that degree of central direction of economic affairs that the Labour Party regards as essential to the maintenance of full employment and to economic growth. This economic philosophy stands alongside the political justification offered for nationalization, namely that it is required to achieve the economic equality that is at the centre of the Labour Party's aims. More specifically, State monopoly is regarded as desirable by the Labour Party in the case of those industries that are deemed inefficient or over-cautious, those with a history of bitter industrial relations and those dominated by giant concerns, which are seen as possessing a concentration of economic and political power incompatible with democracy. The policy of the Conservative Party, on the other hand, is based on the view that private ownership is generally essential to political freedom and economic efficiency, that the State can direct economic affairs without the creation of State monopolies, in which economic power may remain unduly concentrated, and that the remedy for undesirable private monopolies is State action designed to encourage competition or State regulation of prices. The Conservative governments that followed the electoral defeat of the Labour Party in 1951, however, have left coal, railways and the Bank of England, to name the most important cases, in State ownership.

### THE POLICY OF A MONOPOLY

Monopolies operating under government supervision are generally allowed to follow a policy that will earn them a reasonable rate of profit on capital employed or, as in the case of most nationalized corporations, are enjoined to balance current costs and revenue 'taking one year with another'. Unregulated private monopolies may also forbear from exploiting their power to the full, because of a sense of fairness, or because of the fear of incurring public or government hostility, or because of the monopolist's desire to avoid tempting new firms into the industry.

An uncontrolled monopolist can charge whatever price he pleases, but he cannot sell as much as he would like at whatever price he chooses. If a monopolist chooses a high price he must be content with a lower volume of sales, depending on the elasticity of demand. This applies to any firm, but the advantage of a monopoly lies in its ability, because of the absence of significant competition within a certain range of prices, to choose a level of output and a price that provide profits higher than those earned in competitive industry. It is by restricting his output and by raising his price to a level just short of that at which demand eventually becomes dangerously elastic that a monopolist earns high profits. One further difference from the situation in a many-firm industry is that the monopolist may have to bear in mind the effect of his own scale of output on the prices of the factors of production he uses, so that by restricting output he may be able to keep factor prices low. Against these tendencies making for the restriction of output, however, may be set the possibility that a monopolist, unlike the individual member of a many-firm industry, may expand production in order to benefit from what would be external economies of scale in a many-firm industry.

### DISCRIMINATING MONOPOLISTIC PRICES

Price discrimination is the practice by which a seller charges different prices to different buyers of exactly the same product, after allowing for differences in transport and selling costs. For price discrimination to be possible two conditions must prevail. First, the seller must have some degree of monopoly power, in order to prevent those buyers to whom he sells at relatively high prices from transferring their custom to low-price competitors. Secondly, a monopolistic seller must be able to sell his product in markets sufficiently isolated from one another to prevent it being bought in the cheaper market and resold in the dearer.

The discriminating monopolist may charge different prices to different classes of buyers in the same locality, or he may charge different prices in different areas. It will pay a monopolist to charge different prices in separate 'markets' when the conditions of demand are different; he can thus charge low prices in the market where higher ones would cause an unprofitable reduction in sales, without at the same time spoiling his other markets where higher prices are more remunerative. Thus price discrimination is a means of charging 'what the traffic will bear' in different markets. The ability of a discriminating monopolist to charge high prices in the market where demand is relatively inelastic is one incentive for him to separate his markets in this way. Another is that price discrimination may make it possible for a monopolist to raise his total output, and where he is able to spread expensive overheads as a result or to obtain economies of scale, price discrimination will appear particularly attractive.

One example of price discrimination occurs when producers attempt to sell their goods in foreign markets at prices below those they charge at home. This practice of 'dumping', as it is called, is particularly profitable where foreign demand in overseas markets is rendered very elastic by the existence of competition, but where demand at home can be kept inelastic by holding off foreign competition with the help of stiff import duty. Needless to say, this device has aroused much resentment in international trade, and it has been less frequently used than before the war.

### THE CASE FOR AND AGAINST THE SINGLE-FIRM MONOPOLY

The case for a single-firm monopoly is strongest where economies of scale result in lower costs if production is combined in the hands of a single producer. A monopoly may also profit by full-capacity operation through 'rationalization', that is by closing down plants that would be run below capacity in conditions of many-firm competition. Economies may also be obtained by concentrating each plant on a narrower range of products.

Outside the field of public utilities the question of whether monopoly may be more efficient than a multi-firm industry is controversial, and it is not easy to generalize. The distinction must be made, for example, between the advantages of large firms and those of large plants. A monopoly may consist of a number of large plants each of which is at its most efficient size; and the public interest might be better served by breaking up the monopoly into its constituent units, providing the advantages of both large-scale production and competition. The case for competition is strong where there are no important economies in unified marketing or purchasing, and in those instances in which the large size of a monopoly creates more problems for management than it removes by the absence of competition. Whether monopoly is to the advantage of consumers if it secures its economies by reducing the variety that would have prevailed in a freely competitive industry is not easy to decide. The argument in favour of competition is clearest when a monopoly consists of a very loose organization of separate units formed to exploit their combined bargaining power rather than economies of scale.

A monopoly can take into account the external economies ignored by competing concerns; it may be able to spend large sums on training skilled labour or scientific research workers that competing firms would be unable or unwilling to do because of their fear of losing part of the benefit of their own expenditure. A monopoly may also gain by the pooling of knowledge that would be guarded jealously by competing concerns. In this argument there is some force, but in itself it is not sufficient justification for monopoly, and certain benefits of this sort may be secured through the action of the State or trade associations.

Nevertheless, to many observers of the industrial world the great financial resources possessed by successful monopolies appear to be a source of technical innovation that smaller competitive firms could not afford to undertake. In some industries only the largest concerns can risk the great sums on research and development on which the introduction and marketing of new products depend today, for only large firms can afford to set off what they gain on the roundabouts the substantial sums they may lose on the swings, so that the psychological and financial obstacles to innovation may be smaller in a monopolistic industry. However, whilst the financial barriers to innovation may be reduced if competition is abolished, so may the incentive. The arguments for and against monopoly in its effect on innovation and efficiency are neither clear-cut nor capable of universal application.

The contention that the existence of monopoly introduces a valuable element of stability into the economy is also open to dispute. It has often been said that by preventing its prices from falling sharply during a trade depression a monopoly can maintain its profits and therefore pay higher wages and higher prices for materials and spend more on new capital equipment than a competitive industry could do. It is certainly true that many monopolies have been formed during conditions of depressed trade, and there is no doubt that many a monopoly has succeeded in maintaining stability of prices during a slump. But if it does so, the volume of its output, and therefore the level of employment it offers, might be lower than if prices had been reduced.

The gains of a monopoly that does not have any special justification by way of technical efficiency or boldness are made at the expense of the customers that it charges high prices and the factors of production that it buys at low ones. However, monopoly power is frequently unaccompanied by monopoly profits. The large monopolistic concern may refrain from exploiting its ability to earn excessive profits for the sake of a quiet life, and to this end it may erect an expensive barrier to keep out competition by means that do not meet with public criticism; it may shelter behind heavy advertising or an expensive selling organization or pay unusually high wages and salaries. In other cases the absence of monopoly profits may be explained by the fact that a large firm's monopoly power is more apparent than real, owing to the existence of substitutes or powerful buyers.

The crux of the case against monopoly is not that the monopolistic firm may earn high profits, although this is a legitimate cause for criticism if it is not the result of efficiency and innovation, but that it may be only too ready to rest content with a peaceful existence, safe in the knowledge that it cannot suffer heavy penalties for any failure to reduce costs and improve its products; the monopolist may be too complacent to make use of whatever advantages by way of research and rationalization his position affords him.

### AGREEMENTS TO RESTRICT COMPETITION

Some economists contend that the gap that has emerged between productivity in the U.S.A. and that in this country over the past eighty years is attributable partly to the fact that in many industries free competition in this country has been replaced by some form of restriction, whereas in the U.S.A. government legislation since 1890 has helped to maintain business life in a state nearer to that 'full and free competition' which it was the object of the Sherman Act of that year to secure.

Economists who applaud the existence of a more vigorous state of competition in the U.S.A. find cause for concern in British business life not so much in those rare cases of single-firm monopolies, which may at least possess economies of scale, but in the more frequent occurrence of agreements between a number of firms to limit competition in one way or another. The most important of these concern the maintenance of minimum prices.

Such agreements are not new; they existed in medieval England, when the associations of employers and craftsmen known as guilds were common, and they were widespread in the first stages of the industrial revolution. After the Napoleonic wars, however, the development of rail transport destroyed the protection that isolation had afforded local monopolies, and the rapid changes in industrial techniques were often responsible for breaking up monopolistic powers of both employers and craftsmen. By the second quarter of the nineteenth century the effect of extensive industrial growth in a social climate in which the political philosophy of individualism had become acceptable was to establish unrestricted competition as the general rule, outside the field of the statutory monopolies like the railways. Agreements to limit competition had become unpopular, unnecessary and vulnerable.

In the final quarter of the century restrictive practices once more became an important if not a dominant feature of the industrial scene. The institution of limited liability and the economies of large-scale operation, consequences of the very industrial development that had begun by destroying monopolistic practices, combined to favour a pattern of industry in which oligopoly was becoming more common. In some fields the development of the 'holding company', in which are vested a sufficient proportion of the voting shares of other firms to give it effective control, was the means by which large concerns could extend their influence, using the resources of their partly-owned subsidiaries to acquire control over a broadly-based pyramid of companies perhaps extending beyond the boundaries of a single industry. The network of non-competitive industrial relationships could be extended without formal agreement to limit competition by the practice of interlocking directorates, with or without the support of an exchange of shares between companies.

The main stimulus to joint action was the acuteness of price competition in the years of relatively slack trade, particularly during the 'great depression' of 1874–86. By the outbreak of the Second World War the restriction of competition had been carried still farther. By 1939 there were few manufacturing industries where unrestricted competition prevailed, and the tendency towards combination was strengthened by the war, for government departments encouraged the closer association of businesses in order to meet the special requirements of a centrally-directed siege economy.

Agreements to limit competition have been facilitated by the existence of trade associations, through the medium of which they may be enforced. These, it must be emphasized, need not have been set up for such purposes; most trade associations have been founded to further the common interests of their members in regard to negotiations with the government and trade unions, the exchange of professional or technical knowledge, and the maintenance of standards of quality. The division between these functions and agreements to restrict competition, however, is not always easily drawn. In the cable-making industry, for example, a report of the Monopolies and Restrictive Practices Commission in 1952* approved of the practice of co-operation to maintain quality and to standardize the dimensions of cables. But the Commission was more critical of the Cablemakers' Association's agreements 'for fixing common prices, sharing business in agreed proportions based on sales over previous periods, and, for mains cable, allocating orders and pooling profits'.

Agreements to restrict competition merely to maintain profits, on the other hand, have generally been born in times of relatively unprofitable trade, especially in industries with large fixed costs, and it is not difficult to express sympathy for the objective of maintaining incomes in a slump. But if, as is to be hoped, general trade depression can be mitigated by government policy, a large part of this case for the cartel is destroyed. In any case, it is doubtful to what extent the widespread existence of cartels really helps to mitigate a slump, for prices and profits may be maintained only at the expense of output and employment.

When an individual industry is faced with a declining demand its members may come to agreement to accelerate the process of contraction. The coal, cotton and shipbuilding industries before the war suffered from protracted excess capacity, as a result of the determination of individual firms to hang on in the hope of a return to better times, and but for which profits and wages might have been higher and average costs lower. Various attempts were therefore made, in some cases with the spur of government encouragement or assistance, to secure the reorganization of these industries into a smaller number of fully employed concerns.

* *The Supply of Insulated Electric Wires and Cables* (H.M.S.O., London).

These objectives are praiseworthy in industries where the alternative of prolonged losses and chronic insolvency is at best an uncertain and harsh remedy. But even where agreements to limit competition have been designed to facilitate such reorganization they have not always been followed by such action, and their methods have sometimes been open to criticism. The restriction of competition tends to protect the inefficient at the expense of the able. The profits secured through the formation of a cartel set up to limit price competition rather than to achieve rationalization may not seem 'excessive', but this may be because the survival of the less efficient concerns means that the majority of firms are forced to operate well below full capacity. Industries in which price competition is restricted are often those in which low output means high average costs, so that the maintenance of excess capacity imposes a heavy charge on consumers. The cartel may be too generous to its less efficient members in its selection of what it considers to be a firm of 'average' efficiency by which a 'fair' profit margin is to be earned. The allocation of production quotas to individual firms, usually decided by reference to a 'base period', results in an arbitrary rigidity of the industry's structure, and the incentive to introduce improved products or methods is blunted. Reporting on the rainwater goods trade, for example, the Monopolies and Restrictive Practices Commission remarked that 'the introduction of lower cost methods of production is retarded, since a manufacturer, after signing the Agreements, cannot count on the market expansion which lower costs have secured for him and which may be necessary to justify the commercial commitments involved'.*

## DEVICES TO LIMIT COMPETITION

The restriction of competition has often been based on devices that have been regarded as socially undesirable in themselves. One example is the 'fighting company' or 'fighting brand' designed to operate at a loss, and the 'bogus independent' or 'competition company' has also been used to conceal the existence of monopoly. An even earlier device was the use of price discrimination to destroy competitors. The growth of the Standard Oil Company in the U.S.A., for example, was assisted at the end of the nineteenth century by its ability, derived from its size, to force the

* *The Supply of Cast Iron Rainwater Goods* (H.M.S.O., London).

G

railways to allow it to transport its oil at lower freights than those charged to competitors. Another method is that whereby distributors in some industries receive an aggregated quantity rebate on purchases made from members of a cartel or trade association within the year, irrespective of whether their individual orders afford economies of bulk handling. In its extreme form the pressure on distributors or customers takes the form of 'exclusive dealing' arrangements, which may also be forced on suppliers.

A company that is in a sufficiently strong position may be able to secure exclusive custom without the aid of rebates if it produces some article that is in great demand and without a substitute. By the practice of 'full-line forcing' the supplier may be able to oblige his customers to buy their requirements of other goods from him alone, although these goods may be available from competing sources.

### Resale Price Maintenance

A widespread and controversial practice is that of 'resale price maintenance', by which a manufacturer requires distributors to resell his goods at stated fixed prices or at not less than stipulated minimum prices.

In some trades resale price maintenance is intended to prevent the use of the 'loss-leader', by which some retailers sell popular goods below cost in order to attract customers into their shops to buy other articles. It is held that the use of the loss-leader would result in the public's having to pay more for these other goods bought in shops taking advantage of the practice, and it is contended that it is in the interest of manufacturers to prevent the use of loss leaders in order to avoid incurring the resentment of those retailers who refrain from indulging in the practice. Manufacturers of branded goods may also enforce resale price maintenance because they fear that if some retailers sold their product at lower prices than others the public might attribute to it a quality inferior to those goods whose prices were fixed. It is thus argued that the prestige of a proprietary article is bound up with maintaining fixed prices.

The supporters of resale price maintenance also believe that consumers generally prefer to know that they can get certain goods at the same price irrespective of the shop in which they are bought. For certain types of article consumers do not seem to be prepared to compare prices charged by competing shops until they have found the best bargain; in the case of cigarettes, beer and petrol, for example, which are bought relatively frequently at low unit prices, the decision on where to purchase may depend mainly on the mere proximity of a retailer. In cases such as these, therefore, the manufacturer may believe that he can achieve the highest level of sales by inducing the largest number of shops to stock his goods, irrespective of whether they are forced to charge a slightly higher price through being assured an attractive retail mark-up. Moreover, the less capable are consumers of recognizing differences in the intrinsic merits of rival brands the greater appears the advantage to the manufacturer of persuading the greatest number of retailers to stock his products; the loyalty of retailers is thus substituted for that of consumers. Resale price maintenance serves this end by offering the retailer a profit margin that he knows will not be undercut by more vigorous competitors. Resale price maintenance is always applied where distributors agree to stock only the goods of a certain manufacturer, as in the case of the 'tied' garage. Finally, resale price maintenance may be the means by which manufacturers in certain trades ensure that the retailers who stock their goods are able to offer a high level of service. Until the Restrictive Trade Practices Act of 1956 manufacturers in some industries, such as the motor industry, combined to enforce resale price maintenance, usually penalizing the price-cutter by the 'collective boycott' or 'stop list'. By this means all manufacturers who were parties to the agreement, usually members of a trade association, would refuse to supply the distributor who had sold the goods of any one of them at below the stipulated price.

The critics of resale price maintenance assert that its general effect is to protect the inefficient retailer and to divert competition from price to that of service, which consumers, if given a free choice, might not prefer. By maintaining the existence of retailers who could not survive if price competition were free, resale price maintenance leads to the existence of a larger number of shops and higher unit costs. The practice may in some trades hinder the development of more efficient forms of retailing, such as the chain-store and the self-service shop, which require a large turnover and therefore, it may be, low unit profit margins.

Whether the successful development of branded products really depends on the practice is arguable, and some branded goods are not subject to any such provisions. The unwillingness of manufacturers to allow efficient distributors to sell at lower prices, based on their desire to retain the support of small retailers, has led some chain-stores to manufacture their own products, which are then sold at prices lower than those fixed for price-maintained goods. The practice of resale price maintenance has sometimes been circumvented by distributors by means such as the provision of favourable terms for second-hand goods offered as part of the purchase price. The benefits that resale price maintenance brings to small shopkeepers may be reduced by the fact that competition may be diverted to the provision of services which the small retailer is in no position to provide.

### ATTITUDES TOWARDS COMPETITION

Apart from the fifty years spanning the middle of the nineteenth century it is probably fair to say that the general public attitude has always been to accept some degree of restraint in competition. From the early days of commerce vigorous price competition has often been regarded as being detrimental to craftsmanship, and producers have been at pains to express their 'identity of interest' and to consider 'excessive' or 'unfair' competition as both selfish and harmful to the interest of their trade 'as a whole'.

The climate of opinion may be based on considerations that are not easily susceptible to economic analysis. Competition as a form of human behaviour may be condemned by some as the expression merely of 'selfishness' and 'greed' and may be contrasted with the ideal of 'social harmony', a view of the world that is often taken by those who see nothing but 'chaos' in the competitive economy as opposed to the 'order' to be secured by 'rational planning'. Technical change has almost always been resisted by those groups who have feared its consequences; and the restriction of competition, even at the expense of checking innovation, has been regarded with benevolence in times of depressed trade.

Economists who value competition for the spur that it applies to economic development also do so, as a rule, because in an economy dominated by monopolies or monopolistic combinations there can be little scope for the individual initiative that is valuable for its own sake, and political liberty may be weakened. In the opinion of economists to whom competition, in its widest sense of meaning freedom of action for both producers and consumers, does not appear merely as the expression of selfishness, it is the existence of change that gives rise to those problems that appear to be solely the result of some fundamental discord in society. The balance of interests between different groups is bound to be disturbed periodically as the course of economic development favours first one and then another. Unless the prevention of change is generally acceptable the tendency for monopolistic practices to resist change may create only the temporary illusion of stability and harmony, compressing what might otherwise be a continuous and comparatively temperate adjustment into concentrated and explosive reactions as the bonds of monopoly are finally broken.

The unfortunate choice of the words 'perfect' and 'imperfect' as applied by economists to competition should not be interpreted to convey a contrast between a desirable and an undesirable type of business behaviour. The imperfection of competition due to the variety of products that the modern economy showers upon its members is generally welcomed rather than deplored, and the productivity attained in industries where economies of scale leave room only for a small number of firms is not usually a cause for regret; it is in the field of oligopoly that technical innovation is often most eagerly pursued. The imperfections caused by the geographical isolation of some markets or by ignorance on the part of consumers are facts of economic life, but not incapable of being influenced by improvements in transport, in education and in laws relating to advertising. The important thing is that forces of competition should be free to act as a spur to innovation and efficiency and to operate so as to shift resources in the right direction; in a complex world of continual but barely predictable change this is a tremendous achievement.

That some firms may make 'abnormal' profits is both inevitable and desirable. It is inevitable because the adjustment to changes in demand and costs cannot be instantaneous, and the frequency of change may prevent the theoretical 'long run', in which profits are forced nearer to 'normal' levels, from ever being attained; it is desirable because in a competitive economy the attraction of abnormal profits is a stimulus to efficiency and innovation and the mainspring that sets the economic mechanism in motion to shift resources to where they can be of the greatest social value at the least cost. It follows that the possibility of loss is also part of a properly functioning competitive economy, which is not just a profit but a profit *and* loss system. It is because the economist regards the incurrence of loss, at a time when the economy generally is prosperous, as a necessary penalty for inefficiency and the misuse of scarce resources that his valuation of the social benefits of free competition is so often different from that of the individual businessman or employee.

But among neither economists nor businessmen is there unanimity as to the exact degree of competition that is needed to achieve the efficiency, the growth and yet the stability that are now generally expected from the modern industrial economy. Some are inclined to discount the adverse effects of monopoly and restrictive business practices, because they regard them as a price that must be paid to obtain the benefits of private ownership and large-scale business or because they believe that, in the absence of government support, monopolistic behaviour will be limited in extent and temporary in duration.

On one view certain types of monopoly and restrictive practices are a form of 'insurance' necessary where large-scale businesses face large-scale risks that might discourage heavy capital investment and costly development projects in the absence of some limitation of competition. It is sometimes argued that some restraint on competition may actually speed up the pace of economic growth—'there is no more paradox in this than there is in saying that motor cars are travelling faster than they would otherwise do *because* they are provided with brakes.'*

On this view certain tendencies towards monopoly are seen not as the enemies but as the allies of economic change, whilst in turn the power of monopoly is eventually limited by the process of change itself. The attraction of high profits tempts businessmen into paths that lead to innovation and the emergence of 'pioneer' monopolies based on new products or techniques; these may destroy entrenched positions that in turn had previously been built on the ruins of formerly secure businesses, 'This process of Creative Destruction is the essential fact about capitalism.'† This

* Joseph A. Schumpeter, *Capitalism, Socialism and Democracy* (Harper & Brothers, New York).
† Schumpeter, op. cit.

assessment adopts a tolerant and even benevolent attitude towards the role of the monopoly established through the power of a new production technique, a new form of organization or a new product, even if achieved by the aid of methods that in themselves seem undesirable; but it is not an opinion that can be applied to those forms of monopolistic practice that resist change.

The power of a monopoly or dominant concern may also be limited by the opposition of equally large and powerful organizations. In the United States the giant U.S. Steel Corporation is faced by the powerful General Motors Corporation; the influence of the large food processors and packers is limited by the equally large chain-stores through which they have to sell; while in general the powerful trade unions and the employers' associations offset one another. Whether or not any inherent tendency can be discerned in the capitalist economy for large organizations to develop in self-defence against the power of others, it is certainly true that the ability of a large concern or combination to exploit its position may be checked by the existence of 'countervailing power'. To some observers it is through this rather than through the more traditional forms of competition within the same industry that the most important checks and balances now operate.

### GOVERNMENT POLICY

An analysis on these lines, however, leaves unanswered the question of just what policy should be adopted by the State in regard to single-firm monopolies or restrictive practices. Some economists maintain that government policy itself has been the most important cause of the conditions in which monopoly positions remain unchallenged. The encouragement of trade associations in wartime has already been mentioned, and so has the blessing given to rationalization schemes during the inter-war slump. The imposition of import duties or quotas, too, operates over a much wider field to limit competition from overseas that would otherwise be present as a continual threat to monopoly, and the high level of personal and company taxation may be an important obstacle to the growth of new businesses. If government policy did not so frequently have the effect, deliberately or otherwise, of bolstering monopolistic positions, it can be argued, their existence might be precarious enough to be ignored. The position of the cartel or looser combination might be particularly insecure; restrictions on their competitive power are irksome to low-cost producers; and competition can be disguised in many ways.

Nevertheless, perhaps the majority of economists and both Labour and Conservative governments have come to support the view that State action in this field should not be limited to refraining from policies that assist monopoly. Attention has been concentrated on the spur that competition can apply to efficiency and innovation and in particular on the limitations imposed on the producer of efficiency and initiative by the devices used to restrict competition.

However, sweeping generalizations command little support. A definition of the 'public interest' that can be applied to the variety of conditions in which industry operates is not easily formulated. Above all, it must be admitted that, whether or not the 'public interest' can be satisfactorily defined, it may be extremely difficult to prove that, out of a multitude of perhaps vague and conflicting possibilities, a particular practice will on balance have effects in the future that are either clearly favourable or detrimental to it.

### RESTRICTIVE PRACTICES AND THE LAW IN BRITAIN

Since the middle of the nineteenth century until quite recently the legal protection of the community from monopoly rested largely on the common law, under which absolute monopoly was illegal and contracts 'in restraint of trade' had generally been void as being contrary to 'public policy'. As the years passed, the common law came to be interpreted by the Courts with increasing liberality. Absolute private monopolies, complete, permanent and countrywide, are rare; and, broadly speaking, by the nineteen-thirties the Courts were generally prepared to enforce contracts of trade if 'restraint' could be shown as being 'reasonable' as between the contracting parties and, where a third party suffered injury as a result, not founded on malice. By and large the Courts came to regard the sanctity of contract and the right of employers and traders to protect their own interests from competition as being sufficient justification for agreements in restraint of trade and would not explore the wider economic consequences of the restraint of trade for the public interest.

### The Monopolies and Restrictive Practices Commission

In the inter-war years opinion hardened in favour of the establishment of some specialized body to consider the economic aspects of restrictive practices passed over in the operation of the common law, but it was not until 1948 that the first general step back to the statutory protection of the public interest from the possible evils of monopolistic practices was taken. In that year the Monopolies and Restrictive Practices (Inquiry and Control) Act set up a Monopolies and Restrictive Practices Commission, whose duty it was to investigate and report upon cases referred to it by the President of the Board of Trade.

By the end of 1957 the Commission had issued reports on some fifteen cases, one of which, on Matches and Match Machinery, related to a single-firm monopoly. In this the main recommendation of the majority report was the imposition of price control. The Commission felt monopoly to be 'probably the natural organization of this trade'.

The general attitude of the Commission proved empirical; practices that it condemned in some industries it approved in others. In general, however, the Commission deplored practices that imposed restrictions on entry into any field of business activity. Devices such as exclusive dealing arrangements, trade association rebates and the use of 'fighting companies' were condemned as having little purpose but to prevent outside competition, and the Commission also viewed with disfavour resale price maintenance supported by collective boycott. Agreements between manufacturers to fix minimum prices, on the other hand, were regarded by the Commission as not harming the public when they were associated, for example, with the exchange of technical information or with the maintenance of quality. Where a combination of sellers was or could be faced with an equally powerful organization of buyers, the Commission was disposed to look to the effect of countervailing power to safeguard the public interest—it recommended, for instance, that the Central Electricity Authority, the Admiralty and the G.P.O. should cost the factories of the Cable Makers' Association in order to negotiate 'fair' prices.

In 1955 the Commission issued its first general report, that on Collective Discrimination.* The report covered collective discrimination by sellers and buyers, resale price maintenance and practices that are supported by preferential treatment—discounts, rebates and exclusive dealing arrangements—or by collective penalties. It declared that the general effect of such practices was against the public interest. It found that in most cases these devices were not necessary to secure whatever desirable results they were ostensibly intended to achieve, and it concluded that the general tendency of such practices was to 'lead to the creation of a privileged group subject to relatively little outside competition' and to deter manufacturers and traders from experiment and innovation. The majority report of the Commission recommended outright prohibition of these practices, subject to certain exceptions. A minority group, on the other hand, was unwilling to agree that the evidence put before the Commission justified 'so sweeping a condemnation' and proposed instead that such practices should be made subject to registration and individual cases prohibited if then found to be against the public interest.

### The Restrictive Trade Practices Act, 1956

The Restrictive Trade Practices Act, 1956, which applies only to the production or supply or processing of goods, implements the main proposals of the minority report. Under the Act a Registrar of Restrictive Practices is charged with maintaining a register of agreements subject to registration. The Board of Trade names the classes of restrictive agreements which contracting parties must register. The Act also sets up a Restrictive Practices Court to which agreements may be referred by the Registrar, on the order of the Board of Trade, or by a person contesting their validity. Such agreements may be declared void if they are deemed contrary to the public interest, and they are deemed to be so unless the Court is satisfied that certain circumstances apply, e.g. that the restriction is reasonably necessary to protect the public against physical injury. Under the Act agreements for the collective enforcement of resale price maintenance are prohibited, but an individual supplier remains able to enforce

---

* *Collective Discrimination: A Report on Exclusive Dealing, Collective Boycotts, Aggregated Rebates and Other Discriminatory Trade Practices* (H.M.S.O., London, 1955).

conditions of resale. The Act confines the functions of the Monopolies Commission to the investigation of single-firm monopolies, of the result of restrictive practices for exports and of the general effect of restrictive practices.

The 1956 Act is less ambitious than the legislation of the United States; it represents a logical extension of the philosophy of the 1948 Act in seeking to build up a body of case law that will serve as a guide to business policy. Like all such forms of negative legislation, however, it cannot force businesses to compete freely in those industries where agreements to limit competition are informal or where competition is restricted without any agreement at all.

# CHAPTER 7

# THE MARKET FOR LABOUR AND TRADE-UNION ACTION

Only a brief reference to some of the main features of the labour market can be made here. The machinery of wage negotiation and settlement varies from industry to industry. Out of a total of 22 million wage- and salary-earners in 1957, about $9\frac{1}{2}$ million were organized in trade unions, covering wage-earners in most of industry, transport and distribution. In this field minimum or basic wage-rates are negotiated mainly by collective bargaining between trade unions and employers' organizations. Wage-rates are still influenced by market forces of supply and demand, but the degree of competition between individual employers and wage-earners is limited, and strike action, or the threat of it, has become a potent factor.

In certain industries wage negotiation is carried out through the medium of Joint Industrial Councils, consisting of representatives of employers and employees; they provide a means of discussion on matters such as welfare and safety as well as wages and hours of work. Joint Industrial Councils, which arose out of the report of the Whitley Committee (Committee on Relations between Employers and Employed) in 1918 and are thus sometimes referred to as Whitley Councils, operate in the field of central and local government and in flour-milling, wool textiles, printing, chemicals and shipping, for example. In certain other trades wages are settled through the machinery of Wages Councils, which before the Wages Council Act of 1945 were described as Trade Boards. These were set up to protect the interests of employees in a number of industries where trade-union organization was weak, mainly in industries consisting of a large number of small concerns. The Councils are appointed by the Ministry of Labour and include independent members as well as representatives of both sides of industry. The Councils decide minimum wage-rates, which are legally binding if confirmed by the Minister of Labour; they operate in retail trade and in the clothing industry, and in the chocolate and tobacco trades, where a number of large firms predominate. In some industries, e.g. building and footwear, wage-rates are adjusted according to an agreed sliding-scale if retail prices change.

## MARKET FORCES

On the side of demand, the wage-rates that business employers are prepared to pay depend on the contribution they expect different quantities of each type of labour to make to the profits of their businesses. The market productivity of labour reflects both the increase in physical output obtainable by adding to the quantity of labour employed and the value placed on that output by buyers, so that the demand for labour is a derived demand. The pattern of wage-rates is determined not by the total productivity of different classes of labour but by their *marginal* productivity. Manual labourers as a whole may be indispensable to the economy; but if one manual labourer were removed the loss of his services, as assessed by those who pay for them, would be smaller than that incurred if one engineer less were to be employed.

The demand for different types of labour at different wage-rates is influenced by the possibility of substitution between them at the margin and by the possibility of substituting other factors of production—capital or land—for labour that becomes relatively expensive. Other things remaining unchanged, the lower the wage-rate the more of a particular type of labour will find employment, reflecting the elasticity of demand for it. The latter will be influenced by the possibilities of substitution, the proportion of total costs represented by the labour concerned, and the elasticity of demand for the goods or services which it helps to produce. Whether more labour in the economy as a whole will be employed at lower rather than higher wage-rates is a different question that is deferred to a later chapter.

The conditions on which labour will be supplied depend both on the ability and the willingness of workers to undertake different forms of work. The country's social and educational structure and its training facilities determine the potential supply of labour of different degrees of skill, and the attitude of individual workers to different occupations will reflect their assessment of relative 'net advantages', including subjective factors as well as wage-rates and other terms of employment, such as conditions of work. Certain types of unpleasant or arduous work do indeed earn low wage-rates, but this is because the work concerned is unskilled. As unskilled labour is relatively plentiful, the contribution of the marginal unskilled worker to production is relatively small, owing to diminishing returns.

Generally, more of a particular type of labour will be supplied at a high wage than a low one, high wages inducing workers to give up leisure for overtime working and shift from other jobs, and attracting a larger number of women into the labour force. On the other hand, a rise in wage-rates beyond a certain level, particularly in those occupations where work is arduous or unpleasant, such as coalmining, may lead workers to feel that they can afford to work fewer hours and increase their leisure instead.

The supply of a particular type of labour, or the supply of labour to an individual industry, will generally be more elastic than the supply of labour as a whole. In the short run the flexibility of the supply of labour to an industry may be a matter of the willingness of the workers concerned to work overtime, but in the longer period the important consideration is the ease or difficulty of inducing workers to transfer from one trade or industry to another. The mobility of labour is of profound importance to the flexibility of the whole economy. Mobility of a particular type of labour may be fairly high within a limited area, for there is generally a continual turnover from firm to firm. The important obstacles to mobility, however, lie in the transfer of labour from one district and from one type of trade to another, obstacles that are both psychological and material.

If there were no restrictions on competition between employers or workers, wage-rates would fluctuate according to the pressures of supply of and demand for each type of labour. As in the field of business behaviour, a theoretical model of perfect competition could be constructed in which there would always be a wage at which all workers seeking employment in a particular trade or industry would be given jobs; wage-rates there would fall under the force of unemployment until all employers were induced to take on those offering themselves for work, or would rise until the demand for labour by employers was satisfied. Whether full employment in the economy as a whole would necessarily be maintained by fluctuating wage-rates is another matter; what is true of the part may not be true of the whole, and the question is considered at a later stage.

SOME EFFECTS OF COLLECTIVE BARGAINING

As a result of collective bargaining, however, wage-rates are much more rigid than this, at least as far as the possibility of a fall in wage-rates is concerned. Under the surface of wage negotiations there is, it is true, more flexibility than might appear at first sight; competition for labour extends to matters other than wage-rates; overtime and bonus arrangements can be varied, and in times of labour shortage wage-rates above the minimum may be offered. But the extent to which effective wage-rates can fall in an industry suffering from declining demand is limited, so that in this situation the success of trade-union action in maintaining the level of wage-rates may be obtained only at the expense of unnecessarily depressing the level of employment in that industry. In the same way, if a trade union succeeds in raising wage-rates above a certain level the result will be to cause unemployment in the industry concerned, depending on the elasticity of the demand for labour.

Trade unions developed in the nineteenth century with the prime object of protecting wage-earners against what they considered to be the superior bargaining power of employers, with their greater material wealth. But it would be extremely difficult to assess the extent to which collective bargaining has succeeded in raising the general level of real wages above what it would have been in its absence; in prosperous times free competition between employers would lead them to bid up wage-rates even if there were no trade unions. In industries dominated by monopoly, on the other hand, it is indeed probable that trade-union action can lead to higher wage-rates than would otherwise be obtained, and without causing a fall in the number of workers employed. Apart from this, however, the question is not easily answered; although it may well be that by making employers more conscious of the advantages of installing capital equipment the pressure for higher wages has tended to accelerate the long-term growth of national output. But against this stimulus must be set the effect of restrictive trade-union practices in discouraging employers from purchasing equipment that is costly unless fully utilized.

Trade-union action can and certainly does alter the pattern of wage-rates between different occupations. Strong unions can obtain high wage-rates for their members at the expense of other unions, whose members are thereby obliged to pay higher prices for the goods they buy. Certain trade unions are able to strengthen their bargaining power by the enforcement of stringent apprentice regulations or by obliging employers to accept a 'closed shop'. If, as a result of the pressure for high wages in these strongly organized trades, workers are displaced and therefore compete for jobs in other industries, wage-rates in the latter tend to be relatively depressed as the very consequence of the success of the stronger unions.

However, in the conditions ruling since the war, at least, the determination of wage-rates has not been decided merely on the basis of the short-term self-interest of employers and trade unions. The operation of the machinery of arbitration—the Industrial Court, the Industrial Disputes Tribunal and *ad hoc* boards of arbitration—has tended to create an atmosphere in which 'justice' and 'fairness' have been appealed to as factors in their own right worthy of equal treatment with 'economic' considerations. The case for wage increases submitted by trade unionists has not been based on purely market factors such as a shortage of labour or an increase in labour productivity in a particular trade. The most frequent argument submitted in support of a wage claim has been the 'necessity' for wage-rates or earnings to keep pace with the increase in the cost of living, without any clear analysis of the economic effect of a rise in wage-rates in the industry concerned; the assumption has generally been made, explicitly or otherwise, that the 'necessity' for maintaining the purchasing power of wage-earners is a moral as well as an economic one. Secondly, reference has sometimes been made to the 'necessity' for maintaining the standard of living of a particular group of workers at a level regarded as 'proper' in view of their social or professional status. Thirdly, wage claims have often been submitted to maintain or restore a pattern of relative wage-rates regarded as desirable. Skilled workers in a particular industry might seek to maintain a certain margin over the earnings of unskilled employees within the same industry; clerical or administrative workers in a range of industries might demand a certain relativity with the earnings of civil servants, for example. That changes in such 'differentials' may have desirable or undesirable economic effects—for example, in influencing the supply of skilled as opposed to unskilled labour—is undeniable, but economic factors may be relegated to the background of such wage claims, in which the force of custom is usually strong.

The influence of trade unions cannot be assessed in relation to their effect on wage-bargaining alone. They have become a valuable feature of the operation of large-scale modern industry; they facilitate joint consultation on working conditions, and wage-earners may derive satisfaction from membership of a trade union as an expression of group loyalty, and through the medium of union subscriptions welfare benefits may be financed.

Perhaps the most controversial aspect of trade-union action has been not so much the desire to secure higher earnings as the means which unions sometimes use. The weapon of the strike is abused if drawn on in order to fight on minor issues which in a more sensible industrial world could be settled by discussion, and one symptom of this has been the frequent occurrence of unofficial strikes and those set off by inter-union disputes. Restrictive practices encouraged or tolerated by trade unions, although understandable in times of economic depression, are just as much against the interests of the country as a whole as many such practices pursued by employers. The unwillingness to accept the introduction of labour-saving machines except on uneconomic terms regarding the number of workers to be employed with them; the discouragement or open boycott of men who work 'too hard'; the undue restriction of the supply of apprentices; the rigid insistence on 'demarcation', by which certain jobs may only be performed by specified workers; these practices are out of harmony with a progressive economy in full employment and facing the opportunities as well as the challenge of change. In slowing down the growth of national output they ultimately conflict with the interests of trade-union members themselves.

H

# CHAPTER 8

# GOVERNMENT POLICY AND THE PRICE MECHANISM

The operation of monopoly and restrictive practices is one way in which the working of the price mechanism as a guide to what should be produced and as a spur to efficiency and innovation may be frustrated. The object of this chapter is to introduce briefly other matters in which government intervention may be needed to supplement or modify the operation of the price mechanism within the framework of a predominantly private-enterprise economy.

## PRIVATE AND SOCIAL COSTS AND BENEFITS

To the extent that consumers and producers take into account only costs that they alone incur and benefits that they alone receive, which we can describe as private costs and benefits, the price mechanism may fail to register the costs incurred and the benefits received by society at large, which we can call social costs and benefits. The inability of competing firms to take into account external economies of scale is one example of the possible divergence between private and social costs or benefits. Another is that of the factory-owner who does not include in his costs the effect that the smoke of his plant produces on the surrounding district. Soil erosion and the denudation of forests are other examples. We can extend the category to include owners of private property who may not take a long-enough view of the future needs of the community in considering at what rate to use up natural resources. But this is an argument that is often overworked; the value of private property reflects its future and not just its current earning capacity, and private owners are usually concerned to maintain the value of their property by good husbandry, at least when it is marketable.

Expenditure will not be undertaken by private enterprise if it is not considered to yield an adequate profit. Nevertheless, some projects that do not yield a profit may be worth undertaking on behalf of the community if the benefits they bestow are spread beyond those who could be induced to meet their cost as a private venture. A classic example is that of the lighthouse; there is no way in which the private builder of a lighthouse can collect payment from all those whom it benefits. Most lighthouses could therefore be built by private enterprise only at a loss. Nevertheless, lighthouses are worth constructing by the community, whose members are taxed to pay for their cost. Other cases include defence, education, the enforcement of law and order, fire services, and public libraries and parks.

Where private and social costs and benefits do not coincide, there is a prima-facie case for State intervention in the economy. Many such problems, however, are border-line cases and arouse controversy because they call for political judgement. Support for State intervention is far from unanimous in the case of education, social insurance, health and town-planning. In these there are no simple rules by which economics can show whether State action is justified. Least of all is it possible to generalize as to the type of government intervention that may be required and to what degree.

### METHODS OF STATE INTERVENTION

The State has a choice of methods by which to intervene in economic affairs. Compulsion is one. The emission of 'dark' smoke from factory chimneys, for example, has been made an offence. Alternatively, the government may attempt to secure the voluntary co-operation of the public in some fields. The method that is perhaps of special interest to economists is that which works through the price mechanism and not against it. By the imposition of taxes on goods and services the use of which is to be restricted and by the provision of subsidies on those which are to be encouraged the government can secure the modification of private action in conformity with its own policy in a manner that avoids compulsion or exhortation.

Economically, if not always politically, taxes and subsidies are flexible instruments; they can be raised or lowered, and certain classes of the community may be granted partial or total exemption. The use of taxes to modify private action allows those individuals who receive an especially high degree of satisfaction from pursuing a course that is to be discouraged to continue to do so if they are prepared to pay the additional cost to the community in the shape of a tax.

## THE STATE'S JUDGEMENT OF PRIVATE BENEFITS

Consumers might act differently if they possessed all the facts regarding the consequences of their actions. Needless to say, the problem of whether the government knows better than the individual what is good for him is one that arouses controversy of the most vigorous kind. Economics alone provides no answer to these questions, for the issue of whether the individual should be allowed a free hand in planning his expenditure for himself or on behalf of his family is largely a political one. But such matters may also involve social costs or benefits where State action is more acceptable. In these fields, again, taxes and subsidies exist as an alternative to compulsion and exhortation. Some measure of taxation on alcohol, for example, can be justified not only on the grounds that an excess of alcohol is harmful to personal health but also because the whole community may have to bear part of the cost of drunkenness. But those who do not drink to excess can claim that this charge should not be levied on them, and in practice expediency has played a much larger part than the consideration of social costs in shaping the pattern of taxation.

In general, since economic growth depends on change and change springs from experiment, on economic grounds alone interference with individual judgement is not without its possible cost to the community. When the alleged inadequacy of the individual's judgement as to his own interests is attributed to his lack of information, an obvious policy is for the government to ensure that the information required is readily available.

## THE STATE AND THE FORESIGHT OF PRIVATE PRODUCERS

The State may supplant or restrict the operation of private producers when the government is confident that it has a clearer view of the economic future. Since the public sector of the economy is now so large the government may reasonably hold the view that its own plans, or the information it possesses, call for certain policies to be pursued within the private sector. The government might be convinced, for example, that the capacity of certain private industries was not being extended with sufficient rapidity to meet the demands which the nationalized industries would be placing upon them. The government might feel justified in introducing some measure of State control, which may or may not proceed as far as State ownership, over those heavy fixed-cost industries where private owners, preoccupied with memories of past fluctuations in demand, seem over-cautious and where the expansion of the industry concerned is regarded by the agreement as being vital to the country's prosperity.

Naturally, this type of issue involves the question of government versus private foresight, and an obvious danger attached to intervention by the State is that its errors are likely to be on a large scale, whereas the smaller unit of decision that exists in most private industries results in investment policies that can be more readily modified if events differ from expectations.

PRICE CONTROL AND INELASTIC SUPPLY OR DEMAND

The price changes needed to balance supply and demand when these forces are inelastic may have to be very large. Large price changes may be regarded as undesirable when they cause hardship to groups of consumers or producers whom the State wishes to protect.

*In Conditions of Excess Supply*

In many countries before the last war the fact that supply or demand in the case of certain raw materials and foodstuffs tended to be inelastic made it difficult for the industries concerned to adjust themselves to conditions of falling demand. In those areas which specialized in the depressed commodity hardship was often acute and prolonged. Regional specialization may itself be a cause of inelastic supply, in that alternative opportunities for the employment of factors of production may not be available in the short run. In these cases some form of State assistance has often been given.

State intervention may take the form of fixing the price of the commodity concerned at a level above what would otherwise have been the market price. In order to prevent this higher price from re-creating conditions of excess supply, therefore, price control of this sort has to be accompanied by measures designed to restrict production, and such action may have to be on an international scale if it is to be effective. Hence the success of schemes such as these depends very much on their ability to secure support from all potential producing countries. A similar difficulty may be created by the existence of substitutes, to which demand may be transferred if the price of a commodity is held up by the restriction of output.

On the side of production, too, there may be obstacles to success; the restriction of output requires a decision as to what share of the total market is to be granted to each producer or group of producers, and low-cost producers tend to be dissatisfied with what they may consider as a burdensome restriction on their ability to compete. Schemes of this sort must also face the basic problem of having to fix a price appropriate to long-run conditions of demand and supply. There can be little reassurance that the price chosen is the 'right' price.

### 'Shortages'

During and after the war the difficulty which the operation of the price mechanism had to deal with was not so much one of excess supply but one of 'shortages' of certain commodities. The rationing of foodstuffs, for example, was necessary because the restriction of imports considerably reduced their supply, which the shortage of shipping space rendered inelastic. Demand for many foodstuffs tends to be relatively price-inelastic, so that had supply and demand been allowed to have been brought into balance only by the operation of the price mechanism, the result would have been a very sharp rise in prices, causing particular hardship to the poorer groups of the community, who spend a large proportion of their income on food. Since prices were fixed below what would have been their free market level, rationing was necessary to ensure 'fair shares'.

After the war price control was maintained on many commodities in this country; but a distinction must be drawn between the shortages of individual goods due to the difficulty of expanding supply and a general shortage of goods that may prevail because of a general excess of monetary demand during an inflation. The appropriate remedy for inflation is not universal price control but the removal of the conditions that cause it. We are here concerned only with the former category. If the commodity concerned is not regarded as 'essential', there is less reason to control its price;

a high market price will induce consumers to economize in its use and encourage an expansion of output. In these cases, if the temporarily high level of profits that results from the free play of supply and demand is regarded as undesirable, the government can impose a tax on the commodity concerned. The tax can keep the price high enough to balance supply and demand, but the 'excess' profit will go to the government.

The use of price control to deal with particular shortages suffers from two important difficulties. First, if it is to be effective, price control must be accompanied by the specification of the quality of the good or service to which it is to apply. Price control may therefore be impracticable unless producers are compelled to limit their output to certain standard types, so that control may result in uniformity. Secondly, price control may be self-defeating. Price control is satisfactory if the price fixed, although below the market level that would otherwise prevail in the short run, is high enough to provide a sufficient margin of profit to make it worth while for producers to expand output and thus eventually to remove the original cause of the shortage. Unfortunately, since price control is applied most frequently to 'essentials' the government may attempt to earn popularity by fixing prices at too low a level to encourage the rapid expansion of output. When this happens the effect of price control may be to prevent the removal of the 'shortage'. Thus the control of rents after the war made it unprofitable for many private landlords to keep working-class houses in a state of good repair, with the result that some landlords preferred to neglect or abandon their property, contracting the supply to the poor of houses in good condition.

Whether the object of limited price control is to deal with a shortage or a surfeit of supply its success cannot be ensured unless sufficient inducements are given to remove the cause of the problem. The fundamental solution is to increase the mobility of resources.

### ECONOMIC INSTABILITY

It is now generally accepted that the maintenance of general economic stability and of a satisfactory balance of international payments cannot be left to the free play of market forces. But agreement as to principle does not necessarily carry agreement as to practice; and both are the subject of later chapters.

### THE INEQUALITY OF INCOMES AND WEALTH

Here, of course, political considerations are explicit. The government may support the view that equality or inequality of incomes and wealth is politically desirable in itself. Or it may believe that the free operation of market forces would result in an ethically more acceptable pattern of incomes and wealth if only the social framework within which they operated were equitable. The latter view, that 'equality of opportunity' is desirable, would probably command a wide measure of assent in this country.

This raises the question of the degree of equality of opportunity made possible by the community's social structure and the provision of educational facilities. The size of the gap between the earnings of an engineer and a dustman, for example, given the community's demand for each type of service, depends on the relative numbers of people who are capable of becoming engineers and dustmen. With the effective extension of higher education, for example, the supply of potential engineers would increase in relation to that of dustmen, so that, if the demand for each remained unchanged, the gap between their earnings would be narrowed. Indeed, over the past fifty years 'differentials' have tended to close because of the improvement in education. The possession of wealth, too, confers on its holder the advantage of bargaining power and manoeuvre and the opportunity to take advantage of chances of gain that cannot be exploited without finance. The distribution of inherited wealth is therefore another element in determining the equality of opportunity.

Inflation and rising prices favour the business community, 'strong' trade unions, borrowers, and owners of certain types of property; those with fixed money incomes are penalized. Deflation, involving widespread unemployment and falling prices, favours lenders and those with fixed money incomes, penalizing the unemployed and the weaker businessman. In either extreme, therefore, the price mechanism can be said to be economically biased. But in their absence, and if there are no monopolistic or restrictive practices, the mechanism is neutral. Within the framework of the social structure it provides rewards according to the distribution of scarcities—the scarcer the supply of any service in relation to the demand for it, the higher the price it will command. If the pattern of scarcities were different the pattern of incomes would also be different. It is quite true, of course, that the distribution of incomes could be made more or less equal by interfering with the operations of the market. Profit margins and prices could be controlled, minimum levels of income could be prescribed for certain occupations and maxima for others. The economic case against disrupting the price mechanism in this way has already been indicated. Rationing interferes with the freedom of choice of the poor as well as the rich. If it is held desirable to redistribute incomes and wealth more equally the most economical method is to allow consumers freedom of choice but to influence by means of taxation policy the amounts that different groups *can* spend. Thus the rich are taxed more heavily than the poor through the medium of taxes on income; death duties reduce the inequalities caused by inheritance; 'essential' goods consumed mainly by the poor can be subsidized, and 'luxuries' bought by the rich can be taxed.

How incomes and wealth should be distributed is mainly a political question, since it rests ultimately on ethical judgement. It is not one, however, on which economic analysis has absolutely nothing to say. In the first place, through the exploitation of monopoly or restrictive practices certain producers may charge prices high enough to earn unfairly high incomes. In these cases State intervention is justified if free competition cannot be satisfactorily restored. Secondly, it is usually thought that, even apart from ethical considerations, a more equal distribution of incomes will increase the total satisfaction derived by the community as a whole. This will be so if the loss of satisfaction incurred by the rich in having their incomes reduced, by whatever means, is less than the gain received by the poor whose incomes are increased. This may be held to follow from the principle of diminishing marginal utility; the higher a man's income, the less will be the satisfaction lost or gained through having his income lowered or raised, if 'other things', e.g. his tastes and environment, remain unchanged. It may therefore be true that the marginal pound of income provides less satisfaction to a rich man than to a poor one.

Unfortunately this conclusion does not necessarily follow; all that the principle says is that the marginal satisfaction of income for each individual will decrease as his income rises—it does not say anything about the satisfaction derived from the marginal pound of income by one individual as compared with that obtained by another. A rich man may derive so much more pleasure from his income than a poor man that the loss of even a small part of it may mean more to him than the gain of satisfaction obtained by the poor man to whom it is transferred. However, there must also exist poor men who also obtain an abnormally high degree of satisfaction from income, so that the current presumption that the community's total satisfaction from income can be increased if great extremes of inequality are reduced is not necessarily invalid. But just how far the process of redistribution can be pushed without socially undesirable economic consequences is a controversial problem, and certain aspects of the issues it raises are introduced in subsequent chapters.

PART II

PRIVATE FINANCE AND
THE CAPITAL MARKET

# CHAPTER 9

# MONEY AND FINANCE

## LEGAL TENDER

Certain forms of money are legal tender, that is a means of payment which creditors are compelled by law to accept in settlement of a debt. Bank of England notes are legal tender up to any amount, but the coins in circulation in the United Kingdom are legal tender only for small sums—'copper' up to one shilling, threepenny pieces up to two shillings, and 'silver', or cupro-nickel, up to two pounds. But legal-tender money forms only a small part of the total quantity of what we know as money, and the fiat of the State is neither necessary nor sufficient to determine what forms money shall take. By far the greater part of what we use as money today consists of bank deposits, in other words balances held with a commercial bank or, to a small extent, with the Bank of England.

## FORMS OF MONEY TODAY

What these three forms of money, coin, paper notes and bank deposits, have in common is neither source of issue nor intrinsic value nor the backing of some other substance which does possess a value in its own right. Coin is produced by a government department, the Royal Mint, and sold to the Bank of England in return for a balance held with the Bank. Notes are issued by the Bank of England, which has been a nationalized corporation only since 1946; up to 1921 notes could be issued also by private banks in England, and the right to issue notes is still possessed by banks in Scotland today. Bank deposits, the liabilities of banks to their customers, are held with both private and State banks, e.g. with one of the 'Big Five' or the Bank of England. The market value of the metal of which coin is made today represents only a small part of its face value, so that coin is a form of 'token money'; so, of course, is paper money, and a bank deposit can be exchanged only for notes and coin.

A Bank of England note, it is true, carries on its face a declaration signed by the Chief Cashier of the Bank of England to the effect that the Bank 'Promise to pay the Bearer on Demand the Sum of One Pound'. But this is a fiction; the 'pound' is only a word describing a unit of account, and a man who exchanges his pound note for a poundsworth of coin has little of value apart from that which resides in the pound note as well. The Bank of England's 'promise' is a relic from the time when the pound sterling was on the gold standard, a system in which the Bank of England and commercial banks would exchange notes and their deposit liabilities for gold coin or bullion.

Gold bullion is still a form of international money; together with the still more important bank deposit it is one of the means of payment used by the monetary authorities of different countries to settle their debts with each other. But the passing of the domestic gold standard in 1931, leaving behind it only a promise to pay a promise, reveals clearly the essence of money, whatever its form, whether it be notes, gold, or cowrie shells. The essence of money is its acceptability to those who use it; and the distinction between what we all recognize as money and the many forms of near-money in use today, such as a bill of exchange, is one that concerns only the degree and area of acceptability. In their time, and in certain areas, cowrie shells, tea, salt, tobacco, cattle and even nails have been used as money, as well as gold and silver.

### FUNCTIONS OF MONEY

Money derives its acceptability from the efficiency with which it performs certain functions. The miser may gloat over money for its own sake, but, this rapidly diminishing class apart, money is acceptable because it gives its users command over goods and services, now or in the future. This quality is based on the prime function of money as a *medium of exchange*, and as such it also serves the purpose of a common standard of value, a *unit of account* or common denominator by which the price of wheat can be expressed in terms of coal; but it is conceivable, when prices are rising rapidly, for a country's currency to serve as the medium of exchange but for a foreign currency, or gold, to act as the unit of account. This was the case, for example, in the violent inflation experienced by Germany after the First World War, when some goods were priced in dollars but paid for in marks, the number of marks needed to buy a loaf of bread increasing almost every hour while its price in dollars remained unchanged.

This brings us to the third function of money, namely that of serving as a *store of value*, giving command over a definite quantity of goods and services in the future. The obverse of this is the use of money as a standard for deferred payments, in which contracts to pay future sums can be fixed. The use of money as a store of value depends partly on its physical durability and safety and partly on the danger that the State may repudiate existing types of money as far as its own willingness to accept them is concerned; but in a country free from disorder and revolution the efficiency of money as a store of value depends almost entirely on money's maintaining its value in terms of goods and services, that is on the stability of the general price-level.

For if prices rise, those who hold money or claims to a fixed amount of money lose a corresponding part of their real wealth, that is their command over goods and services; whereas, if prices fall, those who hold goods or owe fixed sums of money lose. Therefore if prices are expected to rise substantially people may prefer to hold more of their wealth in the form of gold, physical property or claims to property, rather than money. As a shift from money into goods tends to accelerate the rise in prices, the process may become cumulative if inflation gets out of hand, and eventually the monetary system may break down.

### OTHER REQUIREMENTS OF EFFICIENT MONEY

The efficiency of money, in all of its functions, also depends on its being sufficiently durable, divisible, standardized and convenient to use. Originally, when cattle or cowrie shells served as money, money had a value derived from the use to which these goods were put as commodities in their own right; but they were not very efficient forms of money. Gold and silver, which were valuable originally for their ornamental use, and perhaps for a certain mystic aura, filled these requirements much more satisfactorily. But the precious metals suffer from two defects as money: their lack of convenience, including the risk of loss or theft if handled in large sums, and their scarcity. Money must have a certain scarcity to function as such at all, but if it is too scarce other forms of money are likely to be developed. Both factors have contributed towards the replacement of gold and silver by the bank-note and the bank deposit, both of which originated in the practice whereby merchants deposited their gold and silver in the strong-rooms of the goldsmiths for safe keeping, as Chapter 28 describes.

## THE NEED FOR FINANCE IN BUSINESS

Finance is the provision of money for some purpose or other. Finance is required in business because receipts and payments are not always synchronized; some businesses will find that over the period that lies ahead planned expenditure exceeds expected receipts. The divergence may be the result of an inevitable discontinuity of payments or receipts, including those due to seasonal fluctuations. In other cases a gap between receipts and expenditure may be sustained over a fairly long period as a matter of policy. Finance is required to set up a new business, and for some time afterwards losses may have to be incurred by the young concern. Outside the field of business, the government may deliberately budget for a gap between receipts and payments for the financial year as a whole.

A growing business requires finance because it takes time for capital equipment to earn its purchase price. A business that maintains a steady level of output also requires finance, however, even with a synchronized flow of expenditure and receipts. Finance will be needed if there is a time-lag between each successive act of expenditure and the receipt to which it gives rise. The process of production is time-consuming; some time must elapse between the input of factors of production and the stage at which the goods thereby created are ready for sale, during which time the cost of production must be financed.

Let us suppose, by way of illustration, that a manufacturer is to commence operations in a new factory. For some time he will have to finance the cost of labour and materials purchased until they pass through the process of manufacturing to emerge at a later date as some product ready for sale, during which period production takes the form of work in progress. We can assume that the manufacturer borrows in order to finance this stage of the work. When the goods are sold the businessman will be in a position *either* to repay his debt *or* to buy fresh materials and labour in order to start the cycle of production anew; for money will once more be needed to finance the next round of production. If the level of operations became continuous and reached a constant magnitude the cost of production in any period would equal the value of sales in the same period (setting aside the question of profit). But finance would still be required for the work in progress that, in these conditions, would remain at a constant level.

Finance is also required because the modern economy does not operate on a solely 'cash and carry' basis. Credit is given by one business to another and by the Exchequer to business, since business taxes are paid on profits earned in the past. Businesses also receive credit from wage-earners and salaried workers, who are paid in arrears. In any period, therefore, some businesses are net receivers while others are net givers of credit.

### FINANCE IN THE MODERN ECONOMY

The character of finance has changed with the development of productive methods requiring large amounts of physical capital. Earlier, finance would have been needed largely to tide the borrower over some misfortune, such as a crop failure or the loss of a ship, or to provide for some festive occasion on which society expected an appropriate scale of expenditure; it was also required, of course, to finance war or extravagance. The point is that in these early times, and even today in primitive regions, finance was needed to a great extent for purposes that were defensive or materially unproductive. In these circumstances the high rates of interest that could often be exacted by the money-lender were, not unnaturally, regarded as a form of exploitation.

With the growth of the capitalist, or capital-using, economy, the proverbial injunction against lending and borrowing has been replaced by the acceptance of both as virtuous in a world in which the main reason for wanting finance is to provide for some productive enterprise, from which the expected rate of return is sufficient to pay a rate of interest settled by a bargaining process in which the act of borrowing is no longer regarded as an admission of economic weakness. That the borrower looks forward to a profit from his enterprise has two important consequences. First, it gives to both borrower and lender a more reliable standard by which to judge the rate of interest the former can afford to pay; secondly, by enhancing the probability of repayment it gives to a claim on an honest borrower qualities necessary for its being used as a negotiable asset.

I

## FINANCIAL INSTITUTIONS

The development of the capitalist economy has therefore both depended on and stimulated the growth of financial markets, through which persons, businesses and government bodies that require funds can find some means of making contact with those that have a surplus over immediate requirements. It would obviously be impossible for these marriages of surpluses and deficiencies to be arranged directly; and finance has reflected the course of economic development in general, in that the demand for and the supply of finance are brought together through the medium of many types of institution, which may pass funds through many hands before they are actually spent.

These institutions shoulder some of the risks of finance, which are mainly of three kinds. First, there is the risk of default due to the dishonesty of a borrower. Secondly, there is the risk of default, or loss of capital, due to adverse economic conditions. Thirdly, there is the risk of loss of capital value due to a rise in market interest rates, for this implies a fall in the market value of a capital asset bearing a fixed nominal rate of return.

Financial institutions naturally guard against the risk of default or adverse economic experience by the exercise of due caution in the selection of transactions. The banks, for example, will generally require their loans to be supported by some form of security, and building societies lend on the security of the property whose purchase they finance. Some institutions specialize in matters in which their skill and knowledge is a safeguard against loss. But many seek to minimize these risks by spreading their assets over a wide field. Liabilities, too, can be pooled, as in the case of the life-assurance company, which is able to calculate the flow of payments which it will be called on to make to its policy-holders by transacting a sufficient volume of business, so that the incidence of mortality can be forecast with sufficient accuracy for premiums to be set at a prudent level.

The holder of a security has to bear the risk of a fluctuation in its price due to a change in the market rate of interest or yield. In general the longer the term to redemption of a fixed-interest security the greater is the risk of loss of capital value during its life due to a rise in market rates of interest; in the case of a bond with little time to run before redemption, the knowledge that a given redemption price is soon to be received acts as a stabilizing force on the current price. Therefore, institutions which do not consider it prudent, having regard to the nature of their business, to bear the risk of wide fluctuations in market values will hold a greater proportion of short-term assets. Some institutions, such as building societies, can take advantage of the fact that the greater security of capital value attached to short-term assets may lead to a pattern of interest rates in which longer-term assets carry higher yields. They may seek to earn a profit by borrowing 'short' and lending 'long', if they are willing to face the risk of loss due to a rise in the rate of interest payable to their short-term creditors that is not matched immediately by a corresponding increase in the interest receipts on their long-term assets. In some respects hire-purchase finance houses and the banks act in this way.

### MARKETS IN NEW AND EXISTING ASSETS

The complex of financial markets serves three purposes: to collect the surplus funds of large numbers of lenders; to channel them to business, government and other spenders; and to enable holders of existing financial claims to transform them into money. Through the medium of the Stock Exchanges, businesses and the government can raise funds in the form of new issues of securities for public subscription, and the Exchequer can also borrow from the public through the National Savings movement. The banks accept large numbers of deposits and lend in the form of bank advances and overdrafts to business and other spenders. Building societies issue shares and accept deposits and lend their proceeds for the purchase of property. Hire-purchase finance companies issue securities and also accept deposits in order to obtain the funds they use to lend on hire-purchase transactions. Life-assurance offices and pension funds collect the savings of millions of policyholders and contributors and use their mounting reserve funds to invest in many forms of financial and real assets.

The passage of funds to spenders could not have developed on this scale were it not for the fact that holders of existing claims are enabled by the operation of financial markets to 'disentangle' themselves from the role of creditor at any time, or after a stated interval of time, and to hold their wealth in the form of money instead of claims to future sums of money. There is no need for an investor to 'lock up' savings for the whole period of the physical capital formation which they are used to finance. Bank deposits can be withdrawn on demand or at short notice, and similar facilities exist in the case of short-term assets held with building societies, hire-purchase finance companies, local authorities and the National Savings movement. Holders of Stock Exchange securities, on the other hand, do not usually have the right to turn them into money at any time on stated terms, but can sell them at whatever price these assets fetch in the market provided by the operation of the Stock Exchange. This price will depend on the willingness of *other* investors to hold securities.

In the case of marketable securities the balance between the desire to hold claims and that to hold money is maintained through variations in the prices of securities, high prices inducing some holders to sell and low prices tempting potential holders to buy. But the distinction between the two forms of 'marketability' is not clear-cut, for if banks or building societies, for example, experience a sustained withdrawal of deposits they, too, can resort to the price mechanism in order to safeguard their business, by raising the rates of interest payable to depositors and so stemming the outflow and attracting new deposits.

In its widest sense the marketability of many financial assets is part of the foundation of the financial system, and it rests ultimately on the ability of market forces to keep the supply of and demand for funds in balance, for would-be sellers cannot dispose of their assets unless purchasers can be found. There can be no market if the pressure of transactions is 'one-way'.

### THE CHOICE OF ASSETS

The range of assets chosen by different individuals and institutions will be influenced by their particular financial circumstances and by the characteristics of different classes of assets. The latter can be grouped according to liquidity, income, risk and certainty of real value.

### Liquidity

Liquidity refers to the facility with which an asset can be exchanged for a *known* amount of money and depends on ease of marketability and certainty of capital value. Liquidity and income tend to be alternative characteristics of assets. Those that are less liquid have to offer a higher income to compensate holders for this disadvantage. The way in which people—as well as companies and financial institutions—will deploy their wealth will thus be closely related to their desire for liquidity rather than income on the one hand and the rates of return they can obtain from different classes of less liquid assets on the other. By definition the most liquid of all assets is currency—banknotes and coin. Deposits held at a commercial bank—as long as it is solvent—are also exchangeable into an equal value of currency, but they suffer from two slight defects as liquid assets. Banks are not open at all hours of the day, and bank charges usually have to be paid on cheque and other transactions. On the other hand, bank deposits are more convenient than currency for transactions of large amounts and are not subject to the same possibilities of loss or theft. The choice between bank deposits and currency as a form of asset is therefore mainly one of convenience and habit; in the United Kingdom bank deposits withdrawable only after a period of notice also earn interest.

Complete certainty of capital value is also afforded by the various forms of National Savings, but these vary as to convenience and income, and the amount of investment in each is subject to a statutory maximum. Deposits and shares in building societies are also relatively liquid assets, the risk of default being slight in the case of the well-managed societies; they earn income but are subject to the disadvantage that a period of notice may be needed for withdrawal. Other forms of deposit are those made with hire-purchase and similar types of finance houses; these generally offer a higher rate of return than building societies but, in addition to similar provisions regarding notice of withdrawal, are generally considered by the public to be subject to a somewhat higher risk of default. Deposits can be placed with some local authorities; these are subject to a low risk of default and yield interest, but their advantages as to liquidity will depend on the conditions attached to the notice of withdrawal. Shares in retail co-operative societies are another avenue for personal saving; they are comparatively safe as far as capital value is concerned and afford income in the form of 'dividends', which are refunded discounts on purchases made 'at the Co-op'.

### Market Imperfections

The risk of default is not the only, or in practice the most important, form of risk attached to certain financial assets. Many assets are liable to uncertainty as to market price, that is uncertainty as to the price at which they can be sold to other potential holders.

This uncertainty will always be present in the case of those types of assets for which no organized market exists or in which the market is grossly 'imperfect'. For in these cases there will be a risk that the purchase or selling price of an asset may not be representative of its type, a difficulty that would be magnified if the asset concerned was not one of a highly standardized class. Furthermore, in a highly imperfect market a comparatively small volume of sales may reduce the market price—in the financial world a market subject to this disadvantage is often described as 'narrow'. In these circumstances the price at which an asset can be bought or sold may not be ascertainable until the transaction is attempted; the price at which a similar transaction was last carried out may not be a reliable guide to that at which another can be effected. Many physical assets fall to a greater or lesser extent within this class. At any point of time some degree of uncertainty will exist as to the price at which a piece of jewellery, a second-hand motor-car or a house, for example, can be sold; but among financial assets shares in companies that are not quoted on the Stock Exchange are also subject to the same disadvantage.

### Fluctuations in Interest Rates

The most important forms of uncertainty as to the market price of assets, however, concern alterations in interest rates and in the prices of variable-income assets. Alterations in the rate of interest earned by some assets do occur, it is true, with no resultant change in market value, as in the case of National Savings assets and building society deposits. It is to the broad class of marketable securities—government bonds, company stocks and shares—that uncertainty of capital value caused by changing interest rates is most closely related. Purchasers of securities have to face the risk that when the time comes to sell their security the market price will have fallen to below the purchase price because of a rise in the market rate of interest. Even if resale is not contemplated, the risk of a fall in price will cause many prospective investors to exercise caution; in the case of some institutions the presentation of annual accounts, in which fluctuations in security values may have to be recorded, may be an important consideration.

The simplest example is that of a security issued with interest payments fixed in perpetuity. One hundred pounds by *nominal* value of 2½ per cent Consolidated Stock, a government security, for example, provides interest at £2 10*s.* per annum in perpetuity. (This stock is actually redeemable at any time on notice from the Treasury, but as long as the market rate of interest on long-term stocks is above 2½ per cent it can be assumed that the option will not be exercised, for nothing would be saved by the Exchequer in redeeming the stock.) At a market rate of interest of 5 per cent the price of 'Consols' would be only £50 for each £100 of nominal value. The annual contractual interest payment is sometimes described as the *nominal* or *coupon* rate of interest and the market rate of interest as the *yield* of an asset. Given the price as set by the market, the yield on any stock depends on its coupon rate of interest; conversely, given the coupon rate and the yield, the price of any stock is determined.

For a perpetual stock the calculation, ignoring the question of interest accruing since the last date of payment, is as follows:

$$\text{Yield } \% = \frac{\text{coupon rate } \%}{\text{market price}} \times 100$$

$$\text{e.g. } 5 = \frac{2\frac{1}{2}}{50} \times 100$$

Over the past century the yield on perpetual government securities has varied from approximately 2½ to about 5½ per cent, so that the full price range of a 2½ per cent coupon stock has been from about 45 to 100. Long-term rates of interest do not usually change sharply over short periods of time, but the risk of some adverse movement is always present.

Of course, it is true that there is also the possibility of a rise in the market price of the asset. But uncertainty of this sort, even though the chances of gain and loss may be equal, tends to act as a deterrent to many possible purchasers. If the chances of a given loss or gain are thought to be equal, those who do not enjoy risk-taking for its own sake will only commit their wealth to this form of uncertainty if the yield of the asset concerned is regarded as adequate compensation, bearing in mind that the balance may be tilted by the fact that interest income is generally subject to tax, whereas loss of capital may be a net loss.

### Yields on Dated Securities

In the case of a security with a limited period to redemption two yield calculations can be employed. The simplest, and least informative, is the 'flat' or 'running' yield, relating the coupon rate of interest to the current market price. The other is the yield to redemption. A bond with ten years to run, redeemable at a price of 100, may bear a coupon rate of 5 per cent and have a current market price of 95. The flat yield is 5·26 per cent, but the yield to redemption takes into account the capital appreciation of £5 per £100 (nominal) of stock, spread over ten years, which can also be expressed as a rate of interest, allowance being made for compounding. The yield to redemption (ignoring all questions of taxation on interest or capital) is 5·56 per cent, which is in excess of the running yield because the stock is standing at a discount; if the market price were above the redemption price the yield to redemption would be lower than the running yield. In the rest of this book the expressions 'rate of interest' or 'yield', if unqualified, are intended to denote yield to redemption.

In general, the shorter the period to redemption the smaller is the fluctuation in market price, expressed proportionately, for any given change in yield. This may not always be true of stocks standing at a very large discount or premium and which are more than a certain distance from maturity. With this reservation, however, we can say that the shorter the term to redemption the greater is the equivalent change in yield represented by a given change in price and, therefore, the more stable will the price tend to be. A change in price involves a change in the discount or premium at which the stock is standing; the shorter the term the greater is the change in yield per annum represented by a change in the element of appreciation or depreciation to redemption. If the price of a ten-year stock with a coupon rate of 5 per cent falls from 100 to 95, the yield would increase from 5 to 5·56 per cent. A similar price movement in the case of a stock with fifty years to run would involve an increase in yield from 5 to only 5·29 per cent, because the element of capital appreciation to redemption is spread over a longer period of time.

If yields were the same on all stocks irrespective of their term to redemption, therefore, it is clear that fluctuations in the level of yields would allow the prices of short-term securities to remain *relatively* stable, and although the historical range of fluctuations in the yields on short-term securities has been greater than the range of fluctuation in long-term interest rates, the difference has not been sufficient to destroy the conclusion that the shorter the term to maturity the less prone will an asset be to fluctuations in market prices during its life.

Nevertheless, a short-term security may be unattractive to some investors even though the risk of capital loss is slight and temporary and even though, in certain circumstances, its yield may be higher than that obtainable on longer-term stocks. For the proceeds of a stock maturing in one year's time, unless needed for immediate expenditure, will have to be reinvested in another security, by which time the yield obtainable on the latter may be relatively low. Certainty of capital value for one year may be obtained only at the expense of uncertainty of the income obtainable over a more lengthy period. Short-term assets other than securities, such as interest-bearing deposits, on which the rate of interest is alterable at the option of the borrower, are also subject to this uncertainty.

In general, investors who are unwilling to accept the risk of uncertain capital values, such as those who hold assets against short-term liabilities and those institutions which are reluctant to show temporary book losses in published accounts, will be deterred from holding long-term assets, whilst those who dislike uncertainty of long-term income even more will tend to avoid short-term assets. On the whole, the risk of capital loss operates so as to deter the greater part of the community from committing its wealth directly in the form of marketable securities at all. The willingness to risk capital loss shows a marked relationship, not unnaturally, to the size of a man's wealth.

### Risk of Default

Certain assets may carry the right to a fixed annual interest payment, but their market value will be influenced not only by the movement of market rates of interest on default-free securities but also by the market's assessment of the risk of default on the annual interest payment or on the eventual repayment of principal. Securities issued by companies fall into this class, which also includes loans issued by domestic semi-governmental bodies and by overseas governments. Thus the market prices of fixed-interest industrial securities may fluctuate more widely than those of government securities, according to the general state of trade. Their greater variability therefore makes them even less attractive to those investors who will not accept uncertainty of capital value.

### Variable-Income Assets

Finally, we come to the greatest cause of uncertainty of capital values, namely the risk of variation of the annual income provided by those assets to which no legal commitment of a fixed annual payment is attached. Ordinary shares, for example, provide a right only to a dividend that may be altered from year to year as the directors of the company concerned consider prudent. Market prices of ordinary shares respond to the market's fears and hopes regarding future dividend changes, and fluctuations in these are both stronger than and superimposed upon the effect of changes in the market rate of interest on fixed-interest securities, with which they compete for investors' funds. Thus ordinary shares offer still less attraction than fixed-interest securities to those investors averse to accepting the risk of capital loss. Similar considerations apply to investment in other assets that offer a variable annual income—for example, property that is open to the risk of periodical lack of tenants or to low rents.

### Certainty of Real Value

In an economy in which prices remain stable investors are likely to identify real with monetary values. But the experience of large price fluctuations, particularly of rising prices, may destroy this identity. If continually rising prices are expected, money and fixed-interest assets become inferior forms of wealth, and investors will turn instead to those assets whose value rises more in step with the increase in prices, such as physical property and ordinary shares, which are a form of claim on the income of physical property. The desire to hold such assets will be particularly strong in the case of those investors whose financial commitments also keep pace with the rise in prices.

### A Summary

To sum up, we can say that, given an investor's psychological attitude to risk-taking, his investment in different classes of asset will depend on a number of factors. The total value of his wealth will influence his willingness to undertake any form of risk. The nature of his liabilities, for example, the size and timing of possible future outlays as compared with future income, will influence the importance he attaches to certainty of capital value as compared with certainty of long-term income. The extent to which high-yielding but capital-uncertain assets can be pledged as security for future borrowing, a factor we have not yet mentioned, will also be a consideration in the case of an investor the nature of whose liabilities would otherwise require him to keep a reserve of potentially liquid assets. Given the character of his liabilities, his psychological propensity to undertake risk, and the size of his wealth, the investor will naturally assess the relative rates of return currently obtainable from different types of asset that can be set off as compensation for differences in the degree of liquidity and risk. Finally, his policy will depend on his expectations regarding the future movement of yields and capital values. The investment policy of financial institutions will be subject to similar considerations.

### THE VARIETY OF ASSETS AND THE FINANCIAL SYSTEM

The variety of financial assets available has greatly facilitated the operation of the financial system by allowing investors to hold wealth in the form most appropriate to their own financial circumstances, thus making them more ready to part with surplus funds. The investor who is willing to give up the chance of a high but uncertain income can obtain a lower but more certain return on a fixed-interest asset backed by the good name of the borrower or by real property. A certain long-term income can be obtained from a long-term asset with no risk of default. The investor who is not willing to bear the risk that the capital value of his wealth may fluctuate widely can choose a short-term asset.

The less cautious investor can chance his arm in the uncertainties of business experience by accepting the greater degree of risk attached to the variable-dividend ordinary share, which also carries by way of compensation some measure of control over the business concern in the form of a vote at its shareholders' meetings, which may or may not be exercised, according to choice.

Those who seek funds have a corresponding range of selection. A business may raise finance in the form of fixed-interest debt, perhaps secured on its physical assets. This form of liability has the advantages of carrying a relatively low rate of interest and of retaining the control of the business in the hands of existing owners as long as the liability is met. Finance by variable-dividend shares, on the other hand, passes a greater part of the risks of business to those who supply funds, but at the cost of sharing with them a greater part of the gains of a profitable concern and of allowing them some measure of control. The operation of the market enables a balance to be found between these considerations and a bargain to be struck between those who seek and those who supply finance.

### FINANCE, SAVING AND INVESTMENT

Finance for capital investment may be made available from the current saving of persons, businesses or the government; or from money balances accumulated from saving performed in the past; or from money created by the government and banking system. Neither the user nor the supplier of finance need distinguish between these sources, but it is essential for us to do so if we are to look behind what has been called the veil of money to the real goods and services of which capital investment is composed.

For capital investment to take place, resources must be withheld from current consumption. For this condition to be satisfied, an equivalent volume of current saving is required. Saving is the withholding of income from expenditure on consumption, and income is derived from production, so that by saving today we allow production to be used for capital investment today. The resources represented by what we saved last year have already been used for capital investment, so that finance supplied from last year's saving does not make available the real resources required today. Thus ultimately it is the current act of saving and not the provision of finance alone that makes capital investment possible.

To this vital principle there is one exception, if the economy is fully employed. The real resources for capital investment in this country may be provided by a reduction in our exports or by an increase in our imports. But for this to happen we must allow our foreign assets to decline, or we must borrow abroad, or we must receive grants from abroad, in the form, for example, of inter-governmental assistance. If the economy is not fully employed, however, the principle that it is saving and not finance alone that makes capital investment possible need not apply. If a country has sufficient idle resources, these can be put to work to produce capital goods without requiring the community to give up part of its existing consumption. But as long as full employment exists, saving and not finance remains the ultimate limitation on capital investment.

# CHAPTER 10

# INVESTMENT AND FINANCE IN THE PERSONAL SECTOR

### THE ONE-MAN BUSINESS AND PARTNERSHIP

Of the 51 million people in the United Kingdom, about 40 million are over the age of fifteen. Of these, more than 21 million are wage- and salary-earners. Rather more than $1\frac{1}{2}$ million are self-employed; they are to be distinguished from companies, which have a corporate legal identity distinct from the individuals who own them, for the identity of the unincorporated business is inseparable from that of its owners. The importance of this distinction exists in the ability of the company to bring an action at law in its own name as opposed to those of its owners; in the difference between the incidence of taxation on companies from that on their owners as persons; and, above all, in the fact that owners of unincorporated businesses are liable, if necessary, to the full extent of their personal property for debts incurred in the course of their business, whereas owners of a limited-liability company are liable only up to their share in the capital of a company as defined by law.

## Legal Requirements of the One-Man Business

No legal permission is required to commence trading, and accounts may be kept in such form as is thought prudent, subject to the requirements of the Inland Revenue authorities for taxation purposes. The income earned by one-man businesses and partnerships is merged with any other form of income received by their owners for the assessment of income tax and surtax; unincorporated businesses are not liable to profits tax. Not only is the owner obliged to meet outstanding business debts from his own personal resources; all the assets of his business will be merged with his other property for the assessment of estate duty in the event of his death, thus increasing the tax liability on his estate and, because business assets may have to be sold to meet this liability, rendering more difficult the passing of his business to his heirs.

## Legal Requirements of Partnerships

Partnerships are subject to closer legal supervision. The number of partners must not exceed twenty (ten in banking), and partners can only sue or be sued in their own name. In the absence of arrangements to the contrary, any partner can end a partnership merely by giving notice to the others; a partnership is also dissolved automatically by the death of one partner.

Each partner is entitled to a share of profits in agreed proportions. Each is entitled to take part in the direction of the business, so that each may bind the others in any contract falling within the scope of the concern's business; and each may be liable, after meeting his own debts, for those of the partnership, to the full extent of his private wealth. A partner can avoid the risk of unlimited liability by becoming a limited or 'sleeping' partner in a limited partnership. In this case his liability is restricted to the sum he has brought to the business, but he can take no part whatsoever in the direction of the business. This is not a common form of partnership, for the private company offers greater advantages in both convenience of operation and scope of finance.

The partnership is a cumbersome business unit; its success depends on harmonious personal relations between partners, and its duration may be uncertain. The death or withdrawal of a partner may oblige the others to sell business assets or incur debt in order to repay his share, and the entire personal property of each is bound up with the integrity and skill of his associates. As a result, partnerships now play little part in industry and trade; they numbered only 200,000 in 1957 and are important only in the professions.

## The Decline of the Unincorporated Business

Until the close of the nineteenth century family businesses were predominant in trade and many manufacturing industries. They had developed from very modest ventures, growing on income ploughed back into the business, or had been established at the outset on a more substantial scale out of the private fortune of some comparatively rich man. The main limitation on the development of the one-man business or partnership, however, was that of finance. Even before the industrial revolution led to the development of large-scale manufacturing and mining industry, the financial requirements of certain types of business began to exceed what the unincorporated concern could deploy. First in overseas trading and then in railways, the capital needed was more than individuals or partnerships could provide. Even where a number of men were in a position to supply adequate finance as a partnership, their reluctance to bear the risks of unlimited liability would be increased by the difficulty of control. Two, three or even four men in a partnership might each feel confident of possessing sufficient powers of control over a manufacturing enterprise to which their whole wealth was committed: twenty such men could hardly do so.

After the middle of the nineteenth century, when legislation removed the existing legal obstacles to the development of limited-liability companies, the unincorporated business began to decline in relative importance. Still, before 1914 many manufacturing businesses could be set up with the aid of finance provided in the form of loans or participation in limited partnerships, through the medium of advertisements in newspapers or through the assistance of solicitors. Where the business was to be established in a prosperous district and its founder was known personally to wealthy people—he may, for example, have been one of their employees—the chance of securing sufficient finance was still relatively high.

With the redistribution of incomes and wealth brought about by the increase in taxation on income and property, however, this source of finance has been severely reduced, and because of the severity of taxation on high incomes many rich people tend to seek tax-free capital gains in the use of their fortunes rather than a heavily taxable return in the form of income.

The financial limitations on the establishment and growth of unincorporated businesses and the disadvantage of unlimited liability today restrict this form of enterprise to those fields where comparatively little capital is needed; in manufacturing it is limited to a very minor role, such as subcontracting in the clothing industry. In 1955–6, according to the report of the Inland Revenue Commissioners for 1956–7, there were about 560,000 unincorporated businesses assessed for income tax in retail and wholesale distribution; 325,000 in farming and fishing; 140,000 in building; 155,000 in professional services; 295,000 in entertainment, sport and other services; and in clothing, food and road transport some 105,000 between them. All other industries accounted for about 100,000. The number of unincorporated businesses is large, but in 1956 capital formation in the personal sector, other than houses, represented only some 9 per cent of capital investment in the economy as a whole.

### THE FINANCE OF HOUSE-PURCHASE

Apart from expenditure by unincorporated businesses, housing is the main form of investment in the personal sector. Of the total of 15 million houses and flats in existence, some 3 million are owned by the local authorities; of the remainder, 8 million are rented, leaving some 4–5 million occupied by their owners. In the post-war years both the total and the composition of the number of houses built have undergone important variations due in the main to government policy and in particular to the government's attitude towards the number of houses to be built for private rather than local authority ownership.

TABLE 3. *Houses built in the period 1934–1957*

| | Total | For local authorities | For private owners | Others* |
|---|---|---|---|---|
| 1934/5–1938/9† | 361,142 | 85,945 (23·78%) | 275,186 (76·19%) | 11 (0·03%) |
| 1948 | 232,463 | 193,548 (83·26%) | 34,390 (14·79%) | 4,525 (1·95%) |
| 1957 | 307,590 | 169,629 (55·15%) | 128,784 (41·87%) | 9,177 (2·98%) |

Source: *Annual Abstract of Statistics* (H.M.S.O.)

\* Mainly construction by government departments and housing associations.
† Annual average.

A very high proportion of new private houses built each year are financed by their purchasers through some form of mortgage loan. The main lenders in the field of house-purchase are the building societies, followed by life-assurance offices. As a result of an inquiry made in 1954 the Building Society Association estimated that two-thirds of the houses built for private ownership were financed by building society advances. At the end of the year there were 1¾ million borrowers on the books of building societies.

### PERSONAL INCOMES

The main changes reflected in Table 4 have been the maintenance of full employment since the war, rent control, the

K

relatively slow increase in rents, dividends and interest, and the development of what has come to be known as the 'Welfare State'. As a result, the proportion of total personal income received in the form of wages, salaries and public grants has increased, while the share of income from property has fallen. In the process the inequality of gross personal incomes has been reduced.

TABLE 4. *Personal Income in 1938 and 1957*

|  | 1938 £m | 1957 £m |
|---|---|---|
| Wages | 1,920 | 7,720 |
| Salaries | 910 | 4,060 |
| Pay in cash and kind of the Forces | 66 | 397 |
| Employers' contributions |  |  |
| National Insurance | 54 | 308 |
| Other | 72 | 457 |
| Total | 3,022 | 12,942 |
| Total income from self-employment | 647 | 1,787 |
| Rent, dividends and interest | 1,134 | 2,001 |
| National Insurance benefits and other current grants from public authorities | 275 | 1,257 |
| TOTAL PERSONAL INCOME | 5,078 | 17,987 |

Source: *National Income and Expenditure* 1958 (H.M.S.O.)

The incidence of income tax and surtax has worked in the same direction. Because even before the war the proportion of income taken by these taxes rose in steps up the scale of incomes, the general rise in money income per head that has occurred since 1939 would have been sufficient to cause a more equal distribution of incomes *after* tax. But the increase in rates of tax has borne most heavily on the higher incomes, so that net money incomes after tax have been equalized to a remarkable degree. Because of the steep rise in retail prices since 1938 the reduction in the real net incomes of those people with high incomes has been severe indeed.

Some idea of this redistribution can be obtained simply from the statement that whereas the gross earnings of the average male adult manual worker rose from £180 in 1938 to about £640 in 1957, representing an increase after tax of about one-quarter in real terms, the number of people in receipt of a net income after tax greater in real terms than that afforded by the minimum surtax level of £2,000 in 1938 can be estimated to have fallen from about 105,000 to a mere 9,000–10,000 in 1957. The share of total net personal income represented by this diminishing class declined from 8 per cent in 1938 to under one-half of one per cent of the total in 1957. It is not known whether tax avoidance, legitimate or otherwise, materially weakens this contrast.

## INCOMES AND SAVING

This redistribution has been of great importance to finance and investment. Although generalizations about spending habits must be treated with caution, because of the wide dispersion within any income group, it is clear from the evidence available* that the distribution of incomes and property dominates the pattern of personal saving. On average, the proportion of personal income, after tax, that is saved rises with the size of income. People with very low incomes, who include the retired and unemployed, tend to dissave, that is to spend in excess of their incomes, and even in the range of income earned by the majority of adult male manual workers the average rate of personal saving is low, perhaps of the order of 2 per cent in 1953; nearly two-fifths of all households are thought not to save at all from one year to the next. Above an income of £1,000 per annum the proportion saved rises steadily. It was estimated by Lydall that in 1953–4 the top 3½ per cent of income recipients, with incomes of more than £1,000 per annum gross, were responsible for more than one-quarter of all the personal saving done in this country.

It is because of this link between size of income and the proportion saved that some observers of the post-war economic scene fear that the redistribution of personal incomes has reduced the volume of capital investment that this country can undertake. The proportion of total net personal income saved has actually risen since before the war, mainly as a result of full employment and the growth of contractual saving; but those who express concern at the equalization of incomes believe that, but for the heavy burden of taxation now borne by the rich and not-so-rich, the level of personal saving would be higher still. On the other hand, this increase in taxation has been the means whereby saving by the government, that is the excess of current receipts over

* See H. F. Lydall, *British Incomes and Saving* (Basil Blackwell, 1955).

current government expenditure, has risen. But even if it is true that taxation has merely shifted saving from persons to the Exchequer, the diversion may have been to the detriment of enterprise, for wealthy individuals are usually more ready to finance novel and risky projects than the State. But this is part of a wider, political question.

### CONTRACTUAL SAVING

The main types of personal contractual saving are performed through life assurance, pension schemes and the repayment of building-society mortgage advances. Repayment of hire-purchase debt is excluded here because of its greater variability from year to year. About 70 per cent of all income recipients are believed to pay life-assurance premiums,* and about 8 million people were thought to be members of pension schemes in 1953.† Building society mortgages, on the other hand, are limited to about one-eighth of all households. Roughly three-quarters of all households appear to engage in one or more of these forms of contractual saving, and throughout the whole range of incomes people who make these contractual payments save more than those who do not.

In 1957 about 7 per cent of net personal incomes, or some £1,200 million, was devoted to life-assurance premiums, pension contributions (including those made by employers) and the repayment of building society mortgages. This figure is perhaps misleading, in that employers' contributions to pension funds include payments to make good certain capital deficiencies as well as normal annual payments, and perhaps one-half of all building society repayments, or roughly £100 million, may be advances repaid in lump sums out of the proceeds of the sale of old houses. But the part played by contractual payments is undoubtedly substantial.

The net contribution of contractual saving must take account of payments by life-assurance offices and pension funds to policy-holders and contributors and new building society mortgages granted each year, for these sums help to swell the volume of spending by persons. The expenses of these institutions must also be deducted. On the other hand, the investment income

* Lydall, op. cit.
† *Report of the Committee on the Economic and Financial Provision for Old Age.* Cmd. 9333 (H.M.S.O. 1954).

received by these institutions can be included, for it represents income earned on behalf of persons. In the case of building societies we are then left with an excess of new advances over repayments, but the net increase in the funds of life-assurance and pension schemes represents positive saving. The latter has grown from about £80–90 million in 1938 to £557 million in 1957, representing a rise from about 30 per cent of all personal saving in 1938 to about 37 per cent in 1957. The latter year was one in which other forms of personal saving were probably running at abnormally high levels; between 1953 and 1957 net saving through life-assurance and pension funds averaged about 45 per cent of all personal saving.

In recent years pension funds have been growing more rapidly than life-assurance funds, and their combined rate of increase of about £600 million per annum is probably now divided evenly between them. In the context of the redistribution of incomes, life assurance in particular has been of great significance as a medium of saving in the post-war years, because it is the largest single form of saving favoured by the wage-earner, the main beneficiary of the process of redistribution

## THE DISTRIBUTION OF WEALTH

The distribution of wealth is far more uneven than the spread of net incomes. But the impact of death duties on the estates of two generations and the especially severe taxation of high incomes since the Second World War have had the effect of considerably reducing the degree of inequality. The movement in this direction is likely to continue if only because the rates of both income tax and estate duties rise in steps, and the general level of incomes and wealth increases in money value.

Estimates of the total value of the wealth owned by persons and its distribution are difficult to construct with any great degree of accuracy. It has been calculated* that 1 per cent of people over the age of twenty-five owned 70 per cent of all private property in 1913 and 55 per cent in 1936. No reliable estimate has been made for the post-war period, but a comparable figure would now be of the order of two-fifths or less. These estimates exaggerate the degree of inequality somewhat in that they include women

* H. Campion, *Public and Private Property in Great Britain* (Oxford University Press).

who are not heads of households, and a further difficulty is that they exclude estates too small to rank for death duties, that is those below £2,000. A more useful statement of the present position, perhaps, is that 10 per cent of all families own something like two-thirds of all property assessed for estate duty. However, although about one-third of the value of estates above £2,000 consists of those in excess of £50,000, at the bottom end of the top two-thirds we find estates of the more modest value of £5,000, including house property.

## THE CHOICE OF FINANCIAL ASSETS BY PERSONS

### Liquid Assets

The choice of financial assets, and particularly that between liquid and less liquid or capital-uncertain assets, is closely related to the distribution of wealth; the distribution of capital-uncertain assets is even more unequal than the range of personal wealth as a whole. The proportion of wealth held in liquid form is highest at the bottom of the scale of wealth and falls as we ascend it. Currency and National Savings assets, especially deposits with the Post Office or Trustee Savings Banks, are the usual forms of liquid asset held by wage-earners. Deposits with a building society or a commercial bank are held only by a small minority.

About one household in five is believed to hold a bank account, but the total of personal bank deposits is concentrated on the relatively wealthy. The estate-duty statistics indicate that holdings of net bank deposits (less overdrafts) fall from more than 20 per cent of gross capital value in estates of £2,000–£10,000 to 7 or 8 per cent in those of £100,000–£300,000; but three-quarters of all personal net bank deposits, or more than £1,500 million, appear to be held by persons with property in excess of £10,000. The concentration of bank deposits in the hands of the relatively rich provides a reservoir of funds from which a Stock Exchange boom can be fed when fear of capital loss is replaced by hope of gain.

### Stock Exchange Securities

Stock Exchange securities are held mainly by the wealthy. According to one estimate,* only 5–7 per cent of households hold stocks and shares, apart from National Savings Certificates and

* H. F. Lydall, op. cit.

Defence Bonds, and nearly one-fifth of their total value is believed to be held by only one-tenth of one per cent of households. Because of their capital-uncertainty the ownership of company securities is even more closely concentrated. According to the estate duty statistics industrial securities form only about 5 per cent of gross capital value in estates of £2,000–£5,000, and it is not until the £20,000 level is reached that industrial securities, including fixed-interest stocks as well as ordinary shares, represent more than 20 per cent of total wealth. Almost one-half of the total value of company securities disclosed by estates assessed in 1953–5 was held in estates of more than £50,000, that is in only 3 per cent of the total number of estates assessed.

## 'Risk' Finance

It is because the willingness to accept the risks incurred in holding company securities appears very nearly to be restricted to the wealthy that the continual redistribution of incomes and wealth has aroused the fear that the result will be to dry up one of the sources of finance for the more adventurous forms of business, which raise capital in the shape of risk-bearing ordinary shares. The effect may also be to tempt prosperous companies to rely much more for their finance on retained profits, depressing the incomes of their shareholders and thus restricting their ability to subscribe to new issues of capital, to which less strongly entrenched concerns are obliged to resort. The pattern of company investment may therefore be distorted to the disadvantage of newer firms and those unsupported by monopoly positions and thus, perhaps, to the detriment of economic growth. It is partly because of considerations such as these that the plea has been made over the past twenty years for greater participation by the government and financial institutions in the provision of 'risk' finance and for an attempt to be made to interest people of modest means in industrial securities in one way or another.

# CHAPTER 11

# LIMITED LIABILITY COMPANIES

## THE GENERAL NATURE OF CORPORATE BODIES

The company, unlike the unincorporated business, possesses a legal identity that exists apart from that of its owners and continues irrespective of changes in its individual members. A company can sue and be sued in its own name and thus seek enforcement of and suffer responsibility for the contracts into which it enters. The company has a *corporate* identity; it is one of a class of corporate bodies that includes organizations as diverse as building societies and nationalized concerns.

Corporate bodies are subject to certain common obligations. In general, to obtain legal recognition they must define the objects for which they were founded, their contractual capacity being thereby established. Secondly, the rights of members must be defined, both as between each other and between themselves and the corporation, so that the delegation of authority to the executives of the corporate body must also be clearly provided for. These features are expressed in detail in the statute, charter or establishing documents by which the corporate body is formed.

## THE DEVELOPMENT OF JOINT-STOCK COMPANIES AND LIMITED LIABILITY

The joint-stock principle refers to the participation of a group of people in an enterprise by means of joint contributions to its finance. As a form of commercial organization it is not new; in medieval England individual members owned shares in ships and mines. The first expressly corporate bodies were the medieval boroughs and guilds, but in the sixteenth century the corporate body took firmer root in England's commercial life because of the large-scale financial requirements of overseas trading ventures, and concerns like the Muscovy Company and the Hudson Bay Company, for example, were formed. But until the middle of the nineteenth century incorporation was basically a privilege, and until 1837 could be conferred only by Royal Charter or Act of

Parliament; at common law joint-stock ventures were regarded as partnerships. It was not until the Limited Liability Act of 1855 that the principle of limited liability was finally established by statute.

For a long time company promotion had been associated with fraud. With the bursting of the 'South Sea Bubble' in 1720 a period of speculation came to an end that had brought the joint-stock company into disrepute—schemes such as that 'for an undertaking which shall in due time be revealed' hardly commend themselves to English law. Despite the growing need for the principle of limited liability, it was still opposed by sections of both industrial and legal opinion one hundred and thirty years later, although the principle was in successful operation in the United States and France. The vested interests of established traders and manufacturers and the distrust of what was described as the 'Rogues Charter' combined to delay the introduction of general limited liability until the Act of 1855 was secured by the efforts of a comparatively small number of determined men. Today we take the principle for granted.

### SOME EFFECTS OF THE LIMITATION OF OWNERS' LIABILITY

The Act of 1855 limited the liability of a member of a company to the amount, if any, not paid up on his shares. In 1862 a further Companies Act consolidated the legislation of the previous thirty-seven years. The consequence of the legislation of 1855–62 was greatly to broaden the flow of finance to industry and commerce and thus to smooth the way for the rapid economic development that was to follow. It enabled investors to minimize the risks of finance by spreading their holdings over a number of businesses, a policy which in the days of unlimited liability would only have magnified the hazards of investment. Limited liability was thus the instrument by which the field of investment in companies was enlarged for both the very wealthy and those of more modest means, as well as for the growing financial institutions of the second half of the century. By widening the sources of finance, limited liability assisted in the development of large-scale business organization and facilitated the development of the inter-company network.

By decreasing the degree of risk attached to ownership, limited liability has not only extended the field of ownership but has also reduced the need for close control by shareholders. Limited liability has made possible the further development of specialization by facilitating the emergence of a skilled class of business managers, for the principle enables the business of a company to be conducted without the need for detailed or day-to-day supervision by its owners. This has undoubtedly conferred great benefit upon the community as a whole, but the growth of a class of specialized 'managers' and the weakening of the link between ownership and control have attracted much critical attention. The large company of today is owned by numerous shareholders, who may be unwilling or unable to exercise close control, so that it is directed by salaried executives whose motives may not be those of the businessman who, as both owner and manager, was typical a century ago. This is a large question, on which further comment is deferred.

The innovation of limited liability was naturally open to abuse, and since the mid-nineteenth century a succession of inquiries and statutes has been directed to minimizing the possibilities of fraud, injustice and financial weakness. The conditions on which finance can be raised have been made more stringent, the rights and obligations of directors and shareholders have been more clearly defined, the accounts that companies must keep have been prescribed in greater detail, and the range of information that companies must make public has been extended. The last such inquiry of major importance was that of the Cohen Committee on Company Law Amendment, which issued its report in 1945 and was followed by the Company Act of 1947 and the consolidating Act of 1948.

### THE COMPANY AND ITS MEMBERS

The attitude of the law towards the separation of identity between the company and its members has not proved unequivocal. A court decision of 1897 (Salomon *v.* Salomon & Co.) seemed finally to affirm in absolute terms the distinct identity of the company as existing apart from that of its members. But neither legal nor business opinion proved entirely satisfied as to the possible implications for the rights of creditors in certain circumstances. The 1897 decision, for example, meant that a man who was both the dominant shareholder and director of a company could lend to a company on the security of its assets and thus claim priority of repayment over other creditors with no security, his own liability as a shareholder being limited to the amount, if any, not paid up on his shares.

Provisions in the 1948 Act mark some retreat from this position, making it more difficult for a person to evade payment of debts on the grounds that they are the liability of a company that happens to be under his control and not the liability of himself as an individual.

The legal distinction between company and members has also been modified in regard to taxation. Since 1922 the shareholders of certain private companies may be liable to surtax on their *undistributed* profits if these are deemed by the Inland Revenue authorities to have been withheld from distribution in order to evade surtax to which shareholders, as persons, might be liable on the income they would have received had the profits of the company been distributed. This provision has proved necessary in order to deal with extreme cases where persons might evade surtax by operating as companies in which the joint-stock principle, the basis of incorporation, is no more than a pretext; but it has also been applied to genuine trading companies.

### PUBLIC COMPANIES

Since 1908 the Companies Acts have distinguished between *private* and *public* companies. Legislation, it is true, does not actually define a public company, being directed at 'companies'; but special provisions are made for 'private' companies where applicable.

A public company may raise capital from the general public by means of advertisement, but in return for this facility it must comply with certain statutory requirements. It must file with the Registrar of Companies, an official of the Board of Trade, a copy of its annual balance sheet and auditors' report, together with an annual return showing details of its capital and a list of its members. These documents are open to public inspection at the office of the Registrar. If it seeks capital from the public, the prospectus through which its offer is advertised must provide detailed information of the company's affairs as prescribed by statute. In order to enable the public company to raise funds from the public there is no limit to the number of its shareholders; but the memorandum of association of a public company—one of its basic documents of incorporation—must be signed by at least seven persons.

## PRIVATE COMPANIES

The institution of the private company was given legal recognition to meet the needs of the smaller business, which, it was felt at the beginning of the century, might be put at a special disadvantage by the obligation placed upon public companies to publish their accounts and thus to disclose information to trade rivals.

A private company, if certain conditions are fulfilled, need not file its balance sheet with the Registrar. It may not, however, invite the public to subscribe to its capital. Like the public company, it must file an annual return listing its capital and members and its outstanding indebtedness. The maximum number of shareholders in a private company is limited to fifty (apart from employee-shareholders), but its memorandum of association need not be signed by more than two persons. The directors of a private company must have the right to restrict the transfer of shares between members.

Because of the ease with which they can be formed, private companies are numerous, and at the end of 1956 approximately 290,900 were on the Register, excluding those in course of liquidation and those, mainly non-profit-making, bodies with no share capital. In addition to their advantage over the unincorporated business in respect of limited liability, private companies are free from two obstacles placed by the weight of taxation in the path of the unincorporated business. Because the rate of tax borne by companies has been less than that to which wealthy persons are subject it is easier, or, as many would express it, less difficult, to build up reserves out of the annual profits of the company than out of the surtax-stricken income of the one-man business or partnership. Secondly, the private company is less open to the danger of dismemberment through the death of one of its principal owners than is the partnership, which is automatically dissolved in such an eventuality. The private company also possesses the advantage of being able to raise additional capital with greater ease than the partnership.

## EXEMPT PRIVATE COMPANIES

The facility with which the private company might withhold its operations from public scrutiny has been the subject of certain restrictions. To prevent the possibility of abuse the 1948 Act exempts the private company from the obligation to file its balance sheet with the Registrar only on the following main conditions:   .

(a) Subject to certain exceptions* no corporate body may be the holder of its shares or debentures. (A debenture is a form of indebtedness carrying a right to a fixed return and secured by a charge on the company's assets.)

(b) The limit of fifty on the number of shareholders must be accompanied by a similar limit on the number of debenture-holders.

(c) No person other than the holder may have an interest in its shares or debentures (other than a beneficiary under a family trust, for example).

(d) No corporate body may be a director.

(e) No arrangements may be made to allow outside interests to control its policy.

Private companies that comply with these conditions are known as 'exempt private companies'; others, while they continue to enjoy most of the remaining advantages of the private company, may no longer withhold their balance sheet from the Registrar of Companies. In 1957 about 80 per cent of private companies on the Register were able to secure exemption.

### THE RELATIVE IMPORTANCE OF PRIVATE AND PUBLIC COMPANIES

The inability of the private company to seek finance from the public limits the scale of its operation, so that it is to be found mainly in the distributive trades and in those branches of manu-facturing where the smaller business is able to prosper. There are, however, still in existence some private companies which, through skilled management and the retention of family holdings, have grown to a size exceeding that of many public companies.

To compare with the 304,271 private companies having a share capital and in existence in Great Britain, there were only 10,994

* For example, where certain financial institutions are shareholders.

public companies on the Register at the end of 1957. About two-fifths of these had capital quoted on the Stock Exchange, but the dominant role of the public company is made clear by the fact that the 2,500 largest public companies account for over half of the total profits recorded by all companies, both public and private. The predominance of the public company continues despite the fact that their number has been falling while private companies have been growing more numerous. The private company has come to hold an increasing share of the field formerly occupied by the unincorporated business, while the number of public companies continues to dwindle through amalgamations.

TABLE 5. *Companies Having a Share Capital on the Registers in Great Britain*

|  | Public companies | | | Private companies | | |
|---|---|---|---|---|---|---|
|  | 1928 | 1939 | 1957 | 1928 | 1939 | 1957 |
| Number (ooo's) | 16·7 | 13·9 | 11·0 | 89·0 | 146·7 | 304·3 |
| Paid-up capital (£m.) | 3,517 | 4,117 | 4,537 | 1,461 | 1,923 | 2,607 |
| Average capital per company (£ooo's) | 210 | 296 | 412 | 16·5 | 13·1 | 8·6 |

Source: *Companies; General Annual Report by the Board of Trade* (H.M.S.O.)

This divergence between the numbers of private and public companies has occurred despite the conversion of many private companies. The ability of the public company to seek finance from the public has always been an attraction to the growing private company faced with difficulty in raising sufficient funds to feed its expansion, and since the war the benefits of conversion have been augmented by the effect of death duties. The private company is less vulnerable than the partnership in this respect, but difficulties may still occur when the executors of the estate of a large shareholder are obliged to sell his shares in a private company. Directors are at liberty to refuse to approve the transfer of shares, and in any case the statutory limitation on the number of shareholders may make it difficult to sell the shares at a satisfactory price. A further stimulus to the conversion of private companies has been the opportunity of obtaining tax-free capital gains by the offer of part of the existing owners' shares to the public.

# CHAPTER 12

# THE CAPITAL OF JOINT-STOCK COMPANIES

At the end of 1957 there were about 16,000 companies on the Register in Great Britain without a share capital. These are mainly companies 'limited by guarantee', whose members undertake to discharge their company's outstanding debts by some form of subscription other than by way of an issue of shares. They are generally non-profit-making concerns such as professional bodies. The capital issued by the 315,000 companies which did not come within this category can be divided for convenience into three classes: loan capital; preference capital; and equity capital. In relation to equity shareholders the holders of loan and preference capital have prior claims on the company's resources; the equity shareholder is a residual legatee, his claims ranking only after those of the holders of loan capital (and other creditors) and those of preference shareholders have been met. In the U.S.A., however, the term 'equity capital' includes preference shares.

## LOAN CAPITAL

The term 'loan capital' is used here for convenience, and it is doubtful whether the securities that are often described as representing 'loan capital' should properly be regarded as part of the company's 'capital', in the strict sense, at all. For 'loan capital' does not form part of what can be described as 'owners' capital'. The holders of a company's loan capital have rights ranking with those of creditors; unlike preference and ordinary shareholders, over whose claims they take priority, they are not members of the company and have no influence on company management except in the event of default. They are usually entitled to a fixed rate of interest, and as a rule loan stocks are redeemable by the company. Depending on the conditions of issue a company may also buy up its issue of loan stock on the Stock Exchange, if it is a quoted stock, by means of what are known as sinking-fund purchases. There are broadly three types of loan capital—*debentures, mortgages* and *unsecured loans*.

*Debentures* are secured by a general charge on the remaining assets of a company, i.e. by a 'floating' charge, after accounting for the claims of prior creditors, including those secured by a charge on specified assets, or 'fixed' charge. In certain circumstances, e.g. if the company defaults on its debenture interest, the debenture-holders have the right, with the consent of the court, to appoint a receiver to administer the company's assets on their behalf until the default is made good or the principal repaid.

A *mortgage* (in England) is secured upon company assets that are specified by name, normally on its land or property. In the event of default on interest, the income of the mortgaged assets may be appropriated for the benefit of the mortgagees, and if necessary the specified assets may be sold to repay principal. In view of the risk that the value of the mortgaged assets may prove insufficient to meet the claims of the mortgagees, the protection of the mortgage is usually reinforced by attaching to it a floating charge on the remaining assets; this form of capital is usually known as a *mortgage debenture*.

The claims of the holders of *unsecured loans* rank before those of the preference shareholders but, unlike the other two classes of loan capital, are not secured by a charge on assets. In the event of the company's defaulting on the interest on its unsecured 'notes', in which form this type of capital is generally issued, the notes fall due for repayment. Holders may apply to the court to have the company wound up, but in this respect they are at a disadvantage in view of the low priority of their claim vis-à-vis debenture- and mortgage-holders.

A *convertible debenture* gives its holders the right to convert their stock into the company's ordinary shares at stated prices, an option they will usually exercise only if the prosperity of the company causes the market price of its ordinary shares to rise above the price of conversion. The debenture-holder thus gets the benefit of security if the company does badly and the right to capital appreciation if it does well. This advantage is obtained at the expense of the existing ordinary shareholders, who have to meet a prior charge in the first eventuality and share part of their equity in the second. This type of issue may be appropriate in certain circumstances, e.g. when the financial outlook is highly uncertain, or when the project to be financed is not likely to bear fruit for a considerable time.

Finally, we may note a subsidiary form of debenture, the *income debenture*. On this type of stock the maximum rate of interest specified becomes payable only if sufficient profits are available.

Owing to their relatively high degree of security, yields on loan stocks are generally less than those on preference or equity capital, and when the rate of taxation is high their status as an allowable business expense for taxation purposes brings a further advantage to companies. Because the holders of loan stocks are creditors and not members of the company, the interest on loan stock ranks as part of the company's expenses and not as distribution of profits to members. Interest on loan capital is therefore deducted as an expense in arriving at profits subject to taxation. But because of the priority of the claim exercised by the holders of loan capital upon the company's assets in the event of default, large issues of loan stocks are only suitable for those concerns which do not experience wide fluctuations in profits and which have highly marketable assets for realization in the event of liquidation. For these reasons loan stocks are most favoured in companies like breweries, retail stores, property companies and investment trusts. Loan stocks that are secured upon highly specialized assets whose market value falls sharply in the event of a recession in trade may prove to possess little by way of real security. The standing of any loan stock must also be qualified by the possibility of the company's issuing further securities ranking in priority to it; whether the company has the right to do this will be specified in the terms of issue.

## PREFERENCE CAPITAL

Preference shares carry priority over equity capital in regard to dividends or the repayment of capital, or both. They may be 'cumulative' or 'non-cumulative'. In the case of the former, arrears of preference dividend must be made good before any dividends are paid to 'junior' capital. However, the 'senior' class of preference capital in a company may be non-cumulative, its claims ranking in priority to those of a 'junior' cumulative stock.

Some companies issue a hybrid form of preference share, generally known as a 'participating preference' share. In addition to a fixed rate of preference dividend these shares carry some right to participate in surplus profits, if any. Some forms of

L

participating preference capital have no rights to any additional dividend but share in the distribution of surplus assets in the event of winding-up. The value of this right has to be considered against the possibility that the company's directors may declare very high dividends to equity shareholders on the approach of the company's liquidation, thus reducing the assets available for the repayment of preference shareholders.

Because the risk that preference shareholders bear is less than that of ordinary shareholders, preference shares generally carry no vote, except in certain eventualities, e.g. when preference dividends are not paid. Compared with those of debenture-holders their protection against the non-payment of dividend or capital is less secure, being limited as a rule to the stay of payments to junior shares and to increased voting power. The balance of the voting power within a company may be crucial to the status of preference shares in the event of winding-up or the reconstruction of capital, and the voting power of preference shareholders may in time be affected by a fresh issue of ordinary shares, so that the security of preference shares may be liable to encroachment by both 'junior' and 'senior' forms of capital.

Since 1929 companies have been able to issue redeemable preference shares, and if the price of redemption is fixed at the par value of the share, preference shareholders will be subject to a loss in the event of their shares being redeemed at a time when their market value is standing above par. A preference share carrying a coupon rate of dividend of, say, 6 per cent, may be quoted at a price of 120, providing a yield of 5 per cent. It would therefore be in the interests of equity shareholders to redeem these preference shares, for example, out of the proceeds of a further issue of preference capital if this could be floated at a price of 100 but carrying a coupon rate of interest of 5 per cent. Conversion would save the company the 1 per cent difference in preference dividends, but existing preference shareholders would suffer a loss of 20 on each share held.

The redemption of preference shares on similarly unfavourable terms has also been known to occur when a company has gone into voluntary liquidation despite its possession of surplus assets over and above those needed to meet the claims of creditors, as did certain coalmining companies which used the proceeds of their compensation awards following nationalization after the war to repay their capital. Preference shareholders suffered a loss represented by the excess of market value at the time over the price at which their shares were redeemed. Equity shareholders can claim the residue of surplus assets; the law places upon the preference shareholders the onus of establishing their claim to surplus assets in the event of a winding-up. More attention has therefore been paid in recent years to safeguarding the rights of preference shareholders when drawing up the terms of a new issue of preference capital.

### EQUITY CAPITAL

Equity shareholders exercise the residual rights as to dividends and the repayment of capital, as defined by reference to the rights of senior classes of capital. That is to say, their right to dividends and their claim on the company's assets may only be exercised after the claims of creditors and preference shareholders have been met. *Ordinary* capital is the most common name for a company's issue of equity capital, but existing nomenclature includes, for example, 'deferred' shares and 'deferred ordinary' shares or stock. (In Canada and the U.S.A. 'common stock' is the title generally used.) Some companies have two classes of equity capital differing in voting power; votes may be vested only in the ordinary shares issued to the company's founders or original proprietors, whereas its 'A' shares may, except in certain eventualities, possess no vote. In recent years the non-voting ordinary share has been subject to some criticism on the grounds that it weakens the moral position of ordinary shareholders generally and widens the gap between ownership and control.

Equity shareholders bear all the immediate risks of ownership and possess a full claim on its rewards after prior charges have been met. The burden of company taxation, for example, falls ultimately upon earnings available for distribution to ordinary shareholders, since there is no way whereby a company may pass on its charge for profits tax to preference shareholders entitled by contract to a fixed rate of return. If the profits of a company fall, the existence of prior charges means that the level of earnings available for distribution to ordinary shareholders will be reduced by an even greater proportion; conversely, a rise in company profits means a proportionately larger increase in these 'equity earnings'.

The statement that equity shareholders carry 'residual' rights, however, requires some modification. The decision as to what proportion of equity earnings shall be distributed to equity shareholders rests with a company's directors; ordinary shareholders have no way of exercising their claim on a company's surplus profits unless they are in a position to influence its board or replace it by another more amenable to their wishes. In law the assets of a company, including its retained profits, belong to the company and not to its shareholders as such, so that the extent to which equity shareholders are able to enforce their claims will depend on circumstances. The tendency for directors to pursue conservative dividend policies, of course, also limits the risk borne by equity shareholders, in that many companies may be in a position, in the event of a fall in profits, to maintain their existing equity dividend at the expense of a decline in undistributed profits.

# CHAPTER 13

# THE INTERNAL AND EXTERNAL RELATIONS OF COMPANIES

Company legislation as embodied in the Companies Act of 1948 is directed at three sets of relationships involved in the operation of the joint-stock company: between shareholders and directors; between different classes of shareholders; and between the company and third parties, namely creditors and potential shareholders. It is not always possible, however, to consider company legislation in regard to any one of these three aspects alone; many legal provisions, and indeed the procedures adopted by companies themselves, affect more than one side of a company's affairs.

## MEMORANDUM AND ARTICLES

All companies, whether private or public, must file with the Registrar of Companies two basic documents that form its constitution—the *Memorandum of Association* and its *Articles of Association*; there is, however, one exception to registration concerning the latter that is noted below. These documents define the identity of a company, setting out respectively its relationship with the outside world and that between its members. Only when all the legal formalities have been completed—and these are more stringent in the case of public companies—will the Registrar allow the company to commence business.

The memorandum proclaims the name of the company, which (except in the case of non-profit-making companies) must end with the word 'Limited'. It lists the amount of and subdivision between different classes of its nominal or authorized share capital, states whether its registered office is in England or Scotland, and describes the objects of the company. The latter are usually drawn so widely as to embrace almost every possible form of business activity, whether or not the company's founders intend to pursue them. For similar reasons of prudence the authorized capital is usually fixed at a figure higher than the amount to be issued in the near future. The provisions of the memorandum relating to the objects of the company can be altered if authorized by a special resolution approved by the members of the company.

The articles of association provide for matters such as: shareholders' meetings; voting rights; the appointment and powers of directors; the rights of different classes of capital; and the conditions under which alterations of capital may be made. A company's internal rules are governed by what are in effect a standard set of articles prescribed by the 1948 Companies Act unless its own articles expressly exclude or modify the provisions contained in Table A of the Act. The exception to the obligation placed upon companies to register their articles applies to a company adopting Table A without modification. Articles may be altered if approved by special resolution at a company meeting.

## COMPANY MEETINGS

The control exercised by shareholders over the directors of a company operates through the instrument of company meetings. Company legislation prescribes certain matters on which directors cannot act without the consent of the company's members and also gives to shareholders the power to take the initiative and put forward resolutions which, if passed, are binding on directors. There are three classes of company meeting—the annual general meeting, extraordinary general meetings, and meetings composed of particular classes of shareholders. All business conducted at company meetings is special business, other than the recurrent routine matters that usually make up the main part of the agenda of the annual general meeting. An ordinary resolution is passed by a simple majority of those shareholders present and voting; extraordinary or special resolutions require a three-quarters majority. Although each voting share is entitled to one vote, resolutions are passed by show of hands unless a recorded poll is demanded.

Before each annual general meeting, which must take place at least once each calendar year and within fifteen months of the previous annual general meeting, directors must send the annual balance sheet and profit and loss account to each member, duly audited, together with a report by the directors on the affairs of the company. The latter must show the way in which the year's profits have been appropriated to reserve and other allocations.

The balance sheet and profit and loss account must be audited by independent professional auditors. The rules governing what persons may serve as auditors are less strict in the case of exempt private companies.

At the annual general meeting shareholders are asked to adopt the company's accounts and the ordinary dividend declared by the board. Shareholders have the right to vote a reduction but not an increase in the ordinary dividend. The initial appointment of auditors is made by the board, but any variation in appointment must be approved by shareholders at the annual general meeting, at which the auditors' report must also be adopted.

### THE POWERS OF DIRECTORS AND SHAREHOLDERS

Every public company registered after 1929 must have at least two directors, and every company registered before that date must have at least one. The directors of a company are appointed in the manner prescribed by its articles; it is usual for directors to retire in rotation after three years, approval for their reinstatement or for the appointment of a new director being required from the shareholders at the annual general meeting. The Companies Act empowers members to remove a director before the expiry of his term of office by ordinary resolution, of which special notice has to be given. Directors' fees may be fixed by the articles and amended by general meeting; the company's accounts must show the total emoluments paid to or on behalf of directors, and any payment to a director as compensation for loss of office must be approved by shareholders. The articles may prescribe that only persons holding a certain minimum number of shares may qualify as directors, and the Companies Acts place two statutory restrictions on the selection of directors. Directors must retire on reaching the age of seventy, unless shareholders in general meeting decide otherwise. Secondly, no undischarged bankrupt may act as director without permission of the court, with certain exceptions. Each company must keep a register of directors' holdings of shares and debentures in the company and subsidiaries.

So far we have outlined only those matters which are normally dealt with at the annual general meeting. Other questions on which the directors cannot act without the consent of shareholders but which require an extraordinary general or a special meeting are: a change of auditors; the alteration of the objects of the company; changes in the company's articles; reconstruction of its capital; a proposed amalgamation with another company; a proposed agreement with creditors; and winding-up. In these matters shareholders are empowered also to take the initiative. An extraordinary general meeting may be called by shareholders possessing not less than 10 per cent of the paid-up shares with voting rights. Directors must facilitate the submission of a members' resolution by circulating it to all shareholders.

In the event of directors deliberately or negligently mismanaging a company's business, shareholders, if they have a majority, may sue the directors in the name of the company, to whom the directors owe responsibility. But the need for this is rare, as a majority of shareholders can remove directors from office. The power of the individual shareholder to sue the company for misconduct in his own name is limited to cases where he has been treated fraudulently by shareholders with a majority of votes, whether they are directors or not, or where directors have been guilty of a deliberate breach of duty to the company and are in a position to prevent the company from suing them because they control its voting power.

Directors are subject to the general criminal law in the event of fraud. But the ability of the shareholder to seek redress by civil action is in practice limited. However, the Companies Act, in the event of alleged misconduct by directors, also gives to the Board of Trade the power to appoint inspectors to investigate a company's affairs on application by two hundred shareholders or those possessing one-tenth of the company's issued shares, or on the request of a special resolution, or on the order of the court, or on its own initiative. The Board may consequently petition for a winding-up, refer its findings to the Director of Public Prosecutions for criminal proceedings or institute civil action against the directors, suing them for damages in the company's name.

Where the articles of a company provide that it is to be wound up in certain events members may pass a resolution in general meeting requiring that the company be wound up voluntarily. In certain other cases the company can petition the court for a winding-up order.

Finally, shareholders are protected by the obligations placed upon companies by the Companies Act to comply with the many provisions concerning the drawing up and auditing of accounts and the publication of a prospectus on the issue of capital to the public. Penalties are imposed on directors, for example, for false statements made in a prospectus.

### THE RELATIONSHIP BETWEEN SHAREHOLDERS

The rights of each class of shareholders are defined by the company's articles, governing questions such as: the right to dividends; the right to repayment in the event of winding-up; voting powers; the prior right, if any, to subscribe to new issues. In general, rights of shareholders vary with the risk they bear. It has already been stated that loan-stock holders are not members of a company (although they have certain powers of control in the event of default), preference shareholders have votes as a rule only in special cases, and some so-called ordinary shares also have no vote. The rights of any class of shareholder may be varied if, in accordance with the terms of a company's articles, the resolution is agreed by a meeting of the shareholders concerned and as a rule by other classes of shareholders as well. But shareholders who do not consent to such variation may apply to the court to have it cancelled if they are supported by holders of 15 per cent of the capital affected.

In the event of a reconstruction of the company's capital, if an application is made by the company or its members, the court may order a meeting at which the proposed arrangements are to be explained. The material interests, if any, of the directors of the company must be disclosed. Reconstruction of capital must have the support of a three-quarters majority of the company's members and must be sanctioned by the court. The rights of minority members are further strengthened by the ability of any member who complains that a company's affairs are being conducted in an oppressive manner to apply to the court, which may take such action as it thinks fit.

The value of a shareholder's right to participate in the repayment of capital or surplus assets generally depends on the imminence of such an eventuality, so that capital rights in the event of liquidation differ in importance from their material value while the company remains a going concern. The variation of members' rights most often occurs as a result of the reconstruction of a company's capital, especially as a consequence of its inability to pay a dividend to preference shareholders.

In these cases the balance of voting power assumes great importance; for example, ordinary shareholders as a class may feel that their interests are being insufficiently considered by a proposal to convert preference shares into ordinary capital, thus enlarging the claim on surplus profits. As a rule, voting power resides with those who bear the most risk, so that ordinary shareholders usually predominate in these circumstances. It should also be observed that the interests of any class of capital may be affected by the exercise of the company's powers, under its articles, to create some senior class of capital or indebtedness, so that these powers are usually closely defined, with a more liberal dispensation in the case of bank overdrafts needed for ordinary trading purposes.

### THE COMPANY AND THIRD PARTIES

The third parties who are protected by company legislation are creditors, actual and potential, and potential investors. In the first place no company, as has been stated, can start trading as a company until it has complied with the necessary legal formalities. Both the memorandum of association and the articles of a company, whether public or private, are open to public inspection at the office of the Registrar. The list of the company's members must also be filed for public inspection, and the restrictions on the appointment of directors serve to protect third parties as well as members. Furthermore, the Companies Act empowers the Board of Trade to refuse to register a company's name that it deems undesirable, on the ground of similarity with the name of an existing company, for example. In the case of the public company the requirements of the law, of course, go much farther by making it necessary for the company to file with the Registrar its annual report and balance sheet, and the requirements governing the issue of a prospectus are strict.

The claims of creditors fall upon a company's assets in the following order of priority:

> Creditors secured by a charge on specified assets.
> Inland Revenue for taxes and local authorities for rates; clerks, workmen for wages and salaries.
> Creditors secured by a floating charge.
> Unsecured creditors.

Creditors secured by a 'fixed' charge are in the most well-protected position, but the Companies Act includes provisions intended to safeguard the claims of creditors who are less favourably placed. Each company must file with the Registrar a statement of the charges created on its assets, and a number of provisions are designed to ensure that a company has available the capital represented as having been issued by it. A reduction of capital requires the consent of the court, and dividends may not be paid 'otherwise than out of profits'. Special provisions govern the issue of shares other than for cash, and any premium received on an issue for shares at above their nominal value must be treated for certain purposes as paid-up capital. Shares may be issued at a discount only if authorized by a general meeting of the company and sanctioned by the court. The desire to protect creditors is responsible for the requirement that each share must have a par value; although creditors do not seem to be in any weak position in those countries, e.g. the U.S.A., Canada and Belgium, where no-par-value shares are permitted. The Companies Act also states that preference shares should be repaid only out of the proceeds of a fresh capital issue made for that purpose or from surplus profits which have been capitalized in a capital redemption reserve fund.

The Companies Act provides for the winding-up of an insolvent company on the order of the court. Creditors may petition the court for a winding-up order, and even a voluntary winding-up is deemed a creditors' winding-up unless the directors of the company have made a statutory declaration of solvency. There are various penalties for the misappropriation of funds in the event of a winding-up. The court has the power to appoint and remove liquidators of a company, and the general operation of winding-up proceedings is supervised by the Board of Trade. Any arrangement between the company and its creditors is binding only if it has the support of three-quarters of the creditors and is sanctioned by the court.

The interest of the potential investor is affected by many provisions here outlined under all three headings. It may also be noted that since an Act of 1939[1] the touting of shares, or 'share-pushing', has been illegal, and the Companies Act makes it illegal to allot shares offered to the public for subscription unless there has been subscribed a certain minimum amount named in the prospectus.

## OWNERSHIP AND CONTROL OF THE
## JOINT-STOCK COMPANY

Those who see in the development of company operation since the Limited Liability Act of 1855 the separation, if not the actual divorce, of ownership from control contend that company legislation still does not compel boards of directors to publish information about a company's affairs sufficient to enable shareholders and creditors to make an accurate appreciation of its progress. First, companies are under no obligation to publish information regarding sales. Secondly, the publication of an annual report may be of little assistance to members of a company which experiences a sharp turn in fortune during the course of its financial year. Thirdly, boards are not compelled to file with the Registrar, for the benefit of interested parties other than existing members, their comments on the year's trade or the annual address of their chairman. Fourthly, the possibility of holding shares through a nominee may reduce the protection afforded to creditors by the requirement upon companies to file the list of their members. Fifthly, the treatment of asset values and allocations to reserve in a company's accounts may in certain respects obscure the true state of a company's affairs.

In practice many companies go further than the requirements of the Companies Act, because of the pressure of public opinion, including the standard set by more progressive managements, and the influence of the Stock Exchange. The requirements of the Stock Exchange imposed upon a company seeking a quotation for its shares or making a new issue of capital are more stringent than those of the Companies Act with regard to the volume of information to be published. The practice of retiring directors in rotation is also a Stock Exchange requirement, and the independence of shareholders as against directors has been strengthened by the obligation to use a 'two-way' proxy form. The Companies Act enables shareholders to assign votes to a proxy, who may be a director, without stating in which direction the vote is to be exercised; the form of proxy that companies with Stock Exchange quotations are obliged to use is designed so as to place upon the shareholder the onus of deciding how the resolution under consideration should be voted. Beyond this, public opinion and the example of more advanced practice have gradually extended the range of information provided in company quarterly or half-yearly reports.

Whether or not the information published by companies is sufficient to enable shareholders to exercise that degree of control envisaged by the architects of company legislation, it is evident that the power of shareholders is restricted. The Companies Act does not empower shareholders to control the business management of a company but merely gives them certain rights to appoint and dismiss directors, to approve or disapprove of certain directorial action and, in certain matters, to enforce resolutions upon the board. In practice the effect of these rights is limited, even if shareholders wish to use them to the full. To attempt to change the management of a company by dismissing its whole board is a formidable undertaking for shareholders not possessing a compact majority of votes, and even in these circumstances the problem of substituting a new and acceptable set of directors might prove extremely difficult. As for the rotation of directors, it is usual for shareholders, if only because of their limited knowledge regarding alternatives, to accept the appointment recommended by the board. The ability of members to initiate action by the submission of company resolutions has to be assessed in the light of the fact that they are liable for the expense involved unless a general meeting of members decides to the contrary.

Shareholders and creditors are protected against fraud on the part of directors by the criminal law, but civil action is difficult. The law confers responsibility on directors only as individuals, able to plead ignorance or good faith. The problem of the responsibility of directors towards the interests of shareholders starts well short of the possibility of deliberate fraud or malice. Directors may hold qualifying shares, and to this extent their interest may be regarded as being identical with that of the general body of shareholders. But as a rule directors of large companies hold only a tiny proportion of the capital of the companies on whose boards they sit, and their individual holdings may be small. The responsibility of directors towards the members of a particular company may be influenced by their interests in other concerns. In any case the danger cannot be ignored that directors may allow considerations of prestige and the maintenance of their own position to influence their policy unduly. It is true that the Board of Trade has the power to investigate company affairs and the record of directorial stewardship, but the Board appears to intervene only if requested or if the case for inquiry appears irrefutable.

### The Passivity of Shareholders

If the extent to which company legislation protects the right of members is strictly limited, this appears in the main to be the result of the willingness of the large body of shareholders to accept the present state of affairs. The proportion of shareholders who attend company meetings is small indeed; most are content to leave company management in the hands of existing directors without impediment as long as the condition of their company is obviously not critical. There is, of course, much justification for this attitude. Most shareholders possess neither the time nor the experience required for a more positive supervision of company affairs. The member of a company with shares quoted on the Stock Exchange has the facility of being able to sell his holding if he feels that his company's affairs are not proceeding to his advantage; by spreading his investments over a number of companies he can limit the risk of bad management in any one. The competition of companies for finance and the publication of accounts by other companies in the same industry place upon directors the necessity for showing their stewardship in a favourable light.

Although the majority of individual shareholders may perhaps be accused of comparative indifference to the management of companies of which they are members, freedom of action of directors may be constrained by the presence of large shareholders. Large shareholders may be effective although they possess only a small percentage of the total vote; and beyond this circle the influence of stockbrokers and the financial press, in providing advice to investors, may be more widely felt. The large financial institutions, in their capacity as shareholders and subscribers to new issues, hold a watching brief over the progress of companies. The Investment Protection Committee of the British Insurance Association, like the Association of Investment Trusts, was set up to safeguard the interests of its members. But these bodies rarely take the initiative at company meetings; their intervention is restricted to cases where their own interests are seriously and directly threatened, e.g. by the variation of the rights of a class of capital in which they are represented.

## Dividend Policy

The problem of the relationship between directors and shareholders is most complex when directors of companies *in general* seem to be acting in a manner contrary to the interests of shareholders. In this respect the conservative dividend policy pursued by most companies since the war is noteworthy. To some extent this has been the result of government requests, but the emphasis placed by boards on the necessity to plough back funds into the expansion of their own companies rather than pay higher dividends is not entirely above criticism. It lends some support to the view that preoccupation with the prestige or other benefits that directors derive from the growth of their own companies has pushed the necessity for the free circulation of finance among companies according to the choice of shareholders too far into the background. Cases can be found, indeed, where surplus profits have been withheld from distribution not for the purpose of enlarging productive capacity but merely so as to increase a company's liquid reserves well beyond the demands of reasonable prudence.

In law the claim of equity shareholders upon surplus assets or profits of their company has proved doubtful. The principle of limited liability has, in effect, evoked its complement of limited claims. In law the assets held by a company are held to belong not to its shareholders but to the company as a separate body, and it may be that the subordination of the interests of shareholders to what directors regard as those of 'the company', while giving yet new substance to the idea of a company as an identity apart from that of its owners, has done so in a manner that was probably not envisaged a century ago.

## The Company as a Complex

One reason for this apparent dichotomy, perhaps, is that the identity of a company is now more widely accepted as involving more than the relationship between its directors and its shareholders; the nexus of responsibilities has been consciously extended to include more and more the interests of employees and of consumers. Since the war, explicit recognition has been given to the former over a widening field in the shape of profit-sharing schemes and arrangements for systematic joint consultation. But the main safeguard of the rights of the consumer is provided by the working of the competitive market economy. However, although it is true that in its broadest sense competition provides a continuous measure of protection of the rights of all who make up the abstraction we call a company, the necessity for a succession of statutes concerned with the prevention of abuse in company operation indicates that, in this field at least, laissez-faire, even if based on competition, is no guarantee of justice and harmony.

CHAPTER 14

# HOLDING COMPANIES

The majority equity shareholder in a company may be yet another company, the latter being known as the parent company or, as the Companies Act describes it, the holding company; the company whose shares are held is the subsidiary company.* Subsidiaries may in turn hold shares in other companies, so that the holding company may form the apex of a pyramid of companies.

### ADVANTAGES OF HOLDING COMPANIES

The use of subsidiary companies to achieve diversification offers advantages where the different activities pursued by the group are unsuitable for direct unification under one management; and the profitability of each line of business may be more clearly assessed in this form of organization. Subsidiaries can be left free from detailed day-to-day interference by the parent company but can share in certain economies of scale, for example in selling, buying or finance, that only the group as a whole can realize. Such economies may thus be obtained without incurring many of the problems of large-scale control. Alternatively, an especially skilled management is enabled to direct a group the size of whose individual units is too small to exploit its skill to the full.

### SOME PROBLEMS

Where subsidiaries are not wholly owned by the holding company the rights of minority shareholders must be considered. A holding company may tend to frame its policy in the interests of the group as a whole or of itself, at the expense of a subsidiary company. The profits of a subsidiary company may be restricted by a pricing policy favouring other members of the group with whom it trades, or its surplus cash may be made available to other subsidiaries too cheaply. The minority shareholders of a subsidiary company may suffer even though the parent company is acting in good faith. This problem still exists despite the

* According to the Companies Act a company is a subsidiary if the shareholding company holds more than half of its equity capital or if it "controls the composition of its board of directors".

M

obligation placed by the 1948 Companies Act upon holding companies to publish information of the group's activities in clearer detail. The device of a holding company has also been one of the methods by which companies have been able to establish or reinforce their monopolistic position. But this question is part of the larger problem of monopoly.

### Gearing of Income

One danger of the holding company is the possibility of excessive 'gearing' of its income; that is to say, changes in the income of the holding company may be magnified by changes in the income of its subsidiaries. This may occur when the holding company owns only part of the capital of its subsidiaries and prior charges have to be met. A holding company may control a larger subsidiary; and, if the subsidiary company uses its capital to acquire a holding in a 'sub-subsidiary' even larger than itself, the holding company at the apex may be in control of a group many times its own size.

The sensitivity of the income received by the holding company may be illustrated by a simple example. Let us suppose that the holding company possesses an equity capital of £100,000 and preference capital of a similar amount, making a total of £200,000. This is used to acquire one-half* of the ordinary shares of a subsidiary with equity capital of £400,000 and preference capital of £400,000. The total capital of the subsidiary company of £800,000 is in turn used to obtain a 50 per cent equity holding in a sub-subsidiary with an equity capital of £1,600,000 and preference capital of a similar value, making a total capital for the group of £4,200,000. Let us assume that the trading operations of the group are undertaken solely by the sub-subsidiary company, which earns 10 per cent net on its total capital, and, like the other companies in the group, pays 6 per cent on its preference shares and distributes the whole of its residual income to its ordinary shareholders.

The profits of the sub-subsidiary amount to £320,000; of this, £96,000 is required for preference dividends, leaving £224,000 for its equity capital. Of this, £112,000 represents dividends payable to minority shareholders, leaving £112,000 as payment to

* The proportion of one-half, rather than a larger percentage, has been chosen for the sake of arithmetical simplicity.

the subsidiary company. This in turn has to pay £24,000 on its preference shares, leaving £88,000 for its equity dividends. After deduction for dividends to minority shareholders, £44,000 remains by way of payment to the holding company. The latter pays £6,000 on its preference capital and is able to declare an ordinary dividend of 38 per cent.

The income available for the ordinary shareholders of the holding company, however, would be highly unstable. In the event of a fall in the earnings of the sub-subsidiary company from 10 per cent to 7 per cent of total capital, the dividend on the holding company's ordinary shares would be reduced from 38 per cent to 14 per cent; another reduction of 1 per cent in the sub-subsidiary company's income would reduce the ordinary dividend of the parent company to 6 per cent.

# CHAPTER 15

# INTRODUCTION TO COMPANY ACCOUNTS

The 1948 Companies Act requires every company balance sheet to give 'a true and fair view' of the state of affairs of the company as at the end of its financial year and every company's profit and loss account to give 'a true and fair view' of the profit and loss of the company for the financial year. Each company's accounts must be audited and the auditors' report annexed to the balance sheet; in this report the auditors must say whether they have to the best of their knowledge obtained all the information necessary for their audit, whether proper books have been kept, whether these are in agreement with the balance sheet and profit and loss account, and whether, in their opinion, the latter give the 'true and fair view' required by law. Auditors cannot be changed except by resolution of the shareholders, and so are now in a strong position to maintain an independent view, free from directorial pressure; any qualification in an auditor's report must be accorded careful scrutiny, and in practice any departure from the orthodox phraseology usually constitutes a qualification.

## TRADING ACCOUNTS AND TRADING PROFITS

The Companies Act requires every company to keep proper books of account with respect to: all sums of money received and expended and the matters to which they relate; all sales and purchases of goods; and the company's assets and liabilities. Details of many of these accounts are rarely published; but banks and other lenders may be in a position to obtain the right of inspection.

The company's trading profit, which appears in its profit and loss account, is the balance of its trading accounts. These are not published and differ considerably in detail according to the nature of the company's business, but their essentials can be indicated by the following highly simplified example.

Table 6 represents a highly condensed summary of what in the modern company is likely to be represented by a number of accounts, dividing the business into product groups. Many companies separate these accounts into production and sales accounts, striking a profit balance for each stage. This practice may involve difficult questions of allocating overhead charges common to different product groups and stages; many of these problems arise in any case because the company's products have to be 'costed' in order to arrive at a satisfactory pricing policy and to calculate the profit actually earned on each. Setting aside these matters, Table 6 can be expanded to throw more light on

TABLE 6. *A Specimen Trading Account*

'XYZ Manufacturing Company Ltd.' Trading Account year ending
31 December

| Debit | £ | Credit | £ |
|---|---|---|---|
| 1 Jan.  Stock in hand | 500,000 | 1 Jan.–31 Dec.  Sales | 2,700,000 |
| 1 Jan.–31 Dec. | | 31 Dec.  Stock in hand | 600,000 |
| Materials purchased: | 2,200,000 | | |
| Wages; Salaries; | | | |
| Fuel; Rent and Rates | | | |
| Sundry expenses | 100,000 | | |
| 31 Dec. Gross Trading | | | |
| Profit | 500,000 | | |
| | 3,300,000 | | 3,300,000 |

the accounting process of striking the trading profit balance; in Table 7 the items are placed in narrative form.

The items of Table 7 combine to form Table 6. The 'profit' on factory operations might be based on the prices at which similar goods could be bought for resale or on some estimate of a 'reasonable' rate of return on capital employed.

THE TREATMENT OF STOCKS

In Table 7 opening stocks are shown in effect as part of the costs of production or of sales, and closing stocks are deducted from these costs. An estimate is thus made of the cost of producing and marketing only those goods that are sold, the trading profit being the difference between this and the value of sales. The result is identical with the simpler version of Table 6, where closing stocks are not deducted from purchases but are treated as if they were 'sales' to the next financial year. Purchases of materials for stock do not reduce a company's profit, as long as the stock is deemed resaleable at the cost of acquisition.

This treatment is based on the principle, in computing the profit of the current financial year, of charging against the year's sales only that part of the year's purchases of materials that is

TABLE 7. *Specimen Production and Sales Accounts*

'XYZ Manufacturing Co. Ltd.'

| Production Account | £ | Sales Account | £ |
|---|---|---|---|
| Raw material stock Jan. 1 | 100,000 | Transfer from Factory | |
| Raw materials purchased | 1,000,000 | Account | 2,375,000 |
| | | Stock of finished goods | |
| | ———— | Jan. 1 | 100,000 |
| | 1,100,000 | Wages, salaries etc. | 200,000 |
| Less raw material stock | | | |
| Dec. 31 | 125,000 | | |
| | ———— | | ———— |
| Raw materials consumed | 975,000 | | 2,675,000 |
| Wages, salaries and | | Less stock of finished | |
| other expenses | 1,100,000 | goods Dec. 31 | 125,000 |
| Work in progress Jan. 1 | 300,000 | | |
| | ———— | | ———— |
| | 2,375,000 | Net cost of sales | 2,550,000 |
| Less work in progress | | 'Profit' on sales | 150,000 |
| Dec. 31 | 350,000 | | |
| | ———— | | ———— |
| Net factory cost of | | Sales proceeds | 2,700,000 |
| finished goods | 2,025,000 | | ———— |
| Factory 'profit' on | | | |
| finished goods | 350,000 | | |
| | ———— | | |
| Transfer to Sales Account | 2,375,000 | | |
| | ———— | | |

deemed attributable to those sales, the remainder—as far as stocks are concerned—being carried forward in the shape of the closing stock figure. The latter forms the opening stock entry of the following financial year.

In making this allocation of production costs between one year and the next the convention is usually followed in this country whereby the opening stock is deemed to be used up first before materials purchased during the year are drawn into production and sold. When material prices have risen, therefore, the 'costs' to be debited against the year's sales will be the opening stock, valued at the earlier, lower level of prices, plus that part of the year's purchases deemed to be used up in sales and valued at the cost of acquisition. The closing stock is thereby deemed to be made up of those materials purchased most recently and accordingly valued at this higher level of prices.

In effect, this practice is based on the theory that the year's profit can be struck as if the expense of acquiring the closing stock had never been incurred, for it is assumed reasonable to suppose that the year's sales could still have been made even if the opening stock had been run down to zero and purchases of materials confined only to quantities needed for embodiment in current sales. On the face of it, this is perfectly logical, but the assumption regarding the 'cost' of the closing stock will be shown in Chapter 18 to result in what may be a misleading increase in profits when costs and selling prices are rising, because the purchases that are excluded from the current year's expenses are deemed to be those made at the more recent and higher prices. Further discussion of this matter, however, is postponed to the later chapter, for although questions of accounting theory are involved the most important practical consequences lie in the effect on company finance.

### Stock Valuation and Falling Prices

This method of stock valuation is in practice qualified by expediency and by the desire for conservative valuation. Prices of most raw materials and even of many finished products fluctuate, and those ruling at the end of a company's financial year may well be transient. The desire for cautious accounting, therefore, has led to the convention of entering closing stocks at a figure of cost or current market value, whichever is the lower.

When prices have been falling the practice of entering the closing stock at the cost of acquisition (based on the assumption that the closing stock consists of articles 'last' bought) thus gives way to that of valuing them at their, now lower, market values. The result is that, when prices have fallen, the current year's profits, in order to acknowledge the possibility that part of the year's outlay may be irrecoverable, are made to carry the burden of what may be a very sharp drop in stock values indeed, following, perhaps, a year in which book profits have been augmented by a rise in prices.

In the case of work in progress and stocks of finished goods, direct labour and other prime costs incurred are included in stock values, but there is no single treatment of overheads, which may or may not be added to prime costs for the purpose of stock valuation. As a general rule, however, no element of operating profit is included in stock values, except in the cases of contract work spanning two accounting periods and of 'forward' sales, that is, in the case of goods sold for delivery in the future, such as those produced by plantation companies. In the matter of stock valuation auditors are rarely in a position to conduct a physical inventory, and, except in the event of obvious error, are in practice obliged to accept the directors' estimates. Since some allowance must be made for physical deterioration and marketability, stock valuation is—in addition to the question of accounting theory introduced above—a question of judgement, the soundness of which investors and creditors are unable to assess.

### THE PROFIT AND LOSS ACCOUNT

The trading profit computed in a company's trading account is transferred to its profit and loss account, where it is combined with a number of other items for the calculation of the company's net profit for the year. The profit and loss account also shows how the year's net profit after tax has been appropriated.

Table 8 is a profit and loss account embodying the main entries encountered in practice. It could equally well be arranged in the narrative form which has become increasingly common, presenting its material as a series of additions and deductions, starting with the year's trading profit and ending with the balance carried forward to next year.

Corresponding figures from the previous year's profit and loss account must be recorded. Certain matters, if not otherwise shown, must be included in the profit and loss account as separate notes, e.g.: whether and how depreciation is provided for if a normal charge is not made; exceptional or non-recurrent transactions; and any material respect in which items shown have been affected by a change in the method of accounting.

Most of the items included in Table 8 are self-explanatory, but a few preliminary remarks concerning certain of them may be useful. The first part of the profit and loss account is generally the simpler of the two. Certain items are added to the year's trading profit, while certain 'non-trading' expenses are deducted to arrive at the figure for net profit before tax. If a company is subject to taxation overseas this, too, must be shown, after deducting any relief thereby granted by way of abatement of the U.K. tax liability. The appropriation account shows the disposal of the year's net profit after provision for taxation. To the balance transferred from the first part of the profit and loss account is added the balance brought forward from the previous year's appropriation account.

Also included in the total available for disposal are any transfers made from reserves or any withdrawals from provisions.* These occur when previous transfers to reserves, etc. are subsequently deemed to be unnecessary or excessive or when a reserve is applied to the purpose for which it was established. Several examples of transfers to reserve have been shown in Table 8. The first of these augments the reserve set up for the redemption of the company's preference shares. The second refers to a transfer made to provide for the obsolescence of fixed assets and for any replacement expenditure that may prove necessary over and above that allowed for in the provision for depreciation shown in the first part of the account.

*Capital reserves* are those regarded as not free for distribution through the profit and loss account, e.g. by way of dividends. The expression covers reserves which cannot legally be distributed and those which, because of their origin or the purpose for which they are retained, are placed in this category on the decision of the company's directors.

*Revenue reserves*, on the other hand, may be distributed by way of dividends if the directors see fit to do so. In Table 8 another transfer to revenue reserve could be included. A stock contingencies reserve might be applied to the replacement of stocks at

---

* The 1948 Companies Act requires the term 'provision' to refer to any amount written off or retained by way of providing for depreciation, renewals or diminution in the value of assets, or retained by way of providing for any *known* liability, subject to its limitation to cases where the known liability cannot in amount be determined with substantial accuracy. Since the Act states that the term 'reserve' shall *not* be used for depreciation, etc., or any amount retained by way of providing for any known liability, it follows that a known liability of known amount is, according to the Act, neither a reserve nor a provision! It is usual to group such items with 'creditors' in the balance sheet.

TABLE 8. *The Profit*

XYZ MANUFACTURING

Profit and Loss Account for

| 1957 £ | | | | 1958 £ |
|---|---|---|---|---|
| 19,824 | Directors' Emoluments, etc. | | | 20,100 |
| 7,321 | Payments to Staff Pension Funds | | | 13,075 |
| 12,938 | Debenture Interest (net of tax) | | | 12,938 |
| 3,106 | Remuneration of Auditors | | | 3,202 |
| 63,084 | Depreciation | | | 70,213 |
| 399,631 | Net Profit before tax (carried forward contra) | | | 413,272 |
| 505,904 | | | | 532,800 |
| | Taxation on net profit for the year: | | | |
| | *238,400* U.K. Income Tax | *255,375* | | |
| | *50,041* U.K. Profits Tax | *42,022* | | |
| | *Less*: | | | |
| | Overprovision in past | | | |
| | *3,600*   years | *7,043* | | |
| | Relief in respect of | | | |
| | *2,724*   Initial Allowances | *2,218* | | |
| 282,117 | | | | 288,136 |
| | Net Profit after Taxation (carried forward to | | | |
| 117,514 | Appropriation Account) | | | 125,136 |
| 399,631 | | | | 413,272 |

*Appropriation*

| | Transfers to Reserve: | |
|---|---|---|
| 20,000 | Capital Redemption Reserve Fund | 25,000 |
| | Capital Reserve—Obsolescence and Replacement of | |
| 20,000 | Fixed Assets | 20,000 |
| | Revenue Reserves— | |
| 10,000 | —Dividend Equalization | 10,000 |
| 30,000 | —General | 48,375 |
| | Dividends (net of tax): | |
| 8,375 | Preference Shares | 8,375 |
| 30,150 | Ordinary Shares | 33,500 |
| 18,209 | Balance carried forward to next year | 16,129 |
| 136,734 | | 151,379 |

The bold figures might be printed in red on an actual example.

## *and Loss Account*

COMPANY LTD.

Year ending 31 December 1958

| 1957 £ | | | 1958 £ |
|---|---|---|---|
| **482,072** | Trading Profit for Year | | 505,585 |
| | Income from Investments: | | |
| *14,104* | Trade Investments | *15,210* | |
| *9,728* | Other Investments | *12,005* | |
| **23,832** | ——— | ——— | 27,215 |
| | | | |
| **505,904** | | | 532,800 |
| | | | |
| **399,631** | Net Profit before tax (brought forward) | | 413,272 |
| | | | |
| **399,631** | | | 413,272 |

*Account*

| | | |
|---|---|---|
| **117,514** | Net Profit after Taxation (brought forward) | 125,136 |
| **16,805** | Balance brought forward from last year | 18,209 |
| | Transfers from Reserves: | |
| | Equalization of taxation in respect of Initial | |
| **2,415** | Allowances | 8,034 |
| | | |
| **136,734** | | 151,379 |

rising prices, a matter which will become clearer from the discussion in Chapter 17; alternatively, a stock contingencies reserve might be used to reduce the impact on book values and the year's book profit of the writing down that would otherwise be the result of a fall in the market value of stocks. The purpose of the dividend equalization reserve is to enable the company to pay a steady dividend when fluctuating profits may not justify the dividend in a particular year. The general reserve is earmarked for no particular purpose. In principle the balance of the appropriation account carried forward to the next year is no different from a transfer to general reserve.

### Some Differences in Interpretation

Companies keep books for two statutory purposes: to comply with the Companies Act and to assess their liability for taxation. In the interpretation of the Companies Act there is far from complete uniformity in the way that profit and loss accounts are presented. Differences between one company's accounts and another's arise, for example, over the treatment of items that are not the result of the year's business, such as delayed tax adjustments or windfall gains, and even over the treatment of reserve allocations.

Furthermore, the 'true and fair view' of the year's affairs that a company presents in its profit and loss account and balance sheet need not conform to the assessment of profits liable to tax made by the Inland Revenue authorities acting under the direction of the Income Tax and Finance Acts. The most important distinction is that between deductions made before determining the year's net profit subject to tax and those that are allocations of net profit after tax, however expressed; the former are often described as *charges on* profits, in contrast to an *appropriation of* profits to reserve. Items which a company's published profit and loss account shows as charges on its profit before tax need not, either in form or in amount, correspond to the deductions actually allowed for in the assessment of the company's liability for taxation; in the eyes of the Inland Revenue they may represent an appropriation of and not a charge on profits. Furthermore, the interpretation of the investor or creditor may correspond to neither that of the company's accountants nor that of the Inland Revenue.

The Inland Revenue and a company's directors may disagree, for example, as to whether certain forms of maintenance expenditure shown in a company's accounts as a charge on profits should be reckoned for tax purposes as capital outlays representing an appropriation of profit; and similar differences often occur in the case of what the Inland Revenue will allow as directors' emoluments. But the most important problems in distinguishing between charges on profit and its appropriation arise in the case of depreciation.

### DEPRECIATION AND THE PROFIT AND LOSS ACCOUNT

Recorded provisions for depreciation are often considered in relation to the ability of a business to finance the replacement of its fixed assets when they wear out; but it must be emphasized that depreciation as an occurrence, irrespective of any accounting provision that may be made, constitutes a cost analogous to that incurred in using up, say, a firm's stock of coal.

Fixed assets possess a limited life. They may become physically useless through wear and tear or cease to be used through the exhaustion of other assets from which they cannot be separated, such as machinery that cannot be moved without great expense from a depleted mine; alternatively they may—as in most cases—eventually become uneconomic because of the rising cost of repair and maintenance required to keep them in operation. The value of an asset to its owner is represented by the present discounted value of the net return expected from its remaining economic life. As an asset grows older this value will eventually fall (in terms of the prices of the goods it helps to produce). In their use fixed assets are 'consumed', in effect, as are stocks—hence the expression 'capital consumption' as a more accurate alternative to 'depreciation'—and in principle the measurement of profit requires this cost to be recorded. It should be noted that the fact of depreciation occurs even in those cases where the contribution of the asset to the *current* year's profit is not diminishing at all; for depreciation consists of the fall in the value of the remaining life of an asset.

It is true that in accounting practice it is usual to distinguish between depreciation, as described here, and obsolescence. The latter is the provision for any decline in an asset's value resulting from the impact of competing inventions and other changes in technique or from a fall in the demand for its product. Provisions for obsolescence are shown as an appropriation of net profit after tax to reserve; but the logic behind this distinction, tax law apart, is questionable. However, the statutory allowances for depreciation provide for obsolescence to the extent that, if a fixed asset is sold at a price less than its acquisition cost minus statutory depreciation allowances already received, the difference, known as a 'balancing allowance', is a deduction from taxable profits. In the opposite case, when sale or scrap value exceeds the unallowed value of the asset, the excess, known as a 'balancing charge', is liable to tax.

In its accounts a company may deduct what allowance for depreciation it considers necessary for the computation of its net profit, as long as it uses a consistent method. Indeed, it is entitled to abstain from making any such allowance at all, as is often the case with certain wasting businesses such as mines; but in this event attention must be drawn to the omission in the notes to the profit and loss account. But accurate measurement of the amount of depreciation actually incurred is difficult, involving as it does an estimate of the value of the remaining service likely to be rendered by the asset concerned, including its eventual scrap value; and so rules of thumb are generally adopted. A certain term of life is attributed to each class of fixed asset, and the cost of depreciation spread over that life by methods that are described in Chapter 18.

### Depreciation Allowances and Fixed Asset Values

Accounting practice has traditionally been based on the view of profit as the surplus remaining after providing for the maintenance of the *money* value of capital employed in a business, and the depreciation allowances that income-tax legislation has permitted for the purpose of calculating profit subject to tax have generally related to the 'original' or 'historic' cost at which buildings and equipment have been acquired. A prudent board of directors, on the other hand, may deem it necessary to make further provisions for depreciation, when equipment prices are rising, in addition to those allowed for tax purposes, in order to ensure that depreciation provisions are sufficient to meet the cost of replacement. These supplementary provisions represent deductions from profit that has already borne tax, whether or not they are shown as such in the profit and loss account; they are usually shown as transfers of net (taxed) profit to reserve.

## Statutory Allowances and Adjustments

On the other hand, Finance Acts since the war have attempted to reduce the drain on company finance due to rising replacement costs by permitting statutory depreciation allowances to be concentrated in the early years of an asset's life, and since 1954 it has been possible in certain cases to claim statutory depreciation allowances in excess of original cost. The result is that the statutory allowances in some years may be abnormally high, resulting in a correspondingly low net profit if the entire statutory allowances are charged against the year's gross profit. In these cases, it is the usual practice for a company in its profit and loss account to show a provision for depreciation below that actually claimed for tax purposes.

Since an abnormally high statutory depreciation allowance will cause the year's liability for tax to be abnormally low, the profit and loss account will often include an adjustment to provide, in effect, for the eventual rise in taxation liability that may become necessary if the statutory depreciation allowances decline in the later years of an asset's life. In any case it is sound accounting practice to state in the notes to the profit and loss account the policy adopted.

The allowance for depreciation recorded in the profit and loss account will also be below that allowed for tax purposes when the length of life attributed to an asset by the Inland Revenue for the purpose of depreciation is less than the period over which it is written off in the company's books. In these cases, too, the net profit before tax recorded in the published profit and loss account will thereby be higher than that on which tax is actually charged.

For industrial buildings an annual allowance of one-fiftieth of construction cost is made under the Income Tax Acts; no statutory allowance is given for commercial buildings. Annual allowances granted by the Inland Revenue for plant and machinery range from $7\frac{1}{2}$ to 15 per cent of the written-down value at the end of each year; for motor vehicles the annual allowance is generally 25 per cent. At the other end of the scale the annual allowance for steamships and motor vessels is 5 per cent of the original cost.

The depreciation of freehold land is not normally a charge

against profits. At the other end of the time-scale, assets with a short life, such as loose tools, are generally revalued at the end of each year rather than entered in a company's accounts after deducting depreciation; the profit and loss account will then show a charge for 'renewals' instead of depreciation.

## THE ANNUAL REPORT OF THE DIRECTORS

The Companies Act requires a balance sheet to be accompanied by a report by the directors 'with respect to the state of the company's affairs'. The report must include the declaration of the proposed dividend and the amount to be carried to certain reserves. Furthermore, it must deal, in the words of the 1948 Act, 'so far as is material for the appreciation of the state of the company's affairs by its members and will not in the directors' opinion be harmful to the business of the company or any of its subsidiaries, with any change during the financial year in the nature of the company's business'. The report will often include an explanation of unusual items in the profit and loss account beyond that required to be included in the notes to the account. Some companies will use the directors' report as a vehicle for the review of the year's operations, providing details of capital expenditures and sales and a commentary on the course of sales and costs. Others, if they provide such information at all, will include it in the chairman's annual statement, which since the war has grown in the case of an increasing number of companies into an informative supplement to the year's accounts that investors cannot afford to neglect.

# CHAPTER 16

# THE BALANCE SHEET

The two sides of a balance sheet are usually headed 'Assets' and 'Liabilities'. But it is more accurate, as well as a reminder of the method of conventional accounting, to describe them as an arrangement of 'open' book balances.

The books of account kept by a company can be divided into its *current* accounts and those of its *asset & liability* accounts. Its current accounts include, for example, its wages, salaries, current purchases and sales, as well as 'imputed' expenses such as depreciation. The company's asset accounts include those relating to its fixed assets, stocks, and its holdings of cash and securities, as well as its claims on the outside world, i.e. 'debtors'. Liability accounts embrace liabilities to the outside world, e.g. 'creditors' and tax provisions, as well as potential claims on the company by its shareholders, in the form of its issued capital and reserves.

At the end of the company's financial year each current account is 'closed off' and the balance, that is the difference between the sum of the items on each side of the account, is carried to some part of the profit and loss account, if necessary after being 'cleared' through the trading or operating account, whose balance alone is carried to the profit and loss account.

The asset and liability accounts, on the other hand, are left 'open'; their end-year balance is carried to the opposite side of the account to become the opening entry of the new financial year. The contrast between these two methods of treatment is only apparently complicated by the fact that the end-year stock figure appears both in the trading account and the balance sheet; for this is merely another way of expressing the essence of the procedure. In effect the *difference* between the opening and closing stock is carried to the trading account, the end-year stock being carried to the opposite side of the stock account to become the opening figure for the next year.

The balance sheet is a statement of 'open' book balances, together with the balance of the profit and loss account itself,

N

which, like a reserve, is a potential liability to the company's shareholders. So far nothing in this analysis detracts from the description of a balance sheet as a statement of 'assets' and 'liabilities'. The point is, however, that the decision whether to treat a particular account as a 'current' account, or as an 'asset' or 'liability' account, is in some cases a matter calling for careful consideration and one that is open to dispute. Moreover, conventional accounting records as 'assets', for example, certain entries that the layman may not expect to find in a balance sheet, such as the 'preliminary expenses' of forming a company.

### THE IDENTITY OF 'ASSETS' AND 'LIABILITIES'

The essential consideration is that the balance sheet and profit and loss account *between them* are complementary, if summary, versions of the company's entire books; balances that are omitted from the one must be incorporated in the other. Given this, the 'double entry' nature of modern accounting explains why the two sides of a balance sheet must always balance. Every book entry has its twin in some other account, an entry on the left or 'debit' side of one account being matched by one on the right or 'credit' side of another. This matching is to be found in one of the following four identities:

1. Between an entry in a current account and one in some asset or liability account. An entry of £100,000 in the 'Sales' account, for example, must be matched by an equal amount in the asset account 'Cash' or 'Debtors'. The total of 'Liabilities', on the other side of the balance sheet, will also be increased by a similar amount. For when the balance of the 'Sales' account is carried to the profit and loss account (via the trading account), the effect of sales worth £100,000 will be to raise the net profit to £100,000 more than it would otherwise have been. This increase will necessarily be reflected in a rise in one or more of the following: taxation provisions; dividends declared; reserves and provisions; balance of the profit and loss account. All these appear on the Liabilities side of the balance sheet. Thus current account entries that raise profit also increase both Assets and Liabilities; conversely, those that lower profit decrease the total of each side of the balance sheet. The twin to an entry in the 'Depreciation' account, for example, will be found in some fixed asset account, reducing the book value of the asset concerned.

2. Between an entry in one asset account and that in another. The purchase of a factory, for example, will be recorded by an entry

introducing the purchase price in the 'Factory' account and another diminishing the balance in the 'Cash' account. Payments to the company by its debtors, to take another illustration, will reduce the outstanding balance in the 'Debtors' account and swell that of the 'Cash' account. These transactions thus raise the book value of one asset and diminish that of another by an equal amount, leaving total Assets unchanged.

3. Between an entry in a liability account and one in an asset account. When a company obtains a bank advance, for example, the entry in the liability account—'Bank Advance'—is matched by the record of the proceeds entered in the 'Cash' account. The payment of outstanding taxes reduces the balance in the 'Tax Liability' account and that in the 'Cash' account. A less obvious example is that of an increase in the book value of a company's fixed assets due to the decision to record in the balance sheet a major rise in asset prices; the counterpart to this writing up would be found in the first instance as an increase in the 'Capital Reserve' account on the opposite side of the balance sheet. The effect of transactions in this class is thus to increase or decrease both Assets and Liabilities in the balance sheet.

4. Between an entry in one liability account and that in another. The declaration of a dividend, for example, will reduce the balance of the profit and loss appropriation account and, until it is paid, stand in the balance sheet as an 'Outstanding Dividends' account. The transfer of profit to reserve will similarly reduce the profit and loss account balance and augment, instead, the balance in the reserve account concerned. Entries in this class of identities, therefore, raise the balance of one liability account by as much as they lower that of another, leaving the total unchanged.

To sum up, the double-entry system of accounting, incorporating all book balances in the profit and loss account and the balance sheet between them, necessarily ensures the equality of total Assets and total Liabilities. For each pair of entries in the company's books can only increase or decrease both totals by the same amount or leave each unchanged. To say that the two sides of a balance sheet are equal in total is less revealing than to describe them as different aspects of the same transactions, the two sides of the same coin.

### ASSETS

In Table 9 a specimen balance sheet of a manufacturing company with no subsidiaries is drawn up, illustrating the layout of the main features of what in practice may vary considerably in

TABLE 9.

XYZ MANUFACTURING

Balance Sheet as at

| 1957 £ | | Authorized £ | Issued & Paid Up £ | 1958 £ |
|---|---|---|---|---|
| | **CAPITAL** | | | |
| | 6% Cumulative Preference | | | |
| | Shares of £1 each | *500,000* | *250,000* | |
| **1,250,000** | Ordinary Shares of £1 each | *2,000,000* | *1,000,000* | |
| | | | | 1,250,000 |
| | | *2,500,000* | | |
| | | | | |
| | **CAPITAL RESERVES** | | | |
| **75,000** | Capital Redemption Reserve Fund | | | 100,000 |
| **12,225** | Share Premium Account | | | 12,225 |
| **500,000** | First Mortgage Debenture Stock Redemption | | | 500,000 |
| **100,000** | Obsolescence & Replacement of Assets | | | 120,000 |
| **271,472** | Revaluation of Fixed Assets | | | 271,472 |
| | **REVENUE RESERVES** | | | |
| **423,625** | General Reserve | | | 472,000 |
| **50,000** | Stock Contingencies Reserve | | | 50,000 |
| **20,000** | Dividend Equalization Reserve | | | 30,000 |
| | Profit & Loss Account— | | | |
| **18,209** | Unappropriated Balance | | | 16,129 |
| | **FUTURE U.K. INCOME TAX** | | | |
| **210,432** | Estimated Liability 1959/60 | | | 230,242 |
| | Taxation Equalization Reserve in respect of Initial | | | |
| **13,369** | Allowances | | | 45,435 |
| **500,000** | 4½% FIRST MORTGAGE DEBENTURE STOCK | | | 500,000 |
| | **CURRENT LIABILITIES AND PROVISIONS** | | | |
| **42,342** | Bank Overdraft | | | — |
| **169,245** | Sundry Creditors | | | 171,831 |
| **172,124** | Current Taxation | | | 194,200 |
| **4,230** | Debenture Interest Accrued (less tax) | | | 4,230 |
| | Dividends (less tax): | | | |
| **8,375** | Preference | | | 8,375 |
| **20,100** | Ordinary (Final Dividend Proposed) | | | 22,333 |
| **3,890,748** | | | | 3,998,472 |

The bold figures might be printed in red in an actual example.

*The Balance Sheet*

COMPANY LTD.

31 December 1958

| 1957 £ | | | | 1958 £ |
|---|---|---|---|---|
| | FIXED ASSETS | | | |
| | Land & Buildings | | | |
| | At Net Book Value 31st Dec. 1955, less sales, plus acquisitions at cost | | | |
| *721,176* | | *752,346* | | |
| *60,182* | *Less* Depreciation | *78,042* | | |
| **660,994** | | | | 674,304 |
| | Plant & Machinery | | | |
| | At Net Book Value 31st Dec. 1955, less sales, plus acquisitions at cost | | | |
| *944,968* | | *1,034,273* | | |
| *176,218* | *Less* Depreciation | *228,571* | | |
| **768,750** | | | | 805,702 |
| | Loose tools, office furniture etc. at net book | | | |
| **21,046** | value 31 Dec. 1958 | | | 25,321 |
| **25,310** | Goodwill, at cost less amounts written off | | | 25,310 |
| **20,425** | Patents, at cost less amounts written off | | | 11,464 |
| | CURRENT ASSETS | | | |
| **920,432** | Stocks | | | 705,584 |
| **602,051** | Debtors | | | 484,002 |
| **394,375** | Trade Investments, at cost | | | 294,375 |
| | Quoted Investments, at cost (Market value | | | |
| **225,461** | 31 Dec. 1958, £310,235) | | | 302,042 |
| **239,482** | Tax Reserve Certificates | | | 325,126 |
| **12,422** | Cash at Bankers & in Hand | | | 345,242 |
| **3,890,748** | | | | 3,998,472 |

JOHN SMITH ⎱ *Directors*
JAMES BROWN ⎰

detail but generally conform in outline. It is more convenient, as well as an often much needed reminder that only its assets can yield a return to a business, to consider first the main constituents of the Assets side of the balance sheet.

### Fixed and Current Assets

The 1948 Act requires the distinction to be drawn, where practicable, between fixed and current assets. The dividing line is not always easily decided but may be of some importance to the interpretation of a balance sheet. It is usual' to define current assets as those which are held for realization, that is for transformation into cash, in the ordinary course of business, together with those representing a temporary investment of surplus funds. In conjunction with current liabilities, on the opposite side of the balance sheet, current assets form the starting point of any assessment of a company's potential liquidity over the ensuing year. Fixed assets, on the other hand, so runs the usual definition, are held with the definite purpose of earning revenue by their use, not for sale, in the ordinary course of business. Fixed assets endure in physical shape, their contribution taking the form of a flow of service lasting beyond the compass of a single financial year; current assets, on the other hand, 'turn over' or 'circulate' during the course of the year, hence being sometimes described as 'circulating' assets. Stocks, for example, are drawn on and replenished, and the same is true of cash, whereas the blast-furnace or the railway wagon serve for many years. The distinction is blurred, on the other hand, when component parts of machinery, for example, have to be replaced at intervals within the year, like the blade of a cutting tool or the tyres of a much used heavy lorry.

### Differences in Treatment of Fixed and Current Assets

One result of this division is that it classifies assets according to the nature of the business concerned, so that tools that are fixed assets to the firm using them are current assets to that producing them; the point is that the way in which an asset is valued in the balance sheet will depend on whether it falls on one side of the line or the other.

Fixed assets generally appear in the balance sheet at original cost, less accumulated depreciation; it is only a minority of companies that revalue their fixed assets at current prices (less accumulated depreciation also at current prices) when, as in the period since the war, replacement prices rise far above original cost. (In these cases, it has already been noted, the excess of new over previous book values on the asset side of the balance sheet is reflected in an increase in capital reserves on the liabilities side.

Stocks, on the other hand, are generally entered at 'cost' or market value, whichever is the lower, giving rise to frequent fluctuations in book profits. Moreover, when items in stock are sold at above book values the excess appears as part of current profits; when fixed assets are sold at prices above book value, on the other hand, the excess represents a reserve that can be disposed of only if, after a bona-fide valuation, all other assets can be certified to be fully of the value stated in the balance sheet. The assets, less outside liabilities, must also be at least equal to the company's paid-up capital, a requirement which will automatically be met if the balance of the profit and loss account is positive. Alternatively the excess may be used to write down the book value of the remaining fixed assets.

This sometimes arbitrary distinction between the treatment of fixed and current assets is one example of the way in which the balance sheet lacks homogeneity as a statement of the company's condition at the end of the year.

## Current Assets

Changes in the stock figure call for careful interpretation, since much will depend on whether an increase, for example, is caused by an increase in the volume of business or by the pile-up of finished products due to their unsaleability.

The item 'debtors' is open to less uncertainty, but even here caution may be needed. Reasonable provisions may be deducted for doubtful debts without disclosure in the published accounts, and in this respect, as in the case of stocks, the investor's appreciation of the solidity of a company's assets must rest on the judgement of its directors. In times of depressed trade, the proportion of bad debts will rise,[2] and (a contingency which does not generally appear as such in the balance sheet) the costs of collection of outstanding debts will increase. In any event, periods are often encountered when the debtors concerned are, on paper, no less prosperous than usual, but when debts are difficult to collect promptly. Such a situation will occur when business as a whole is running short of liquid funds, through a more stringent overdraft policy on the part of the banks, for example. In these conditions a company trading at a book profit may yet be near insolvency if in opposition to the urgent demands of its creditors, including its employees, it can set only the promises of equally hard-pressed debtors as its main current asset.

The remaining current assets require less qualification. The market value of investments quoted on a stock exchange must be shown as at the balance-sheet date. Prudent directors will ensure that these investments are of a type not subject to sharp fluctuations in market value if they are to serve as a reliable second-line reserve of liquid assets; hence quoted investments generally take the form of short-dated government stocks. Tax Reserve Certificates are a special type of government security. They can be held to meet future tax payments, interest being paid when they are actually tendered in discharge of tax liabilities, the period over which interest is calculated, however, being subject to a limit of two years from the date of purchase. Interest on Tax Reserve Certificates is exempt from income tax and surtax.

### Intangible Assets

The treatment of so-called intangible assets is another example of the limitations of the balance sheet as a statement of asset values and, in particular, illustrates the problems that arise through the accounting necessity for recording values for individual assets or classes of asset. For the value that would be realized by the sale of a firm's assets on the occasion of its winding-up, its true 'break-up' value, is normally well below the price that would be placed upon them by a prospective purchaser considering the acquisition of a company 'as a going concern'.

In the latter sense the value of a business must depend on its expected future earning power and can be formally described as the present discounted value of expected future net profits. The break-up value sets only a lower limit to what assets are worth; if a company is to be regarded as a going concern its asset values *in total* must reflect its prospective earning power; but to attribute values to individual assets is a matter of some conceptual difficulty if the value of the business as a whole is to be derived from their summation.

The limitation of the balance sheet is that it appears to do just this.  It might seem that the cost at which any asset can be replaced at least sets an upper limit to its value, since in isolation no asset can be said to be worth more than the figure at which an exactly identical asset can be acquired.  But when assets are used together in a business their total value to that business or to a prospective purchaser will often be in excess of their aggregate replacement cost; this will occur, for example, when the business concerned possesses some degree of monopoly power, or some other special advantage, for whatever reason, so that the expected rate of profit on the assets employed in the business exceeds that from the use of similar equipment by other concerns, whose demand helps to determine current prices.

The price at which a business changes hands, therefore, may well exceed the aggregate book value of its assets, even when this has been adjusted to take account of current prices.  It therefore follows that when a company acquires another business for, say, £500,000 in cash and brings into its own accounts assets with an existing book value of, say, £300,000 the equality between the two sides of its balance sheet will be disturbed unless the gap can be filled with the entry of another asset valued at £200,000.  Hence the entry 'Goodwill', which is created to meet the difference between the purchase price of a business that has been acquired and the book value of the acquired assets.  It is usual gradually to write off goodwill out of profits, especially windfall profits, on the argument that should the company ever go into liquidation goodwill might well prove to be not only an 'intangible' but a 'fictitious' asset.  It is, nevertheless, something of a paradox that when a firm is making the satisfactory profits out of which the item can be comfortably written off, goodwill can be justifiably regarded as a reflection of the true value of the firm as a going concern; it is only if there are no profits out of which to write down goodwill that the 'asset' can be definitely said to be worthless!

Other examples of intangible assets are patents and trade-marks.  Unlike goodwill, these can be sold separately from the business as a whole, so that their entry in the balance sheets as individual assets is easily understandable.  Patents and trade-marks are shown at their cost of acquisition less amounts written off; many, of course, may be valuable for a short period only, and writing down is a more accurate reflection of the true state of affairs than is often the case with goodwill.

Other intangibles conform less easily to the idea of an asset as viewed by those not acquainted with accounting methods. Certain assets relate to expenditure carried forward into the accounts of later years; for example, when a company is formed, the so-called 'preliminary expenses' of formation are treated not as a current charge on profits but as an 'asset' and entered as such in the balance sheet. The justification for this is that the expenses of company formation are not attributable to its operations in its initial year alone but can be regarded as the price paid for the lasting 'asset' of incorporation, the cost of which is logically chargeable to the whole life of the business. Like goodwill, however, preliminary expenses are generally written off out of profits as early as possible. A similar example concerns expenses incurred in connexion with an issue of share capital or debentures. Another such intangible asset is sometimes to be found in the shape of 'advertising expenditure'. When a company undertakes a major advertising campaign part of the outlay may initially be withheld from the profit and loss account and entered in the balance sheet as another intangible asset on the grounds that it, too, should not be regarded as a constituent of the cost of one year's operations alone if its benefits are expected to stretch well into the future. A similar case is provided by development or prospecting expenditure.

The practice of treating certain abnormally large outlays temporarily as assets rather than as current costs may be open to criticism when its justification is sought only in the need to avoid 'undue' fluctuations in profits. The appearance in the balance sheet of these values for which no real counterpart can be found is, of course, another reflection of the problems raised by modern accounting in being less than a valuation of the future but more than a mere record of the past in its treatment of assets and liabilities. The treatment of intangible assets is not without its logic, but their true status as assets, that is to say as prospective earning power, depends entirely on whether the expectations entertained regarding their profitability are sound. It is in this sense that their occasional description as 'fictitious' assets may be fitting.

Finally, perhaps the most curious intangible 'asset' that may appear on the right-hand side of the balance sheet is the balance of the profit and loss appropriation account when this is a deficit. The most obvious course would be to deduct an equivalent amount from the reserves of the company, but in the eyes of the Companies Act this would be tantamount to writing down the book value of the company's capital. Such a step would require the consent of the court, in the absence of which the item appears as an 'asset'. This should not be allowed to obscure the fact, however, that if a business makes a loss its resources have been depleted by this amount.

### LIABILITIES

In Table 9 'Liabilities' are arranged in the manner which the provisions of the 1948 Act and the need for ease of interpretation between them have made common.

### Capital

The 1948 Act requires the amounts of both *authorized* and *issued* capital to be stated. The former is that authorized in the company's Memorandum of Incorporation (and on which capital duty has been paid). The latter refers to the number and nominal value of the preference and ordinary shares that have actually been issued. The full nominal value of these shares may not have been payable at the time of issue, or the calls for payment on a recent issue of capital may not have been completed at the balance-sheet date, so that the balance sheet must show how much has been paid up on issued capital.

### Capital Reserves

The general nature of capital reserves has already been described. The Capital Redemption Reserve Fund and the reserves for 'Obsolescence and Replacement of Assets' and 'Revaluation of Fixed Assets' have also been explained. The Share Premium Account, on the other hand, has not yet been met. It arises when shares have been issued at a price in excess of their nominal value. The ordinary shares first issued, for example, might have been issued at their nominal value, but by the time of a subsequent issue of the same class of share the Stock Exchange quotation for the original shares might well be in excess of their nominal value, owing to the progress of the company in the intervening period. The new issue of shares, identical as to dividend rights and other respects with the original issue, would thus be made at prices comparable with the current quotation of the original issue, and the excess of the issue price over nominal value—owing to the statutory requirement that all shares must carry a nominal or 'par' value—would have to be shown separately in the Share Premium Account. This account is often used for writing off 'preliminary expenses' and other intangible assets.

The First Mortgage Debenture Stock Redemption reserve appears to be self-explanatory; the terms of redeemable fixed-interest issues may provide for the regular allocation of net profits to such a reserve. But the book entry may be deceptive, for whether the allocation in any way facilitates ultimate redemption depends entirely on whether the company possesses sufficient cash at the date of redemption, a state of affairs that in no way depends on the entry under consideration. It is true, of course, that a company with a good financial status in the eyes of investors may be able to redeem a maturing stock out of the proceeds of a new issue floated for the purpose. The establishment of a redemption reserve, however, does possess some merit in making it clear that part of the company's assets are not available for distribution to shareholders. In some cases the terms of a debenture issue may go further and provide for the annual purchase on the Stock Exchange of part of the stock outstanding; such purchases must be stated in the balance sheet.

### Revenue Reserves

Revenue reserves represent allocations of profit that may be reversed through a company's profit and loss account; if the company possesses sufficient cash, additional dividends can be paid to ordinary shareholders from a balance in the profit and loss account augmented by transfers from such reserves. The distinction between the different forms of contingency reserve is unimportant. There is nothing to prevent indirect transfers from one revenue reserve to another, and there is something to be said for the view that transfers of profits to contingency reserves, as against the general reserve or balance carried forward in the profit and loss appropriation account, may be intended more as a check to pressure by shareholders for higher dividends than as convincing evidence of the need for retaining profits within the business.

## Reserves and Cash

Revenue reserves arise through the retention of profits, but they are in themselves no reliable guide to the soundness of a company's finances at a particular time. Dividends can be paid 'out of' reserves only in the book-keeping sense; whether a company can distribute more than the year's net profit depends on whether it has the necessary cash. Even if it has a sizeable cash balance (or liquid assets such as government securities that can easily be realized), the directors may not use it to pay dividends if other claims take priority, for example current liabilities or longer-term capital commitments. Revenue and capital reserves represent no more than accounting records; if a company has used its retained profits to acquire factories, machines or stocks it is their contribution to earning power that is vital while the company remains a going concern, and in the event of a company's liquidation the values at which physical assets stand in the books may not be those at which they can be realized.

Reserves, it has been stated, are accounting records of the retention of profits or a mixed bag of certain so-called capital entries. In certain cases the accounting method adopted may understate a company's reserves; but the cautionary remarks that have been directed to their interpretation as a distributable 'fund' still apply.

## Hidden Reserves

These occur when reserves or provisions created in the company's books by transfers from the profit and loss account are not disclosed in amount, even if their existence is indicated. They might be included in the balance sheet as part of some comprehensive entry, e.g. 'Sundry creditors, including provisions for contingencies'. Except in the case of shipping concerns, life-assurance companies, banks and discount companies, this practice is no longer permissible as a result of the 1948 Act.

## Secret Reserves

These arise through the deliberate undervaluation of assets or the overstatement of liabilities. If capital expenditure on fixed assets, e.g. the purchase of machinery, is charged to revenue the result is to reduce the year's recorded profit (and perhaps the taxation thereon) and also to understate the value at which assets appear in the balance sheet. A similar result is obtained if excessive provision is made for depreciation, obsolescence or bad debts, or if the tax liability is overestimated. Although the Companies Act aims at preventing the establishment of secret reserves in the detail of its provisions and its general requirement of a 'true and fair view', the Act has not resulted in their complete abolition, even in regard to transactions arising since 1948; secret reserves already in existence when the Act came into force remained broadly unaffected by the Act.

## Taxation Provisions

Provisions for taxation in our imaginary balance sheet appear, it will be noted, under two headings: 'Future Income Tax' and 'Current Liabilities and Provisions'. Apart from the questions raised by the effect of special statutory depreciation allowances (the reserve for deferred liability due to Initial Allowances) the distinction arises because the income tax payable in the coming financial year of a company is not necessarily that assessed on the profits of the year that has just ended. Income tax is assessed in the Exchequer income-tax year, which runs from 6 April to 5 April, and is assessed on the profits of the trading year that precedes the year of assessment. The tax itself is payable on 1 January of the Exchequer year of assessment and in some cases may be paid in two instalments, on 1 January and 1 July.

The interval between the end of a company's trading year and the time at which the tax liability must be met will thus depend on the date on which the company's trading year ends. The following examples make this clear.

| Company trading year | Year of assessment 6 April–5 April | Income tax payable 1 January |
|---|---|---|
| 1 January 1957–31 December 1957 | 1958–59 | 1959 |
| 1 April 1957–31 March 1958 | 1958–59 | 1959 |
| 6 April 1957–5 April 1958 | 1958–59 | 1959 |
| 1 July 1957–30 June 1958 | 1959–60 | 1960 |
| 1 October 1957–30 September 1958 | 1959–60 | 1960 |

Thus for all companies except those whose trading year ends between 1 January and 5 April, the income tax liability in respect of the latest year's trading will not be payable within the coming year and is therefore usually shown apart from the current liabilities; except in these cases current liabilities will normally include only the tax due in respect of the profits of the last trading year but one. The Companies Act requires the basis of the provisions made for income tax to be shown, including the way in which the previous year's 'Reserve For Future Income Tax' has been applied to the entry 'Current Taxation' in the latest year's accounts.

The allocation for income tax that is not payable within twelve months is really an appropriation of profits to reserve; if the company were to cease trading, the payment might never have to be made. As long as the company stays in business the excess of tax charges over the current year's tax liability represents retained funds available for normal use.

Assessment for profits tax is made on the profits of the latest trading year, and the estimate of profits tax due on these profits will generally be entered together with the income tax payable within the coming year, that is generally as a current liability.

The remaining current items call for little comment. The provision for debenture interest and preference dividends is on account of those accrued but not yet paid; that for outstanding ordinary dividends represents those declared but not paid.

Finally, to the balance sheet must be appended in note form the amount of capital expenditure outstanding which the company has contracted to make. Other notes would include, for example, details of any arrears of cumulative preference dividends. The balance sheet must be signed by two directors.

# CHAPTER 17

# TOWARDS THE INTERPRETATION
# OF COMPANY ACCOUNTS

Some of the limitations of company accounts, particularly the balance sheet, as a statement of the year's trading and the company's condition at the end of the year, have already been mentioned. They merit a brief repetition. The profit and loss account may present some difficulty because of the distinction between the requirements of the Companies Act and those of the Inland Revenue, and the policies adopted by companies in regard to this and other problems are found to vary. The balance sheet is homogeneous neither in its aims nor in its method. It is not just a straightforward record of transactions, since practically all of its asset components, with the main exception of cash, involve some estimate as to the future. On the other hand, it is not, and does not claim to be, a valuation of the business as a going concern; but as a guide to break-up values the usual balance sheet is handicapped by its reference to original rather than replacement costs as far as fixed assets are concerned. The distinction between fixed and current assets, which *are* sometimes entered at current market values, may not be clear or consistent. Even on their own chosen ground, the significance of company accounts may still be obscured by secret reserves, the provisions of the Companies Act in practice acting as a safeguard only against the grosser form of abuse. Finally, as long as company accounts make no reference to turnover and order-books, give no indication of changes in conditions within a period shorter than a year, and make no apportionment of profits between the different sides of a business, the student of company affairs must at the outset recognize the paucity of the information put at his disposal.

Bearing these qualifications in mind, it is nevertheless possible to rearrange the components of the balance sheet in the form of groupings and ratios so as to assist the interpretation of the account and its changes from year to year. These calculations may provide few answers, but they do at least serve to raise questions that might otherwise have been overlooked. They also have a certain conventional value, for in so far as other investors are known to use them in their appraisal of the relative merits of different securities it pays any investor to give them some attention. Since it is not part of the aim of this book to enter into a detailed study of the interpretation of company accounts, only a sample of the possible groupings and ratios will be given.

## NET ASSETS

These can be defined as the total book value of assets in which the shareholders of a company have rights, after deducting the liabilities of the company to 'outsiders', including debenture-holders. The term is often used to refer to 'tangible' assets only, goodwill, etc., being excluded. The calculation is as follows:

TOTAL ASSETS *minus* Debenture liability
          Bank overdraft
          Other creditors
          Tax reserves and provisions

Leaves NET ASSETS (including intangibles)—
          which are represented by SHARE CAPITAL *plus* RESERVES.

To obtain net tangible assets the intangibles are simply deducted from this total.

## NET ASSETS PER ORDINARY SHARE

Taking the calculation one stage farther, the net assets 'attributable' to the ordinary shareholders alone, or 'net worth', can be found by deducting from net assets (or net tangible assets) the redemption value of any preference shares. If in turn this residual is divided by the number of ordinary shares in issue, a figure equivalent to net assets (or net worth) per ordinary share is obtained.

## BREAK-UP VALUE PER ORDINARY SHARE

If intangibles are excluded the result is often expressed as the break-up value per share. When some estimate of the realizable value of a firm going into liquidation is required, the reserve for future taxation, which may not be needed, is often added back; on the other hand, the book value of physical assets and debtors must be treated with caution.

o

## RETURN ON CAPITAL

The profitability of a company's operations may be considered in regard to the return on its resources as a whole or from the point of view of the ordinary shareholders alone. The former would be the criterion used, for example, to examine whether a monopoly was earning an excessive rate of profit, calculated by expressing gross profits after depreciation but not deducting directors' remuneration or interest on loan capital and other debts, as a percentage of gross tangible assets, that is before deducting 'outside' liabilities. But to the ordinary shareholder it is the return on the assets used on his behalf that matters.

An assessment of this return can be based on the calculation of annual equity earnings (that is the residual of profits after interest on debentures and preference dividends) expressed as a percentage of net worth. To debenture holders and preference shareholders, on the other hand, it is their degree of security, the margin of available assets and earnings over their claims, that is relevant.

## SOME PROBLEMS IN COMPARING ASSET VALUES

The main difficulty encountered in comparing the return on net assets (or on assets as a whole) between one company and another is that the divergence of book values from the current values of fixed assets will be found to vary widely from company to company after a period of marked price instability. The calculation of the return on assets employed is perhaps of greater value in tracing the profitability of one company from year to year, particularly in examining the use of retained profits or new capital.

In choosing between shares of different companies, investors often compare tangible net worth per share with the latter's market price; here again the divergence between book and current values presents a difficulty. Many cases have been encountered in practice where net worth per share is in excess of the market price of the share and would be even more so if current market values could be assigned to fixed assets.

One explanation for this discrepancy between share price and asset values is that the former may have been depressed by a fall in profits. In this case the question must be asked whether the period of adverse trade is likely to be of short duration; for otherwise the figure attached to the book value of the firm's assets might deserve a somewhat sceptical assessment. Another likely cause of the discrepancy is the conservative dividend policy of a company that is prospering, for investors naturally value the dividend bird in the hand more highly than that in the bush. By way of contrast, in the case of companies whose dividends are expected to show a marked increase in the near future, the market price of ordinary shares may be pushed well above the figure of net worth per share. This is another reflection of the fact that the aggregate of the values assigned individually to physical assets, even on the basis of replacement cost, may be much less than their collective value when used in a particular business concern, as represented by the present discounted value of expected future net earnings. If profits were entirely distributed to shareholders, we could expect market values per share to fall short of net worth per share only in the case of those companies whose operations were expected to contract. In the case of companies that were approaching liquidation the market value of the ordinary capital would depend on what could be expected from the realization of fixed assets and on the liquid assets accumulated as a result of past operations; break-up values calculated from balance-sheet figures might be a poor guide.

### CURRENT ASSETS AND LIABILITIES

The usual current assets are stocks, debtors, marketable investments, Tax Reserve Certificates and cash. An examination of these items often provides a clue as to the course of a company's operations. A marked rise in the ratio of stocks to debtors may mean either the piling up of unsold goods or the building up of work in progress prior to a major increase in sales; which inference is to be drawn cannot usually be decided without additional information, for example, from trade reports or the chairman's statement. The ratio of stocks to production, when known, may give some indication of the relative efficiency of comparable firms in regard to the economy of resources. The balance of current assets as between liquid and non-liquid items is frequently a matter for careful consideration when the ability of a company to pay higher dividends or expand output is under examination.

A review of current assets alone is less revealing than their consideration together with current liabilities, usually bank overdraft, creditors, current taxation and outstanding interest and dividends. The difference between current assets and current liabilities, described as *net* current assets or working capital, provides a clearer view of the year to year—or more precisely the year-end to year-end—experience of the firm than do current assets alone. For in the course of net current assets may be found a guide to the firm's solvency and its ability to withstand the stresses and strains of changing financial conditions, as well as its financial capacity for enlarging the scale of its operations.

The comparison of the net current assets possessed by different companies is often expressed as so much per ordinary share, against which the market price of the share can be considered.

### LIQUID ASSETS

Sometimes current assets are described as 'liquid assets', but it is advisable to reserve this term for cash and realizable investments, since stocks and trade debts may not in certain circumstances be saleable at their book values, especially if cash is required quickly. Liquid assets are sometimes expressed as a percentage of gross current assets, total tangible assets or net worth, or simply as an amount per ordinary share. *Net* liquid assets, the excess of cash and securities over bank loans and current tax, interest and dividend liabilities, are a more useful indication of liquidity.

The ratio of net current assets to production or profits, if current dividend and interest liabilities and current taxation are deducted from liabilities and an equivalent amount excluded from current assets, may throw up significant variations in the financial requirements of different companies. One difficulty here, however, is to decide how to treat what is obviously a surplus of liquid assets held by firms unwilling either to expand output or increase dividends.

While calculations such as these are often of much value, the limitations of the balance sheet, with its succession of static portraits of a company's affairs at a single point of time, must always be borne in mind. Where seasonal factors are important, many of these methods of comparing one company's accounts with another's lose a great deal of their usefulness in cases where balance-sheet dates differ; the make-up of the working capital of a retail store immediately after Christmas, with stocks low and cash at a high level, will be quite unlike that of one whose financial year ends on 31 March, just before an Easter sale period.

## OVERTRADING

The condition known as 'overtrading' consists of a level of operations that is too high in relation to liquid assets possessed. When over-expansion takes place, net current assets are depleted as current liabilities, mainly bank overdraft and trade creditors, rise rapidly to support the company's ambitions after its liquid assets are exhausted. The financial stringency that results is itself a cause of a loss of profits; stocks may be too low for prompt delivery to be assured, the shortage of cash means that favourable buying opportunities may have to be forgone, further credit facilities may be expensive, and pressure on trade debtors may damage a firm's goodwill. Sooner or later the competitive ability of the overtrading concern may be weakened by its tendency to defer the replacement of old plant and machinery. It is the loss of profits that causes current liabilities to rise by *more* than current assets; expenses increase by more than the inflow of cash from sales, plus claims on customers and saleable stock. The remedy is either a lower volume of trading or an issue of long-term capital.

## EARNINGS AND COVER

The course of profit margins, that is the ratio of profits, before or after depreciation, to sales, is obviously of major importance to the understanding of company operations. Unfortunately, statistics of turnover are rarely published by individual companies in this country; although some reference to profit margins is often made, in a general fashion, in the chairman's statement.

The security of interest and dividends provided by the current level of profits can be measured more directly by examining the profit and loss account. Profits have to meet interest on loan stocks and taxation, then the claims of the preference shareholders, the ordinary shareholders' rights being vested in the remainder. The company's profit after depreciation, less profits tax but before deducting income-tax or debenture interest, can be expressed as 100, and debenture interest, preference and ordinary dividends can be calculated gross as successive percentages of the total. This is the 'priority percentage' method of assessing the income cover for interest and dividends. As expressed here it will slightly underestimate the cover for the debenture interest, as income represented by the amount of profits tax paid would be available to meet debenture interest, which ranks as an expense for tax purposes. In practice, however, this complication may be ignored if the rate of profits tax is light. The calculation will also be more complicated if in the imposition of profits tax a distinction is made between distributed and undistributed profits.

### Priority Percentages

Suppose a company earns £200,000 after profits tax but before deducting debenture interest and that the gross debenture interest is £20,000, gross preference dividends £20,000 and gross ordinary dividends £80,000; this gives priority percentages of:

| Gross debenture interest | Gross preference dividends | Gross ordinary dividends | Gross 'residual' |
|---|---|---|---|
| 0–10 | 10–20 | 20–60 | 60–100 |

In this case debenture interest is covered ten times by profits. Just how the cover for the preference dividend should be expressed is sometimes a matter for dispute. On the simplest calculation the preference dividend can be said to be covered nine times, that is $(100-10)/10$ times. But in order to give full weight to the claims of prior charges a common practice is to relate earnings to the cumulative requirements of different stocks. In this case the preference dividend would be said to be covered five times, that is $100/(10+10)$ times. The amount remaining after meeting debenture interest and preference dividends is sometimes described as being 'available for ordinary shareholders' or, more usually, as 'equity earnings'; when the context is clear the word 'equity' is often omitted. The ordinary dividend in this example is usually described as being twice covered by earnings, that is $(100-20)/(60-20)$ times.

Another company might provide twofold cover for its ordinary dividend, but in the following priority percentages:

| Gross debenture interest | Gross preference dividend | Gross ordinary dividend | Gross 'residual' |
|---|---|---|---|
| 0–30 | 30–80 | 80–90 | 90–100 |

In this case it would take only a 10 per cent fall in profits to uncover the ordinary dividend; the position of the ordinary shareholders is obviously less secure than that revealed in the first example despite the fact that in the second the apparent gross cover for the ordinary dividend is no less. The explanation is that in the second example the income of the company is more highly 'geared', that is a greater proportion of the year's income is taken by the prior charges. When the outlook for profits is unfavourable, therefore, the shareholders in a highly geared company are at a disadvantage. On the other hand, high gearing means a proportionately greater expansion in earnings available for distribution when profits are rising.

Priority percentages show a clearer picture of the security for debenture interest and preference dividends as well. A simple 'times covered' method of description, unsupported by priority percentages and omitting to combine debenture interest with the preference dividend, may appear to imply that current earnings provide greater security for the preference dividend when this is smaller than debenture interest. This, of course, cannot be the case; a similarly misleading comparison might be given as between the different classes of preference shares alone.

### Capital Cover

The margin of cover for debenture interest or preference dividends—'income cover'—may be widely different from the margin of assets available for the repayment of principal—'capital cover'. Capital cover consists of that portion of net assets that would be available for repayment, usually after the deduction of intangibles from book assets and, of course, after adjustment for any claims ranking prior to that in question. Thus a debenture may carry income cover of, say, ten times and capital cover of five times. But in regard to the latter the qualifying remarks made regarding reserves must be borne in mind; the ability of a company to repay depends on its cash resources, which will usually form only a small part of total net assets, and in the event of liquidation the proceeds of realized assets may differ from book values.

### CONSOLIDATED ACCOUNTS

Most large companies today operate through subsidiaries, which the 1948 Act defines as companies in which they hold more than half of the ordinary capital or in which they are members and determine the composition of the board. A distinction must be made between a subsidiary and an associated company; the latter is one in which some interest less than control is held, usually as part of a business agreement. Holdings in associated companies are often shown in the balance sheet as 'trade investments'; although there is something to be said for the reservation of this term to cases where only a small part—say less than one-quarter —of the ordinary capital is held, for a larger stake can enable considerable influence to be obtained in the other company, which is thus an 'associate' in the usual sense of the word. As there is no legal obligation to disclose the earnings of the associated company, over and above the dividends received from it, or the asset values in excess of the book value of the shares held in the associated company, considerable secret reserves may exist behind the balance-sheet entry 'trade investments' or 'holdings in associated companies'.

A company that has subsidiaries (and is not itself a wholly-owned subsidiary of another British company) is required by the Companies Act to publish accounts for the group as a whole unless, broadly speaking, group accounts are deemed by the holding company's directors to be impracticable, misleading or harmful to the business. These group accounts are generally presented as *consolidated* accounts—that is, the separate accounts of the companies concerned are merged into one set of accounts item by item to show the relationship of the group with the outside world, transactions between one company and any other within the group cancelling out for the group as a whole. As far as is possible the dates of the financial year of the companies in the group must be synchronized.

Where the subsidiaries are all wholly owned by the holding company the analysis of consolidated accounts can proceed along the lines already introduced. Where subsidiaries are only partly owned, however, the consolidated balance sheet and profit and loss account of the group includes among the liabilities an item showing the 'interest of minority shareholders', or simply 'minority interest'. In the case of the balance sheet this is more than the amount of issued capital held by the minority shareholders; it must include the claim of the latter to the reserves of the subsidiary companies, calculated proportionately. The appropriate deduction from the year's income must also be made in the consolidated profit and loss account; part of the undistributed income of the subsidiary must be allocated to its minority ordinary shareholders. When calculating net assets, etc. attributable to the ordinary shareholders of the holding company allowance must be made for the minority interest; it is the consolidated rather than the holding company's account that must be examined. However, where only the non-participating preference shares of the subsidiary are held by outsiders the 'minority interest' is merely the book value of the preference shares alone and need not be described as such.

Although the accounts of a holding company and its subsidiaries are published in group form, the group as such has no legal identity; and creditors have to look for satisfaction to the individual companies to which they may have supplied goods, services or cash. Like those of the minority shareholders, their interests may be damaged by the conduct of affairs between one member company and another; unsecured creditors of a subsidiary suffer from the danger that part of its resources may pass out of their potential control, by way of sale or loan, on possibly unfavourable terms, to another company of the group. Creditors of the holding company are in a stronger position, for a receiver appointed on their behalf could sell the shares held in subsidiary companies; but it is generally impossible for a receiver to go further and force subsidiaries into liquidation to meet the claims of parent-company creditors.

# CHAPTER 18

# ASSET VALUES AND BUSINESS FINANCE

### HISTORIC AND REPLACEMENT COSTS

A business must resolve two important problems when the costs of its raw materials and components are changing. If it has any control over its own prices, it has to decide whether they should be based on the cost at which these materials were actually acquired, that is on 'original' or 'historic' costs, or on the costs at which the firm's existing stock of materials will have to be replaced when they are used up, i.e. 'replacement' costs. Secondly, whatever the way in which selling prices are formed, a firm's directors have to decide how to calculate in the annual accounts the costs actually incurred if the materials consumed during the year were bought at different times and at different prices; this is the problem of stock valuation.

Over a wide range of businesses prices are often based on historic costs. Frequent price changes may weaken a firm's goodwill, and alterations to catalogues may be costly and inconvenient; the sheer uncertainty of the course of material prices favours the use of historic costs as a pricing standard. This policy also conforms to the view of profit as the surplus left after maintaining intact the money, as opposed to the real, value of a firm's capital, an interpretation that, at least until the recent years of rapidly rising prices, has been accepted by most businessmen and accountants, to say nothing of the Inland Revenue authorities. The adjustment to changes in wage costs, on the other hand, is more direct, since these are both less frequent and less transient.

### SOME EFFECTS OF ORIGINAL-COST PRICING

When material prices are rising but selling prices are based on original costs, the apparent prosperity of business may be deceptive. Consider, for example, an imaginary scrap-metal merchant who buys and sells ten tons of metal each month; ignoring handling costs, etc., he can be supposed to sell at a margin of 20 per cent above original cost. If in the first month he buys ten tons at £100

per ton and sells ten tons at £120 per ton, his sales proceeds of
£1,200 will be sufficient to yield a profit of £200 and leave £1,000
to replace his physical capital—ten tons of metal at £100 per ton
—for his next month's trading.

If in the following month the replacement cost of his scrap
purchased rises to £110 a ton but the merchant continues to sell
his existing stock of ten tons at its original cost of £100 a ton plus
20 per cent, his sales proceeds of £1,200 will not be sufficient to
yield a consumable profit of £200 and provide for the replacement
of ten tons of metal, which would now cost £1,100. The money,
but not the real, value of his capital would be maintained; and to
keep intact his real capital the merchant would have to deplete
his cash resources for the purchase of materials at higher prices.
Thus, when costs are rising, pricing policies based on historic
costs deplete a firm's liquid resources if the volume of trading is
maintained.

When prices are falling, on the other hand, the pressure of
competition will make it difficult in some industries to maintain
the normal profit margin as a proportion of historic costs. The
proportionate margin over replacement costs, however, may not
fall at all, so that despite the appearance of reduced profits
(aggravated by the writing down of stock values to the lower of
cost or market values), real capital can be kept intact if the scale
of operations is maintained, and an increase in liquidity will
develop.

CHANGING PRICES AND THE VALUATION OF STOCKS

The second, and not unrelated, question is the calculation of
costs during a period in which materials have been bought at
different prices. The accounting problem is to decide how to
value the closing stock when identical physical units of material
bought at different prices have been used up in the productive
process, leaving in stock a number of units whose individual
purchase prices are unascertainable and, indeed, irrelevant to any
conventional definition of profits. The valuation of the closing
stock in effect determines the cost to be attributed in the company's
accounts to the materials actually used up. Since the figure for
materials purchased is a straightforward cash entry, the cost of
materials used up during the year is represented by the difference
between the cost of materials purchased, on the one hand, and the

increase in the accounting value of material stocks between the beginning and the end of the year, on the other.

By way of illustration, let us assume that our merchant maintains a stock of 120 tons at the end of each month, first selling and then buying ten tons during the course of each month. Let us suppose, furthermore, that at the end of his first financial year his stock of 120 tons had all been bought at a cost of £100 a ton, but that in the following year the price he has to pay for his metal purchases rises by £10 a ton in each successive month. We can again assume that the price at which he sells each month is equal to the cost of the previous month's purchase plus 20 per cent. Ignoring other costs, his sales and purchases in his second year can be recorded as follows:

### TABLE 10. *Monthly Purchases and Sales*

1 Jan., *Stock*—120 *tons bought at* £100 *a ton*—*Book Value* £12,000

| | Sales | £ | | Purchases | £ |
|---|---|---|---|---|---|
| Jan. | 10 tons @ £120 value | 1,200 | 10 tons @ £110 value | 1,100 |
| Feb. | ,, ,, ,, £132 ,, | 1,320 | ,, ,, ,, £120 ,, | 1,200 |
| Mar. | ,, ,, ,, £144 ,, | 1,440 | ,, ,, ,, £130 ,, | 1,300 |
| Apr. | ,, ,, ,, £156 ,, | 1,560 | ,, ,, ,, £140 ,, | 1,400 |
| May | ,, ,, ,, £168 ,, | 1,680 | ,, ,, ,, £150 ,, | 1,500 |
| June | ,, ,, ,, £180 ,, | 1,800 | ,, ,, ,, £160 ,, | 1,600 |
| July | ,, ,, ,, £192 ,, | 1,920 | ,, ,, ,, £170 ,, | 1,700 |
| Aug. | ,, ,, ,, £204 ,, | 2,040 | ,, ,, ,, £180 ,, | 1,800 |
| Sept. | ,, ,, ,, £216 ,, | 2,160 | ,, ,, ,, £190 ,, | 1,900 |
| Oct. | ,, ,, ,, £228 ,, | 2,280 | ,, ,, ,, £200 ,, | 2,000 |
| Nov. | ,, ,, ,, £240 ,, | 2,400 | ,, ,, ,, £210 ,, | 2,100 |
| Dec. | ,, ,, ,, £252 ,, | 2,520 | ,, ,, ,, £220 ,, | 2,200 |

*Total Sales* 22,320          *Total Purchases* 19,800

The question is: what value should be given to the closing stock of 120 tons?

### *First In First Out Valuation*

The conventional accounting method in this country of 'First In First Out' (FIFO) assumes, in effect, that the quantities of material first bought will be the first to be sold so far as the above example is concerned (or used up in the production process in the case of a manufacturing business). In our example the opening stock of 120 tons would thus not be deemed to have been completely exhausted—if sales were ten tons a month—until the final month of the year. The closing stock on 31 December, therefore, would be deemed to be composed of the 120 tons purchased during the second year and valued at the actual cost of acquisition to total £19,800. On the basis of FIFO our merchant's trading account for his second year would be as in Table 11.

The profit of £10,320 is equivalent to sales of £22,320 *minus* the 'cost' of materials used up, which FIFO accounting has put at £12,000. The latter figure is the difference between purchases and the increase in the value of stocks, i.e. between £19,800 and £7,800. In our example, of course, the metal sold in the year is deemed to have been the opening stock.

TABLE 11. *Trading Account (Second Year)*

|        |           | £      |         |       | £      |
|--------|-----------|--------|---------|-------|--------|
| Jan.   | Stock     | 12,000 | Dec. 31 | Stock | 19,800 |
| Jan.–Dec. | Purchases | 19,800 | Jan.–Dec. | Sales | 22,320 |
|        | Trading Profit | 10,320 |      |       |        |
|        |           | 42,120 |         |       | 42,120 |

This profit of £10,320 in the merchant's second year would contrast with one in the previous year of only £2,400, derived from 120 tons purchased at £100 and sold at £120 per ton, opening and closing stock values having been the same. The quantity of metal sold, the quantity in stock and the percentage profit margin in his second year have remained unchanged; what has happened is that the cost debited to the year's trading has been based on the low prices of the past, while the rise in replacement prices has been withheld from the year's cost and embodied in the closing stock figure instead. The effect has been to produce a total profit equal to the difference between purchases and sales (£2,520) *plus* the increase in the book value of an unchanged quantity of stock of £7,800. This latter component is known as *stock appreciation* or, by the somewhat misleading American expression, *inventory profit*.

### Stock Appreciation

Stock appreciation consists of the recorded increase of the closing stock figure over the opening stock due entirely to a rise in price and is thus the increase in the value placed upon the physical quantity of opening stock. But it should be noted that the closing stock is entered not at the market value prevailing at the end of the year (£220+20 per cent per ton), nor at the purchase price of metal that prevailed at the end of the year (£220 per ton), but at a 'cost' defined by the method of accounting.

The element of stock appreciation will depend not only on the course of prices but also on the timing of material purchases and sales, that is on the course of physical stock 'turnover'. In our simple example, with prices rising by a constant amount, the merchant's stock being turned over evenly throughout the year and the year's purchases and sales being equal in volume to a constant stock, stock appreciation per ton is equal to the difference between the opening price of £100 a ton and the *average* price of purchases made throughout the year, which is £19,800/120, or £165 per ton. If the merchant's purchases and sales had been concentrated on the months towards the end of the year, or if he held a smaller stock that, as in practice, would be turned over more than once during the year, the element of stock appreciation, as well as the other constituents of his book profits, would have been different.

### Stock Appreciation, Profits and Liquidity

The bearing of stock appreciation on the problem of business finance is that if the total recorded profit of £10,320 were paid in taxation and distributed in dividends our merchant would be able to finance the replacement of his stock of 120 tons only by drawing on his cash resources or by raising additional capital. His sales receipts of £22,320 would not be enough to pay out £10,320 in taxation and dividends and provide for his metal purchases costing £19,800, so that a cash deficit of £7,800—equal to the stock appreciation—would have to be met despite the appearance of high profits given by his accounts. To calculate true distributable profits, therefore, the element of stock appreciation must be deducted from his book profits after tax.

FIFO accounting thus exaggerates the 'true' rise in profits when prices are rising, if we define 'true' profits as those calculated after providing for the maintenance intact of real as opposed to money capital; and in so far as businesses tend to base their dividend and capital expenditure policies on the course of book profits its use aggravates the shortage of finance due to the formulation of prices by reference to historic costs. Moreover, inventory profits are inherently unstable, and when a period of rapidly rising prices comes to an end, stock appreciation falls sharply, and if prices actually decline stock depreciation is recorded.

If prices were to fall in our trader's third year, stock depreciation would be aggravated by the practice of entering closing stocks at the lower of 'cost' or market value, no matter how 'cost' is defined. If in the third year the replacement price of scrap were to recede by £10 a month to £100 at the end of December, our merchant's closing stock would, on conservative accounting criteria, be entered at its market value (but excluding profit margin) of £12,000, recording stock depreciation of £7,800 from the opening stock figure of £19,800. This would mean a swing in the stock element in recorded profits of £15,600 (from +£7,800 to −£7,800), which would produce a net loss in the trader's accounts, even in the unlikely event of his maintaining a 20 per cent mark-up on a falling market, an assumption which, for the sake of simplicity, is maintained in Table 12.

TABLE 12. *Trading Account (Third Year)*

| | | £ | | | £ |
|---|---|---|---|---|---|
| Jan. 1 | Stock | 19,800 | Dec. 31 | Stock | 12,000 |
| Jan.–Dec. | Purchases | 18,600 | Jan.–Dec. | Sales | 22,320 |
| | | | | Trading Loss | 4,080 |
| | | 38,400 | | | 38,400 |

His third is apparently an unprofitable year for our trader, but in fact, before paying taxes or dividends, his liquid resources have increased by £3,720, the difference between his purchases and his sales, presenting a contrast with his accounts that shows how unstable is the link between the course of financial resources and published profits in conventional accounts. When commodity prices decline, recorded gross profits may fall sharply owing to the swing in stock appreciation; but 'true' undistributed profits may actually rise, reflecting the diminished cost of financing stocks. The incidence of stock appreciation is greatest in those industries where raw material costs form a large part of total costs and substantial stocks are held, e.g. in cotton and wool textiles, electric cables, and non-ferrous metal fabrication. Fluctuations in the element of stock appreciation, exaggerated by FIFO accounting, have been an important cause of oscillations in published company profits, aggravating swings of confidence in the financial and business world, in the board-room as well as on the Stock Exchange, and causing fluctuations in business liquidity that seem to be at variance with the appearance given by profit and loss accounts and the course of trading.

In recent years greater awareness of the true situation produced by the unstable element of stock appreciation seems to have been shown on all sides. But company taxation is still levied on book profits containing an element of stock appreciation, despite the fact that this is tantamount to the taxation of real capital when, as in most of the post-war years, prices have been rising; in a period of rapidly increasing prices, as in 1950–51, the effect is to deplete company liquidity just when it is most needed for stockholding. The existing system of taxation weighs heavily on the problem of financing business expansion in these conditions, and a departure from the policy of FIFO accounting has been suggested as a remedy.

### Base Stock Valuation

Although methods other than FIFO are fairly common in the U.S.A., for example, their use in this country is still limited. One such system is the base stock method, which has been used by some concerns in the non-ferrous metal fabricating industries, for example. In these trades a certain minimum stock of metal, carried in the form of work in progress, is absolutely essential for the functioning of the business. This minimum stock, under base stock accounting, will be entered in the books year after year at a constant price, the cost of its original acquisition. The result is that profits will be unaffected by changes in the replacement price of this part of a firm's stocks. Where the system was customary it had been approved by the Inland Revenue for the calculation of tax liabilities until a Court decision of 1953.

### Last In First Out Valuation

Another alternative would be to replace the traditional adoption of FIFO accounting by that of 'Last In First Out' or LIFO, a method that is used in the U.S.A. and Canada. Instead of the assumption that the part of a firm's stock of materials that is first sold or used up in production is that which was bought first, the computation of profits can be made on the not necessarily more arbitrary supposition that the latest unit withdrawn from stock for processing or sale is that which was bought last. Returning to the example of our metal merchant, the accounts of the second year's trading would be as follows under the LIFO system.

TABLE 13. *Trading Account (Second Year), LIFO*

|  | £ |  |  | £ |
|---|---|---|---|---|
| Jan. 1 Stock | 12,000 | Dec. 31 Stock | | 12,000 |
| Jan.–Dec. Purchases | 19,800 | Jan.–Dec. Sales | | 22,320 |
| Trading Profit | 2,520 | | | |
| | 34,320 | | | 34,320 |

With the LIFO method the trading profit in this year of rising prices is shown as £2,520, against the £10,320 produced by FIFO accounting. The value of the closing stock in our example is equal to that of the opening stock, but only because the assumption has been made that each month's sale of ten tons is replaced by a purchase of an equal amount and that the equivalent of just one year's stock is sold within the year. The 120 tons sold during the year is thus deemed by the LIFO method to have been the 120 tons purchased in the same period, leaving the 'original' 120 tons in stock at the 'original' price of £100 per ton. Because of the simple assumptions regarding stock turnover, it will be observed that LIFO accounting has produced the same result as would the base stock method if a base stock of 120 tons were maintained.

### LIFO Valuation and Price Changes

It our example were altered so that no purchase of metal was made until the opening stock had been completely exhausted, then the 120 tons purchased for replacement would all have been bought in December of the second year, and the LIFO profit would be the same as under the FIFO system. In practice few businesses allow their stocks of individual items to be entirely depleted before replacement, so that LIFO accounting would produce a smaller profit in times of rising prices; but the complete

P

elimination of stock appreciation would in practice be rare, as few businesses approximate to the conditions of our previous example. In times of falling prices, on the other hand, the practice of recording stocks at market values takes precedence over either LIFO or FIFO methods if the fall in prices is severe enough. If LIFO were used in these circumstances stock depreciation would be smaller than under either the FIFO or market value method of accounting, thus restricting the depressing effects on business confidence and on the Stock Exchange of heavy book losses, but at the expense of a tax liability in times of declining prices that would be higher than that calculated under the FIFO or market value methods of valuation.

## Other Valuation Methods

One argument held against LIFO accounting is that it is more difficult to apply conveniently to work in progress, and other methods are to be found in use. In some industries it is possible to attribute to particular articles their actual individual cost—the 'unit cost' system. A not uncommon method of valuing work in progress is that of 'standard cost', by which a standard budgeted cost per unit is entered, usually varying with the selling price, which is itself altered after large changes in raw material prices. Under the 'average cost' system, on the other hand, the book cost of the opening stock is averaged with the cost of materials added within each of a number of periods during the year, the cost of materials used up in the production process being charged at the average price. But none of these methods completely disposes of the element of stock appreciation.

### FIXED ASSET VALUES

## Provision for Depreciation

Apart from any receipts from the scrapping or sale of fixed assets, the provision for depreciation will be just sufficient to enable a firm to replace a constant stock of fixed assets as they wear out, if the following conditions are satisfied:

(1) If the firm does not make losses.
(2) If the life of the fixed assets and their flow of service have been correctly valued.

(3) If any movement in the replacement price of fixed assets has been taken into account.

If a firm makes losses its provision for depreciation will be insufficient to replace its fixed assets even if the other three conditions are satisfied, for the incurrence of a loss means an excess of current costs over current receipts which can be met only by drawing on some form of asset if no fresh capital can be raised. If sufficient liquid assets are not available the loss will entail the running down of stocks or of fixed assets, either by sale or failure to replace as used up. In the absence of losses, on the other hand, depreciation provisions that satisfy conditions (2) and (3) will enable a firm to replace its fixed assets year by year, for they will amount to the correct withholding, after all other current expenses have been deducted, of current receipts from dividend distribution and from liability to tax. A company need not replace its fixed assets as they are consumed if the return from them is inadequate; the point is, however, that accurate depreciation provisions would enable it to replace fixed assets if desired.

Depreciation provisions can only hope to approximate to the second of the above conditions, and one of three methods of calculating depreciation is generally used: the sinking-fund or annuity method, the diminishing balance and the straight-line method.

### The Sinking-fund Method

This is most appropriate to an asset that yields the same net return year after year until it ceases to be used. A common example is that of leasehold property; in this case the process of writing down the book value of the asset is more usually known as 'amortization' (the term also being used for the principle of providing for the ultimate repayment of a loan), and in accounting terminology there is a tendency to reserve the word 'depreciation' for the loss of value due to use—in the income-tax codes depreciation allowances are described as representing 'wear and tear' But there is no difference in principle.

If an asset yields the same net return year after year until it is discarded, then all that the provision for depreciation has to account for is the element of time, that is for the fact that the length of the asset's unexpired life is reduced year by year and that at any moment of time the asset's value is dependent on the number of years of use that remain. The difference between the value of a new asset with twenty years of life ahead and that when it is one year old, when it has only nineteen years to run, lies in the fact that in the latter case one year's net income, *nineteen years ahead*, is no longer to be enjoyed; in both cases the same net annual return is available for nineteen years. The loss of value during the first year of life is represented by the present discounted value of the twentieth year of income; the loss of value in the second year of use will be the present discounted value of the nineteenth year of income and so on. Because of the effect of discounting equal parts of an asset's initial value over successively shorter periods of time, the provision for depreciation rises year by year, along the path of a sinking fund accumulation. If each year's instalment of the sinking fund is invested to yield a rate of interest equal to that used in the discounting calculation, the sum of the sinking fund provisions and the interest (itself reinvested each year) will be equal to the initial value of the asset.

### The Diminishing-balance Method

Where the loss of present value due merely to the passage of time is only one of the causes of depreciation of an asset the sinking-fund method may not be appropriate. Where loss of efficiency or increasing costs of maintenance are important, the net income produced by the asset year by year may follow a falling path. In these conditions the loss of value will be greater in the asset's earlier years, as the period of comparatively high net annual income passes. In the case of an asset with a relatively short life the effect of discounting may not be sufficient to offset this factor, so that the annual provision for depreciation should itself follow some downward curve. A convenient if rough-and-ready method is to compute depreciation each year as a constant percentage of the written-down value of the asset, so that a machine costing £1,000 depreciating by the diminishing balance method at 10 per cent per annum would be written down in the first year by £100, in the second year by £90, and so on. The common use of this method in Britain is to be explained only partly by its logic: separate depreciation provisions need not be made for individual assets in the company's books. It is only necessary to reduce the book value of each class of asset to which a given percentage rate of depreciation is to be applied, irrespective of its age or previous depreciation.

## The Straight-line Method

A third method, common in North America, but until recently comparatively rare in this country, partially restores the effect of discounting, thus compromising between the sinking-fund and diminishing-balance methods. The straight-line method allows for depreciation by assuming that the effect of discounting in increasing the loss of present value year by year, as the remaining period of life becomes shorter, is exactly offset by the effect of decreasing efficiency in lowering the annual loss of value as the years of high net income pass. The asset is simply written down annually by a fixed percentage of its initial value—the depreciation of an asset costing £1,000 written off over ten years would be £100 in each successive year.

## Depreciation and Changes in Asset Prices

Since the war the choice of one of these three methods has been less important to the problem of maintaining physical capital intact than the difference between original and replacement prices. Rising prices render inadequate for the purpose of replacement the simple application of the methods described if based on original cost, and the deficiency is enlarged if taxation is levied on profits defined with reference only to original cost, so that supplementary depreciation provisions to fill the gap have to be made out of undistributed profits that have already borne tax. If a company's directors were to distribute to shareholders the whole of their company's net profit after tax, without first making these additional provisions, they would be running down the firm's capital in real terms, although the consequences might be obscured for some time until replacement expenditure fell due.

In periods of falling prices, on the other hand, depreciation allowances based on original cost are more than sufficient for replacement and swell a company's surplus liquid assets; but the apparent fall in net profits, with depreciation charges based on original cost taking an increasing share of gross profits, may react adversely on business confidence, so that the increase in business liquidity may not be used to finance capital expenditure. In these conditions the accrual to business of surplus and idle depreciation funds diverts money from the flow of expenditure and incomes, to the detriment of the general level of economic activity and employment. It is true that in times of falling prices the provision of allowances for depreciation based on original cost results in a lower tax liability than does a system based on replacement costs, but this factor may not compensate for the deflationary effects of a fall in net book profits.

Since the war the impact of high taxation on money profits swollen by rising prices—a period in which a high level of capital investment has been increasingly regarded as being of prime national importance—has brought to the fore the disadvantages of defining depreciation with regard to original costs only. Depreciation funds might, it is true, be invested in new physical assets on which the return was high enough to provide profits sufficient to fill the gap between historic and replacement costs on existing assets, but this would still mean that net profits normally regarded as being available for distribution to shareholders or to finance expansion were being reserved for the purpose merely of replacement.

### Replacement-cost Depreciation

After the war the suggestion that depreciation should be linked to replacement cost received increasing support. Two methods of accounting have been put forward. One would compute depreciation allowances in terms of the original cost of the asset and then adjust the figures each year so as to reflect current values; the additional allowance, which would be a charge on profits before tax, would be shown as a special capital reserve, leaving the book value of assets on an original cost basis. The other would first adjust the original cost or book value of the written-down asset, entering the adjustment to the asset value as a capital reserve, before calculating the allowance currently due; in this case the book value of the fixed assets would be entered at replacement prices less depreciation at replacement prices. Each method would result in a change in the provision for depreciation each year equal to whatever was regarded as the change in replacement costs in the year.

At first sight it might appear insufficient, in order to ensure replacement, merely to increase only the current year's provision for depreciation by, say, 10 per cent if prices have risen by this amount in the year, without raising past allowances in the same proportion. The answer is that the method would be adequate if an amount equal to each year's depreciation were each year invested in the physical assets whose values were rising. This can be seen if a business with ten machines each originally costing £1,000 is considered. As long as replacement costs do not rise and if the machines have a life of ten years, a provision for depreciation of £1,000 per annum will allow one machine to be replaced each year. If replacement costs increased by, say, 10 per cent in a particular year a proportionate increase in the year's depreciation would raise the year's provision to £1,100, which would equal the now higher replacement price of the one machine to be purchased in the year.

The adjustment of depreciation allowances in this manner would not be sufficient, on the other hand, if replacement were not made continually year by year, so that depreciation funds had in some years to be held in money or in securities whose yield after tax was less than the increase in the cost of replacement.

The deceptive impact of price changes on profits has led some economists and accountants to the conclusion that profits should be redefined to take account of alterations in prices, so that, among other things, the incidence of taxation can be made less onerous than in the present situation, in which rising prices alone may cause large increases in taxable profits, possibly endangering a firm's liquidity. Opinions differ, however, as to what criteria should be used for a redefinition of profits.

Some economists maintain, for example, that what is at stake is the ability of a business to continue as an aggregation of physical assets; they argue, in other words, that profits should be defined only after providing for the maintenance of the real as opposed to the money value of capital, a problem that has been approached here only from the point of view of stocks and fixed assets, ignoring other assets and all liabilities.

Others argue along different lines, maintaining that taxable profits should be measured after provision for keeping capital intact in terms not of replacement prices but of some cost-of-living index. What this line of approach seeks to do is to ask whether the value of a firm's assets has increased in relation to retail prices in general; if so, the argument runs, its owners have improved their position in real terms and should thus bear a greater share of the tax burden.

These questions were considered by the Royal Commission on the Taxation of Profits and Income.* In its final report the Commission did not support as a principle of taxation the contention that profits should be defined in terms of maintaining real capital intact, whether in terms of replacement costs or prices in general, as this would protect businesses from forces from which other taxpayers are not immune. The Commission doubted whether the full implications of such a redefinition of profits, involving the recalculation of other accounting items, such as debtors and creditors, would be acceptable to the business community.

In the case of stocks, the Commission observed that FIFO is not the sole method permitted under the existing law. It concluded that any of the commercially acceptable methods should be permitted, as long as it was applied consistently over a period of years and not in an arbitrary fashion; it did not appear, however, to view the LIFO method with much favour. Proposals for the adjustment of depreciation in accordance with replacement costs, or in proportion to prices in general, were rejected by the Commission. The Commission found no evidence to support the contention that any general erosion of physical capital had taken place in industry since 1939; but it recognized that the maintenance of physical assets might have been difficult in the absence of certain special supplementary depreciation allowances granted by the government.

Since the Commission had to assume no change in the general level of taxation its concern was with its form, and it did not favour any alternative to depreciation provisions in their current form, on the basis of original cost. Although the Commission admitted that in the future shortage of finance might restrict investment by companies, it did not accept the view that it would be necessarily wrong for industry to be obliged, because of the

* Cmd. 9474, 1955 (H.M.S.O.).

incidence of taxation, to turn to outside finance merely to preserve its productive capacity. This argument follows from the conclusion of the Commission that, as a matter of accounting principle, a trader's profit should be computed with reference to the replacement of his money and not his real capital.

The Commission quoted with approval the opinion expressed by the Institute of Chartered Accountants in England and Wales that: 'An important feature of the historic cost basis of preparing annual accounts is that it reduces to a minimum the extent to which accounts can be affected by the personal opinions of those responsible for them.'* Those who give less weight to this observation would reply that at least part of the undesirable effect of the historic-cost basis would be removed if, as in France, the government were to announce annually or at longer intervals an index of fixed-asset prices to be used in revaluing assets and depreciation on a replacement-cost basis. But one important difficulty in computing the change in prices to be applied to fixed assets arises from the need to distinguish between changes in prices due merely to alterations in money costs and those reflecting changes in the productivity of new physical assets.

It is sometimes difficult, in examining the fears expressed by businessmen and others during this period, to distinguish between the condemnation of a high level of company taxation as such and, in regard to depreciation allowances, the particular form in which it is cast. It cannot be said that in all cases the considerations expressed concerning the practical question of finance are those applied to the principles on which profits should logically be computed. The suggestion that depreciation should be linked to replacement costs has been made both by those who consider the proposition to be essential to a valid definition of profits and those who, while doubtful about the theory, regard more generous depreciation provisions as a practical necessity of business finance. As a result it is probable that the fears of many businessmen on the subject of depreciation would be quietened if the general level of taxation were lowered, even though the original-cost basis of depreciation were retained. It is useful to bear this point in mind when considering the measures actually adopted by the government to meet the problem.

* Institute of Chartered Accountants in England and Wales, *Recommendations on Accounting Principles*, XV, para. 287.

INITIAL AND INVESTMENT ALLOWANCES

The Royal Commission was able to observe that the government had in fact helped to ameliorate the problem since the end of the war. Even before the war some assistance was given by increasing the percentage rates to be applied to original cost in computing annual allowances, thus allowing more rapid writing down. In 1946 there came into force, as a result of the Income Tax Act of the previous year, the device of the 'Initial Allowance', which was designed to facilitate re-equipment.

The allowance applied to expenditure on plant and machinery, mining works and industrial buildings and advanced part of the total depreciation allowable for tax purposes in respect of these classes of assets by granting a disproportionate allowance on the acquisition of an asset. The 1945 rates of Initial Allowance were 20 per cent for plant and machinery, 10 per cent for industrial buildings and 10 per cent for mining works; since 1945 these rates have been altered in order to encourage or restrict investment.

The Initial Allowance was granted independently of the normal statutory allowances, but together depreciation for tax purposes was still limited to 100 per cent of original cost. In the Finance Act of 1954 the Initial Allowances were superseded by the Investment Allowance, which was in turn withdrawn in 1956, except for ships, fuel-saving equipment and expenditure on scientific research.

### Effects of the Initial Allowances

The incidence of the Initial Allowances as between one firm and another depends on the fixed assets actually acquired during the year, since it is on these and not on the existing stock of assets that the allowance is granted. For some firms, therefore, the Initial Allowances could bring the year's total depreciation provisions to a level in excess of the figure that would be computed on a replacement-cost basis in respect of previously acquired assets, while other firms would still show a deficiency. Moreover, since the total tax-allowable depreciation provision for each piece of equipment amounts to no more than the cost of the asset's acquisition, the effect of the concentration of a disproportionate depreciation charge on the year of purchase is merely to postpone the payment of tax, in so far as the acquisition of each individual asset is concerned. The Initial Allowance represents a remission of taxation, reclaimable against future tax, approximating in effect to an interest-free loan on each asset acquired.

Nevertheless, under this system, a firm investing a constant or increasing sum in eligible assets year by year would, *if the allowance remained in force indefinitely*, receive some tangible benefit, in the shape of the reduction in taxation due to the Initial Allowances on its purchases each year. But, even if the concession were to remain in force indefinitely at the same rates, the benefit currently accruing to a business maintaining a constant level of gross capital investment would gradually fall to nothing. The Initial Allowances on new purchases would eventually amount to no more than the shortfall in depreciation on existing assets as compared with what would have been the normal statutory allowance in the absence of the Initial Allowances. The existence of any benefit at all, other than the interest-free nature of the 'advance', would depend on the concession's not being withdrawn.

Because, by its very nature as a means of influencing capital investment, the Initial Allowance may be withdrawn when the government wishes to restrict investment, the allowance may provide little stimulus to capital investment; the Initial Allowances were withdrawn in 1951, for example, a year of rapidly increasing replacement costs.

### Effects of the Investment Allowances

As an inducement to invest and a supplement to company funds, the Investment Allowance introduced in 1954 was a more potent instrument. The Investment Allowance was indeed granted with a view to encouraging capital expenditure by strengthening the businessman's inducement to invest, rather than as a means of removing a financial obstacle to any *given* business investment policy. The Investment Allowance covered a rather wider field than the Initial Allowances, mainly by including, in addition, agricultural buildings and assets acquired for scientific research; but it excluded motor-cars and second-hand machinery or plant.

The rates of the allowance were 10 per cent on industrial and agricultural buildings and works and 20 per cent on the other eligible assets, the allowance being granted on acquisition. The basic distinction between the Initial and the Investment Allowances was that the latter was provided *in addition to* the total normal allowance. In the case of plant and machinery a business would eventually receive depreciation allowances equal to 120 per cent of the cost of acquisition. Thus part of the profit made would be permanently free from taxation; with income tax and profits tax equal roughly to 50 per cent the concession in effect enabled a firm to buy a machine at a net price approximately 10 per cent lower than before. The benefit already received by a business from the Investment Allowance would not be destroyed if the concession were withdrawn; the Investment Allowance on each asset was a permanent and not a temporary remission of tax. Moreover, if continued indefinitely the total value of the tax concession ultimately accruing to a firm would be greater than that of the Initial Allowance.

Although it is difficult to distinguish between all the factors at work, it is generally agreed that the Investment Allowance played at least some part in stimulating industrial investment in 1954 and 1955; indeed, its very success was responsible for its withdrawal in 1956, when the pressure of orders for capital goods had outstripped the productive capacity of the engineering and building industries concerned. While recognizing its possible efficacy, particularly in regard to small-scale projects that could be put in hand at short notice, the Royal Commission on Taxation, it must be recorded, set its face against this particular means of stimulating investment. Contending that the Investment Allowance was not designed to remove financial hardship caused by the previous system of taxation, the Commission, although not unanimously, expressed the opinion that it was wrong to use an instrument of direct taxation at all for preferential treatment designed to achieve an economic aim. The Commission maintained that direct taxation should be 'resigned to a rather rigid principle of impartiality', as free as possible from 'experiments in discriminatory taxation'. This argument conforms to the Commission's view that replacement-cost accounting for business would be unfair to other taxpayers.

Since the war the adequacy or otherwise of the statutory allowances has varied with the height of the Initial and Investment Allowances. In certain years, e.g. 1949–51 and 1954–5, the total statutory allowances have exceeded the estimates of capital consumption in the company sector that have been published by the

Central Statistical Office in the annual Blue Book on *National Income and Expenditure.* In recent years the fact that an increasingly large part of equipment in use is relatively new has helped to enlarge depreciation allowances based on original cost, and in a rapidly expanding economy, with a growing stock of fixed assets, the provision made for depreciation at any time will, apart from price changes, exceed the amount of replacement expenditure currently required (and depreciation funds will be invested in improved forms of equipment). But individual companies, e.g. in the shipping industry, have been less favourably placed in these respects.

# CHAPTER 19

# TAXATION AND COMPANY FINANCE

Whereas persons, including unincorporated businesses, are subject only to income tax (and surtax), the business profits of corporations, if in excess of £2,000 per annum, are charged not only with income tax but also with a profits tax not levied on other taxpayers. This distinction reflects the legal view of the company as a separate entity.

But the law does not follow this distinction to the extent of first taxing company profits and then subjecting shareholders to income tax on their dividends as a separate source of income; for the payment of income tax by the company at the standard rate upon its profits is taken as discharging its shareholders from any liability to pay that tax on the dividends they receive out of its profits. But shareholders liable to tax at more than the standard rate are subject to the excess upon their dividends, and a rebate can be claimed in the opposite case.

## COMPANY TAXATION AND EQUITY

The distinction between companies and persons as separate taxable entities is not one that is capable of precise application in framing the incidence of taxation so as to preserve equity between persons, as between members and non-members of companies and as between individual members themselves. For a company derives its capital ultimately from the wealth of persons and employs it for their benefit. Shareholders obtain some pecuniary benefit even from profits that are not distributed, but personal wealth in this indirect form is not generally under the control of any individual shareholder and so can be said to represent a lesser form of taxable capacity than direct income itself. This consideration is usually regarded as justifying the preferential treatment accorded to companies, as compared with unincorporated businesses, in not subjecting the former to surtax but imposing upon them a less onerous profits tax instead.

It is, however, impossible to say to what extent this line of reasoning should be pursued, because many shareholders would not be subject to surtax even if company profits were entirely distributed in dividends. Moreover, the development of a system of progressive taxation, whereby rates of income tax and surtax ascend with levels of income, so that the standard rate is only one of a wide range of rates, has made it difficult to weigh the fairness of imposing the standard rate of income tax on company profits, for not all company shareholders would be liable to the standard rate on their marginal income if the profits that are now retained by companies were distributed. It has to be borne in mind that among company shareholders are numbered insurance companies and other bodies subject to income tax at less than the standard rate, as well as surtax payers. The Royal Commission on Taxation, considering the question of justice along these lines, therefore came to the conclusion that, 'in the absence of any clear guidance from principles of fiscal equity, we must expect that the rate will be determined primarily by the current need for revenue and by the economic objects that it may be hoped to achieve by changes in the impact of taxation'.* And so it has proved.

### INCOME TAX AND PROFITS TAX

From the point of view of the company, as a body apart from its members, the ultimate burden of income tax is felt as a charge upon profits placed to reserve. Between 1947 and 1958, the weight of profits tax, on the other hand, varied with the proportion of profits distributed to shareholders, for profits that were distributed attracted a higher rate of profits tax than those which were not.

In 1958 the discrimination of the profits tax between distributed and undistributed profits was removed, and a flat rate of profits tax of 10 per cent was substituted. The degree of differentiation in 1957–8, before this change, was secured by legislation first charging profits tax on a company's profits at the rate of 30 per cent and then allowing 'non-distribution relief' at 27 per cent on profits that were not distributed.

These rates, which were introduced in 1956, followed a succession of changes. At its peak in 1951–2, income tax and profits tax would take between 50 and 65 per cent of net profits if a company paid nothing in dividends, and between 64 and 75 per cent if it distributed all available profits, depending on the incidence of the Excess Profits Levy then in force. The corresponding

* Final Report, para. 57.

percentages arising from the provisions of the 1956 Budget were approximately 46 and 63 per cent. These proportions are expressed as a percentage of profits after deducting depreciation, other allowable expenses and gross debenture interest, the income-tax payable on the latter being regarded merely as a payment made by the company on behalf of the debenture-holders.

Besides United Kingdom taxes, companies that operate abroad may have to pay substantial sums in overseas taxation. Without entering into details, it can be said that, depending on the double taxation relief agreements concluded with overseas countries, these overseas taxes will in some cases be treated as discharging an appropriate part of the company's liability for United Kingdom taxation; in others, overseas taxes rank as expenses deductible before calculating income subject to United Kingdom taxation. The fact that United Kingdom taxation is generally higher than that levied by overseas countries may place British firms operating overseas at a disadvantage as compared with their overseas competitors, and in post-war years there was a tendency for British companies trading overseas to shift their seat of control abroad in order to escape the burden of British taxation. The Royal Commission on Taxation recommended special provisions to ameliorate this burden and thus to lessen the inducement for skilled managements to 'emigrate'.

The 1957 Finance Act implemented these recommendations by defining a special class of company, described as Overseas Trade Corporations, whose trading income would be exempt from United Kingdom taxation except in so far as it was distributed to shareholders in this country. To qualify for this exemption a company must be registered and controlled in the United Kingdom and, broadly speaking, must be wholly engaged in carrying out a trade overseas. Income from securities and other financial investments does not qualify, and shipping, insurance and financial concerns are also excluded, for special reasons.

## SOME EFFECTS OF COMPANY TAXATION

The liability for U.K. taxation only of all companies in this country, after deducting relief arising through taxation abroad, reached a peak in 1951–2 at rather more than one-half of gross income less statutory depreciation allowances, falling to two-fifths in 1956. Compared with pre-war years, when roughly one-quarter of net income was paid in taxation, the weight of company taxation was still heavy eleven years after the war, despite the reductions made after 1952.

### Taxation and the Availability of Company Finance

It cannot be said that since the war the level of company taxation has been such as to cause a shortage of finance for investment by companies as a whole. In most post-war years retained earnings have been more than the amount of investment actually undertaken by companies; the barriers to investment have in general been psychological and material rather than financial.

Despite the increase in taxation, finance has been adequate in the form of earnings retained by companies as a whole, because gross profit margins, at least until 1957, were generally as high as in the less prosperous pre-war years; and thanks to the rise in prices and the volume of output the gross income of companies has risen to several times its level in the less profitable year of 1938. In money terms, however, gross debenture interest and gross preference dividends on the *pre-war* capital structure were more or less fixed at their pre-war level by their very nature as fixed-interest securities. The consequence has therefore been a manifold increase in the margin of company income available after meeting gross debenture interest and preference dividends. Out of this margin must be found gross ordinary dividends, retained profits, the profits tax, and that part of income tax that can be regarded as falling upon the undistributed profits of a company.

Table 14 shows how the burden of taxation since the war has been carried not by undistributed profits, which in 1957 were over six times their pre-war level, but by the ordinary shareholder, whose gross share of the residual has fallen from over one-half to less than one-quarter. If taxation is deducted entirely, the share of net ordinary dividends in the net amount available for equity can be found to have fallen from two-thirds to somewhat over one-third.

It would not be true to say, however, that the incidence of taxation has had no adverse effects on internal business finance at all. For new companies, particularly if they are small concerns, without easy access to outside finance, rely on undistributed

Q

profits to finance their expansion; and with taxation taking up to one-half of net profits in the post-war years, even if no profits at all were distributed, the effect of taxation has been to penalize the new as compared with the established business. In the case

TABLE 14. *Company Profits in 1938 and 1957*

*Combined Appropriation Accounts*[1]

|  | 1938 (£m.) | 1957 (£m.) | Index (1938=100) |
|---|---|---|---|
| Trading profits of companies operating in U.K.[2] | 548 | 2,517 | 459 |
| Trading profits of British companies operating abroad[2] | 106 | 299 | 282 |
| *Non-trading income* | 239 | 651 | 272 |
| TOTAL INCOME[2] | 893 | 3,467 | 388 |
| LESS: |  |  |  |
| Debenture interest, gross | 61 | 71 | 116 |
| Preference dividends, gross | 121 | 109 | 90 |
| Misc. interest and dividends, gross[4] | 66 | 242 | 367 |
|  | 248 | 422 | 170 |
| LEAVES: |  |  |  |
| AVAILABLE FOR ORDINARY SHAREHOLDERS AND TAXATION[3] | 645 | 3,045 | 472 |
| OF WHICH: |  |  |  |
| Ordinary dividends, gross | 368 | 720 | 196 |
| Taxation, inc. overseas taxes[3] | 129 | 1,353 | 1,049 |
| Retained income, net[2] | 148 | 972 | 657 |

Source: *National Income and Expenditure*, 1958 (H.M.S.O., London).

[1] The figures for 1938 relate to some companies that were nationalized in 1957 and therefore excluded from the table.
[2] After depreciation, but excluding stock appreciation.
[3] In this table income tax deducted from payments of interest and dividends is treated as falling not on companies but on the recipients of the interest and dividends, so that interest and dividends are shown gross, before deduction of tax. The figures of taxation recorded here can be regarded, therefore, as falling only on undistributed income. Total U.K. taxation accruing on company income, including income tax on interest and dividends, was £256 million in 1938 and £1,533 million in 1957.
[4] Building society interest and dividends; co-operative society dividends.

of the new business whose outside shareholders look for a high return on their capital, the barrier to growth in the form of a penal rate of distributed profits tax would naturally be even higher. Although the importance of these considerations cannot be measured statistically, and thus stand in danger of being overlooked, the level of company taxation can be said in this way to have accentuated the rigidities in the British economy and to have blunted the forces of competition.

### Some Effects of Low Dividends

The effect of passing the burden of company taxation to the ordinary shareholder, with the encouragement of successive governments who have appealed for restraint in dividend policy in order to restrict wage claims and personal expenditure, has also been to discourage economic flexibility. It is true that it is possible to argue, paradoxically, that the policy of keeping ordinary dividends low in relation to available earnings may actually have raised the status of ordinary shares in the eyes of the financial world, particularly of institutions such as insurance companies and of conservatively-managed trust funds; for the increase in the margin of cover for ordinary dividends reduces the risk that they will be cut when trading conditions become unfavourable. To the extent that relatively low dividends have made investors in general and the institutions in particular less afraid to hold ordinary shares, the result has been to broaden the demand for ordinary shares and thus to widen the field of risky capital investment projects that can be undertaken now that sufficient time has elapsed for the margin of cover for ordinary dividends to have been built up.

Against this must be set the important consideration that the pattern of capital investment is likely to have been distorted by unduly conservative dividend policies. Many individual concerns have found their retained earnings insufficient to finance investment projects that they consider worth undertaking. The main channel through which the surplus funds of one company can be made available to finance the expenditures of another is via the new issue market. If the level of ordinary dividends had been higher it would have been easier for their recipients to subscribe to the new issues of those concerns requiring new money. The distribution of capital investment between different companies and industries, and thus their relative rates of growth, would have been decided to a greater extent by the assessment of their prospects by the investing community and less by the existing pattern of profits and reserves. The latter being influenced by history and by the distribution of monopolistic advantages, a more generous dividend policy would have enabled investment projects to come within a wider scrutiny. It might even have led to a higher level of investment overall, for some companies retained profits excessively in the form of idle liquid resources in the decade after the war.

Low dividends may also tend to discourage capital investment in other ways. By depressing share prices they render the raising of capital from the public more expensive and so make it more difficult to justify raising new equity capital. The earnings yield on ordinary shares is relevant in this context. If existing ordinary shares have a market price of £5 and are backed by equity earnings of £1 per share the earnings yield is 20 per cent. If the company issues new shares at a price of £5 the earnings per share on the augmented capital will fall and previous shareholders will suffer accordingly, unless the project financed earns at least 20 per cent per annum. Low dividends, by holding down share prices, mean high earnings yields.

The same problem can be looked at from another point of view; until 1955, at least, the market value of the ordinary capital of many companies was lower than the current replacement value of the assets which they represented. In this situation a company can only enlarge the assets at its disposal by a new ordinary-share issue if it increases its nominal capital by proportionately more, thus reducing earnings per share for holders of existing shares unless the rate of return on the new project is sufficiently greater than that obtained from existing assets.

In short, dividend restraint encouraged by government exhortation and the incidence of taxation tend to restrict the field of investment projects that some companies can afford to finance out of new capital, in so far as directors give full weight to the interests of their shareholders in framing their investment policy. Here again, taxation accentuates economic rigidity by penalizing the concern faced with a potentially above-average rate of growth and especially the small or new concern, whose shareholders may seek high yields in any event.

A further possible consequence, but one difficult to assess, is that companies may in the long-run react to the high earnings yields required by investors by raising their prices to their customers in order to obtain a rate of profit on their capital projects sufficient to enable them to finance their investment from retained earnings. The general effect would be to strengthen tendencies making for rigidity and monopoly, for it is only the well-established and monopolistic concern that is in a position to pursue such a course.

## The Royal Commission's View

The Royal Commission on Taxation broadly agreed with these views in its final report. It also noted the fact that a system of taxation penalizing the distribution of profits distorts capital structures by making the issue of preference shares generally injurious to the interests of the ordinary shareholders, as the higher rate of profits tax that had to be paid until 1958 on preference dividends as distributed profits could only come out of the earnings otherwise available for ordinary shareholders. For these as well as other reasons it therefore recommended the substitution instead of a single flat-rate tax, to be levied in addition to income tax, in order to end the differentiation between distributed and undistributed profits. This recommendation, it has already been noted, was implemented in the Budget of April 1958.

## Company Taxation and Risk-bearing

The effect of a high rate of tax on risk-taking is not easily judged. The tangle of motives that lead men to undertake financial risks is not such as to enable simple generalizations to be made, especially in the sphere of company finance, where limited liability and the position of managers who are not large shareholders modify whatever conclusions can be applied to the unincorporated business. It is generally accepted, however, that as businessmen are concerned with their *net* income, high rates of taxation inhibit them from undertaking the more risky capital projects. By 'more risky' in this context is meant not those projects with a low expected rate of return—which, after all, may be predicted with confidence—but those whose outcome is more uncertain, in which the rate of return may lie within a comparatively wide range of probabilities.

It is true that taxation, which reduces net gains, also mitigates the net loss of income in the event of a capital project proving a failure. But losses only reduce tax liabilities if they can be set off against income, and they can be carried forward for tax purposes only for a limited period. In a business whose income is known to fluctuate or for which the outlook is in any case uncertain, such as a new business, there may not be sufficient profits forth-coming against which can be charged the possible losses that may be incurred on risky projects. The small firm may be at a special disadvantage in this respect, for the size of the risky project is likely to be larger in relation to its usual level of profits than that of the giant concern; in many industries there is a scale of opera-tions beyond which it is economic to proceed only by means of a comparatively large jump, and it is at this stage that this considera-tion may prove important.

In its effect on risk-taking, high taxation penalizes the small and the rapidly growing concern and strengthens the position of the monopolistic and the well-established business. The con-sequences of high taxation may be particularly serious in regard to the ability of this country to export, for it is in this field, whether investment takes the form of manufacturing or marketing facilities, that uncertainty is generally highest.

### TAKE-OVER BIDS

A take-over bid is an offer to purchase a sufficient number of shares of a company in order to acquire control over it. Since the purchase price offered is generally in excess of the current market price of the shares, it follows that the purchaser expects to obtain a higher return than that to which other investors were previously looking forward. This may be possible through a number of ways which have made 'take-overs' a common feature of industrial life, such as, for example, the integration of a small company with a larger one in order to secure greater operating efficiency or other economies of scale. Sometimes the purchaser may believe that he can arrange for a company to be run more successfully even within the existing framework of operations merely by changing its management; although this sometimes arouses controversy no special issues are involved, for the existing shareholders will only accept the bid if they are positively dis-satisfied with the present management, who are generally given adequate compensation.

### Take-over Bids and Low Dividends

Certain types of take-over bid have been a special feature of the post-war period, however, resulting indirectly from the low level of dividends, which in turn has been partly the result of the system of taxation. The simplest example is that where a purchaser believes that a higher rate of dividend is justifiable even if the business is continued along existing lines, with no redeployment of physical assets. In this case the company to be acquired must have a sufficiency of liquid assets out of which dividends can be raised. The would-be purchaser may be convinced that the existing board of directors, unable to use the company's liquid funds for physical investment, has merely been overpossessive by not distributing part of them to shareholders. The purchaser may perhaps believe that, by writing up book asset values to current prices, he can show that the company's liquid resources are obviously surplus to the company's indebtedness. With government exhortation for dividend restraint and a high rate of tax on distributed profits such cases have not been uncommon in post-war years. They generally resolve into the question of whether the existing shareholders possess sufficient confidence in the current management to accept its assurance that a conservative dividend policy is essential; although in a number of cases the existence of the bid has in itself been enough to prompt directors to raise dividends in order to make it impossible to purchase their company's shares 'on the cheap', suggesting that in the companies concerned an over-cautious dividend policy was certainly being pursued.

## The Redeployment of Assets

The examples of take-over bids that have aroused the most controversy are those where the purchaser believes that some rearrangement of the company's assets will be profitable. In these the essence of the object of a take-over is to acquire control over the company's liquid resources for one of two purposes.

First, the purchaser may, on acquiring control, be in a position to use the company's cash to make a tax-free payment out of capital gains, by first liquidating its fixed assets at current values, for example. The so-called capital distribution may not be free of tax if the take-over is one of several carried out by the purchaser, for the Inland Revenue authorities may deem take-overs to have become his 'trade'; in this case his receipts will be taxed as 'income'. The Royal Commission on Taxation, it may be observed, argued that these 'special capital profits dividends', as they are sometimes called, should not be allowed to escape tax, since they 'do not appear to differ substantially from other dividends' in being a distribution made only after the company's directors have satisfied themselves that its remaining assets will be sufficient to meet all the various claims made upon them.

Secondly, the purchaser may use the company's cash to purchase shares in what will become a subsidiary or associated company. In some cases the company over which the bidder is seeking to gain control may not even possess the cash required to carry out these objects, but the would-be purchaser will hope to be in a position to turn part of the company's physical assets into cash by outright sale or, in the many cases where the physical assets concerned are freehold property, by means of what is known as a *sale and lease-back* arrangement. In this latter case the freehold will be sold, perhaps to a large institution such as an insurance company, and probably at a price in excess of its book value, but the property will be continued to be used in return for an annual rent.

### The Distribution of Cash

In the situation where existing cash balances are distributed as tax-free capital payments, the issue from the company's point of view is again whether the cash is really surplus to its operating requirements. This possibility may make a take-over bid profitable because of two factors. First, the low level of dividends paid may result in the market prices of the company's shares being not much above the value of its liquid assets per share. Alternatively, it is sometimes argued, a purchaser may be prepared to strip a company of part of its necessary working capital when the capital payments can be made free of tax. The first consideration is again a question of prudent dividend policy. The second possibility cannot easily be accepted at its face value. For in bidding for a company's shares the effect is usually to raise its price, not only because of the public announcement of the bid but because in the process the would-be purchaser usually buys a sufficient number of shares to be in a position to influence the board. If the distribution of cash goes so far as to injure the long-run prospects of the company its share prices could ultimately be expected to fall, so that whether the purchaser could afford to carry out such a policy would depend on the comparison between any tax-free receipts on the one hand and the movement of the price of his shares on the other. In fact, the distribution of cash in this way has been rare, and the purchaser has generally retained part of the equity he had acquired and therefore kept an interest in the long-run prosperity of the company.

### The Sale of Physical Assets

In some cases, however, the purchaser may indeed be willing to damage the future earning power of the company over which he acquires control if he can sell part of its physical assets at a really large profit over their book value, perhaps even going so far as to wind up the company. This situation is generally only possible when the profit earned by the company's assets in their present use is simply not high enough to enable dividends to be raised by the existing management. Fixed assets may nevertheless still be sold at a profit if they can be put to better use in another line of business. The social argument in favour of such an action in this case, therefore, is that the take-over bid results in plant and equipment being used in ways which the community, judged by the test of the market, regards as being more desirable.

The sale and lease-back transaction, which in the case of many types of company, such as the multiple retail store, is a common method of economizing in capital, presents no controversy when the proceeds of the transaction are used within the business; obviously if it were not profitable it would not be undertaken. Dispute may arise, however, when the proceeds of the sale and lease-back are used either for a distribution of capital or to purchase assets in another business. It may be contended that the sale and lease-back transaction, by committing the company to paying high present-day rents for the period of the lease, will saddle it with a fixed obligation it will eventually be unable to bear. Furthermore, the operation involves uncertainty as to the terms on which the lease will be renewed and may reduce the security the company may henceforth be able to offer when raising fresh capital. Nevertheless, so runs the usual criticism, the purchaser can take his handsome tax-free profit and then, before sufficient time has elapsed for investors to realize the damage done to the company, and thus for the price of its shares to fall, he can sell his interest, leaving the remaining shareholders to 'hold the baby'.

### The Crux of the Question

This is the crux of the matter in most of these cases. Either the purchaser's policy damages the company's long-term interests or it does not. If it does, the purchaser can only be sure of making a large profit in most cases by selling his shares before other investors realize the facts of the situation; bids that secure their profit by winding up the company's business are the minority. On the whole this would appear to be a dangerous foundation on which to base a transaction of any magnitude, and there is no reason why these operations must necessarily be injurious to the earning power of the company concerned if the proceeds are not distributed. In any case, the purchaser of the freehold in a sale and lease contract will generally make a careful assessment of the ability of the company concerned to meet the rent to which it will be committed. A business that cannot recover the economic rent of its own property by earning a sufficient profit margin, indeed, is making an uneconomic use of its own resources.

The factors involved in take-over bids are obviously complex, and each must be judged on its own merits. No simple answer can be given to the question of whether a take-over bid is socially desirable if, in return for securing a more economic use of a company's resources, the purchaser makes a large tax-free profit, which, because it is tax-free, is regarded by many as inequitable. If the purchaser uses the cash released to acquire an interest in another business, the question to be considered is whether the group is an economic combination, in which scarce business talent is merely being spread as widely as possible. The possibility that a false take-over bid may be engineered in order to buy and then sell shares at a profit is one that may call for Stock Exchange investigation; but the risk that is involved would seem to make the opportunity a rare one. The characteristic common to many take-over bids is that they are made possible by over-conservative dividend policies; if they result, through the defensive action of boards of directors, in a general increase in dividends, they are, of course, open to attack by those who consider that higher dividends are in themselves socially harmful.

Above all, take-over bids often involve changes in the use of resources; if they became more frequent in the post-war years it was partly because after a long period of industrial rigidity caused by easy profits, controls and shortages, rich rewards could be reaped by those willing to undertake change. In so far as change is necessary to economic growth they serve a useful purpose even when certain aspects, such as the existence of tax-free gains, may be regarded as undesirable. They surely cannot, as sometimes is claimed to be the case, be condemned merely *because* they involve change.

# CHAPTER 20

# THE PROVISION OF SHORT-TERM FINANCE FOR COMPANIES

## BANK ADVANCES

Bank credit is not usually given in this country where it is expressly intended to be used for the acquisition of long-term capital assets, except to bridge the time before permanent capital can be raised. In practice, however, the fact that a bank advance may be repayable on demand may not prevent a businessman from regarding his bank loan as a possible form of long-term finance. Bank loans are usually reviewed at intervals, but bankers do not today press many of their customers to repay when business conditions deteriorate, for the consequence might be the failure of concerns that would otherwise survive. New advances, however, may become more difficult to obtain.

Many advances to businesses take the form of unsecured loans, but the lending banker will normally restrict a loan to bear some relationship to a borrower's current assets. In this century bank credit has shown a tendency to grow less rapidly than the national income, probably as a result of changes in the structure of the economy, including business integration, the relative decline of the merchant, economy in stock-holding, and the growth of other credit institutions. In the prosperous period since the Second World War public companies have in general shown little dependence on bank finance, owing to a high level of retained profits and access to a receptive new issue market. Private companies and unincorporated businesses, with more restricted access to permanent capital, rely more on bank credit.

## TRADE CREDIT

Most businesses give credit to one another. In some industries discounts are given for prompt settlement; but in manufacturing trades credit is given as a matter of course, settlement not being due, say, for one month; when money conditions are tight many businesses come to borrow larger amounts and for longer periods, and creditors may be unable to speed up the collection of debts.

Trade credit has grown faster than business turnover since the war partly because the alternative of bank finance has not been easily obtainable in some periods, but at a time when many businesses were sufficiently liquid to extend extra credit to their customers. Finance has been unevenly distributed, moreover, because in certain so-called 'essential' industries firms have been in a favoured position in the matter of obtaining bank credit or permanent capital. In many cases, in order to promote their sales, they have been prepared to pass on part of the proceeds to firms less fortunately regarded by the authorities. Unincorporated businesses and small private companies, without ready access to permanent capital, may at all times find in trade credit a particularly important source of finance.

## BILLS OF EXCHANGE

The bill of exchange can be likened to a post-dated cheque. It takes the form of an instruction to B to pay A, or his order, a certain sum at a stipulated date. The bill is 'drawn' by A, the 'drawer', on B, the 'drawee', who acknowledges his responsibility for payment by 'accepting' the bill, that is by signing it, thus becoming the 'acceptor'. Most bills in use today are of between one and six months' maturity, the three-month bill being the most common, and are described as 'usance' or 'period' bills as against the 'sight' bill, which is repayable immediately on presentation.

The bill of exchange is traceable as far back as the days of classical Greece; but its use for trade within England was hindered until the end of the seventeenth century by the operation of the usury laws. In the eighteenth and nineteenth centuries, following the legalization of the inland bill, the bill of exchange developed as the 'negotiable instrument' of a widespread system of domestic and international credit.

### The Bill as a Negotiable Instrument

The expansion of its use was based not merely on its utility as an I.O.U. but on the fact that, in certain conditions, the bill could be sold, at a discount on the sum due, before being presented to the acceptor on maturity. A three-month bill for £1,000, discounted immediately on being drawn at a rate of 6 per cent per annum, would be sold at a price of £985, for example. For a bill to be discounted, that is sold before maturity, the purchaser must feel sure of final payment. Where the trader on whom the bill is drawn is of first-class financial standing there may be little danger of default, but the difficulty is that his exact financial status may not be known to the third party purchasing the bill; *trade bills*, which are drawn by one trader on another, are therefore not of the highest standing. If a second signature, belonging to a financial house of great repute, can be added to the bill, the negotiability of the bill is greatly increased and the cost at which it can be discounted reduced. The bill may pass through several hands before maturity.

## Merchant Banks

A second signature came to be provided by merchant banks. These originated, in most cases, as merchants, and having achieved a great measure of financial success and possessing an intimate knowledge of trade and traders in many parts of the world, they were able gradually to develop the practice of adding their signature to bills of exchange, i.e. accepting them, in return for a commission. In the course of time they found their merchanting business incompatible with their new role as providers of credit; and gradually their business became one of finance alone. Both their opportunities and their importance to the network of credit greatly increased when in the eighteenth and nineteenth centuries bills accepted by merchant banks became eligible for rediscounting with the Bank of England.

By the end of the eighteenth century the bill of exchange had become the link that held together the network of finance and commerce. An exporter could obtain immediate payment by drawing a bill on the importer for, say, three months and selling it at a rate of discount depending on the supply of and demand for bills and on the creditworthiness of the acceptor. The ultimate security for the bill would be the goods actually consigned. The importer would be given three months' credit and would be able to meet his debt out of the proceeds of his sale in turn.

## Discount Houses

Bills can be discounted with a bank or a discount house; the latter developed out of the bill broker, who originally secured his income in the form of a commission for 'matching' bills of exchange. Suppose an eighteenth-century Bradford wool merchant had drawn a bill on the dealer in Bordeaux to whom he had sold his wool. At the same time another merchant in Bradford might have imported wine from a second dealer in Bordeaux. If the two Bradford merchants could get in touch, the wine importer could pay cash to the exporter of wool in return for the bill 'on Bordeaux'. He could then send this bill to his own creditor in Bordeaux, who would then present it on maturity to the other Bordeaux merchant for payment or discount it with a Bordeaux bank. All parties would thus be satisfied without the need for any cash having to cross the channel.

The bill broker developed almost concurrently with the merchant banker; in addition to their commission business the more adventurous brokers acted as buyers or sellers of bills on their own behalf. Their customers included not only traders but country banks; the demand for credit by the growing industrial areas would be met by the sale of bills to banks in other parts of the country where saving was in excess of capital investment.

## Types of Bill

At the beginning of the twentieth century, despite the great growth of bank advances, the bill of exchange was still a highly important financial medium for the finance of overseas trade, particularly in the case of the import of staple commodities. In home trade it would be used, for example, to finance farmers between the time of harvesting and the sale of their crops and in certain industries where the period of production was particularly long, as in shipbuilding. Perhaps over half of the bills of exchange in use just before the First World War were *finance bills*. These cannot be given a precise definition, but the term is generally used to denote bills drawn for purposes other than the movement of goods; such bills might be drawn to finance the processing of goods, the international movement of securities, or foreign exchange transactions.

By this time the usual practice was for a merchant bank, now more accurately described as an *acceptance house*, to open a line of credit against which either the seller or buyer of goods could draw a bill, depending on one of the several alternative procedures in use. The bill could then be readily discounted with a bank or discount house at the market rate. Bank bills, which are those bearing at least two 'first class' names, one of which is a London bank or acceptance house, are discounted at the lowest rates, for they are eligible for rediscounting at the Bank of England.

Foreign bills, that is bills which are drawn or accepted abroad, tended to be used for imports into this country rather than for exports; but the merchant banks also accepted a great many bills for the finance of trade between two overseas countries. After the First World War, the use of 'reimbursement credits' grew. These are arranged with foreign banks and not direct with foreign importers; it is up to the foreign bank to be responsible for determining the credit standing of the debtor.

Bills that are both drawn and accepted in this country are known as *inland* or *internal* bills, although they might be used to finance transactions involving foreigners.

### The Decline of Bills of Exchange

An estimate made by *The Economist* before the war put the total volume of bills of exchange outstanding in 1913 at £518 million, of which £182 million were inland bills. By 1928, it is thought, the total of bills accepted in this country had risen to over £750 million, of which £210 million were inland bills; these figures are compiled from stamp-duty receipts. By 1936-7, the total of bills accepted in the United Kingdom had fallen to only £275 million, of which inland bills were almost one-half, as a result of the depression in world trade.

The decline of the bill of exchange as a medium of short-term credit was hastened by the slump in world trade and the relative decline of the merchant. The integration of business concerns must have weakened the demand for external short-term finance as a whole, in which the bill of exchange has given way to the bank advance. The latter is less cumbersome; branch banking ties together the geographically dispersed payments and receipts of the large concern; the instrument of the cheque provides the simplest form of transferability; and interest need be paid only on advances that are actually drawn (although before 1939 the practice of granting rebates on prepaid bills was growing).

Some small revival in the use of the inland bill, however, did occur just before the outbreak of the Second World War, partly because of the low level of discount rates prevailing. The provision of finance by specialist houses to traders selling goods on hire-purchase was one field in which the inland bill made new progress.

Messrs. Jessel Toynbee and Co., a discount house, have concluded from the figures of stamp-duty receipts that the use of bills (including promissory notes) reached a peak in the post-war decade in 1951–2, when commodity prices were inflated by the effects of the war in Korea; in this period foreign bills are thought to have amounted to £212 million and inland-drawn bills to £363 million, the highest total since 1929. After a sharp fall in the value of bill finance in the following two years foreign bills recovered to £206 million in 1956–7 and inland bills and notes to £371 million. Although bills in use have recovered to two-thirds of their 1929 value, this represents perhaps only one-quarter of their 1929 volume in terms in 1929 commodity prices.

### The Cost of Bill Finance

Representative market rates of discount are published in the financial columns of leading newspapers, e.g.

*Discount (Bank Bills) (per cent)*

| 60 days | 3 months | 4 months | 6 months |
|---------|----------|----------|----------|
| 4¼–4 5/16 | 4¼–4 5/16 | 4¼–4 5/16 | 4⅜–4½ |

*Fine Trade Bills (per cent)*

| 3 months | 4 months | 6 months |
|----------|----------|----------|
| 5½–6 | 5½–6 | 5½–6½ |

The total cost of bill finance exceeds these rates by stamp duty and acceptance commission. The former, for a bill of £100 or more and of a period in excess of three days, is at present (in 1958) one shilling per £100 or any part thereof. On a three-month bill this is equivalent to 0·2 per cent per annum. Acceptance commissions are a matter for negotiation and at present are from 1½ to 2 per cent per annum.

#### HIRE-PURCHASE FINANCE

Many small businesses, especially new concerns, economize in finance by acquiring equipment on hire-purchase terms, a field that has widened considerably over the past twenty years. Vehicles, machine tools and other forms of expensive equipment can be obtained in this way until the firm has accumulated sufficient funds to purchase outright. Finance for these transactions is provided by specialist houses. It is also convenient at this point

R

to refer to the possibility of hiring certain forms of equipment required for only a small part of their life. This is a common practice in the building industry, in particular. In many industries vehicles may be hired even though they are to be used fully; some firms, especially those with widely dispersed operations, find it costly to undertake maintenance themselves.

### TAX RESERVES

The fact that the payment of taxation by a business is in arrears of the trading year in which the liability is incurred means that an increase in tax reserves, that is in the net excess of accruals of tax over the amount actually paid during the year, may be an important form of short-term finance provided by the Exchequer. In some years this element may be negative, but in 1957, for example, it amounted to £197 million for companies as a whole. In Table 14* the increase in tax reserves is included in the provision for taxation.

* Page 226.

# CHAPTER 21

# THE COST AND CHOICE OF EXTERNAL FINANCE

Some element of uncertainty is attached to every industrial security, namely the risk that the operations of the company concerned may not be sufficiently profitable; investors will not, therefore, be willing to take up unlimited amounts of any one company's securities at a constant price if other factors in the situation do not change. This would be so even if investors had access to an unlimited supply of funds on constant terms, for an increase in the proportion of assets held in the form of any one industrial security means an increase in the concentration of risk and a corresponding increase in the chance of loss. This factor helps to explain why a new issue of securities by a company can ordinarily be made only at a price somewhat below that at which identical securities of the company stand in the market. The effect of this is strongest in the case of an issue of ordinary shares, so that in their assessment of the profitability of a new investment project requiring a new issue of ordinary shares the directors of a company must take this factor into account if they are to pay full regard to the interest of the existing ordinary shareholders.

## THE COST OF FINANCE

### Finance by Ordinary Shares

If the responsibility of directors towards shareholders is to be exercised fully, it is by the ultimate effect on the market value of the company's ordinary shares that an investment project must be judged. This means that if the result of a new issue of ordinary shares is to depress share prices the project to be financed will be worth undertaking only if it is expected to raise actual net earnings per existing ordinary share by an amount sufficient to compensate for this and also for the risk involved in the project.

The earnings yield of existing shares *after* the issue, plus expenses, can thus be regarded as the 'cost' of finance raised in this form, and the expenses of the issue can also be expressed as a rate of interest. Given present earnings per share, a rise in the market price of the existing ordinary shares lowers the cost of equity finance: this is one reason why new issues are sometimes accompanied or preceded by an increase in ordinary dividends out of existing earnings; another is that the increase in dividends signals the confidence of the company's directors in its future earning power.

### *Finance by Loan Capital*

If the project under consideration is to be financed by an issue of loan capital it will be worth undertaking only if it is expected to raise net earnings per ordinary share, after payment of loan interest, by some margin. For, owing to the inevitable uncertainty that surrounds a company's future income, the introduction of a further element of debt in the company's capital structure, resulting in an interest charge ranking prior to dividends on ordinary shares, may cause investors to regard the latter as now subject to greater risk. The market value of the company's ordinary shares could be expected to fall somewhat in consequence if other factors remained unchanged. It is true that *if* the investment project is a success the result of higher gearing will be to increase earnings per share more than proportionately to the rise in net profits after tax, but a change that raises the chances of both gain and loss equally is one that, in the financial world, usually has to be paid for.

In practice, however, the increase in the gearing of capital structure is likely to be of noticeable importance only when it is taken beyond a certain point; and 'other factors' rarely remain unchanged, for the news of a new issue may itself draw attention to the possibility of an expansion of profits. Within the range of prior charges itself, however, differences in the rate of interest that have to be paid on securities of different degrees of seniority will usually be evident. Similar considerations apply to an issue of preference shares.

### *Finance out of Retained Profits*

What should be the test of whether capital investment is worth financing out of retained profits ? Not, surely, that a new project should merely achieve *some* increase in earnings per ordinary share; for a project that yielded any positive return at all would satisfy this condition. If the interests of ordinary shareholders are to be fully served, the return on such a project must provide them with adequate compensation for the earnings yield they could have obtained if retained income had instead been distributed and used to buy ordinary shares in some other comparable concern or, more realistically perhaps, used to purchase a representative sample of ordinary shares in general. Admittedly this criterion cannot be applied precisely. An increase in ordinary dividends might bring an immediate return to shareholders in the form of higher share prices, but the directors of many a company can argue that a certain level of net capital investment is needed merely to keep its position in the industry and thus to maintain the long-run value of its shares; a company that does not attempt to grow is one that is likely to contract.

Whatever the force of these and other qualifications, such as the taxation that might have to be paid by or on behalf of shareholders if dividends were increased, it remains true to say that the cost to the shareholders of retaining profits within the company must bear *some* relationship to the earnings yield available on the ordinary shares of other concerns that could be purchased out of the proceeds of higher dividends. But the extent to which either investors or directors attempt to apply some such standard in practice is a matter for conjecture.

### THE CHOICE OF FINANCE

#### Relative Terms

Several considerations influence the businessman's choice of external finance. The first and most obvious is the relative cost of the methods that are open to a company—the rate of interest required on a debenture, the dividend yield to be provided on a preference share, and the earnings yield on ordinary capital, each adjusted for the expenses involved in the new issue. At the same time the question of whether finance should be sought on a short-term or long-term basis must be considered. It will be worth borrowing on a short-term loan even if the interest charge is greater than that payable on a long-term loan, if on maturity the short-term loan can be re-financed at a sufficiently low rate of interest. In practice, however, uncertainty as to the possibility and the terms of re-negotiation of a short-term loan puts a premium on long-term finance when this is needed for long-term purposes.

The incidence of taxation may be important. Because debenture interest, for example, ranks as an expense in calculating company profits subject to tax, a rise in the rate of taxation will lower the net cost of this form of finance in relation to that of an issue of ordinary or preference shares. A high rate of distributed profits tax, on the other hand, is a particularly strong deterrent to the issue of preference shares.

Several factors have to be examined in conjunction with the direct net costs of different forms of new capital. In the case of loan capital or bank finance, the collateral security required, the restrictions placed on the use of assets pledged as security, and those placed on the issue of capital of equal or senior status are important considerations. The method and timing of repayment of a loan will also be given careful attention.

### The Position of Different Companies

These matters will be assessed differently by different companies. The nature of a company's operations will influence its choice of the different forms of finance and the relative terms on which they can be obtained. A company possessing valuable freehold properties, or one earning a steady income, will find it relatively easy to raise money by way of long-term fixed-interest capital, whereas a business possessing large current assets, e.g. stocks or debtors, will generally be found to rely more on short-term finance. The existing capital structure will also be a critical element in the appreciation of both the cost and the risks of finance. Even when interest rates are relatively low, for example, the management of a company whose capital structure is already highly geared will usually view with caution a proposal to add to its loan capital, especially if trading conditions are unfavourable or uncertain. Thirdly, the existing owners of small companies in particular may be averse to sharing their equity interest with outsiders; but their preference for debt finance is not always matched by the availability of suitable assets that can be pledged as collateral security.

### Reconciliation between the Supply of and Demand for Finance

From the point of view of the potential supplier of finance, many of these considerations will naturally apply in reverse. When interest rates are expected to rise, the borrower will be concerned to secure long-term finance, whilst the lender will be impressed with the advantages of lending 'short'. When trade is depressed, companies are reluctant to resort to debt finance, whereas investors will not favour equity finance. In the course of the bargaining process the price of loanable funds and the other contractual elements of the bargain will vary so as to compensate for these factors and others, bringing the demand for finance into closer equality with its supply. But it does not follow that the conflict between lender and borrower over matters such as these can always be smoothed by a small adjustment in the rate of interest, for either side may stand so firm on certain points that it would require a rate of interest unacceptable to the other party to over-come this. Thus the matching of demand with supply that does materialize and the level of capital investment that is thereby undertaken will be influenced by the attitudes that are adopted by both sides to these financial questions, as well as by the expected rate of return on new projects.

## Debt versus Equity Finance

In this field, perhaps the most important conflict arises over the question of debt versus equity finance. The fixed-interest capital raised by many companies at high rates of interest in the boom that followed the First World War proved a costly burden when profits fell in the years of poor trade that followed. Some of these companies, as a result of the existence of high debt charges at a time of low profits, found themselves unable to pay any ordinary dividends at all, and in some cases even preference dividends were endangered. This unfortunate experience made investors less willing to supply finance by way of ordinary shares except at relatively high yields but made companies equally reluctant to raise loan capital except at very low ones. The general reduction in interest rates after 1931 eased this conflict by reducing the cost of debt finance, but nevertheless one result may have been to curtail the level of capital investment actually undertaken and thus to have retarded the country's recovery from the depression. The shortage of 'risk' capital, which even before the war began to be attributed to the redistribution of incomes and wealth through taxation, may have been as much the result of the unfortunate experience of ordinary shareholders in the inter-war slump.

The general effect of a relatively high proportion of debt finance may be first to intensify the later stages of a boom, since high gearing leads to a proportionately greater increase in equity earnings when profits are rising, and secondly to accentuate any ensuing slump. If losses are incurred the depletion of current assets reduces the capital as well as the income cover for any debt element, and the consequent difficulty in raising equity finance delays economic recovery. The problems involved in raising external equity finance in the unfavourable conditions of the pre-war years may have strengthened the inducement already provided by high taxation to retain a high proportion of earnings. But the persistence of a long period of high money profits, combined with low dividends, has since caused loan capital and other debts, such as bank advances, to fall as a proportion of total assets, and the low gearing that can now be seen to be enjoyed by most companies has given them a much wider range of choice in seeking outside finance.

Companies new to the Stock Exchange generally find it easier to issue ordinary shares. The market in preference shares, particularly if the company is small, is narrow, so that the cost of a preference issue may be high. Secondly, it will usually be possible to issue debentures on acceptable terms only if an adequate layer of preference or ordinary shares is already in existence, providing a substantial margin of income cover for the debenture interest, a consideration that applies to quoted companies as well as to those seeking Stock Exchange quotations. Thirdly, when a company has been nursed by an issuing house, so that the issue of shares is made by the latter as principal, the issuing house will expect to make a substantial profit on successful issues to balance the cost of its weaklings; this is usually only possible if the issue is made in the form of ordinary shares. Fourthly, the type of investor interested in the issue of shares by a company new to the Stock Exchange will generally be more concerned with the chance of gain than with the necessity for safety, at least within limits. A company that promises expansion, even if some measure of uncertainty is involved, will be more popular with this class of investor than one that promises safety but no growth, for even promises of safety are not always redeemed.

ISSUES BY COMPANIES SINCE THE WAR

Table 15 shows how the pattern of new issues has changed under the pressure of events. One clear line of division can be drawn through the year 1949. In the first four post-war years ordinary-share issues formed a larger share of the total than in the pre-war period, with debentures playing a smaller and preference shares a rather larger part than before the war. In this period the attitude of the institutional investors, such as life-assurance offices and pension funds, may have been less than usually receptive towards fixed-interest issues, because their own

TABLE 15. *Types of Securities Issued by Companies\**
(*excluding Railway and Gas and Water Undertakings*)

|  | Debt | | Preference | | Ordinary | | Total |
|---|---|---|---|---|---|---|---|
|  | £m. | % of total | £m. | % of total | £m. | % of total | £m. |
| 1933–8 average | 35·5 | 35·9 | 21·5 | 21·7 | 41·9 | 42·4 | 98·9 |
| 1946 | 20·1 | 15·7 | 30·5 | 23·7 | 77·8 | 60·6 | 128·4 |
| 1947 | 32·3 | 24·1 | 40·5 | 30·3 | 61·1 | 45·6 | 133·8 |
| 1948 | 15·6 | 11·0 | 24·9 | 17·6 | 100·8 | 71·3 | 141·3 |
| 1949 | 34·0 | 29·8 | 30·3 | 26·5 | 50·0 | 43·7 | 114·3 |
| 1950 | 71·5 | 55·6 | 10·9 | 8·5 | 46·2 | 35·9 | 128·6 |
| 1951 | 49·1 | 37·8 | 19·7 | 15·1 | 61·1 | 47·1 | 129·9 |
| 1952 | 36·7 | 28·6 | 4·1 | 3·1 | 87·8 | 68·3 | 128·6 |
| 1953 | 53·1 | 50·4 | 7·9 | 7·5 | 44·3 | 42·1 | 105·4 |
| 1954 | 101·0 | 49·9 | 28·3 | 14·0 | 73·0 | 36·1 | 202·3 |
| 1955 | 65·1 | 27·2 | 18·9 | 7·9 | 154·9 | 64·9 | 238·9 |
| 1956 | 76·0 | 33·8 | 3·1 | 1·4 | 145·7 | 64·8 | 224·7 |
| 1957 | 183·3 | 54·0 | 1·7 | 0·5 | 155·2 | 45·5 | 340·2 |

\* Statistics compiled by the Midland Bank, comprising issues for 'new money' only.

portfolios already carried an abnormally high proportion of government or government-guaranteed stocks as a result of war finance and post-war nationalization. After 1949 the situation changed in several ways. Owing to certain court decisions confirming the right of companies to use surplus cash, if the action is in accordance with their articles, to redeem preference shares at par at a time when their market value is well above par, preference shares lost some of their merit in the eyes of investors and so could be issued only on more expensive terms than previously. Following the outbreak of war in Korea the increase in taxation reduced the net cost of debenture interest in relation to the cost of other types of issue, and the increase in the rate of tax on distributed profits bore heavily against the issue of preference shares. The bias against preference-share issues will be seen never to have disappeared after 1949; but the balance between ordinary-share and debenture issues was once more tilted for a time towards the former after 1954 owing to a rise in interest rates and debenture yields at a time when rising ordinary-share prices held down earnings yields on ordinary shares in 1955 and 1956.

# CHAPTER 22

# THE NEW-ISSUE MARKET

## THE DEVELOPMENT OF THE LONDON
## NEW-ISSUE MARKET

During the last fifty years the new-issue market has been transformed by the change in the country's economic position, the market's adaptation to the needs of those it serves, and by the development of company law. The period before the war of 1914–18 was one in which the dominance of Britain in international trade and finance was reflected in her lending large sums abroad, and foreign investment played a much larger part in the new-issue market than it does today. In the years 1910–14, according to one estimate, four-fifths of the total value of new issues was on foreign account, and even over the period 1895–1914 as a whole the proportion appears to have been as high as three-fifths.*

### Issuing Houses

At the heart of the market in foreign issues lay the great institutions whose development had been bound up with the expansion of this country's foreign trade and commercial finance. The great international banking concerns like Rothschilds, and the merchant banks, whose acceptance business involved close association with foreign business conditions, were thus the leading institutions handling foreign issues. Some of the merchant banks, who by this time had given up most of their merchanting business, specialized in issues for those parts of the world with which they were particularly well acquainted. Several of the great international banks, especially Rothschilds, used their great wealth and influence mainly to handle issues for foreign governments.

These institutions played a relatively small part in the market for home issues, except where railway securities were concerned. Issues for British companies were handled mainly by stockbrokers and other individual promoters, whose concern was sometimes with

* A. R. Hall, 'A note on the English capital market as a source of funds for home investment before 1914', *Economica*, February 1957.

making large profits out of individual operations rather than with acquiring a lasting reputation for integrity and sound judgement. This preoccupation with quick profits, in a period in which a weak company law and the unfamiliar standing of many of the companies coming to the market favoured speculation, was not one out of which the development of a sound new-issue market was likely to grow.

### The 1928 New-Issue Boom

After 1918 there was a marked expansion in the volume of home issues, for which the rise in taxation and the development of large-scale production were responsible. At the same time the issuing houses themselves grew in both number and variety. As a result of Britain's weakened international position and of the fear, dormant in the nineteenth century, of troubled political and financial conditions abroad, foreign issues had contracted. The merchant banks, whose acceptance business had become subject to the increasing competition of the large deposit banks, adapted themselves to this new need and new opportunity by taking a much greater interest in home issues.

The expansion of home issue business also attracted a relatively new type of institution for which no single accepted name exists— 'investment bank' is a term that is sometimes applied. These, like the merchant banks, accept deposits from a limited field of commercial and financial clients, but most of them, unlike the merchant banks, do no acceptance business. Post-war conditions also favoured the development of a miscellany of financial houses that the official year-book of the Stock Exchange classifies as 'Financial Trusts'. These hold portfolios of industrial securities, for the most part deriving their profits from dealing in securities rather than from the receipt of dividend income or long-term capital appreciation. Finally, the expansion of new-issue business on home account could still provide a rich harvest for the individual company promoter.

In the five years before the new-issue boom of 1928, new securities issued in London, excluding those of the British government, reached about £270 million per annum, of which just over one-half consisted of home issues. These figures are confined to the issue of 'new' shares; if the sale of existing shares to the public through the new-issue market were taken into account the total would be considerably larger. Not only had this country's foreign investment fallen, but the destination of the funds raised for foreign issues had changed, Commonwealth countries now representing between one-sixth and one-third of the total, a larger proportion than that usual before the war. In the boom year of 1928 new capital issues reached a peak of £362 million, of which only about £143 million, or roughly two-fifths, were overseas issues. Of the £219 million raised in home issues, £201 million went to companies.

The year 1928 marks a turning-point in the development of the new-issue market. In the international crisis and trade depression that followed, neither home nor foreign issues regained this level. In the five years that preceded the outbreak of the Second World War, new issues, excluding those by the government, averaged only £162 million a year, less than half their 1928 total, and a mere one-fifth of these were for overseas countries. Of greater long-term importance for the market, for the legal framework in which it operated and for the nature of the institutions of which it was composed, was the fact that the boom was followed by a disastrous slump in share prices, in which the home issues of 1928 suffered most. The position was aptly summarized by the Macmillan Report*:

> How easily he (the individual investor) can be misled in times of speculative fever by glittering—even tawdry—appearances is proved by the experience of 1928, as the following striking figures will show.
>
> In that year the total amount subscribed for capital issues, whether of shares or debentures, of 284 companies was £117 million. At the 31st May 1931 the total market value of these issues as far as ascertainable was £66 million, showing a loss of over £50 million or about 47%. In fact the public's loss has been greater, since many of these shares were no doubt sold by the promoters at a high premium. Still more striking perhaps, seventy of the above companies have already been wound up and the capital of 36 others has no ascertainable value. The issues of these 106 companies during that year amounted to nearly £20 million.
>
> That you cannot prevent a fool from his folly is no reason why you should not give a prudent man guidance. We believe that our financial machinery is definitely weak in that it fails to give clear guidance to the investor when appeals are made to him on behalf of home industry. When he is investing abroad he has the assistance of long established

* Commission on Finance and Industry. Cmd. 3897 (H.M.S.O., 1931).

issuing houses, whose reputation is world wide. When subscriptions to a foreign issue are invited by means of a public prospectus, it is almost certain that the issue will be vouched for by one of these issuing houses whose name will be evidence that it has been thoroughly examined and the interests of investors protected as far as possible. For the issuing houses' issuing credit, which can easily be affected, is involved, and it is very highly to its own interest to make sure that the issue is sound. If, as must from time to time happen, something goes wrong with the loan or the borrower the issuing house regards it as its duty to do everything it can to put matters straight, and indeed, to watch continuously the actions of the borrower to see that the security remains unimpaired. These duties are sometimes very onerous and involve a great deal of labour and expense, as well as judgment, skill and experience.

Contrast this with nearly all home industrial issues. There are, it is true, one or two first-class houses in the City which perform for certain first-class companies the same functions as the older issuing houses perform for foreign borrowers. In addition, these latter are to a limited extent entering the domestic field, though, for the reasons we give later, their direct interest must probably remain limited. Again, the advice of stockbrokers, when asked for, may be a safeguard, but it is scarcely sufficient to take the place of the responsibility of a first class issuing house. With these exceptions the public is usually not guided by any institution whose name and reputation it knows.

These observations serve both so summarize the requirements of a sound new-issue market and to point to the changes that have occurred since. An issuing house must have adequate capital, so that it can, if necessary, tide over a company for a short period in which market conditions are difficult; it must possess facilities for examining with care the needs and the prospects of the companies for which it deals; it must possess close contacts with large investors whose support is essential to the success of issues of any size. None of these facilities can be put to any effect unless the reputation of the issuing house is beyond question. In 1928 few of the small financial institutions and syndicates of individual promoters who had been attracted to the new-issue market possessed these prerequisites.

### The Strengthening of the New-Issue Market

Since 1928 the foundations of the new-issue market have been strengthened by the more rigorous requirements of the Stock Exchange and by the provisions of the Companies Acts of 1929 and 1948 and Prevention of Frauds (Investment) Act of 1939[3]. Among the company promoters and syndicates both the weak and the disreputable were destroyed by the slump itself. The acceptance business of the merchant banks, being a short-term liability, had restricted their participation in new-issue operations, so that the continued decline in acceptances both obliged and enabled the merchant banks to expand their issuing facilities. The continued spread of the interests of the merchant banks and 'investment banks' into new-issue business gave rise to that closer association between finance and industry that the Macmillan Committee regarded as indispensable in a competitive world. On the other side of the new-issue market the growth of the large investment institutions, especially the insurance companies and investment trusts, possessing skilled staffs and aided by a more experienced financial press, has matched the development of the issuing houses themselves.

The close association now existing between the financial world and British industry has been achieved without the disadvantages that the more formal relationship favoured by the Macmillan Committee and others might have involved. In Germany, for example, in France, and to a lesser extent in the U.S.A., the development of industry towards the end of the nineteenth century was bound up with the provision of finance for long-term capital investment by the ordinary deposit banks, a policy from which British banks have always shrunk. During the great depression that followed the crash of 1929 the creditworthiness of many of these banks was endangered by the loss of their investments in industry. 'The British houses sponsor, but, except to a limited extent in preparation for a new issue, they do not in general themselves finance. They risk their reputations and good names but not, in general, customers' deposits. Even the severest economic or financial crisis, while no doubt inflicting losses on investors, would not imperil the security of bank deposits or lead to that collapse of bank credit which utterly paralyses the whole economic system.'*

### The New-Issue Market Today

The new-issue market still presents a varied picture. Issues by public bodies are handled by the Bank of England and other

* F. W. Paish, 'The London New Issue Market', *Economica*, February 1951.

banks. The old merchant banks handle something like one-third of the value of all non-official issues* but a much smaller proportion of their number, since their resources and their wide repute enable them to concentrate on the larger operations. The other members of the Issuing Houses Association—the newer acceptance houses and the 'investment banks', together with some of the 'financial trusts'—are today responsible for nearly one-fifth of the total by value but over one-third by number.† Issues sponsored by stockbrokers alone account for nearly two-fifths by both number and value. Then there are a number of specialist houses, such as the South African finance companies and those handling plantation issues. Many large issues are made through groups of these bodies in combination. Contact is made by the larger institutions with industry and the rest of the financial world at many points. The merchant banks still have their acceptance business and, like the investment banks and financial trusts, control a number of investment trusts; some manage the investment portfolios of rich individuals, private trusts and pension funds. Many of their directors are to be found sitting on the boards of industrial companies, investment trusts and insurance companies. In this way, and through the day-to-day business of new-issue operations, an extensive network of mutual confidence, centred on the City, provides facilities that are now without equal in the rest of the world.

Paradoxically, with this great improvement in the quality of the market has come a decline in the volume of its operations, when account is taken of the rise in prices. Issues of new shares by companies in the decade following the war averaged only some £150 million per annum; if foreign issues and new issues by public bodies, but not the British government, are included the annual average will be found to be about £340 million, which in real terms is only about one-half of the average of the five years before the 1928 boom. As a consequence of the further weakening of Britain's international position, foreign issues have accounted for a smaller proportion of the total than in the nineteen-twenties; although it is not surprising to find that in these days when many overseas countries are eagerly pressing on with ambitious develop-

---

* Paish, op. cit. These estimates and those that follow are based on new issues made 1946–9, excluding conversion issues and free bonus issues.

† Paish, op. cit.

ment programmes the share of overseas issues has been as large as that in the nineteen-thirties. Since the war, overseas issues have undergone a further change as a result of the restrictions placed on foreign lending by the government in order to conserve foreign currencies; they have been limited almost entirely to Commonwealth countries, the greater proportion being reserved for official borrowers.

Table 16, compiled from the statistics collected by the

TABLE 16. *New Issues**

| | ALL ISSUES (£m.) | Public bodies (£m.) | Companies (£m.) | Total (£m.) | % all issues |
|---|---|---|---|---|---|
| | | | HOME ISSUES | | |
| 1933–8 average | 162 | 34 | 97 | 131 | 91 |
| 1948 | 252 | 100 | 114 | 213 | 85 |
| 1949 | 139 | — | 96 | 96 | 69 |
| 1950 | 313 | 154 | 108 | 262 | 84 |
| 1951 | 252 | 76 | 128 | 203 | 81 |
| 1952 | 371 | 206 | 117 | 323 | 87 |
| 1953 | 396 | 246 | 92 | 337 | 85 |
| 1954 | 471 | 225 | 186 | 410 | 87 |
| 1955 | 567 | 306 | 219 | 525 | 93 |
| 1956 | 296 | 54 | 211 | 265 | 89 |
| 1957 | 383 | 27 | 294 | 321† | 84 |

† Including the whole of an issue of £41 million by British Petroleum Ltd., which cannot be divided into 'Home' and 'Overseas'.

OVERSEAS ISSUES
Commonwealth and Empire
Countries

| | Public bodies (£m.) | Companies (£m.) | Total (£m.) | Foreign countries (£m.) | Total (£m.) |
|---|---|---|---|---|---|
| 1933–8 average | 10 | 17 | 27 | 5 | 31 |
| 1948 | 8 | 29 | 37 | 1 | 38 |
| 1949 | 21 | 21 | 42 | 1 | 43 |
| 1950 | 28 | 17 | 45 | 6 | 51 |
| 1951 | 30 | 8 | 38 | 11 | 49 |
| 1952 | 33 | 13 | 46 | 1 | 47 |
| 1953 | 41 | 18 | 59 | — | 59 |
| 1954 | 35 | 19 | 55 | 7 | 62 |
| 1955 | 18 | 22 | 40 | 2 | 42 |
| 1956 | 14 | 18 | 31 | — | 31 |
| 1957 | 13 | 48 | 61 | 1 | 62 |

* Totals and sub-totals may not add up exactly, owing to rounding.

S

Midland Bank, shows how the composition of new issues of marketable securities has altered in this way since the war. The figures exclude issues made by the government and attempt to exclude sales of existing securities which do not add to the resources of the company whose securities are being offered and other issues that do not bring 'new money', such as conversion issues.

New issues by companies in this country averaged £157 million between 1948 and 1957. The Blue Book on National Income and Expenditure shows that net capital investment by companies in this country averaged £470 million over this period. This latter figure includes net investment by private companies and public companies too small to take advantage of the new-issue market. The contribution of the new-issue market to the net domestic investment of public companies alone in these years must have been over one-third. Of the new issues by public bodies in this country between 1948 and 1957, excluding those made by the central government, nearly 90 per cent were those made by the nationalized industries; until 1953 practically the whole of local-authority borrowing was made from the central Exchequer. If the issue of shares already in existence but without any previous quotation on the Stock Exchange and other issues, such as conversion issues, that provide no 'new money' are included, the total of all issues made through the Stock Exchange in London would be found to average nearly £400 million per annum in the four years between 1947 and 1950 inclusive, more than ten times the volume of new issues made outside London.*

### THE CAPITAL ISSUES COMMITTEE

New issues had to be submitted for Treasury consent as early as the First World War, the purpose of control being to prevent capital expenditure on projects not deemed to be in the public interest and to restrict competition with government borrowing. The government hoped thus to block any loopholes in the system of direct controls over the use of scarce materials and to keep down the level of interest rates on government loans. Between the wars supervision by the Treasury was confined to foreign issues, the purpose being primarily to conserve foreign exchange (with the

* These figures were given by Sir John Braithwaite, chairman of the Stock Exchange Council, in a lecture to the Institute of Bankers in March 1951.

chief exception of 1932, when the object was to clear the path for the huge War Loan conversion operation), and Treasury control in this period was intermittent and at times only informal. In 1936 the Foreign Transactions Advisory Committee was set up to advise the Treasury on its control over foreign issues, and in 1939 this body was succeeded by the Capital Issues Committee, whose terms of reference extended to domestic issues.

Since the war applications for issues of more than a certain minimum size, except those by public bodies, have had to be submitted to the Capital Issues Committee[4], which advises the Treasury as to the desirability of the issue within a framework of criteria prescribed by the Treasury, on whom the final decision rests. Between 1945 and 1956 issues of £50,000 and over had to be submitted to the C.I.C., the limit being lowered to £10,000 in 1956 but raised again to £50,000 in 1958; official permission is required[4] if the new issue, together with other issues or borrowings over the previous twelve months, exceeds this sum. Broadly speaking, the C.I.C. regulations concern issues of share capital and all forms of borrowing other than that for purely temporary purposes. Thus most bank loans in the ordinary course of business are generally exempt from these regulations; they are, however, subject to the directives and requests of the authorities in various respects.

From time to time the Chancellor of the Exchequer instructs the C.I.C. as to the broad objects of expenditure that it is to regard as nationally desirable or undesirable. These instructions have usually given priority to capital investment for the enlargement of export capacity and until 1955 forbade new issues by hire purchase finance houses. Direct supervision by the Treasury of issues by public bodies, e.g. local authorities and nationalized industries, depends on the legislation governing their operations; in this field the government has wide powers. A third channel of official control passes through the Bank of England, which marshalls the 'queue' of new issues in order to ensure an orderly market, with particular reference, no doubt, to the imminence of government loans.

## TYPES OF NEW ISSUE

The new-issue market deals in two classes of security, those being offered for the first time and those already in existence but previously without a Stock Exchange quotation. The proceeds of the first type of issue are available for the finance of physical investment, for the acquisition of interests in other companies, for the finance of an amalgamation of two companies, for the repayment of existing debt or preference capital, or for the strengthening of liquid resources. The second category of issue provides for a change of ownership of existing paper assets, a change for which there may be several reasons: the owners of existing shares may wish to acquire funds in order to provide for death duties or to have their hands free for further physical investment in their own business; or the major shareholders of a company whose shares are not yet quoted on the Stock Exchange may be making them available as part of the process of securing a Stock Exchange quotation, including perhaps a change of status from that of a private to that of a public company.

The new-issue market thus has to provide for the issue of securities of two types of company; those which already have a Stock Exchange quotation and those which, although possibly long established, have never previously had their securities quoted on the Stock Exchange. The activity of the market may also include the sale of shares already possessing a Stock Exchange quotation but previously 'tightly' held by a small number of shareholders. In considering the importance of the new-issue market it would be wrong to direct attention at 'new' shares alone. The issue through the market of existing shares of established companies serves the purpose of enabling them to achieve a financial status that in the future will make it possible for them to raise capital more cheaply. The sale of existing securities by large shareholders in businesses that previously had no Stock Exchange quotation is also part of the wider function of the capital market of providing liquidity, at a price, whenever it is required. In addition the public are enabled to acquire an interest in a previously unquoted company after a 'trial period' in which the bulk of the risk has been borne by those most closely associated with the business.

The variety of needs that the new-issue market meets is reflected in the variety of forms in which new issues may be made. The London new-issue market is noted for its flexibility of operation; by shaping each issue to reconcile the requirements of industry and investors it enables capital to be raised at a lower cost than would be possible if new issue operations were more standardized.

New capital issues may be divided into the following classes:

Issues for public subscription.
Offers for sale.
Stock Exchange placings.
Stock Exchange introductions.
Issues to shareholders.

TABLE 17. *Types of Issue: 1950–7*

| Year to 31 March | TOTAL £m. | No. | Public issues and offers for sale £m. | No. | Placings and introductions £m. | No. | Issues to shareholders £m. | No. |
|---|---|---|---|---|---|---|---|---|
| 1950 | 167 | 402 | 67 | 45 | 44 | 164 | 56 | 193 |
| 1951 | 176 | 456 | 45 | 44 | 52 | 186 | 79 | 226 |
| 1952 | 151 | 362 | 34 | 20 | 37 | 150 | 80 | 192 |
| 1953 | 183 | 306 | 80 | 21 | 63 | 129 | 40 | 156 |
| 1954 | 309 | 424 | 134 | 49 | 47 | 201 | 128 | 174 |
| 1955 | 302 | 583 | 93 | 31 | 83 | 309 | 126 | 243 |
| 1956 | 276 | 498 | 69 | 21 | 61 | 156 | 146 | 321 |
| 1957 | 301 | 305 | 65 | 10 | 64 | 106 | 172 | 189 |

Source: The Times Issuing House Year Book. These figures cover a wider field than those in Table 16, by including issues of existing shares, conversion issues and others that do not provide 'new money' for companies; free bonus issues are excluded.

## Issues for Public Subscription

Public issues are those made of newly-created securities for which the issuing house acts only as an intermediary. The public are invited to subscribe to a fixed number of securities at a published price. The basis of the issue is the prospectus, which must be published in at least two leading London daily newspapers for a quotation to be granted on the London Stock Exchange.

The Companies Act requires the prospectus to set out in detail matters such as: the rights of various classes of capital; the latest balance sheet and profit and loss account and a five-year dividend record; the pecuniary interest of directors and promoters in the issue; and a description of all material contracts. In the case of very small issues, the expenses of which would otherwise be prohibitive, the Stock Exchange is empowered to grant a certificate of exemption.

The process of a public issue involves many stages. Preliminary discussions will be held between the company and the issuing house, which will examine the company's history, assess its prospects and advise as to the terms of the issue. A preliminary prospectus will be drawn up, and the arrangements for the physical handling of applications, allotments and subscriptions planned. At an early stage details will be submitted to the Stock Exchange Council, whose approval of the issue has to be given before a quotation can be granted, and time will be required to obtain the approval of the Capital Issues Committee.[4]

### Underwriting

The issuing house will also arrange to have the issue under-written. Underwriting is an agreement to take up part of the issue, in return for a fee, if it is not fully subscribed; if an underwriter agrees to underwrite, say, 100,000 shares and the issue is only three-quarters subscribed at the issue price, he will be obliged to take up 25,000. The issuing house is responsible to the company for underwriting, but in order to reduce its own risk it will arrange to pass out part or whole of the issue to sub-underwriters; in this case its own part of the underwriting commission is known as its 'overriding commission'. Sub-underwriters are institutional investors such as life-assurance companies, and it is here that the reputation of the issuing house, on which depends its being able to rely on having the issue underwritten, is of first importance. Conversely the institutional investors make a useful income from underwriting and value their place on an issuing house's list of underwriters. As a result, the attitude of these bodies to under-writing an issue whose success is uncertain is influenced by their desire to obtain an adequate share of the underwriting when a really popular issue is made.

The underwriting commission for a particular type of security therefore does not vary much from issue to issue in normal times. In recent years the total commission on first-class debentures has usually been between 1 and $1\frac{1}{2}$ per cent. Issues of ordinary shares carry higher commissions, usually of 2 per cent, depending on their quality. Overriding commissions, which are included in these figures, are generally 1/2 per cent.

### The Operation of the Issue

Particulars of the issue have to be advertised at least forty-eight hours before the Quotations Committee of the Stock Exchange Council meets to give a final decision on the request for a quotation, which allows time to elapse for members of the public who wish to give information about the company or its personnel to write to the Committee.

In the case of public issues and offers for sale the lists of application may not open until three days have elapsed since the advertisement—if the prospectus is advertised on Monday the list of applications will not open until Thursday. With their applications to the issue the public have to send the cash instalment specified in the terms of the issue; these applications, which may run into many thousands, will be handled by the issuing house or by a bank. Then comes the process of allotment after the application lists have closed. If the total value of the application is in excess of the size of the issue some applications will have to be scaled down; smaller applicants will often be allotted a larger proportion of their application. In some issues existing shareholders are given some measure of priority. The allotment letter is the legal title to the stock until certificates are issued; it can be transferred to another person by the act of 'renunciation'. Finally, the process of handling the new issue will go on for several months as share certificates are prepared and any further cash instalments or 'calls' are paid.

Because public issues are expensive to handle and because these expenses do not rise proportionately with the size of the issue, they are generally confined to the larger operations.

### Issues for Tender

One variation of the public issue is the *issue for tender*, in which the public are invited to subscribe, not at a fixed price, but at prices that applicants judge will secure for them the allotment they desire. The difficulty of arriving at the right bid makes this an uncommon method of issue in this country; but it has been used in the case of some issues by public utilities, and the Treasury bill issue is in this form.

### Offers for Sale

These are issues of securities already in existence, and the issuing house or stockbroker handling the issue acts as principal and not as intermediary. The issuing house will have acquired the shares from the company some time earlier, and the net proceeds received by the latter will depend on the price paid by the issuing house and the division of costs of the issue between the two. The amount paid to the company must be disclosed in the contracts set out at the end of the press advertisement; offers for sale are based on a prospectus in the same way as an ordinary public issue, and the responsibility for the facts in the prospectus is borne by the company in the form of a published 'chairman's letter' to the issuing house.

Whether an offer for sale should be regarded as providing funds for the company whose shares are being sold depends partly on how long before the issue the shares were bought from the company by the issuing house. Details regarding issues of shares made within the period of two years prior to the publication of the prospectus have to be disclosed therein. In some cases, especially where a small company is involved, the issuing house may have bought its shares years earlier, having nursed the company until it was in a condition fit for an issue to the market. The shares offered for sale may alternatively have been purchased by the issuing house not from the company but from its principal shareholders; in these cases the company concerned will often be found to be a private company entirely controlled by its directors.

Offers for sale are generally underwritten. But because the issue price determines the amount received by the issuing house and not by the company or its principal shareholders, the issuing house bears a risk as principal that the company assumes in the case of a public issue. Offers for sale are therefore useful for companies previously without a Stock Exchange quotation and so without an existing following among investors. Like public issues, offers for sale are relatively expensive and are generally confined to large issues. Occasionally offers for sale may be made directly by the initial owner of the securities, possibly a 'financial trust'.

The arrangements that have to be made for an offer for sale are similar to those in a public issue.

### Stock Exchange Placings

These are sometimes described as Stock Exchange introductions, a term that is here reserved for a different type of issue.

In a Stock Exchange placing the issuing house places the shares directly with institutional and other investors who are on its placing list; part of the placing may be made through the intermediary of stockbrokers, who will have their own placing list. In a Stock Exchange placing the issuing house may be acting merely as intermediary or may have bought the shares itself in the first instance.

A Stock Exchange placing must be accompanied by the issue of a prospectus, and arrangements have to be made, in securing the approval of the Stock Exchange Council, for providing at least two jobbers with sufficient stock to create a market in the issue. The expenses of a placing are lower than those of a public offer; printing costs are less, as the number of prospectuses and application forms required is small, no expenses of allotment or bank charges for handling application moneys are involved, no underwriting commissions are incurred, and newspaper advertisement charges are lower than for public offers. In all, a saving in expenses of between one-quarter and one-third may be made as compared with a public issue.

Because the placing is not an offer to the general investing public no underwriting is necessary, but some of the subscribers to the placing may sell their securities within a comparatively short space of time. Certain institutions are in effect dealers in securities, and for them the issue will be a success only if the price at which dealings open is in excess of the price at which the placing was made; long-term holders will similarly be dissatisfied if the opening price is below the placing price, for by waiting they would have been able to buy their shares more cheaply. Some excess of the opening over the issue price is therefore necessary for placings to be successful. There need be no single price of sale for all the subscribers to a placing, but the vendor of the shares to the issuing house must be informed of the prices at which the operation is carried out.

Because they confer upon a limited number of applicants the possibility of some immediate gain, placings were frowned on by the Stock Exchange before the war, and after the war the Stock Exchange Council adopted a policy of requiring reasons to be given why an issue should be made in this form rather than by way of a public offer. Nevertheless, about two-fifths of all issues made in the pre-war years, other than issues to shareholders, were Stock Exchange placings, and in the early post-war years this proportion rose to nearly three-quarters.* Part of the explanation

* F. W. Paish, *Business Finance* (Pitman).

is that the Stock Exchange Council has looked on placings with more favour in the case of issues for small companies, and in the immediate post-war years issues associated with the conversion of private to public companies were common. The placing is a cheaper method for a small company than an offer for sale or a public issue, and the possibility of success is enhanced by the reputation of the issuing house.

### Private Placings

In these a company's shares are placed directly with large institutional investors such as insurance companies. As the securities placed are unquoted, the arrangements for acquiring a Stock Exchange quotation do not have to be made. The expenses of a private placing are therefore particularly small, as neither advertising nor prospectus is necessary. Private placings have been the subject of some criticism on the grounds that the rate of interest attached to a private placing would be higher were it not for the excellent Stock Exchange facilities provided for marketable stocks, the yields on which form a basis for those on placings. The point of this argument is that private placings, if they were to become more common, would reduce the activities of the new-issue market in particular and the Stock Exchange in general.

The case for private placings, on the other hand, is that any capital market must adapt itself to changes in the needs of both companies and investors; private placings are undoubtedly cheap, because the lack of marketability of the securities involved is not a serious loss to the large institutional investor such as the insurance company or pension fund, of whose total portfolio these shares constitute only a small proportion. Institutional investors such as these have undoubtedly assumed great importance in the new-issue market and, indeed, provide the major part of the annual flow of savings going into new issues; it is therefore only natural, those in favour of private placings contend, that the capital market should reflect the changing requirements and preferences of its largest customers. Furthermore, in the case of relatively small private placings of debentures or preference shares, alternative methods would be difficult because even quoted fixed-interest securities may have a narrow market.

Quantitatively speaking, private placings are still relatively unimportant.

## Stock Exchange Introductions

A Stock Exchange introduction, sometimes described as a 'permission to deal', is similar to a Stock Exchange placing except that in the majority of cases existing rather than 'new' shares are involved. Unlike a Stock Exchange placing, the number of shares introduced to the market need not be made public. But a certain minimum number of shares will have to be made available under Stock Exchange regulations in order to create an adequate market, so that special arrangements have to be made with the jobbers. Legally the advertisement that accompanies a Stock Exchange introduction is not a prospectus, but often a similar statement is deposited with the Registrar of Companies. Introductions are more common when the shares brought to the market are those of a small company.

## Issues to Shareholders

An issue to shareholders (a 'rights' issue) is an offer by a company to take up shares made direct by circular to the existing shareholders. It has several advantages. First, the expenses of the issue are low, as no financial intermediary is required for vetting; legal fees are small, the administrative machinery required for handling the issue is relatively simple, and underwriting may be dispensed with. A rights issue may be made relatively cheaply because there is some presumption that existing shareholders are favourably disposed towards the company concerned. To shareholders a rights issue of ordinary shares brings the advantage of enabling them to maintain their share of the equity of the company.

A rights issue is obviously most appropriate for a company whose existing shares are already quoted on the Stock Exchange and widely held. In the years before the war two-thirds of the ordinary share issues made by quoted companies were in this form.* In the early post-war period, when new issues included a greater proportion of those made by companies coming to the Stock Exchange for the first time, rights issues formed a smaller part of the total of ordinary share issues, but in recent years their share has increased once more.

If the current market value of the company's existing shares is substantially above their nominal value, the issue can be offered to shareholders at a price well below that of the current price, that

* R. F. Henderson, *The New Issue Market* (Bowes & Bowes).

is to say, on what are usually described as 'bonus terms'. As a result, the price of the company's shares, including the new shares, will be lower after the issue than the market price of the old shares before the issue. But the price after the issue, if market conditions do not change, will also be above the figure at which new shares were offered to old shareholders, who are therefore compensated for the fall in the value of their old shares, a form of protection they would not enjoy if the issue were made without such preferential rights. This is the chief attraction of the rights issue for the existing shareholder.

Some time after the announcement of the issue is made, existing shareholders (or, more precisely, those on the company's register at a certain date) will receive their provisional letter of allotment. When this occurs their old shares, which in the interval will have been quoted 'cum-rights', will now fall to an 'ex-rights' value. But existing shareholders, if they do not wish to subscribe to the new issue, can obtain compensation for this by completing a Form of Renunciation and selling their 'rights' to the new shares, until a date stipulated in the allotment letter. The value of their 'rights' is expressed by the 'premium' represented by the excess of the market price of the new shares over their issue price. This value may be calculated as so much per old share, a figure that will differ from the former according to the ratio of new to old shares.

### The Effect of a Rights Issue on Investors

We must distinguish between three elements—the price at which the new shares are being offered to existing shareholders as compared with the price of old shares before the issue; the ratio of new to old shares; and the appreciation of the situation made by investors as a result of the issue.

If one new share were issued for every one old share, an existing shareholder would gain when the period of the issue ended if the final market price of each new share over the issue price of the new share were greater than the fall in the price of the old share. If one new share were offered for every *two* old shares the existing shareholder would gain only if the excess of the final market price of each new share over its issue price were more than *twice* the final fall in the price of each old share. For the gain on each new share would have to bear the loss on two old shares.

Putting the matter in another way, the existing shareholder will gain if the final price of his shares exceeds the price at which the total market value of old and new shares, when they finally merge into one class, would be equal to that of the old shares alone before the issue *plus* the money that has to be put up to buy the new shares.

## The Value of Rights

For example, if one new share is being offered to shareholders at 30*s*. in the ratio of one new to two old shares quoted before the issue at 45*s*., the calculation is as follows:

| | | |
|---|---|---|
| 2 old shares quoted at 45*s*. each .. .. | 90*s*. |
| 1 new share issued at 30*s*. .. .. .. | 30*s*. |
| 3 shares, at 40*s*. each .. .. .. | 120*s*. |

If the market price of the new and old shares after the issue settled down at 40*s*., which we can call the 'equalization' price, the shareholder would be all square, having lost 10*s*. on each pair of old shares and having gained 10*s*. on each single new share.

When the provisional allotment letter is received dealings in the new shares begin at a premium over their issue price, and usually around a level equivalent to what in the above example is the 'equalization' price of 40*s*. This will be the figure on which the prospective value of the 'rights' is based in the prior calculations of stockbrokers, financial journalists, etc. If, in the above example, the new shares opened at 40*s*., they would be quoted at '10*s*. premium', i.e. 40*s*.—30*s*., and 10*s*. would be the value of the rights per new share. This can also be seen to be (45*s*.—30*s*.)/ (1+0·5), where 0·5 is the ratio of new to old shares, which is an alternative method of calculation.

If the 'rights' are expressed per old share, their value would be 5*s*. per old share if the final market price were 40*s*., the figure of 5*s*. being equal to the fall in the value of each old share from 45*s*. to 40*s*.

## The Course of the Premium

How the premium will move after a rights issue has opened will depend on how the sale of rights by existing shareholders compares with the demand by would-be shareholders and speculators. The current ex-rights price of the old shares during the period of the issue, after first falling to something like 40s. in the above example, would reflect any movement in the premium, diverging from the latter only up to the amount of the 2 per cent stamp duty that has to be paid on the purchase of the old but not on the new shares. Clearly the final price of the issue should depend on how investors assess the effect of the issue on the earning capacity of the company, and in this respect an issue to shareholders is in principle no different from, say, an ordinary public issue if the same amount of money is raised and on the same net terms to the company.

Rights issues, it is true, do have certain advantages, such as the lower expenses of issue. Apart from these, however, and particularly when share prices in general are buoyant, investors often appear to consider a rights issue as necessarily involving some potential gain to the shareholder not present in a straightforward public issue. Some investors may consider a rights issue to be the more attractive the larger is what is sometimes described as the 'bonus element', namely the difference between the initial price of the old shares and the price at which the new shares are offered, despite the fact that this means that, other things being equal, the fall in the value of the old shares will be all the greater. It is sometimes contended that the chance of the final price being higher than the 'equalization' price—40s. in the above illustration—is greatest when the number of shares to be issued is small in relation to the number of existing shares. In this case a smaller number of shareholders will be obliged to sell their shares, and less risk will exist that the new scale of operations will prove too large for the company's management to handle. But similar considerations apply to a straightforward public issue the smaller its size in relation to existing capital, the less wide need be its support.

The popularity of a rights issue of ordinary shares must therefore be attributed to the conventional belief that they *are* inherently different. The basis of this convention may be that, when the new issue is relatively small, investors assume that this particular method has been chosen because the directors expect to maintain the old rate of dividend on the enlarged nominal capital, so that the final price might be hardly less than the initial price of the old shares and therefore well in excess of the 'equalization' price.

Occasionally a rights issue may be made of shares of a different class, such as when preference shares are offered to ordinary shareholders on bonus terms, that is at a price below their nominal value. In this case the effect on the market value of the ordinary shares may be slight; the proceeds of the new issue can be expected to earn more than the rate of preference dividend, and the increase in the degree of gearing may be regarded as unimportant. When an issue of preference shares is made on bonus terms to preference shareholders, on the other hand, a direct benefit is given to these at the expense of the ordinary shareholders, who will have to face the eventual repayment of the preference shares at a price above their issue price. Such cases are therefore rare.

## *Preferential Allotment*

When a company wishes to raise an amount much larger than can be obtained from existing shareholders, it can make a public issue but grant existing shareholders preferential treatment in allotment, by circulating to them the traditional pink preferential application form. The price at which such issues are made will generally be above that at which an issue to shareholders would be offered but sufficiently below the current price of existing shares to compensate them for any fall in the latter.

### FREE BONUS, SCRIP OR CAPITALIZATION ISSUES

The extreme case of an issue to shareholders on bonus terms is that in which additional shares are issued to shareholders free of charge, in proportion to their existing holdings; this is known as a free bonus, scrip or capitalization issue.

The usual purpose of such an issue is to capitalize a company's reserves. After several years of ploughing back profits into the business, the issued capital of a company may be small in relation to its revenue reserves and to its total assets. The market value of its ordinary shares will be considerably in excess of their nominal value, and the dividend paid will appear high when expressed as a percentage of the latter. A capitalization issue therefore serves to bring the company's issued capital 'into line' with its assets and destroys any possible illusion that its revenue reserves represent accumulated funds available for distribution. In other cases the new ordinary capital may be substituted for existing capital reserves. On the liabilities side of the balance sheet, therefore, there is merely a reduction in some reserve figure corresponding to the creation of new ordinary shares, without any change in the total of book assets or liabilities. Alternatively, a capitalization issue may be made to synchronize with the revaluation of fixed assets, in which case total book assets and liabilities would be increased in the process.

If the total amount of ordinary dividends paid is not increased the result will be merely to reduce proportionately the rate of dividend per share on the enlarged capital. A capitalization issue may therefore help to still the criticism of those who, looking only at the rate of dividend calculated on nominal capital and not on actual capital employed, regard the dividend paid as excessive. Post-war Labour governments have frowned upon bonus issues for fear that they would make it easier for companies to avoid dividend restraint by combining an increase in dividends with a bonus issue, thus holding down the *rate* of dividend declared on nominal capital. Bonus issues, including rights issues, were subject to a bonus duty between 1947 and 1949, and the Capital Issues Committee was instructed to reject applications for free bonus issues between 1949 and 1951 except when these could be said to further objects declared to be in the public interest, such as enlarging export capacity, a curious qualification in view of the fact that free bonus issues produce no new money for a company.

## The Effect of a Capitalization Issue on Investors

If a capitalization issue were not accompanied by an increase in the total amount of dividend, so that the rate of dividend per share was reduced, the price of the old share might be expected to fall proportionately. One minor qualification to this proposition is that shares with a high market price are often unpopular because they are 'heavy' and so are avoided by investors who are averse to purchasing in small numbers. A capitalization issue may therefore increase a share's marketability, an advantage that will be reflected in its new price. The same benefit could have been obtained, however, by splitting the denomination of each share, thereby turning the existing nominal capital into a larger number of shares. Apart from this relatively minor point, the crux of the matter is the question of the total amount of dividend to be paid. If this is increased, the price of the enlarged number of shares will not fall proportionately with the capitalization issue, so that the total market value of the company's ordinary capital will rise, with a consequent gain to the ordinary-share holder.

It must be emphasized that in this case it is the fact of an increase in the total amount of dividend paid, and not the capitalization issue, that is responsible for the rise in the total market value of the shares, and the same result could simply have been achieved by a straightforward increase in the rate of dividend without the accompaniment of a capitalization issue at all. Because of the obvious implication that a capitalization issue, as such, does not necessarily bring any tangible benefit to the shareholder, the attempt by successive governments to restrict the practice has been strongly criticized as a misdirection of attention.

At the same time, however, there is little doubt that in practice many investors tend to regard a free bonus issue as a signal for an increase in the market value of a company's ordinary capital, so that the market price per share does not fall proportionately. Once more we must turn for an explanation to the existence of convention, the facility with which each investor can convince himself that *other* investors regard a bonus issue as bringing some tangible benefit, and in the last resort the convention may be said to spring from the hope that the directors have made an issue because they intend to increase the total amount of dividend. Paradoxically, however, the larger the number of new shares issued in relation to the existing capital, the less is the likelihood that the dividend per share will be maintained.

Sometimes a company will choose to issue a small number of bonus shares each year to correspond with the profit it has been ploughing back, and the increase in the total amount of dividends will then take the form of a constant rate declared on an increasing nominal capital. Apart from registering the fact that capital employed is expanding, this method has some advantage in that it enables existing shareholders who do not wish to increase the total market value of their holdings in a company to sell their rights to additional shares, a less complicated process than selling a small number of shares. Furthermore, the purchase of the rights by the buyer is not subject to the 2 per cent stamp duty payable on the transfer of 'old' shares, and this will be reflected in their price.

It is sometimes contended that a capitalization issue is of special value to the surtax payer and correspondingly against the interest of shareholders paying less than the standard rate of tax, because capital appreciation is not subject to tax whereas dividends are.

T

This is misleading in that it is the retention of profits and not the bonus issue that substitutes a capital for an income gain.

Finally, a capitalization issue of voting ordinary shares will obviously be disadvantageous to the interest of the preference shareholders unless provision to the contrary is made in the company's articles, for the effect will be to increase the number of votes possessed by the ordinary shareholders. A company's articles may therefore provide for the voting power of preference shares to be rated up in such a situation.

## STAGGING

The 'stag' is a form of speculator. He hopes to profit from the fact that a successful issue must be made at a price below that of comparable securities, and his technique is to apply for shares with a view to a practically immediate resale at a profit. He will have to put up the application money, but his other expenses are small, since stamp duty does not have to be paid on a new issue until share certificates are circulated. Until the 1948 Companies Act he could even withdraw his application if the issue looked like being a failure, but now the application constitutes legal acceptance for three days. It has been said that 'the stag is a nuisance to the company, to the genuine investor with whom he competes and who does not know what proportion of his application will be allotted to him, and to the market whose good functioning is hindered by the stag's erratic and useless intervention. He has no friends, and if his life has been made miserable for him, there is nobody to sympathize.'*

This judgement may be somewhat harsh, in that the stag helps to smooth the way for an operation that would otherwise involve the raising of a large sum of money on one particular day; the effect of stagging is to help to spread new-issue operations over a period of time in which a more extended assessment of the issue may be made by many investors. The stag, of course, takes the risk of an unfavourable change in market conditions.

The case against the stag is that he tends to be most active when the risk is least; stagging is naturally most common during a boom. His activities can be restricted, however, by increasing the amount required to be paid on application when market

* M. S. Rix, *Stock Market Economics* (Sir Isaac Pitman & Sons, London, 1954).

conditions are favourable, and if this fails to deter him, an attempt can be made to reduce his share in the issue at the allotment stage by identifying the various devices he usually adopts—for example, the completion of application forms on behalf of the several individual members of his family.

## NEW ISSUES BY THE NATIONALIZED INDUSTRIES

Parliament's general intention has been that the nationalized industries should finance the bulk of their capital investment, in excess of replacement, by outside borrowing; at least there is no express statutory instruction to these bodies to meet their capital requirements out of surplus revenue. In recent years, however, the scale of new issues by the nationalized industries has given rise to certain problems from which issues by ordinary commercial concerns are free. Nationalized industries, when they come to the market, do so for very large sums—in 1955, for example, the Central Electricity Authority made an issue of £200 million, and issues of £100 million have been common. Issues of this size cannot be absorbed by the investing public at one gulp. It is not just a matter of terms, for if the rate of interest to be offered on an issue of £200 million were raised in an attempt to attract more funds, the result would probably be for the prices of comparable stocks to be marked down on the date of the announcement, forestalling any large-scale 'switching'.

The effect of a new issue on the market prices of comparable stocks, given the terms of the issue, depends on its size, but it is not certain that the general problem would be solved by the nationalized industries' coming to the market much more frequently for smaller sums. For the knowledge that a steady stream of still-sizeable issues was likely to impinge on the market over the near future might lead investors to the conclusion that ordinarily there was no great urgency about subscribing to any one. The general effect might therefore be to raise the rate of interest at which the nationalized industries—and the Exchequer— could raise capital.

### The Role of the 'Departments'

Until 1956 this problem was resolved by the operation of the authorities, that is various government 'departments' such as the National Debt Commissioners and the Bank of England, in support of the new issue. The bulk of the new stock would first be taken up by the 'departments' and subsequently sold on the market as conditions allowed. This is a perfectly legitimate procedure, in that underwriting is an indispensable requirement for any large public issue, but the difficulty is that if the flow of tax and other receipts into the Exchequer is not large enough the issue can only be taken up by official hands if new money is deliberately created for the purpose. This is economically undesirable when the creation of new money is inflationary.

### The Arrangements of the 1956 Budget

In the Budget of 1956 the Chancellor of the Exchequer announced a change in these arrangements. For two years the capital requirements of the nationalized industries were to be met out of the Exchequer, up to a limit of £350 million a year for industries other than coal, which was already financed directly in this way, and the new procedure was continued in 1958. In one respect this method is no different from the previous system, in that, under both, the creation of money will be avoided only if the authorities succeed in drawing on the community's saving, by taxation or by selling government securities to the public. The government hoped for one improvement, however, in regard to the condition of the market in government stocks, for a steady stream of discreet security sales is less unsettling than the effect of large new public issues. Moreover, the timing of public-corporation issues in the past has not been entirely within the control of the Treasury, for nationalized industries may have been forced to come to the market at a time inconvenient to the authorities by virtue of their having reached the borrowing limits accorded to them by the banks, on advances from whom they relied during the intervals between new issues. Following the 1956 Budget only normal short-term requirements were to be met by bank finance.

CHAPTER 23

# INVESTMENT BY FINANCIAL INSTITUTIONS

## 'THE MACMILLAN GAP'

The London new-issue market came in for serious criticism in the years following the war of 1914–18 on the grounds that it placed unnecessary obstacles in the way of investment by small firms, in the form of excessively high new-issue expenses. Small concerns will usually have to make some extra payment to investors to compensate them for the extra risks the latter run, or believe they run, as compared with investments in large concerns. The critics contended either that this risk was exaggerated in the mind of the investor or that whatever hazard did really exist would be minimized if institutions could spread the risks of investment in small firms over a number of such holdings. This line of reasoning received support from the Macmillan Committee in 1931.

That the cost of a new issue does not rise proportionally with its size is due partly to certain expenses being fixed practically for any size of issue; these include the cost of the advertisement and the prospectus. Then there are the costs which reflect differences in the element of risk, so that an issuing house may charge a proportionately larger fee for a small issue on this account; and in the case of a placing or Stock Exchange introduction the price at which securities are sold will fall short of the proceeds received by the company by a greater amount. A company that is going to the Stock Exchange for the first time will have to be even more carefully vetted by an issuing house than is usual, and the costs of such examination do not rise in proportion to the size of the issue. As a result the expenses of small issues in the inter-war years, particularly for companies new to the market, were undoubtedly relatively costly, as much as 15 per cent for issues below £200,000.

## THE INDUSTRIAL AND COMMERCIAL FINANCE CORPORATION

The Macmillan Committee contended that no suitable facilities existed for the small company to raise permanent capital outside the new-issue market, and its recommendations were eventually implemented in 1945, when the Industrial and Commercial Finance Corporation was established. The publicity that this organization has received may create the impression that this was the only body established after the 'Macmillan gap' received widespread attention, but in fact a number of institutions were set up after 1930 that provided finance for small firms, both with and without official financial support. The establishment of I.C.F.C. nevertheless marked a new stage in the provision of finance for small concerns, if only because of the size of its resources. Whereas the *Charterhouse Industrial Development Company*, for example, a private institution that was set up in 1934 to invest in small companies, has an authorized capital of £7,400,000, I.C.F.C. was formed with an authorized capital of £45 million, to be provided by the main English and Scottish banks and by the Bank of England.

I.C.F.C. possesses the large expert staff of accountants, financial experts and engineers that this type of business requires. By 1957 its portfolio had been expanded to a total of £33 million, spread over nearly 600 firms and distributed over a wide range of industries. The Corporation has paid dividends on its ordinary shares since 1952–3.

### NO POST-WAR MACMILLAN GAP ?

The operations of I.C.F.C. have undoubtedly been attended by a large measure of success, but not much more than one-half of its authorized capital has been used, from which the inference might perhaps be drawn that the 'Macmillan gap' has been filled. Another body set up by the government to aid small businesses, the *National Research and Development Corporation*, which was established in 1948 to provide funds for the development and exploitation of inventions for which commercial finance had not been forthcoming, is also in a similar position in that only a small part of its borrowing powers has been exploited.

Such a conclusion may be unwarranted. The earlier post-war years, at any rate, were those in which many small companies possessed ample funds in the shape of unspent profits and Excess Profits Tax refunds, and the general buoyancy of Stock Exchange conditions in most years favoured the issue of capital by small concerns. For nearly a decade after the end of the war material shortages and government controls were the main obstacle to expansion, and in this regard small firms may have been under a special handicap.

The policy of I.C.F.C. itself has been conservative; at 31 March 1957 only 9 per cent of its investments were in the form of ordinary shares, and the fact that some 50 per cent of its portfolio took the form of issues exceeding £100,000 indicates that a number of quite substantial concerns were in its portfolio. The scope of the Corporation's lending may also have been restricted by undue concentration in the London area; businesses in the London area amounted to 37 per cent of its total portfolio. That some closer regional contact may be needed is suggested by the formation of the *Glasgow Industrial Finance Company*, set up by a group of Glasgow investment trust companies to sponsor local new issues; this development was followed by the establishment of a development company aimed at financing local concerns before the public issue stage. Another such company is *Northumbrian Finance*, set up in 1954 to facilitate the provision of finance for firms in the North of England.

Whether adequate facilities are now provided for the concern too small to come to the new-issue market is still a debatable question. On this market itself, however, the facilities for smaller issues have been improved since the Macmillan Committee published its complaint. Issues of £600,000–£700,000, which is the present-day real equivalent of the £200,000 lower limit mentioned in the Macmillan Committee's report, are now easily arranged; the minimum size of issues now handled without much difficulty may be as little as one-quarter of the real equivalent of the Macmillan Committee's figure. The attitude of institutional investors towards securities of relatively small concerns, especially if vetted by I.C.F.C. or one of the finance houses, has become much more receptive, partly because of the strengthening of these financial intermediaries that has occurred since 1928 and partly because of the relatively favourable experience of investment in growing firms enjoyed in the profitable conditions of the post-war period. The expense of small issues, too, seems to have fallen over the past twenty years.

This, it must be stressed, applies to the company whose size is not too far from that at which recourse to the London market is practicable. In comparison with the industrial giants of today these are certainly small concerns, but even the smallest company that in the more favourable conditions of the post-war years can float a new issue is still large compared with the bulk of *new* businesses, and it is to these that the supply of finance must have contracted as a result of the increase in taxation on personal incomes. It is at this early stage that the difficulty of outside assessment of a relatively untried management and perhaps a new product brings the risks of finance to their peak. It is not a field into which even the large institutional investors can enter with confidence, despite their ability to spread their risks over a large number of companies; for whether the return on such investments in a period of more difficult trading conditions than those experienced in the relatively favourable years since the war would be sufficient to meet the cost of the investigation and supervision that would be needed and yield a return commensurate with the risk is not a question that can be answered easily. It is worth noting, for example, that between 1950–1 and 1956–7 I.C.F.C. made offers to only one-fifth of the 3,500 applications received.[5] The rejection rate of the Charterhouse Industrial Development Company has been even higher.

Where new businesses are concerned, management ability may be even more scarce than finance, and outside supervision is needed as a rule because it is difficult to sell such investments if things go wrong. In many cases the owner of a promising young business may be averse to allowing outside shareholders to participate at all in his equity, but the problem for the institutional investor considering this type of business is that some proportion of equity finance is essential so that losses on unprofitable ventures may be recouped from the gains on those that succeed. Fixed-interest investment, backed by the perhaps specialized assets of a small concern, may offer little real security in the event of unfavourable trading conditions.

### 'Edith'

The years since the war have seen a proliferation of financial institutions set up to meet specific needs. *Estate Duties Investment Trust Limited* was formed in 1953 to purchase shares in private companies to provide for the payment of death duties, which might otherwise cause the disintegration of family businesses. Edith aims at avoiding any element of control or interference in the management of the business. Its shareholders consist of I.C.F.C. and a number of insurance companies and investment trusts, and it is able to draw on the expert technical services of I.C.F.C. in selecting its investments. Its issued capital at March 1957 amounted to £1½ million in ordinary shares and £500,000 in debenture stock. The book value of its investments at that date had reached almost £1,800,000; but Edith's business has been larger than this figure alone would imply, for some of the shares offered to it have been placed with its shareholders.

Edith, while still the *prima donna* in the field, is no longer the sole institution doing this type of business. In 1953 *Private Enterprises Investment Company Limited* was formed for a similar purpose by four well-known institutions* and an investment trust, and in the same year *Safeguard Industrial Investments Limited* was set up by London and Yorkshire Trust. The *Charterhouse* group is also active in this sphere.

### F.C.I.

The new issue market provides adequate facilities for the larger concern. It may therefore seem surprising that in 1945 a special organization was set up to provide medium-term finance for comparatively large firms on the grounds that in some respects the new issue market was still deficient. *Finance Corporation for Industry Limited* was established in 1945 with an authorized capital of £25 million, subscribed by the Bank of England (30 per cent), insurance companies (40 per cent), and investment trusts (30 per cent). It was formed mainly in order to finance large-scale projects that, although profitable in the longer-run, could not by their very nature be expected to yield an immediate return. At the end of the war it was feared that projects of this type would not receive support in the financial world because of the unfavourable pre-war experience of investors in heavy industry, which would be the field of activity most likely to come within the category. The Corporation, under the terms of its charter, was only to make advances on new projects considered to be in the national interest, and then only when the required finance could not be obtained from any other source.

By 31 March 1957 only £500,000 of the authorized capital of

* Samuel Montagu & Co. Ltd., M. Samuel & Co. Ltd., N. M. Rothschild & Sons, and S. G. Warburg & Co.

F.C.I. had been issued, but with the aid of bank advances totalling more than £40 million it had built up a portfolio with a book value of £42 million. The Corporation normally provides only loan finance, repayable as a rule within seven to ten years; it may also take options on share capital, but it is the Corporation's intention that its advances should be replaced by normal external finance as soon as possible. In its early years F.C.I. made a series of losses, and it was not until 1955 that a dividend (of 6 per cent) was paid on its issued capital. Whatever might have been the attitude of investors in the immediate post-war period, the low return obtained by its shareholders and the more realistic but not unsympathetic appraisal made by the new issue market of long-term ventures have since weakened the case for the Corporation's existence.

### COMMONWEALTH FINANCE

Another government-sponsored body is the *Commonwealth Development Finance Company*, incorporated in March 1953. Its object is to promote the development of Commonwealth resources, and subscribers to its authorized capital of £15 million include the Bank of England and leading industrial, commercial, mining, shipping and financial interests.

The *Colonial Development Corporation*, on the other hand, is an official body, established in 1948 in order to speed up economic development in the Colonies. It was not a commercial success in its early years, in which it seems to have paid little attention to direct financial considerations. After a period of reorganization the Corporation made its first annual profit in 1955, and now seems to be operating on commercial principles.

### SPECIALIST INDUSTRIAL INSTITUTIONS

These institutions have one characteristic in common, in that they aim to spread their risk over a wide variety of industrial enterprises; indeed, variety is essential to their security. Since the war, however, a number of bodies have been established for the purpose of financing a particular industry.

The *Ship Mortgage Finance Company* was founded in 1951 with an issued capital of £1 million by an association of shipbuilding concerns and various insurance and other City interests. The objects of the company are to make medium-term loans (normally five or six years) on mortages on ships constructed in the U.K. and to raise money for this purpose by the issue of medium-term debentures. The limit of the debenture debt is ten times the issued capital and reserves. Loans are normally limited to 50 per cent of the cost of the ship concerned. At 30 June 1957 advances outstanding totalled £3,000,000, and £2,000,000 of debentures had been issued, while short-term debt to the banks and the F.C.I. stood at £400,000.

The heavy demand for funds to finance the building of oil-tankers and the restriction of lending by the Ship Mortgage Finance Company to medium-term loans made only on completion were responsible for the formation of two companies in 1957 whose object is to finance the tanker-building programmes of the Shell group and British Petroleum Limited. These two companies, *Tanker Finance Company* and *Tanker Charter Company*, with resources of £30 million and £40 million respectively, have their medium-term finance (up to eight years) provided by a group of banks and their long-term resources by a number of insurance companies and pension funds. Their formation is an interesting example of the way in which the operations of the capital market can be adapted to the special requirements of lenders and borrowers.

Another of these specialist bodies is *Air Finance Limited*; with an authorized capital of £1 million, it was formed in 1953 by three City merchant-banking companies in co-operation with F.C.I. and a number of leading aircraft manufacturers. The objects of the company are to help finance British aircraft exports by making short-term loans (normally up to three years) to foreign purchasers to cover up to about 40 per cent of the purchase price. F.C.I. has made available loan facilities to the company up to a value of £10 million, and the co-operation of the Board of Trade's Export Credits Guarantee Department (whose guarantee is normally required in connexion with foreign orders financed under Air Finance arrangements) has been obtained.

The Ship Mortgage Finance Company and Air Finance Limited are private institutions. The *National Film Finance Corporation Limited*, which was set up by the government in 1948, derives its total resources—at present about £8 million—from the Treasury. It makes loans to film producers, but although it was intended merely as a form of temporary finance aimed at placing British film production on a firm footing, it has developed into a subsidy on which film producers appear to depend.

### EXPORT CREDIT INSURANCE

The *Export Credits Guarantee Department* of the Board of Trade was set up in 1919. It insures credit given to finance British exports, covering both the commercial risk of default by the overseas importer and the now more common hazard of currency restrictions. The insurance of export credits is usually essential if bank or acceptance house finance is to be obtained for export business, and E.C.G.D. insures between one-fifth and one-sixth of Britain's export trade. Normally the Department covers an exporter to the extent of 85 per cent of any loss caused by insolvency of the buyer and up to 90 per cent of losses caused by the imposition of import or currency restrictions.

In recent years E.C.G.D. has been handling about £500 million of business per annum, the large bulk of which is of under two years' duration. Since the re-entry of Germany and Japan into world markets, the view has often been expressed in business circles that British export credit facilities are insufficient to meet the growing challenge of foreign competition, and since 1953 the policy of the Department has become more liberal.

Besides these government facilities some export credit business is also insured privately—the *Trade Indemnity Company*,[6] for example, is active in insuring short-term transactions with the Commonwealth. But because E.C.G.D. not unnaturally insists on insuring against both the lesser risk of insolvency and the more unpredictable hazard of currency restrictions, private export credit insurance can only be undertaken on a small scale, since very large funds are required to cover political risks.

### A Shortage of Export Credit?

The E.C.G.D. only provides insurance cover for export credit, and the availability of credit for export transactions constitutes a separate problem. In recent years the banks have shown a willingness to provide export credits for more than short-term contracts, but no conclusive answer has yet been given to the question whether the credit facilities available in Britain for financing sales of heavy equipment, in which the importer may insist on several years' credit, compare badly with those provided in other countries.

Similar complaints can be heard even on the part of exporters in Germany and the U.S.A. Since the war the main buyers of heavy equipment in many overseas markets have been governments or public corporations, and these have been able to demand generous credit terms from suppliers. Whether it is really in this country's interests to struggle to sell this type of product if long credit terms have to be granted is not a simple question, and it might be thought that if the large manufacturers of such products are confident that the provision of long-term credit to, say, Brazilian importers is a sound proposition, they should finance it themselves out of capital raised in the ordinary way. The difficulty, however, is that individual manufacturers would rarely be able to achieve a wide-enough spread of risk; and the average export credit contract is of too short a duration to be a suitable investment for long-term investors such as insurance companies and pension funds. For reasons of political policy, on the other hand, other countries, such as the U.S.A. and Soviet Russia, can provide credit through their official agencies on a scale that Britain cannot match.

### THE 'INSTITUTIONAL INVESTORS'

The term 'institutional investor' is used in a number of ways. It may embrace government institutions such as the Bank of England and the National Debt Commissioners; it may take in the whole of the banking system and the institutions just described, or it may be confined to those private institutions whose funds are drawn from personal savings throughout the community. It is in this third sense that the term is used here. The most important of these institutional investors are the life-assurance offices, pension funds, building societies and investment trusts; but other examples include the Ecclesiastical Commissioners, trade unions and other friendly societies, and a variety of trust funds.

### INSTITUTIONAL INVESTORS AND THE NEW-ISSUE MARKET

Life-assurance and pension funds, which have a preference for long-term Stock Exchange investments, have been growing at a rate of over £500 million per annum. This was equivalent to roughly one and a quarter times the annual value of all capital issues (for 'new money') made in 1955–7 other than by the government, whereas in 1938 the corresponding proportion was only one-half. Taking this comparison back to the five years up to the new-issue boom of 1928, the increase in the funds of life-assurance offices and pension schemes, at about £50 £55 million per annum, was equal to only one-fifth of the value of new issues at that time; and in the years just prior to the First World War the proportion was only of the order of 7–8 per cent. Although these institutions invest only a part of their accruing funds in new issues, it is now a commonplace of the capital market to say that no large new issue can succeed without their support.

It is also true to say, however, that as the annual growth of their funds is now large in relation to the net increase in the total supply of securities, life-assurance offices and pension funds, or at least the more substantial of their class, depend on new issues as convenient investment outlets. In normal times only a tiny proportion of the existing stock of industrial securities changes hands in sizeable blocks, and this usually through the liquidation of deceased estates. As it is not economical for the leading life-assurance offices and pension funds to buy securities in amounts of less than a certain minimum size, they are always active supporters of the new-issue market out of self-interest as well as through an awareness of their new responsibility for the finance of industry.

Neither pension funds nor life-assurance offices are subject to any statutory restrictions on the type of investments they may hold, and their growing appetite for industrial securities has maintained the flow of external finance to companies large enough to make use of the new-issue market, thus counteracting the constriction of personal finance due to the heavy taxation of the rich. This freedom contrasts with the restrictions placed upon institutional investment policy abroad, for example in India and Norway. The avowed purpose of these limitations, as in the United States and Canada, is generally to safeguard the interests of contributors and policy-holders; but in some cases their object also appears to be to reserve life-assurance and pension funds for government borrowing or for projects approved by the government. The result has been that high taxation of personal incomes has eaten into the supply of industrial finance without any compensating flow of institutional funds. In some countries where institutional funds are siphoned off in this way the government has had to adopt special and not altogether consistent measures aimed at reviving the market in industrial finance.

## INSURANCE COMPANIES AS INVESTORS

### *Income Rather than Liquidity*

The funds invested in this country by British life-assurance offices have recently been growing at the rate of about £250–£300 million a year, and the total book value of their assets has risen to about £5,000 million. These assets are held to honour the commitments of the life-assurance industry to its policy-holders, but as long as we do not experience a trade depression of a depth and duration unprecedented in our history the annual accrual of premiums and interest can be expected to exceed the annual outgo by way of current payments to policy-holders and other charges. Because the inflow of receipts year by year enables life-assurance offices to meet maturing policies without liquidating existing investments, only a small part of their portfolio need be held in cash or highly liquid short-term assets, and at the other extreme their assets will generally include some proportion of unquoted securities as well as those quoted but without an active market.

The fact that the well-managed life-assurance office can normally disregard the fear of having to sell investments on a weak market in order to meet its commitments, together with the necessity for earning a steady and adequate income, gives to its investment policy a measure of continuity not shared by that of the personal investor. With their eyes on the more distant future, the managers of life-assurance funds can invest steadily. They will alter the direction of their policy according to their assessment of the financial outlook, but they are not likely to be heavy net sellers of industrial investments through the fear of a temporary fall in security prices. Variations in investment policy, particularly in the case of the larger office, for which the availability of suitable investments is an important consideration, are more likely to take the form of a change in the type of security being acquired than of the large-scale substitution of securities for cash, or vice versa. Because the investment of life-assurance funds is free from the wilder swings of hope and fear about the immediate outlook to which the ordinary personal investor is sometimes subject, it brings to the capital market an element of stability and long-term judgement that cannot but foster the ultimate object of enlarging the flow of finance to the most worthwhile capital projects.

In the investment of life-assurance funds the aim of actuarial solvency is paramount; an investment income must be secured at least equal to that assumed in the calculation of premiums. The investment manager of a life-assurance office is therefore concerned with obtaining a wide spread of assets of which the foundation consists of reliable fixed-interest securities. Because the need for

TABLE 18. *The Changing Composition of Assets*

*The Assets of Life-Assurance Offices\* 1880–1956*

| | | 1880 | 1913 | 1927 | 1937 | 1948 | 1956 |
|---|---|---|---|---|---|---|---|
| TOTAL ASSETS | £m. ... | 155 | 530 | 1,064 | 1,655 | 2,724 | 4,757 |
| Mortgages (%) | | 46 | 21 | 12 | 11 | 7 | 12 |
| Loans on public rates, British municipal and county securities, public boards (U.K.) (%) | | 13 | 6 | 5 | 7 | 4 | 3 |
| Loans on policies and personal security (%) | | 6 | 6 | 5 | 3 | 1 | 1 |
| British government securities (%) | | 3 | 1 | 26 | 22 | 40 | 24 |
| Commonwealth government provincial and municipal securities (%) | | 5 | 8 | 8 | 7 | 4 | 4 |
| Foreign government and municipal securities (%) | | 3 | 7 | 7 | 5 | 4 | 4 |
| Debentures (%) | | 7 | 25 | 15 | 16 | 9 | 13 |
| Preference shares (%) | } 5 | | 6 | 5 | 8 | 8 | 7 |
| Ordinary shares (%) | | | 4 | 5 | 10 | 11 | 16 |
| Real property (%) | | 8 | 9 | 5 | 5 | 5 | 8 |
| Agents' outstanding balances and accrued interest (%) | | 3 | 3 | 4 | 3 | 5 | 6 |
| Cash (%) | | 3 | 2 | 2 | 2 | 3 | 2 |

\* Offices established in Great Britain only, but including their assets held against overseas and non-life business; the figures relate to balance-sheet and not market values.

income is normally greater than that for liquidity, the life-assurance company's portfolio will consist largely of long-term investments.

Beyond these considerations, the pressure of competition between different life-assurance offices, in regard to premium rates and to the bonuses declared on with-profits policies, is able to seek an outlet in the field of investments promising greater returns, but subject to greater risks.

The composition of life-assurance investment portfolios has reflected both the development of the capital market and the changing economic background against which it must always be related; in twenty years' time, no doubt, these figures will have undergone further important alterations. Before the First World War the volume of long-dated government securities outstanding was small in relation to the annual flow of saving seeking investment outlets, and reliable ordinary shares, outside the field of railways and public utilities, were even scarcer. Mortgages, in this period, in which the building society movement was still young, provided the chief source of reliable long-term income. By 1913, however, important changes could already be discerned; the boom in foreign capital issues and the growth of the market in good-class industrial securities had extended the range of investments. As a result of the First and then the Second World Wars, the great increase in the supply of government securities was responsible for a striking change in the composition of life-assurance portfolios, and the growing availability of suitable ordinary shares in the inter-war years can also be traced in Table 18. In the immediate post-war years nationalization augmented yet again the life-assurance companies' holdings of government-guaranteed stocks, and it is only comparatively recently that the proportion of industrial securities has returned to its immediate pre-war level. The growing part played by the ordinary share, however, is especially noteworthy in view of the fear that the replacement of the rich man's saving by personal thrift channelled through life-assurance and pension funds might lead to the eclipse of equity investment.

Over the past forty or fifty years the growing importance of British government stocks and ordinary shares in life-assurance portfolios has been counterbalanced by the decline not only of mortgages but of loans to local authorities, personal loans and overseas securities. The development of the central Exchequer's finance of local government expenditure brought a contraction in the supply of local authority loans, while the growth of the building society movement, the banking system and of hire-purchase has caused a parallel decline in the relative importance of loans made by life-assurance offices on policies and on personal security. The contraction in the share of overseas securities is less sharp, but perhaps even more significant. It reflects the inability of this country to invest large sums abroad and the much greater risk attached since 1929 to overseas lending than in the

U

comparative stability of the pre-1914 era. The bulk of the overseas investments now held by British life-assurance companies serves as backing for their liabilities in the same currency, the counterpart of the growing business conducted by their overseas branches; and the principle of matching assets and liabilities in the same overseas currency is rarely departed from.

### MUTUAL LIFE-ASSURANCE OFFICES

It is convenient at this point to distinguish between life-assurance offices that are limited-liability joint-stock companies and those that are known as mutual life-assurance offices or societies. In mutual life-assurance societies there are no share-holders; the profits belong entirely to the holders of those life-assurance policies that participate in profits. Directors are elected by the policy-holders, generally the participating policy-holders alone, and to qualify for office they must usually effect on their own life a participating policy for a certain minimum sum. Most mutual life-assurance offices were incorporated by special Acts of Parliament, and their powers and rules are defined in those Acts. By their nature mutual offices are difficult to set up; some began on the basis of an outside guarantee, and others were founded originally as joint-stock companies before being transformed. As far as their investment policy is concerned, there is no evident difference from that pursued by joint-stock life-assurance companies.

### NON-LIFE INSURANCE COMPANIES

Table 18 includes assets held against the non-life insurance liabilities of those companies that conduct general branch business (fire, accident, motor and marine insurance, for example) as well as life assurance. These assets, which amounted to about £375 million of the total in 1955, in addition to some £420 million held by purely non-life offices, are not channels for personal saving, being analogous to the stock-in-trade of an ordinary business concern. Since the payment of general branch claims fluctuates from year to year, liquidity is a highly important consideration in the investment of these funds, so that cash forms a high proportion of total assets. At the end of 1955, one-tenth of the total assets of companies transacting non-life business only took the form of cash and a further one-fifth was held in agents' balances and outstanding premiums; mortgages represented only 2 per cent and all industrial securities only 20 per cent of the total. British companies are notable for the fire, accident and marine insurance business they transact abroad, and a large part of their funds is therefore held overseas to meet liabilities payable in foreign currency; Commonwealth and foreign government and municipal securities therefore represented almost one-fifth of total assets at the end of 1955, and a considerable proportion of the cash deposits possessed by these insurance companies is held in foreign currency.

### THE INVESTMENT OF PENSION FUNDS

Pension funds are growing rapidly. It has been estimated* that at the end of 1953 their accumulated funds amounted to at least £1,678 million, divided in the following way:

|  | £ million |
|---|---|
| Public services | 237 |
| Nationalized industries | 261 |
| Life-office schemes | 450 |
| Internally-administered schemes | 730 |
| Total | 1,678 |

This total can be guessed to have reached £2,500 million by the end of 1957. The investment of pension funds is governed by the terms of the trust under which they are set up. If no stipulation to the contrary is made in the trust deed, however, a pension fund, like any other trust fund in a similar position, virtually cannot invest in other than trustee securities; otherwise the trustees are personally responsible for any loss. Trustee investments are those in which the Trustee Acts empower a trustee to invest any trust funds. They include† U.K. government and government-guaranteed stocks, real or heritable securities in the U.K., including the security of a charge on freehold land, most local authority loans and certain Commonwealth government securities. In certain cases, e.g. local authority and Colonial government loans, restrictions are placed on the power of trustees

* *Report of the Committee on the Economic and Financial Problems of the Provision for Old Age* (Phillips Committee). Cmd. 9333 (H.M.S.O., 1954).

† Under the Trustee Act of 1925, which applies to England and Wales only, and subsequent amendments.

to purchase redeemable securities standing more than 15 per cent above the redemption price.

In recent years the need to provide for pensions at money income levels that threaten to rise year by year with the general increase in prices has caused the trust deeds of many pension funds to be amended or established within much less narrow limits. This consideration, together with the country's experience of prosperous economic conditions since the war, has been responsible for an increase in the share of pension fund portfolios held in the form of ordinary shares.

Statistics of the distribution of pension fund assets are not generally published. An inquiry made by Professor E. V. Morgan* into a sample of over 360 funds with total assets of £510 million in 1955 revealed the following distribution of assets:

TABLE 19. *Pension Fund Assets*

|  | % |
|---|---|
| Mortgages | 4·6 |
| Government securities | 32·6 |
| Local authority, public board and other government securities | 10·4 |
| Debentures | 12·8 |
| Preference shares | 7·7 |
| Ordinary shares | 27·3 |
| Real property | 1·7 |
| Cash, etc. | 2·9 |

Other evidence suggests that the proportion of pension fund assets held in the form of ordinary shares has been growing; five years earlier, in 1950, it was not much in excess of 10 per cent. Pension funds are usually steady long-term investors; and, if their trust deeds permit, they can be expected to invest rather more heavily in ordinary shares than life-assurance offices because they are more concerned with securing protection from rising price-levels; and as they do not have to publish their accounts they are less embarrassed if their balance sheets show a temporary fall in capital values.

## BUILDING SOCIETIES

The total assets of the building society movement have grown from £60 million in 1900 to about £2,400 million at the end of

* 'Pension Funds and the Market', *Financial Times*, 9 May 1957.

1957. Their funds are drawn from the issue of shares and from deposits made by the public, but the amount they are able to invest over any period will be augmented by the flow of mortgage repayments, which is usually well in excess of the annual increase in shares and deposits. The prime outlet for building society funds is in the field of house mortgages, and, to a small extent, of mortgages on commercial premises.

## The Problem of Liquidity

The necessity for always being in a position to meet its short-term liabilities to the holders of shares and deposits renders it important for the building society to have a good slice of liquid assets in its portfolio. Its mortgage repayments, in the absence of widespread default, return a flow of cash to the building society that can be used to repay shares and deposits simply by contracting the provision of new mortgage advances. But liquid resources have to be held because withdrawals of share and deposit funds can in certain circumstances become particularly large, and the risk of default on mortgages cannot be ignored.

Building societies have to compete with alternative outlets for short-term funds, such as government securities, deposits with the banks and local authorities, and the National Savings Movement, as well as with the attraction of using funds for personal or business expenditure. When the force of this competition gathers strength, building societies may have to meet a sustained outflow of funds, particularly those previously held on deposit. The need for liquidity is increased still further by the general reluctance of the building society movement as a whole to raise its own interest rates, either those it offers to shareholders and depositors or those it charges on advances, in order to check an outflow of funds not of serious proportions. Building societies consider that general stability of rates is in their best long-term interest, on the grounds that in the long-run the prospect of fluctuating rates would deter both the prospective house-purchaser and the potential depositor. Complete stability is not practicable, but variations in building society rates tend to lag behind changes in the supply of and demand for their funds.

The need for adequate liquidity, apart from the annual flow of mortgage repayments, is met in several ways. First, the Council of the Building Society Association recommended in 1950 that 'free liquid funds', in the form of cash and investments, should not be less than $7\frac{1}{2}$ per cent of total liabilities to shareholders and depositors and $33\frac{1}{3}$ per cent of deposit liabilities alone. In fact, liquidity ratios are usually well in excess of these. Secondly, apart from first mortgages and cash, building societies are allowed to invest only in trustee securities and savings bank deposits. Thirdly, a large part of the building society's non-mortgage assets will usually be of a relatively short-term nature, such as loans to local authorities and short-term government securities.

### INVESTMENT TRUSTS

Investment trusts are not 'trusts' in the legal sense but are joint-stock companies that use their capital to hold a range of securities, mainly industrial securities. The shares of investment trusts can be bought or sold on the Stock Exchange, and offer to their holder an interest in a wide spread of securities and in the skilled management of the trust. These facilities have some appeal to the non-professional personal investor with neither special investment knowledge nor the large funds required to obtain a spread of securities. Companies that can properly be described as investment trusts are mainly long-term investors, purchasing securities with an eye to long-term income rather than immediate capital appreciation. If they satisfy the Inland Revenue authorities that they are not merely dealers in securities, buying and selling at frequent intervals, they are subject to tax only on their income and not on capital appreciation. A distinction can thus be drawn in this way between the investment trust and the finance company whose capital gains and losses are brought into its tax assessment; the latter generally holds a much narrower range of investments, some of which may give it a controlling interest. The Stock Exchange criterion goes further, limiting the term investment trust to those companies whose articles of association preclude the distribution of capital gains to its shareholders.

### *Sources of Finance*

The volume of securities held by investment trusts is limited to their capital and reserves, plus what they can borrow from other sources such as the banks and other institutions. From the outbreak of war until July 1953 the Capital Issues Committee was instructed by the Chancellor of the Exchequer to refuse permission to investment trusts seeking to issue new capital above the C.I.C. limit of £50,000 in any one year. This prohibition was thought to reflect the official view that any expansion of the capital of investment trusts would divert funds from the finance of industry, on the grounds that the money subscribed for the increase in investment trust capital would otherwise have been used to purchase a greater proportion of new issues than is the practice of investment trusts. This is a doubtful proposition and without much relevance to a period in which the annual supply of new industrial issues failed, by and large, to match the appetite of the market. Other considerations influencing the government may have been the fear that new investment trust capital would also divert savings from government issues and would be used to a large extent to buy overseas stocks available for purchase from other British holders, a policy that the authorities may have feared would cause leakages in the exchange control.

About one-third of all British investment trusts, by both number and capital value, and including the largest, are Scottish. Many of these are operated in groups under a holding company, because the most economical size of a skilfully operated investment portfolio is fairly large. The capital of an investment trust is usually highly geared; the existence of a broad spread of marketable investments provides security of both income and capital for its debentures and preference shares, and the high gearing itself magnifies the return provided for the ordinary shareholders of a successful investment trust. Partly because little new investment trust capital could be raised until 1953, and partly because they are bought as long-term investments, shares in investment trusts are not easily obtainable in large amounts.

### Investment Trusts as Investors

Investment trusts hold between 60 and 95 per cent of their assets in ordinary shares, averaging approximately three-quarters, and in some investment trusts as much as two-fifths of the total portfolio takes the form of American and Canadian securities. Investment trusts, as long-term investors, can afford to hold shares which do not have an active market, and some investment trusts hold a small proportion of their portfolio in unquoted shares.

Their holdings of debentures and preference shares contribute a dependable margin of income towards the service of their fixed-interest capital.

Like all institutional investors, investment trusts have adapted their portfolios to changing economic conditions since their period of rapid growth in the last two decades of the nineteenth century. Whereas their investments in the expanding North American continent have increased since before the war, the part played in their portfolios by other overseas investments, notably South American and European securities, has dwindled so much over the past thirty years that United Kingdom securities now occupy a much larger share of the total. In the nineteen-twenties investment trusts held not much more than one-third of their assets in U.K. securities, and before the First World War, when investment trusts were enthusiastic subscribers to foreign issues, the proportion was even smaller. The change from trade depression to the active and generally prosperous conditions enjoyed by business since the war, on the other hand, has been accompanied by an increase in the proportion of U.K. ordinary shares in the total assets of investment trusts. Because of their gearing, their management expenses and their allocation of part of their income to reserve, the share capital of investment trusts will generally be found to have a market value well below that of the underlying assets.

## UNIT TRUSTS

Unit trusts were developed in the nineteen-thirties to enable the small investor to acquire securities representing a spread of assets that he could not hope to obtain by direct purchases on a small scale. Unit trusts are legal trusts, set up under a trust deed and managed by persons who have to be registered under the 1939 Prevention of Frauds (Investment) Act. The securities purchased on behalf of the trust are deposited with trustees, usually a bank.

The portfolio of the trust consists of a block of investments, vested in the trustees, who will divide these into titles described as 'units'. Units are available for purchase by the public, and a holder is entitled to a proportionate share of the beneficial interest in the underlying securities. The number of units held depends on the volume of purchases by the public, whereas the portfolio of an investment trust is limited to the size of its capital and reserves plus outside borrowing.

In a 'fixed' trust the securities held are specified by the trust deed; in a 'flexible' trust investments will not be subject to such restrictions. This second type is now the usual form of unit trust. As the whole of the interest or dividend receipts, less management expenses, is distributed to members, the price of a unit will stand close to the market value of the underlying assets. The market in units is provided generally by the trust managers, who undertake to re-purchase units at any time. Unit trusts are usually created for a definite period, after which members are given the value of the assets underlying their units or the option to convert into the units of a new trust.

The majority of unit trusts hold only high-grade ordinary shares. In 1940 some ninety unit trusts were in existence with units possessing a total value of £81 million. The prohibition of new issues by investment trusts until 1953 applied equally to the creation of new units, and the subsequent expansion of the unit trust movement has been small until recently; but it is now evident that a new period of growth is beginning.

# CHAPTER 24

# THE STOCK EXCHANGE AND COMMODITY MARKETS

### THE PROVINCIAL EXCHANGES

There are twenty-two Stock Exchanges in the large towns of the United Kingdom, those outside London being affiliated in a body known as the Associated Stock Exchanges. Securities in many local companies are dealt in on the provincial markets, and some of the provincial Exchanges are especially noted for their active market in certain types of share associated with local industry. A network of private telephone lines links the provincial Exchanges with each other and, of course, with London, so that any of the thousands of securities traded on the London Stock Exchange can also be dealt in on the provincial Exchanges. Stockbroking facilities are available to the investor living in a town with no Stock Exchange of its own, through the operations of the Provincial Brokers' Stock Exchange, which has members in a further one hundred and forty towns in the British Isles and its headquarters in York. Would-be investors can usually be put in touch with a broker by a solicitor or can leave it to their bank to arrange for their transactions.

### THE LONDON STOCK EXCHANGE—A BRIEF HISTORY AND CONSTITUTION

Foremost among the Stock Exchanges of Britain is, of course, the London Stock Exchange. Like so many successful British institutions whose efficiency and integrity we now take for granted, 'the' Stock Exchange was born in obscurity and nurtured in crisis. Dealing in stocks and shares developed in the last quarter of the seventeenth century following the expansion of the overseas trading companies, the less obvious growth of British industry, and the regularization of government borrowing under William III. There were no rules, and the risks were high. Over-optimism and over-extended speculation, combined with the inevitable scope for sharp practice, soon brought the first crisis when the 'South Sea Bubble' burst in 1720. In the train of the ruin caused by this tragic fantasy followed the first clumsy improvements in company law and the strengthening of the credit status of the government, without which the Stock Exchange could never have reached its present respectability. Further storms, however, had still to be weathered. The development of Britain's industrial economy in the nineteenth century proceeded by a series of onrushes, like the railway boom of the eighteen-forties and the advance into the hazardous fields of overseas finance, many of which brought similar excesses of speculation and subsequent collapse. The growth of banking and finance houses was subject to its own fevers. In the second half of the century, however, the force of these recurrent outbreaks gradually subsided, and in 1878 the Royal Commission appointed to inquire into the operations of the Stock Exchange was able to reach a generally favourable if not unqualified verdict. The Commission acknowledged the integrity of the bulk of the Exchange's members and the sense of responsibility of its governing body, and could not support the view that the Stock Exchange encouraged, let alone produced, speculation.

By 1878 many changes had occurred. In 1773 the stockbrokers and stock jobbers who formerly crowded out the coffee-houses of 'Change Alley', off Cornhill, decided to set up a building opposite the site of the present 'House', and the Stock Exchange had arrived as a formal if still colourful organization. Outgrowing this accommodation, the Stock Exchange moved in 1802 to a new building on its present site in Capel Court, its constitution reshaped in a deed of settlement from which its present organization and rules have developed, the last major reconstruction of its constitution taking place just after the last war.

Although the Stock Exchange possesses a share capital it is legally an unincorporated body established under a deed of settlement and operating in accordance with its own constitution. While they must naturally comply with the general legal framework, members of the Stock Exchange do not have to be registered with the Board of Trade under the Prevention of Fraud (Investments) Act, and the Stock Exchange is not subject to any detailed code of government regulations, having put its own house in order.

Since 1945 the Stock Exchange has been controlled by a single governing body, the Council of the Stock Exchange. The Council is elected by the members of the Stock Exchange and has full authority over all aspects of its operations. The establishment of the Council in 1945 ended the system of dual control whereby a Committee for General Purposes had authority over the Stock Exchange as a market and the trustees and managers ran it as a business. Two years later a further change removed any trace of the possibility that the element of profit-making in the payment of dividends on the share capital of the Stock Exchange would conflict with its wider responsibilities, by converting the 20,000 shares of £36 each into shares of only 1s. each, carrying voting rights but no claim to dividends.

Every effort is made by the Stock Exchange to recruit its members only from persons of personal and financial integrity, but without narrowing its limits to that of an exclusive inward-looking society. Membership may be obtained by a man without approved Stock Exchange experience by acquiring a nomination *vice* a retiring or deceased member. Since nominations are scarce they command a price: as high as £2,000 in 1937 and as low as £45 in 1948. He must also find three members to act as surety to the extent of £500 each for four years and pay an entrance fee of 1,000 guineas and an annual subscription of 105 guineas. Even if he can meet these financial requirements he has still to secure a three-quarters majority vote of approval by the Stock Exchange Council and, like all members, has to be re-elected annually.

A more common and less expensive road to membership of the Stock Exchange is that open to any employee of a Stock Exchange firm of brokers or jobbers who has been allowed to work on the 'floor' of the 'House' for four years, getting quotations and carrying messages as an 'unauthorized' clerk or actually dealing as an 'authorised' clerk. He must still acquire a nomination and pay the full annual subscription, but need find only two members to stand surety and pay only half the maximum entrance fee. In practice part of the cash will often be provided by his employers. The third and cheapest route is also the longest. Clerks with four years' experience in the 'House' may become members without acquiring a nomination if they join a special waiting-list.

## BROKERS AND JOBBERS

In March 1958 membership of the Stock Exchange numbered 3,432, grouped into 434 firms, each of which is a partnership or, in a handful of cases, an unlimited-liability company. Of these,

316 were stockbroking firms and the remainder jobbers. The distinction between brokers and jobbers is one in which the London Stock Exchange is unique.[7] Only stockbrokers deal direct with the public; if an investor wishes to buy or sell securities it is the broker with whom he must get in touch. The broker will then execute his order by a transaction with a jobber.

Stockbrokers can thus be described as intermediaries in a market that is 'made' by the dealings of jobbers, but this would not be strictly accurate, in that it is the broker and not his client from whom the jobber will expect settlement in due course; it is up to the broker to collect the cash or the shares from his client. Stockbrokers obtain their income from the commission chargeable on the purchases and sales of securities they make on behalf of their clients, and a minimum scale of commissions for different types of security and for transactions of different amounts is prescribed by the Stock Exchange Council. The skill they can bring to bear in order to obtain the best terms for their clients and the investment advice they can offer will help to determine the success of brokers in their own field.

The jobber stands ready to buy or sell stocks and shares, dealing only with brokers or other jobbers. His income is obtained from the jobbers' 'turn', that is the spread between the price at which he stands prepared to buy a particular stock and that at which he will sell. If he quotes a price of 48s.–48s. 6d. for the ordinary shares of a company, for example, this means that he is prepared to buy at 48s. and sell at 48s. 6d. If he commits himself to buying, say, 1,000 shares at a price of 48s., he must be able to provide the broker with title to the shares by the time of settlement day. He can meet his commitment in a number of ways. He may be able to draw on his own holdings of the shares; in the case of securities in which there is an active market this would not be the jobber's usual source of stock unless he had been taking a deliberate view of the future course of share prices. Usually the jobber will hope to provide the necessary stock by 'marrying' the transaction with one already made in the opposite direction, or will hope to attract marginal sellers by slightly adjusting his prices, thus drawing out the transaction that will 'balance his book', that is leave him with no net liability in either direction. In the last resort the jobber may turn to other jobbers in order to purchase the stock he has agreed to supply.

Certain jobbers specialize in certain types of security, such as government securities, or oil shares, or steel shares, and the existence of keen competition normally keeps the prices quoted by one jobber closely in line with those 'made' by others. When a jobber is asked for a quotation by a broker or his clerk, he does not know whether he is being approached as a buyer or seller, and his skill lies in so judging the state of the market that he can meet his commitments at prices that leave him with a profit on his turn. A jobber may always keep his books in balance, or he may take a definite view and 'take on' stock, if he thinks prices are going to rise, or commit himself as a net seller if he believes he can 'cover' later on by acquiring stock at a significantly lower price.

If a jobber finds the tide of the market running too strongly for him in one direction he will raise his prices if he is obliged to choke off demand and lower them if he wishes to attract buyers. At times of acute uncertainty, when the situation is such that either strong buying or strong selling pressure may suddenly emerge, the jobber will attempt to protect himself by widening the spread between his buying and selling prices. Furthermore, in normal times the size of the spread or jobbers' turn on different stocks will depend on how active a market they command. Transactions in securities that are being bought and sold at frequent intervals will make it much easier for the jobber to balance his books than those in which dealings occur only infrequently. Thus the jobber's turn is smallest in the field of government securities and largest in the case of the shares of a small company in which dealings are rare.

An efficient market is one in which prices do not react violently to small variations in the pressure of demand or supply. If this condition is met, potential buyers and sellers will have the assurance of being able to deal at prices close to those previously quoted; the market will not be unduly constricted by uncertainty as to the hour-to-hour, or day-to-day, course of prices; and potential buyers or sellers need not fear that their own intervention in the market will turn prices against themselves. A narrow market on the other hand, with prices fluctuating violently and with a broad spread between buying and selling prices, is obviously inimical to the holding of securities and ultimately unfavourable to industrial finance.

The advantage of having the London Stock Exchange's separation between broker and jobber is that it enables the latter not only to specialize in knowledge but to devote all his capital to the business of 'making a market', to holding stock and thus cushioning a fall in prices when demand declines and subsequently braking the rise when demand recovers. But the ability of jobbers to act as shock-absorbers is thought now to be restricted by a shortage of finance due to high taxation. Jobbers are prevented by the rules of the Stock Exchange from turning themselves into limited companies and raising outside capital, and the imposition of a high rate of surtax on their income may tend to deter them from running the risk of keeping their book unbalanced. As a result, occasions have in post-war years become regrettably frequent when a small shift in supply or demand, or a sudden wave of sheer uncertainty as to the immediate future, has been enough to cause marked fluctuations in prices or a sharp increase in the spread of prices from which even government securities have not been immune.[8]

Jobbers are able to supplement their own financial resources by borrowing from the banks, but this source of funds is liable at times to become constricted when the banks feel obliged to cut down their lending. They also borrow money on short notice from certain financial concerns known as money-brokers, who in turn obtain the bulk of their funds by borrowing at slightly lower rates of interest from institutional investors and from large business firms with a temporary surplus of cash. But this supply of finance, too, is likely to dry up when money is short.

## STAMP DUTY

Deeds or certificates transferring securities from one holder to another must, with certain exceptions, bear an Inland Revenue stamp duty of 2 per cent, related to the money involved in the transfer and payable by the purchaser. The chief exceptions are United Kingdom and Commonwealth government and municipal securities, allotment letters on new issues, bearer securities, and American and Canadian securities passing merely by endorsement; other securities bought and sold for the same settlement day are also exempt.

## THE MECHANICS OF TRANSACTIONS

Dealings in United Kingdom and Commonwealth government and municipal securities are 'for cash', which in practice means that settlement must be completed on the following business day. Transactions in other securities are governed by the timing of the Stock Exchange 'Accounts' within the year. With the exception of the three-week accounts spanning public holidays, these run for fourteen days, opening on Monday and closing on Friday. Business transacted within the account is for settlement on what is known as account or settlement day, which is the Tuesday but one following the end of the account. The intervening business days allow the brokers and jobbers to carry out the work involved in settlement, and form part of the next account. If securities are bought and sold within the same account no stamp duty is payable, and broker's commission is usually charged only on the initial transaction. In this respect dealing 'for the account' offers more scope for speculation than longer-term transactions, on which expenses are higher.[9]

To soften the concentration of purchases or sales that might be occasioned by the opening of a new account, dealing for 'new time' is allowed. This refers to the last two business days of one account; if a broker is instructed to buy shares on any of these two days 'for new time', settlement will not be due on the next account day but on the one after that, that is on the account day following the coming account. Purchases for new time are not charged with stamp duty, but share prices quoted for these transactions are slightly less favourable to the buyer or seller.

When an order is placed with a stockbroker he will send his client a contract note immediately on completing the 'bargain', showing details of the transaction and its expenses, which include in addition to stamp duty and commission the cost of the contract stamp affixed to the contract note and the registration fee payable to the company whose securities are being bought for registering the stock in the name of the new owner. Both contract stamp and registration fee are small costs, and the latter, like the 2 per cent stamp duty, is not payable on a purchase that is reversed within the same account, for no transfer deed is then prepared. The contract note will also show the date for settlement, by which payment must be made or the transfer certificate or other document of title to the stock delivered.

These transactions are cleared through the settling-room of the Stock Exchange, after the buyer's name and address has been 'passed' on a name-ticket by the broker to the jobber, so that at the other end the deed of transfer can be prepared by the broker of the seller. As the jobber may have bought the stock concerned from another jobber, the name-ticker may pass through several jobbers before the other end of the chain is reached. The selling broker must obtain his client's share certificates or other documents of title, after first preparing the deed of transfer, which must be sent to the seller for signature. The selling broker will pass the completed transfer deed together with the appropriate stock certificate or bearing a 'certification' that the certificate has been deposited with the Share and Loan Department of the Stock Exchange. The latter will be required, for example, when two or more transfer deeds to separate buyers have to be prepared against one share certificate. The transfer deed (or deeds) must then be sent to the purchaser for signature before being lodged with the registrar of the company concerned and a stock certificate thereby obtained by the purchaser.

Although the seller must deliver the transfer deed or other document of title by settlement day, in practice considerable delay may be involved. The seller may be ill or on holiday, or the signatures of several joint sellers or buyers may be required on the transfer deed, as in the case of trustees or executors; the mechanism of the Stock Exchange cannot operate more quickly than its clients. Payment by the purchaser is nevertheless due on settlement day, unless special arrangements are made with his broker, but delay in delivery of the transfer deed cannot be made grounds for repudiating the contract.

The London Stock Exchange publishes a Daily Official List, with the full authority of the Stock Exchange Council. Besides containing information on individual securities, such as interest or dividends paid, the Official List sets out the prices at which transactions are recorded under a system whereby brokers and jobbers provide clerks of the 'House' with a note of the prices at which business is transacted. This system is not compulsory, but it is thought that normally the majority of transactions are recorded by members. For each price at which dealings take place

x

only one 'mark' occurs in the Official List, and there is no way of telling how many bargains were transacted at that price or what volume of securities changed hands at any one price recorded.

## EX-DIVIDEND

Shortly before a dividend payment is due a company will 'close' its register of shareholders in order to prepare dividend warrants in the names registered at that moment. For the time being, therefore, transfers cannot be registered, and if a shareholder was on the register at the time of closure the company would pay the dividend to him even if he were to sell his shares after the company's register had been closed. To prevent confusion as to the right to dividends, a Stock Exchange rule requires securities to be quoted 'ex-dividend' usually on the first business day of the account in which the register of the company is closed. Before this the share is quoted 'cum-dividend'. The ex-dividend price will be lower than the last cum-dividend quotation, if market conditions do not change, approximately by the amount of dividend due less income-tax at the standard rate.

If a security is bought cum-dividend (or cum-interest in the case of a debenture or government security) the dividend belongs to the buyer; if it is purchased ex-dividend the seller has the right to the payment. If a share goes ex-dividend shortly after purchase but before enough time has elapsed for the transfer to be registered, the brokers concerned have the duty of ensuring that the dividend payment is passed from the seller to the buyer.

## CONTANGO DEALING

If a stock is purchased in the belief that its price is going to appreciate in a short space of time the buyer may hope to resell the stock within the same account. If successful, he will have made a profit without having to put up any purchase money and will have saved the expense of stamp duty and brokerage on the resale. If, on the other hand, the account closes without the expected increase in price, the buyer may still adhere to his view but may not be able to take up his stock. He may, on the other hand, be able to 'carry over' his operation into the next account if his broker can find someone else, usually a jobber, to pay for the stock and hold it through the next account. For this the buyer will have to pay interest at a rate depending on market conditions.

Similar carry-over facilities may be available in the case of someone who has sold stock that he may not yet have bought, in the hope of closing his operation by purchasing the stock within the same account at a price lower than that at which he has contracted to sell it. If the price of the stock has not yet fallen by the end of the account the seller may be able to carry over into the following account if his broker can find someone to deliver the stock to the purchaser on his behalf.

Usually the seller will receive interest on the operation, for he will have relieved someone else of the necessity for paying for stock for the time being. If, on the other hand, there are more sellers wanting to 'borrow' stock for continuation dealings than there are buyers wanting to 'borrow' money, the sellers may have to *pay* interest for the service. In this case the interest payment is known as 'backwardation'.

Whether continuation facilities can be arranged at all will obviously depend on the state of the market in the stock involved in the operation. They are generally difficult to obtain when pressure in the market is all 'one-way', and even in more normal times they can usually be effected only in securities in which dealings are frequent. Some brokers do not arrange continuation facilities at all.

### THE ROLE OF SPECULATION

It is clear that in this outline of continuation dealings we have been introduced to speculative transactions. It is not easy to define 'speculation' to cover all the many shades of meaning with which the word is endowed in practice. The man who buys a share that he hopes to sell at a profit within the same or following account and thus avoid payment—the 'bull' of Stock Exchange jargon—is obviously speculating; so is the man who sells for the account stock that he has not yet bought—this is the action of the 'bear'. Account dealing is a clear example of speculation. But what of the man who purchases shares in the belief that their price is going to appreciate over, say, the next six months? If his view proves correct, shall we call him a speculator if he 'takes his profit' and resells, but merely an investor if he does not? Which course seems the more profitable to him will depend on the market outlook when the time comes. Similarly, what of the man who sells his shares in the belief that their price is about to fall?

The desire to protect oneself against loss clearly does not deserve criticism, but are we to call the seller a speculator if he repurchases the same shares after their price has fallen but not if he buys some other stock ? In this situation again, the most profitable policy will depend on the market outlook.

Thus, although in practice the word 'speculation' is generally used to refer to those transactions where the buyer or seller hopes to reverse his action within some short space of time, the term has no precise application except in one class of operations, for initial intentions are apt to be modified by the course of actual events, and securities purchased with an eye to resale within, say, three months may have to be held for very much longer. The special category where the term 'speculation' has a clear meaning comprises those transactions based on borrowed money or on borrowed stock, in which the buyer or seller must reverse his operation in order to meet his commitments.

Speculation, whether used in this narrow sense of the word or extended to embrace all transactions where purchases or sales are made in the hope of a capital profit that is intended to be realized in the not too distant future, is often a term of opprobrium. But it cannot be too strongly emphasized that a stock market completely free from speculation would be one in which prices fluctuated erratically. There can be no assurance that so-called non-speculative purchases and sales would offset one another, and prices would react sharply from day to day. It is the speculator who can act as a shock-absorber in a free market, taking on stock when a sudden bout of selling causes what he believes to be a merely temporary depression of prices, and selling when demand sends up prices to levels that he considers unrealistic. The useful role of speculation can be seen most clearly in the action of the jobber, who is a 'technical' day-to-day speculator, but his task is eased if speculation by other operators has a similar cushioning effect.

Speculation acts most successfully to damp down major fluctuations in prices when speculators have in their mind a picture of a long-term or 'normal' level of prices, deviations from which they expect to be temporary. It is true that speculation may also be the cause of fluctuations in share prices, for speculators may react to a fall in share prices by selling securities in the belief that the fall is likely to continue owing to impending sales by other investors; and similarly they may act so as to extend a rise. In these cases the actions of forward-looking operators will advance movements in security prices, but in their absence similar changes in prices might still have occurred, but at a later stage. It is also true that in a market in which speculation is based on guessing the actions of *other* speculators share prices are likely to follow the curious rhythms common in the market for ordinary shares. Whatever inconveniences are inflicted by speculation on the long-term investor are part of the cost of having a free and active market; in the last resort they are part of the price that must be paid for a free economy. Attempts have been made to reduce the scope for short-term speculation; during the war settlement on the Stock Exchange had to be made within five days, and continuation facilities were theoretically withdrawn. But when Stock Exchange activity revived after the war the disadvantages of these restrictions were soon realized. Option dealing was forbidden by the Council in 1939. In 1958, however, members of the Stock Exchange voted for its restoration. Option dealing provides facilities for buying an option to sell or buy shares, usually described as 'put' or 'call' options, at a fixed price by a certain date; if the option is not exercised, only the cost of the option need be discharged.

Generally speaking, the action of 'professional' or 'semi-professional' speculators is much less likely to cause violent fluctuations in share prices than the marked swings of hope and fear by which the enthusiastic amateur is periodically overcome. The most important danger lies in the possibility that speculation may get out of hand through too-easy resort to borrowed money, when purchases can be financed on 'margin', that is when the shares bought form the security for the loan by which their purchase is financed. In this situation not only might share prices rise to excessively high levels, but any subsequent collapse might be particularly violent, because the fall in the market value of the securities standing as collateral would force speculators dealing 'on margin' to sell other securities as well in order to repay their loans. The immediate cause of the collapse in share prices itself might well be a sudden restriction in the supply of loans to speculators. In the U.S.A., where such operations greatly aggravated the 1929 stock-market boom and ensuing collapse, margin dealing is subject to strict government regulation, and in Britain the rules of the Stock Exchange limit that form of

dealing possible on borrowed money through the system of fortnightly accounts and continuation facilities. Beyond this the
supply of bank credit to speculators is subject to the influence of
the government's credit policy, and the extent of margin dealing
has been small since the war.

## SPECULATION AND COMMODITY MARKETS

The role of speculation on the Stock Exchange has its parallel
in the part it plays in the organized commodity markets, to which
an introduction can therefore usefully be effected at this point.
Commodity markets have grown up in the City of London over
the centuries for products of many kinds, and each is subject to its
own rules of operation. Some work by auction; others by private
dealing. Those where speculation takes its most interesting and its
most intricate form are the Terminal Markets, where trading takes
place in *futures*. These are contracts for delivery at some time in the
future at a price fixed now, the bulk of the payment not being due
until delivery, which is usually from three to twelve months ahead,
with three months' forward transactions being the most common.

Futures markets are only possible in the case of commodities
of easily identifiable grades; and futures contracts, although made
in terms of a single grade, can generally be satisfied by the delivery
of one of a number of specified grades, the price payable on delivery
being adjusted according to a schedule drawn up by the market
authorities. The rules of each market also stipulate the minimum
quantities for which futures can be bought or sold and the standard
places and times of delivery. In London, futures markets exist
for copper, lead, zinc, tin, rubber, cocoa, wool, sugar, maize,
and barley; before the war and the introduction of exchange
control over payments in dollars, wheat would have been included
in the list. The famous cotton exchange is to be found in Liverpool, and in Dundee there is an organized market in jute.

Futures markets have developed in response to the need to
minimize the risk attached to price fluctuations. The period of
time over which this risk must be 'covered' may arise in a number
of ways. An importer may seek cover for the period between
purchase overseas and sale in the United Kingdom, and a farmer
may want an assured price for his crop due to be harvested several
months ahead. The processor of raw materials may seek protection
against a fall in the price of his stock of raw material because it will

cause the market price of his product to fall as well; or he may have committed himself to future production without having yet purchased his raw materials, so that in this case he will need cover against a rise in his raw-material costs. In agricultural commodities production is concentrated at harvest-time, whereas consumer demand is generally spread over the whole year, so that someone has to hold stocks after the harvest.

In the organized commodity exchanges there are therefore two related markets—the 'spot' market (alternatively called the 'cash' market), where purchases and sales are for immediate delivery, and the futures market, in which forward contracts are transacted. Through the adjustment of spot and forward prices dealers, merchants and manufacturers can choose between spot and forward transactions according to their needs, their assessment of future prices and their willingness to undertake the risk of an adverse movement of prices.

To hold a commodity involves certain costs—storage, insurance and interest—so that as a rule forward prices stand above spot prices, for someone with supplies to hand will only sell forward rather than spot if the forward price is sufficiently above the spot price to compensate for these expenses. The existence of a forward price that is abnormally high in relation to the spot price can be taken to mean that a sufficient number of operators are expecting a rise in the spot price due, for example, to a poor harvest, so that merchants will have bought forward to meet their commitments rather than wait and buy spot; speculators will have bought forward in the hope of selling spot at a price sufficient to discharge their forward purchase and yield a profit. Spot prices can rise in relation to forward prices, on the other hand, when there is a temporary scarcity of spot supplies.

Buyers and sellers can either take the risk of an adverse movement of prices or 'hedge' by combining opposite spot and forward transactions. The merchant or processor who buys spot can cover the risk of a fall in the price of his stock before he sells, by combining his spot purchases with a forward sale of the same amount. When he comes to sell spot he will close his operations by buying back his futures contract.* If prices in the spot and

---

* He will close his commitment to sell forward in this way, because in most cases the 'spot' stock will be sold in the ordinary course of business and so will not be available to meet the forward contract when it matures.

forward markets have moved in the same direction and to the same degree, any loss or profit on his spot transactions will be exactly offset by a profit or loss on his futures contracts. In practice, while spot and forward prices generally move in the same direction, they may not change by the same amount, so that the hedge may not be perfect. But the risk of adverse price movements will generally be reduced sufficiently for short-term business operations to proceed on a more assured basis and for bankers and others to provide finance against the security of the commodity in question.

The counterpart to a commercial spot or forward sale or purchase may be another commercial transaction. The forward sale by an importer seeking an assured price for goods due to arrive in three months' time may be matched by the forward purchase of a manufacturer who is seeking a firm raw-material price on which to base his production programme. But no market can eliminate the existence of risk for its buyers and sellers as a whole; it can only transfer it, from those unwilling to bear it, and thus prepared to pay to be free of it, to those ready to stand it, at a price. 'Commercial' transactions are therefore only a part of the operation of a futures market; in the last resort it is the speculator who stands the risk that the merchant or manufacturer is unwilling to bear and who broadens the market so that day-by-day transactions can be accommodated without violent price fluctuations.

If speculators are correct their operations have the effect of damping down price fluctuations, as long as their action is not based on the belief that a recent movement in one direction will continue. If they take the view, for example, that the coming crop is going to be a poor one they will buy forward, in the hope of selling spot when the time comes at a price high enough to show a profit. A rise in the forward price of sufficient magnitude will make those holding stocks more reluctant to sell spot, so that spot prices also tend to rise. The result will therefore be to diminish immediate consumption and for stocks to be carried forward to the period of scarcity, checking the rise in spot prices when this emerges. Seasonal fluctuations can also be absorbed in this manner. Of course, if the speculators are wrong the consequence of their action will be to aggravate price fluctuations; in the above example the increase in the carry-over of stocks would cause a severe fall in prices should the new crop turn out to be unexpectedly large. But the usefulness of the specialist speculator turns on the reasonable assumption that his skill at forecasting will be greater than that of the manufacturer or merchant whose main concern lies elsewhere. The specialization made possible by the existence of organized produce markets also extends to the existence of commodity brokers, who, as in the Stock Exchange, act as skilled intermediaries and advisers.

Futures markets have been hindered since the war by factors from which pre-war markets were relatively free. Government attempts to influence commodity prices, in the U.S.A., for example, by means of various controls supported by stockpiling, have tended to cause periods of price rigidity to be punctuated by spells of highly unstable prices. During the former 'hedging' has been less necessary; during the latter it has been more expensive than would otherwise have been the case. Speculators are generally less willing to take risks when the market is dominated by relatively arbitrary government action, and when large surplus stocks are known to exist forward prices may stand below spot prices. This 'backwardation' in prices will make it costly for a trader or manufacturer to cover a spot purchase by means of a forward sale.

# PART III

# INTRODUCTION TO PUBLIC FINANCE

CHAPTER 25

# INTRODUCTION TO PUBLIC FINANCE

## GOVERNMENT EXPENDITURE

### *Some Basic Objectives*

While we continue to argue about their application there is a wide measure of agreement about the broad principles governing the proper objectives of government expenditure. Nearly two hundred years ago the 'duties of the sovereign' were classified by Adam Smith* in terms that would now command even more general assent than they received in his own day. The first duty of the State, he said, is to defend society from 'the violence and invasion of other independent societies'. The second is that of 'protecting, as far as possible, every member of the society from the injustice or oppression of every other member of it'. The third has a remarkably modern ring about it: it is that of 'erecting and maintaining certain public works and certain public institutions, which can never be for the interest of any individual, or small number of individuals to erect and maintain; because the profit could never repay the expense to any individual or small number of individuals, though it may frequently do much more than repay it to a great society'.

Adam Smith had in mind the provision of things like lighthouses and drainage, the cost of which could not be recouped by charging a price for their benefits as in a normal trading venture, or where the benefits to society as a whole extended beyond the limits of those who were prepared to pay for them. What we have come to regard as basic services, such as education, street lighting, drainage, parks and roads, fall for the most part in this category; but in some cases, such as toll roads, the expense can be charged directly to those who use them. Adam Smith's third duty has in the course of time come to be interpreted with increasing liberality as the role of the State has grown. The State now undertakes expenditure that we believe it can perform at less cost than private

* Adam Smith, *The Wealth of Nations*, Book IV, Chapter IX.

agencies because of the economies obtainable from large-scale operation; the telephone and telegraph services are examples.

Of much greater significance, however, is the fact that considerations of economy have come to be merged in the much more complex problem of the State's responsibility for ensuring equity or 'social justice'. It is the belief that the State can at least mitigate what is regarded as the hardship and social injustice arising from the gross inequality of wealth that, more than any other single factor, has been the cause of the great increase in government civil expenditure in the twentieth century. The social services now occupy the central place in what has come to be known as the 'Welfare State'.

The attempt of the State to provide, through National Insurance, the National Health Service and other amenities, some measure of social security is directed towards three objectives of modern public finance. First, to secure *equity*. Secondly, to meet a need with *economy*, in the belief that such services can be provided most efficiently by the State. Thirdly, to increase national *productivity*, for the hope that the social services will enhance the prosperity of the nation as a whole by encouraging effort and improving industrial relations is another of the causes of their extension.

To these three objectives must be added a fourth—*economic stability*—that has more recently been accepted as one of the paramount aims of public finance. The Budget has ceased to be a simple matter of making the Exchequer's ends meet now that the State has undertaken the ultimate responsibility for maintaining economic stability, that is for ensuring full employment, conserving our reserves of foreign exchange, and preventing an intolerable rise in prices.

Within these broad terms government expenditure has come to be applied to a variety of purposes that are focal points of political controversy. As the government has such powers of conferring fiscal benefits and penalties on certain groups within the community, it is not surprising that public finance has become an important, if not the main, battlefield of domestic political dissention.

### The Growth of Central Government Expenditure

That the growth of the role of the State, for good or evil, has been the most important feature of the economic and political development of the twentieth century is now a trite observation. In 1890, for example, the current expenditure of the central government and local authorities was not more than 10 per cent of the national income. With the spread of the social services this proportion had reached 15 per cent by the outbreak of the First World War, but during the war itself no less than three-quarters of the nation's total expenditure was made by the State. In the 1930's the continued growth of the social services brought the proportion of State spending to about one-third, and after the Second World War, in which the figure reached four-fifths, public current expenditure, excluding that of the nationalized corporations, has settled down at nearly two-fifths of the national income.

During the past two generations the centre of gravity of public expenditure has shifted more and more to the central government as the growing social services have been unified. Nominally, however, the National Insurance Funds, although administered by one of the central government departments, are outside the finance of the central Exchequer itself, except in so far as they receive Exchequer grants or contribute towards the cost of the National Health Service. Other parts of the social services are direct charges on the Exchequer, and one result of the growth of the Welfare State is that only part—about one-half—of the current expenditure of the central government, excluding the so-called 'extra-budgetary' National Insurance Funds, consists of payments made in return for the receipt of goods and services. The remainder consists of what are sometimes described as *transfer* payments and include subsidies, grants made to persons and the local authorities, and interest paid on loans contracted by the Exchequer, that is on the national debt. The proportion of the nation's output of current goods and services used by the government itself has grown from about one-seventh in 1936 to about one-fifth in recent years; transfer payments have grown even faster. The lion's share of current expenditure is taken by defence, which at one-third in 1958 compared with 15 per cent before rearmament began in the 1930's and about two-fifths of a very much smaller figure before the First World War.

The capital outlays of the central government include expenditure on the acquisition of fixed assets for the Post Office and other government departments and on stocks of materials held by the various Ministries; loans made to local authorities and public corporations; and the repayment of debts incurred by the Exchequer in the past. If we include the sterling that the authorities may have to provide as the counterpart of an increase in our reserves of gold and foreign currency, the total capital disbursements of the central government can be said to have fluctuated between £600 million and £1,000 million per annum in recent years. Only a small part of this, about £200 million per annum, will normally be direct expenditure on physical assets.

## THE CLASSIFICATION OF CENTRAL GOVERNMENT EXPENDITURE AND REVENUE

The classification that is generally accepted as that most relevant to the impact of government finance on the economy distinguishes between its direct use of real resources and its transfer payments and divides current from capital outlays. This is the classification presented in the official National Income statistics, but it is not the way in which government expenditure is grouped in the Financial Statement and similar financial summaries of the Exchequer's operations that have been developed as part of the government's accountability to Parliament. In these the distinction is made between 'above-the-line' and 'below-the-line' expenditure, the latter consisting of items that may be financed by borrowing, such as grants and loans made to local authorities, public corporations and overseas governments. This is only a poor approximation to the distinction between current and capital outlays.

Corresponding to above- and below-the-line expenditures are above- and below-the-line revenues. Above-the-line revenue consists mainly of taxes; receipts below the line arise largely through the repayment of loans to the Exchequer and also include 'interest outside the Budget'. The latter is a bookkeeping entry occasioned by the application of receipts from the operation of various statutory funds and is balanced by an identical item on the opposite side of the account.

The Financial Statement and annual Finance Accounts also isolate those above-the-line items that constitute what is described as Ordinary Revenue and Expenditure. These make up the bulk of the account above the line; what is not Ordinary

Revenue or Expenditure above the line is Self-Balancing Revenue or Expenditure, of which the most important example is to be found in the receipts and payments of the Post Office.

## THE SOCIAL SERVICES AND THE NATIONAL INSURANCE FUNDS

Social security is not the dispensation of the State alone; life-assurance, private pension and private medical insurance schemes, to say nothing of the voluntary organizations that were the pioneers of most of the social services, are an integral part of the community's defences against hardship and insecurity. The State first intervened to supplement private action, but in many ways the role of the State and that of private bodies has been reversed over the past two generations.

There is no room here to trace the growing field of State social services from the Poor Law Act of 1601 and the quickening of State activity in the Factory, Education and Public Health Acts of the nineteenth century to the comprehensive system that is their object today. Two generations ago about nine-tenths of government social service expenditure was directed at education and the relief of the destitute, but this proportion has now fallen to about one-quarter or one-third. The relief of poverty began to be extended beyond the field of pauperism with the assistance for industrial injuries provided under the Workmen's Compensation Act of 1897, and this more positive approach to the prevention rather than the relief of poverty took an important step forward in the Liberal reforms of the early years of this century. The shift of responsibility for the provision of the social services from the varied and often unavoidably inadequate standards of the local authorities to the central government, together with the change in their underlying philosophy from the relief of acute hardship to the attainment of some minimum standard for all, can be traced to the Minority Report of the Poor Law Commission of 1909. Many recommendations of this Report were put into effect by the legislation of the Liberal government of 1906–11. Pensions date from the Old Age Pensions Act of 1908, and the National Health and Unemployment Insurance Schemes were commenced on a limited scale with the National Insurance Act of 1911.

Y

Since 1911 progress has been made in all branches of the social services. Their general framework was erected by a number of Acts embodying the desire for a comprehensive nationwide system that found its full expression in the stimulus to State action given by the war. The main lines of present educational policy were set by the Education Act of 1944, and the aim of social security 'from cradle to grave' was the inspiration of the post-war legislation that implemented many of the proposals made in the Report of the Interdepartmental Committees on Social Insurance and Allied Services of 1942 (the Beveridge Report). Their basic philosophy, to quote an official pamphlet,* is that 'every child or citizen of Britain whatever the circumstances of his birth shall be assured freedom from want and insecurity, and equal opportunities in regard to health, education and employment'.

The main problems encountered along this road have changed with the alteration in economic conditions. The development of educational policy has been relatively steady; but the chief question facing the social services before the war was the relief of hardship caused by heavy unemployment, which put a great strain on local authority finance until legislation in 1934 first transferred the greater part of the financial responsibility to the central government. With the attainment of full employment this has become a minor question, and the most important problems that have emerged from the post-war legislation have been the cost of the health services and of the State pension scheme.

The cost of the social services, like government expenditure as a whole, consists of two elements: expenditure incurred in the purchase of goods and services, and the provision of money grants to persons. The first constitutes a direct charge on the country's real resources; the other involves the transfer or redistribution of income from one person to another. Total current expenditure on the social services in 1957 was divided almost equally into these two classes. The problem facing policy, in framing the size and nature of benefits, has been to limit the 'real' cost of the social services to what the community can afford in view of the other competing claims upon its resources and, broadly speaking, to maintain the burden of transfer payments at levels that are regarded as equitable and tolerable as between those who make them and those who receive them.

* *Social Services in Britain* (H.M.S.O., London, 1956).

## The Actuarial Contribution and Capital Deficiency

The 1946 National Insurance Act followed the principle established by the Act of 1911 and the Contributory Pensions Act of 1925 in prescribing rates of contribution based on an 'actuarial contribution'. This is the weekly amount that would have to be paid by or on behalf of an insured person in order to provide, on average, for the cost of the benefits to which he and his dependants would become entitled. The Exchequer meets part of this in the form of supplements of fixed amounts to the weekly contributions of employer and employee. The liability of the Exchequer, however, is not limited to this. The actuarial contribution relates to a person entering the scheme at the initial age of sixteen, but every time the level of benefits is raised—usually because of a rise in prices—and rates of contribution are revised on the principle of the actuarial contribution, a 'capital deficiency' is created in respect of existing beneficiaries and contributors; this capital deficiency exists in the sense that discounted future contributions and interest fall short of discounted future benefits. There has also been a capital deficiency in the case of every person brought into the scheme over the age of sixteen. In fact, the retirement contributions paid by or on behalf of a man who retired at sixty-five in 1957 after having been a contributor since the inception of the contributory scheme in 1926, if interest at 3 per cent had been earned, would have represented less than one-tenth of the pension payable to him and his wife.

## The Problem of Solvency

In private pension schemes which aim at actuarial solvency this problem is met by one or both of two methods. The capital deficiency is financed by special payments into the pension fund by the employer, or correspondingly high contributions have to be paid by those in respect of whom the capital deficiency is incurred. In an actuarially solvent scheme a fund is established which can meet all future liabilities with the aid of interest and the future contributions of existing members. The National Insurance Scheme is not actuarially 'funded' in this way, and its deficiency eventually emerges in the form of an excess of expenditure over normal income, including interest and the normal Exchequer supplement; this excess will have to be met by special payments from the Exchequer or by an increase in the contribution rate.

About three-quarters of the benefits paid under the National Insurance Scheme are retirement pensions, and it is in regard to these that the main capital deficiency will emerge as the number of pensioners increases in relation to the working population. The 1946 National Insurance Act went beyond the Beveridge Report in not postponing the operation of a comprehensive scheme until part of the capital deficiency could be met by the accumulation of sufficient funds, and benefits have had to be increased several times since the Act came into force in 1948, because of rising prices. The report by the Government Actuary on the first Quinquennial Review of the scheme in 1954 estimated that the capital deficiency already incurred would emerge in the form of an excess of expenditure over income, at current contribution rates, of £364 million in 1979–80. If contributions were not increased, the Exchequer would have to provide a total of £434 million, including the normal supplement. As a result of improvements in benefits necessitated by the rise in prices the Government Actuary subsequently estimated, in 1957, that this future charge on the Exchequer had been increased to £598 million.

This deficiency will have to be met out of general taxation or by an increase in contributions in relation to current benefits; in both cases the liability will fall on the working population. In the 'real' sense, of course, the goods and services bought by the pensions of the retired can only, for the overwhelming part, be provided by their working contemporaries, for we cannot in our working life store the food, clothing and services we shall consume when we retire. It might appear, therefore, that the fact that the retired are, in real terms, an unavoidable charge on the working population reduces the question of how the National Insurance Scheme is to be financed to the order of a minor financial technicality.

### The Function of 'Funding'

This is a short-sighted view of the function of 'funding', that is of creating a fund whose capital value is related to the present discounted value of future net liabilities. For in the process of building up a fund, saving is performed that enables real investment to be increased and thus makes possible an increase in the future output of goods and services that would not otherwise have occurred, so lightening the real burden of future pensions. This real 'backing' to an actuarial fund is the means whereby the promise of future pensions is transformed into performance without placing an unfair weight upon the next working generation, and it is not lightly to be dismissed. Private pension schemes play a part in putting more tools into the hands of the next working generation, but the saving performed by the National Insurance Funds—their current surplus—had dropped from £169 million in 1950 to £24 million in 1957.

This implied criticism of the National Insurance Scheme should not be interpreted to mean that existing beneficiaries should never have their benefits increased if prices rise. For the very object of the scheme is to relieve hardship incurred through no fault of its members, and such a harsh judgement would be doubly unjust in that beneficiaries may have paid their fair share of contributions in real terms even though in money values a rise in benefit rates made necessary through a rise in prices will have set up a money deficiency on their behalf. Neither should the advantage attributed here to 'funding' imply that a capital deficiency that is set up in the National Insurance Scheme requires an immediate increase in the Exchequer supplement financed by taxation or in contributions, irrespective of the impact on government finance as a whole. When excessive unemployment exists, it is economically undesirable to levy the sharp increase in taxation or in contributions that might be required to maintain actuarial solvency, unless, as will usually be the case, compensating reductions in taxation can be made in other directions.

Furthermore, the true incidence of National Insurance contributions, in real terms, may not fall entirely on those legally liable; and it is not clear just how much extra real saving by the community as a whole occurs when the National Insurance Funds show a current surplus. For an increase in employers' contributions, in falling upon all employers, may be met out of higher prices, and this may also be the result when an increase in the rate of employees' contributions leads to a successful claim for higher wages and salaries. In these cases it is not contributors but those members of the community whose incomes do not keep pace with prices who are obliged to reduce their real consumption and provide real 'backing' to the National Insurance Fund, and these less fortunate people may to a large extent consist of the retired themselves. Alternatively, an increase in contributions may be paid partly at the expense of existing business or personal saving and so may not make possible an increase in real investment at all.

Nevertheless, even if these qualifications are given full weight, a scheme that aims at lightening the burden of future working generations must at least attempt to perform an adequate level of saving; the basic argument against merging the finance of the National Insurance Scheme in the operations of the Exchequer as a whole is perhaps that, politically, the hope that governments will maintain a large surplus of current revenue over expenditure for any length of time is unrealistic unless the scheme has at least a nominal autonomy. Those who are even more pessimistic about the ability of governments to restrict their expenditure, or promises of future expenditure, may, however, argue that the existence of *any* current surplus, even in a fund with a formal autonomy, is bound to tempt the government to raise benefits to the point at which, even though the current surplus is not immediately extinguished, a large capital deficiency is created, causing a corresponding current deficit to emerge in the future.

Finally, there is the important question of the assets in which a State fund is to be invested. The existing National Insurance Funds are invested only in government and government-guaranteed securities and other forms of loans to the government. In 1957 the Labour Party proposed the establishment of a new Superannuation Scheme, on a partially funded basis, the assets of which would include private industrial securities, especially ordinary shares. To those who view with concern the formation of a State fund that might dominate the private capital market and so prevent its operation as a free and flexible institution, recourse to an unfunded scheme may appear as the lesser of evils. However, it is by no means essential that a funded scheme of State pensions should invest in private securities in order to make possible the increase in real investment that must be its real object.

TAXATION—SOME GENERAL QUESTIONS

Ideally, in general terms that amount to tautology, taxes intended to raise a given revenue should be levied so as to cause the minimum of disturbance to the aggregate satisfaction enjoyed by the community out of its net income. This criterion has three important aspects that can also be stated broadly but briefly. First, the marginal pound of tax burden borne by any individual should be no more painful, in terms of satisfaction forgone, than that paid by any other. Secondly, a tax should disturb freedom of consumers' choice between different goods and services as little as possible. Thirdly, it should not distort a man's choice between work and leisure. Add to these the requirement that taxes should be impartial as between individual citizens in identical circumstances, and so easy to calculate and collect and clear in their application, and we have a collection of rules few of which can be viewed as absolute in the modern economy. A hundred, even fifty, years ago, when the total revenue that had to be raised was comparatively light, and when fiscal policy was not directed to a multiplicity of social and economic ends, this prescription might have been more helpful to the Chancellor of the Exchequer.

### 'Ability to Pay'

In broad outline, however, their influence can be discerned, if only in the manner in which the announcement of a new tax is assessed by economists, financial journalists and all others who are called upon to pronounce if not to pay. In the first place, 'ability to pay' has long been one of the canons of British taxation and the way in which the first of our rules has been interpreted. Even in its early history after its introduction in 1799, income tax, although levied basically at one standard rate proportional to income, was charged at a reduced rate on low incomes and was subject to a total-exemption limit.

Towards the end of the nineteenth century 'ability to pay' came to be interpreted with much more sophistication. It was in 1894 that the principle of *progressive* taxation was first applied with any formality, to the death duties recast by Sir William Harcourt, and in 1909 the principle was extended in the shape of the super-tax, later renamed surtax. A progressive tax is one where the proportionate rate of tax increases as we move up the scale of income or wealth; its opposite is said to be *regressive*. The progressive principle is usually justified by the postulate that the sacrifice of satisfaction entailed in the loss of a marginal pound of income or wealth is smaller the richer the taxpayer. This question has already been referred to.*

* See page 105.

### Direct and Indirect Taxes

Traditionally the distinction has been drawn between *direct* and *indirect* taxes. The former are those where the collecting authorities are in direct contact with the taxpayer, a rough-and-ready description that has to be modified to take into account Pay-As-You-Earn and other tax payments at source. Indirect taxes are those which are legally payable to the authorities by the retailer, wholesaler, or manufacturer. In the latter case, however, the effective incidence, as we shall see, may fall on the final consumer and not on the trader legally responsible for making the payment. Direct taxes include income tax, surtax, profits tax, local rates and motor-vehicle duties; among the main indirect taxes are Customs and Excise duties, including purchase tax.

### Taxes on Income and Outlay

A more useful distinction is that between taxes on income (and capital) and those levied on the purchase, hire or use of goods and services; the latter can be described as outlay or sales taxes. A man is subject to a certain measure of income tax depending on his income, but his payment of outlay taxes is a matter of choice, depending on the pattern and the level of his consumption. This distinction is not far removed from the traditional dividing line, except that motor-vehicle duties and local rates (the latter being levied, broadly speaking, on the consumption of house room) are outlay taxes.

For many years taxes on income were generally regarded as being potentially progressive, and outlay taxes, once the revenue to be raised had approached the formidable total that the modern Chancellor must find, as tending towards the regressive. The former were therefore favoured by those who emphasized the equity of progressive taxation. Until the war, at least, the case for taxes on income (or capital) rather than on outlay was further strengthened by the argument that the former allowed the taxpayer full freedom of choice in his spending, whereas outlay taxes lead consumers to alter the pattern of their expenditure. Discriminatory outlay taxes open a gap between the relative satisfaction received by consumers from different goods and services and their relative costs to the community. If outlay taxes are at low levels this may not be serious, but in order to keep the weight of indirect taxation off the shoulders of the poor, food and clothing have borne little or no tax while a limited number of commodities have been subject to very high rates since the war.

## The Incidence of Outlay Taxes

The effect of an outlay tax on prices will depend on the conditions of demand and supply in the industry concerned. If the demand for the produce of a competitive industry is elastic, the price of the commodity will not be raised by the full extent of the tax, part of which will therefore fall on the producers' profits. High-cost firms, or those in a better position to transfer to other lines, will reduce their output of the taxed article.

If the supply of the good is very elastic, on the other hand, as will be the case where producers can easily switch to making other goods, businessmen will only continue to make the same quantity of the taxed article if they can pass on the whole of the tax to the consumer by raising prices; but their ability to do so will depend on the elasticity of demand for their goods. Except in the extreme cases of completely inelastic demand or supply, in which the tax will be fully absorbed by consumer or producer respectively, the imposition of an outlay tax will cause some increase in price and some reduction in sales, output and profits. Given the supply conditions, the rise in price will be smaller and the fall in profits more the greater is the elasticity of demand. Given the demand conditions, the rise in price will be smaller and the fall in profits greater the less elastic the supply.

The economic as distinct from the legal incidence of the tax will thus depend on market conditions, and so will the tax revenue raised. For where demand or supply are elastic the greater will tend to be the reduction in sales and output and the smaller will be the total tax receipts secured by a tax of a certain level. From the point of view of the Exchequer, the article most suitable for taxation, when the object is to raise revenue, is one where demand or supply is very inelastic, so that production and sales are not affected, and one which forms a large part of total consumers' expenditure without bearing too harshly on the poor, so that the rate of tax need not be high. For many years the tax on tobacco seemed to come close to this ideal position. Where the object of an outlay tax is to check consumption, on the other hand, it will be achieved at a moderate rate of tax only if demand or supply is sufficiently elastic.

An assessment of the incidence of an outlay tax is difficult to make in the case of goods used in a wide variety of industries. Furthermore, this sort of analysis is really applicable only to taxes on goods and services that form a small part of total consumers' expenditure. For when outlay taxes are sufficiently high or widespread and so affect the retail price-level as a whole, they may ultimately be passed on to consumers in their entirety, or very nearly so, if consumers are able to obtain a rise in wages and salaries sufficient to compensate for the rise in prices caused by the outlay taxes themselves. In this situation the imposition of outlay taxes will result in a multiple increase in prices, the real burden of which will be borne by those sections of the community whose incomes do not keep pace. This is a very bald statement of what in practice is likely to prove a complicated sequence of events.

### Outlay Taxes as Checks to Consumption

Outlay taxes may be imposed to check the sale of certain goods rather than to raise revenue; the duties on imported goods are examples of fairly long standing. More recently, purchase tax has come to be used to restrict the demand for certain consumer durable goods, such as motor-cars. The intention of the government in the latter case has been to divert sales away from the home market to exports and to restrict the use of materials in particularly short supply, such as steel. No single criterion can be applied to these problems; the question of import duties is a matter of foreign-trade policy as well as of public finance in the narrower sense, and certain restrictive taxes, including perhaps the tax on alcoholic drinks, may be said to serve some generally accepted social end. The discriminatory taxes levied in order to stimulate exports or conserve particular scarce resources are bound to be the subject of greater controversy, for they act against the principle of freedom of consumers' choice and, when their coverage has been extended to household and other goods not the monopoly of the rich, may seem to have no clear foundation in equity.

From the point of view of the Exchequer, discriminatory outlay taxes have the advantage that they can be concentrated on goods for which demand tends to rise faster than consumption as a whole; from the point of view of the trader and the consumer, they are subject to the disadvantage not only of interfering with freedom of choice but of being liable to sudden and drastic changes because of the administrative ease with which these can be made. In economically less advanced countries, and in those where income tax evasion is more serious than it is in Britain, outlay taxes on a small number of goods, especially imported goods, often make up the bulk of tax revenue, owing to the greater facility with which they can be assessed and collected.

### THE DISADVANTAGES OF HIGH TAXES ON INCOME

Traditionally the distortion of consumer choice caused by outlay taxes has been one of the reasons for regarding taxes on income as superior fiscal instruments. More recently, this view has come to be modified as a result of the high level at which income tax and surtax have been maintained since the war.

Three disadvantages of high rates of income tax and surtax can be discerned. First, there is the probability that a high rate of income tax will reduce private saving; in Victorian times this was one of the main reasons for the slow development of the use of income tax. With this can be combined the criticism that the heavy taxation of the rich will militate against the purchase of more risky investments in particular and so inhibit enterprise. Secondly, the maintenance of income tax and surtax at high rates inevitably leads, if not to illicit evasion, to a diversion of effort in an attempt by people to arrange their affairs so as to avoid tax, for example by the excessive use of expense accounts and untaxed emoluments and by the quest for tax-free capital gains. Thirdly, high rates of income tax may distort the choice between work and leisure.

This may occur if the *marginal* rate of tax, that is the proportion of an extra pound of income that is paid in tax, is high, for in this case the effect may be to make the marginal pound of gross income seem hardly worth working for. A high *average* rate of tax, on the other hand, may have the opposite effect, by making a man feel that it is all the more necessary to earn an extra pound of income, even though part of it will be taken in tax. But it seems to have become generally accepted that the marginal rates of income tax and surtax on high incomes constitute an important deterrent to extra effort. During the war the operation of P.A.Y.E. in causing weekly fluctuations in the tax liabilities of skilled factory operatives according to the number of hours worked or the amount of piece-work performed was thought to have had a similar effect on overtime and to have been responsible for absenteeism, but the increase in allowances at the lower income levels, with a consequent reduction of the marginal rate of tax, has since reduced the effect of the Pay-As-You-Earn system on weekly wage-earners.

Since the war, when the choice between work and leisure became a national as well as a personal question, the incidence of income tax and surtax on the exercise of professional and managerial skills has become the subject of some concern. Various alternatives to the heavy weight of direct taxation have been suggested, but have been open to criticism either because of the difficulty of administering them or because they act against the principle of progressive taxation. Generally speaking, however, some swing of opinion can be discerned towards taxes on expenditure rather than on income, in the hope of stimulating both effort and saving.

### A GENERAL SALES TAX

One possible alternative to discriminatory outlay taxes bearing heavily on certain goods would be a general sales tax, imposed at a uniform rate over as wide a range of goods and services as possible. If the tax were collected from retailers this would prevent the possibility of any 'pyramiding' that might occur if the tax were levied at the manufacturing or wholesale level and included in the cost on which profit margins were based at subsequent levels of purchase. It would also avoid the problems caused by claims for relief from the tax by firms making goods for export. But one obvious difficulty of a general sales tax collected from the multiplicity of retail outlets would be that of administration. Another is that a uniform sales tax would be regressive; the proportion of income consumed tends to move inversely with income after a certain point. For this reason it has sometimes been suggested that foodstuffs and perhaps clothing should be excluded from the operation of a uniform sales tax.

However, if a uniform tax were substituted for the present structure of discriminatory outlay taxes, it is doubtful whether their impact on the poorer sections of the community as a whole would be much more severe, because of the weight of taxes on beer and tobacco already borne by the working class. These greatly reduce the redistribution of real income that would otherwise be brought about by the incidence of income tax and surtax, the high rates of purchase tax on 'luxuries', and the operation of the social services. However, it is of little value to discuss the effect of public finance on broad economic groups designated by income or wealth in a situation such as that which has existed since the war, in which important differences in tax payments and in the receipt of social service benefits exist as between individual members of the same income group, according to their consumption habits, their access to tax-free emoluments and gains, and their receipt of subsidized goods and services such as housing.

## AN EXPENDITURE TAX

Another possible alternative to both penal rates of income tax and the present system of discriminatory outlay taxes, but one that could be designed to preserve the progressive principle, is the expenditure tax. This would operate in gradations similar to those applied to the progressive scale of income tax and surtax, but would be levied on consumers' expenditure. The latter would have to be calculated from returns made by each individual to the authorities showing his income and other receipts and his capital assets held at the beginning and end of each fiscal year. The idea of a tax on expenditure rather than on income, and designed to stimulate saving, is a clear hundred years old, but in recent years it has received support from those who believe that the standard by which economic inequality is to be assessed is inequality of consumption rather than of income or wealth. The supporters of an expenditure tax argue that 'it is only by spending, not by earning or saving, that an individual imposes a burden on the rest of the community in attaining his own ends'.*

This point of view has an obvious attraction in an economy in which a high level of saving is regarded as nationally desirable, but the expenditure tax has yet to receive widespread support as a practical proposition. The difficulty of administering a tax on expenditure remains its clearest drawback, in view of the complexity of the returns that would have to be filed and the possibilities of evasion; the transitional stage, for example, might require

* N. Kaldor, *An Expenditure Tax* (George Allen & Unwin Ltd.).

the withdrawal of all existing bank-notes to prevent people from building up secret cash hoards in anticipation of the introduction of the tax.

It is not clear whether an expenditure tax would create greater equality of consumption and stimulate saving to a very much greater extent than the present system of taxation. The advantages of having access to untaxed allowances such as expense accounts would continue; the stimulus to saving would be blunted by the heavy tax that would have to be paid when savings are finally spent or become subject to death duties. Neither is it clear that an expenditure tax would remove the deterrent to risk-taking if the fruits of enterprise could not be spent without bearing tax.

### TAXES ON CAPITAL
#### Death Duties

The case for death duties is largely political: they are necessary if inequality of opportunity is to be minimized. Their economic utility is small, in that they do not result in the restriction of consumption and therefore cannot be used to check excessive spending in times of inflation. They may even deter a man from saving and accumulating capital during his lifetime, a possibility that will depend on the rates at which death duties are levied. Those who believe that estate duties are a deterrent to saving but agree that gross inequality of inherited wealth is incompatible with equality of opportunity contend that for the estate duty should be substituted a legacy duty, which could be levied at progressive rates, but varying with the size of individual bequests, so that there would be an incentive to minimize total liability to duty by dividing one's estate between a large number of legatees.

#### Capital Levies

A capital levy is a tax on wealth usually declared as a 'once and for all' tax. This is because the prospect of a succession of capital levies would cause people to reduce their future liability to tax by dissaving heavily.

Usually the economic object of a capital levy is to mop up part of the existing stock of money when this is regarded as a cause of inflation through being excessive in relation to the nation's output of goods and services. In the United Kingdom a small capital levy—the 'special levy'—was made in 1948, and a widespread capital levy was involved in the substitution of a new currency in Germany and elsewhere after the war. Whether a capital levy will achieve its object of reducing the stock of money and checking expenditure will depend very much on whether it is really accepted by taxpayers as a non-recurrent measure. A capital levy that is not part of a general currency reform also runs the risk of tempting people to exchange domestic for foreign assets, and the outflow of capital may put pressure on the rate of exchange and thereby on the price-level. The sale of capital assets that may be necessary to secure funds for meeting the levy may disrupt the market for securities and real property unless taxpayers can be tided over by means of bank credit, but any such assistance would be inconsistent with the levy's object of reducing the quantity of money.

## A Capital Gains Tax

A capital gains tax, on the other hand, is a continuing tax. A capital gain arises when an asset is sold at a price greater than its cost of acquisition. At present capital gains are taxable only when they come within the legal concept of 'income'. The latter is interpreted by the Income Tax Acts as arising when property has been committed to a trade or to an 'adventure or concern in the nature of trade' and is then realized in the course of trading operations. A capital gain that arises from the realization of property not so committed is not income, and so is not subject to tax. A capital gain from a trading venture will be taxable even though it may not be the general line of business of a trader and is a completely isolated act. At the other extreme, Stock Exchange gains accruing to ordinary persons are not taxable.

The case for a capital gains tax (which operates in the U.S.A., for example) is usually based on three propositions. The first is that the present definition of taxable income is held by its critics to fail to assess fully the 'ability to pay' that can be said roughly to make up the foundation upon which the British tax structure rests. The supporters of a capital gains tax pay particular attention to gains arising from transactions in securities, which, they argue, are indistinguishable from profits secured in the normal course of trade. They contend that only the wealthy can protect themselves from rising prices through the purchase of ordinary shares and other forms of property whose market values tend to appreciate, if not proportionately, as retail prices increase. Secondly, the view may be expressed that as the existence of a high rate of income tax tends to reduce effort or to divert it towards transactions yielding tax-free capital gains, it would be economically more desirable to use the proceeds of a special capital gains tax to reduce the level of income tax. Thirdly, some economists believe that capital gains lead to excessive spending in times of boom.

The arguments against a capital gains tax can be listed with corresponding brevity. First, supporters of the private-enterprise system generally hold the view that risk-taking is the essence of its progress, and many of them contend that capital gains play a part as a reward for risk-bearing that it would be economically undesirable to restrict. Parallel with this attitude is the view that it is desirable to stimulate the ownership of Stock Exchange securities over a wider field in order to give people a more direct stake in British industry and enlarge the supply of industrial finance; a capital gains tax might act against this. Thirdly, *realized* gains, which are the only capital gains that would rank for tax, may bear no close connexion with personal expenditure or the redistribution of wealth involved when the prices of certain forms of property increase. Fourthly, some economists would not support the argument that capital gains are an important source of excessive spending, and many contend that the check to expenditure that its supporters look for in a capital gains tax could be achieved more directly, and with less administrative effort, by monetary and fiscal policy. Fifthly, the year-to-year proceeds of a capital gains tax can hardly be forecast with accuracy. Such a tax cannot therefore be used as a major instrument of budgetary policy to replace the more predictable yield of income tax and surtax.

To avoid being unfair, a tax on capital gains would require the allowance of capital losses to be offset against capital gains. But the result would not be to hold the balance evenly as between capital gains and losses, for whereas a gain would be chargeable even if there were no realized loss, a loss would not be allowable except so far as there was a realized gain; special provisions would be required to cover this case. More generally, a capital gains tax would penalize the investor who showed a profit on the security or asset he realized but a loss on others he did not, as against a man in the opposite situation. The reinvestment of a capital gain, moreover, may not constitute a 'profit' in any true sense. This is clear in the case of a man who has to pay a high price for a house after having sold his old house at the same high market value; a tax on the realized profit on the sale of the old house would amount to a tax on his real capital. A similar problem arises in regard to a person who, after a fall in the rate of interest, takes a capital profit; he may be obliged to accept a lower yield on his money and may therefore need to reinvest most of his gain to maintain the same nominal income.

To allow for these and other matters an equitable system of taxing capital gains would be administratively costly, and the net yield might be low. If high rates are imposed there will be a tendency for investors to minimize the weight of the tax, e.g. by delaying realization if reduced rates of tax, as in the U.S.A., apply to long-term gains, and by marrying gains with losses in any particular year of charge. A capital gains tax would also reduce the yield of estate duty and perhaps that of the stamp duty at present levied on security transactions. Politically, it would probably be thought necessary to exempt realized profits on transactions in houses when purchase and resale take place outside some minimum period of time. The Inland Revenue authorities suggested in their evidence to the Royal Commission on Taxation that the net long-term yield of a capital gains tax in this country would probably not exceed £50 million a year even if all realizations were treated as occasions for a charge to tax, including death, gifts and an owner-occupier's sale of his house. This estimate assumed that the charge would be at income-tax and surtax rates and that there would be no persistent inflation. It was made before the marked rise in security prices between 1952 and 1955, but even if the net long-term yield turned out to be twice or three times this figure, it would still be very small by comparison with the £2,200 million raised in income tax and surtax in 1957–8.

Finally, a capital gains tax might have the effect of narrowing the market in stock exchange securities, by deterring holders from realizing their profits.

z

# CHAPTER 26

# EXCHEQUER FINANCE AND THE NATIONAL DEBT

It is useful to think of the Exchequer's operations in two parts, those of its current and its capital accounts, corresponding only approximately to the above- and below-the-line categories adopted in the standard financial statements. The capital accounts of the Exchequer will generally show a deficit, with capital outlays exceeding the repayment of past loans made by the Exchequer. But this deficit will not have to be met by borrowing, to the extent that the Exchequer's current account is in surplus, which can be applied to the finance of the deficit on capital account. It is thus only the Exchequer's *overall* deficit, if any, that will have to be financed by funds raised from extra-budgetary operations.

The Exchequer can finance an overall deficit through funds obtained from a current surplus in the National Insurance Scheme, through foreign exchange operations, or through borrowing from the public, the banks or the Bank of England.

## NATIONAL INSURANCE FUNDS

A surplus in the National Insurance Funds provides the Exchequer with finance. The National Insurance Funds are invested by the National Debt Office under the authority of the National Debt Commissioners, a body appointed by statute to dispose of funds accruing for the reduction of the national debt. The Commissioners include the Chancellor of the Exchequer and the Governor and Deputy Governor of the Bank of England, who form a quorum, but one which has not met since 1860.

The National Insurance Funds are invested by the National Debt Office, with the advice of the Ministry of National Insurance as to the purposes of the Funds, in securities deemed most suitable for these purposes, having regard to the need for the respective claims of liquidity and income. The general direction of official monetary policy is followed by the National Debt Office in investing these funds only if consistent with the purposes for which they were set up, so that they are not used to finance the Exchequer deficit as a matter of course. However, if suitable securities are on offer from the Exchequer they can be purchased for the National Insurance Funds. The investment of various other trust funds undertaken by the National Debt Office is also subject to the same constraints, whereas the investment of the funds of the Post Office and Trustee Savings Banks, being guaranteed as to capital and income by the Exchequer, is not so restricted. It is possible, however, that in practice the National Insurance and other trust funds may be used to purchase suitable securities from the 'guaranteed' funds, the proceeds of which can then be passed over to the Exchequer; unfortunately, little is known about the precise policy followed.*

### FOREIGN EXCHANGE OPERATIONS

The Exchequer obtains funds in sterling through the country's foreign exchange operations when the country's central reserves of gold and foreign currency are run down through an excess of imports over exports or a net outflow on foreign capital account. When, for example, a British trader imports goods from overseas and has to meet his bill in foreign currency he will have to pay the British authorities for the latter in sterling, in the form of a deposit with a United Kingdom bank. The process is similar if a British resident wishes to invest abroad or if foreigners decide to withdraw funds from this country held in the form of bank deposits. An increase in our gold and dollar reserves, except that resulting from a foreign loan to the British government, requires the Exchequer to pay out an equivalent amount of sterling.

### BORROWING FROM THE PUBLIC

In the simplest case the government may borrow directly from the public by selling existing securities to the public or by issuing new securities for public subscription. The latter can be divided into securities offered in a specific amount on a particular occasion and those, like National Savings Certificates, Defence Bonds and Tax Reserve Certificates, which can be purchased by the public at any time on stated terms. The increase in Post Office savings deposits is also a form of Exchequer borrowing from the public;

---

* This section is based on evidence given before the Committee of Public Accounts in 1954. (*First, Second and Third Reports from the Committee of Public Accounts. Session* 1951–52 (H.M.S.O., London, 1952), paras. 5697–5821.)

the assets of this institution are invested in government securities in the name of the National Debt Commissioners.

When the government's spending is financed through borrowing from the public, the latter as a whole releases money in exchange for securities purchased from the Exchequer, but this money is returned to the public as the government spends the proceeds of its loans, so that in the end the finance of the Exchequer's deficit will have increased the security holdings of the public but will have left its total holding of money unchanged. It is this important fact that distinguishes the economic effects of the finance of the Exchequer deficit through securities sold to the public from those of government spending financed by borrowing from the banks and the Bank of England.

### BORROWING FROM THE BANKS

#### *Treasury Bills*

The main channel through which the Exchequer borrows from the banks is by the issue of Treasury bills. Each Friday the Treasury offers a stated amount of these securities for sale by tender. Treasury bills have a life of 91 days* but carry no stated rate of interest; instead, would-be purchasers bid for a quantity of bills at the weekly tender at a discount, that is at a price below the redemption price of, say, £5,000, which is the smallest denomination that can be obtained at the tender. Part of the week's offer of Treasury bills may be allotted to the Bank of England acting on behalf of clients such as the central banks of other Commonwealth countries. The rest of the week's offer goes to the highest bidders.

At the weekly tender bids will be made by discount houses, overseas banks with branches in London, and United Kingdom banks tendering on behalf of clients such as large industrial companies. United Kingdom banks have not tendered directly for the Treasury bills they wish to hold since 1934; instead they purchase, or lend against, Treasury bills acquired in the first instance by the discount houses, but as the latter are essentially intermediaries dependent on bank finance, we can think of the major part of the bills acquired by the discount houses as loans made to the Exchequer by British banks.

* Since 1955, 63-day bills have also been offered at certain times.

The issue of bills through the weekly tender must be distinguished from the sale of Treasury bills to government departments, including those made to the Bank of England on its own account. These are usually described as 'tap' bills, and their rate of discount, if any, is not known.

An alternative method of borrowing from the banks is for the government to offer longer-term securities for sale, in the hope that their terms are sufficiently attractive for them to be purchased by the banks. Although these alternatives differ in several respects as to their effect on the operations of the banks they have one important consequence in common. When the Exchequer borrows money from the banks in order to finance its deficit, the spending of that money by government departments puts money into the hands of the public that was not there in the first instance.

### BORROWING FROM THE BANK OF ENGLAND

The only alternatives once open to a monarch or a government that could not meet expenditure by taxation or borrowing were to print more notes and, before the use of bank-notes, to debase the coinage, that is mint more coins from a given quantity of gold or silver. Both would increase the number of money units in circulation and raise the community's spendable money income in relation to its real output, thus causing prices to rise. Often this rise in prices would in turn enlarge the deficit of the spendthrift government, forcing it to speed up the operations of the printing-press, and so on. The cumulative effect of such a process on the price-level could lead ultimately to a general financial crisis.

Nowadays the role of the printing-press has been replaced by that of a deposit with the central bank, acceptable to the commercial banks in discharge of the government's debts. In the modern monetary system the effect is similar. If the government finances its spending by drawing cheques on the central bank to pay wages and salaries, etc., the immediate consequence is to increase the deposits held by the public with the commercial banks when the public pay these cheques into their own accounts.

### THE NATIONAL DEBT

#### *The Economic Role of Budget Deficits and Surpluses*

The Victorian prescription for economic health was to recommend the government to spend and borrow as little as possible.

One reason why this has been discarded is that government expenditure may be necessary to cure unemployment. Idle men and idle tools can be put to work if someone is prepared to pay for what they can but do not produce. The State can do just this; for it can place contracts for new roads and schools, and it can create a demand for goods and services at one remove, by paying higher social service benefits to people who in turn would use them to buy food and clothing. But it follows that if this government expenditure is to cause a *net* increase in the flow of purchasing power, it should not, as a rule, be financed by taxation, for taxation generally depletes the income that the public could otherwise spend on unemployed resources. The government can spend in excess of its tax receipts and finance its deficit by borrowing from the banks or the Bank of England. A Budget deficit is also expansionist, if less so, if financed by loans raised from the public. It is true that this method merely takes money out of the pockets (or, more accurately, out of the bank accounts) of the public and puts the same amount back again; but the same pockets are not involved. For most of the money used to subscribe to the issue of government securities would otherwise have been held idle, whereas in the hands of the Exchequer it will be used to purchase goods and services or, as transfer payments, passed to others who will do the spending.

Budget deficits (sometimes described as unbalanced Budgets or deficit spending) can therefore be powerful weapons against unemployment, and conversely Budget surpluses can play their part in preventing inflation.

### Attitudes Towards the National Debt

Budget deficits on capital account incurred in the acquisition by the State of real capital assets such as roads and buildings have usually been tolerated as a proper subject for borrowing, but it was once widely thought that Budget deficits on current account were undesirable just *because* they increased the national debt, that is the debt incurred by the Exchequer, for the national debt was in some way regarded as a measure of national insolvency. It is true that government, or for that matter private, loans raised abroad, if considered apart from the uses to which they are put, place a real burden on the economy as a whole, for the community has to set aside resources to provide exports that will earn the foreign currency required for meeting interest and capital liabilities. But as far as the domestic debt is concerned, that is the overwhelming proportion of the debt which is contracted by the Exchequer with British citizens, this identification of national debt with national insolvency can be seen to be misplaced. For this internal national debt merely represents the liability of one section of the community—the Exchequer—to another, to the banks and the public.

The anxiety felt by previous generations towards an increase in the national debt was due partly to the failure to appreciate that, in the event of unemployment, Budget deficits could lead to a rise in production and thus increase the real wealth of the community. The growth of the national income along with the national debt would hold down the *proportion* of Exchequer revenue required to meet interest charges, and in years of boom a Budget surplus could be used to redeem debt incurred in the slump. Nevertheless, although they are merely transfer payments, the interest charges on the national debt have to be met out of Exchequer receipts, and, if after a long succession of deficits interest charges necessitate a high level of taxation, it is through the economic undesirability of high taxation that the main disadvantages of a large national debt are felt.

There may, however, be some disadvantage in having too small a national debt, in that the existence of a sizeable stock of government securities, spread over a wide range of redemption dates, offers outlets for saving free from the risk of default and suitable for a variety of investors. If the national debt is too small the development of an active capital market may be hindered.

### The Growth of the National Debt

The national debt of the United Kingdom can hardly be said to fall short of this requirement. It was born as the twin of the Bank of England in the finance of the war of William III against France. In 1697 it totalled £15 million, and since then its upwards bounds have been largely the result of war finance. The main alternative to heavy government borrowing in wartime is a level of outlay taxes so high as to cause an intolerable rise in prices or rates of income tax so drastic as to cripple the working effort of the people. Even in the limited wars before the twentieth century the difficulty of finding fresh taxable capacity made government borrowing inevitable. By the end of the war against Louis XIV in 1714 the national debt had more than doubled to £36 million, and the Napoleonic wars a century later caused an even sharper rise from £240 million to £830 million. The Victorian policy of budgeting for a small surplus succeeded in reducing the debt over the following century, and at the end of 1914 its total was only £650 million, equivalent to about one-quarter of the national income.

With its formidable financial requirements the First World War involved a tenfold rise in the debt to almost £7,500 million at the end of 1919, and the Second took it from £8,000 million to £22,500 million at the end of 1945. Nationalization and a series of overall Budget deficits have since carried the national debt to £27,000 million, equivalent to more than one-and-a-half times the national income.

Of this total, rather more than £2,000 million is payable in foreign currencies, representing mainly the loans received from the U.S.A. and Canada after the war. The remainder of the debt is described in the official accounts as 'internal debt', although part of it is owed to overseas holders.

Of the total of £27,000 million, about £3,800 million consists of the 'funded' debt, made up of those securities with no fixed redemption date; 2½ per cent Treasury Stock, for example, is redeemable '1975 or after'. Of the remaining 'unfunded' debt of £23,000 million, the 'floating' debt amounted to £4,900 million at 31 March 1958, consisting of Treasury bills to the extent of £4,600 million; temporary Ways and Means advances made to the Exchequer by government departments, including, to a small extent, the Bank of England, constitute the rest of the floating debt.

The increase in the total debt has naturally been accompanied by a rise in its annual interest cost, from £233 million in 1938 to approximately £750 million in 1957. But as a proportion of the national income this represents a fall from 4¼ to 4 per cent; as a proportion of government current revenue the fall has been even sharper—from 22 to 13 per cent—for government revenue has increased more than the national income. Rising prices and incomes help to hold down the burden of national debt interest, but rising interest rates increase the charge on new debt, including that created to redeem maturing securities. In this respect the debt is more vulnerable to high interest rates than in 1938, for a larger proportion consists of short-term debt. The floating debt, for example, has risen from 12 to 18 per cent of the total (in 1958), and other debt that must be redeemed within five years has increased in importance from 1½ per cent in 1938 to approximately 18 per cent. This change in the structure of the debt, as well as the increase in its size, has given the Exchequer an incentive to keep interest rates low, despite the fact that part of the interest paid out by the Exchequer returns to it by way of income tax and surtax.

# CHAPTER 27

# LOCAL GOVERNMENT FINANCE

The traditional case for local rather than central government is that the needs and conditions of localities vary and that the close contact between citizens and government deemed to exist in the local councils is a political virtue. The forces operating against local autonomy, on the other hand, have been the development of urban industrial society, the desire by Parliament to see certain services provided for on a minimum or standard scale throughout the whole country, and the experience that social services can be centrally financed and administered provided that there is some decentralization of operation to bodies in touch with local needs.

In the twentieth century the rising tide of central government finance has reduced the relative importance of local authority expenditure. Before the National Insurance Act of 1911 the expenditure of the local authorities amounted to just over half of all government spending. With the diversion of the finance of the growing social services from local to central government and the loss to the nationalized corporations of local trading services such as gas and electricity, the share of current government expenditure undertaken by the local authorities fell from between one-third and two-fifths between the wars, varying mainly with the burden of unemployment relief, to only one-sixth in 1957. About two-fifths of local authority current expenditure in recent years has been devoted to education and one-third to basic and other local services, including the police.

Inevitably these changes have been reflected in the finance of local authorities. The obligation placed upon the local authorities by Parliament to undertake certain 'onerous' local services led to the provision of grants-in-aid by the Exchequer in the first half of the nineteenth century, and these have been steadily increased as a proportion of local authority current receipts from about one-tenth at the beginning of the twentieth century to nearly two-fifths just before the Second World War and just over two-fifths in more recent years. This growing dependence on Exchequer funds is to be explained by the desire of Parliament for minimum or standard services on a countrywide scale. 'Specific' Exchequer grants promote local authority spending on designated services, and 'general' grants are deemed to assist authorities with sub-average resources.

The local rate can be traced back to the twelfth century and became universal in England and Wales on the introduction of the Elizabethan Poor Law. The local rate is a tax levied on each 'heriditament' of land and buildings upon it, in the form of an amount 'in the pound' of rateable value, the poundage varying from council to council. Rateable values are traditionally intended to be equivalent, subject to certain deductions, to the yearly rent that would prevail in a free market if the tenant paid rates and taxes and the landlord the cost of insurance and repairs. Since 1929 agricultural land and buildings have been entirely exempt and industrial premises have been relieved of three-quarters of the liability for rates.

### Local Rates as Instruments of Finance

Rates provide roughly two-fifths of local authority current receipts. The utility of the rate as an instrument of local authority finance lies in its locally defined incidence and in the fact that the relative stability of rateable values protects the revenue against conditions of depressed trade; furthermore, the standard of rateable values was once held to approximate to the consumption of basic services by the occupiers of different properties. On the other hand, one disadvantage of the rate is that the very stability of rateable values means that receipts from rates do not increase automatically in times of rising incomes and prices, so that the improvement in the quality and the increase in the cost of local services from year to year has necessitated an almost continuous rise in rate poundage. Local councils are politically highly sensitive to this disadvantage. A second disadvantage is that it is doubtful whether services consumed now correspond closely to the relative scale of rateable values, in view of the varied nature of local authority expenditure. Thirdly, rates tend to be regressive, especially as against large families; although their weight on the poor can be easily exaggerated and should be regarded in the broad perspective of taxes and benefits as a whole. Lastly, the incidence of rates has been distorted by the insufficient frequency of changes in rating valuations and by the effect of rent control, as well as by the relief given to industry and agriculture. In many other countries local authorities levy income and outlay taxes to replace or supplement local rates.

### Rating Valuations

Until 1948 local authorities were responsible for fixing rateable values. However, since 1929, when certain Exchequer grants came to be related to rateable value per head of population as the criterion of regional wealth, the disadvantages of varying and inconsistent valuing standards have become a national concern. The Local Government Act of 1948 transferred the responsibility for valuation to the Inland Revenue authorities, and a new countrywide valuation, the first for over twenty years, was completed in 1956. For a number of reasons, especially the uneven impact of rent control, current market rents could not be used as the standard for domestic property, for which Parliament fixed instead the temporary but arbitrary standard of the 1939 level of free market rents. The valuation of 1961 is to revalue houses and flats on the basis of prevailing market rents.

Apart from generally raising rateable values the main effect of the 1956 valuation was to reduce the share of residential property from 60 to 50 per cent of the total and to raise that of shops and commercial property. Owing to complaints raised by shopkeepers and commercial interests the government agreed to give shops and commercial premises a 20 per cent relief.

Under the Rating and Valuation (Apportionment) Act of 1928 industrial premises were derated to the extent of 75 per cent and agricultural property was completely derated, in order to mitigate the effects of the trade depression. The prosperity enjoyed by industry and agriculture since the war has considerably weakened this justification for derating, and in 1957 the government announced its intention of raising the assessment of industrial premises from 25 to 50 per cent at some unspecified date.[10] To abolish the derating of industry altogether would add about £120 million, or roughly one-fifth, to rateable values but would provide little assistance to the rural authorities that are generally the most deficient in rating resources, and the Exchequer would lose part of the gain in taxation accruing to the authorities that did benefit, as rates count as an allowance against income tax payable by companies.

## Exchequer Grants

Specific grants, which are given for designated services only, may be unit grants, such as fixed subsidies for each house built or for each child of school age, or percentage grants, in which an agreed proportion of local government expenditure on improved services is provided by the Exchequer, 50 per cent in the case of education, for example. A third type of specific grant is the special grant paid from time to time for some particular purpose such as flood relief. Specific grants account for over four-fifths of the assistance provided by the Exchequer to local revenues. Specific grants were relatively most important before the introduction of the 'block' grant in 1929, when they amounted to nearly 95 per cent of all Exchequer grants, their growth since the beginning of the century being due to the expansion of services encouraged by the central government and to the fact that percentage grants are a powerful inducement for local authorities to undertake the services concerned. However, the percentage grant suffers from the disadvantage that only the richer authorities may be in a position to use it fully.

In 1929 the provision of general grants was extended in the form of the block grant (the National Exchequer Contribution) aimed mainly at compensating for the loss of revenue due to the derating of industrial property. It was also intended, if to a smaller extent, to assist the poorer local authorities; these suffered a cumulative disadvantage in that their low rateable value per head of population necessitated a high poundage (particularly when their burden of unemployment or poor relief was relatively high). A high rate of poundage and inadequate local services in poor areas tended to drive away businesses and individuals from these districts, depressing rateable values still further. The block grant was not a great success as an equalizing instrument, but it was responsible for raising the share of the general grant in the following decade. Since the war, on the other hand, the relative decline in the general grant has continued, being the counterpart of the rise of the specific grant on education necessitated by the expansion of the school population and the desire for higher education standards. In recent years, however, this swing of the pendulum back to the specific grant has come in for some criticism on the grounds that percentage grants tend to make local authorities extravagant and, in thereby necessitating close central government control, reduce still further the autonomy of local councils.

In 1948 the Local Government Act replaced the block grant by 'equalization' grants. These are paid to county and county borough councils in England and Wales if their rateable value per head of population, after certain adjustments, is less than the average, the adjustments being based on the number of children under fifteen and, in the case of county councils, on sparsity of population in relation to road mileage. Equalization grants make no attempt to rob the richer authorities to pay the poor and are not intended to equalize rate poundage.

## LOCAL AUTHORITY BORROWING

In the post-war years the erection of houses for letting has accounted for the bulk—about three-fifths—of local authority capital expenditure, with schools taking a further 15 per cent. Only a very small part of the total has been financed by Exchequer capital grants. The current surpluses of the local authorities themselves, including depreciation, seem to have covered about one-fifth of the total in recent years, compared with one-half in 1938, so that the major element in the finance of local government capital outlays has had to take the form of borrowing.

Local authorities are empowered to raise loans, on the security of their local revenue as a whole, for certain items of capital expenditure, such as the acquisition of land and the erection of works and buildings. Before the war the main form of borrowing was by the issue of long-term securities on the Stock Exchange. Authorities too small to resort to this channel borrowed from the Public Works Loans Board, a body appointed by the Crown and financed, since 1946, out of the current revenue of the central Exchequer. The Local Authorities Loans Act of 1945, however, prohibited borrowing from any source other than the Board, with certain minor exceptions; the purpose of this restriction was mainly to prevent an excessive demand for capital and to clear the market for government issues. This restriction was modified first at the end of 1952 and again in October 1955, when the government announced that no further loans would be granted by the Board unless councils could satisfy the Board of their inability to raise loans elsewhere. The object of this reversal of policy was to bring local authority expenditure under the discipline of market rates of interest and to ease the burden on the Exchequer. Before this change about two-thirds of the outstanding gross debt of local authorities in England and Wales had been contracted with the Board, against less than one-fifth at the outbreak of war.

In Scotland all, and in England and Wales most, local authority stocks rank as trustee securities. Issues of stock by local authorities on the Stock Exchange, which accounted for nearly two-fifths of outstanding debt in 1940 but only one-eighth in 1956, enable large amounts to be raised at a time, but they are suitable only for the larger authorities. An alternative source of finance is the mortgage market. Local authority mortgages in England and Wales are trustee securities if the authority is empowered to issue housing bonds; in Scotland all local authority mortgages are trustee securities. Before the war, borrowing by mortgage, usually arranged as private placings through specialist mortgage brokers, was a common method of finance, accounting for nearly two-fifths of all local authority debt in 1940. By 1945 their share had fallen to only 16 per cent, but experienced some recovery after the change in the regulations in 1955. Local authority mortgages before the war were usually of three to five years' duration, but from 1947 to 1956 could not be issued for a term of less than seven years. The shorter-dated mortgages are often taken up by industrial companies, and those between, say, seven and ten years are suitable for building societies and Trustee Savings Banks.

The interest charges paid by local authorities in 1956 were equivalent to one-third of their revenue from rates. Councils are sensitive to high interest charges on long-term loans because they find them awkward to pass on as a rise in rates; local authorities will, if possible, attempt to avoid committing themselves to high interest rates on long-term loans by borrowing 'short', in the hope of re-financing temporary borrowing on more favourable terms at a later stage. In England and Wales temporary borrowing is permitted under the Local Government Act, 1933, to finance capital expenditure pending the raising of a loan; in Scotland it may be adopted as a renewable and thus permanent form of finance if not exceeding 15 per cent of total borrowing. Both before the war and after it, because of low interest rates in the former period and government policy in the decade after 1945, temporary borrowing provided only a small part of local authority funds, but its importance increased noticeably when interest rates rose in 1955–6. Temporary loans are obtained from the banks, the surpluses of other local authorities, and from the money market, in which councils borrow in the form of bills or deposits for fixed periods. This market is fed by the liquid resources of financial concerns, industrial companies and foreign institutions, as well as the surpluses of the local authorities themselves; interest rates are influenced by conditions in the larger money market consisting of the banks and discount houses. Councils may also seek to attract deposits for short periods by advertising to the public.

# PART IV

# THE BANKING SYSTEM
# AND MONETARY POLICY

# CHAPTER 28

# THE BANKING SYSTEM OUTLINED— COMMERCIAL BANK ASSETS AND LIABILITIES

## THE DEVELOPMENT OF BANKING

The great institutions that we know today as banks have their origin in the goldsmiths of the Middle Ages, when their strong-rooms became a convenient place in which the money-bags of traders could be deposited for safety; from this practice derives the description 'deposit' for the present-day banker's liability to his customers. As from day to day old deposits were withdrawn and new ones made, a certain amount of gold always remained in the goldsmiths' care, and the crucial step from what has been described as 'cloakroom' banking was taken when the goldsmiths turned to lending some of this residue. Eventually the goldsmiths found it profitable to offer interest to attract deposits.

What was lent could with safety consist only of part of the goldsmith's 'idle' stock; for there could be no certainty as to just how the balance of deposits and withdrawals would run from day to day. Prudence demanded that loans should be made only for short periods and on some form of security that could be sold for gold without much difficulty. Even so, this business would be jeopardized if there were a flood of simultaneous withdrawals that the goldsmith could not meet by pressing his debtors or by drawing on his own wealth.

The receipt given by the goldsmith in acknowledgement of deposits came to be used to settle debts, entitling the new holder of the document to make the actual withdrawal of coin if required, and so we have the bank-note, a statement of indebtedness of the banker to his customer used as money. Among people who trusted the ability of the goldsmith whose signature it bore to meet his liabilities, the receipt could be used as a means of payment. To traders this practice offered convenience; but of greater significance was the fact that the use of his receipt in this way had the result of leaving a larger stock of gold in the goldsmith's vaults, hence increasing what could be safely lent. By the end of the seventeenth century this practice was growing appreciably, and banking had ceased to be a side-line of the goldsmiths.

It was also in the seventeenth century that the cheque originated, in the form of an order made by a depositor to his bank to pay part of his deposit to someone else. As a result a bank could create a 'deposit' in the form of an entry in its ledger, merely by making a loan to a trader on which cheques could be drawn. This added further elasticity to the credit structure, limited, for the prudent banker, by the additional claim on his reserve of gold.

From these beginnings the modern banking system has developed, and the elementary lessons of sound banking remain as then: that at all times a bank must match some minimum proportion of its liabilities in a form that is acceptable, or can be made so without question, to its depositors. In short, viable banking must balance income with liquidity, and the history of banking in most countries is marked by bank failures due to inadequate liquidity.

Without the confidence of his depositors a banker cannot function. This might be of limited significance were it not for the fact that a banking failure is not a matter private to the bank and its customers. When the claims of depositors cannot be met by a bank they are valueless for any purpose, and the worthlessness of an insolvent bank's notes would reduce the ability of their holders to meet *their* debts to others, and so on. If the bank were important the spread of insolvency, or the fear of insolvency, would radiate doubt about the state of other traders and other banks. In the process goods would be unloaded on the market to obtain gold and prices would tumble, causing losses to other traders and destroying the backing of other debts. A run on otherwise sound banks could spread ruin, although, apart from the collapse of the pyramid of credit, nothing substantial in the economy might have altered.

Over the past two centuries the lesson has been painfully learned that in the world of credit trust is indivisible, and the foundations of credit have been strengthened so as to make it plain that this type of crisis can be overcome; in the process the very possibility of crisis has dwindled, and the character of money has undergone its ultimate transformation from a claim to gold, itself valuable as a commodity, to 'pure' money, a claim to nothing more valuable than the claim itself.

## THE BANK OF ENGLAND

The base upon which the financial structure of the country rests is the Bank of England. 'The Bank', as it is often described, was founded in 1694 by a number of City merchants to raise funds for the war of William III against France. By virtue of the privileges awarded to it in return under its Charter and the skill and caution with which it was managed, it soon earned the respect and the custom of the growing mercantile community; the acceptability of its notes spread accordingly. 'As safe as the Bank of England' meant that its notes were 'as good as gold', and their status as a widely recognized means of payment was formally acknowledged when the Bank's notes became legal tender in 1833, giving paper money the same legal standing as gold coin for the first time. In 1844 the Bank Charter Act prohibited new issues of notes by all other banks and provided for the replacement of other bank-notes by those of the Bank of England whenever a bank closed down or, as proved increasingly frequent in the second half of the century, amalgamated with another. In Britain today the only notes issued outside the Bank of England are those of certain Scottish banks, a small proportio. of the total.

Because of its legal privileges, its reputation, and therefore its growing size, the role of the Bank of England within the financial system was already changing by the time its notes became legal tender. It had become the banker to the other London banks and to the bill brokers, or discount houses as they are known today, as well as to the Exchequer. The other banks kept a balance with the Bank of England as their ultimate reserve against their deposit liabilities, and when the demand for Bank of England notes or for gold threatened to outrun the reserves of the banks, the latter, together with bill brokers and merchants, could turn only to the Bank of England for the cash needed to meet their liabilities. The Bank of England, as the nineteenth century unfolded, was gradually obliged to assume the responsibility of supporting the liquidity of the banks, discount houses and merchants, that is their ultimate ability to meet their commitments in gold or Bank of England notes, in order to prevent periods of strain from developing into crises threatening the viability of the whole financial structure.

The Bank of England gradually recognized its position as the ultimate source of support for the financial and mercantile community whenever the demands of internal trade, or the need to settle our foreign trade debts, or a sudden wave of distrust in the pyramid of credit, threatened to exhaust the reserves of the banks.

Until 1914, apart from the years 1797–1821, the Bank of England was legally obliged to redeem its notes on demand in gold coin, and the extent to which the Bank could print notes in excess of its gold holdings was strictly limited after 1844. Because, in the absence of special government dispensation, the extent of the Bank's note-issuing power was limited by its gold reserve, the latter formed the effective basis of the money supply, and the available reserve of notes, backed by gold, that remained in the Bank of England's vaults became the critical element of monetary regulation. The resources of the Bank of England came to be made available at times of strain by the Bank's allowing certain of its customers, private traders and discount houses—the banks, by calling in their own loans to the discount houses, preferred to force the latter to seek recourse to the Bank of England rather than do so themselves directly—to rediscount bills of exchange complying with its requirements of eligibility, thus acting as 'lender of last resort' to the system as a whole. In order to prevent such demands from exhausting its note-issuing power it developed the practice of charging a penal rate of interest, *Bank rate*, aimed at checking such transactions.

The development of this role greatly strengthened the credit structure; it also fashioned the means whereby the central control of the financial mechanism became possible, for ultimately the volume of notes and deposits that could be created was limited by the willingness of the Bank of England, as reflected in the level of Bank rate, to make available its uncommitted gold reserve, that part of its gold holdings not earmarked as backing for its notes already in circulation.

For the third time in its history, the Bank of England was forced to repudiate the obligation to redeem notes in gold in 1931, the two previous occasions being in 1914 and 1797, both in the circumstances of war. The gold standard has not been restored, but the Bank is still the base of the financial pyramid, and the quantity of money is still within its control.

## THE COMMERCIAL BANKS TODAY

The business of the commercial bank is still to balance liquidity with profit, but it now also embraces a wide variety of activities, from clearing our monetary claims on one another to performing the duties of executor and trustee. These ancillary services have come to occupy an increasingly important part in the business of the commercial bank, for the use of the bank account as a monetary 'cloak-room' and medium of payment has spread.

The process of amalgamation, which gathered pace in the second half of the nineteenth century, has greatly reduced the number of banks at the same time as the number of branches has increased. The latter now total 12,000, of which nearly 9,000 are owned by the 'Big Five'—Barclays, Lloyds, Midland, National Provincial, and Westminster—which also account for nearly four-fifths of total commercial bank deposits in the United Kingdom. In addition to the Big Five, a further six banks, one of which is affiliated to National Provincial, use the London Bankers' Clearing House. Three of the seven Scottish banks are also affiliated with members of the Big Five, as are the two main Northern Ireland banks. Concern lest the amalgamation movement should lead ultimately to financial monopoly was the reason for the recommendation made by a committee of inquiry in 1918 that no further bank amalgamations should take place without the consent of the Treasury and the Board of Trade.

## BANKERS' CLEARING ORGANIZATIONS

The use of the cheque has been made considerably less costly by the development of the bankers' clearing organizations. The result of my drawing a cheque on my account, let us say, with the Midland Bank and sending it to my tailor, who banks with Lloyds, is to reduce my deposit at the Midland, increase my tailor's balance with Lloyds and to give Lloyds a claim on the Midland to the same amount. On the same day my tailor may draw a cheque in favour of a cloth merchant who banks with the Midland, thus giving rise to a counter-claim by the Midland on Lloyds. The stamp-duty figures indicate that approximately 800 million cheques are issued every year, and the thousands of claims of one bank on another that arise every day are set off against claims in the opposite direction through the mechanism of the clearing organizations, so that only the daily *net* balance need be settled. This settlement of inter-bank claims takes the form of a transfer from one bank to another of part of the deposits that all the 'clearing banks' hold with the Bank of England. Clearing organizations exist in the main provincial towns and, on a less formal basis, in other large towns; but the most important is the London Bankers' Clearing House.

### HOW BANK DEPOSITS ARISE

A bank deposit is merely the liability of a bank to its customers, an entry in its books recording the right of the holder of the deposit to payment in currency or to transfer the deposit—and thus this entitlement to currency—to somebody else through the medium of the cheque, which is merely an order to a bank to make these payments. The main ways in which commercial bank deposits arise can be enumerated briefly.

(i) A bank will credit my account, that is increase my deposit, with any valid cheques drawn on other accounts that I may pay in. When these are drawn on accounts held with other commercial banks in the United Kingdom this merely redistributes the total of deposits between different holders, leaving their total unchanged. There is one important exception to this concerning the use of overdrafts, which is examined separately in category (v).

(ii) When I pay in to my account in this country a cheque drawn on a bank account overseas my deposit is increased, and this represents a net addition to commercial bank deposits in Britain.

(iii) When a cheque drawn on an account with the Bank of England is paid into the account held by a member of the public with a commercial bank, this, too, represents a net increase in commercial bank deposits held by the public; the result is also to increase the balance of the commercial bank held at the Bank of England. Thus payments by cheque to the public by government departments on their account with the Bank of England involve an increase in commercial bank deposits. In the context of banking operations the 'public', while embracing corporations as well as individuals, excludes the commercial banks themselves, the discount houses and all holders of deposits at the Bank of England.

(iv) A bank will increase my deposit if I pay in notes and coin of exchange.

(v) Deposits expand when banks make loans to their customers. These are either straightforward loans or overdrafts. A bank will enter the full amount of a straightforward loan to its customer's credit at the time it is made, causing an immediate increase in the deposit of the customer concerned. In the case of an overdraft the banker merely agrees to allow his customer to draw cheques in excess of his credit balance up to a certain limit. No deposit is created until the credit balance, if any, has been exhausted; further cheques are then drawn in favour of another account— perhaps at another bank—which is then credited with the amount concerned, while the bank which has given the overdraft merely notes that the borrower is in debt to it to this sum.

(vi) Commercial bank deposits are increased when a bank purchases goods, services or securities from the public, paying by entering the sum involved to the credit of the seller if he is already one of its customers or by a cheque drawn on itself if he has an account with another bank. In monetary analysis it is the purchase of securities by the banks that is of importance in this category.

Transactions in the opposite direction reduce deposits. We can summarize these transactions by saying that the deposits of the commercial banks as a whole will be increased by a net flow of payments by government departments to the public; by the receipt by the public of drafts on bank deposits overseas; through the transfer of notes and coin from the public to the banks; by loans granted by the banks to the public; and by the purchase of securities by the banks from the public. Three factors deserve special attention. The first and fundamental point is that deposits can only arise when banks acquire, or in one case create, assets to an equal amount; in the processes outlined above, these assets are notes and coin, balances with the Bank of England, securities and loans. For the sake of simplicity deposits held by one commercial bank with another have been ignored; these are unimportant except in the field of international payments. Assets of little interest to monetary analysis, such as bank premises, can also be disregarded. The second is that only two classes of transactions come under the direct control of the banks, in that whether banks grant loans or purchase securities are matters for them to decide. In the case of other changes in deposits the banks are passive, except in so far as they can influence the proportion of their wealth that the public choose to hold in the form of bank deposits rather than in notes and coin by altering the rate of interest paid on deposits or by improving the convenience of banking facilities. The third point is that the two classes of asset over which the banks exercise direct control yield interest, whereas notes and coin, or deposits with the Bank of England, do not.

### COMMERCIAL BANK ASSETS AND LIABILITIES

Table 20 refers to the eleven banks that are members of the London Clearing House but does not include the whole of their

TABLE 20. *Assets and Liabilities of the London Clearing Banks. Average of Monthly Figures 1957*

|  | £ million | % of total deposits |
|---|---|---|
| LIABILITIES—DEPOSITS | | |
| Current accounts | 3,972 | 61·8 |
| Deposits and other accounts | 2,460 | 38·2 |
| TOTAL DEPOSITS | 6,432 | 100·0 |
| *Less* Cheques in course of collection, etc. | 295 | 4·6 |
|  | 6,137 | 95·4 |
| ASSETS | | |
| Coin, notes and balances with Bank of England | 526 | 8·2 |
| Money at call and short notice | 439 | 6·8 |
| Treasury bills discounted | 1,143 | 17·8 |
| Other bills discounted | 148 | 2·3 |
| Total 'Liquid Assets' | 2,256 | 35·1 |
| Investments | 2,008 | 31·2 |
| Advances to customers | 1,952 | 30·3 |
| TOTAL OF ASSETS LISTED ABOVE | 6,216 | 96·6 |

assets and liabilities; it omits, for example, the book value of their premises, capital and reserves, in order to concentrate on the main items of monetary importance. The table shows how deposits are matched by the assets acquired.

### *Liabilities*

*Current accounts* are repayable on demand, can be transferred by cheque but, since the war, carry no interest. *Deposit and other accounts* consist mainly of deposit accounts repayable only if notice of withdrawal, usually seven days, is given. For this slight inconvenience their holders receive some compensation in the form of interest, and to the bank their relative immobility has the advantage of a smaller potential claim on its reserve of notes and coin and on its balance with the Bank of England. In other countries, the U.S.A. for example, current and deposit accounts are distinguished by the more descriptive terms 'demand' and 'time' deposits. When business is expanding, a shift from deposit to current accounts can be expected to occur, and indeed the proportion of current accounts has recently been higher than in the slacker years before the war. The ratio will also be influenced by the attraction of alternative assets as a store of wealth and by the distribution of wealth itself between rich and poor, both factors which have also tended to increase the proportion of current accounts since the war.

*Cheques in course of collection, etc.*, consist mainly of cheques paid in by a bank's customers that have been drawn on accounts with other banks but have not yet been cleared through one of the clearing houses. Cheques in course of collection are bank assets but are shown above as a deduction from liabilities, as the deposits of the bank on whom these cheques have been drawn will be overstated. However, as far as the individual bank is concerned, the published figure of cheques in course of collection is somewhat misleading, for no allowance can be made for cheques drawn on itself that have not yet been cleared. In their policy of maintaining certain ratios of different classes of assets to 'deposits', it is the figure of total deposits that is used by the banks.

### The Cash Ratio

*Notes, coin and balances with the Bank of England* constitute the banks' *cash* reserves. The banks hold only part of their cash reserves in notes and coin, for their balances with the Bank of England can be used to augment their 'till money' by obtaining notes and coin from the Bank when required; these balances are also used, as has already been indicated, to settle claims arising between the commercial banks themselves and those between the commercial banks and the Bank of England. As a rule, therefore, less than half of the banks' cash reserves are held in notes and coin.

Experience has shown that in conditions of public confidence in the banking system only a small proportion of deposits need be backed by a cash reserve, which thus supports a much larger structure of deposits brought into existence through the acquisition by the banks of interest-bearing assets, namely securities and loans, from which the banks obtain the greater part of their income. Since 1946 the banks have agreed with the Bank of England to aim at a ratio of cash to deposits of 8 per cent.

With this cash ratio the banks' deposits must be twelve and a half times the size of their cash reserves; the banks adjust their loans and their security purchases until this relationship is achieved. It follows that if the banks can be relied on to maintain a fixed cash ratio, the monetary authorities can influence banking policy and the level of commercial bank deposits as a whole by varying the cash reserves possessed by the banks: hence the critical importance of the fixity of cash ratios to monetary policy.

### Other Liquid Assets

*Money at call and short notice* consists mainly of loans repayable nominally on demand. These loans are made chiefly to the discount houses on the security of Treasury bills, good-quality commercial bills, or short-term government bonds. These assets earn only relatively low rates of interest as a rule, but they occupy a special place in the banking system because of their liquidity, that is because they can be turned into cash easily, quickly and without loss. If a bank has to restore its cash reserves in order to maintain the 8 per cent ratio, it will call in—or refuse to renew—part of its loans to the discount houses.

The latter will attempt to repay by increasing their borrowing from other banks or from other financial institutions. If they succeed, the result will probably be to transfer part of a balance with the Bank of England from one bank to another. If the discount houses cannot obtain funds in this way the effect of the banks' pressure on the discount houses is to force the latter to find the necessary cash by recourse to the Bank of England, by discounting eligible bills, i.e. Treasury bills, with the Bank or by borrowing from it. The result in this case is to restore the balances with the Bank of England of the commercial banks as a whole.

*Bills discounted* play a similar role in banking operations. Commercial and similar bills of exchange now comprise only a small part of the total, rarely more than 10 per cent, the remainder consisting of Treasury bills. Since an agreement made in 1935 the commercial banks do not bid for Treasury bills at the weekly tender except as agents for their customers. Treasury bills discounted by the banks are purchased from the discount houses when they are at least seven days old, a limitation designed to prevent disguised tendering by a bank. Except when the Bank of England takes the initiative in purchasing them from the banks, Treasury bills are not resold by the commercial banks. This is a remnant of a tradition in which resort by the banks to the Bank of England was regarded as a sign of weakness. Commercial bills, of which the best class may be rediscounted at the Bank of England, are always held to maturity by the banks.

When Treasury bills mature, however, the Exchequer makes the repayment out of its balance with the Bank of England, so that the commercial banks can take the initiative themselves when they require cash by not replacing maturing bills, as well as by calling in loans made on the security of bills. Thus bills, together with money at call and short notice, and of course cash itself, constitute the so-called *liquid assets* of the banks; and their bill portfolios are arranged so that maturities run evenly from week to week, with concentrations on those dates when requirements of cash are known to be heavy.

### The Liquidity Ratio

The special significance of call money and bills discounted, which together are sometimes described as the banks' money-market assets, is two-fold: they form the usual channel of contact between the commercial banks and the Bank of England, and their high degree of liquidity, which is only the result of this contact, gives them a degree of importance second only to that of cash itself. The banks have developed the practice of conforming to a minimum liquidity ratio as well as to a cash ratio. The banks aim as a rule at a minimum ratio of cash, loans at call and short notice, and bills discounted to total deposits of about 30 per cent. More precisely, their liquid-asset ratios will not be allowed to fall below this for any length of time except in special circumstances, and the fact that liquid assets earn a relatively low return normally deters the banks from letting their liquidity ratios rise much above 30 per cent if non-liquid assets are available on attractive terms.

This figure applies directly to the period of heavy tax payments in the first quarter of the year, when cash reserves are consequently under pressure; during the rest of the year the minimum liquidity ratio is somewhat higher and less precise, rising to roughly 35 per cent in December.

When liquidity ratios suffice, the banks can expand deposits by acquiring other income-yielding assets, if these are available on suitable terms, until the ratio of liquid assets to total deposits falls to something nearer 30 per cent. When liquidity ratios are too low, on the other hand, the banks will restore them by contracting their holdings of other assets, thus reducing total deposits in relation to their liquid assets. It will be observed that the banks cannot raise their liquidity, as opposed to their cash, ratios by calling in loans to the money market or by letting their Treasury bill holdings run down in order to draw cash out of the Bank of England, for this would only increase their cash reserves at the expense of their money-market assets, leaving their liquidity ratios unchanged.

### Earning Assets—Investments

The 'other assets' referred to above are investments and advances, sometimes described as the 'earning assets' of the banks, for rates of interest on these generally exceed those on money-market assets. *Investments* consist very largely of British government and government-guaranteed stocks. The attitude of the banks towards these assets, like that of most investors, will be influenced by the market outlook; when they expect a fall in security prices they will refrain from adding to their investments even though their liquidity ratios can support an increase. Although the banks purchase investments with the object of holding them to maturity, they are sensitive to the risk of a fall in gilt-edged prices; until 1952 the banks entered investments in their annual accounts at market values or below, but the depreciation of security prices experienced in that year was greater than the inner reserves of some of the banks, and a policy of recording investments at book value but above total market value, which was shown separately, had to be adopted. Although such a situation would normally be purely temporary, in that the market values of the securities held would usually be below their redemption values, it is one that the banks wish to avoid. In order to minimize the risk of even paper losses, the banks appear in recent years to have concentrated their holdings on short-term securities with a life of less than ten years and with an average term to maturity of very much less.

The risk of capital loss is increased by the possibility that a situation in which any one bank is obliged to sell investments may also be one in which other banks are also sellers, so that the pressure of sales on a weak market will have a serious effect on bond prices. The instability of bond prices, however, is only one reason why government securities other than Treasury bills cannot be considered as liquid assets. An attempt by all banks to sell investments to the public does nothing to add directly to the absolute level of their cash reserves. Only assets that can quickly be turned into cash with little or no loss, that is into a balance with the Bank of England, can be regarded as liquid; hence the vital difference between the banks' holdings of money-market assets and their investments.

## Advances

Advances, loans other than those made at call or at short notice, are usually overdrafts.[11] Although in recent years medium-term loans have been becoming less rare in banking operations, the banks still adhere to the traditional view that only short-term loans are suitable banking assets. Traditionally, bankers regarded what were described as 'self-liquidating' loans, secured usually against some consignment of goods due for sale within a short period, as the ideal form of bank credit. But what has been said about investments and liquidity is true also of bank advances, even those secured on goods approaching sale. The banks as a whole cannot obtain cash by calling in their advances, and to do so in the name of a policy aimed at confining loans only to the most secure borrowers would risk forcing traders to unload their goods at low prices in order to repay their bank loans. The consequence might be to weaken the security of traders in general, for one man's bank loan is the source of his purchases and thus of another's sales receipts.

This does not mean that the general policy of limiting advances ostensibly to short periods is unjustified, for it is more difficult for a bank manager to assess the credit-worthiness of an individual trader or manufacturer in the more distant future, and although most advances are backed by some form of security the banks are naturally reluctant to consider the enforced sale of business assets, or even of securities, as anything but a last resort. One consequence of making long-term, non-marketable loans would be to oblige the banks to intervene more closely in the management of business, which in this country they greatly prefer to avoid. Nevertheless, the line between temporary advances and long-term loans to business is in practice somewhat indistinct, for bankers are reluctant to call in advances, on which many concerns have come to rely as a form of almost permanent finance.

Advances are generally more profitable assets than investments, for although the higher rate of interest they yield is partly compensation for the risk of default, the incidence of loss on a bank's advances as a whole is normally very small, and advances usually bring in ancillary receipts, such as bank charges. The banks are anxious to follow a policy of lending only to evidently sound borrowers; they are not prepared to soften their standards of credit-worthiness in return for higher rates of interest. But the element of competition between the banks enables the very largest concerns, and of course the nationalized industries, to secure relatively favourable terms, while at the other end of the scale personal borrowers and many small private businesses may have to pay relatively high charges. The banks have developed the policy of linking the rate of interest charged on advances to Bank rate, a common formula in recent years being 1 per cent above Bank rate with a minimum of 5 per cent, but the largest borrowers can generally expect to pay less and the smallest rather more in some cases.

### The Scissors-movement of Advances and Investments

The banks' policy of not lending to 'risky' borrowers, no matter what rate of interest the latter may offer, brings to bank lending an element of passivity, in that the level of advances is very much a reflection of the demand for bank accommodation by credit-worthy businesses; the banks do not actively raise their charges when this demand increases or lower them when it falls. As a result advances tend to rise spontaneously when business conditions become more buoyant and to fall when they become slack. If liquidity ratios are at their minimum the profitability of advances, particularly when booming business conditions reduce the risk of default, together with the fear of losing good customers to other banks, normally leads the banks to accommodate an increase in the demand for credit by selling investments, so that a 'scissors-movement' of investments and advances may be a distinct feature of bank asset ratios; it may be extremely difficult for the banks to hold down advances when borrowers seek to take full advantage of unused overdraft facilities agreed on in the past. But this switch from investments to advances or back again will not be entirely unaffected by the state of the market for government securities. When the sale of investments means incurring heavy capital losses, or giving up assets with a relatively high yield, the rising demand for advances will not be so readily accommodated. When the demand for advances is falling, the banks will be less willing to expand their security portfolios if the outlook for security prices is unfavourable, preferring instead to run up their liquidity ratios.

### Treasury Deposit Receipts

Between 1940 and 1952 bank balance sheets included one class of asset no longer to be found there, namely Treasury Deposit Receipts. These were the result of the wartime emergency; they were compulsory, ran mainly for six months and could not be sold, except to the Bank of England at a discount equivalent to Bank rate or in payment of subscriptions to government loans. At the end of the war they represented 40 per cent of total deposits, falling to roughly 8 per cent in 1950 and finally disappearing in February 1952. They were less liquid than Treasury bills, but this was of little disadvantage in a period in which cash could be obtained from the Bank of England, in sufficient quantities and without loss, in other ways. However, their inflexibility and their compulsory nature made them unwelcome members of the banks' assets when the special needs of war had passed.

#### DISCOUNT HOUSES

The discount or money market consists of the banks[12] and the discount houses, together with several small firms of 'running brokers' who do some dealing in bills and act as agents for 'non-clearing' banks and other concerns. Amalgamations have reduced the discount houses to twelve in number. Although the decline of the commercial bill and the tremendous extension of government

2 B

finance have transformed their activities the commercial bill still plays a part in their business. The discount houses act mainly as intermediaries between borrowers and the banks; they perform for the latter the useful function of sorting commercial bills into 'parcels', well spread as to risk but concentrated on maturity dates which the banks may be seeking.

Over the last fifty years dealings in Treasury bills have become the mainstay of the activities of the discount houses. Since 1934–5, when the trade depression, the direction of monetary policy, the policies pursued by the banks, and the demand for sterling bills from overseas, threatened to undermine the profitability of dealing in bills by driving rates down to levels that produced no net return to the discount houses, above the rates at which they were obliged to borrow, the discount houses have submitted a joint bid at the weekly tender. From this period also dates the abstention of the clearing banks from the tender.

The exact arrangements of the so-called 'syndicate' are not known, but it is understood that the bid is made for all the week's Treasury bills on offer and that the syndicate's share of the weekly allotment is divided among the individual houses in a prearranged fashion. The internal mechanism of the syndicate is not completely rigid, however; the share of each discount house can be adjusted within limits, and bids may be submitted to some extent by individual members in addition to that made by the syndicate as a whole. As the syndicate bids for the whole amount on offer, bids placed at higher prices by other bodies are accepted in full, while those at lower levels are completely unsuccessful; the syndicate's bid thus constitutes the maximum rate of discount of the tender. On average the syndicate seems to aim at obtaining about one-half of the bills on offer.

The discount houses' earnings from Treasury bills are obtained in three ways. They hold Treasury bills for at least seven days until they are purchased by the commercial banks; during this period bill holdings will be financed by borrowing from the banks and other institutions, and the net income from carrying bills will depend on the difference between the rates at which the discount houses have to borrow and the rate of interest earned on their bills; if the rate on borrowed money rises sharply in this period the discount houses may, of course, suffer a loss.

Secondly, owing to the fact that bills close to maturity are in most demand by the banks the rate of discount on a one-month bill, for example, will generally be less than that on a three-month bill, so that an additional profit is to be made on holding bills if the pattern of rates does not change. If the three-month rate is 4 per cent per annum, a £1,000 bill of this period to maturity can be bought at £990; if the one-month rate is 3½ per cent per annum, it can be sold for £997 2s. two months later, a gain of £7 2s. in two months.

Thirdly, if the level of bill rates as a whole falls further, a capital profit will be made on resale (whereas, if a rise occurs, more than the whole of the interest on the bill may be lost).

The rate at which the discount houses are prepared to bid for any given volume of Treasury bills will thus be influenced by their views on the immediate future of the banks' call-money rates, on the competition of 'outside' tenderers, on the market rate at which they can sell Treasury bills to the banks, and on the risk of being forced to obtain funds from the Bank of England at a penal rate.

Government bonds amounted to about two-fifths of the total assets of the discount houses in 1956–7. Dealings in bonds by one or two of the discount houses began in the nineteen-twenties, in an attempt to offset the decline in their commercial bill business, but until the years prior to the Second World War were frowned upon by the authorities and other houses alike. The great expansion in the national debt during the war created both the opportunity and the need for an extension of these activities, however, and the discount houses were enabled to take the prior steps of strengthening their position by amalgamation and by raising additional permanent capital. The discount houses carry government bonds against money borrowed from the banks and elsewhere. The margins on which they work are narrow, so that bonds carried against short loans or call money are limited to those of not more than five years to maturity and in the aggregate amount to some multiple of the total of their capital and reserves. The bond purchases of the discount houses serve the useful function of broadening the market in short-dated stocks, which are not satisfactory investments for many financial institutions other than the banks.

The basic utility of the discount houses to the monetary system has sometimes been questioned. From the point of view of the banks, however, they play a valuable part in providing a reservoir into which surplus cash can be poured or from which it can be withdrawn from day to day; the facility with which cash reserves can be adjusted through the medium of the discount houses enables the banks to maintain stable cash ratios on a daily basis. To the Bank of England the discount houses appear as a channel through which its policy can be transmitted to the banking system as a whole or, to vary the metaphor, as a sensitive nerve acting on the monetary system. Alternative arrangements could no doubt be devised to perform the present functions of the discount houses in both the money and bond markets, but whether they would be any more economical may be doubted, and the experience of the discount houses in the field of commercial bill finance is not lightly to be discarded. The chief weakness of the discount houses is that they may be extremely vulnerable to sharp increases in short-term interest rates.

# CHAPTER 29

# THE BANKING SYSTEM
# AND MONETARY POLICY

Monetary policy is action taken by the authorities to influence the quantity of money and its distribution, the level and pattern of interest rates, the availability and terms of different types of loans, or the structure and distribution of the national debt. Our concern here is with the impact of monetary policy on the banking system, on some of what may be regarded as its short-range effects. As for 'the authorities', this is a term whose vagueness reflects the fact that, whereas ultimately the responsibility for monetary policy lies with the government, in practice most of its day-to-day operations are carried out by the Bank of England.

## THE BANK OF ENGLAND, THE GOVERNMENT, AND THE COMMERCIAL BANKS

The role of the Bank of England as the central bank was given full statutory recognition by its nationalization under the Bank of England Act of 1946. This formalized the shift of responsibility for monetary policy from the Bank to the government, acting through the Treasury, that had already occurred when Britain went off the gold standard in 1931 and was confirmed later in the needs of war finance. Before the war the experience of the Bank and the personality of its Governor accorded to the Bank of England a special voice in the direction of monetary affairs, but the authority of the Treasury was paramount; on the other hand, the views of the Bank still carry great weight in the rooms of the Treasury. The Governor, Deputy Governor and Directors of the Bank of England are now appointed by the Crown, and the legal authority of the Treasury over the Bank under the 1946 Act is limitless.

The 1946 Act has also given the Bank some measure of statutory power over the affairs of the commercial banks. Clause 4 states that 'the Bank, if they think it necessary in the public interest, may request information from and make recommendations to bankers, and may, if so authorized by the Treasury, issue directions to any banker for the purpose of securing that effect is given to any such request or recommendation'. As far as the 'recommendations' that the Bank may make, without the express direction of the Treasury, it is equally doubtful whether the Act has added

TABLE 21. *Assets and Liabilities of the Bank of England*

The Weekly Return of the Bank of England—
Return for Wednesday, 27 August 1958

ISSUE DEPARTMENT

| | £ | | £ |
|---|---|---|---|
| Notes issued: | | Government debt | 11,015,100 |
| In circulation | 2,046,987,460 | Other government | |
| In Banking Depart- | | securities | 2,085,203,826 |
| ment | 53,372,840 | Other securities | 768,501 |
| | | Coin other than gold | |
| | | coin | 3,012,573 |
| | | | |
| | | Amount of fiduciary | |
| | | issue | 2,100,000,000 |
| | | Gold coin and bullion | 360,300 |
| | | (at 250s. 5d. per oz. | |
| | | fine) | |
| | 2,100,360,300 | | 2,100,360,300 |

BANKING DEPARTMENT

| | £ | | £ |
|---|---|---|---|
| Capital | 14,553,000 | Government securi- | |
| Rest | 3,896,361 | ties | 224,204,550 |
| Public deposits | 12,032,887 | Other securities: | |
| Other deposits: | | Discounts and | |
| Bankers | | advances | |
| £206,005,132 | | £8,175,700 | |
| Other accounts | | Securities | |
| £70,127,808 | | £18,937,522 | |
| | 276,132,334 | | 27,113,222 |
| | | Notes | 53,372,840 |
| | | Coin | 1,923,970 |
| | £306,614,582 | | £306,614,582 |

much to the authority of the Bank, whose influence within the banking system, based ultimately on its power as lender of last resort, has long been exercised through the medium of informal consultation.

The Bank Charter Act of 1844 made the division between the Issue Department and Banking Department that can be seen in the Bank return, a summary of which is reproduced in Table 21. This division, which was made in order to separate what was intended to be an automatic process of issuing notes from the 'banking' operations of the Bank of England, is now unimportant, but the form of the return has remained broadly unchanged since 1844. The return is prepared every Wednesday and published on the following day; the fact that the Governor and Directors meet on Thursday morning to decide on the level of Bank rate is due traditionally to the need to consider this weekly statement, but the link between them is tenuous indeed now that practically all of the country's gold reserve has been transferred to the Exchange Equalization Account.

The liabilities of the Issue Department consist of Bank of England notes. The greater part of these are already in circulation with the banks and the public, but in addition some notes are held in the Banking Department; in a consolidated balance sheet these internal cross-entries would be eliminated. Against these liabilities the Issue Department now holds only a tiny amount of gold. The main assets of the Issue Department held against the note issue are 'Other government securities', including Treasury bills, ways-and-means advances and government bonds of different maturities. 'Government debt', on the other hand, is merely a book entry recording loans made by the Bank to the Exchequer in its early years. 'Other securities', another small item, consists mainly of loans made to Commonwealth governments and similar first-class borrowers. The assets of the Issue Department are grouped into two—gold and the assets that support the fiduciary issue, reflecting the legislation by which notes may be issued only up to an amount equal to the Bank's holdings of gold plus the fiduciary issue.

The liabilities of the Banking Department include the Bank's capital, now owned by the State, and the item 'Rest', which represents its undistributed profits; the profits on the note issue are now passed to the Exchange Equalization Account and these items are of only historical interest. 'Public deposits', on the other hand, are of considerable importance to monetary analysis, for they are the balances held by government departments. In 'Public deposits' are included the balances of the Exchequer and those of the Post Office Savings Bank and the National Debt Commissioners.

Of the item 'Other deposits', the component 'Bankers' deposits' is of special importance, as it represents the balances of British banks which operate mainly in this country. The last asset item, 'Other accounts', consists of the deposits with the Bank of England of overseas governments and banks, including overseas central banks, together with the deposits of the small number of industrial and other firms that are still customers of the Bank.

The largest of the items on the assets side of the Banking Department's accounts—'Government securities'—consists again of Treasury bills, government bonds and ways-and-means advances to the Exchequer. No statistics are published as to the relative proportions of the separate components of this group, but it is likely that Treasury bills constitute the larger of the security items as a rule.

The distinction between the two constituents of 'Other securities' is of considerable importance. 'Discounts and advances' consist of bills discounted by the Bank for its customers, especially discount houses, and advances made to them, *both on their initiative*, and include the assistance given by the Bank to the money market when it comes to the Bank when money is tight. 'Securities', on the other hand, are made up of miscellaneous securities bought by the Banking Department on its own initiative from overseas governments and certain commercial concerns, together with commercial bills bought from the discount houses as a regular arrangement designed mainly to enable the Bank to check the quality of the bills discounted by the market.

The item 'Notes' is a counterpart of the liability item in the accounts of the Issue Department. 'Coin', like the notes in the Banking Department, is held in readiness to meet the requirements of the commercial banks, and today consists almost entirely of silver coin purchased from another government department, the Royal Mint.

### THE NOTE ISSUE

The Bank Charter Act of 1844 permitted the Bank of England to issue notes only up to an amount equal to the value of the gold held by the Issue Department plus the fiduciary issue. Apart from the fact that the Issue Department's gold is now valued at the current market, and not at a fixed, price, this is still the situation, but with a vital exception that has effectively reversed the position. The Act of 1844 fixed the fiduciary issue at the *constant* figure of £14 million, apart from small increases in partial replacement of the lapsed note issues of the private banks, so that the allowable note issue, except when special steps were taken to permit an expansion of the note issue beyond these limits during the banking crises of the nineteenth century and in 1914, could be increased only to the amount of any rise in the quantity of gold held by the Issue Department.

Today, in contrast, the Issue Department holds little gold, and the limit to the note issue instead varies with the size of the fiduciary issue. The Currency and Bank Notes Act of 1954—the latest of a series of statutes concerned with the regulation of the note issue—provides for a basic fiduciary issue of £1,575 million and empowers the Treasury, after representations by the Bank, to vary this amount; but except under the authority of a statutory instrument (subject to annulment by a resolution of Parliament), the fiduciary issue may not remain above this figure of £1,575 million for more than two years. Although this provision appears to echo one object of the gold standard in placing some statutory limit on the note issue, once regarded as the vital regulator of economic activity, the consent of Parliament to a rise in the note issue has become something of a formality, and by 1958 the fiduciary issue had reached £2,000 million.

The Bank tries to anticipate an increase in the public's demand for notes—for example, at holiday times—by augmenting the stock held in its Banking Department; when necessary, additional notes are obtained from the Issue Department, which is 'paid' by a transfer of government securities from the Banking Department. When notes come to be withdrawn from the latter by the commercial banks payment is made by them in the form of a reduction in their balances held with the Banking Department, that is in 'Other deposits—Bankers'. As long as Parliament can always be relied on to give its sanction to an increase in the fiduciary issue, the regulation of the note issue is not a critical element in the monetary system. The commercial banks can meet the demand for notes by the public by running down their balances with the Bank of England.

It will be observed that an outflow of notes from the commercial banks to the public, by reducing bank deposits and cash reserves by the same absolute amount, causes a reduction in the cash ratio of the banks. This can be made good by the Bank of England if it acts so as to increase 'Other deposits: Bankers' to the required extent. If the Bank of England has control over 'Bankers' deposits', changes in the public's demand for notes rather than deposits can always be accommodated without any change in the *total* quantity of money held by the public, that is without any multiple alteration in the level of deposits due to a loss of cash by the banks. Conversely, if the Bank can control the cash reserves of the commercial banks it need not fear that any change it is seeking to bring about in the level of deposits will be frustrated by the effect on bank cash ratios of the public's demand for notes.

### THE BANK OF ENGLAND AND 'BANKERS' DEPOSITS'

Apart from a return of notes and coin from the public and the minor question of transfers from 'Other deposits: Other accounts', the balances of the commercial banks with the Bank of England can be increased only as a result of two types of operation. One is a transfer to 'Bankers' deposits' from 'Public deposits' due to net payments made by government departments to the public or to the banks themselves. The other must be associated with an increase in the total assets of the Banking Department, so that the control of bank cash reserves by the Bank of England lies in its ability to expand or contract its total assets.

The assets acquired or released by the Bank to influence the cash reserves of the commercial banks can be gold, foreign exchange, or securities. With the passing of the gold standard and the transfer of our foreign exchange reserves to the Exchange Equalization Account, dealings in securities—Treasury bills and government bonds—are now the normal method of control.

These transactions can be grouped broadly into two classes: action taken by the Bank of England to relieve pressure on bank cash ratios, in which the Bank supplies cash to relieve stringency, i.e. in order to bring bank cash ratios up to 8 per cent, so as to support whatever level of deposits arises from the other actions of the authorities; and operations undertaken by the Bank as part of a positive policy of influencing the level of bank cash reserves in order to change the volume of deposits that the banks can support. The dividing line does not always seem distinct, for, paradoxical as it may seem at this stage, action in the first category is often the consequence of operations in the second, and there is the fact that the Bank may act not only to relieve stringency but also to absorb excess cash in the banking system. The division is important, however, and it can be said to be that between the actions of the Bank as *lender of last resort* (or, in effect, as borrower of last resort) and those undertaken as *open market operations*.

### THE BANK AS LENDER OF LAST RESORT

The Bank of England is always ready to supply cash to the banking system *at a price*. It will rediscount, that is purchase, bills of exchange that meet with its requirements, or make loans to the discount houses against eligible bills and bonds. This role, however, can be played in two ways, depending on what the Bank is hoping to achieve. The Bank is *always* prepared to discount eligible paper, that is Treasury bills (usually not far from maturity) and first-class commercial bills, *at its published Bank rate*. The essential point is that this is intended to be a penal rate, standing above rates current in the money market, so that a loss is suffered by a discount house that is obliged to rediscount at a Bank rate of 5 per cent bills that it has bought at a rate of 4 per cent. A similar result ensues when a discount house comes to the Bank for an advance on the security of a bill; the rate which it is charged will be higher than the running yield it obtains on the bill over the period, usually seven days, for which the loan by the Bank is granted. In the past these advances have been granted at Bank rate or at published rates fixed $\frac{1}{2}$ per cent above or below Bank rate, according to the strength of the penalty the Bank wanted to impose.

When the discount houses are forced 'into the Bank' at the penal rate for large amounts or for a prolonged period, they will react by raising the rates at which they are prepared to buy new Treasury bills, in order to minimize their losses. They may also be obliged to do so as a result of a rise in the call-money rates of the banks due to the very stringency that forces the banks to oblige the discount houses to seek assistance from the Bank of

England. Moreover, the banks and discount houses are sensitive to what they believe the Bank of England's intentions to be, and if the Bank of England forces the discount houses to seek such assistance at the penal rate for large amounts they may interpret this as a desire on the part of the Bank to see higher market rates. Thus the effect is for market rates—bill rates and the commercial banks' money-market loan rates—to rise.

From time to time the Bank may force the market to seek assistance at the penal rate for very small amounts, just to keep the discount houses alert and to remind them that the penal rate remains an instrument not to be ignored; in these cases there will be little effect on market rates.

If the Bank of England wishes to act as lender of last resort *without* forcing up money-market rates it will rediscount bills *at the current market rate* through the purchases made by its special buyer, a small discount house, in the market, so that no loss is incurred by the seller. The decision as to whether relief should be given at the penal rate or at the market rate lies entirely with the Bank. When the Bank purchases bills at the market rate it is often described as dealing through its 'back door', its 'front door' being its Discount Office, at which such transactions are carried out at Bank rate.

The Bank may supply cash at market rates by purchasing bills from the discount houses or from the banks. In the former case the Bank's assistance is usually described by convention as 'direct' and in the latter as 'indirect'; purchases from the banks will generally occur when the Bank will take only those bills close to maturity, for most of these will have found their way into bank portfolios. This distinction between 'direct' and 'indirect' assistance is a topsy-turvy description of operations designed fundamentally to restore the cash ratios of the banks, the discount houses being merely intermediaries when the Bank supplies so-called 'direct' relief.

## SMOOTHING OPERATIONS

The use of the 'back door' makes it possible for the Bank of England to prevent erratic disturbances of the banks' cash reserves that would otherwise result in purposeless fluctuations in money-market rates, if fixed cash ratios were maintained. Today the main potential source of these day-to-day shocks is government finance. Government expenditure and receipts are now large in relation to the cash reserves of the banks, and in the absence of smoothing operations could cause frequent and sharp changes in bank cash reserves and thus in money-market rates from day to day. In the absence of offsetting operations by the authorities the only way in which these disturbances to market conditions could be avoided would be for the banks to allow their cash ratios to vary, as may have been the case at times before the war. The maintenance of a fixed cash ratio on a daily basis without frequent fluctuations in market rates requires cash ratios to be stabilized other than through the medium of assistance at Bank rate.

### The Treasury Bill Issue and Bank Cash Ratios

As the government's balance with the Bank of England is normally kept to a minimum working level, the form in which any net excess of government expenditure over receipts is financed, after making use of any inflow of extra-budgetary funds, including those accruing from the sale of gold and foreign exchange reserves, is by means of an issue of Treasury bills through the tender; and a surplus of receipts over expenditure is used to decrease the volume of bills outstanding by reducing the weekly offer of bills below the volume maturing.

The course of Exchequer receipts is marked by a distinct seasonal hump in the last quarter of the fiscal year, when income tax and surtax receipts are at their peak. In a year over the whole of which the Exchequer may be in balance, therefore, it will incur a deficit in the first three-quarters and a surplus in the fourth. Finance by the issue of Treasury bills has the effect of offsetting the change in the banks' cash ratios that would otherwise result. When the Exchequer is in deficit, in which case its net payments would otherwise be increasing bank cash ratios (by raising bank cash reserves and deposits by the same amount), the increase in the Treasury bill issue draws off the rise in the banks' cash reserves that would otherwise occur and adds to their money-market assets instead, in so far as the new Treasury bills are taken up by the discount houses, who finance their purchases by loans from the banks. In the final quarter of the fiscal year the outstanding volume of Treasury bills is reduced, and the excess of maturing bills over those on offer prevents the cash reserves of the banks from being depleted, for the proceeds of maturing bills held by the banks are paid into 'Bankers' deposits'.

Except when the authorities deliberately pursue a different policy, expressly aimed at expanding or contracting the level of deposits, the main course of government outlays and receipts is felt by the banks not in the form of a change in their cash reserves but as movements in their liquid-asset ratios as a whole. When the Exchequer is in deficit the consequent rise in bank deposits is accompanied by a rise in the liquid-asset ratios of the banks, and the slight deficiency of cash that results from deposits having increased while cash reserves remain unchanged can be made good at the Bank of England's 'back door'. The annual rise in liquid-asset ratios between the end of March and the end of December is normally accepted by the banks as a seasonal movement and, as such, does not lead the banks to expand their earning assets, apart from a seasonal increase in bank advances in the autumn.

### Residual Discrepancies

The Treasury seeks to adjust the weekly bill issue in accordance with its knowledge of the future course of government outlays and receipts, but this cannot be done with perfect precision. Day-to-day discrepancies are bound to occur, especially when large payments have to be made on a single day, such as those made to farmers by the Milk Marketing Board twice a month and to doctors by the Ministry of Health. When net government expenditure outruns receipts from Treasury bills taken up from the previous tender the Exchequer finances itself by borrowing from the Bank of England; the consequent transfer from 'Public deposits' to 'Bankers' deposits' can be offset by the sale of existing bills by the Bank in the money market, sometimes described as 'reverse selling', and the Exchequer's borrowing from the Bank can be repaid at a later date. Similarly, when the Exchequer's surplus exceeds the reduction in the Treasury bill tender issue (or more precisely the reduction in the holdings of the banks and discount houses) the banks' cash ratios can be restored by the purchase of bills by the Bank of England through its 'back door'. Similar tactics can also be employed to offset fluctuations in bank cash ratios due to seasonal swings in the volume of notes in circulation.

### Smoothing Operations and Money-market Rates

The Bank of England is thus in daily contact with the banks and discount houses by virtue of its smoothing operations. Superficially the greater part of these will appear to be directed at the discount houses. Each day by three o'clock the discount houses must 'balance their books', that is settle the net difference between funds being called in from the banks (and other institutions) and those being made available, leaving themselves with no net cash and no loans still to be repaid on that particular day. To do this the discount houses obtain cash from the Bank of England when there is a net balance to be repaid or buy bills (or bonds) whenever, on balance, the banks and other institutions are net lenders to them on the day. In the former case cash will always be made available by the Bank at a price; in the latter, existing bills will be sold by the Bank in sufficient quantity to mop up excess cash.

This daily contact between the money market and the Bank of England enables the latter to exert a measure of continuous control over money-market rates of interest that can be used, within limits, without altering Bank rate itself. By adjusting the quantity of cash that it is prepared to make available through the 'back door' the Bank is in a position to influence the day-to-day movement of money rates. The necessity for smoothing operations provides a useful opportunity for causing a shift in market rates in relation to Bank rate, especially as the market is always anxious to gauge the Bank's intentions.

### OPEN MARKET OPERATIONS

Open market operations are purchases or sales of securities undertaken by the central bank in order to influence interest rates, the level of bank cash reserves, or the volume of deposits held by the public. Although in their broadest sense open market operations include smoothing transactions, it is useful to regard the latter as a readjustment of cash reserves to a 'change' in the monetary situation and the former as one possible type of change itself. This distinction has perhaps only become significant since the war.

### Operations to Fix Interest Rates

The ability of the Bank of England to influence interest rates depends ultimately on its willingness and its ability to supply cash or securities in sufficient amounts. If the Bank wishes to prevent the rate of interest yielded by a particular class of security from falling below a certain level, it has to be ready to sell sufficient quantities whenever the demand for that security threatens to drive its yield below this. If the Bank wishes to place an upper limit on the rate of interest, it has to stand prepared to buy. In the extreme case, in which the Bank wishes to hold or 'peg' the rate of interest at a constant level, it has to be prepared to act as either buyer or seller if necessary, according to the pressure of the market. In all cases the policy of the Bank will be made easier if other operators are convinced of the Bank's determination and ability to carry out its intentions.

The Bank has taken action to 'peg' the rate of interest at a constant level in the case of Treasury bills, between 1940 and 1945 and again between 1945 and 1951. In these years the Bank of England kept its 'back door' always open. It was always willing to buy or sell bills at the fixed discount rate of 1 per cent per annum between 1940 and the end of 1945 and at $\frac{1}{2}$ per cent thereafter until October 1951. During this period Bank rate, which stood at 2 per cent, had no influence as a penal rate, and the authorities had effectively pegged the market rate of discount.

At other times Bank rate provides an example of a *maximum* rate of interest set by the Bank, in that, as long as the Bank is always willing to rediscount eligible bills at a stated Bank rate, the rate of interest on these cannot exceed bank-rate, since no holder need sell them at a higher rate (that is at a lower price) if the Bank will give him better terms.

### Objectives of Open Market Operations

Within these limits a range of objectives may be pursued by the Bank in the money market or in the market for government bonds. The Bank may wish to shift the whole pattern of interest rates up or down in order to influence the supply of and demand for loans; or it may wish to alter the shape of the pattern, buying short-term securities and selling long-term stocks, for example, so as to ease a coming conversion operation by bringing the maturing stock into its own portfolio. It may, on the other hand, operate only in one class of security in the hope that the effect on its yield will be transmitted to shorter- or longer-term stocks. Whatever its object, intervention by the Bank can usually be expected to be assisted by the effect of its initial steps on the expectations of other operators, many of whom will try to anticipate the authorities' further actions in the hope of making a profit or avoiding a loss.

The emphasis of open market operations may, however, be placed on changes in the banks' cash reserves. For example, if the authorities wish to induce the banks to expand their 'earning' assets, the Bank of England can buy securities from the public. Here, too, the immediate effect will also be to tend to lower interest rates on the class of security purchased—the rise in the price of the security being needed to tempt existing holders to sell—and the impact of the banks will take the form of an equal increase in cash reserves and in the deposits of the public.

### Open Market Operations and Bank Cash Reserves

The sequence of events can be illustrated by considering their effect on an imaginary consolidated balance sheet of the commercial banks, but ignoring 'non-monetary' assets and any changes in the public's demand for notes that might be caused in the process. The latter could modify the course of bank cash reserves in either direction.

STAGE I

*Cash ratio 8 per cent. Liquidity ratio 30 per cent*

|  | £m. | % of deposits |
|---|---|---|
| Cash | 80 | 8 |
| Money market assets | 220 | 22 |
| Liquid assets | 300 | 30 |
| Earning assets | 700 | 70 |
| Deposits | 1,000 | 100 |

*Stage II.* The Bank of England buys £30 million of government bonds from the public. In its own accounts 'Bankers' deposits' rise by this amount, and there will be an identical increase in 'Government securities' in the Banking Department or in the

2 C

'Other government securities' of the Issue Department—in the latter event the Banking Department would be 'paid' by a transfer of notes from the Issue Department. The balance sheet of the commercial banks would be as follows:

STAGE II

|  | £m. | % of deposits |
|---|---|---|
| Cash | 110 | 10·6 |
| Money market assets | 220 | 21·3 |
| Liquid assets | 330 | 31·9 |
| Earning assets | 700 | 68·1 |
| Deposits | 1,030 | 100·0 |

Thus in Stage II the cash ratio has been increased to 10·6 per cent and the liquidity ratio to 31·9 per cent. The banks cannot restore their cash ratio to 8 per cent by adding to their 'earning' assets alone, for this would bring their liquidity ratio well below 30 per cent; if the banks increased their 'earning' assets to £1,045 million so as to cause deposits to rise to £1,375 million, or 12½ times £110 million, their liquidity ratio would fall to only 24 per cent.

In other words, for the banks to restore *both* their cash and their liquidity ratios, they must be enabled to increase their money-market asset holdings. This might be possible to some extent if the increased bank demand for money-market assets led them to reduce their rates on money at call and short notice. For this might enable the discount houses to raise their bid for Treasury bills and so increase their share of the total issue, and perhaps to add to their bond holdings; in practice the Bank will generally regard such a reduction in money rates as consistent with the expansionist aims of its initial purchases from the public. But if the latter were on a large scale, it is unlikely that the fall in money rates would enable the banks to restore their money-market asset holdings with sufficient speed—initially 'money' would be 'un-lendable' and rates would behave erratically at very low levels. It follows that the Bank of England, in order to enable the banks to restore both their cash and their liquidity ratios, would have to supply the banks with part, at least, of their additional money-market assets, by selling bills (or short-dated bonds) to the discount market. The final equilibrium stage would be as follows:

STAGE III

| | £m. | % of deposits |
|---|---|---|
| Cash | 88 | 8 |
| Money market assets | 242 | 22 |
| Liquid assets | 330 | 30 |
| Earning assets | 770 | 70 |
| Deposits | 1,100 | 100 |

The initial injection of cash in the form of security purchases of £30 million, with an equal increase in the banks' total liquid assets, has thus enabled the banks to add £70 million to their 'earning' assets to support a total increase in deposits of $\frac{100}{30} \times £30$ million, i.e. £100 million. If, as is likely, the increase in deposits was accompanied by a rise in the public's demand for notes, the final expansion in deposits would have to be correspondingly smaller unless the Bank injected further cash into the system in a similar way.

It is instructive to compare the process as represented by Stages II and III with what would be the sequence if the Bank bought £30 million of securities, not from the public, but from the banks or discount houses, in the form of Treasury bills. In this case Stage II would be as follows:

| | £m. | % of deposits |
|---|---|---|
| Cash | 110 | 11 |
| Money market assets | 190 | 19 |
| Liquid assets | 300 | 30 |
| Earning assets | 700 | 70 |
| Deposits | 1,000 | 100 |

The rise in the banks' cash reserves would thus take place at the expense of their money-market assets, leaving their liquid-asset ratios unchanged. No direct change in the level of 'earning' assets or in deposits could ensue as long as the 30 per cent liquid-asset ratio were maintained; instead the Bank's purchases, the glut of cash and the corresponding shortage of money-market assets in the banks' portfolios would drive down money rates and oblige the Bank of England to 'mop up' the excess cash in the system to enable the 8 per cent cash ratio to be restored. The Bank would be in a position to supply bills at lower rates of discount. But unless the commercial banks could acquire bills from other holders by bidding up their price, which would enable them to raise both their liquid assets and their deposits, the only equilibrium position would be that of Stage I, the original situation.[13]

In the situation in which the Bank's open market operations took the form of a sale of bills to the discount market, Stage II would be as follows:

|  | £m. | % of deposits |
|---|---|---|
| Cash | 50 | 5 |
| Money market assets | 250 | 25 |
| Liquid assets | 300 | 30 |
| Earning assets | 700 | 70 |
| Deposits | 1,000 | 100 |

Here the cash ratios of the banks have been shown as being depressed to a mere 5 per cent, but liquidity ratios are unchanged owing to the increase in money-market assets. Before this process was a day old, however, the banks would restore their cash ratios by calling in their loans to the money market, and we should be back to Stage I again. However, the initial sale of bills would raise money rates, and by forcing the market to come to it for assistance the Bank of England would be in a position to call the tune, dictating the terms on which it was prepared to act as lender of last resort. In practice the whole operation, if on a large scale, would only be undertaken in order to force the market 'into the Bank', that is to accept help at the penal rate and so cause market rates to rise. There would, however, be no *direct* change in bank deposits.

### Cash Reserves and Money-market Assets

Is there a paradox here? We have said that the banks work to a cash ratio of 8 per cent, implying that a change in their cash reserves of £X million involves a change in deposits of £12·5X million. But in these two examples of bill operations, the impact effect of which was to change cash reserves by £30 million, the Bank of England is shown as having been obliged to restore the original situation, leaving cash reserves and deposits unchanged. What has happened to the argument that the Bank can control the level of deposits by acting on bank cash reserves?

The explanation is that the 8 per cent rule says what the change in deposits will be *IF* the banks' cash reserves are changed by a given amount 'permanently', that is to say after they have taken whatever action is necessary from day to day to maintain their cash *ratios*. The 8 per cent rule does not say *how* the necessary change in cash reserves is to be enforced in a system in which the Bank is always prepared to act as lender or borrower of last resort, mopping up in the afternoon surplus cash that it has created in the morning, or restoring cash that it has just withdrawn.

The banks will respond to a reduction in their cash ratio to below 8 per cent by calling in loans to the discount houses or by reducing their bill holdings, but as long as their money-market assets are sufficient to maintain the 30 per cent liquidity ratio, *after their cash ratio has been restored*, the banks need take no further action. Given the 30 per cent convention, therefore, if the authorities wish to reduce the level of deposits, they must somehow or other cut the supply of money-market assets to the banks to below 22 per cent of deposits with the cash ratio at 8 per cent. In other words, in order to secure a reduction in bank cash reserves as a 'permanent' feature the authorities must somehow draw down the banks' money-market assets *without* giving the banks cash in return.

Similarly, to increase the level of deposits by acting on the banks' cash reserves the authorities must supply the banks with sufficient liquid assets *in addition to* cash.

Thus it is true that the Bank of England can control the level of bank deposits and the volume of bank 'earning' assets as a whole by its powers of control over the banks' cash reserves; but under the present system, in order to secure a change in these and yet permit the Bank to act as lender (or borrower) of last resort, the authorities must also be able to bring about an appropriate alteration in the supply of money-market assets to the banks.

A reduction may occur almost automatically if the Exchequer has an overall surplus, or if the country's gold and dollar reserves are declining at a rate in excess of any overall deficit in the

Exchequer accounts. For the result is to cause a transfer of cash from the public to the authorites, enabling a reduction in the issue of Treasury bills to be made. Apart from this, the supply of money-market assets to the banks can be diminished by 'funding' operations or by influencing the demand for Treasury bills by the public. For the sake of simplicity the Exchequer can first be assumed to be in balance.

### Funding Operations

Although the 'funded' debt of the Exchequer consists only of securities with no fixed redemption date, the term 'funding' has come to be applied to the sale of government bonds of any maturity to the public in order to replace Treasury bills held by the banks and discount houses. For its opposite, 'unfunding', there is an even less authentic lineage.

Suppose the Bank of England sells bonds to the public to the amount of £30 million and uses the proceeds to purchase Treasury bills from the banks or discount houses. The picture, shown as an artificial series of 'stills', would be as follows:

|  | I | | II——————III | | | | IV | |
|  | £m. | % | £m. | % | £m. | % | £m. | % |
|---|---|---|---|---|---|---|---|---|
| Cash | 80 | 8 | 50 | 5·2 | 80 | 8·2 | 72 | 8 |
| Money market assets | 220 | 22 | 220 | 22·7 | 190 | 19·7 | 198 | 22 |
| Liquid assets | 300 | 30 | 270 | 27·9 | 270 | 27·9 | 270 | 30 |
| Earning assets | 700 | 70 | 700 | 72·1 | 700 | 72·1 | 630 | 70 |
| Deposits | 1,000 | 100 | 970 | 100·0 | 970 | 100·0 | 900 | 100 |

In practice, Stages II and III would be simultaneous. The reduction in the liquid-asset ratio in III leads the banks to contract their 'earning' assets and their deposits until the 30 per cent ratio is restored. In the process, other things being equal, the sale of government bonds by the Bank of England would tend to raise interest rates on such securities, and this effect would be strengthened as the banks sold investments or called in advances, forcing borrowers to seek other methods of finance. In the money market, on the other hand, the desire of the banks to exchange surplus cash for money-market assets following Stage III would bring down money rates, including bill rates, between Stages III and IV.*

The effect on money rates has been expressed in this way rather than by saying that the Bank's purchase of bills has been the cause, because the greater part of this purchase (namely, £22 million) has had to be made in order to prevent a shortage of cash that would otherwise have caused a sharp rise in money rates. Given the pattern of market expectations about the future of rates, money rates can be said to depend on the relationship between the supply of bills and the supply of cash from the banks (and other lenders), and it is only in the movement from Stage III to Stage IV that the balance of supply and demand is altered in this way.

It is worth looking at the final result*[14] of these operations as reflected in the Bank of England's assets and liabilities. The Bank has sold bonds to the amount of £30 million, decreasing the item 'Government securities' in the Banking Department or 'Other government securities' in the Issue Department. It has also bought £22 million of bills, which would increase one of these two asset items, so that the Bank's assets have fallen on balance by £8 million. This is exactly equal to the reduction in the banks' cash reserves, which are liabilities of the Bank of England. When the Treasury bills purchased by the Bank mature, they can be replaced by an issue of tap bills to the Bank. Alternatively, the maturing bills can be replaced by other securities newly issued to the Bank or by securities sold to the Bank by another government department, which in turn can take up new tap bills.

Whatever the exact arrangements the process of funding would result in a reduction in the issue of tender bills. The government's accounts as a whole, however, would remain in balance. The £22 million decrease in the Exchequer's indebtedness to the banking system in the form of Treasury bills has been offset by an increase of £30 million in its indebtedness to the public and a reduction of £8 million in the Bank of England's indebtedness to the commercial banks; the net indebtedness of the complex of government departments as a whole to the non-government sector has not changed.

---

* It must be stressed, once more, that the probability of a change in the note circulation has again been ignored.

### 'Unfunding'

'Unfunding' would work in reverse. If the Bank of England simultaneously sells bills to the discount houses and buys bonds from the public the effect is to raise bank deposits and liquid asset holdings by the same amount, the increase in the banks' liquidity ratios making possible an expansion of 'earning' assets and therefore an increase in deposits.

In one respect, however, the sequence of events need not be exactly the opposite of the funding process. The banks are under no compulsion to prevent their liquid-asset ratios from rising above 30 per cent if they are unwilling to risk a future fall in gilt-edged prices or dilute their standards of credit-worthiness.

The addition to the volume of bills in the hands of the banks and the discount houses produced by 'unfunding' would have to be repaid on maturity out of the proceeds of new bills issued through the weekly tender. If the operation were carried out by a department other than the Bank of England the pattern of events would be somewhat different, although the result would be the same. The department would buy bonds from the public out of the proceeds of tap bills specially repaid by the Exchequer, which could finance these repayments by an increase in the issue of tender bills.

### Funding via the Banks

These examples of open market 'funding' and 'unfunding' operations have been described in terms of bonds sold to or bought from the public. The final effect on the banks' cash reserves will be similar if transactions are conducted by the authorities with the banks instead, but the assets held by the public will not be directly affected. The sale of bonds to the banks, the proceeds of which are used to reduce the money-market assets of the banks, will not immediately reduce the level of deposits but, by substituting bonds for money-market assets, will reduce the liquidity ratios of the banks. In practice, of course, the banks would be unwilling to purchase bonds if at the outset their liquidity ratios were already at a minimum. If liquidity ratios were well above 30 per cent, however, this implies that the banks *preferred* not to add to their investments at the current level of interest rates, so that if the authorities wished the banks voluntarily to purchase bonds at the expense of their money-market assets they would have to adjust the pattern of interest rates so as to make bonds relatively more attractive than bills.

In November 1951 liquidity ratios were at the very high level of 39 per cent when the authorities began to change the direction of monetary policy towards a more positive control of deposits. To do this it was first necessary to bring bank liquidity ratios much nearer 30 per cent; the measure adopted by the Bank of England was that of 'inducing', by means of informal pressure, the banks and discount houses to subscribe to special issues of Serial Funding Stocks with lives of one, two, and three years and amounting to £1,000 million, payment being made in the form of Treasury bills. In consequence liquidity ratios were cut to 32 per cent, not long before the period of seasonal pressure on bank liquidity, and in the event the banks were forced to sell some £100 million of investments. This 'forced funding' was generally accepted as an emergency once-and-for-all measure needed to clear the ground for a radical change in policy, but some concern was expressed in the financial world at the repetition of such tactics a year later, in October 1952. In the next round of conversion operations, in the autumn of 1953, the element of compulsion was not reintroduced.

Voluntary funding in 1951 and 1952, whether conducted with the banks or the public, would have required higher interest rates on government bonds, and this the government was not prepared to accept; in 1953, on the other hand, interest rates were tending to fall, making voluntary funding easier to achieve.

OTHER OBJECTS OF FUNDING

In this section funding operations have been presented as a means of controlling the level of deposits. This is not their only use. The main object of the government's policy in pursuing such tactics might be to raise long-term interest rates, the effect on deposits being a secondary consideration. It may also be noted that the first impact of official sales of bonds to the public will be to reduce the deposits held by the public, who can be induced by a sufficient increase in the rate of interest to exchange bank deposits for bonds. The authorities may not press their sales to the point of forcing bank liquidity ratios below 30 per cent, so that there is no *multiple* contraction of deposits. The authorities may be content with a modest reduction in the liquidity of the public as part of a policy aimed at preventing inflation, in the hope of making it rather more difficult for people to spend in the future, for a further rise in interest rates, involving a fall in security prices, might deter people from selling their bonds at a loss in order to finance expenditure in excess of their current income. Alternatively, open market operations may be carried out primarily with the aim of absorbing *excess* bank liquidity, making it difficult for the banks to expand deposits in the future.

Traditionally, funding, in the sense of lengthening the average term to maturity of the national debt, has always seemed a desirable long-term policy to Chancellors of the Exchequer, because a national debt that consists to a large extent of Treasury bills or short-dated bonds is much more vulnerable to a rise in interest rates, particularly to a rise in Bank rate, the historic monetary weapon. Indeed, the reluctance of the government to pursue a policy involving high short-term interest rates in order to check excessive spending during the earlier years of the post-war inflation may be attributed, if only in part, to the size of the short-term debt. As part of the floating debt is in the hands of overseas holders a high Treasury bill rate imposes a 'real' burden on the country. Unfortunately, while funding itself tends to lower money rates, the increase in long-term rates that new government issues, whether in the form of special funding issues or conversion stocks, have to bear is a burden that has to be borne over the whole life of the securities concerned. Therefore a period in which issues of government bonds are falling due for redemption in large quantities and in which the market rate of interest on bonds is higher than that on Treasury bills is not usually regarded by the Treasury as a favourable opportunity for lengthening the term of the national debt, unless the present long-term rate is significantly below that at which the authorities expect it to remain over the future.

### THE DIVERSION OF TREASURY BILLS TO THE PUBLIC

If the main object of funding is to reduce bank liquidity by removing both cash and Treasury bills (or loans against Treasury bills) from the assets of the banks, the same purpose will be served if a larger part of the Treasury bill tender issue is taken up by the public, whose payments to the Exchequer draw on the banks' cash reserves. Large commercial concerns and financial institutions such as insurance companies and building societies may be induced to hold a greater proportion of their liquid resources in Treasury bills if their yield is sufficiently more rewarding than other assets that can easily be turned into cash.

The chief alternative to holding Treasury bills is the use of deposit accounts. In order to induce large companies and financial institutions to take up bills instead, the authorities must therefore raise the yield on Treasury bills relatively to that offered on deposit accounts. For about a century the London banks have linked their deposit rate to Bank rate, so that such a policy involves raising market rates in relation to Bank rate, by open market sales of Treasury bills or by use of the Bank's power in smoothing operations. A rise in bill rates in this way had some effect in reducing bank liquidity in the nineteen-twenties and again during the tight-money policy of 1955.

A reduction in bank liquidity will also take place if the public take up any assets sold by the authorities, including Tax Reserve Certificates, Post Office deposits and other instruments of National Savings, all of which enable the issue of Treasury bills to the banks to be curtailed.

### BANK RATE AND THE BANKING SYSTEM

A change in Bank rate, the traditional weapon of the Bank of England, can be said to have three types of effects on the banking system—semi-automatic, psychological, and indirect.

#### *Semi-automatic Effects*

Its semi-automatic effects derive from the arrangements whereby certain lending and borrowing rates of the banks are linked to Bank rate. The London banks have agreed as to a maximum deposit rate since the middle of the last century, when competition between the banks for deposits and the high rates that ensued led the banks to discount doubtful commercial paper in order to cover their costs, a policy whose risks were exposed in the banking crisis of 1857. In 1921 the banks reached formal agreement on a minimum rate for loans to the money market, the arrangement having the blessing of the authorities, who were at that time anxious to keep market rates up to Bank rate.

The margin between these two rates and Bank rate and the gap between the deposit rate and minimum call-money rate (which is an important element in the banks' profits) are by no means fixed permanently. Changes have occurred in their relationship from time to time, the spread being compressed when Bank rate has been low and extended when it has been high. In the short-run, however, these margins have been relatively stable, so that changes in Bank rate have generally been followed by movements in the deposit rate and call-money rate in the same direction and, except at the extreme limits of Bank rate, to the same extent. The minimum short loan rate has a direct influence on other money-market rates, including the Treasury bill rate, which can fluctuate between this level and Bank rate itself, according to the pressures of the market and the actions of the authorities.

Only part of the money lent by the banks to the discount market is offered at the minimum rate; in practice there have been a number of rates to which different conditions are attached, such as 'overnight' money and 'privilege' money, the latter always being made available up to certain amounts; money 'at call' may be genuinely at call, or understood, by the discount houses at least, to be more in the nature of a 'fixture'. The proportion of money lent at rates fluctuating from day to day has varied. Neither the level of marginal rates nor the bill rate itself will change by as much as Bank rate if the market has already anticipated, or been forced to anticipate, the change in Bank rate.

Movements in the rates charged by the banks on their advances, which do not appear to be subject to open agreement, may perhaps be described as 'demi-semi-automatic'. For many years the banks are believed to have been guided by the formula of '1 per cent above bank-rate; minimum 5 per cent', but competition between the banks, and between the banks and the new-issue market and other sources of finance, leads in practice to flexibility at both ends of the scale of borrowers.

### Psychological Effects

The psychological effectiveness of bank-rate depends on the reliability of a change in the rate as a guide to future monetary policy. If the banks and discount houses regard a rise in bank-rate after a period of stability as the prelude to a further increase or as a warning of open market operations, market rates can be expected to move up sharply close to the new Bank rate. The banks may be led to the conclusion, moreover, that it would be prudent not to let their liquidity ratios fall below a level which in easier circumstances they would regard as ample. If they are convinced that official policy will lead ultimately to less profitable business conditions, they may go so far as to prune their advances, by trimming marginal amounts off loans to weaker borrowers.

## Indirect Effects

The ability of a change in Bank rate to influence indirectly the level of 'earning' assets which the banks regard as safe lies in the possibility that the movement in the rate will cause a change in the condition of the gilt-edged market through the actions of *other* operators. If a rise in Bank rate causes uncertainty as to future bond prices the reluctance of the banks to add to their 'earning' assets may be strengthened, and in a situation in which the banks are none too sure of the adequacy of their liquidity ratios this indirect result may take the form of a voluntary reduction in 'earning' assets. The weaker the gilt-edged market the greater the likelihood that the restrictive consequences of a rise in Bank rate will be felt by advances. Correspondingly, a reduction in Bank rate can be expected to induce the banks to adopt a less austere policy regarding their 'earning' assets.

## Bank rate and the Floating Debt

The effectiveness of Bank rate *alone* as a means of controlling bank deposits now depends largely on what the banks regard as a safe liquidity ratio. This link is very different from that which helped to make Bank rate a powerful weapon before the First World War. The contrast lies in the fact that the greater part of the banks' holdings of money-market assets consists of Treasury bills or of loans against Treasury bills; a rise in Bank rate has no effect either on the credit-worthiness of the Exchequer or on its immediate willingness to borrow. Before 1914, on the other hand, the banks' money-market assets were almost entirely commercial bills, or loans against commercial bills, and a rise in Bank rate could operate with greater potency, for the quantity of commercial bills in the banks' possession, and thus the level of deposits, could respond to changes in the degree of credit stringency and to changes in expectations on the part of both lenders and borrowers regarding the business outlook, on which substantial movements in Bank rate could be expected to have an influence. Both the supply of and the demand for commercial bills, especially those not of the first quality, would tend to react to sharp changes in Bank rate in an economy in which the maintenance of prosperous business conditions, such as those we have now experienced for almost twenty years, was not to be taken for granted.

The growth of the floating debt therefore takes its place with other repercussions of the growth of government expenditure as a factor that has taken one edge off the weapon of Bank rate just as Britain's decline in the world of international finance has blunted the other. Before 1914 part of the loss of gold that was the cause of a rise in Bank rate was usually reversed by the effect of the increase in money rates in London in diminishing the flow of short-term lending by this country in other financial centres. As a result the contraction of ordinary business operations in Britain which had to be secured for Bank rate to succeed in its object of restoring the Bank's gold reserve was itself usually small in the period before 1914.

### Keeping Bank rate 'Effective'

The power of Bank rate as a penal rate lies in its standing above market rates. When action is taken by the Bank to make its rate 'effective', that is to force money rates closer to Bank rate, by driving the market to seek assistance at the penal rate, its effect as a penalty is reduced if money rates have settled down close to Bank rate. In this case open market operations in the bill market can have a marked effect on money rates only if Bank rate is raised still higher.

A rise in money-market rates may have psychological and indirect effects on the banks similar to those of an increase in Bank rate itself. If open market operations in bills are undertaken by the Bank to drive up bill rates the banks may interpret this as a sign of a general change in official policy towards greater stringency and act accordingly. The gilt-edged market may also be affected through the reaction of other investors, inducing the banks to remain content with a higher liquidity ratio than previously.

### MONETARY CONTROL BY COMPULSION

Since the war, governments of both parties have made use of their powers of compulsion, largely in the form of directives or 'requests' issued to the banks by the Chancellor or by the

Governor of the Bank of England. Their main object has been to check the growth of advances. Not until 1955 did the government instruct the banks to make an actual reduction in the aggregate of advances; this was also the year in which the authorities are first thought to have ordered the banks to adhere to what was previously only a conventional minimum liquidity ratio of 30 per cent. Official control over advances has for the most part been exerted by requests to the banks to restrict the provision of credit to certain so-called non-essential borrowers.

Instructions to the banks may be thought desirable by the authorities in order to prevent the former from taking advantage of ample liquidity ratios to expand advances. The authorities may tolerate excessive bank liquidity if the banks add to their holdings of investments instead, on the grounds that, although both an expansion of advances and an increase in bank investment portfolios add to deposits, those created by bank advances are more inflationary, being used directly for spending, whereas deposits created by purchases of securities by the banks are more likely to remain idle. The authorities may alternatively expect the banks to use surplus liquidity to take up bonds sold by government departments; or directives may be aimed at ensuring that the banks react to a *shortage* of liquid assets by reducing advances rather than investments.

Instructions to reduce advances are necessary only if the authorities are unwilling to accept the higher level of interest rates that might result if they used open market operations or a rise in Bank rate to reduce excess bank liquidity, to induce the banks to work with liquidity ratios above 30 per cent, or to restrict advances rather than investments. Directives do not always prevent the growth of bank advances, for bankers find it hard to turn away insistent and credit-worthy borrowers when their liquidity is ample. The task of discriminating against business transactions deemed by the government to be national luxuries is not one that, considering the generality of the criteria offered by the authorities and the actual complexity of the economic fabric, is likely to be pursued without some arbitrariness and inconsistency; and the suspicion of undue generosity to large concerns is not easily dispelled. Discrimination in favour of 'essential' borrowers may be insufficient to prevent excessive credit creation, for in a vigorous boom the aggregate of even 'essential' investment planned by industry may outrun the economy's resources. It is not even certain that industrial borrowers turned away by the banks (or the Capital Issues Committee) need be deprived of finance at all if the economy is sufficiently liquid, for the substantial growth in trade credit since the war indicates that those concerns looked on with favour by the banks (and the C.I.C.) may be able to share their augmented liquid resources with those outside the official pale. Loans may also be obtainable from institutions outside the ordinary banking system, such as hire-purchase finance houses and similar concerns.

### 'Special Deposits'

In July 1958 the government announced a scheme whereby the Bank of England could require the banks to put into special deposits at the Bank of England a stipulated percentage of their gross deposits. Special deposits are to be treated as non-liquid assets and will earn interest equal to the rate on Treasury bills. This scheme was stated to be a temporary one pending the recommendations of the Radcliffe Committee on the working of the financial system, but it evidently reflects the view of the authorities, based on their experience of the past few years, that some such compulsory arrangement will continue to be necessary. The operation of special deposits will not markedly differ from the effect of open market operations in government securities if they are to be used to cause an actual reduction in bank deposits, by depressing liquidity ratios to below 30 per cent, but their use would allow the authorities to mop up excess bank liquidity, and thus to forestall a rise in deposits, without pressing sales of government securities on a weak market. It is therefore the reluctance of the authorities to cause the sharp increase in interest rates that a vigorous funding policy may entail that underlies the decision to return to a system that is basically similar to that of the Treasury Deposit Receipt. It has no special value, on the other hand, as a means of expanding deposits.

### OPEN MARKET OPERATIONS AND 'CHEAP MONEY'

The ability of the authorities to use departmental funds facilitates the implementation of a 'cheap money' policy, that is one aimed at producing low interest rates. Purchases of bonds by the authorities, followed by the addition to the banks' own holdings made possible by the consequent expansion of their cash reserves,* will normally raise gilt-edged prices. Open market operations in bonds are not the only method of reducing long-term interest rates, however. Before 1932 the traditional approach of the Bank of England to a situation in which lower interest rates seemed desirable was to concentrate on bill rates, by purchasing bills in the market and by reducing Bank rate, leaving the effect to be transmitted to longer-term securities through the reaction of investors. Sometimes these operations, while sharply reducing bill rates, had little effect on long-term yields. Although it is now more widely accepted that a policy aimed at causing substantial movements in long-term interest rates may require official intervention directly in this section of the market, the view that the authorities should act so as to bring about changes in long-term interest rates directly does not command universal assent, particularly in the U.S.A. Opposition to direct official intervention is usually based on the view that it would be detrimental to the free working of the gilt-edged market as a market and that the long-term rate should be left free to reflect what in some quarters are described as fundamental natural forces.

One difference between open market purchases of bills and the process of 'unfunding' is that the latter may cause money rates to rise, by analogy with the movement between Stages III and IV shown in the illustration of funding; the enlarged supply of bills presses on the banks' cash reserves. To prevent this the Bank would have to make open market purchases of bills. Alternatively, bills held by the banks could be paid off out of the proceeds of loans to the Exchequer by the Bank of England, for this would provide the banks with surplus cash and thus make them eager to purchase Treasury bills. The policy would also be assisted by a reduction in Bank rate.

## CONVERSION OPERATIONS AND BANK LIQUIDITY

Switches from one security to another within official portfolios, leaving their total values unchanged, often play a part in the conversion of maturing stocks. A government department can buy up a bond approaching maturity by selling a longer-dated stock, thus making a 'successful' conversion more likely.

---

* The authorities would have to supply the requisite increase in money market assets as well.

2 D

When conversion operations necessitate payments to existing holders of the maturing stock who decline the offer of a new stock in exchange, however, the Exchequer will normally provide the necessary cash by an increase in the Treasury bill issue. If these holders are members of the public the effect is exactly as if the authorities had pursued an open market policy of 'unfunding', causing an expansion of deposits and an increase in bank liquidity ratios. Conversion operations may therefore loosen the control of the authorities over the banking system unless surplus bank liquidity can be drawn off, for example by open market sales of bonds.

When the cash payments involved in conversion operations are made to discount houses, which will often be the holders of the maturing stock, the result of the increase in the issue of Treasury bills needed to provide the cash is merely to substitute bills for the bonds maturing in the portfolios of the discount houses, leaving the liquidity of the banks unchanged if the additional bills are all taken up by the discount houses.

# PART V

# THE DETERMINATION OF SECURITY PRICES

CHAPTER 30

# THE DETERMINATION OF
# THE RATE OF INTEREST

### AN INTRODUCTORY SUMMARY

It is a useful first approximation to consider the complex of interest
rates as a whole, by pretending that there is only one class of
security, an irredeemable fixed-interest stock with no risk of
default. This brings into sharper focus forces bearing on all
fixed-interest securities. It is in this sense that the term 'the rate
of interest' is used throughout this and the following chapter,
which aim at making a broad survey of the factors influencing the
rate of interest in the modern industrial economy where capital
is for the most part in private hands.

### THE RATE OF INTEREST AS A PRICE

The rate of interest yielded by an irredeemable fixed-interest
security, or bond, is inversely proportional to its price, so that we
can examine the behaviour of the rate of interest as we would
that of any set of prices, in terms of the supply of and demand for
bonds. An increase in the demand for bonds relative to their
supply tends to raise their price, but as a rise in price means a fall
in the rate of interest we can speak of the rate of interest as being
determined by the supply of and the demand for bonds.

If the total demand for bonds when the rate of interest was, say,
4 per cent, exceeded the volume that operators were supplying,
that is trying to sell, the rate of interest would fall below 4 per cent.
It would remain stable when the volume of securities on offer at
the current rate of interest exactly balanced the volume demanded.

In one sense, of course, supply and demand are equal at any
moment of time, for the value of actual purchases must equal the
value of sales; but this is merely equality by definition. What is
meant by 'supply' is the volume that people would offer at a
given price, and by 'demand' the volume that investors would
attempt to take off the market at that price. If 'demand exceeds
supply', this must mean that some investors would be willing to

pay a higher price than that ruling at that moment, and in a competitive market the pressure of demand would cause prices to rise until those who were not willing to sell at the initial, lower, price were finally induced to meet this unsatisfied demand through being able to sell at a higher one, or until some investors who were prospective buyers at the lower price curtailed their demand as security prices rose.

### THE DEMAND FOR SECURITIES

Let us assume that the total quantity of money of the community, which substantially means the level of bank deposits, remains constant and that we are examining a community with no international transactions.

### The Deployment of Existing Wealth

First, demand in any period will be fed by those people whose total wealth has not changed but who wish to hold a greater proportion of it in the form of bonds rather than money or goods, such as paintings or real property. Fixed-interest securities compete with money and real assets as a form in which wealth can be held, and each form has its own possible advantages and disadvantages that will be assessed differently by investors in choosing how to hold their wealth.

*Money*, on the simplest assumptions, would earn no interest. In practice, interest is earned on a deposit account with a bank, but the holder suffers some slight loss of liquidity in return, in that notice of withdrawal is required. Notes, coin and current-account balances earn no interest but provide greater convenience in regard to the possible need for future expenditure than either securities or real assets; they have the virtue of offering a certain and immediate command over goods and services if the general level of prices remains unchanged. If the price-level rises, holders of money lose in real terms; if it falls, they gain.

*Real assets*, on the other hand, protect their holder from a real loss if their prices rise with the general price-level, but involve him in a real loss if their prices fall more than the general price-level. Some real assets yield an annual income, e.g. in the form of rent, and all are subject to possible changes in capital value due to a variation in the supply of or demand for them.

*Fixed-interest* securities, like money, suffer a loss of real value if prices in general rise, assuming that their money value does not increase. Against this, securities earn interest. They are also open to the chance of a rise or fall in capital value, in money terms, due to a fall or rise in the market rate of interest itself.

Thus the demand for fixed-interest securities as a form of wealth turns on the force of the different qualities of the three classes of assets, as they appear to investors. The greater is the demand for the convenience offered by money as a means of payment, the stronger will be the desire for money rather than real assets or bonds. The greater the fear of a rise in the general price-level, the stronger will be the demand for real assets rather than money or fixed-interest securities. Given the demand for monetary convenience and expectations regarding the price-level, the demand for fixed-interest securities will be greater the higher is the rate of interest and the smaller seems the risk of a further rise. Expectations about the future of the rate of interest play a crucial part in determining the current rate of interest.

### The Demand for Securities from Current Saving

The stream of demand in any period will be fed by those investors who are in the process of *adding* to their total wealth by saving out of their current income and who wish to use part of their current saving to purchase bonds, that is, who wish to hold part of the *addition* to their wealth in this form.

Of course, in practice there will be a demand for bonds by investors who are both saving and trying to change the proportion of their existing wealth held in the form of bonds. We can allocate these mixed actions to both elements of demand. If members of the community as a whole are saving at the rate of £20 million a week and wish to use only half of this to purchase securities and the other half to add to their money balances instead, the situation is exactly the same as if one half of the community, saving £20 million a week, was using the whole of its current saving to purchase securities while the other half, neither saving nor dissaving, wished to add £10 million to its money balances at the expense of its security holdings. Thus the whole of current saving can be included in the demand for securities if we take account of any *net* desire to increase or reduce existing money balances as an alternative to holding bonds, including the desire to do so on the part of current savers.

### THE SUPPLY OF SECURITIES

These two sets of factors can be matched on the other side of the market. First, there is the supply of bonds by operators who, at the ruling rate of interest, would prefer to hold a greater proportion of their existing wealth in the form of money or goods. Secondly, there is the supply of bonds on the part of businesses and public bodies which are raising money in order to spend it on capital investment. The securities offered may be new issues or those being sold by businesses out of their portfolio of existing securities.

When one business merely buys equipment from another, investment by the first is set off by disinvestment by the second, so that no investment* has taken place by business as a whole. When we speak of the supply of securities for the purpose of investment, we mean those supplied in order to finance the *construction* of capital equipment and the addition to stocks on the part of the community as a whole, including that by the government. If businesses or the government are able to finance their capital investment by running down existing money balances, without having to sell securities, there is no *direct* effect on the rate of interest. The situation is as if business or the government first bought securities through a desire to increase the proportion of their wealth in this form and then sold them to raise finance.

The factors behind the supply of bonds are thus the desire to reduce the proportion of wealth held as bonds and capital investment.

### DEMAND, SUPPLY AND THE EQUILIBRIUM RATE OF INTEREST

The determination of the rate of interest can therefore be summarized in the statement that the equilibrium rate, tending neither to rise nor fall, is that at which the supply of and the demand for bonds are equal. When demand exceeds supply the rate of interest will tend to fall until it reaches a new equilibrium through its interaction with the desire to hold existing wealth in securities, with the willingness to save, or with investment. When

---

* The term 'investment' in this and the following chapters will be used to mean the acquisition of a physical asset; the verb 'invest' and its subject the 'investor', on the other hand, will be used to mean the acquisition of a financial asset, as in everyday speech.

supply exceeds demand the rate of interest will tend to rise until a new equilibrium level is reached. The process by which this equilibrium is achieved is discussed in the following chapter.

Any discrepancy between the community's desire to save and its capital investment will have no direct effect on the rate of interest if the willingness to hold existing wealth in securities changes in the appropriate direction. If, for example, the investment that the community attempts to undertake exceeds the volume of saving that it is willing to perform, the direct upward pressure on the rate of interest that would otherwise result will be avoided if the excess supply of bonds involved is matched by an equal demand on the part of investors who, at the ruling rate of interest, wish to raise the proportion of their existing wealth held in bonds. But, as we shall eventually see, this is in the nature of a short-term equilibrium only, for unless, in a sense that we have still to define, saving and investment are equal *and* the community as a whole is satisfied with the composition of its existing wealth, the economy will not be stationary and the rate of interest will not be in final equilibrium.

The assumption of a fixed quantity of money need not be maintained. An excess supply of securities may be met, at the initial rate of interest, by an increase in demand by the monetary authorities or the banks, which in the process of adding to their assets will raise the level of deposits. An increase in the volume of advances reduces the need for borrowers to sell securities. Once the community has decided what part of its wealth it wishes to hold in the form of money, an increase in the quantity of money arising through the purchase of securities from the public by the banks or the authorities will usually be acceptable to the public only if there is a fall in the rate of interest sufficient to induce it to part with securities and hold the newly-created money instead. When the increase in the quantity of money does not occur at the expense of the public's security holdings, as will be the case when a budget deficit is financed by government borrowing from the banking system, for example, we can expect part of what will then be an increase in the *total* wealth of the public to be used to purchase securities.

To sum up, the rate of interest is determined by saving, investment, the strength of the desire to hold existing wealth in the form of securities rather than real assets or money, and the size of the quantity of money to be held somewhere in the economy, the latter being the consequence of the actions of the monetary authorities and the banks. In this analysis, the size of the stock of real assets and the size of the stock of bonds in existence at any moment need not be taken into account as such, for they are the result of *past* investment and the past actions of the authorities, which are brought into the analysis at the time they occur. Here the demand for and supply of securities are expressed as a 'flow' over a period of time; but some economists prefer to describe the process in terms only of 'stocks' of real assets, bonds, and money in existence at successive points of time.

This summary implies that when demand exceeds supply, the consequent fall in the rate of interest tends to restore equilibrium between them because it leads to the gap being filled by stimulating the supply of securities or by curtailing the demand for them (and conversely when the discrepancy is in the opposite direction). The decline in the rate of interest may lead those who are holding bonds to sell them and hold money instead, as long as the fall is not expected to be followed by a further fall. A decline in the rate of interest may stimulate capital investment or it may induce people to save a smaller proportion of their income; it is generally held that both investment and the desire to save respond to changes in the rate of interest in this way, if only to a small extent. The lower the rate of interest, the wider the range of projects that it will be profitable to undertake; the lower the rate of interest, the less worthwhile it will seem to some people to sacrifice current consumption for the future, for the smaller will be the financial return available from the assets purchased out of current saving. But just how sensitive to changes in the rate of interest are the willingness of businessmen to undertake investment and the desire of the public at large to save out of a given income is open to dispute.

The more sensitive are the constituents of supply and demand in response to a change in the rate of interest, the smaller will be the adjustment in the rate required to maintain equilibrium (except in the situation where a *continued* movement in the rate of interest is expected). In other words, we are back to the problems of *elasticity* of supply and demand, and the question of how interest-elastic are saving, investment and the desire to hold bonds in different circumstances is at the heart of the problem of the determination of the rate of interest. It is also a matter of some dispute among both economic theorists and economic policy makers.

### SOME PROBLEMS OF DEFINITION

If ambiguities that have beset theories of the rate of interest in the past are to be avoided, it is unfortunately necessary to consider some questions of definition at length. These are more than of mere academic interest; differences of opinion as to whether 'saving must equal investment', for example, will in some situations lead investors in quite opposite directions and in the past twenty years have been responsible for some of the fiercest conflicts in monetary economics. By and large these conflicts have now been resolved, in that differences of definition have been distinguished from differences of argument as to facts.

#### *'Saving Equals Investment'*

In this chapter both saving and investment have been represented as being among the direct determinants of the rate of interest. This implies that there is a sense in which saving and investment need not be equal in value, for if they were they could have no direct effect on the rate of interest. For some time after the publication of the *General Theory of Employment, Interest and Money* by John Maynard Keynes in 1936, a book which has had a great influence on the development of economic thought, it was indeed held by his most uncompromising supporters that saving and investment were necessarily equal at all times. A change in investment was considered simultaneously to involve an equal change in the amount saved, so that the supply of and demand for securities due to these two factors would always remain in balance.

It was contended, for example, that if people tried to reduce their expenditure on consumer goods and to increase the amount they saved out of a given level of income, the result could only be a fall in the total national income to a level at which the amount people were willing to save was just equal to the (unchanged) level of investment. The amount actually saved was held to remain constant throughout the whole process. The only exception would occur if businesses remained content to see stocks of unsold consumer goods pile up, this increase in stocks due to the fall in consumers' expenditure being defined as an increase in investment, which would necessarily equal the increase in saving.

But in no case, it was once argued, could the rise in the desire to save have any *direct* effect on the rate of interest; a rise in the desire to save could only influence the rate of interest if the fall in the national income that was held to be its only direct consequence made businesses and ordinary individuals more willing to hold securities rather than money, of which less would be needed as a means of payment at a lower level of income and expenditure. Similarly, a rise in investment was held to act *directly* on the national income only and not on the rate of interest; the latter might rise, it is true, but only if, with a higher national income, people wished to hold more money for the sake of convenience.

Before these views were expressed, on the other hand, it would usually be said that an increase in saving might reduce the rate of interest and that the fall in the rate of interest might stimulate capital investment by business, thus leaving the level of total output and income more or less unchanged. The first half of this statement—that a change in saving can directly influence interest rates—was held by the 'saving equals investment' school to be quite erroneous.

The heart of the matter lay in the way in which saving and investment were defined and in the treatment of the element of time. Certain economists always defined both saving and investment as the amount actually saved and actually invested in a given period, like the past quantities measured by national income statisticians. Total income received in that period was defined as being equal to the value of production in that period. Production —assuming for the sake of simplicity that there is no foreign trade —must take the form of consumer goods sold to the public, those added to producers' stocks, and capital goods. The value of consumer goods sold is necessarily the same as the amount bought. As saving was defined as income earned in the period under consideration minus expenditure on consumer goods in that period, saving must always, it would appear, be equal to investment, that is to say, to that part of production not in the form of consumer goods sold in the period.

Thus, in a given period:

| | | |
|---|---|---|
| Production | = | consumption plus investment |
| Income | = | consumption plus saving |
| Income | = | production |
| Saving | = | investment |

This equality between saving and investment is an accounting identity, reflecting the choice of definitions. It is analogous to the 'equality' of 'supply' and 'demand' for any commodity when these are expressed in terms of the amount actually bought and sold in any given period. The problem of definition arises from the attempt to express in discontinuous periods a process that is continuous and determined by constantly changing and mutually interacting forces, in the manner of problems of dynamics encountered in physics. The amounts of saving and investment that are actually performed in any given period are the *consequences* of the forces operating on each other in that period, including the rate of interest, and it is to the forces and not to the consequences that we must look.

## The Interaction of Saving, Investment and the Rate of Interest

The problem can be exemplified by considering the effects of an increase in the willingness to save. If, for whatever reason, part of the population decides to increase the proportion of income saved and to use the whole of its new saving to buy securities what are the possible results ? Some economists who claimed that saving *must* equal investment seemed to argue that no actual increase in the total amount saved could possibly occur.* All that would happen, they appeared to contend, was that the people who tried to increase their saving, by reducing their expenditure, would merely reduce the incomes and thus the saving of those from whom they had previously bought their goods. The amount saved would remain throughout the whole process at a level exactly equal to investment, and there is no reason why the latter should rise once the increase in producers' stocks of consumer goods due to the fall in sales had been worked off. The result would then be a fall in total income equal to the fall in consumers' expenditure. As for the rate of interest, a *direct* change was thought impossible —the new purchases of securities by those who had been increasing their saving would be offset by the reduction in security purchases by those whose saving had to be cut owing to the fall in their incomes. This may, *in fact*, be the actual sequence of events, but

---

* This should not be taken to imply that economists who choose to express saving and investment as accounting identities today argue about the *process* of economic *events* in this way.

if so, it follows not from any 'necessary' equality of 'saving' with 'investment' but from certain assumptions regarding the behaviour of the rate of interest and the reaction of investment.

The correct statement of the problem is that *if* the increase in the willingness to save lowers the rate of interest, and *if* this sufficiently stimulates investment, the decline in the incomes received in the consumer goods industries will be offset by the increase in incomes in the capital goods industries. Similarly, the reduction in security purchases out of the former set of incomes may be made good by new purchases out of the latter. *If* this happens, the desire to save a higher amount is achieved, and the total national income is unchanged—consumption has fallen but investment has increased. We can only say that an increase in the desire to save will cause an equal fall in the total national income *if* something happens to prevent the rate of interest from falling, or if the fall in the rate of interest that does materialize has no effect on investment.

A fall in the rate of interest would not occur, for example, if existing holders of securities were convinced that the rate of interest ruling at the beginning of the period was already at its lowest possible level in the circumstances prevailing, so that any tendency for the rate of interest to fall would be defeated by the sales of nervous investors. Alternatively, those who were in the process of increasing their saving might choose to hold part of this addition to their wealth in the form of money rather than securities, in which case not all of the new saving would be offered through the capital market for the finance of additional investment. Thirdly, the fall in the rate of interest might be too small to induce businessmen to expand their investment expenditure. In these circumstances, it is true, the increase in the willingness to save would be self-defeating.

## PERIOD ANALYSIS

There are a number of ways in which this problem of defining saving and investment can be met. One is to discuss the process of cause and effect in terms of *attempted* saving and investment, which need not be equal. Through interaction with the rate of interest, attempted saving and attempted investment can be said to lead to certain identical quantities of saving and investment actually materializing in a given period. This is sometimes described as the difference between *ex ante* and *ex post* saving and investment.

## The 'Week'

An alternative and in many ways more fertile method of expression is that usually described as 'period analysis'. The time factor is dealt with by supposing that time can be split into a succession of very short periods usually described as 'weeks'. A 'week' is defined so that at the beginning of each the members of the community make a plan to save a definite amount during the week and to purchase a certain quantity of securities during the week, while businesses and the government make their plans as to how much capital investment they are going to carry out during the week.

A 'week' is defined to be too short for plans for saving and investment made at the beginning of the week to be changed during that same week—any changes in response to the situation developing during the week can only be made in the following weeks. Investors make their plans to purchase securities during the week, out of planned saving or out of money balances held at the beginning of the week, their plans being made with reference to the ruling rate of interest. The latter, however, may change during the week, so that the willingness of investors to hold their existing wealth in the form of securities may be modified immediately. Thus the rate of interest will be such as to keep the supply of and demand for securities in equilibrium during the week.

### Planned and Unplanned Saving and Investment

We can speak of the *planned* saving and the *planned* investment of any week. As saving and investment are performed by different members of the community, there is no reason why these two sets of plans should necessarily be equal.

The method of period analysis also uses the magnitudes of *realized* saving and *realized* investment, these being the levels of saving and investment that actually materialize during each week. They are defined so as to be always equal. That is to say, in any week total income equals the total value of production, income equals consumers' expenditure plus saving, while production is used for consumption or investment, so that saving equals investment as realized quantities. But planned saving need not equal realized saving and planned investment need not equal realized investment; so that in any week *unplanned* saving and *unplanned* investment may occur.

Whereas planned saving may be accompanied by plans to purchase securities with part of the proceeds, it is an important part of the construction that the unplanned saving of any week is too much of a surprise to be used to buy securities in that week, and so is held in the form of money until new plans are drawn up in the following week. This is a realistic assumption, for in practice there is probably some time-lag between unplanned saving and new security purchases. Unplanned investment occurs in any week in which actual business sales fall short of planned sales, so that an unplanned accumulation of stocks takes place, financed, by analogy with unplanned saving, by business drawing on its money balances, not by the sale of securities in the same week.

### An Illustration of the Process

By way of illustration, suppose that in week I the level of income is 100, with consumption equal to 80 and realized saving and investment equal to 20. Let us assume that in week I planned saving equals realized saving and planned investment equals realized investment, so that planned saving and planned investment are also equal. We measure planned saving in relation to the income of the *previous* week; planned saving in any week is the *previous* week's income minus consumers' expenditure in the *present* week.

In week II, what happens if businessmen raise their planned investment to 30 and are able to put their plans into effect by issuing new securities and using the proceeds to purchase capital goods which the equipment industries construct during the week? If planned saving remains at 20 and consumption at 80, then there is an excess of planned investment over planned saving of 10. The implementation of investment plans during week II means that wages, salaries and profits are increased by 10 in week II as the new plant and equipment are constructed, resulting in an increase in income in week II equal to the increase in realized investment. Thus in week II the income of the community rises from 100 to 110, but as, by hypothesis, consumption remains at 80, realized saving has increased from 20 to 30, compared with planned saving of only 20. Thus in week II unplanned saving of 10 will result.

We now have realized investment exceeding planned saving by 10, which is also equal to unplanned saving of 10, which is also equal to the increase in income between week I and week II. This relationship is inherent in our definitions. Any excess of realized investment over planned saving means an equal increase in income and an equal amount of unplanned saving during the week, for we have said that planned saving is related to the income of the previous week, so that unplanned saving is always the result of an increase in income. (Conversely, if in week II realized investment had fallen by 10, income would have fallen by 10 and there would have been unplanned *dissaving* during the week.)

What about the rate of interest in week II ? Let us return to week I, in which planned saving equalled planned investment and at the end of which the rate of interest was such that people were content with the distribution of their wealth between money, securities and real assets. In week II the increase in planned investment, as already described, is financed by an increase in new issues of securities to the amount of 10. This represents an increase in the supply of securities over and above that which the market was willing to absorb in the previous week at the ruling rate of interest. We have already said that at the end of week I people were content with their existing disposition of assets and that unplanned saving is held in the form of money; it therefore follows that the excess of planned investment over planned saving involves an excess supply of securities and exerts some upward tendency on the rate of interest sufficient for this increase in supply to be absorbed during the week by the inducement given to investors to raise the proportion of their wealth held in securities.

What happens in week III will depend on matters of fact, not of definition. The rise in the rate of interest in week II may diminish planned investment in week III, while the receipt of unplanned income, in the form of unplanned saving, will almost certainly induce people to revise their saving plans and increase their consumption. These reactions will in turn lead to new levels of income, saving, and investment and a new rate of interest; businessmen and households will respond to unplanned saving

2 E

and investment until at last the whole system is once more in balance, with plans being exactly realized, at which point there is no further change.

Our illustration would have been modified if the excess of planned investment over planned saving had been financed out of the existing cash balances of businesses or out of an increase in the quantity of money, in the form of a rise in bank advances, for example, or if investors had experienced a change of expectations at the beginning of the week and had decided to use their existing money balances to purchase more securities and so had taken up new issues at an unchanged rate of interest. In these cases no increase in the rate of interest would have occurred in week II, and the sequence of events in week III and so on would have been different.

### The Process if Planned Saving Changes

The model can also be used to describe the situation in which planned saving changes. Suppose in week II planned investment had remained as in week I but that planned saving had fallen by 10 because consumers decided to increase their consumption from 80 to 90. The reduction in planned saving in this case means a fall in plans to purchase securities not offset by plans to issue fewer securities, so that equilibrium in the market for securities is restored by a rise in interest rates. The increase in consumption, on the other hand, does not lead to an increase in production or incomes in week II because, by definition, all producers have already made their week's plans. What happens, as in real life, is that the increase in consumption is met first by an unplanned fall in the stocks of consumer goods held by businesses, that is by unplanned disinvestment; and business receipts from unplanned sales, like unplanned saving, are not used to purchase securities in the same week. This reduction in stocks means a fall in realized investment equal to the increase in consumption, so that in week II total income does not change.

In week III businesses might react to the rise in their sales by expanding output; there is a time-lag between an increase in consumption and an increase in production and income, whereas there is no such lag between an increase in investment and an increase in income.

Period analysis of this sort is one way in which economists can attempt to describe what in practice is a more or less continuous process, and, like all abstract descriptions of a complex and mutually interacting flow of events, it suffers from certain artificialities. It does, however, possess the virtue of making its assumptions sufficiently clear for the many alternative possible consequences that may follow a change in the magnitudes employed to be identified.

# CHAPTER 31

# THE DETERMINATION OF THE RATE OF INTEREST—THE INTERACTION OF SUPPLY AND DEMAND

### PLANNED SAVING AND THE RATE OF INTEREST

Variety is the keynote of the free economy, and 'the' level of planned saving is the result of a multitude of decisions, influenced by many forces, of which the rate of interest obtainable is only one. In order to analyse the behaviour of the rate of interest, however, we must consider the response of planned saving to a change in the rate of interest on the assumption that other factors affecting planned saving, such as tastes, the level and distribution of incomes, remain unchanged.

A rise in the rate of interest makes future consumption 'cheaper' in terms of present consumption, so that some people may decide to save more if interest rates increase; but others may even decide to save less, if their saving is aimed at producing a *given* level of income in the future, for a rise in the rate of interest makes it possible to provide for a given future income—or a given future capital sum—with a lower level of saving in the present. But some people may be induced to spend less as a result of the fall in the capital value of their wealth held in bonds. On balance, most economists believe that an increase in the rate of interest is likely to strengthen the willingness of the community to save out of a given income; but a small change is not likely to have a marked effect, at least in the short run.

Business saving in the form of depreciation provisions is insensitive to changes in the rate of interest. Business saving in the form of undistributed net profits 'planned' is an illusive concept, as profits may vary considerably from year to year. Dividend policy is unlikely to be altered in response to small changes in the rate of interest, but large changes may have some influence on the willingness of directors to increase dividends, for when interest rates are high, companies may be anxious to retain profits in order to avoid having to raise funds on the open market to finance their capital investment.

Planned saving by the government is the surplus on current account that the government expects to achieve, in relation to its previous level of current revenue; it reflects political as well as economic considerations, and the rate of interest normally has little direct influence.

Something like one-quarter of the nation's non-personal saving takes the form of depreciation provisions, and the proportion of personal saving flowing through the steady streams of contractual saving has been two-thirds or more in recent years. If we set aside these two channels of saving and that of the public authorities and public corporations as being insensitive to the rate of interest, we are left with a residue of rather less than one-half of all saving, consisting largely of retained business profits. On the whole, therefore, saving cannot be regarded as 'interest-elastic'.

### INVESTMENT AND THE RATE OF INTEREST

#### Business Investment

Investment by private industry tends to move in the same direction as the rate of profit that businessmen expect to earn. The higher the expected rate of profit, the higher the rate of interest that businessmen will be prepared to pay on their new issues of capital or forgo by selling their holdings of government securities to finance their investment. When the outlook for profits becomes more favourable, therefore, the stimulus to business investment will tend to raise the rate of interest, in so far as businesses cannot finance their investment out of their existing money balances or through an increase in the total quantity of money.

Given the expected rate of profit, the level of business fixed investment will tend to some extent to vary inversely with the rate of interest. But just how sensitive business investment is in practice to changes in the rate of interest is not clear. Where a piece of equipment to be bought possesses a short life, or is written off over a short period, the interest element in its cost may seem insignificant in relation to the provision for amortization and obsolescence. If a machine costing £2,000, for example, is to be replaced in five years, amortization charges amount to £400 per annum. If the rate of interest is 4 per cent, the annual interest charge on the securities issued to purchase the equipment is £80, making a total annual charge of £480. If the rate of interest were to rise to 5 per cent when the businessman was considering his purchase, the annual interest charge would then be £100 and the total charge £500 per annum, an increase of only 4 per cent. Many businessmen take account of uncertainty regarding the distant future and the threat of obsolescence by calculating the profitability of their planned investment over a period shorter than that during which their equipment is likely to function. The effect of this is to diminish the part played by interest charges in their calculations.

Where the capital equipment to be purchased is intended to last for a long time the annual amortization charge will be smaller in relation to the annual interest charge, but its profitability, as predicted over the whole of its life, may be highly uncertain, just because its earning life stretches so far into the future. In this case a wide range of possible rates of profit will exist, and the mean expected rate may have to be very much larger than the rate of interest for the investment to be undertaken at all. A change in the rate of interest from 5 to 6 per cent will usually appear unimportant to a businessman who is basing his invest-ment on the assumption that he will be able to earn 20 per cent per annum if things go reasonably well. The tendency for many businesses to rely to a large extent on retained profits to finance their investment also reduces the potency of a change in interest rates. When the rate of taxation is high, moreover, the cost of an increase in gross interest charges in terms of net profits after tax is correspondingly reduced.

How business investment in stocks and work in progress reacts to changes in the rate of interest is a matter of some dispute. Except in cases where the level of stocks is very large in relation to the capital employed in the business, such as in some merchant-ing concerns, moderate changes in the rate of interest, of no more than, say, 1 per cent, may have no appreciable effect on plans to hold stocks. Stocks are closely geared to the level of output and sales, and variations in the rate of interest in practice may be small in relation to the total cost of carrying stocks.

The type of business investment most likely to be interest-sensitive is the construction of buildings, for these are long-lived, so that annual amortization is relatively small, and in many cases the yield over their life may be predicted with some assurance. Commercial building in particular can be expected to provide a steady stream of office rents and therefore may prove a highly interest-elastic form of fixed investment.

Because in practice so many considerations affect the businessman's decision to invest, it is difficult to isolate the effect of changes in the rate of interest alone, and reliable evidence as to the formation of business decisions is unfortunately not plentiful. A number of inquiries into business behaviour undertaken in several countries, however, lead to the conclusion that on the whole, with the exception of building work, business investment is not sensitive to moderate changes in the rate of interest within the limits we have experienced since the war. But this conclusion is quite consistent with the view that there is *some* level of interest rates at which businessmen will sharply reduce investment.

Moreover, a rise in interest rates of even a moderate order may lead businessmen to curtail investment by affecting their expectations as to the future of trade. This may be the response to a sudden tightening of monetary policy, which may therefore succeed in cutting planned investment because businessmen expect it to succeed, and they may do so if it has succeeded within the span of their own experience. Businessmen may also interpret a change in the rate of interest, particularly in Bank rate, as a sign of impending changes in other constituents of government economic policy. But the strength of such reactions to a change in the rate of interest will depend on the nature of the situation at the time; a given change in the rate of interest is least influential in conditions of vigorous boom and severe depression.

In a vigorous boom the expected rate of profit on the great majority of investment plans is likely to be well in excess of the rate of interest, and businessmen may be confident of their ability to pass on higher interest charges to their customers. Because prices of capital equipment are today rarely raised to the point at which a vigorous demand is held down to the capacity of the capital goods trades, the latter are likely to have long order-books in such conditions. During a vigorous boom, therefore, moderate changes in the rate of interest may be particularly ineffective in curtailing investment and the demand for finance, for if one business drops out of the queue for capital goods another will merely move up to take its place, and the actual volume of work put in hand may not fall even though an increase in interest rates may have deterred the more cautious businessman from putting his plans into action.

In a slump, long-term investment on which the return seems fairly certain will be encouraged by low interest rates. But for many types of business investment, such as machinery and even factories, the availability of cheap finance in a slump will be a very weak stimulus to investment if there is substantial excess capacity or if much of existing equipment is far from being due for replacement. In a severe slump the pessimism of businessmen is a stronger force than cheap and plentiful finance.

Although business investment as a whole may not prove to be very sensitive to changes in the rate of interest, the method and timing of finance may well be affected. If businessmen expect an increase in the long-term rate of interest to be only temporary, there will usually be some tendency to defer recourse to the new-issue market and to draw on cash resources to finance expenditure until interest rates fall, or to turn to short-term borrowing, in which case the effect is to redistribute the demand for finance within the pattern of interest rates as a whole. (The government may also react to changes in interest rates by borrowing 'short' or 'long', as the case may be.)

### Interest Rates and Public Investment

Capital investment by the central government and by the nationalized industries does not seem to be based on decisions that pay much regard to the rate of interest. Local authorities, on the other hand, are not so favourably placed, sometimes finding it politically difficult to pass on higher interest charges in the form of higher rates. Civil engineering works undertaken by semi-official bodies dependent on outside finance may also be sensitive to the level of interest charges.

One important field in which changes in the rate of interest are likely to affect the pace of investment is that of housing, whether private or local authority. For here the annual 'return' is relatively certain, and the element of durability makes the annual amortization charge sufficiently small to elevate interest charges to a position of importance.

## THE RATE OF INTEREST IN THE SHORT RUN

If important sections of investment are not sensitive to interest rate changes, at least in the short run, an increase in investment in one part of the economy to a level in excess of planned saving is not likely to lead to a fall in investment elsewhere merely because the additional demand for finance has the effect of raising interest rates. Conversely, if planned saving exceeds planned investment, the consequent fall in interest rates is not likely to prove a strong stimulus to investment in the short run, except perhaps in the field of building. To this extent, therefore, the rate of interest cannot be regarded as a very effective short run regulator for keeping planned saving in balance with planned investment. It follows from this that it is largely through the interaction of the rate of interest with the desire to hold bonds rather than money or goods that movements in the rate of interest keep the supply of and demand for bonds in balance in the short run.

## THE RATE OF INTEREST AND THE CHOICE BETWEEN MONEY AND BONDS

The choice between bonds and goods as a store of wealth needs no amplification; if the general price-level is strongly expected to rise, both money and bonds become inferior assets. For the rest of this chapter we shall assume that the proportion of its wealth the community wishes to hold in goods remains constant, so that it is only the choice between money and bonds that has to be considered.

### Working Balances and Contingency Reserves

Habit and inertia play their part in this choice, but making allowance for this it is possible to identify three reasons for holding money and thus for relinquishing the opportunity of earning interest. The first is the need for holding a working balance, to finance any excess of expenditure over receipts from day to day. The second is the need to hold money as a reserve against future contingencies; this is often described as the 'precautionary motive'. If there were no risk of a fall in security prices such a reserve could be held in bonds, but the uncertainty of security prices makes it prudent to hold it in the form of money (or, in practice, in very short-term assets). The third reason for holding money rather than bonds is related to the uncertainty of future security prices alone, in that money will be held in excess of any requirements by way of a working balance and contingency reserve if the holder is afraid of the risk of a fall in security prices, i.e. of a rise in the rate of interest.

The important distinction between these factors is that the size of the quantity of money required as working balances and to meet future contingencies is related to the level of national income and expenditure. If the national income increases, that is to say, most members of the community will want to hold more money for these purposes, and if the total quantity of money in existence is fixed, the effect will be to put some upward pressure on the rate of interest in so far as persons and businesses seek to add to their working and contingency balances by selling securities or by refraining from purchasing them. Conversely, if the national income falls, less money will be required to be held for these purposes, so that, if the total quantity of money in existence does not change, the holders of money that is surplus to their requirements will be more ready to purchase securities.

### Idle Money Balances

Given the total quantity of money and the size of working balance and contingency reserve requirements, there remains part of the money stock that has to be held somewhere in the economy as 'idle' balances, idle in contrast to the 'active' nature of working and contingency balances, which are turned over more frequently. The important point is that the distribution of these surplus or idle money balances will depend on the expectations of investors; they will be held by those investors who are afraid of the risk of a fall in security prices, whereas other investors will be holding more of their wealth in bonds. This does not mean that investors have to choose between holding nothing but bonds and nothing but money, for investors are rarely absolutely certain in their own minds as to the future of security prices, but merely that idle balances will be held predominantly by those investors to whom the chance of a rise in the rate of interest appears relatively high.

### Investors' Expectations

In principle, the expectations of investors regarding the *future* rate of interest must pay regard to the course of saving, investment, the movement of prices and the national income, and the operation of banking and monetary policy. But as the rate of interest will be affected more by the actions of his fellow investors than by his own, each investor, in formulating his own expectation of the course of the rate of interest, will also have to hold some opinion regarding the expectations of others. Strictly speaking, the sophisticated investor must try and guess their expectations concerning the course of saving, investment, monetary policy, etc. and *their* expectations of *other* investors' actions, for all investors can be thought of as engaging in the same guessing game regarding the future action of their fellows.

The problem of such collective expectations is thus a complex one, but in practice investors are likely to pay great regard to those economic factors which their experience tells them play an important part in influencing the opinions of other investors, such as the state of the balance of payments, or the tendency towards inflation or deflation, or the trend of government thinking. Few investors can make a direct assessment of other investors' opinions regarding the future rate of interest, but past experience enables a conventional judgement to be made on many occasions. In many post-war years, for example, it was reasonable for any one investor to expect 'the market' to react to a sharp fall in the country's gold and dollar reserves by raising the rate of interest, partly because he would be aware that such a development might be followed by government action involving higher interest rates, and partly because 'other' investors would be expecting 'other' investors to consider a rise in the rate of interest likely in such a situation.

'Convention' therefore helps the market to resolve uncertainty regarding future security prices, and the experience of the past is of great importance in appearing to set limits to the range within which the rate of interest is likely to fluctuate in the future. In this country the long-term rate of interest has rarely been above $5\frac{1}{2}$ per cent or below $2\frac{1}{2}$ per cent in peacetime over the past century, so that there is a strong temptation for each investor to assume that *other* investors will continue to regard these as the limits in the future. In acting on this assumption investors collectively justify their own individual reliance on imputed opinions.

### The Variety of Expectations

Investors can sell only if others are willing to buy, and can buy only if others are willing to sell. It is the existence of a variety of expectations as to the future course of security prices that brings forward buyers to absorb sales. The variety of opinions is the result of the uncertainty of the course of security prices.

A convenient simplification is to define those investors who, at the current rate of interest, are willing to buy securities as 'bulls' and those who are willing to sell as 'bears', with a host of 'hesitaters' in between. As long as we assume that expectations do not alter, using the word 'expectations' to embrace the whole complex of views about the future course of the rate of interest and the confidence with which these views are held, a rise in the rate of interest will induce some investors who were previously 'bears' to join the 'bull' brigade or the much larger army of 'hesitaters'. Similarly, a fall in the rate of interest will induce some 'bulls' to move into the ranks of the 'bears'. This follows from the knowledge that the rate of interest *does* fluctuate. For as the rate of interest moves towards its likely limit as envisaged by investors, the greater will appear the chance that it will return towards a level that they regard as most probable in the long run. In these circumstances a rise in the rate of interest will cause an increase in the demand for securities or a reduction in their supply, and conversely, until the rate of interest is once more such that the 'bulls' and 'bears' cancel each other out, and idle balances are held only by those who wish to hold them for some time.

If we drop the assumption that expectations remain unchanged, quite different results may follow. Expectations may alter, for example, in response to the movement in the rate of interest itself, or as a result of the reaction of investors to the economic events to which the change in the rate of interest is attributed. A fall in the rate of interest may lead some investors to assume that other investors are growing 'bullish', so that some investors may revise their own expectations; the result will be for a fall in the rate of interest to cause a further fall. The necessity for guessing as to the course of other investors' actions often tends to make expectations become infectious for a time, prolonging a movement in interest rates.

### THE INTERACTION OF SUPPLY AND DEMAND— SHORT-RUN EFFECTS

To illustrate the way in which the rate of interest may behave, a quick sketch of a number of situations can be drawn in which the market, after a period of stability, may be imagined to be disturbed by changes in one of the categories of supply or demand.

### When Planned Saving Exceeds Planned Investment

In this situation the rate of interest will tend to fall. If neither planned saving nor planned investment reacts significantly to a fall in the rate of interest in the short run, the movement will continue until checked by the working of investors' expectations. In the extreme case, if investors as a whole were convinced that the level of interest rates prevailing when the movement began was already at its lowest practical limit, then an excess of planned saving over investment could not cause any appreciable fall in the rate of interest. Any incipient tendency for the rate of interest to decline would be destroyed by the effect of security sales by those investors who believed it was likely to recover to its previous level.

If investors' expectations do not remain unchanged, the market will be more unstable. The tendency of the rate of interest to fall may lead some investors to believe that *other* investors hold the opinion that it will continue to do so. The knowledge that planned saving is increasing, or that investment is declining, may itself cause investors to expect the fall in the rate of interest to continue. The pressure of demand in the market for securities due to the excess of planned saving over investment will thus be increased, and the rate of interest will continue to fall until it is low enough to check saving, stimulate investment, or reduce the number of 'bulls' once more.

If planned saving exceeds investment, the implication is that the level of national income is falling. Apart from the probability that investors will associate a slump with low interest rates and that the authorities may pursue a policy of cheap money in such a situation, there is thus an inherent tendency for the rate of interest to decline during a slump, especially as the desire to hold money in working and contingency balances will fall with the national income. Initially, however, uncertainty as to the course of business activity and the credit-worthiness of debtors may give rise to a strong desire for liquidity in the early stage of a slump that can be regarded as an increase in the demand for money balances to meet contingencies. For some time this may actually force up the rate of interest.

### When Planned Investment Exceeds Planned Saving

In this situation the rate of interest will tend to rise, if not checked by the response of planned saving and investment, or by an increase in the quantity of money, until a sufficient number of erstwhile 'bears' or 'hesitaters' become 'bulls' and absorb the excess supply of securities by running down their idle cash balances. The rise in the rate of interest will also be reinforced by the necessity for holding larger active cash balances owing to the increase in the level of the national income that is the consequence of the failure of the rate of interest to keep planned saving and investment in balance. The rate of interest thus tends to increase during a boom.

The tendency for interest rates to rise in a period of inflation is especially strong, for investors expect interest rates to increase in such a situation, and their reluctance to hold bonds will usually be strengthened by the desire to hold more of their wealth in the form of real assets, for fear of a further rise in the general price-level. The authorities may also be expected to pursue a policy of high interest rates in such circumstances.

### Changes in the Quantity of Money

An alteration in the total quantity of money, other things being equal, will cause a movement in the rate of interest in the opposite direction; this will continue until checked by the response of planned saving and investment and the operation of investors' expectations. The existence of these checks implies that there are limits to a change in the rate of interest that can be brought about even by official intervention in the market, despite the resources which the authorities command; and the limit exists in both directions.

If the rate of interest is already considered by investors to be near its lower limit in the economic circumstances prevailing, the authorities will find that a policy aimed at lowering the rate of interest will be countered by sales of securities on the part of investors concerned at the risk of capital depreciation should the fall in the rate of interest not be maintained; and the risk of capital loss will be regarded as particularly serious by those investors paying a relatively high rate of tax on their interest income but none on capital transactions, for a given capital loss will mean correspondingly greater loss in terms of gross income. The rate of security purchases by the authorities, and thus the rate of expansion of the quantity of money, will have to be progressively increased as the rate of interest moves towards what the market believes to be its lower limit. If the expansion in the quantity of money involved in the attempt to lower interest rates stimulates planned investment or diminishes planned saving, the resistance to the fall in the rate of interest will be all the greater.

The authorities may be faced by corresponding obstacles to a policy intended to drive up the rate of interest. Investors may believe that the current rate of interest is so far above a 'normal' rate, to which the market will return sooner or later, that they may be eager to run down their cash balances to absorb the securities sold by the authorities, thus checking the rise in the rate of interest. But the barrier to a rise in the rate of interest is more likely to crumble under a determined attack by the authorities. The possibility of gain is not as influential as the risk of loss, our notion of an upper limit to the rate of interest is vague, and there is a limit to which 'bullish' investors can run down their balances.

A change in the rate of interest due to monetary policy may also be checked directly by the reaction of planned saving and investment, but in the very short run the response of these factors will usually be less effective than investors' expectations.

Among causes of a change in the quantity of money other than official policy, the most important is probably a movement in the level of foreign exchange reserves. An increase in these will probably tend to lower long-term interest rates, by raising the level of bank liquidity and deposits, and the movement may be extended if it strengthens the confidence of investors or if it leads the authorities to relax a restrictive monetary policy. On the other hand, one effect of a surplus of exports over imports, or of an influx of foreign capital, may be to stimulate investment; if the economy is already at full employment the government may take the view that a policy of dear money aimed at preventing an increase in domestic expenditure is needed. An influx of short-term capital from abroad, in particular, may be prevented by official sales of securities from causing excess liquidity in the banking system.

### Changes in Investors' Expectations

In practice, changes in expectations can often be founded only on the broadest of views. The checks and balances within the market will operate as before. If the expectation grows that the rate of interest is about to fall, the expectation is likely to be justified. Jobbers may even mark up security prices in anticipation of a strong demand, so that few transactions may actually take place. If expectations are unanimous, no investor can act on his view; it is only the existence of a variety of expectations that enables an investor to obtain a profit by purchasing securities if he is of the opinion that their price is about to rise.

In the short run neither planned saving nor planned investment may react with sufficient vigour to check a movement in the rate of interest initiated by a change in expectations, and the policy followed by the authorities will depend on the nature of the situation. If they do not intervene, the movement in the rate of interest will continue until the 'bulls' and 'bears' are once more of equal force. If the interaction between the rate of interest and expectations becomes cumulative, however, the movement in the rate of interest will be prolonged. This is more likely to occur when there is a scramble for liquidity, which may be intensified by the knowledge that other investors are seeking it, and the rise in the rate of interest may accelerate so strongly that official intervention may become necessary to prevent the utter demoralization of the market. Such was the situation, for example, following the devaluation of sterling in September 1949.

#### LONGER-RUN EFFECTS

In the short run, investors' expectations play a leading role in determining the rate of interest. In the longer run, on the other hand, it is the forces of saving and investment and the relationship between the size of the national income and the quantity of money available to meet working balance and contingency reserve requirements that stand in sharp relief. As Fig. 1 shows, the movement in the long-term rate of interest since 1921 has broadly followed the course taken by the liquidity of the economy, expressing this as the percentage of the national income represented by the quantity of money, movements in the rate of interest occurring through changes in either or both of these magnitudes.

However, the interaction of economic forces makes accurate prediction difficult, for its effect may be either to extend or check, and even reverse, a movement in the rate of the interest. An improvement in the balance of payments, for example, may tend in the first instance to lower the rate of interest; but if higher domestic expenditure results from the increase in exporters'

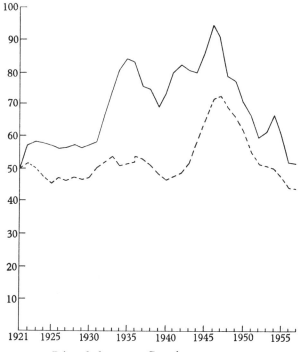

—— Price of 2½ per cent Consols
– – – Net bank deposits, plus currency in circulation, as a percentage of the gross domestic product

Fig. 1. The price of 2½ per cent Consols and the liquidity of the economy 1921–56.

incomes, the rate of interest may be forced upwards. Similarly, an expansionist monetary policy, or a Budget deficit financed by bank credit, may begin by reducing the long-term rate of interest; if it generates inflation, the rate of interest may well rise to a much higher level than the original one if the authorities are not willing to increase the quantity of money at an expanding rate.

2 F

As long as planned saving and investment are not equal, the economy will be either expanding or contracting, and even if the gap between these two constituents of the demand for and supply of securities is filled by an equal and opposite flow of demand or supply resulting from the interaction of the rate of interest with investors' expectations, or from a change in the quantity of money, the market in securities may not remain stable. For expansion or contraction in the national income is likely to give rise to a series of mutually-interacting developments that will bear on the rate of interest in one direction or the other. For the rate of interest to be firmly anchored, investors as a whole must be content with the proportion of their wealth held in bonds, planned saving and investment must be equal, and the quantity of money must be constant. Needless to say, this stationary state of affairs rarely occurs.

If a very long view is taken of the history of the rate of interest, broad cyclical movement can be identified with the alternation of what some economists have described as 'capital-hungry' and 'capital-sated' periods. Wars; discoveries and inventions; the development of new goods and productive techniques; population movements—these may create conditions in which planned investment will be sustained at a relatively high level for many years, causing high rates of interest about which secondary fluctuations occur. As the outlets for profitable investment become more fully exploited, the intensity of investment then falls off, and the tendency towards lower rates of interest may be strengthened by the fact that the rise in real incomes produced by the investment of the 'capital-hungry' period may increase the proportion of its income that the community is able and willing to save.

These 'capital-hungry' and 'capital-sated' periods may last for as much as twenty or thirty years. Colin Clark, for example, in *The Economics of 1960*, has distinguished the following sequence over the past century.

(1) 'Capital-hungry' period from about 1850 to about 1875—the long-term rate of interest moving within the range of $3-3\frac{1}{2}$ per cent.

(2) 'Capital-sated' period from 1875 to 1900—with the long-term rate of interest varying between $3\frac{1}{4}$ and a little under $2\frac{1}{2}$ per cent.

(3) 'Capital-hungry' period from 1900 to 1930—with the long-term rate of interest rising to $5\frac{1}{4}$ per cent in 1920.

(4) 'Capital-sated' period from 1930 to the outbreak of war—the long-term rate of interest falling to under 3 per cent and not rising again above $3\frac{3}{4}$ per cent.

(5) 'Capital-hungry' period since the war. The long-term rate of interest has already been as high as $5\frac{1}{2}$ per cent.

These 'long waves' of economic fluctuation do not stop at the shores of any one country. Within them there could be discerned before the war the 7–10-year oscillations associated with trade cycles, with their similar movements in the rate of interest within the larger swings. But just how far the rate of interest will rise in the boom and fall in the slump, history alone will not tell us.

## THE RATE OF INTEREST AND THE LEVEL OF TAXATION

Other things being equal, an increase in the rate of taxation tends to cause a rise in the rate of interest. A decrease in the rate of interest *net* of tax reduces the attraction of bonds compared with that of money as a form in which wealth can be held to meet future contingencies and may also reduce the willingness to save. But 'other things' are rarely equal, and the full effect of a change in the rate of taxation cannot be readily discerned, for it may react on capital investment and on the expectations of investors as well; the use of fiscal policy may also modify the extent to which the authorities draw on monetary weapons instead in order to check a boom or prevent a slump.

The net rate of interest at the standard rate of income tax has remained remarkably low since the war, increasing from roughly $1\frac{1}{2}$ per cent in 1946 to not much more than 2 per cent in 1954, and rising to 3 per cent only in 1956. In the decade 1919–29, before the onset of world-wide depression, the net rate fluctuated between $3\frac{1}{4}$ and $3\frac{3}{4}$ per cent. Taking into account the rise in retail prices, the net interest return on government bonds in real terms in most post-war years has actually been negative. This suggests that inertia and habit play an important part in the capital market and that the expectations of investors concerning the likely upper limit to the rate of interest remain based for a long period on historical notions dominated by the record of interest rates gross of tax.

### YIELDS ON DEBENTURES AND PREFERENCE SHARES

Yields on debentures and preference shares follow the general direction of the long-term rate of interest. As these securities are not entirely free from the risk of default, there is some tendency for their yields to increase somewhat, in relation to 'the' rate of interest, when industrial or political conditions become uncertain or when the supply of industrial fixed-interest securities in the form of new issues presses upon the market. But the extent to which yields on first-class debentures have diverged from the

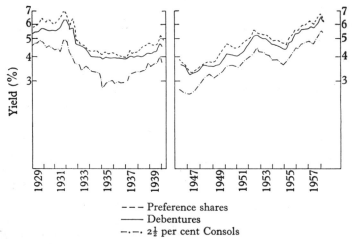

- - - Preference shares
——— Debentures
—·—· 2½ per cent Consols

Fig. 2. Yields on preference shares, debentures and 2½ per cent Consols 1929–57, based on constituents of Actuaries' Investment Index. Logarithmic vertical scale. The pre-war and post-war series are not strictly comparable.

rate of interest since the war has been small. Preference shares, which are subject to a rather greater risk of default than debentures, may prove somewhat more sensitive to industrial conditions.

The status of redeemable preference shares was damaged in 1949, when court decisions confirmed the right of a company to redeem its preference shares when their market value stands above par. The effect this had in inserting a thicker wedge between yields on preference shares and the long-term rate of interest was reduced somewhat in subsequent years owing to the fall in the volume of new issues of preference shares caused mainly by the incidence of the tax on distributed profits.

The yield on any individual debenture or preference share, of course, will depend on the market's assessment of its security. Investors will pay regard to the standing of the company, the asset and income cover for its fixed-interest stocks, and the degree of priority possessed by the claims of the holders of the debentures or preference shares concerned on income and assets. The yield of *redeemable* fixed-interest industrial securities will also be influenced by expectations regarding the future pattern of interest rates, as in the case of any dated stock; this question is the subject of the following chapter.

# CHAPTER 32

# THE PATTERN OF INTEREST RATES

## SHORT-TERM AND LONG-TERM YIELDS

Because of the existence of securities with different terms to maturity, investors' expectations cannot be considered simply as influencing the choice between one class of securities and money or goods. The expectation of changes in interest rates may instead justify switching from one class of security to another, from short-term to long-term stocks, or vice versa. When rates of interest on stocks of different maturities are expected to rise to the same degree, it is clear that investors will be justified in switching 'short', and conversely.

If the yield on $2\frac{1}{2}$ per cent Consols were to rise from 4 to 5 per cent, for example, the price of this 'perpetual' stock would fall from $62\frac{1}{2}$ to 50, a drop of almost one-fifth. If the yield to redemption on a $2\frac{1}{2}$ per cent coupon stock with only one year to maturity were to rise from 4 to 5 per cent, its price would decline from approximately 98·5 to 97·6, a reduction of only 1 per cent. This is because the yield to redemption of a dated stock consists of two elements, the annual interest payment and the difference between the current market price and the redemption price, which can be expressed as compound rate of interest per annum. The nearer the redemption date, the closer must be the current price to the redemption price for a security with a given coupon rate and a given market yield. Thus, for any given change in yield, prices of securities close to their redemption date will change less than those with longer to run.*

Having said this, however, we are not much nearer the relationship between rates of interest on securities of different terms to maturity, for in practice the pattern of interest rates does not move up or down by the same amount throughout its length but experiences greater fluctuations in yield at the 'short' end than at the 'long'. This is inherent in the operation of investors' expectations in the uncertainty as to future rates of interest that prevails in the real world.

* An exception to this principle has been noted on page 120.

SOME IMPLICATIONS OF UNCERTAINTY

*Capital and Income Uncertainty*

The problems raised by uncertainty can be approached by comparing the respective penalties incurred as a result of an 'unfavourable' movement of rates in the case of a purchase of short-term and long-term stocks respectively. In general the purchase of a fixed-interest security carries a greater risk of capital depreciation for any given rise in yield, the longer is its term; but whereas a short-term stock is relatively immune to the risk of depreciation in the event of a rise in interest rates, the purchase of a short-term stock involves a different risk from which the longer-term bond is free for a correspondingly longer period. This is the risk that when the stock matures interest rates will have fallen, so that its proceeds can be reinvested only at a rate of interest which will produce a yield over the whole term of investment lower than that which could have been obtained by purchasing a longer-term stock in the first place. Even if the short-term rate is in excess of the long-term rate in the first instance, some disadvantage may therefore be incurred in buying a short-term rather than a long-term stock. In brief, the degree of 'capital uncertainty' increases with the term of the stock, but what can be described as 'income uncertainty' diminishes.

The risk of capital depreciation of a long-term stock is not removed by the knowledge that in practice long-term yields fluctuate less than short-term yields. In comparing the possible price fluctuations of a five-year and a twenty-year stock, for example, each with a coupon rate of 3 per cent, a rise in yield from 3 to $4\frac{1}{2}$ per cent in the longer stock would entail a fall in price from 100 to 80.* In contrast, it would require an increase in the five-year rate from 3 to $7\frac{3}{4}$ per cent to subject a five-year stock to this degree of capital depreciation. In the past century the full range of fluctuation in very short-term rates, as measured by the yield on a first-class bill with three months to run, has been from about $\frac{1}{2}$ to 10 per cent, whereas the yield on a perpetual stock has varied roughly between $2\frac{1}{2}$ and $5\frac{1}{2}$ per cent. The full range of price fluctuation in the case of $2\frac{1}{2}$ per cent Consols has been roughly twenty times as great as that on a three-month bill.

* With half-yearly interest payments.

The choice between income and capital risk is thus one between short-term and long-term bonds. However, it may be asked, if an investor were quite uncertain as to the future of interest rates, why should he prefer one to the other ? For although it is true that a rise in yields would penalize the holder of a long-term bond, he would gain if interest rates fell; and conversely in the case of a holder of a short-term stock. If investors were completely uncertain as to the future, or if they believed that the probabilities of a rise and a fall in interest rates were equal, why should they not be indifferent between short-term and long-term bonds if they carried the same yield to redemption, irrespective of whether investors were influenced by considerations of income or capital ? If investors were indifferent between stocks of different maturity in conditions of complete uncertainty, they would merely select stocks providing the highest yield until all stocks yielded the same amount. In the same way borrowers would issue securities for the term showing the smallest cost, again leading to a set of uniform yields.*

### Income- and Capital-consciousness

In real life, however, uncertainty produces not indifference, but caution; some investors are conscious of the risk of capital depreciation, while others are more conscious of the necessity for maintaining a steady income over a longer period. If stocks of different periods to maturity provide the same yield to redemption, the investor who values certainty of capital will choose shorter-dated stocks if he is quite uncertain as to the future, whereas the 'income-conscious' investor will put his money into longer-term stocks. The capital-conscious investor will require a higher yield on a long-term bond than on a shorter stock as a 'risk premium' to compensate him for the fact that, if the yield were to rise by the same amount on each, his capital would depreciate by more if held in the form of the long-term security. The predominantly income-conscious investor, on the other hand, will prefer the longer-term bond unless the short-term stock provides a risk premium above the yield on a long-term bond, to compensate him for the possibility of a fall in interest rates.

---

* If investors are subject to different rates of tax, however, the same stock will provide different net yields to different investors. The incidence of tax will therefore influence the shape of the yield pattern.

This caution, a bias against loss in conditions of uncertainty, or when the chances of loss and gain are thought to be equal, exists in many guises. To the business concern, in its widest sense, the need for solvency is absolute; and most investors are faced with liabilities which must not be compromised. Even where such liabilities are unimportant, the bias against loss exists in the form of what we can describe, crudely, as the diminishing marginal importance of wealth: the importance to us of the marginal $£X$ of our income or our capital, as the case may be, diminishes as the size of our income or capital increases, if 'other things' remain equal. The result is that the loss of $£X$, at any point, constitutes a loss of satisfaction greater than the increase that would be derived from a gain of $£X$. The principle is perhaps the justification of the bias towards caution in what is generally described as 'sound' investment and helps to explain why investment advice when the outlook is uncertain often stands a better chance of being accepted if it strikes the note of pessimism rather than one of hope.

If uncertainty leads the income-conscious investor to be biased in favour of long-term stocks and the capital-conscious investor to favour short-term stocks, the shape of the yield pattern will depend partly on which of these types of investor predominates. Other things being equal, if capital-consciousness is dominant the pattern of yields will be such that yields rise with the term to maturity when the market outlook is very uncertain, for the capital-conscious investor would choose a shorter-term stock if a long-term stock did not provide a higher yield. Conversely, if income-consciousness rules the market, short-term stocks will carry higher yields than long-term stocks when investors are quite uncertain as to the future, for income-conscious investors would choose long-term securities unless these yielded something less than the 'shorts'.

## The Institutional Framework

It is not possible to say, however, what the exact structure of yields would be if all investors were absolutely uncertain as to the future, for this would depend on the psychological qualities of investors individually and on certain institutional factors. It is probable, however, that in the present capital market uncertainty would produce some upward-sloping yield curve, if yields of different stocks were plotted against the vertical axis of a graph and their term to maturity against the horizontal. The discount houses are limited in their policy for the most part to stocks with a life of up to five years, and the banks, if uncertain as to the future, are as a rule unwilling to advance beyond stocks of a certain maturity, with some tendency to concentrate, like the discount houses, on very short-dated bonds. Business concerns, too, have to preserve capital values for future contingencies and hold their liquid reserves in the form of cash or short-dated stocks. At the other extreme are the growing life-assurance and pension funds, which are income-conscious investors; the importance of their annual purchases of securities would probably arrest the upward slope of the yield pattern in conditions of uncertainty.

There is also some dispersion of interests among different types of borrowers. Perhaps only the State would be indifferent between borrowing 'short' and borrowing 'long' if there were no difference in cost. But among other borrowers there will be some who prefer to borrow 'short' only, if they require funds for a short period of time, while those borrowers who wish to obtain funds for a longer period will prefer to borrow 'long', if the cost is no higher than the cost of borrowing 'short'. To the borrower, uncertainty as to the terms on which a short-term loan can be refinanced or a long-term loan liquidated will justify matching the term of his loan with the term of the asset which the loan is required to finance. The borrower who issues a short-term loan to finance a long-term project also faces the risk that in certain circumstances he may not be able to raise fresh funds to re-finance his loan at all. On the whole, the action of borrowers reinforces the conclusion that the curve of yields would slope upwards, at least over a substantial part of its length, in conditions of great uncertainty.

The pattern towards which yields would tend, however, also depends on the supply of stocks of different terms. In those countries where long-term bonds form an unusually small propor-tion of the national debt, for example, the curve of yields will slope upwards less steeply for any given set of preferences on the part of investors. The shape of the yield pattern will also be influenced by taxation. If interest only were subject to tax an increase in the rate of taxation, by raising the penalty of capital depreciation in terms of net income, would tend to strengthen any bias in favour of short-dated stocks. In practice, the varying incidence of taxation cannot be summarized with any precision.

The shape of the yield curve will also be flattened by the operations of financial intermediaries that earn their income by borrowing at a low rate of interest and lending the proceeds at a high one. By borrowing 'short' and lending 'long', when the curve of yields is persistently upwards, they take the risk of a rise in short-term interest rates. To some extent the banks are in this position.

### A 'Usual' Yield Pattern?

In short, the precise shape of the yield curve in conditions of great uncertainty cannot be predicted. Nevertheless, market operators sometimes seek a 'usual' pattern in their interpretation of what 'the market' has come to regard as usual in conditions when no definite expectations about the future exist. The predominant attitude seems to be that only some ascending pattern of yields can be regarded as usual.

Apart from its roots in the basis of capital-consciousness, this view can claim to be founded on fairly recent experience, namely the general upward pattern that has prevailed until recently since 1932. But it cannot be stressed too often that between 1932 and 1952 the pattern was that based on a policy of 'cheap' money, the major part of the period being dominated by either depression or war, none of which, we hope, should be regarded as usual. In the years 1825–1932 the curve of yields was downwards in no fewer than 580 months, so that a long historical view does not reveal any predominant pattern. The longest time for which the short-term rate, in this case the bill rate, has been above the yield on Consols without interruption since 1825 is forty-two months, and periods of more than twenty months were not infrequent before 1932. If we exclude 1932–52, the years of depression and cheap money, the longest period in which long rate has stood above the bill rate is fifty-four months.*

It is true that before 1914, when downward-sloping yield curves were not unusual, the capital market bore little relationship to that today, in regard to the range of stocks available and the influence and policy of different types of investor, but this observation only

* F. A. Lutz, 'The Structure of Interest Rates', *Quarterly Journal of Economics*, Volume LV, 1940–41.

strengthens the case against the idea of a 'usual' yield pattern. Given the character of the capital market and the relative volume of stocks of different terms, the pattern of yields must be explained with reference to expectations, vague though the latter may be, and there is no apparent reason why any set of expectations should be considered 'usual'.

### EXPECTATIONS AND THE PATTERN OF INTEREST RATES
*Mathematical Relationships*

If an investor holds definite expectations about the future of interest rates his choice between stocks of different terms to maturity can thereby be determined. A man willing to tie up his funds for two years will prefer a one-year stock yielding 5 per cent to a two-year stock yielding 4 per cent, if he believes that he will be able to reinvest the proceeds of the former in a year's time at a certain minimum rate of interest. In practice he will be able to reinvest in a security with many years to run, for he can hold it for a year and sell it before maturity. But for the sake of simplicity we can suppose that his choice lies between a succession of two 1-year stocks and one 2-year stock, to be held to maturity.

The choice between them is clear if we ignore the compounding of interest. The two-year stock provides a certain interest return of 8 per cent over the two years, so that the purchaser of the one-year stock yielding 5 per cent must be confident of being able to reinvest in another one-year stock in a year's time with a yield of more than 3 per cent for the (initial) one-year stock to appear a more attractive purchase; if he expects the one-year rate of interest to be below 3 per cent in a year's time, the two-year stock will seem the more profitable security.

The investor would be indifferent between the two stocks if he confidently expected the one-year rate of interest to be 3 per cent in a year's time, that is if the yield per annum on the two-year stock was expected to be equal to the arithmetic average of the two successive one-year rates of interest.

With the compounding of interest the relationship is much more complicated. On the one hand, an initial capital sum of, say, £100 can be continuously invested 'short', to earn a stream of interest receipts growing as a result of compounding through reinvestment at the 'short' rate prevailing in each successive period. On the other hand, the same initial capital sum can be invested 'long' to earn a stream of interest receipts that will grow through compounding at the long-term rate of interest. An investor will be indifferent between these two courses of action if, on using the long-term rate of interest prevailing on the long-term stock to discount the stream of short-term interest receipts foreseen over the life of the long-term stock, the present discounted value obtained is also £100, the initial sum investable in both cases. Discounting takes account of the time factor, giving more weight to high short-term rates of interest prevailing in the relatively near future, for example.

As a rough approximation, however, we can say that the yield on a long-term stock would have to equal the geometric mean of the succession of short-term rates foreseen during the span of its life for an investor sure of his forecast to be indifferent between short-term and long-term stocks.

Ignoring taxation and expenses of dealing, then if all borrowers and lenders had complete mobility as between loans of different terms, and if all investors held the *same* view of the future of interest rates and held it with absolute certainty, the pattern of yields at any time would have to be consistent with that view; yields would be such that investors were indifferent between stocks with different terms to maturity. On the principle just outlined, the yield on any long-term stock would be approximately equal to the geometric mean of the short-term yields foreseen as occurring over the duration of its life. Long-term yields could stand above or below current short-term yields, depending on whether the current short-term yield stood below or above the mean of future short-term yields. Yields would be uniform for all terms only if rates of interest were known to remain quite unchanged for an indefinite time ahead.

Short-term yields would fluctuate more than long-term yields, because the average of a series of yields must be more stable, as a mathematical proposition, than the individual short-term yields that prevail at each successive point of time. The extent to which long-term yields followed the movement of short-term yields would depend on the extent to which the latter at any point of time departed from their future average.

In these circumstances the knowledge that the price of a security was about to fall would not deter an investor from holding it, for the holder would be compensated by his interest payments;

if he held a stock with a different term to maturity, or if he held money instead, he would be no worse and no better off. Holding money for one year would merely deprive an investor of the yield obtainable on a one-year stock, which would also be equal to the yield obtainable from holding any stock for one year. Correspondingly, the knowledge that the price of a security was about to rise would not justify switching into it from another stock.

It does not matter whether we describe such a hypothetical situation by saying that long-term yields would be determined by the expected course of short-term yields or that short-term yields would be determined by expected long-term yields. The point is that if all investors held the same opinion with complete confidence the yields on stocks with different terms would have to be *consistent*. In technical language, the pattern of yields would be governed by the 'reinvestment' rates of interest between different stocks. The reinvestment rate of interest between stocks of $X$ and $Y$ years to run, where $Y$ is greater than $X$, is the yield that in $X$ years' time will have to be obtainable on a stock with $(Y-X)$ years to maturity for an investor to obtain the same yield over the full period of $Y$ years no matter whether he chooses the stock with $X$ or that with $Y$ years to run.

*Expectations and the Pattern of Interest Rates in the Real World*

In the real world expectations are not unanimous or held with complete conviction or clarity. The pattern of interest rates can rarely be regarded as being 'consistent' with a single market view of its future, for investors hold a variety of blurred and conflicting opinions; and the existence of uncertainty deters most investors from altering the composition of their portfolios frequently. Nevertheless, the considerations outlined so far in this chapter can be adapted, within limits, to throw light on the varying pattern of rates in real life.

1. When the bulk of investors have no strong views about the future the pattern will be that of some upward curve. The upward slope of the curve will be less steep at the 'long' end when the long-term rate of interest is at a level which investors have come to regard as being not far from normal, because of the bias of income-conscious investors for long-term stocks.

2. When the curve is downward-sloping over the whole of its length, it can be inferred that the majority of investors believe

that short-term rates of interest, at least, are about to fall. For it is the probability of a fall—which would entail lower yields on reinvestment—that deters income-conscious investors from switching into short-term stocks. It can also be inferred, although with less certainty, that on balance long-term rates are also expected to decline; the more-confident investors will already have switched 'long'.

In a period in which Bank rate has been altered frequently, the downward yield curve will usually be found to result when Bank rate has been raised to what is regarded as an abnormally high level, as in 1957, when Bank rate stood at 7 per cent, and in

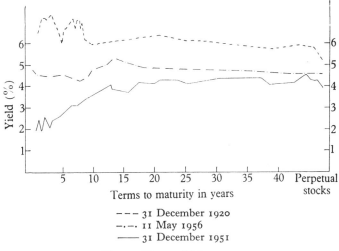

Fig. 3. Three yield curves.

--- 31 December 1920
−·−· 11 May 1956
—— 31 December 1951

1931, when it was raised to 6 per cent. The downward curve can perhaps be regarded as a 'crisis' curve—rates are high but are not expected to remain so indefinitely.

The slope of the curve will depend on how long investors expect the high level of interest rates to continue. It follows that when Bank rate is raised for some obviously temporary purpose, yields on long-term bonds may be hardly affected at all. For example, if a rise in Bank rate causes the rate on Treasury bills to be increased by 1 per cent, an investor who is confident that this new level will not last for more than a year will be deterred from switching into Treasury bills from 2½ per cent Consols if the price of the latter falls by a mere 1 per cent (or by less if he pays tax on his interest). For the return of the price of Consols to its previous price within one year would completely offset the extra yield derived from investing in Treasury bills for one year. In the nineteenth century, when alterations in bank-rate were numerous, the yield on long-term stocks frequently hardly changed at all even when movements in Bank rate were sharp.

That long-term yields do not fluctuate as widely as the yield on shorter-term stocks can be explained either by considerations regarding the comparison of present with expected future short rates, or merely by the knowledge that this has usually been so in the past.

3. There is nothing in principle to prevent short-term and long-term yields from moving in opposite directions, if a movement in short-term rates is widely held to be temporary. If long-term rates have been following the course of short-term rates, long-term rates may eventually move counter to short-term rates when sufficient investors come to the conclusion that the series of changes in short-term rates is coming to an end and that there is a chance of a reversal of the whole movement of rates.

4. When the yield curve slopes upwards over the whole of its length and the curve is steep, so that short-term yields are very low, it can be deduced that the low level of short-term rates, at least, is widely regarded as temporary; capital-conscious investors will have already switched 'short' for fear of a capital loss due to a rise in long-term yields, while income-conscious investors will have switched 'short' in response to expectations of the higher yields likely to be obtained from reinvestment when interest rates rise. A vigorous cheap money policy, particularly when undertaken at a time that investors fear to be inopportune, will, as in 1946–7, result in a curve of this shape.

5. A humped curve may have several explanations. It will occur when sufficient investors have recently switched from medium-term stocks to short-term stocks because of the risk of some rise in short rates, but at a time when long-term yields look rather high, so that few investors have sold long-term stocks to buy medium-dated or short-dated stocks. This situation may exist either when the risk of a rise in short-term yields is not very strong or when the rise is expected to be too short-lived to have much effect on long-term yields.

The development of a hump in the yield curve can also be attributed in situations such as these to the fact that certain institutions, depending on their degree of income- or capital-consciousness, will generally confine their holdings to certain sections of the yield curve. Thus when there is even a small risk of a rise in short-term rates the discount houses, who are very capital-conscious, can be expected to switch short, and the banks may also be induced to act in a similar if less decisive fashion. The actions of these two groups of institutions will thus cause an upward-sloping curve in that part of the yield structure stretching as far, say, as ten-year or fifteen-year stocks. At the other end of the scale, however, income-conscious investors such as insurance companies and pension funds will not be tempted out of their long-term stocks if long-term yields are high, especially if the rise in short-term yields is unlikely to be large or long-lived. A humped curve can therefore sometimes be regarded as two separate curves, one rising and the other falling, each dominated by institutional capital-consciousness and income-consciousness respectively.

A humped curve may also be the result of a situation in which long-term yields are thought to be above their long-term average but in which short-term yields are not particularly high. There may in this case be no definite expectations of a movement in short-term rates one way or the other, so that the capital-consciousness of banks and discount houses will produce a rising curve over part of the yield structure, but income-conscious investors may have switched from medium-dated to long-term stocks. They may have done so because long-term yields were sufficiently high, in relation to yields previously ruling on medium-dated stocks, to lead to the conclusion that the reinvestment of the proceeds of medium-term stocks in, say, fifteen years' time would probably be done on too unfavourable terms, that is to say at too low a rate of interest, to justify accepting a high yield for fifteen years rather than a somewhat lower one for thirty.

6. A saucer-shaped curve is a humped curve with these possibilities reversed.

### Interest Rates and the Impact of Economic Events

Expectations will be influenced by factors such as the course of saving and investment, banking and monetary policy, as well

2 G

as by the possible actions of 'other' investors. The interaction of expectations regarding the pattern of rates with these forces can be analysed in terms similar to those used in the examination of the behaviour of 'the' rate of interest in the abstract.

The pattern of rates may change in the first instance, not because investors' expectations have altered, but because saving or investment, or the policy of the authorities or the banks, has changed. If planned investment increases, for example, the first impact on the security market will depend on just what form is taken by the attempt of industry to obtain extra finance. The demand for additional working capital may put pressure on short-term bond yields, if a rising demand for bank advances can only be accommodated if the banks sell securities. Sales of short-term bonds may also emanate from business portfolios. An increase in the volume of new issues will bear more on long-term security prices; if the proceeds of new issues are held by companies in short-term stocks until required to finance expenditure, short-term yields may even fall for a while.

When the pattern of rates is first influenced by monetary policy, the immediate effect will depend on the form this intervention takes. If Bank rate is changed in a period in which such alterations are frequent, the first impact will be felt by money-market rates and by yields on short-term bonds; there may be little change in long-term yields. If the change in Bank rate, as in 1951-2, comes after a long period of disuse, or if, as in that period, a change is interpreted as a recasting of the whole basis of monetary policy, long-term rates of interest may experience sharp changes immediately. Long-term yields will be affected directly if monetary policy takes the form of open market operations in long-term stocks. The authorities themselves may undertake switching operations for one reason or another.

The consequences of these forces on the pattern of yields will depend on how they react on investors' expectations about the future pattern of interest rates, but expectations may be altered by the knowledge of economic events. The longer the period under review, the less can the effects of any one set of factors be considered in isolation.

# CHAPTER 33

# ORDINARY SHARE YIELDS AND PRICES

In practice there is a half-way house between holding fixed-interest securities and holding goods, namely ordinary shares, which are a cross between a fixed-interest security and a title to goods. Ordinary shares can be purchased out of planned saving and are issued by businesses that finance their investment in this form. To this extent the prices of ordinary shares and of fixed-interest securities are influenced by saving and investment in a similar fashion. But the effect of the actual or expected course of ordinary-share dividends is superimposed upon the forces that determine the prices of fixed-interest securities and ordinary shares alike, so that the prices of ordinary shares and fixed-interest securities can move in different directions; shifts in both supply and demand occur between the two types of asset.

## VARIABLE DIVIDENDS AND RISK

The growth of productivity raises all incomes, including profits, so that, government fiscal action apart, profits and ordinary-share dividends per unit of capital employed follow a rising curve over the long run. In this respect ordinary shares are superior to fixed-interest securities. But because the fear of loss is apt to be a more potent force than the chance of gain, especially when the gain may be distant and the loss not far ahead, the risk that ordinary dividends may one day be reduced to below their current level, or the risk that on liquidation the assets of a company will not realize enough to repay the purchase price of an ordinary share, attaches a disadvantage to equity investment in the eyes of both income-conscious and capital-conscious investors. Wars, high taxation, nationalization, dividend restriction and trade depression are enemies of the ordinary share whose disappearance cannot be taken for granted. 'The' long run increase in profits and dividends which an expanding economy promises is, after all, a statistical average in which individual companies may not participate. Economic expansion is the result of economic change, which has its victims as well as its favourites.

## WHAT IS THE YIELD OF AN ORDINARY SHARE?

### Apparent Yield

At any point of time all that the investor *knows* regarding the yield of an ordinary share is its current market price and its last interim and final dividend. Its yield so calculated can best be described as its *apparent* yield. The fact that many shares show an apparent yield of 10 per cent at a time when others register one of only 4 per cent indicates that apparent yields are as much the result of investors' actions as their cause. At any existing market price it is the pattern of *expected* yields that determines the actions of sellers and buyers.

### Expected Yield

The expected yield is the relationship of the current price of a share to expected future dividends plus or minus any change in price which an investor expects over the future; the expected yield attached by any one investor to a given share may outrage the credulity of another. The term 'expected yield', like the 'expectations' of an investor, is again a form of shorthand, a symbol for the perhaps vague and only half-formed thoughts that an investor harbours concerning future dividends and share prices. He may, consciously or otherwise, have in his mind's eye a range of yields for any one share, with its corresponding range of probabilities. We could, therefore, be more precise by speaking of a most likely or mean expected yield, to which can be related another factor representing the spread of his forecasts around this, the 'standard deviation' of the statistician.

These are useful refinements of analysis, but precision of expression is swamped by uncertainty in the mind of the investor himself. It is doubtful whether many investors are able to place a numerical value on the expected yield they attach to a particular share. Nevertheless, the fact that an investor may not be able to say exactly what yield he expects from an ordinary share need not deter him from saying that the yield he expects from one is greater or less than that which he expects from another or from a fixed-interest security, any more than the fact that we are not mechanically equipped accurately to measure distances and speeds need prevent us from deciding whether to risk a dash across a busy road. We invest for the future and must act on our expectations;

even a refusal to act at all must be based on some view of what lies ahead. In the last resort, if an investor cannot say whether he expects the yield of one security to be greater than that of another he must be indifferent between them, as long as he is similarly undecided about the probable range within which the yield of each will fall.

It should be observed, however, that the prudent investor will not consider the expected yield of a security in isolation from his portfolio as a whole. Strictly speaking, it is by the effect on the expected yield of his whole portfolio and on the confidence with which his expectation can be held that the sensible investor will judge the purchase or sale of a security. Thus he will be reluctant to purchase an ordinary share in a company or industry in which he already has a substantial holding, if he fears that the result will be to expose his portfolio excessively to one type of risk. On the other hand, he will look with favour on a share whose acquisition diminishes the risk attached to his total portfolio, by permitting a greater spread of risk and particularly by allowing different risks to be offset one against another (that is, by reducing the 'standard deviation' on the expected yield of the whole portfolio). Thus, different investors will act differently, according to the existing composition of their portfolio, even though their assessment of the yield to be expected from particular shares, if considered in isolation, may be exactly the same.

### EXPECTED YIELD AND RISK

The expected yield of an ordinary share is blurred because of the uncertainty of future dividends and because the price at which it is likely to stand in the future cannot be predicted with confidence. Here, too, a distinction may be drawn between income-consciousness and capital-consciousness. Equity prices fluctuate more than those of fixed-interest securities, and so the ordinary-share market is not a safe hunting-ground for the capital-conscious investor when the outlook is uncertain. The foundations of the ordinary-share market are built by the transactions of the income-conscious investor, content to accept the risk of temporary fluctuations in share prices for the sake of the expected income yield that the dividends of an ordinary share may provide in the long run. Of course, when expectations are more definitely optimistic, investors who would be preoccupied with the risk of capital loss in times of uncertainty will also be numbered among the 'bulls'.

Ordinary shares are more uncertain investments than fixed-interest securities with no or little risk of default both because ordinary dividends may vary and because ordinary-share prices fluctuate more than ordinary dividends. The expected yield attached to an ordinary share by an investor, whether he is income-conscious or capital-conscious, must therefore exceed the expected yield on a fixed-interest security in order to compensate for this greater degree of income and capital risk. The investor, in other words, will demand a 'risk premium', in order to justify the purchase of an ordinary share rather than a fixed-interest security. For the purchaser of an ordinary share cannot predict with the same confidence that his mean expected yield will be realized.

The size of this 'risk premium' attached by an investor to ordinary shares will reflect the assurance with which he looks forward to his expected yield materializing. The size of the 'risk premium' will therefore be influenced by the risk of fluctuations in business activity, by the marketability of ordinary shares, by the protection afforded by company law, and by the adequacy of company accounts, all of which have some bearing on the uncertainty of realized yield for which investors require to be compensated.

The degree of risk attached to a small holding of ordinary shares is greater than that incurred by a large and widely spread portfolio, whose experience can be expected to be more representative of the ordinary-share market as a whole. The advantage of holding a large diversified selection of ordinary shares does not consist of spreading adverse experience over a number of shares in the mathematical sense alone, as a life-assurance company is able to predict the average mortality of a large group of people for all of whom mortality is inevitable. The difference is that, in economics, many risks are not independent; one industry contracts because another grows, and one business fails because another succeeds. A sufficiently varied portfolio reflects the gains that are the causes of its own losses and so bears some, at least, of the roundabouts as well as the swings of economic change. But because ordinary shares as a whole are open to a general risk, above all that of a decline in business activity, most investors believe it prudent to include in their portfolio some element of fixed-interest investment.

## THE GENERAL LEVEL OF ORDINARY-SHARE PRICES AND YIELDS

### The Long-term Rate of Interest

The rate of interest on irredeemable government securities sets a datum for the determination of ordinary-share yields and prices, in that to any investor too small to influence the market the rate of interest on irredeemable government securities appears as a standard, free from income risk, by which the merits of an ordinary share can be judged. But at any time a movement in the rate of interest may be the result of forces that bear on the market in ordinary shares in a different manner.

### Published Earnings and Dividends Declared

Given the long-term rate of interest, ordinary-share prices reflect published equity earnings and dividends declared. The earnings cover for dividends gives some indication of the security of dividends and the chance of an alteration if trading conditions change; but jam tomorrow is not valued as highly as jam today, so that, other things being equal, dividends declared carry more weight than published earnings.

Viewed in isolation, a conservative dividend policy, or a heavy weight of company taxation, tends to depress ordinary-share prices. But the full effect is less clear. For it is conceivable that retained profits might be used to finance such a high level of capital investment that the value of the national income and that of the general level of profits might be raised above those which would have materialized if dividends had been on a more generous scale but their recipients more abstemious in their personal expenditure. Similarly, in so far as the proceeds of company taxation are spent by the government, gross incomes and profits may be increased in money terms, if taxes are paid at the expense of the current saving of companies or shareholders. In short, both the allocation of profits to reserve and the taxation of profits depress share prices by reducing the *proportion* of gross profits that is distributed, but in so far as retained profits in the one case or tax receipts in the other are spent, the *level* of gross profits will be maintained and even increased.

### Expected Dividends and Earnings

Share prices will be influenced by changes in expectations regarding future dividends and earnings. At any moment of time the level of share prices reflects the predominant state of hope or fear regarding these factors, and the response of the market to dividends declared and earnings published will depend on the extent to which they match expectations. If a change in dividend has been fully anticipated, the news of the change will leave the price of the share concerned more or less unaltered, merely causing a corresponding adjustment in the apparent yield. If an increase in dividends proves to have disappointed a sufficient number of investors, its announcement will be accompanied by a fall in share prices; and the failure of dividends declared to be reduced as much as had been feared will be accompanied by a rise.

### 'Second- and Third-degree Guessing'

Fluctuations in ordinary-share prices have generally been more severe than the movement of the rate of interest and the course of equity dividends and earnings would signify. Part of the explanation is that 'the market's' expectations regarding the course of dividends are not always accurate, but except on occasions such as the slump of 1929–32 and the boom of 1953–5, dividends and earnings do not usually experience fluctuations wide enough for us to attribute swings in share prices mainly to this. The oscillation of share prices is partly the result of changes in expectations regarding future share prices that are to some extent based on the anticipation by investors individually of *other* investors' actions.

'Second-degree guessing' is the belief that *other* investors are on the point of buying or selling because of their forecasts regarding 'objective' factors, such as the future course of dividends and earnings. In principle there is also the need for 'third-degree guessing', i.e. for attempting to assess what 'other' investors' forecasts of 'other' investors forecasts happen to be, but whether many investors go this far explicitly is doubtful. As it is impossible to buy if all investors are seeking to buy, or to sell if all are seeking to sell, however, the capital-conscious investor, including the speculator, must attempt to anticipate purchases and sales by the rest of the market as a whole, so that to each investor the actions, and therefore the expectations, of other investors are highly important.

The behaviour of the equity market in the short run will depend on the extent to which it is influenced by short-term capital-conscious investors or by long-term, mainly income-conscious, investors. For it is the latter who bring to the market the long-run stability and the discriminatory appraisal of industrial prospects that the market requires in order to act efficiently as a signpost to the relative merits of different capital projects and as a means of providing liquidity to investors who wish to turn shares into cash for reasons other than the fear that other investors are on the point of doing the same. It is true that there is a need for the speculator to assist the operation of a free market, as long as he acts so as to cushion fluctuations, absorbing the sudden shocks of purchases and sales; but the speculator will act in this manner only if he, too, has his eye on long-term considerations, or if he is convinced that other investors are willing to remove the responsibility from him within a short space of time. Unfortunately, it is because speculation is so often dominated by the infectious quality of expectations that it frequently aggravates rather than cushions price fluctuations.

For one result of second-degree and third-degree guessing is that share price movements may be geared to themselves for a time. A rise in share prices may lead some investors to take the view that other investors will believe the movement to be extended and so join in themselves. As a rise in share prices gathers pace, the example of easy capital gains may lead to the substitution of wishful thinking, and even sheer greed, for prudence, and in the later stages of a vigorous 'bull' market the ranks of the speculators may be swollen by the influx of inexpert and casual investors, tempted by the capital profits of others to take the plunge themselves.

Sooner or later the necessity for 'beating the gun', for not being caught out if share prices do fall, induces an increasing number of investors to 'take their profit' by selling. The signal for the first phase of weakness may be some 'objective' factor, such as an ominous slackening in the rise of profits or dividends, or merely a vague feeling that the rise in share prices has been 'overdone'. The need to avoid being caught by an eventual fall in share prices makes it all the more likely that a sharp rise in share prices will eventually be reversed, and the fear of incurring capital losses due to the actions of *other* investors will hasten the pace of sales and thus drive down share prices perhaps to very low levels, especially if erstwhile 'bulls' are forced to sell stock in order to find the cash to meet their commitments. As prices begin to fall, the decline may be aggravated for a while by the action of the 'bears', who sell stock they have not yet got in the hope of being able to deliver by purchasing at a lower price.

The knowledge that share prices have fluctuated in the past strengthens the likelihood of fluctuations in the future, and although the timing of vigorous swings in share prices has been a reflection of economic and political developments, their violence has been in large measure due to the ease with which wishful thinking leads the optimistic investor to believe that he can capitalize on other investors' expectations in the boom and to the fear that causes investors to undertake the self-defeating path in reverse, pressing sales on a market in which other investors, too, are guided by the same motives. The succession of swings of hope and fear thus magnifies the effect of fluctuations in profits and dividends.

### The Institutional Framework

In the course of time the demand for ordinary shares reflects changes in the nature of the capital market. The redistribution of incomes and wealth in the direction of greater equality is a development that would tend to reduce the demand for ordinary shares, but for the growth of life-assurance and pension funds. These income-conscious institutions hold a much larger proportion of their assets in the form of ordinary shares than would individuals if their saving were not passed through these institutional channels. The development of investment and unit trusts has also widened the demand for ordinary shares. Changes of this sort have a deeper significance, for the willingness of institutional investors to hold on to their shares at times of uncertainty helps to provide the stability needed to attract other, more capital-conscious investors into the field of equity investment.

On the side of supply shifts may occur in the relative weight of ordinary shares as opposed to fixed-interest securities. In the short run new issues amount to little in relation to the stock of ordinary shares already in existence, and the effect of changes in the level of new ordinary-share issues is often lost in the purchases and sales of existing shares. But when the market in existing shares is otherwise in balance, such as when the market outlook is uncertain, the weight of new issues will be an important determinant of share prices. In the long run the supply of different types of industrial securities by way of new issues tends to adjust itself to shifts in demand, damping down changes in security prices that the latter would otherwise cause. The volume of ordinary shares in existence can also undergo important changes as a result of nationalization.

### THE COURSE OF ORDINARY-SHARE PRICES

Figs. 4 and 5 show two pictures of the course of ordinary-share prices, dividends and equity earnings between 1929 and 1957.

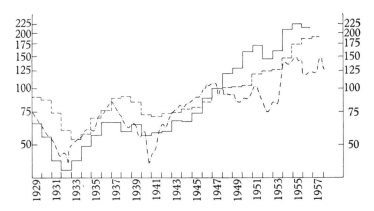

   – – –  Moody's Services index of ordinary dividends, 1947 = 100
   –.–.  Moody's Services index of ordinary-share prices, 1947 = 100
   ——  Moody's Services index of equity earnings, 1947 = 100

Fig. 4. Ordinary-share prices, dividends and earnings 1929–57. Dates refer to the year in which profits were earned and dividends declared. Logarithmic vertical scale.

Both are based on the experience of 150 companies selected by Moody's Services to represent the whole equity market, excluding mines and plantation companies. The indices of dividends and earnings relate to the years in which dividends were declared and earnings published and are therefore in arrears of the period of trading to which they refer. Fig. 4 is a straightforward comparison of the three indices, but in Fig. 5 the index of share prices has been adjusted to take account of the long-term rate of interest, as represented by the price of 2½ per cent Consols. The index of share prices, in other words, has been divided each year by an index of the price of Consols (based on 1929=100), in order to remove the direct effect that a change in the long-term rate of interest may have on ordinary-share prices. Making this adjustment, the long-term course of share prices can be seen to have followed the general trend of dividends more closely than would otherwise appear to be the case. In assessing the part played by

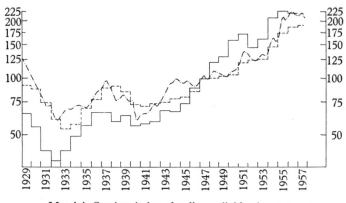

--- Moody's Services index of ordinary dividends, 1947=100
--- Moody's Services index of ordinary-share prices, 1947=100
—— Moody's Services index of Equity earnings, 1947=100

Fig. 5. Ordinary-share prices (adjusted), dividends and earnings 1929–57. Dates refer to the year in which profits were earned and dividends declared. Logarithmic vertical scale.

reported earnings, it must be remembered that published profits are unduly depressed by stock depreciation when commodity prices have fallen, as between 1930 and 1932 and between 1951 and 1952, and inflated by stock appreciation when they have risen sharply, as in 1950–51. Fig. 6 shows that the margin between *apparent* ordinary-share yields and the rate of interest narrows in a boom, as in 1954–5, but that it may also be very narrow after the worst of a slump, as in the years 1931–2, for in both situations investors will be looking hopefully for some not-too-distant improvement in dividends and share prices.

## Equity Prices and Business Activity

Fig. 7 overleaf presents a broad view of ordinary-share prices since 1919, smoothing month-to-month changes. The course of share prices over the years has followed the general direction of business activity, especially in the inter-war period. The boom periods of 1919–20 and 1927–9, and the recovery from the slump of 1929–32, were all marked by an upswing in share prices; and the slumps of 1920–21 and 1929–32 and the minor recession of 1938 brought a corresponding fall. The approach of

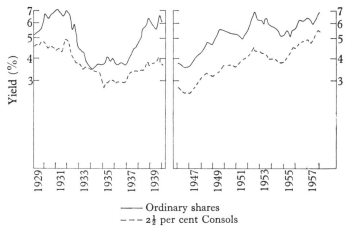

——— Ordinary shares
– – – 2½ per cent Consols

Fig. 6. Yields on ordinary shares and 2½ per cent Consols 1929–57. Based on constituents of Actuaries' Investment Index. The pre-war and post-war series are not strictly comparable. Logarithmic vertical scale.

war can be seen in the failure of share prices to rise as vigorously as production in the later nineteen-thirties.

In the early post-war years the link between industrial activity and ordinary-share prices proved weaker. The fall in share prices between 1946 and 1948 occurred at a time when production and equity earnings were rising strongly. For this divergence three factors were responsible—the rise in interest rates, the generally hostile attitude of the Labour Government to the world of finance, and the increase in company taxation in particular, and the uncertainty generated by our balance-of-payments problems. Since

1949 the course of ordinary-share prices has been more closely related to that of industrial production, with peaks in 1951 and 1955 and a dip during the minor business recession of 1952.

That ordinary-share prices should reflect the current level of business activity, which influences current earnings and dividends, is not surprising, but because investors look ahead share prices may turn down before a fall in industrial production and turn up before a recovery from a slump. Before a fall in business activity is recorded by a downturn in industrial production as a whole its approach will be felt by those businessmen quick to sense a

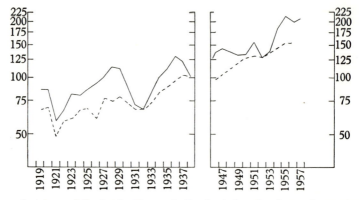

—— London and Cambridge Economic Service index of ordinary-share prices, 1938=100
- - - London and Cambridge Economic Service index of industrial production, 1938=100

Fig. 7. Ordinary-share prices and industrial production
1919–57.  Logarithmic vertical scale.

change in the situation.  Before production declines orders drop away, and rising costs and competition commence to press on profit margins.  The experience of a succession of booms and slumps in the past keeps businessmen and investors with whom they are in touch on the look-out for a repetition of these oscillations.  But, although the record does show that a swing in share prices has preceded a swing in industrial production on many occasions, the greatest fall in business activity ever experienced, that in the U.S.A. from 1929 to 1932, began some months before the fall in share prices.  There have also been times when a fall in ordinary-share prices has proved a false industrial alarm. Nevertheless, the National Bureau of Economic Research, an American organization that has made a detailed study of business fluctuations in the U.S.A., regards ordinary-share prices as one of the indicators of an impending swing in business activity. In the twenty-two swings between 1899 and 1938 in the U.S.A., industrial ordinary-share prices preceded the general business upturn or downturn on sixteen occasions, with an average lead of six or seven months.

### Ordinary Shares and the Price-level

Share prices fluctuate more than retail prices from year to year. But, in the long run, ordinary-share values can be expected to

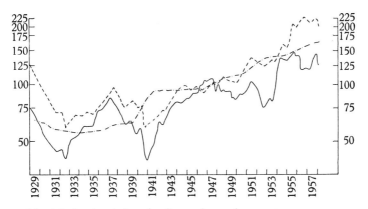

— Moody's Services index of ordinary-share prices, 1947 = 100
– – – Moody's Services index of ordinary-share prices, 1947 = 100. Adjusted for change in price of 2½ per cent Consols
–·–· Index of retail prices, 1947 = 100

Fig. 8. Ordinary-share prices and retail prices 1929–57.
Logarithmic vertical scale.

benefit from rising prices of goods and services, as long as the course of production is not adversely affected by the rise in the price-level itself, as would be the case if exports were depressed by an increase in costs greater than that experienced abroad. Experience shows that profit margins eventually move in line with the general rise in money incomes, however, if the maintenance of full employment is the major object of government policy; for in the last resort the devaluation of the exchange rate may seem a lesser evil than prolonged economic stagnation caused by excessive domestic costs.

If businesses succeed in matching the prices of their products with an increase in variable costs, gross trading profits will rise more than proportionately, for certain overhead costs, such as rents, are fixed in money terms, or lag behind other prices. Moreover, because of the existence of fixed prior claims on a company's profits in the shape of debenture interest and preference dividends, net earnings apparently available for distribution to the ordinary shareholder rise even faster than net profits after tax by a measure depending on the gearing of a company's capital structure. Whether 'true' distributable earnings rise at a similarly rapid rate depends on whether depreciation provisions allowed for tax purposes reflect the rise in the replacement cost of physical capital. A company's distributable resources will also be prevented from receiving the full benefit of inflation if a heavy tax is incurred on stock appreciation in a period of a relatively rapid rise in prices.

Heavy company taxation or conservative dividend policies, on the other hand, may hold back the growth of dividends, which may not keep pace with gross profits, as in the post-war period. The long-term trend in share prices may fall behind a long climb in retail prices for these reasons, unless the experience of inflation draws a wider circle of investors into the equity market. If inflation becomes serious, the scramble for real assets and claims on real assets causes share prices to rise strongly, and apparent yields may even fall below the rate of interest on government securities. But, as Fig. 8 indicates, the rise in the general level of ordinary-share prices between the boom years of 1929 and 1955, when adjusted for the rate of interest, did not keep pace with the more steady ascent of retail prices, as a result of the relative smallness of the increase in dividends.

### YIELDS AND PRICES OF INDIVIDUAL SHARES

The forces described as operating on the general level of share prices and yields act on transactions in individual shares. The pattern of share prices and yields changes with the varying fortunes of the individual companies within each industry and of each industry within the economy. Accurate knowledge of how industrial developments bear on sales and profits of individual concerns is given to few, so that share price movements in the short run may bear little relation to the facts; rumour and accident both play their part.

In their assessment careful investors will consider many aspects of a business: its profit and dividend record; the earnings cover for the current dividend; the little that may be known of its management and its products; the concentration or diversification of its interests; its degree of dependence on exports; the implications of its chairman's statement and its accounts; its vulnerability to political action or to industrial unrest; its gearing; and the marketability of its shares. An investor may be confident that he has made the best appraisal possible of these factors, but he has still to decide whether the current price of the share concerned is worth paying; this is often the most difficult part of his task.

The likely course of *other* investors' actions will influence especially the transactions of those investors to whom short-term capital gains and losses, whether realized or not, are important. The speculative investor in particular is constantly scanning the scene for some indication of a shift in other investors' opinions, for some sign, for example, that a company or industry is going to become a 'fashionable' field for investment because of the publicity given to certain industrial or technical developments. These changes of 'fashion' may only too easily be found to have raised the prices of the favourites too high and to have left too low those that are neglected, when the actual course of industrial profits becomes apparent.

### The Timing of Individual Share Price Movements

The timing of ordinary-share price movements is often in advance of the publication of the facts justifying them, particularly when the facts are published statistics. When the profits of an industry or a company show signs of falling off to those in the know, sales of shares by the latter may affect prices at a time when to the uninformed investor all is favourable on the statistical surface. Economic statistics are published only after some unavoidable delay, and the public revelation of a change in trend may present no suitable opportunity for slower investors to buy or to sell on favourable terms, if only because jobbers may adjust prices in order to prevent themselves from being swamped with orders.

2 H

The time-lag between a shift in trading conditions and in the public knowledge of such a change is followed by a further interval before the publication of the accounts of a company showing the extent to which it has been affected by the change in trade. When the fortunes of companies diverge, therefore, the pattern of their apparent earnings and dividend yields may bear little relationship to that revealed by a comparison of their last published accounts. Differences in apparent yields recorded by the shares of similar companies within the same industry when trading conditions are changing may to some extent be due to the timing of their accounts and dividend declarations.

### Safe and 'Defensive' Stocks

High earnings cover gives some assurance of security of the current level of dividends and some promise of growth; were 'other things' equal, therefore, a high earnings cover would justify a relatively low apparent dividend yield. Shares in industries which have a reputation for stability may also be found to stand on a relatively low apparent yield basis, whereas those thought to be vulnerable to economic fluctuations, to unfavourable developments in overseas markets, or to hostile political action, will record their unpopularity in the form of relatively high apparent dividend yields, if the earnings cover for dividends is no greater than the average. When an industrial boom is suspected of being on the point of petering out, capital-conscious investors may switch to so-called 'defensive shares' in unspectacular but safe industries thought capable of weathering the storm, while others more vulnerable to a slump may be neglected even though their long-term prospects are more favourable.

### 'Growth Shares'

Over the last few years, on the other hand, the search for 'growth' shares has attracted great attention as a result, perhaps, of the belief that scientific and industrial research, in an economy apparently free from serious economic recession, hold out the promise of both vigorous and secure expansion in certain industries. 'Growth shares' are those where profits and dividends are expected to increase faster than the average, as measured from the peak of one boom to another. 'Growth' is usually reflected in especially low apparent yields, but there is little to tell most investors whether today's high level of prices is worth paying for jam not tomorrow but the day after tomorrow, especially when 'growth' is obtainable only at a high cost in terms of profits retained for capital development or scientific research. Because uncertainty is so powerful a factor in these cases, the prices of so-called growth shares may fluctuate more than ordinary shares in general, as the prospect of rapid growth appears to wax and wane. For similar reasons shares in companies not yet in the producing stage, such as mining concerns, also tend to be subject to wide price fluctuations.

# PART VI

# NATIONAL INCOME AND
# ITS FLUCTUATIONS

# CHAPTER 34

# NATIONAL INCOME STATISTICS

National income statistics are indispensable to the study of many aspects of the economy. They are conveniently introduced at this point because they are based on concepts relevant to the analysis of factors determining the general level of economic activity.

'The national income is a measure of the money value of goods and services becoming available to the nation from economic activity. It can be regarded in three ways: as a sum of incomes derived from economic activity, which can be broadly divided for example between incomes from employment and incomes from profits; as a sum of expenditure, the main distinction being that between expenditure on consumption and expenditure on adding to wealth (investment); as a sum of the products of the various industries. These three aspects help to explain both the ways in which the statistics are normally presented and the ways in which the estimates are compiled.'

This quotation from the official guide* to the national income accounts is a convenient summary of the concepts underlying the accounts. The *Blue Book on National Income and Expenditure* that is now published each summer by the Central Statistical Office presents the accounts in extensive detail; provisional estimates of the main components are published in a White Paper before the Budget. In both, the estimates relate to the money value of goods and services 'becoming available' over periods of a calendar year, but since 1957 quarterly estimates of the main summary accounts for national expenditure have been published in the *Monthly Digest of Statistics*.

## 'FROM ECONOMIC ACTIVITY'

The key phrase 'from economic activity' has to bow to the practical difficulty of following the definition to its limits. In the language of economics generally 'income' is linked to the concept of economic activity in the form of 'production', being the

---

* *National Income Statistics—Sources and Methods* (H.M.S.O., 1956). This book has been drawn on extensively in this chapter.

reward of a factor of production for its contribution to output. In the task of measuring 'production' it is by and large practicable only to consider the flow of those goods and services that are customarily exchanged for money. This restriction results in the exclusion of personal services that are given without money payment in return but that are nevertheless part of the country's 'economic activity' in its widest sense. The services of that indispensable member of the economy, the housewife, are therefore omitted.

The national income accounts are not entirely confined to the flow of goods and services actually exchanged for money, for in some cases where money transactions are customary it is possible to 'impute' money values to those goods and services for which no money has actually been paid. Market rents are used to impute a value to the annual 'income' derived by an owner-occupier from his house, so that the annual 'service' provided by the house is placed on the same footing as if the occupier had paid rent. Other imputed values in the national income accounts include food and lodging for domestic servants and the Forces and farm produce consumed by the farmer and his household. These are counted as part of the 'income' of the recipients, but as national income accounts define 'national income' to equal 'national expenditure', imputed incomes must be matched by imputed expenditures, so that in the expenditure category 'consumption' the recipients of imputed incomes are shown as 'spending' these on the goods and services of which they are composed.

National income, as a measure of production, does not include the receipt of gifts or other grants for which no goods and services are given in return; such 'transfer payments' are therefore excluded from the aggregate of national income. Certain transfer payments, such as taxes, National Insurance benefits and interest on the national debt, which only redistribute the national income, nevertheless form an important part of the money receipts of certain sections of the community and, while excluded from the aggregate of national income, are brought into the accounts of the personal sector and the government, cancelling out for the economy as a whole. Interest and dividends paid by business enterprises, including public corporations, are not transfer payments but are shown as rewards for production. Interest on the national debt, on the other hand, has arisen largely through the finance of war expenditures and cannot be regarded as being matched by currently produced goods and services.

## INCOME = PRODUCT

The national income is defined as to be equal to what at this stage can be described as the national product, because both production and income, the return to factors of production, are by definition merely different aspects of the same economic activity. 'Factor incomes' are divided in the Blue Book into the following categories:

> Income from employment
> Income from self-employment
> Gross trading profits of companies
> Gross trading profits of public corporations
> Gross trading profits of other public enterprises
> Rent

Their aggregation gives the same result, if stock appreciation is deducted, as the sum of the products of the various industrial and other productive categories, if 'imputed' products, such as the ownership of dwellings and domestic service, are included, and if, as we shall see, adjustment is made for subsidies and taxes on expenditure. The product of any industry or sector of the economy is also necessarily equal to the factor incomes generated by it.

## PRODUCT = EXPENDITURE

'Expenditure' is also defined in the national income accounts so as to be merely another expression of the economic activity we call production, because the term is applied whether products are sold to final consumers, exported, embodied in capital goods, or retained as an increase in stocks and work in progress. An increase in stocks also forms part of the 'income' of the business in whose hands they accumulate, thus maintaining the identity of 'expenditure' with 'income' as well as with 'product'. In everyday language, it is not straining the concept too far to regard the nation as 'spending' part of its 'income' on adding to its stocks.

## INTERMEDIATE AND FINAL PURCHASES

We therefore have, by definition, an identity between income, product and expenditure. But national income is not an aggregate of *all* recordable factor incomes; national product is not an aggregate of *all* the recordable sales values of goods and services produced; and national expenditure is not the aggregate of *all* recordable purchases. In order to prevent counting the same income, expenditure and product more than once in computing the total for the whole economy, *intermediate* purchases must be excluded in measuring the contribution of each productive unit; national income product and expenditure are the aggregate of *final* purchases.

Final purchases and expenditure in an economy without international transactions are consumption, including that by the government, and capital formation, including the addition to stocks; international transactions make it necessary to extend this definition to include exports and, for reasons that we shall consider, to exclude imports. Intermediate purchases are purchases of goods and services for use in production and subsequent resale.

What is involved in the identity of income, product and expenditure with final transactions can be illustrated by the simple example of a loaf of bread sold by the baker to the housewife for one shilling. The baker may have paid eightpence for his flour and the miller sixpence for his wheat; the farmer may be assumed to have bought no materials. The final purchase or sale is consumer expenditure of one shilling, and the intermediate purchases eightpence and sixpence. If these producers employed no labour or other factors of production, the operating accounts of the three businesses would be as in the following table. The national income accounts are constructed from the various operating accounts.

OPERATING ACCOUNTS

| Bakery | | | | Flour-mill | | | | Farm | | | |
|---|---|---|---|---|---|---|---|---|---|---|---|
| Purchases | 8 | Sales | 12 | Purchases | 6 | Sales | 8 | 'Profit' | 6 | Sales | 6 |
| 'Profit' | 4 | | | 'Profit' | 2 | | | | | | |
| | 12 | | 12 | | 8 | | 8 | | 6 | | 6 |

The 'national income accounts' for this community would show:

NATIONAL INCOME ACCOUNTS

| Income | | Product | | Expenditure | |
|---|---|---|---|---|---|
| Bakery 'profit' | 4 | Bakery | 4 | Consumption | 12 |
| Flour-mill 'profit' | 2 | Flour-mill | 2 | | |
| Farm 'profit' | 6 | Farm | 6 | | |
| Total | 12 | Total | 12 | Total | 12 |

The sum of the products, net of intermediate purchases, equals final expenditure; in each 'industry' income equals product, by definition.

Now suppose that all three businesses employed labour enabling them to double their output and sales.

OPERATING ACCOUNTS

| Bakery | | | | Flour-mill | | | | Farm | | | |
|---|---|---|---|---|---|---|---|---|---|---|---|
| Purchases | 16 | Sales | 24 | Purchases | 12 | Sales | 16 | Wages | 3 | Sales | 12 |
| Wages | 2 | | | Wages | 1 | | | Profit | 9 | | |
| Profit | 6 | | | Profit | 3 | | | | | | |
| | 24 | | 24 | | 16 | | 16 | | 12 | | 12 |

The 'national income accounts' now show:

NATIONAL INCOME ACCOUNTS

| Income | | Product | | | Expenditure | |
|---|---|---|---|---|---|---|
| Bakery profit | 6 | Bakery industry | | | Consumption | 24 |
| | | Profit | 6 | | | |
| Flour-mill profit | 3 | Wages | 2 | | | |
| | | | — | 8 | | |
| Farm profit | 9 | Flour-mill industry | | | | |
| | | Profit | 3 | | | |
| Bakery wages | 2 | Wages | 1 | | | |
| | | | — | 4 | | |
| Flour-mill profit | 1 | Farm industry | | | | |
| | | Profit | 9 | | | |
| Farm profit | 3 | Wages | 3 | 12 | | |
| Total | 24 | Total | | 24 | Total | 24 |

In each 'industry' the product equals the sum of the incomes of the factors of production, and the total is again equal to final expenditure. The total would be the same if the 'appropriation accounts' of the three businesses showed the division of 'profit' into dividends and undistributed profits.

Now suppose that our farmer buys a newly constructed tractor. The important point is that a tractor ranks as a capital good, and the farmer's purchase is not entered as a cost in his operating account, where it would reduce the figure for farm output, but in his capital account, where it ranks as final expenditure in the form of capital formation. Corresponding to this would be the product of the 'tractor industry', which, together with the products of the suppliers to the industry, would equal 'capital formation' and thus preserve the balance between income, product and expenditure. Assuming that the whole of the income of the tractor and auxiliary industries were spent on bread, our model could be summarized as follows:

FARM CAPITAL ACCOUNT

| Reduction in financial assets | 6 | Acquisition of tractor | 6 |
|---|---|---|---|

OPERATING ACCOUNTS

| Bakery | | | | Flour-mill | | | |
|---|---|---|---|---|---|---|---|
| Purchases | 20 | Sales | 30 | Purchases | 15 | Sales | 20 |
| Wages | 2 | | | Wages | 1 | | |
| Profit | 8 | | | Profit | 4 | | |
| | 30 | | 30 | | 20 | | 20 |

OPERATING ACCOUNTS

| Farm | | | | Tractor Industry | | | |
|---|---|---|---|---|---|---|---|
| Wages | 3 | Sales | 15 | Wages | 3 | Sales | 6 |
| Profit | 12 | | | Profit | 3 | | |
| | 15 | | 15 | | 6 | | 6 |

NATIONAL INCOME ACCOUNTS

| Income | | Product | | Expenditure | |
|---|---|---|---|---|---|
| Profits | 27 | Bakery | 10 | Consumption | 30 |
| Wages | 9 | Flour-mill | 5 | Capital formation | 6 |
| | | Farm | 15 | | |
| | | Tractor industry | 6 | | |
| | 36 | | 36 | | 36 |

The introduction of capital formation implies the existence of a new item that can be discerned by comparing income with expenditure. For we now have total income of 36, but consumers' expenditure of only 30. The difference between income and consumers' expenditure is saving, which at 6 is equal to capital formation. This is another of the identities arising from the definitions used; in national income accounting the capital formation carried out in any period—including investment overseas— must be equal to the saving performed in that period.

Finally, the size of the total product will be affected according to where the line between current operating costs and capital formation is drawn. For if our farmer had not bought a tractor but had instead spent 6 on fertilizers used up in the period, we should, it is true, have a product of 6 for the fertilizer industry to replace that of the tractor industry. The net product of the farm, however, would have been not 15 but 9. If the total expenditure on bread had remained the same, the aggregate income and expenditure of our community would have been only 30, devoted entirely to consumption.

## DEFINITION OF THE 'UNITED KINGDOM'

The national income of the 'United Kingdom', as defined in the official accounts, is that accruing to persons, enterprises and institutions regarded as United Kingdom *residents*, wherever that income may arise. The activity of certain foreigners in this country, such as foreign embassy staffs and military personnel, is excluded, but the national income includes the income of our own government officials and armed forces stationed abroad, our merchant fleet overseas and the income accruing through the overseas operations of a business 'resident', that is managed and controlled, in this country.* The overseas income of the resident business is included whether or not it is actually remitted to this country. Thus the national income, product and expenditure are not identical with the economic activity carried on within the geographical boundaries of the United Kingdom, a concept that is sometimes described as the 'geographical product' of the country.

The national income or product can therefore be divided into the United Kingdom's *domestic product* and its net income from

* This is the usual criterion for taxation purposes.

abroad. The former is the product of United Kingdom residents that arises within the country. It includes the product of those British companies operating chiefly in the United Kingdom, including that generated here by foreign companies operating in this country, for these too are United Kingdom residents, and also for practical reasons the product of all British insurance and shipping companies.

Net income from abroad is the difference between two sums, between the total property income of United Kingdom residents received from abroad and property income paid abroad. The former includes, for example, the total profits arising from the overseas operations of United Kingdom resident companies, interest and dividends received from investments in non-resident enterprises, and interest received on the securities and loans issued by overseas governments. In property income paid abroad are to be found profits transferred abroad by foreign companies operating in the United Kingdom and interest paid on the loans made to this country by the United States and Canadian governments.

We can say that:

National income=domestic product *plus* net income
from abroad.

### NATIONAL INCOME AND DEPRECIATION

We can distinguish between 'gross' and 'net' aggregates of income, product and expenditure according to whether we define them before or after deducting depreciation. 'National income' is defined as the aggregate of incomes after deducting depreciation; but, owing to the difficulty of making reliable estimates of depreciation at current replacement prices, the official accounts present all the aggregates on a gross basis. Thus a figure for the national income is the one measure not to be found in the so-called national income accounts. However, in this field honesty is the best statistical policy, and tables of the Blue Book present both depreciation provisions permitted for tax purposes, an unstable series of little value outside the study of company finance, and more realistic if crude estimates of capital consumption in the true sense.

We can continue to build our framework with the following definitions:

National income *and* depreciation=*gross* domestic product plus net income from abroad
=*gross* national product
=*gross* national expenditure.

Naturally, whereas gross national expenditure shows gross capital formation, net national expenditure, the counterpart of national income, would include only net capital formation.

### FACTOR COST AND MARKET PRICES

In postulating an identity between expenditure and incomes generated by that expenditure the official accounts depart from everyday language in one respect. The expenditures actually made by final purchasers in the real world are made at prices that include taxes on expenditure, largely on consumer goods and services, which do not enter into the incomes of producers, being merely collected by them and paid to the government without any specifically identifiable product being exchanged in return. In the same way the money values of some final purchases are less than the receipts of producers, owing to subsidies. Expenditure taxes are paid by final purchasers but are not received as factor incomes; subsidies are received as factor incomes but are not paid by final purchasers. Therefore the market value of the flow of goods and services exceeds the total sum received by factors of production by an amount equal to taxes on expenditure minus subsidies.

The national income accounts therefore distinguish between values expressed *at market prices* and those *at factor cost*. The convention adopted is to confine the terms 'national income', 'national income and depreciation' and 'gross national product' to values expressed at factor cost, without actually appending any such label. In cases where values at market prices are more useful, such as in the study of personal incomes and expenditure, the market price basis is used for the components of expenditure. In the study of the relationship between different classes of national income or of the share of the national product taken by investment or defence, on the other hand, values at factor cost are generally more appropriate. But the identity of the aggregates can always be preserved by deducting from a total shown at market prices the amount of taxes on expenditure less subsidies, to bring it into line with the factor cost basis of the others.

One further modification has to be made to arrive at true factor cost values: stock appreciation must be excluded from incomes to preserve the concept of national income as identical with product and expenditure measured at the prices current in the period for which the accounts are prepared.

We thus now have:

> Total domestic income before providing for depreciation and stock appreciation
> *Less* Stock appreciation
> *Equals* Gross domestic product at factor cost, which, together with net income from abroad,
> *Equals* National income and depreciation
> *or* Gross national product
> *or* Gross national expenditure at factor cost

### Income, Product and Expenditure

If the only international transactions of the United Kingdom, that is transactions between residents and non-residents, took the form of payments and receipts of property income, the relationship between national income, product and expenditure could be expressed as in Table 22.

TABLE 22. *Income, Product and Expenditure*

| Income | Product | Expenditure |
|---|---|---|
| | | Consumption at market prices |
| | | PLUS gross domestic capital formation at market prices. |
| | | Total domestic expenditure at market prices |
| | | LESS taxes on expenditure |
| | | PLUS subsidies |
| Total domestic[1] factor incomes | = Gross domestic product at factor cost | = Total domestic expenditure at factor cost |
| | PLUS NET INCOME FROM ABROAD | |
| GROSS NATIONAL INCOME AND DEPRECIATION | = GROSS NATIONAL PRODUCT | = GROSS NATIONAL EXPENDITURE AT FACTOR COST |

[1] After deducting stock appreciation from an intermediate total described in Table I of the Blue Book as 'Total Domestic Incomes Before Providing for Depreciation and Stock Appreciation'.

In Table 22 the community's consumption (including that by the central and local government) and its domestic capital formation, the increase in the physical assets held by United Kingdom residents in this country, would consist only of goods and services produced entirely by United Kingdom residents in this country. Conversely, on these assumptions the whole of the gross domestic product would be made available to United Kingdom residents. In this scheme, net income from abroad would be equal to the change (positive or negative) in the overseas assets of United Kingdom residents, that is to say to the overseas investment of the United Kingdom.

In real life our participation in international trade upsets this equality between domestic product and domestic expenditure. Part of the domestic product is not made available to the community, being exported to pay for our imports. The latter, on the other hand, raise the total of our consumption, our domestic capital formation and our exports to a level exceeding that which could be provided by our domestic product alone. Consumption, domestic capital formation and exports all include some import content.

We can therefore say that, at factor cost, the gross domestic product must be equal to consumption, *plus* gross domestic capital formation, *plus* exports, *minus* imports, or, in other words, to total domestic expenditure at factor cost *plus* exports *minus* imports. Add net income from abroad to each side of this equation and we are once more back to the aggregates of gross national product and gross national expenditure at factor cost. This is summarized in Table 23.

TABLE 23. *Income, Product and Expenditure*

| Income | | Product | | Expenditure |
|---|---|---|---|---|
| Total domestic factor incomes[1] | = | Gross domestic product at factor cost | = | Total domestic expenditure at market prices |
| | | | | PLUS exports |
| | | | | LESS imports |
| | | | | LESS taxes on expenditure |
| | | | | PLUS subsidies |
| | | PLUS NET INCOME FROM ABROAD | | |
| GROSS NATIONAL INCOME AND DEPRECIATION | = | GROSS NATIONAL PRODUCT | = | GROSS NATIONAL EXPENDITURE AT FACTOR COST |

[1] Excluding stock appreciation.

2 I

## THE SIGNIFICANCE OF THESE EQUALITIES

This equality between the three aggregates has a significance extending beyond its use as a method of accounting. Together, consumption, domestic capital formation and exports cannot exceed home production except to the extent of imports; and this is one of the economic facts of life. Our desire to consume and add to our physical equipment can only outrun our performance as producers if we are able to import more than we export, financing a deficit in our foreign trade out of our net property income from abroad or by running down our overseas financial assets, if the deficit is not covered by gifts from abroad.

Another aspect of this identity is equally important. In a market economy the level of production, employment and prices depends on the flow of expenditure by consumers, government and businesses, including that made by our overseas customers. If aggregate expenditure is not sufficient, output will fall short of what the nation's equipment can produce, resulting in unemployment. When national expenditure tends to outrun the value of home production plus imports the effect is usually to force up the level of prices when resources are fully employed. As imports are affected directly by home demand and exports indirectly, through our ability to divert goods from the home market for sale at competitive prices abroad, the regulation of home expenditure —'total domestic expenditure'—is thus of vital importance to the preservation of both a healthy balance of payments and full employment.

### TABLE I OF THE BLUE BOOK

The framework of Table I of the Blue Book reproduced here in Table 24 is basically that constructed in the previous sections. The treatment of stocks, however, deserves special attention. The inclusion in gross domestic capital formation of the 'value of the physical increase in stocks and work in progress' records the fact that it is the *change* in the level of stocks that helps to determine the level of output. If in year I, in which part of the period's production is used to raise the *level* of stocks held by 50, is followed by year II in which the level of stocks remains unchanged, the 'value of the physical increase in stocks' or, more briefly, stockbuilding, will have fallen from 50 to zero. If no other component has altered, the gross product will also have fallen by 50.

TABLE 24. *National Income and Expenditure*

| | 1938 £m. | 1949 £m. | 1951 £m. | 1953 £m. | 1955 £m. | 1957 £m. |
|---|---|---|---|---|---|---|
| *Expenditure generating gross national product* | | | | | | |
| *At market prices* | | | | | | |
| Consumers' expenditure | 4,394 | 8,847 | 10,085 | 11,235 | 12,826 | 14,174 |
| Public authorities' current expenditure on goods and services | 772 | 1,978 | 2,443 | 3,052 | 3,213 | 3,583 |
| Gross fixed capital formation at home | 656 | 1,606 | 1,921 | 2,392 | 2,858 | 3,402 |
| Value of physical increase in stocks and work in progress | — | 65 | 575 | 125 | 300 | 450 |
| Total domestic expenditure at market prices | 5,822 | 12,496 | 15,024 | 16,804 | 19,197 | 21,609 |
| Exports and income received from abroad | 976 | 2,691 | 4,008 | 3,915 | 4,578 | 5,244 |
| *Less* Imports and income paid abroad | −1,038 | −2,635 | −4,388 | −3,799 | −4,625 | −4,932 |
| *Less* Taxes on expenditure | −622 | −1,984 | −2,274 | −2,373 | −2,626 | −2,956 |
| Subsidies | 37 | 525 | 468 | 364 | 346 | 413 |
| Gross national expenditure at factor cost | 5,175 | 11,093 | 12,838 | 14,911 | 16,870 | 19,378 |
| *Shares in the gross national product (factor incomes)* | | | | | | |
| Income from employment | 3,022 | 7,220 | 8,459 | 9,608 | 11,203 | 12,942 |
| Income from self-employment[1] | 647 | 1,389 | 1,450 | 1,557 | 1,674 | 1,787 |
| Gross trading profits of companies[1] | 690 | 1,848 | 2,489 | 2,323 | 2,922 | 3,265 |
| Gross trading surpluses of public corporations[1] | 10 | 156 | 258 | 317 | 310 | 333 |
| Gross profits of other public enterprises[1] | 64 | 106 | 120 | 66 | 112 | 131 |
| Rent[1] | 470 | 423 | 511 | 639 | 743 | 862 |
| Residual error | — | −11 | 84 | 163 | −71 | −68 |
| Total domestic income before providing for depreciation and stock appreciation | 4,903 | 11,131 | 13,371 | 14,673 | 16,893 | 19,252 |
| *Less* Stock appreciation | 80 | −200 | −750 | 75 | −200 | −100 |
| Gross domestic product at factor cost | 4,983 | 10,931 | 12,621 | 14,748 | 16,693 | 19,152 |
| Net income from abroad | 192 | 162 | 217 | 163 | 177 | 226 |
| Gross national product | 5,175 | 11,093 | 12,838 | 14,911 | 16,870 | 19,378 |
| Capital consumption | 359 | 936 | 1,146 | 1,364 | 1,545 | 1,774 |
| National income | 4,816 | 10,157 | 11,692 | 13,547 | 15,325 | 17,604 |

[1] Before providing for depreciation and stock appreciation.
SOURCE: *Blue Book on National Income and Expenditure 1957*, Table I.

In the lower half of Table 24 there is one item that requires explanation. The calculation of the national income can be undertaken by measuring incomes or expenditure, and the 'residual error' is the discrepancy between the computed totals reached by these two routes. The 'residual error' is included in the income and not the expenditure account purely for convenience; its position does not imply that the estimates of expenditure are necessarily more accurate than those of income.

## THE SECTORS OF THE ECONOMY

The component tables of the Blue Book divide the economy into four main sectors:

> *Persons*
>
> *Corporate enterprises*
> Companies
> Public corporations
>
> *Public authorities*
> Central government
> Local authorities
>
> Transactions with the *rest of the world*

The general scheme followed by the accounts is to include for each sector a current account showing the main elements of income and how they are appropriated or used for current expenditure. An operating account, showing costs and sales, cannot be prepared except for public corporations, since private business enterprises do not publish the necessary information. A capital account indicates for each sector the uses to which current saving has been put in acquiring assets or repaying liabilities. A number of more general accounts examine in detail the composition of the national income, product and expenditure, and several tables are devoted to the analysis of capital formation and its finance. The 'social accounts' of Table 9 in the 1956 Blue Book are a form of reconciliation account, bringing the current and capital transactions of the sectors together in a double entry system of recording. In the sections that follow, some of the problems encountered in interpreting the main accounts will be introduced.

## THE PERSONAL SECTOR

'Persons' include unincorporated businesses and private non-profit-making bodies, such as trade unions and Churches. 'Income' includes sums not actually received by individuals, such as employers' contributions to National Insurance and superannuation funds, which are treated as supplements to wages and salaries and therefore figure as intermediate purchases in the operating accounts of businesses. The constituents of income before tax are shown on a gross basis, although in practice income tax may have been deducted at source. Personal saving is the difference between personal incomes, less taxes on income and National Insurance contributions, and personal expenditure.

One conceptual difficulty regarding personal expenditure concerns the 'quality' of certain services such as distribution and transport. When expenditure on retail goods increases, no account can be taken of any deterioration in the quality of retailers' 'output' that may result, in the form, for example, of slower service. Similarly, no adjustment is practicable for an increase in the degree of congestion in trains and buses. Another difficulty is that, whereas the acquisition of houses is counted as capital formation, purchases of other durable consumer goods, such as furniture and motor cars bought for non-business use, are not; these goods are treated as being 'used up' in the year of acquisition, despite the fact that, like many consumer goods not even classed as durable, they may yield a service over many years. This is the conventional treatment of 'consumer capital' in most countries' national income accounts, but it may exaggerate the change in the standard of living of the community due to a change in its annual purchases of durables, which are small in relation to its stock of such goods.

### The Treatment of Life-assurance and Pension Funds

Life-assurance and superannuation funds are treated as the collective personal property of policyholders and members. A life-assurance company's accounts are thus divided into two: its profit and loss and appropriation accounts are included as part of the company sector, whereas the revenue account of its life-assurance fund takes its place in the accounts of persons. The increase in life-assurance funds—the excess of premiums, rent, dividends and interest received over taxation, payments to policy-holders, expenses of management and shareholders' profits—is counted as part of personal saving.

The rent, dividends and interest received by life-assurance funds are included in the combined figure for these items in the accounts of the personal sector; so is the taxation paid by life-assurance funds. Expenses of management and shareholders' profits, like other forms of productive 'expenditure', augment total incomes, being regarded as the cost of a service bought by life-assurance funds for their policyholders; to match income with expenditure these items are included in total consumers' expenditure.

As life-assurance premiums are paid out of the balance of personal incomes after tax and consumers' expenditure, and are therefore already included in personal saving, payments made to policyholders, which are derived partly from these premiums, must be regarded as negative saving, in order to avoid duplication. If persons spent on consumption an amount equal to the whole of their incomes after tax, including the net rent, dividends and interest received by life-assurance funds on their behalf, but paid life-assurance premiums out of their Post Office Savings Bank deposits, their personal saving would be zero even though life-assurance funds might show a large surplus on current account. Personal saving through the medium of life assurance would merely be exactly balanced by dissaving through other channels, in this example through the Post Office Savings Bank.

The increase in private superannuation funds is treated in a similar manner, with employers' contributions included in personal income from employment, but pensions currently received not being added to personal incomes. Some employers, on the other hand, including the government in the case of its Civil Servants, pay non-contributory pensions to their retired employees. Theoretically it would be proper to include in personal income from employment the increase in the accruing actuarial liability incurred by employers in respect of future pensioners, but in practice no measure of this exists. Instead, pensions paid are included in personal income from employment; like employers' contributions to funded schemes, they are part of the current expenses of the employers' operating accounts.

Whereas employers' contributions to National Insurance are also treated as part of income from employment, being counted as employers' business expenses in the same way as employers' contributions to private pension schemes, they are then withheld from personal saving by their inclusion in personal consumers' expenditure, along with the National Insurance contributions of employees. This method is necessary because the National Insurance funds are included in the central government sector and thus contribute to the saving of the government, not of persons.

### THE CORPORATE SECTOR

The product of business consists of its 'value added'—the excess of sales receipts, plus additions to stocks, over current purchases of goods and services. Company income, therefore, usually consists of gross profits as ordinarily understood. One important conceptual difficulty, however, arises in the case of financial concerns only a small part of whose income is derived from the charges they make to customers for identifiable services and whose main revenue is received from financial assets. Examples in this category are banks, investment trusts, issuing houses and insurance companies. The usual principle of measuring an industry's product leads to curious conclusions when applied here. The banks, for example, provide important services to their customers, but their 'sales receipts' take the form mainly of bank charges, which are the only identifiable receipts for specific services. The excess of these over the banks' current operating costs—wages, materials and depreciation—which form their only 'purchases', may actually be negative. In the everyday sense, however, the banks undoubtedly operate at a profit, derived mainly from net receipts of interest.

One solution might be to count as 'sales' the excess of interest received by the banks over what they pay depositors. In order to match product with expenditure, this would necessitate imputing to the rest of the economy corresponding expenses; it would mean reducing the product and income estimates for the rest of the economy as far as businesses are concerned but increasing the final purchases of personal customers of the banks in their consumer expenditure accounts. These imputed expenses, as in the United States' accounts, might be allocated according to the bank deposits held by each industry or sector, but the Central Statistical Office takes the view that, even if this information were available, it would not necessarily provide a basis for a realistic allocation; it therefore confines bank operating receipts to bank charges. An alternative method, adopted in the Australian accounts, would be to treat the banks as suppliers of final services to the whole community, like the government sector, defining their product not as operating surplus but as the total of wages and salaries they pay; this would mean higher levels of national product and expenditure.

Life-assurance offices are treated differently from the remaining sections of 'insurance, banking and finance'. The transactions of their life fund are regarded as taking place within the personal sector, but management expenses plus shareholders' profits are treated as personal expenditure on 'life-assurance services'. Management expenses and shareholders' profits are viewed as the product of life-assurance companies as corporate stewards of their life funds. This presentation is justifiable because the transactions of life funds are almost entirely with or on behalf of persons.

### THE GOVERNMENT SECTOR

Government current expenditure and receipts can be divided broadly into three categories. Transfer payments and receipts of the central and local government merely redistribute the national income and, whereas they can be included in any individual sector's accounts, cancel out for the economy as a whole, apart from international grants. Secondly, certain government departments, for example the Post Office, act as trading enterprises. In these cases the usual distinction must be made between operating costs and final product, so that payments on operating account are deducted in arriving at the figures of trading and rental income, which are shown as part of government current receipts. In a third group of purchases of goods and services the central government and local authorities render services to the public free, or nearly free, and these do not appear in consumers' expenditure. Nevertheless, in computing national income and expenditure, it is clearly desirable that the work done by teachers, judges and policemen, etc., should not be excluded. This is achieved by regarding public authorities as collective bodies providing free public services for collective consumption by the community. Because these services of public authorities are not sold, they can be valued in money terms only by adding up the expenditure by the public authorities incurred in buying the services of teachers, judges and policemen, etc., together with materials used.

Some of these free services, it is true, could be regarded more in the nature of the 'cost' of producing other categories of output, particularly in the case of services provided free to business enterprises, which might alternatively be treated as the imputed expenses of business, diminishing their product. In the last resort many items of government expenditure, including defence and police, could perhaps be regarded as intermediate national 'operating' costs; but this is not a helpful interpretation of the practical problems facing the national income statisticians.

TRANSACTIONS WITH THE REST OF THE WORLD

International transactions, as defined in the national income accounts, are those between so-called 'residents' of the United Kingdom and non-residents, whether the transactions take place within the political boundaries of the United Kingdom or abroad. Purchases of fuel and ships' stores abroad by British shipping companies operating abroad, for example, are treated as imports into the United Kingdom although they do not enter into this country and are therefore not recorded in the monthly Trade and Navigation Accounts published by the Board of Trade. The latter record *shipments* of imports and exports in the month in which arrivals and departures are registered by the Customs authorities. The national income accounts (and the balance-of-payments White Papers) record transactions at the point of time at which ownership passes. Certain imports are normally paid for and pass into United Kingdom ownership well before they arrive in this country, but payment for United Kingdom exports does not usually take place until they arrive in foreign ports. The timing of imports and exports in the national income accounts is generally made with reference to the time when payment normally becomes due, that is on a 'payable-receivable' basis. This means that if our overseas customers delay paying for British exports, or our creditors press for prompter payment of goods shipped to the United Kingdom, a course they may follow if they expect sterling to become cheaper in terms of foreign currencies, this country's net receipts of foreign currency will fall relatively to the figure implied by imports and exports in the national income accounts.

Another result of the timing of transactions adopted in the national income accounts is that a sharp increase in imports, on a 'payable-receivable' basis, may cause an increase in the figure of investment in stocks shown in the accounts before the goods concerned have arrived in this country.

Both imports and exports are valued f.o.b. (free on board), that is excluding the cost of insurance and freight; in the monthly Trade and Navigation Accounts, on the other hand, imports are valued c.i.f. (cost, insurance, freight), because this is the method generally used for the calculation of import duties. Shipping and insurance services are therefore shown separately in the national income accounts.

### GROSS CAPITAL FORMATION

Since 1951 the national income accounts have defined gross capital formation so as to exclude ordinary repair and maintenance expenditure, which is regarded as a current cost chargeable to operating account and thus held back from the gross national product.

One important table shows the 'financing of investment'. For the United Kingdom as a whole the 'financing of investment' can be expressed in the following way.

| | |
|---|---|
| Gross domestic capital formation | Saving |
| Plus net increase in U.K. assets abroad | Plus net capital transfers from abroad |
| Total investment | = Total Finance |

The above table records the fact that the increase in our domestic and overseas assets in any period must have been matched by saving plus net capital transfers from abroad. This is an accounting identity, although one that echoes the fact that we cannot add to our total wealth more than we can save out of our production, supplemented by gifts from overseas. This accounting identity does not apply to any one sector of the economy, for one sector can invest more than it has saved, as long as another has saved more than it has invested.

### INTER-INDUSTRY RELATIONS

For selected industry groups the 1958 Blue Book shows the estimated value of *gross* output for 1954, that is including intermediate purchases from other industries. It sets out these figures in the form of purchases between industrial groups, excluding duplication within each. The destination of gross output, supplemented by imports, is then recorded in the form of final purchases. The study of such inter-industry relations is usually described as 'input-output' analysis. The input-output table of the Blue Book (Table 18 in the 1958 Blue Book) divides the industries of the economy into eleven groups. It records the value of sales by each industrial group to every other industrial group and also its sales to final 'buyers', in the form of current purchases of persons and public authorities, gross domestic capital formation, and exports. For each industry the input of goods and services purchased from other industries plus the input of its own factors of production add up to its 'total output'; in 1954 the figure for intermediate output in the economy as a whole formed more than half of total output.

Input-output analysis is limited by the amount of information available but provides an interesting insight into inter-industry relations if recorded in sufficient detail. The figures can be adapted to show for each industry group what output is required from that group and from others for each £100 of final demand for its own products. Thus, in 1954, £100 million of final demand for the output of building and contracting would have required the following levels of output from building and other industries.

| From | £m. |
|---|---|
| Mining and quarrying | 3 |
| Chemicals and allied trades | 5 |
| Metals, engineering and vehicles | 17 |
| Textiles, leather and clothing | 2 |
| Other manufacturing | 19 |
| Building and contracting | 101 |
| Gas, electricity and water | 2 |
| Other production and trade | 15 |
| Total | 164 |

Input-output data offer a useful tool for analysis. They can be used, for example, by governments that seek to form detailed plans of economic development or mobilization, such as those drawn up in some 'underdeveloped' countries or more generally in wartime. In this respect input-output data are closely related to the concept of 'linear programming', a mathematical expression of the problem of allocating resources to the best advantage in certain limited circumstances. Input-output statistics, however, would not necessarily make possible economic forecasting by slide-rule even if they could be presented in great detail. Changes in relative prices lead industries to substitute one material for another, or capital for labour, etc., and the statistical 'grid' may not be sufficiently fine to allow for alterations in the variety of an industry's products. Even if relative prices could be forecast, it would still be necessary to know the 'elasticity of substitution' between different materials and different factors of production for any given price change.

A further difficulty is that an input-output table for any one year shows only those relationships appropriate to a given level of production. Inter-industry relationships may not, however, be proportional or 'linear'. A 5 per cent increase in the output of the chemical industry, for example, may not necessitate a 5 per cent increase in the volume of its purchases from the engineering industry. Inter-industry purchases and the use of primary input may not be proportional to final output even if prices remain constant. An industry that is operating well below full capacity, for example, will be able to raise its output without increasing the scale of its equipment purchases and without a proportionate increase in the size of its labour force. An industry straining the limits of its capacity, on the other hand, may incur unusually heavy expenditure on repairs and may be forced to employ labour of inferior quality. A further complication is that inter-industry relationships are bound sooner or later to be disturbed through changes in design and technique.

## THE SOURCES OF NATIONAL INCOME STATISTICS

Most of the data used in the national income accounts are obtained from Inland Revenue tax assessments for incomes, the annual censuses of production for the estimates of industrial output and capital formation, and the accounts of the public corporations, local authorities and central government. These are supplemented by statistics drawn from a variety of sources, such as other data of production and sales of different commodities, the foreign trade statistics of the Board of Trade and the Treasury, and the results of regular sample inquiries into consumers' expenditure, manufacturers' stocks and fixed investment. Little of this information is collected specifically for the compilation of national income statistics, so that the sixty or so tables of the Blue Book represent a considerable achievement. The reliability of the estimates has improved over the years, but the extensive revision of past estimates cannot be avoided in a conceptual system where an alteration in one category, e.g. consumers' expenditure, will necessitate changes being made in others, e.g. personal income or personal saving.

The official guide to the national income statistics attempts to grade the reliability of the main components. The chief weaknesses lie in the estimates of income from abroad, investment in stocks, stock appreciation and in proportionately small 'residuals' such as personal saving; in these there is, roughly speaking, a 90 per cent chance of an error of more than 10 per cent. Unfortunately, investment in stocks and personal saving are fields where accuracy is of great importance to the analysis of short-term economic change, and the possibility of error in other analytically important components, such as gross domestic fixed capital formation, although smaller, is still significant. Recorded changes from one year to another, however, are of greater reliability than the annual figures themselves, and in a number of instances analysis can proceed on this basis.

# CHAPTER 35

# THE LEVEL OF ECONOMIC ACTIVITY— CAUSES OF UNEMPLOYMENT

## EXPENDITURE THE KEY TO EMPLOYMENT

In the short run, in which the state of productive technique can be regarded as fixed, expenditure, or what is often described as 'effective' demand, is the key to the general level of production, employment and incomes. Involuntary unemployment occurs when national expenditure is not sufficient to generate a volume of output at which all those who are willing to work at current wage-rates can find jobs. Some unemployment is unavoidable in a free society, because some workers are always in the process of changing jobs, but this 'frictional' unemployment can be ignored at this stage. Production will be insufficient for the employment of the available labour force when sales by business, including the nationalized industries, are too low; and sales will be too low if expenditure is too low. Expenditure would be greater if incomes were higher, but in the absence of government intervention spendable incomes can only be higher if production rises, and production will not be increased if sales do not keep pace. The vicious circle would seem to be complete.

## THE EQUILIBRIUM LEVEL OF PRODUCTION, EXPENDITURE AND INCOME

The nature of the problem can be most easily examined by first assuming that there is no international trade and that government expenditure and revenue are at such low levels that they can be ignored. National expenditure will then consist substantially of outlays on private consumption and investment.

In the accounts of the national income statisticians, national income, product and expenditure are always equal. But what is of interest to us here is the consideration of those forces that lead to a change in income and expenditure towards or away from their so-called 'equilibrium' level, at which they will remain stable in the absence of further disturbances. For this purpose we must return to the concepts of planned saving and planned investment, which were introduced in Chapter 30. When planned saving equals planned investment, income and expenditure are stable, and planned expenditure equals production, so that there is no unplanned accumulation or reduction of producers' stocks to induce businessmen to contract or expand output.

Involuntary unemployment arises when equality between planned saving and planned investment occurs only at a level of national income, production and expenditure that is too low for full employment. The national income will not remain above this if, at a higher level of income, planned saving would be more than planned investment, in which case unsold stocks would accumulate, leading businesses to reduce production and so diminishing incomes until planned saving and investment—and therefore production and sales—were once more in balance. The national income will not remain below the equilibrium level if at a lower level of income planned saving would be less than planned investment, for the excess of planned investment over planned saving would set in motion forces of expansion.

TABLE 25. *Levels of National Income and Expenditure*

| National income and product | Planned saving | Planned investment | Consumption (1 − 2) | Total planned expenditure (3 + 4) |
|---|---|---|---|---|
| 1 | 2 | 3 | 4 | 5 |
| 2,000 | 600 | 500 | 1,400 | 1,900 |
| 1,900 | 513 | 413 | 1,387 | 1,800 |
| 1,800 | 432 | 357 | 1,368 | 1,725 |
| 1,700 | 357 | 307 | 1,343 | 1,650 |
| 1,600 | 288 | 263 | 1,312 | 1,575 |
| 1,500 | 225 | 225 | 1,275 | 1,500 |
| 1,400 | 168 | 193 | 1,232 | 1,425 |
| 1,300 | 130 | 180 | 1,170 | 1,350 |
| 1,200 | 120 | 160 | 1,080 | 1,240 |
| 1,100 | 110 | 150 | 990 | 1,140 |
| 1,000 | 100 | 150 | 900 | 1,050 |

By way of illustration, Table 25 sets out against hypothetical levels of national income and production the consumption, saving and investment that might be undertaken at those levels. Only with the national income at 1,500 would the economy be in equilibrium, with planned saving equal to planned investment and with production equal to planned expenditure. At national income levels above 1,500, planned saving rises by more than planned investment, so that planned expenditure falls short of production; at levels of national income below 1,500, on the other hand, the excess of planned investment over planned saving, implying an excess of planned expenditure over production, leads businessmen to increase their output, so raising the national income towards the equilibrium level. At this level, however, full employment might not be achieved; the full-employment level of income and expenditure might be, say, 2,000.

There is no reason inherent in the operation of a market economy why planned saving and planned investment should find equality at just the level of national income and production at which full employment is achieved, as saving and investment are performed by different members of the economy and for different motives. But it is evident from Table 25 that the explanation for the existence of involuntary unemployment can be sought in the relationships between income and saving or consumption, and between income and investment. As we move above a national income level of 1,500 in Table 25, the tendency towards unemployment arises because an increase in national income leads to a rise in planned saving, leaving a gap between national product and consumption that is not entirely filled by planned investment. Below 1,500, on the other hand, there is an excess of planned investment over planned saving at each level of income; an increase in product and income would cause planned investment to rise sufficiently to keep ahead of planned saving, which itself moves in the same direction as income.

In the language of economics, what is important is the relationship between the community's propensity to save, that is the proportion of income that the community wishes to save, and its propensity to invest. The higher the propensity to save, the higher would planned saving be at any given level of income, and the higher would planned investment have to be at that value of the national income to maintain full employment.

In this sense it would be true to say that excessive saving is responsible for unemployment. But it is equally true to say that the cause of unemployment is insufficient investment, for a higher level of investment would mean a higher level of planned expenditure, making possible a higher equilibrium level of income and production for any given propensity to save. It is the relationship between planned saving and planned investment and not the level of either alone that matters.

The interaction between saving, investment and the national income is more appropriately examined in the study of economic fluctuations; at this stage we are merely concerned with the question of why a particular level of national income at which the economy may settle need not be that of full employment. In their analysis of the causes of unemployment some economists have been inclined to lay greater stress on the behaviour of consumers, and others on business investment.

Thriftiness, great inequality of incomes, the absence of attractive new products, or the possession by consumers of large stocks of durable goods and clothing can lead the community to save a proportion of its income that is too high in relation to the level of investment that businessmen are prepared to undertake. Some economists used to emphasize the possibility that the proportion of income saved would tend to rise with the national income, so that the gap between production and consumption, which has to be filled by planned investment to prevent unemployment from developing, would increase disproportionately, but this is not essential for unemployment to occur, and in practice the effect of changes in income has proved more complex.

Alternatively, we may consider the level of investment to merit more consideration in certain situations, and the fact that the proportion of national income devoted to capital investment has fluctuated widely in some periods in the past has led many economists to seek the 'main' cause of unemployment here. Given the rate of interest and the pattern of costs and prices, planned investment may be too low in relation to planned saving because businessmen do not think it profitable to expand capacity at more than a certain rate. Or it may be too low to maintain full employment because there is already excess capacity in existence or because businessmen expect sales to fall. Of course there may be excess capacity just because the economy is in a state of unemployment, and businessmen are most likely to fear a fall in sales when one has already begun.

These considerations serve to emphasize the interdependence between income and investment; when planned investment is low in relation to planned saving the national income will tend to fall, but when the national income is below its full-employment level investment is likely to be 'too low' as a result. Like planned saving, the level of planned investment is both a cause and an effect of the size of the national income. This interdependence also helps to explain why movements in the level of income and expenditure may become cumulative for a time; a change in planned investment, for example, causes the national income to change in the same direction, and this in turn will react on consumption and saving and ultimately on planned investment itself.

### UNEMPLOYMENT AND THE SELF-ADJUSTMENT OF THE ECONOMY

What has not been explained is why the economy is not self-regulating. Many economists would once have looked for self-regulation in the form of the flexibility of prices and wages. If involuntary unemployment occurred, they would contend, full employment would be restored if the excess of supply over demand in the labour market were allowed to cause a fall in rates of wages and salaries in relation to prices, the increase in profit margins inducing employers to increase the level of output and employment. The fall in wage-rates would proceed until all those who would accept work at the ruling wage were employed; according to this analysis it is the unwillingness of the trade unions to accept wage reductions that is basically responsible for unemployment that is not merely frictional.

If an individual is willing to accept a lower wage his chances of employment are increased, and the same may apply to the unemployed workers of a single industry. But what is true of the part is not necessarily true of the whole economy, and the simplicity of the theory is deceptive. Wage-earners are purchasers of goods and services as well as factors of production, and a fall in wage-rates greater than the fall in retail prices reduces the real incomes of those already in work when the adjustment begins. For the level of consumption as a whole to be maintained the reduction in the volume of real expenditure by employed workers must be offset by a corresponding increase on the part of businessmen and shareholders, out of the higher real profits that are the counterpart to the reduction in the real wages of the employed. A redistribution of real income in this direction is unlikely to have this effect.

A further redistribution of real income also takes place in favour of past lenders at the expense of past borrowers, for the real value of fixed-interest payments and of the principal of money debts is enhanced by the fall in prices. In so far as lenders tend to be savers and borrowers tend to be spenders, the change is likely to work against the restoration of full employment.

The operation of expectations may also be unfavourable. If unemployment is known to lead to lower prices and wages, purchases of both consumer goods and capital equipment are likely to be deferred when unemployment begins to develop, accelerating rather than checking the decline in business activity until the fall in prices and wages has gone far enough to convince consumers and businessmen that their current level is abnormally low. Unemployment could be seriously increased in the process.

Against these adverse effects of a fall in prices can be set more favourable repercussions. A fall in the price-level due to the existence of unemployment might eventually stimulate consumption and investment by enhancing the real value of the community's holdings of money and near-money assets. It might eventually revive business investment because a fall in prices would reduce the size of the active money balances required to satisfy the transactions and contingencies motives, thus lowering the rate of interest.

Many economists now agree that *eventually* full employment can be restored if only prices fall far enough when planned saving exceeds planned investment, but the rigidity of wages and prices in the real world of imperfect competition in the markets for both labour and goods makes the point an academic one. Moreover, if *low* prices eventually cure unemployment by augmenting the real value of the community's liquid assets and by reducing the rate of interest, the same result can be achieved by budget deficits and by monetary policy without the depressing effects of *falling* prices.

## The Operation of the Rate of Interest

In the world of relatively inflexible prices we are left with the rate of interest as the main automatic regulator set in operation by a discrepancy between planned saving and planned investment. As such, however, spontaneous changes in the rate of interest have not proved potent enough to maintain full employment or even to prevent the extremes of prolonged depression and serious inflation. For if the community's willingness to save outruns its planned investment, the increase in planned saving may not be used wholly to purchase securities. Part may be retained in the form of money balances, and to this extent funds are not offered for potential investment to an amount fully equal to the increase in planned saving. Moreover, neither saving nor investment is sufficiently interest-elastic for moderate changes in the rate of interest to restore equilibrium in the short run, and the range within which the rate of interest fluctuates is restricted by the operation of investors' expectations. The rate of interest cannot fall below the level at which investors as a body are convinced that the rate is dangerously low, and this level may be too high to induce businessmen to undertake sufficient investment, if their expectations are pessimistic, or to bring forth a sufficient volume of consumption to prevent a serious slump.

The failure of the operation of the rate of interest to guarantee full employment does not mean that the economy is without any measure of overall self-adjustment. The proportion of income saved may well fall in a recession, and a decline in investment will be checked by the necessity for replacement expenditure and by the relative stability of those forms of investment, such as certain public works, that are geared to the long-run growth of the economy.

If businessmen are willing to disregard a minor recession and to base their investment plans on the prospect of long-run economic expansion, the consequent element of stability given to business investment will make a major slump much less likely and, in the event, justify the boldness of such a policy itself. When a decline in business activity is international, raw material prices, which are less 'sticky' than wage-rates and manufacturing profit margins, may fall enough to bring down the prices of finished goods. In the process the decline in the incomes of raw-material producing countries may aggravate the problem of maintaining employment in the manufacturing countries, by forcing the former to reduce their imports of manufactured goods; but eventually consumption and investment in the manufacturing countries may be stimulated by the consequent increase in the real value of their liquid assets and by an expectation of a return to a more normal price-level.

## UNEMPLOYMENT AND GOVERNMENT FINANCE

Outlays by the government on current goods and services are a form of 'consumption'. Planned saving is augmented when the government budgets for a surplus on current account and is diminished if it budgets for a current deficit. A planned surplus thus reduces national expenditure and a planned deficit increases it, other things being equal.

The structure of government finance works in the direction of checking a decline in business activity. Even if there is no change in the *rate* of taxation on different incomes, the government's total tax receipts fall proportionately more than the national income if the tax structure is progressive. Because government current expenditure is directed to political objectives, there is no reason why it should decline automatically in real terms during a recession in trade; indeed, the provision of unemployment and other social security benefits helps to sustain the volume of personal consumption during such conditions. An economy with a progressive tax structure, a high level of government expenditure and an extensive system of social security benefits possesses a useful automatic brake—a 'built-in' stabilizer—in the event of a decline in business activity.

## UNEMPLOYMENT AND INTERNATIONAL TRADE

Exports augment national income without a corresponding addition to the supply of goods; imports represent outlays that do not add to home income. An excess of exports over imports (foreign investment) is therefore similar to domestic investment as a determinant of national income and production. As nearly one-quarter of the United Kingdom's national income is derived from exports of goods and services the balance of our overseas trade has an important influence on domestic business activity, magnified through the repercussions of a change in exports or imports on the fortunes of home industries supplying equipment to the export trades or to those which compete with imports.

The state of the balance of foreign trade has been found to have initiated most of the spells of seriously depressed trade in this country over the past hundred years. An international trading economy like that of the United Kingdom is vulnerable to fluctuations in the level of world trade, but it is also true to say that as long as the purchasing power of our overseas markets is maintained no serious slump is likely to occur as a result of a decline in our domestic expenditure alone. For if our consumption or our domestic investment falls when international trade is buoyant, the result is likely to be a substantial increase in the volume of our exports if our factors of production are sufficiently mobile and our prices are competitive in overseas markets.

## UNEMPLOYMENT AND POST-WAR ECONOMIC CONDITIONS

Between 1919 and 1938 the average number registered as unemployed in any one year never fell below 450,000, and in 1932 reached 3 million. Between 1946 and 1952 unemployment never exceeded 537,000, out of a larger population of working age, and in the boom year of 1955 averaged only 265,000, or 1·2 per cent of the working population. The increase in industrial production between 1919 and 1938 was 47 per cent; between 1946 and 1956, a period only half as long, the increase was 56 per cent.

In these few statistics lies a major economic transformation which has fulfilled the desire of people in many countries to see an end to the useless and cruel unemployment of the slump. The extent to which this radical change in the state of the economy has been the result of a conscious and logical reorientation of government policy directed towards maintaining full employment, as opposed to the automatic consequences of war and its aftermath, leaves much room for dispute. But in contrasting the widespread unemployment which persisted during the decade following the First World War with the high level of activity that was maintained in the decade following the Second, it is impossible to be unaware of the recasting of both economic theory and political philosophy that has occurred over the intervening years. That the maintenance of full employment requires and justifies positive intervention by the State is a view which is now commonplace; thirty years ago it was the conviction of only a minority.

This intellectual reorientation is attributable largely to the economic writings of Lord Keynes and in particular to his *General Theory of Employment, Interest and Money*, which was published in 1936. In the *General Theory* Keynes set out to show the inadequacy of the rate of interest as a spontaneous mechanism for maintaining full employment. He was not the first to express some of the ideas that are now embodied in 'Keynesian' economics; and he might disown others, were he still alive. On certain important issues his analysis has even been refuted. But since the publication of the *General Theory* the world of economics has never been quite the same. In the way in which economists explore the causes of unemployment, and in the concepts they use, the *General Theory* stands as a landmark in economic thought. It is no longer usual for economists to regard a slump as fundamentally a necessary correction of previous economic maladjustments, or to call for higher saving as its cure, or to regard State intervention in order to cure a slump as a dangerously inflationary policy made necessary only by the unwillingness of the trade unions to allow wage-rates to fall in conditions of unemployment. There is a wide measure of agreement, in this country, at least, as to the measures which the government might adopt in order to maintain expenditure in the event of a serious recession in trade.

Nevertheless, the absence of serious unemployment in this country since the war has been due not only, or even mainly, to action taken by the government with the deliberate object of reviving national expenditure, for the number of occasions when this has been necessary has been small, at least until 1958. Economically, perhaps the most important contrast between the post-war and inter-war years is to be seen in the field of international trade. In the nineteen-twenties international trade was subject to the stresses and strains left by the First World War and the political changes that resulted. This country's share of international trade was unnecessarily diminished by the decision to return to the gold standard at a rate of exchange that was too high in relation to our domestic costs. In the following decade the international depression, centred on the United States, was the cause of a severe dislocation of international trade to which many countries could react only by adopting defensive policies which, if they succeeded, did so partly at the expense of others. Since the Second World War, on the other hand, the level of international trade in manufactured goods has shown an almost unbroken and remarkably high rate of expansion. For this the internal prosperity of the individual trading nations has been partly responsible; we have taken in one another's washing in increasing quantities. But the desire of governments to maintain a measure of international co-operation directed towards the achievement of liberal trade and internationally harmonious financial policies has been of great assistance.

To the stimulus provided by the growth in our exports has been added a buoyant level of home demand. The physical shortages inevitable during the war left behind them arrears of demand for many consumer goods and many forms of capital equipment, together with a high level of liquid assets in the hands of both business and consumers. The redistribution of incomes by means of taxation and the development of the Welfare State have both operated in the direction of reducing the propensity to save on the part of the public as a whole to below what it would have been in their absence. Government expenditure on defence has been maintained at a record peacetime level, and the expansion of the social services has augmented personal consumption.

Capital investment has increased in order to provide for the expansion in consumption, government expenditure and exports. It has also been high because of the introduction of new techniques and products based partly on a high level of research expenditure and because of a new awareness on the part of businessmen of the potentialities of a growing economy in which a serious fall in business activity is likely to be the signal for prompt and determined government support. The operation of the economy at a high level of employment and output has resulted in a situation in which capital equipment that was being operated at below full capacity during the pre-war slump has proved insufficient to meet the demands placed upon it in industries such as steel, fuel and power.

In short, government economic and social policy has helped to build the framework within which full employment has been maintained, and the knowledge that the government would be both willing and able to act so as to check a slump has been of great psychological importance. But the forces making for prosperous economic conditions have proved so strong that government action has had to be directed more often towards checking national expenditure than to stimulating it. Prosperity has brought its own problems, and the continuing difficulty facing post-war economies all over the world has been that of preventing full employment from developing into inflation.

# CHAPTER 36

# INFLATION

Between 1919 and 1938 retail prices fell by 28 per cent; between 1945 and 1957 they rose by 70 per cent. This increase in the price-level has been the consequence of a number of factors, including the delayed response to changes in costs that were masked by subsidies and controls during the war and the rise in the prices of commodities imported from abroad. Basically, however, the contrast between the two periods lies in the persistent inflation experienced since 1939.

Inflation occurs when the community's aggregate expenditure, or demand, exceeds what can be supplied at unchanged prices. When idle capacity is widespread and labour is mobile, an excess of demand over current supply can be met by a corresponding increase in output with no rise in prices. Sooner or later, and before the whole economy reaches what can crudely be described as 'full capacity' or 'full employment', excess demand can no longer be met by an equal expansion of output at unchanged prices in the short run. An increase in production may still occur, but ultimately the operation of diminishing returns leads first to price increases in individual industries and then to a cumulative and general increase in costs and prices if the pressure of demand continues to grow. There is no single boundary between inflation and stability of prices, but a zone into which further penetration is marked by the spread of inflationary pressure over the economy as a whole.

## INFLATION AT FULL EMPLOYMENT IN A CLOSED ECONOMY

Inflation is fully grown when aggregate demand exceeds aggregate supply in an economy operating at full employment, which we can define loosely as one in which unemployment is at no more than a frictional or seasonal level. As a start it is convenient to assume that we are examining an economy with no foreign trade. We can consider the possible course of events if, following a period of full employment, in which national product and expenditure have been running at 1,000, the community attempts to increase its expenditure by 100. To isolate the problem we can suppose that no general increase in production is possible.

Initially the increase in demand may be met by a reduction in stocks throughout the economy, but this cannot continue indefinitely. Beyond this stage prices may still be held relatively steady, but the excess of demand over supply will lead to an increase in unfilled orders and to some form of rationing. As a result, 'plans' to spend cannot all become effective. This is the case of suppressed inflation, which is examined in a subsequent section.

Alternatively, profit margins and prices may be allowed to rise until the excess of demand over supply at the old price-level is matched by an equivalent supply, unchanged in real terms, but higher in money values. If the pressure of excess demand is slight or is expected to be temporary, businessmen may refrain from raising prices, but if it is strong or persistent the opportunity for earning higher profits is less likely to be ignored. Inflation is usually associated with a rise in prices, and the process calls for more detailed examination.

Returning to our numerical example, demand and supply in money terms will once more be equal if prices rise by one-tenth, so that national product and expenditure are now valued at 1,100. Prices have risen, but *as a result* the inflationary pressure has been absorbed, for demand and supply are once more in balance. At this point, and viewed in isolation, it is not the rise in prices that should be called 'inflationary', for the change in the price-level has been the result of the pressure of excess demand, and the means by which equilibrium has been restored between aggregate demand and supply.

### THE CUMULATIVE NATURE OF INFLATION

If there were no further disturbance discussion could end at this point. But the intractability of the problem of inflation lies in its cumulative nature, in which several forces can be identified. First, there is the tendency of any swing in national demand to feed on itself for a while because of the fact that a rise in one man's expenditure adds to another's income and is thus the means whereby the latter's own expenditure can be raised. Thus the increase in profits that, in our example, was the counterpart to the rise in prices might lead businessmen to spend more on consumption or investment. A rise in their consumption or in their investment would in turn expand the money incomes of those people engaged in the trades experiencing this further round of demand, inducing them to raise their own expenditure, and so on.

A rise in profits and orders on hand will make businessmen ready and even eager to offer higher wages in order to attract labour, and when overall demand is growing, this process, too, can become cumulative as businessmen attempt to conserve their own labour force in the face of a rise in wage-rates elsewhere. On the surface the cause of the increase in wage-rates might appear to be the desire of unions to defend their members from the increase in retail prices, but even if there were no trade unions the competition for labour in such a situation would lead to higher wages.

Thirdly, people whose money incomes cannot be increased may attempt to maintain their real standard of living in the face of rising prices by spending more in money terms, reducing their saving and even running down past savings to do so. Businessmen whose profits do not keep pace with the rise in the prices of plant and equipment may be able to sustain their investment in real terms by drawing on their liquid assets or by recourse to external finance.

All such attempts to maintain or increase expenditure in real terms, whether on consumption or investment, involve an expansion of expenditure in money value, causing fresh inflationary pressures and further increases in prices, profits and wages, and so on. As the expectation of a sustained increase in prices spreads throughout the community the danger of an acceleration of the process becomes even more serious.

## AN END TO THE PROCESS

The upward spiral of prices and costs will come to a halt in a closed economy only when the rise in prices due to a previous excess of total demand over supply is *not* matched by a further increase in money demand emanating from attempts to maintain or increase real expenditure. In the absence of anti-inflationary measures on the part of the government, the expansion of money demand may cease in a number of ways.

First, planned investment may eventually decline in certain sectors of the economy. Many types of investment, even in an economy in which aggregate demand is excessive, tend to follow a cyclical path rather than a steady upwards curve. An economy suffering from inflation is rarely free from discrepancies in the rate of expansion of different industries or from speculative miscalculations, both of which may finally upset the balance of the economy and disappoint expectations of profitability over an increasingly wide area.

Secondly, certain sections of the community may eventually fail to secure a sufficient rise in their money incomes. At some stage or other employers may successfully resist wage claims for fear that the increase in their costs cannot be passed on to their customers. But this is more likely to occur if the pace of inflation is visibly slowing down for other reasons, causing businessmen to become more cautious.

Thirdly, the recipients of fixed incomes will ultimately find it impossible to maintain their real expenditure by reducing their current saving or by drawing on past savings, for with every increase in prices the real value of their saving, past and present, diminishes.

Fourthly, in the process of inflation a redistribution of real incomes and wealth occurs; the average propensity to save of the community as a whole will be increased if those who gain do not attempt to raise their real expenditure by an amount fully equal to the reduction on the part of those who lose. Those who have incurred fixed-interest debts, including the Exchequer, will have gained at the expense of past lenders; those with variable incomes will have gained at the expense of those whose incomes are rigid; those with physical property will gain at the expense of those without; and the stronger trade unions and businesses will have benefited at the expense of the weaker. A marked shift in real incomes and wealth in the direction of greater inequality can be expected to raise the propensity to save of the community as a whole, and the increase in the share of national income accruing to businesses from an increase in profit margins during an inflation may have a similar effect.

In an economy in which taxes on income are progressive and collected speedily, and in which most indirect taxes are on an *ad valorem* basis, a transfer of real net incomes will occur from taxpayers to the State, for taxes will rise faster than incomes. This will strengthen the propensity to save of the community as a whole if government expenditure is not increased to match the rise in the real value of tax receipts. A progressive system of taxation thus acts as a brake on inflation as well as on deflation.

Fifthly, the money supply may not be sufficiently elastic.

### THE MONEY SUPPLY

Inflation requires an increase in the active money supply to finance the excess of planned investment over planned saving and to meet the enlarged demand for active money balances. If there is not a sufficient increase in the total quantity of money in existence, the extra supply of active money can come only from existing 'idle' balances, so that the expansion in the flow of money transactions is made possible by turning over the total quantity of money more rapidly. This process will be reflected in a fall in the ratio of the total quantity of money in existence to national expenditure, that is to say in an increase in the 'velocity of circulation' of the existing quantity of money.

However, unless investors are convinced that no further increase in interest rates is likely, the transfer from idle to active money balances will only be possible if interest rates rise. If the pressure of inflation is persistent the increase in interest rates is likely to be reinforced by the operation of investors' expectations of a further increase and ultimately by a widespread aversion to holding fixed-money-value assets.

If the quantity of money is not sufficiently elastic, rates of interest may eventually rise to a very high level. The willingness to undertake new capital investment may be weakened as a result, and the fall in fixed-interest security prices will correspondingly reduce the spendable value of past savings held in this form. In these conditions, too, there will be a limit to the extent to which the banks are prepared to sell securities to finance an increase in advances, and they may well be disposed to hold larger liquid-asset ratios than are usual. There will be some insecure would-be borrowers who will not be able to obtain finance at any price.

Ultimately, therefore, the pressure of inflation will subside if the total quantity of money does not rise sufficiently. In the past, really violent inflations, as in Germany after the First World War, where retail prices rose by several thousand per cent, have all been accompanied by an elastic money supply, based usually on the finance of a large Budget deficit by loans from the central bank and by increasing resort to the printing-press. For when prices are rising with rapidity and taxes are collected in arrears, the excess of government expenditure over taxes received may be sharply increased, and resort to central bank finance may seem inevitable if, as is likely, the market for government bonds is under continual pressure.

### INFLATION AND THE BALANCE OF PAYMENTS

Finally, a mild inflation may come to an end through its effect on the balance of foreign payments. The excess of home demand and the rise in domestic prices, unless effective import controls are in operation, will raise the level of imports and, unless inflation in overseas markets is sufficiently strong, reduce the volume of exports. The balance of trade will therefore deteriorate.

However, no country's foreign exchange reserves are unlimited, and sooner or later one or more of three things will happen. The government may act to check the loss of foreign exchange reserves by striking at its root cause—the excess of home demand. Alternatively, it may attempt to protect the balance of payments 'directly', by tightening import controls, in which event the pressure of inflation will be intensified as demand is diverted to the home market. Thirdly, the government may be forced to allow the rate of exchange to depreciate.

This third course is also likely to aggravate an inflationary situation. For a while the fall in the exchange rate, it is true, may improve the balance of payments, measured in terms of the domestic currency, by raising the receipts of exporters and checking the demand for imports. But this will add to the level of domestic expenditure and incomes, and if imports are an important element in the price-level the rise in the prices of imports will also intensify the demand for higher wage-rates. By adding to the rise in domestic prices and incomes, exchange depreciation may ultimately be self-defeating, and a repeated adjustment of the exchange rate in a downwards direction may become necessary.

When the reaction of the balance of payments with inflation in a country with a large volume of international trade becomes cumulatively unfavourable and the money supply is highly elastic, inflation can be extremely violent, causing ruin to large sections of the community and ending only in complete financial collapse, with incalculable harm to the political as well as the financial framework of society, as the experience of Germany confirms.

## DEMAND AND COST INFLATION

A rise in prices may be the result of an increase in profits or in costs. The distinction is therefore sometimes drawn between demand and cost inflation. The former occurs when there is an excess of aggregate demand over aggregate supply, i.e. an excess of planned investment over planned saving, when the economy has reached the zone of full employment. Cost inflation occurs when businesses raise their prices directly in response to an increase in costs due to a rise in the money incomes of the factors of production they employ, especially in the form of an increase in wage-rates. In the former situation the rise in prices constitutes an increase in the share of the national income accruing to profits; in the process of cost inflation businessmen raise prices to maintain their share in the national income.

The dividing line is not as clear as it seems, for in most periods of inflation prices rise because of the interaction of both sets of forces, as in the situation discussed in the previous pages of this chapter. A rise in wage-rates will be granted by employers only if they are confident that the demand for their products will be sufficient to support the resulting increase in their prices.

Nevertheless, in some circumstances the distinction may be a useful one. A general rise in wage-rates may be claimed by trade unions and granted by employers at a time when there is *no* excess demand either for final products or for factors of production, including labour. For this to occur there must be no widespread unemployment, so that employers do not feel that they have the upper hand in the bargaining process; and the individual employers and employers' associations who take part in this process must be confident of being able to pass on the increase in costs to their customers. The latter condition will be fulfilled if employers individually feel that an increase in wage-rates will be general. In this situation all employers in the same industry will be similarly affected, and, what is equally important, the rise in wage-rates granted in other industries will generate the increase in purchasing power necessary to absorb the rise in the prices of the products of any one.

The dependence of such a situation on the expectation that wage increases will be general means that a cost inflation of this sort, i.e. when there is no excess demand, is only likely when the driving force behind wage claims is recognized by the majority of employers, for example when trade unions submit wage claims on the grounds that retail prices have increased since the last series of awards. Thus, while most periods of rising prices begin as demand inflation, they may be extended by the process of cost inflation even though, following each round of wage and price increases, aggregate demand and supply are in balance. Cost inflation may occur even though aggregate demand has fallen somewhat below the full productive capacity of the economy, as long as employers individually are willing to retain an under-employed labour force in anticipation of an eventual rise in demand. Cost inflation may also be initiated by a rise in prices following a period in which there had previously been no inflation of any kind; the initial impulse might take the form of an increase in the cost of living due to a rise in import prices or a removal of food subsidies, for example.

Cost inflation is also apt to become cumulative. The rise in prices due to the award to one set of industries of a wage increase in excess of the growth of productivity will induce other trade unions to submit wage claims in order to protect their members against the rise in the cost of living, leading to a further increase in prices and a fresh round of wage claims, and so on. In the process, areas of excess demand are likely to arise as an increase in the incomes of wage-earners in one part of the economy swells the demand for the products of other industries. The process may come to an end for the reasons already introduced.

### SUPPRESSED INFLATION

If excess demand is not allowed to find an outlet in the form of higher prices, the situation is one of *suppressed inflation*. An element of suppressed inflation arises if businessmen prefer to build up their order-books and ration their customers rather than charge what their market will bear when excess demand develops. In its most general form, however, suppressed inflation has usually been the result of the imposition of statutory price controls aimed at limiting the increase in prices during a period of inflation. To prevent queues and under-the-counter transactions, statutory rationing is necessary in such a situation. As a deliberate policy, suppressed inflation suffers from rigidity and administrative clumsiness and necessarily interferes with freedom of choice; it may merely postpone rather than destroy the danger of open inflation.

Suppressed inflation also refers to the situation in which excess demand is deliberately *diverted* into certain channels. Rationing and price controls in the field of 'essentials' may be used to divert unsatisfied demand to luxuries; in this way the force of inflation may be held off the poor, and a cumulative rise in wages and prices mitigated if the increase in the prices of 'luxuries' due to the diversion of demand is disregarded in the formulation of wage claims. The pressure of inflation will be diminished if the rise in prices needed to 'mop up' the demand for unrationed goods takes the form of a stiff increase in indirect taxes, sterilizing purchasing power in the form of a Budget surplus.

In suppressed inflation demand may also be diverted to those industries where there is unused capacity. In an economy engaged in international trade, however, the effect of suppressing demand in one sector may merely be to draw imports and exports into the home market, so that the balance of payments deteriorates. Controls on imports have therefore accompanied such a policy in the past.

A policy of suppressed inflation was resorted to during the war and for some time afterwards. Rationing and price controls limited expenditure on 'essentials', unsatisfied demand was diverted to buy 'luxuries' that were highly taxed, such as cigarettes and alcoholic drinks, and to fill the cinemas and theatres. Unspent income was tempted into National Savings and government bonds, helping to keep down the interest cost of war finance. But the accumulation of liquid assets and the running down of stocks that were inherent in this policy only aggravated the problem of inflation in the post-war years.

# CHAPTER 37

# FLUCTUATIONS IN ECONOMIC ACTIVITY

From the time of the industrial revolution, itself a major ground-swell of economic development, the course of economic activity has been marked by a succession of fluctuations, the repercussions of which have been felt over a large part of the trading world. They have been divided broadly into three categories, according to their typical duration. They are the possible 'long waves' of economic development to which reference was made in Chapter 32, the business or trade cycle of eight to twelve years' duration, and minor cycles whose rise and fall span only two or three years. In addition a variety of rhythms can be discerned affecting some aspect or other of economic activity that may form part of or proceed separately from these three main groups of fluctuation.

## LONG WAVES

The course of economic activity in the industrial economies of Europe and the U.S.A. over the past century and a half is seen by some economists as having followed long rolling waves, taking the form of an alternate intensification and slackening in the underlying rate of economic growth. The first of these long upward waves in the United Kingdom has been identified as lasting from the end of the eighteenth century to the end of the Napoleonic Wars, followed by a succession of long fluctuations about the underlying trend upwards as listed on page 434. During the ascent of the long waves shorter fluctuations have occurred, but over each upwards wave as a whole production has grown relatively rapidly and prices and interest rates have been comparatively high.

One of the most difficult problems in the analysis of economic fluctuations is to decide which events form an organic part of the cyclical character of the economy and which should be regarded as 'extraneous', although historically providing some of the impulses from which the rhythm of economic activity has been derived. Economists are undecided as to whether the bursts of technical innovation, the swings in population growth, even the wars, that some regard as having marked the alternation of rising and falling waves should be thought of as interdependent sets of events forming the very stuff of the economic mechanism or as phenomena bearing on our economic life from 'outside'. Many economists, perhaps the majority, would deny that the historical evidence is strong enough to support the concept of the long wave at all.

It was noted by Professor Kondratieff, a Russian economist, who was the first to put forward in detail the theory of the long wave, that during what he identified as the falling long waves many important discoveries and innovations were made in the field of production and communications that were not applied on a large scale until the next long upswing. Many economists, except those who do not support the concept of the long cycle itself, would agree as to the importance of their role. The economic upsurge that covered the third quarter of the nineteenth century was associated with iron and steam; that which spanned the forty years until the nineteen-twenties saw the rise of electricity, steel, industrial chemistry, and the internal-combustion engine; that which has not yet ended has brought the development of new synthetic fibres, gas turbines, a new metallurgy, control engineering, and atomic energy. The application of these major innovations requires long periods of relatively high capital investment in many industries; and, in the past, periods of rapid growth have drawn into their strong current many contributory streams of economic change.

## BUSINESS CYCLES

Superimposed upon longer-term trends have been fluctuations in the general level of economic activity lasting between eight and twelve years from trough to trough. These cycles in output, employment and incomes, in which commodity prices and interest rates have generally followed the direction of business activity, have been recorded for nearly a hundred and fifty years until the Second World War in the major private-enterprise economies. The channels of world trade have afforded a passage for the spread of the cycle to most of the trading economies of the capitalist world. Table 26 records the fluctuations traced in the United Kingdom before the outbreak of the Second World War. Since the war, activity has remained at a high level and a cyclical pattern is much more difficult to discern.

TABLE 26. *Business Cycles in Britain 1792–1938*

| Crests | Troughs |
|--------|---------|
| 1792 | 1797 |
| 1803 | 1808 |
| 1810 | 1816 |
| 1818 | 1821 |
| 1825 | 1832 |
| 1836 | 1842–3 |
| 1845–6 | 1849–50 |
| 1853 | 1858 |
| 1860 | 1862 |
| 1865 | 1867 |
| 1874 | 1879 |
| 1882–3 | 1886 |
| 1889 | 1893 |
| 1899 | 1903–4 |
| 1906–7 | 1908–9 |
| 1913 | — |
| 1920 | 1923 |
| 1928 | 1932 |
| 1937 | 1938 |

SOURCE : William Beveridge, *Full Employment in a Free Society*. (Allen & Unwin.)

There is no single theory of the trade cycle that commands general assent, and it is by no means clear that we should be justified in speaking of 'the' business cycle, for each cyclical movement has had its unique characteristics. Analysts of the business cycle have to consider which events should be regarded as part of a generalized theory of cyclical fluctuations and which should be thought of as extraneous, although perhaps imparting the initial impulse to certain fluctuations in the past. This is the distinction between the 'endogenous' and 'exogenous' variables that is frequently drawn in theoretical economics. Is the application of a major invention, a change in government policy, or a war to be regarded as 'endogenous' or 'exogenous'?

Historically it is not difficult to isolate special events as being in some way the most important cause of a particular upswing or downturn, and the case for regarding each cycle as a thing apart is strengthened by the statistical record, which shows that different groups of industries lead the way at the turning-point of different cycles.

This leads us to another problem. Whereas we can certainly portray 'the' level of economic activity in the aggregate, by means of an index of production or a statistical measure of the national income, a more discriminating analysis would emphasize the fact that individual industries follow courses that are not identical. Some industries suffer little or no recession during the downwards phase of the cycle; others suffer severely. Certain industries follow cyclical paths whose peaks and troughs do not coincide in point of time, and at 'the' downturn of the economy some industries will still be growing whereas others will have declined some time ago. That the fluctuations we call business cycles have affected a large-enough proportion of all industries to cause sharp swings in the overall level of business activity has not prevented some economists from taking the view that an explanation couched in terms of 'the' level of activity and drawn from the examination of heterogeneous aggregates such as 'consumption' and 'investment' is more superficial, if more easily handled, than one which examines in detail the behaviour of individual industries. Whereas some economists prefer to express the course of individual industries as a reaction to the movement in the general level of activity, others work from the other end of the chain and see aggregates only as a statistical abstraction. The latter economists place greater emphasis on the stresses that develop as a result of the diversity of experience during each phase of the cycle and are more concerned with the *relative* movement of different prices and costs than those who prefer to deal in aggregate measures.

No study of business cycles can disregard the changing institutional framework of the economy and the inconstant propensities of human behaviour. Factors such as the strength of the banking system, the extent of indebtedness, the force of speculation, to say nothing of the role of the government, must be considered when examining the development of fluctuations in different countries or at different times.

CUMULATIVE PROCESSES IN BUSINESS CYCLES

Economists agree as to the sort of factors, if not as to their exact strength, that cause an expansion or a contraction of economic activity to become cumulative. Where they disagree is in their explanation of what makes these extended periods of prosperity and depression eventually go into reverse with, at least until the war, an appearance of some regularity. Three sets of forces, however, help to explain not only why economic change is cumulative, but also why it tends to be cyclical.

### Psychological Factors

The general climate of business opinion, the willingness to take risks and the eagerness to emulate the success of others, tends to swing with the tide of economic activity. Action based on expectations has the collective effect of justifying them, in so far as higher investment by one business increases the profits of another, causing a further increase in investment, and so on. Changes in attitude are important on the part of lenders as well as spenders; in the upswing, businesses find it easier to raise funds by way of ordinary shares, whereas during the downturn the less-secure businesses will be able to raise ordinary capital only on very unfavourable terms but may be unwilling to add to their indebtedness instead.

Psychological factors may also help to bring a boom or a slump to an end, because of the knowledge that booms and slumps in the past have always come to an end. The expectation of a return to 'normal' is likely to become most powerful when there have been marked changes in prices. Today, however, although psychological factors are recognized as being highly important determinants of the force and duration of a boom or slump, most theories of the business cycle tend to cast psychology in a subsidiary role in the analysis of turning-points, in that, whereas a change in business psychology may well bring about a downturn for example, once a boom is seen to be slowing down, the deeper causes of the swing from boom to slump and back again are usually sought in the factors responsible for the loss of impetus to which expectations react.

### The 'Multiplier' Effect

This is the term generally used to describe the process whereby an initial change of expenditure in the form of investment ultimately causes a larger increase in total national expenditure by raising the incomes of those members of the community whose goods and services are purchased for the purpose of investment, thus enabling them to raise *their* expenditure in turn, and so on. The 'multiplier' expresses the size of the final change in national expenditure as a multiple of the initial change, assuming that there have been no other disturbances.

The calculation of the multiplier is derived from the proportion of an increase in their income that people spend on consumption. The obverse of the community's propensity to save is its propensity to consume. If the average propensity to save is one-third, the average propensity to consume is two-thirds. The measure relevant to the calculation of the multiplier, however, is not the average propensity to consume, which relates total consumption to total net income, but the *marginal* propensity to consume, which relates the *change* in consumption to the *change* in income. Thus the average propensity to consume might be nine-tenths, but the marginal propensity to consume might be only three-quarters at a certain level of income; that is to say, only three-quarters of any *addition* to incomes would be spent. The marginal propensity to consume is a measure that can be applied to a change in incomes in either direction, but it does not follow that it need be the same in each case.

The arithmetical relationship between income and the marginal propensity to consume can be shown by a simple example. Suppose that in a closed economy the rate of interest is held steady by official action and that there is widespread unemployment, so that there are no obstacles to an expansion in output, and prices do not change. The consequences of a single increase in investment of £1 million, with a marginal propensity to consume of three-quarters, are drawn in Table 27.

TABLE 27. *Illustration of 'Multiplier' Effect*

|  | Increase in investment (£) | Increase in consumption (£) |
|---|---|---|
| 1st round | 1,000,000 | — |
| 2nd round | — | 750,000 |
| 3rd round | — | 562,500 |
| 4th round | — | 421,875 |
| 5th round | — | 316,406 |
| 6th round | — | 237,305 |
| 7th round | — | 177,979 |

On these simplest of assumptions there would be a diminishing absolute increase in income and output in the form of a geometric progression. Ultimately, strictly speaking after an infinite period of time, the total increase in income arising from the increase in investment would be £4 million. This is equal to:

$$£1 \times \frac{1}{0 \cdot 25}$$

or
$$£1 \times \frac{1}{1 - \text{Marginal propensity to consume}}$$

The term $\dfrac{1}{1 - \text{Marginal propensity to consume}}$ is the 'multiplier'

and is obviously the reciprocal of the marginal propensity to save.

In this illustration the working of the multiplier has been shown at its simplest. In the real world the marginal propensity to consume might not remain constant, and the expansion of aggregate demand might stimulate investment further, thus tilting upwards the whole process of expansion. On the other hand, if the money supply were restricted, interest rates would rise and eventually slow down the process. As full employment was reached, moreover, prices would increase, so that the multiplier would work itself out partly in the form of a rise in prices and in money incomes not matched by an equivalent increase in real output. Taxes on income and expenditure, even if rates of tax remained constant, would also cause 'leakages' in the process of expansion, which would also be checked by any deterioration in the balance of foreign trade.

Nevertheless, the multiplier is a useful concept that helps to explain the cumulative process of expansion or contraction. In this example the initial impulse was a change in home investment; it could equally well be a change in government expenditure not matched by an equal change in taxation, or an initial change in the balance of trade.

### The 'Accelerator' Effect

Whereas the multiplier records the total change in income and expenditure caused by a change in investment, the 'accelerator' refers to a principle that explains one of the processes whereby a change in output may react on investment. The theoretical importance of the accelerator is that it links net investment not to absolute changes in output but to the rate of change, so that investment may actually fall even though the level of economic activity as a whole is still rising.

We can see the operation of the accelerator most simply by assuming away most of the complications of real life, taking as a first approximation an industry, which we can call the motor industry, in which the stock of capital equipment is always a fixed multiple of its annual output. Suppose that the industry uses 1,000 machines, each with a life of five years, to produce 10,000 cars a year. If the lives of the 1,000 machines in use are spread evenly, the maintenance of this level of car output would mean that the industry replaces 200 machines per year.

Suppose that in the second year the sale of motor-cars is increased by 20 per cent to 12,000. On the assumption of a fixed capital–output ratio this will necessitate a similar increase in the stock of equipment, the number of machines in use having to rise from 1,000 to 1,200. In this second year, therefore, as a result of a 20 per cent rise in car sales, the motor industry's purchases of machines doubles. For in addition to the usual replacement of 200, no less than 200 machines have to be bought as net investment to raise the total number in use from 1,000 to 1,200.

In the third year, if car sales again increase, but this time only by 10 per cent to 13,200, the motor industry's purchases of machines will actually *fall* to 320. This figure represents an increase in the stock of machines of 120 plus the 200 machines to be replaced, none of the new machines yet falling due for replacement.

The fact that the rise in car sales in this example necessitated only a temporary bulge in investment can be generalized in the principle that, in so far as the stock of capital equipment tends to be a fixed multiple of the level of output which it is used to produce, the pace of net investment will reflect the rate of change in the output of the industries in which the equipment is employed. If the rate of increase in output of an industry's products slackens, its gross investment may actually fall as a result of a sharp reduction in its net investment, whereas if its output declines the industry's purchases of capital goods may conceivably cease altogether until its stock of capital equipment is reduced by its failure to purchase for replacement. The working of the accelerator will depend, on the simplest assumptions, on the ratio of the stock of capital to annual output and on the length of its usual working life. The former will determine the absolute level of *net* investment appropriate to a given change in output, and the latter will determine the proportion of annual gross investment that takes the form of expenditure for replacement. The longer the usual working life of capital equipment, the more violent will be the relative change in gross investment for any given percentage change in the output of goods and services which the equipment is used to produce.

This illustration greatly over-simplifies the operation of the accelerator. It ignores the effect of possible changes in relative prices of different factors of production, in the availability of finance, and in the rate of interest. It also disregards expectations, for business investment will depend on whether a change in sales is expected to be permanent, and some time-lag is likely to elapse before businessmen respond to changes in sales, so that unfilled orders may accumulate before capacity is expanded. Even so, investment plans will reflect the increase in sales expected by businessmen, which may exceed or fall short of that actually previously experienced. The net investment required to meet a rise in output will be smaller than is implied above if equipment that is wearing out can be replaced by a superior type, and technological developments bearing on production techniques or on the nature of the product may bring about changes in investment that are quite unrelated to the course of sales in the short run.

The assumption of a fixed capital–output ratio is also unrealistic. Up to a certain point the output of many industries can be increased without a proportionate expansion in the plant used, because of multi-shift working or economies of scale, or simply by overcrowding the factory or office building. In the early stage of a revival in trade many industries will possess sufficient excess capacity to deal with a rise in orders without the need for any net investment at all.

The empirical evidence has not produced any clear picture of the working of the accelerator as a short-term instrument of economic change; although its operation as a long-run force is easier to discern. Nevertheless, the imperfections of the concept do not entirely deprive it of its usefulness as part of the explanation why business cycles are associated with relatively large changes in the volume of investment. It is to be noted that, although capital equipment is used ultimately for the purpose of producing consumer goods and services, in any one year part of the community's capital equipment will be used to produce other forms of capital equipment. 'The' accelerator, as an abstract average, does not link the level of investment to the rate of change of consumption alone but to the behaviour of the level of output of the economy as a whole. The result, however, is to blur still more the operation of the accelerator, for different industries have different capital–output ratios, so that the force of the 'average' accelerator will depend on the composition of economic change.

### The Possible Interaction of 'Multiplier' and 'Accelerator' Effects

Together the multiplier and accelerator principles are used by some economists as at least a partial explanation of how a change in the level of output is apt to become extended and how the cumulative processes of expansion and contraction may be reversed.

The operation of the multiplier and accelerator, once an upswing has started, prolongs the process of expansion. The multiplier causes a rise in investment to lead to a larger increase in incomes and output, and the accelerator causes this rise in output to induce businessmen to increase their investment still further, which leads to a further rise in incomes and output, and so on. The course of both boom and slump will be influenced by the strength of both multiplier and accelerator effects.

If both are relatively weak, a recovery from a slump may lead to a more or less steady and slow rise in incomes and output to a new level from which a downturn is not easily set off. But the process of expansion may come to a halt even before full employment is reached; many cyclical upswings have never reached full employment.

If the multiplier and accelerator effects are vigorous, the fluctuations of business activity will be wider. If the accelerator is sufficiently powerful, the pace of recovery from a slump may for a time speed up. The working of a strong accelerator, however, will mean that if, for whatever reason, the rate of expansion is slowed down at some stage in the boom, the result may be a decline in the level of investment. A fall in investment will then cause a fall in incomes and output through the operation of the multiplier, which in turn will act so as to cause a further decline in investment, and so on. If the accelerator worked in both directions the process of contraction would continue until something happened to slow down the rate of decline in output, whereupon the accelerator would initiate a revival of investment and so cause a fresh upswing and so on. In this second type of process, that is to say, a mere change in the rate of expansion or contraction would cause a complete reversal in the movement of the whole economy. In both boom and slump, business expectations would reinforce the cyclical movement.

### TURNING-POINTS IN BUSINESS CYCLES

What has not been considered is how the former type of weak cumulative process may be reversed or what may cause the mere slackening in the rate of expansion or contraction that is required to reverse a cycle with strong multiplier and accelerator effects. The upward swing of a weak cycle might be halted by 'external' factors, such as government action or a fall in agricultural incomes due to the emergence of unsold crops. Even if these disturbances occurred erratically it would be possible for the economy to develop continued and more or less regular fluctuations. Secondly, the reversal of the upswing might come through more endogenous factors. In the past many booms, particularly during the operation of the gold standard, have been accompanied by credit stringency, and in these conditions a weak banking system might develop strains sufficient to cause a collapse of the boom. Alternatively, a rise in investment might come to an end because of its special character: the cluster of innovations which may have sent the economy upwards might lose its expansionist force, or the replacement of capital equipment deferred during the previous slump might tail off, merely because arrears of replacement demand had been overtaken. Miscalculations by unduly optimistic businessmen also play their part.

The downswing of a 'weak' cycle might be reversed for similar reasons; government policy might be applied to maintain aggregate demand, for example, or the exploitation of important innovations might revive investment.

The 'strong accelerator' cycle, reversing itself because of a mere change in the rate of expansion or contraction, may be sent spinning in the opposite direction by similar factors. Of greater analytical interest, however, is the possibility that the reversal may be inherent in the process of expansion or contraction itself.

First, the very fact that a boom may have brought the economy to full employment will mean that physical limitations on supply must eventually slow down the rate of increase in the volume of output and thus diminish both the need and the possibility of an increase in net investment. Secondly, the burst of innovations that may have helped to send the economy moving strongly upwards is unlikely to provide a demand for capital goods at a constant rate of increase; sooner or later the need for additional factories and equipment to exploit innovations will slacken. Thirdly, unless the quantity of money continues to be increased sufficiently, business will eventually become less liquid and interest rates will rise. Fourthly, the rate of increase in consumption may fall off as a result of a decline in the marginal propensity to consume, so that the multiplier effect weakens. This may occur because during the boom consumers rebuild their stock of clothing and durables, making replacements that were deferred during the previous slump. Replacement demand may fall away or 'new' purchases increase at a slower rate as the stock of such goods possessed by consumers increases. The rate of increase in these purchases may decline considerably if consumers have greatly added to their net hire-purchase indebtedness in the process, so that a further extension of indebtedness eventually becomes less acceptable. Fifthly, the marginal propensity to consume may decrease merely because of the growth in real incomes or because of a redistribution of incomes during the boom, in which prices rise and the share of profits in the national income may be increased. Sixthly, the increase in consumption may tail off because the real value of the liquid assets held by consumers falls in relation to real incomes owing to the rise in prices.

The ensuing slump will be sharp if investment falls away suddenly, especially if it is accompanied by a financial crisis. But eventually the rate of decline will slacken as a result of endogenous factors, even if no measures to counter the slump are taken by the government. There is always some so-called 'autonomous' investment that is not dependent on immediate commercial considerations, such as investment by the public authorities and nationalized industries, and this alone will provide a 'floor' to the economy. Government current expenditure on goods and services provides a second element of stability. Although replacement demand for capital goods may be deferred in the early stages of the slump, there will be some replacement that must be undertaken by even the more pessimistic concerns if the current level of output is to be maintained, for some forms of equipment are relatively shortlived, while others will be very old and ready for the scrap-heap; many businesses will find themselves to be more liquid as a result of the recession. Fourthly, innovations born at an earlier period may be brought into operation by the bolder species of businessr an, attracted by low rates of interest, easy access to finance, the availability of labour, and, perhaps, by cheap raw materials and equipment. Fifthly, the marginal propensity to consume may eventually rise during a slump, owing to the fall in total real income, its redistribution, the receipt of social security benefits, or to the rise in the real value of personal liquid assets in relation to current expenditure. Finally, there is some limit to the extent that business inventories can be reduced in relation to any current level of output.

Whereas the slowing down of the rate of contraction during a slump is not difficult to explain, we cannot, however, invoke the operation of the accelerator in order to illustrate how the slackening in the rate of decline gives way to revival. For at this stage many industries will be suffering from excess capacity, and a substantial increase in demand can be met from existing equipment alone, so that net investment does not quickly recover through the working of the accelerator. As an explanation of how a slackening in the rate of contraction is followed by revival the accelerator is a useful concept only in the case of inventories, businessmen may cease to reduce the level of their stocks by the same amount as in the previous period once the decline in their sales slows down. This aspect of business cycles is elaborated in the next section.

To explain the revival, therefore, we have to fall back on a theoretically untidy collection of possibilities. The underlying trend of economic growth, working through technical innovation and perhaps an increase in population, will eventually assert itself; low interest rates may stimulate construction; share prices may start to recover once the decline in output is seen to be slowing down, and an improvement here may gradually lead to a return of confidence among businessmen themselves. With interest rates and perhaps material prices below their 'normal' level, with many businesses in a comfortably liquid position, the revival in confidence will stimulate still further the replacement of equipment deferred in the slump. Once the revival begins, the operation of the multiplier will strengthen the recovery, and as commodity prices move up, businessmen will begin to add to their inventories.

Statistical analysis does not make it possible to put forward any single explanation of the cycle. Some economists of the 'under-consumptionist' school once placed great stress in their explanation of why a boom eventually goes into reverse on the possibility of a fall in the marginal propensity to consume due to the redistribution of incomes, but now many economists tend to concentrate on the volatility of capital investment, which they explain by other reasons, such as the full employment 'ceiling' to output, the satisfaction of deferred replacement demand for capital equipment, or the working of individual industrial 'accelerators' each with its own historical setting. Some economists believe that the business cycle is inherent in the process of economic growth, in that innovations are made continuously but applied in clusters. The psychological resistance towards taking what may be a leap in the economic dark holds up the application of new inventions and productive techniques until at last some 'pioneer' businessman, a Henry Ford, for example, takes the lead, helping to strengthen investment demand, which, together with his own success, creates a more favourable economic climate in which other innovations can be applied by the less bold. It is during the boom that technical change is put into operation on all sides.

## OTHER TYPES OF ECONOMIC FLUCTUATION
### Inventory Cycles

Inventory cycles are fluctuations in output due to changes in investment in stocks of materials, work in progress, or finished products. Their effects may be confined to a single group of industries or may spread to many points of the economy; they may be the chief cause of a short cyclical fluctuation in the economy as a whole, usually lasting two or three years.

Inventory cycles may be caused by a form of accelerator. If businessmen aim at maintaining a constant ratio of stocks to sales the size of the change in the level of stocks, that is of inventory investment, will vary with the rate of change in sales. If an upward movement in sales slows down, therefore, inventory investment in the industry concerned will fall; the absolute level of stocks will continue to rise, but by a smaller amount. If sales fall, the level of stocks, on the simple assumption of a constant ratio to sales, will be allowed to decline; inventory investment will be negative. If a period of inventory investment of, say, 100 is followed by one of −100, a reduction in expenditure of 200 is involved, other things remaining equal. If the rate of decline in sales decreases, the fall in the level of stocks becomes smaller, on these simple assumptions, and this involves an *increase* in inventory investment. For if a period of inventory investment of −100 is followed by one of −50, the result is an increase in

TABLE 28. *Illustration of Inventory Cycle*

| Period | Sales | Level of stocks | Ratio of stocks: sales | Inventory investment | Change in inventory investment from previous period | Production |
|---|---|---|---|---|---|---|
| 1 | 1,000 | 500 | ·50 | Nil | Nil | 1,000 |
| 2 | 1,200 | 300 | ·25 | −200 | −200 | 1,000 |
| 3 | 1,440 | 720 | ·50 | +420 | +620 | 1,860 |
| 4 | 1,440 | 720 | ·50 | Nil | −420 | 1,440 |
| 5 | 1,440 | 720 | ·50 | Nil | Nil | 1,440 |

business expenditure of 50; a smaller part of total demand is met by drawing on stocks.

In practice a constant ratio of stocks to sales is rarely maintained, but the consequence may be to intensify the fluctuation in output. If sales of, say, cotton textiles suddenly increase, the level of stocks of cotton and cotton products held by the industry will be depleted in order to meet the new demand. If the rise in sales continues, a disproportionately large increase in investment in stocks of raw materials and work in progress will then be needed to enable the increase in output to take place. If the rate of increase in sales finally slackens, a fall in inventory investment, usually first in raw materials and then in work in progress and finally in finished products, will occur. The fact that the inventory–sales ratio may not have been rebuilt to beyond its 'normal' figure will not prevent the fall in inventory investment. A simple illustration is given in Table 28.

In period 3, production, including that for stock, exceeds sales by 420, the amount by which the level of stocks has to be increased to restore a 'normal' ratio of stocks to sales of ·50; the swing in inventory investment is 620. In period 4, in which sales are maintained, production falls off by 420, representing a fall in inventory investment by this amount due to the restoration of a 'normal' inventory–sales ratio. In period 5 the fall in inventory investment ceases, and production stabilizes.

Inventory cycles are most important in those industries, like cotton and wool textiles and non-ferrous metal fabricating, in which the normal ratio of stocks to sales is relatively high and in which the raw materials that are used are subject to wide swings in prices, so that the amplitude of the stock movement may be aggravated by the expectation of price changes. The latter may even be inherent in the inventory cycle itself; a restocking movement during a world textile boom may raise the price of, say, cotton to an abnormally high level. The beginning of a downward swing in inventory investment may cause the first break in the cotton market and may be seriously aggravated by the expectation of a further decline.

The combination of swings in inventory investment over a number of industries may cause a minor fluctuation in total output, aggravated by the working of the multiplier, so that an inventory cycle in one group of industries may set up similar forces in others.[15]

## Replacement Cycles

Once sales of durable goods experience a temporary bulge, cycles of demand are likely to perpetuate themselves owing to the timing of replacement, if there is no overwhelming long-term trend of demand. Replacement cycles occur in the field of both durable consumer goods and capital equipment, but the regularity of their movement is often distorted by the fact that replacement is likely to be deferred during the earlier stages of a fall in general activity and incomes and, at least as far as consumer goods are concerned, accelerated when times are growing more prosperous or when new models seem especially attractive.

## 'Indivisibilities'

The 'lumpiness' of many forms of capital investment may cause minor fluctuations in sections of the economy. When a single-track railway is laid down, for example, a steady expansion of traffic can for some time be met merely by gradually increasing the volume of rolling stock in use. Eventually, however, a continuation of the same rate of growth in traffic will become impossible unless another track is laid, causing an upsurge in the demand for steel and building materials. The increasing magnitude in which single economic decisions are made, owing to the development of large concerns and trade unions, nationalization and the role of the State, and even the relatively large size of certain forms of modern equipment, such as a giant ocean liner or a power station, may also tend to make these disturbances more powerful than in the past.

### Time-lags

Time-lags may accentuate economic fluctuations. A lag may occur between an increase in sales and the decision to increase productive capacity, and between the decision to expand and the point of time at which the increase in output emerges. Taken together, these two lags may result in a considerable delay before production is increased in response to the rise in demand which it is intended to meet. If in the meantime demand has fallen off again or has not risen at a sufficient rate, considerable excess capacity may have been installed. As a result, investment will then fall sharply, perhaps causing productive capacity to be too low when demand recovers, so that a fresh 'lagged' cyclical movement begins. Time-lags are likely to cause wide fluctuations in industries like agriculture and mining, consisting of a large number of producers each of which expands his output in response to an increase in demand without taking fully into account the likelihood that his competitors will react in the same way. If demand is relatively inelastic, the expansion of supply which eventually occurs will cause a sharp fall in prices in a competitive industry, perhaps inducing producers to contract their output too sharply, in turn eventually causing prices to rise, and so on.

# PART VII

# INTERNATIONAL TRADE
# AND PAYMENTS

# CHAPTER 38

# INTERNATIONAL TRADE AND SPECIALIZATION

## INTERNATIONAL AND INTRA-NATIONAL TRADE

The basic principles of economics transcend national boundaries. Nevertheless, international trade differs from domestic trade in certain respects. Government regulations impose a considerable degree of restriction on the international movement of labour in addition to the natural barriers of language and distance and may impede the free flow of financial capital and goods from one country to another. International trade is much more subject to the actions of governments in support of what they conceive to be the interests of their own citizens, even if they damage those of other countries in the process.

It is true that the self-interest of South Wales may conflict with that of Lincolnshire, and that the central government, in deciding, for example, that a steel-mill is to be sited in one county rather than another, may modify the working of market forces as does government policy in the international field. However, the degree of self-interested political action in international trade is so much greater as to be almost different in kind from the local economic rivalries of domestic trade, especially as labour and capital cannot easily cross national barriers to share in the fruits of self-interested national action and thus diminish them.

Finally, the settlement of debts accruing from international trade involves the relationship between national currencies with varying degrees of acceptability outside their own national boundaries; in other words, it raises the question of rates of exchange and the problem of how the net balance of payments between one country and another is to be financed.

## GAINS FROM INTERNATIONAL TRADE

The short-sighted observer may deplore Britain's dependence on imports for the bulk of her food and raw materials and a not inconsiderable part of her manufactures, which have to be paid for by exports in a highly competitive and none too reasonable world. It is undisputable that if we had no imports we should have no foreign bills to meet and could cultivate our island garden free from the problems of international trade. But trade brings benefits as well as problems to all countries that participate; in economics, blessed is he who buys as well as he who sells. The gains from international trade lie in variety, economies of scale, and in specialization.

There are some goods and services that this country is physically incapable of producing. We possess no accessible reserves of oil or copper and could hardly grow tropical products. International trade greatly increases the variety of goods and services that any country can enjoy and enables it to share in the natural resources, the special skills, and the knowledge possessed by the rest of the world.

International trade provides economies of scale by enlarging the size of the market open to those industries where average costs are lower if productive units are large or where 'external' economies can be obtained if an industry exceeds a certain size. There are many industries in Britain that would be considerably smaller without their export markets.

Thirdly, international trade enables the benefits of specialization to be obtained by both importing and exporting countries. Our inheritance of natural resources, our supply of labour and capital, and our skills are not those of other countries. We are short of land in relation to our population compared with a country like Canada, but richer in capital and in skill than most. The production of some goods, such as wheat, requires relatively more land than labour, compared with that of motor-cars, which needs relatively more capital and skill. International trade increases productivity and real incomes by allowing countries to specialize in the production of those goods and services in which their relative advantage is greatest; we are thus importers of wheat and exporters of motor-cars.

### COMPARATIVE ADVANTAGES

International trade would still be profitable to those participating in it even if one country had an absolute advantage in the production of everything, as long as its advantage in the production of one good was *relatively* greater than in the production of another.

The gains of specialization are derived from comparative and not absolute advantages.

For a simple illustration imagine two countries in which only labour is scarce. Suppose that the average productivity of labour in the production of wheat and rice is that shown in Table 29.

TABLE 29. *Productivity of Labour in Rice- and Wheat-growing*

|  | Country A | Country B |
|---|---|---|
| Bushels of wheat per day | 8 | 2 |
| Bushels of rice per day | 2 | 1 |

Country A has an absolute labour-productivity advantage in both wheat and rice, but because its efficiency in wheat is four times that of B and its productivity in rice only twice as great, specialization would raise the total output of both countries. If country A shifted one day's labour from rice to wheat this would reduce its production of rice by two bushels and enlarge that of wheat by eight. To make up for this loss of rice, country B would have to shift two man-days of wheat to the production of rice, thus losing only four bushels of wheat. The net result would be that, whereas their combined output of rice is unchanged, their production of wheat would be up by four bushels because of this specialization.

The wheat of country A could be exchanged for the rice of B, the extent of the exchange depending partly on any shift in relative costs that might occur as one country gave up wheat for rice-growing, or vice versa. As country A shifted more of its resources into wheat-growing it would sooner or later find that its efforts yielded diminishing returns, and the same would be true of the diversion of resources to rice in country B. The process might therefore cease before either country was completely specialized in one or the other, for comparative advantages at the margin of output might disappear before this stage was reached. Thus country A might produce part of its rice requirements itself, importing the rest of its supplies. The balance between wheat and rice production would also depend on the relative preference for additional wheat or rice at each level of consumption. If by shifting one man-day from rice to wheat, country A could produce eight bushels of wheat at the expense of two bushels of rice, it would only be rational to do so if its inhabitants gained in enjoyment, and this would depend on their preference for additional wheat or rice and the terms on which they could trade wheat for rice with B. As more and more wheat was produced in relation to rice, the additional satisfaction yielded by the marginal bushel of wheat would fall and so would the price of wheat in terms of rice in conditions of free competition.

### FREE TRADE AND SPECIALIZATION

Free trade, that is trade unhampered by exchange control, by import or export duties or quotas, would tend to spread these advantages of specialization over the trading world as a whole. In each country the mechanism of a free market would cause those factors of production that were relatively scarce to be dear in relation to those that were relatively plentiful. Where land was the relatively scarce factor rents would be high compared with wage-rates and interest-rates; where labour was scarce in relation to land, wage-rates would be high in relation to rents; and where capital was scarce compared with labour, interest-rates would be high in relation to wages. The same principle would apply to different kinds of labour and natural resources.

The free working of market forces would enable each country to concentrate on the production of those goods and services in which its *relative* advantages were greatest, because in these its money costs per unit of output would be relatively low. A country would import those goods and services which used more of the resources with which it was less richly endowed, because in these its money costs per unit of output would be relatively high, and it would be able to import them more cheaply from other countries. Thus countries with a relative advantage in 'land' would concentrate on wheat, those where 'labour' was relatively plentiful would specialize in rice, and those better supplied with capital would concentrate on motor-cars.

Each country as a whole would gain by being able to import more cheaply and to produce more abundantly, the distribution of these gains depending on relative productivities and the terms on which one good could be traded for another. The relationship between the prices of a country's imports and those of its exports is known as its *terms of trade*, and, other things being equal, the lower are its import prices in relation to the prices of the goods it exports, the more a country gains from the exchange. But 'other things' do not remain equal, for trade would benefit country A even if its shift from rice to wheat caused a fall in the price of its wheat exports in terms of its rice imports, as long as its enhanced productivity made up for this.

Free trade would tend to reproduce the general benefits to be gained from the principle of comparative advantages or costs in real terms, but the extent to which it did so would depend on whether the pattern of money costs reflected the relative scarcity of different factors of production. If, by one means or another, money wages are kept at too high a level in one industry in relation to those in another, the principle of comparative real advantages cannot be fully applied, for at a given rate of exchange the cost per unit of output will be too high in the one and too low in the other for the full advantages of specialization to be derived by the country as a whole.

Although international trade is affected by government interference, in the form of import duties, quotas, subsidies, and price support policies, by monopolistic business practices, and by more or less unavoidable structural rigidities, the changing force of relative advantages in determining the pattern of trade is still discernible. The relative advantages once possessed by this country in the production of comparatively simple manufactured goods, such as cotton textiles and the cruder forms of engineering products, have been lost as other countries have also acquired the skills and capital equipment that we were first to accumulate by our early start in industrial development. In these industries, which use a fairly high proportion of labour to capital, our relative advantage has also been narrowed because of the increase in wage-rates that has come about as a result of the more rapid development of other industries in this country with which cotton textiles etc. have to compete for labour. In the case of coal, which was once our staple export, our relative advantage has been steadily eroded as the more accessible seams of our coalfields have been worked out. Today our relative advantages lie with those goods, like electrical machinery, which have a fairly high capital content, but not so high as to put us at a disadvantage vis-à-vis the U.S.A., where capital is relatively plentiful, and in those goods and services in the production of which we possess special knowledge and skills, such as in the manufacture of aircraft engines, ships, and bicycles, and in the provision of shipping, banking, and insurance services.

## TRADE AND SPECIAL INTERESTS

That trade provides benefits to all countries does not necessarily mean that free trade brings to all the best of all possible worlds. Whereas all countries would suffer if they cut themselves off from trade altogether, most economists recognize that something less than completely free trade may be in the interest of individual countries in certain circumstances. But it is important to examine closely any claim that the restriction of trade would be 'in the national interest', for the subject of international trade abounds in fallacies and half-truths expounded on behalf of special interests disguised in national costume. Some are manifestly contradictory. American industry may complain that British manufacturers compete on 'unfair' terms because British wage-rates are lower; here in Britain we may complain that we cannot compete with high-wage American industries because they are more richly endowed with capital equipment.

High money wage-rates do not mean high costs per unit of output if productivity is high. The abundance of her natural resources has given the U.S.A. the ability to equip her industries richly with capital equipment, and the high wage-rates that result from this natural wealth have provided the incentive to use more capital in order to economize in labour. Britain is generally in the same position vis-à-vis Japan. Trade benefits all three countries as a whole if each concentrates on the production of those goods in which the ratio of its productivity to that of the others exceeds the ratio of its money wages to those of the others. If Britain were to restrict the importation of Japanese goods for example, we should be acting against the interests of our consumers, depressing our own total national output by preventing the transfer of resources from cotton textiles to those industries in which we do have a relative advantage and making even poorer a people already much poorer than ourselves. We should also be injuring the interests of our exporters, who would find Japan less able to buy their products.

This argument holds even though Japanese cotton mills might be as well equipped with machinery as Lancashire and have the benefit of low wage-rates besides. As long as wage-rates in the Japanese textile industry were not artificially depressed in relation to those in other Japanese industries we should have no complaint to make about 'unfair' competition, for it is the object of specialization to divert relatively scarce resources—capital and land in Japan's case—to where they can be of greatest value in conjunction with the factor that is relatively plentiful.

Whereas free trade benefits each country as a whole, there is no doubt that, within each, certain groups may lose by trade. If free trade were to cause the cotton-textile industry to contract and, say, chemical production to expand in this country, the shift might result in some reduction in money wage-rates. For the chemical industry uses less labour per unit of output than does the cotton-textile industry, so that the increase in the demand for labour in the chemical industry might not match that released by a contracting cotton-textile industry if wage-rates remain unchanged. To employ all those redundant in cotton textiles, wage-rates in both industries would have to fall. As a general rule, that is, the earnings of any factor of production employed in greater proportion to others by the contracting industry than by the trade that is expanding will be reduced by the change. The extent of this loss will depend on how elastic is the supply of the factor at a disadvantage and how elastic is the demand for it in the expanding industry. If the cotton-textile trade mainly employed women and the chemical industry could employ only men, or labour generally in a fixed ratio to capital equipment, the loss suffered by those redundant in cotton textiles would be relatively severe.

## PROTECTION AND FREE TRADE IN THE UNITED KINGDOM

During the seventeenth and eighteenth centuries the influence of what was known as the Mercantilist philosophy encouraged the State to regulate our foreign trade. The main aims of the Mercantilists were: to achieve an excess of exports over imports, a so-called 'favourable' balance of trade, in order to find markets for what was regarded as 'surplus' domestic production and in order to increase our stock of gold and silver; to favour the production and exportation of manufactures rather than raw materials; to restrict and even prohibit the exportation of those goods, like coal, wool and machinery, that were held to strengthen the competitive position of other countries; to prohibit for similar reasons the emigration of skilled workers; and by means of the Navigation Acts to force British importers to use British ships in order to build up our sea-power in case of war.

In the nineteenth century the Mercantilist philosophy was destroyed and that of free trade enthroned in its place. The transformation was brought about by the combination of the intellectual attack of Adam Smith and other classical economists and the growing influence of the manufacturing classes. The latter had much to gain from the importation of cheap food and materials, which enlarged their domestic market by raising the standard of living of the mass of the people and, by lowering food prices, helped to keep down wage-rates; free trade was seen to expand the market for British exports in those countries from which our imports were obtained. The opposition of farmers and landowners was finally overcome when the Corn Laws, the duties imposed on the importation of corn during the agricultural slump that followed the Napoleonic Wars, were repealed by Peel's Ministry in 1846. Duties on other goods had been reduced by Huskisson as early as 1824, and Gladstone completed the process by 1861. For the next seventy years, until 1931, there were practically no restrictions on imports into Britain, save duties imposed on tobacco and tea, in order to raise tax revenue, and a small number of duties on 'key industries' kept for strategic reasons from the legislation of the 1914–18 war and consolidated under the Safeguarding of Industries Act, 1921.

On the Continent and in the U.S.A., on the other hand, the movement towards the protection of domestic industry gathered force under the impact of increasing international competition after the 1880's. The American tariff of 1890 hastened the return to protection, and the great depression completed the process in the early nineteen-thirties. This country swung into line with the Import Duties Act of 1932, which imposed protective duties on many manufactured goods, generally of 10 per cent *ad valorem* on those imported from outside the Commonwealth, but since ranging up to 30 per cent on motor-cars and $33\frac{1}{3}$ per cent on certain iron and steel products and chemicals. All over the world the desire to reduce unemployment and to protect exchange reserves was the cause of a proliferation of import duties, quotas, and restrictions on financial transactions.

## FREE TRADE VERSUS PROTECTION

The strains of the inter-war period can be regarded as abnormal, and with the return of the world to more stable and prosperous economic conditions progress has been made towards removing some of these restrictions. The imposition of import duties as a means of curing general unemployment does not have much to commend it when other means are available, for if it succeeds it does so partly at the expense of other countries whose exports are reduced and, by interfering with the balance of relative advantages, prevents the most economic allocation of resources. Import duties are not likely to succeed in reducing general unemployment if they lead to retaliation by other countries, in which case the consequence is a general reduction in the level of world trade.

Protection may be claimed to have other advantages, which can be divided into those aimed at benefiting particular groups and those claimed to be in the interest of the country as a whole. Selfishness apart, protection against imports may be claimed for groups that are regarded as being in a particularly depressed position within the community. The import tariffs imposed on manufactured goods by the U.S.A. towards the end of the last century and by Australia in this, for example, are thought by some economists to have increased the share of labour as against landlords in the national income, for labour forms a greater proportion of the value of manufactured goods than of agricultural products, whose production was in effect hampered by the protection of industry. Whether the share of any one group in the national income should be deliberately increased is a political question; but it should not be overlooked that the absolute gain by the one may be less than the loss suffered by the others, for protection may prevent a country from getting the maximum output from its resources.

A second argument for protection as a 'special' case is that a change in economic conditions, such as a series of technical developments, may cause a protracted slump in an industry from which resources cannot easily be transferred. Protection may be resorted to in order to ease the process of adjustment. As land is a relatively 'immobile' factor of production and agricultural workers may be deficient in manufacturing skills, agricultural interests have always been inclined to favour protection.

Thirdly, protection may be claimed for an 'infant' industry, on the grounds that a country's natural resources would favour its development if it were allowed time in which to build up its skills and to reap the external economies obtainable from large-scale operations. This argument is common in countries where the popular view is that 'industry' is the hallmark of an 'advanced' economy and agriculture or mining the stigma of backwardness, irrespective of whether the pattern of relative advantages is such that the standard of living would be higher if agricultural resources were more fully exploited.

In practice it cannot be said that the force and frequency with which these 'special' cases have been presented have been free from special pleading, and it would not be easy to justify the pattern of British duties on these grounds. Infant industries often take a surprisingly long time to grow up, and import duties are politically harder to remove than to impose. As import duties benefit one group by raising prices to another, an alternative form of redistributing the national income would be by taxation and subsidy, a method that makes use of the working of the price mechanism for social purposes and that would have the merit of honesty, for it would make it clear just which groups were being favoured or penalized and by how much. As for assisting a specialized industry in a depressed state, the use of protection alone may retard the transfer of resources; subsidies accompanied by positive measures to encourage mobility are economically superior. The protection of a declining industry is only too likely to be the fence behind which monopolistic practices can be introduced, and to those who value competition as a spur to higher productivity, protection appears as an obstacle to economic growth in general.

The second class of arguments in favour of protection concerns the 'national interest'. The needs of military security may justify assistance to the watch industry, as in the United Kingdom, or to the synthetic-rubber industry, as in the U.S.A., but here, too, subsidies are economically a less harmful form of assistance than import duties, which throw the cost of assistance mainly on the consumers of the product concerned, or on foreign producers, and not on the community as a whole. Claims for assistance on military grounds are only too easily made but rarely reassessed when military requirements change.

The imposition of import duties may appear to be in the national interest to a country that believes that it can thereby improve its terms of trade. An import duty acts as an outlay tax; if demand is elastic or supply inelastic, it may force the exporting country to lower its prices if the country imposing the tariff takes a sufficiently high proportion of its output. If the import duty does succeed in improving the protectionist country's terms of trade it does so at the expense of those countries whose terms of trade are impaired, but whether the gain to the one is greater or less than the loss suffered by the others usually cannot be assessed, and the imposition of import duties may be followed by retaliation on the part of other countries. Retaliation may help to restore a loss of real national income caused by the action of other countries, but if the defensive process leads to a general increase in tariffs to high levels all countries are likely to suffer through a contraction in world trade.

Import duties may be imposed merely to raise tax revenue from 'foreigners'. But whether the effective incidence of the tax falls on overseas producers will depend on the conditions of supply and demand, and if the commodity concerned is produced in the taxing country as well it is difficult to distinguish it from an ordinary protective tariff.

The considerations discussed above also apply for the most part to the restriction of imports by quota, but there are also some important differences between quotas and tariffs. Whereas quotas raise prices to domestic consumers, as do import duties, they provide a windfall gain to domestic sellers and not to the State. Secondly, if the consuming country's demand is sufficiently inelastic and the supply of exports sufficiently elastic, the exporting country may be able to sell the smaller volume at a much higher price and so will maintain the value of its exports, but at the expense of the consumer in the importing country. On the other hand, tariffs can be surmounted by an improvement in efficiency; quotas can not. Quotas also hamper the adjustment of international payments by means of changes in exchange rates, which would otherwise alter the volume of imports or exports by changing the relationship between domestic and foreign costs.

# CHAPTER 39

# INTERNATIONAL PAYMENTS

## INTERNATIONAL BANKING TRANSACTIONS

An international banking network provides the means whereby payments between the residents of one country and those of another are settled. A Liverpool merchant wishing to make a payment in dollars to an American exporter in New York, if he has the permission of the British exchange control authorities, can draw a cheque or draft on his account with a Liverpool bank in favour of the American's account with a New York bank. In the simplest case, where the Liverpool bank has an account with a bank in New York it can merely draw a cheque on its balance there in favour of the American exporter concerned. If the American exporter had an account with the branch of an American bank in Britain, the Liverpool merchant's cheque could have been drawn in favour of the American's account in this country.

Apart from the relatively insignificant use of bank-notes by tourists, 'foreign currency' therefore consists of a balance with a bank overseas. Transactions between British residents and foreigners lead to changes in the balances of British residents and British banks held with banks overseas and to changes in foreign-owned bank balances in the United Kingdom. Central banks are a highly important part of this system; they hold gold and deposits with other central banks and may intervene in the market for foreign currencies. The willingness of central banks to hold foreign currencies helps to determine which currencies are acceptable in foreign transactions.

The importance of the United Kingdom and the United States in world trade and their historical development as foreign lenders have led to the predominance of London and New York as centres of international monetary areas. Banks in many countries hold balances in New York or in London; payments between Cuba and Mexico, for example, may be settled by a transfer of a bank deposit in New York, and those between traders in Amsterdam and Paris by one in London. London and New York thus link those many countries in which the dollar or the pound sterling are acceptable currencies in international transactions; subsidiary financial systems include France and her overseas territories and the U.S.S.R. and Eastern Europe.

## THE BALANCE OF PAYMENTS

A country's international transactions over any period can be divided into current and capital account transactions. Its current receipts form part of its national income; its current expenditure augments the income of other countries. A country's capital account records its transactions in its overseas assets and in its liabilities to non-residents.

### Current Account Items

Included in its current account are receipts from exports of goods and services, property income from abroad, and those gifts whose continuing nature justifies treating them as 'income'. Its current outlays consist of payments for goods and services imported, property income paid abroad, and 'continuing' gifts made abroad.

Exports and imports of goods and services make up a country's *balance of trade*. If the value of its exports of goods and services exceeds that of its imports of goods and services, a country is said to have a surplus in its balance of trade, or a 'favourable' balance of trade. If the balance is in the opposite direction, it has an 'unfavourable' or 'adverse' balance of trade.

Current account items can be subdivided into 'visible' and 'invisible' items. A country's balance of visible trade is the difference between the f.o.b. value of its exports and imports of *goods*, which are its visible exports and imports. Invisible items consist of services, such as shipping, insurance and banking, property income, and current gifts.

### The Balance between Current and Capital Account

The balance of a country's current receipts and outlays, its surplus or deficit on current account, must be equal and 'opposite' to its balance on capital account, if it neither receives nor makes net gifts of a capital nature. Apart from capital grants, the United Kingdom's capital account includes the following items:

| *Assets* | *Liabilities* |
|---|---|
| Gold | Non-resident holdings of sterling currency |
| Overseas currencies | Non-resident holdings of U.K. securities |
| Overseas securities | Other U.K. indebtedness to non-residents |
| Other overseas claims | |

If the United Kingdom has a current surplus and there is no net balance of capital grants, this must have as its counterpart an addition to its international assets or a reduction in its liabilities to non-residents, for the difference between current payments and receipts must have been financed in one way or the other. A current surplus must be matched by the acquisition of gold, overseas currency, overseas securities or other assets, or by the reduction of non-resident holdings of bank deposits in the U.K., or by a decline in non-resident holdings of U.K. securities or other claims on this country. In practice most items in the country's capital account are likely to be affected; it is their *net* balance that must match the balance on current account.

If a country makes or receives net capital grants, on the other hand, this identity will be upset. Grants received may be used, for example, to acquire gold or foreign currencies, which would not be matched by an equivalent surplus on current account, or to finance a deficit on current account, which would then not be reflected in an equivalent reduction in overseas assets or in an increase in overseas liabilities.

### DEFINITIONS OF THE BALANCE OF PAYMENTS

The term 'balance of payments' is usually employed to refer to the state of a country's international transactions on current account.

In recent years, however, an alternative and, for some purposes, more illuminating connotation has been attached to the term, deriving its importance from the fact that a country has to keep a reserve of liquid international assets in order to settle its debts as they fall due. This reserve will consist largely of gold and foreign currencies acceptable to other countries with which it trades, and short-term securities held abroad and payable in a desirable currency. The reserve of the United Kingdom thus consists mainly of gold, United States dollars and short-term securities, whereas that of Australia is held partly in gold and dollars but mainly in sterling bank deposits and securities, especially Treasury bills.

The term 'balance of payments' can therefore be used to refer to the change in the value of a country's gold and foreign exchange reserves. A further refinement would be to take account of any change in short-term indebtedness. For the latter may have to be repaid at short notice and therefore constitutes a potentially immediate claim on its foreign exchange reserves. This leaves as an alternative definition of a country's balance of payments the balance of its transactions on current account and those on *long-term* capital account, that is to say the difference between current and long-term capital receipts on the one hand and current and long-term capital payments on the other. In this sense a balance-of-payments surplus, which would exist, for example, if the surplus on current account exceeded any net outflow of long-term capital, would be used to acquire gold and foreign exchange reserves (including short-term securities) *or* to repay short-term indebtedness to non-residents.

In one sense a change in a country's gold and foreign exchange reserves is a mere residual in its international transactions, but while it should not be regarded in isolation from changes in its short-term indebtedness, the importance of maintaining an adequate liquid reserve often causes attention to be directed at the change in its gold and foreign exchange reserves alone. A country may be said to be in balance-of-payments 'difficulties' when its reserves are falling to what is regarded as a low level (although in fact the situation may be more favourable than this if the fall in reserves has been accompanied by a larger fall in short-term liabilities). The cause of such 'difficulties' might be a deficit on current account, or too large an outflow of capital on long-term account, or a withdrawal by foreigners of their short-term assets from the country concerned, or a combination of these.

The United Kingdom has periodically suffered from one or more of these problems since the war: in some years it has had a current deficit, or its current surplus has been too small to support a high level of net long-term capital payments, or its gold and dollar reserves have been depleted because of the withdrawal of short-term funds by non-residents.

## LONG-RUN BALANCE OF PAYMENTS POLICY

That a surplus on current account is usually described as 'favourable' begs the question of whether the achievement of a persistent current surplus is desirable. The Mercantilists favoured such a policy in order to dispose of what they regarded as 'surplus' domestic production and to accumulate gold. When there is undue unemployment, a favourable balance of payments, it is true, may stimulate business activity and production without inflation. When there is full employment, on the other hand, exports in excess of imports merely represent domestic production shipped to the rest of the world without the receipt of goods and services in return; they deprive the community of part of its current potential standard of living, and the indefinite accumulation of foreign exchange reserves is a form of hoarding. It must be remembered that one country's surplus must be matched by another's deficit, and it would be an impracticable prescription that bade all countries to aim at a surplus as a means to prosperity.

For a country to experience a persistent current surplus and another to record a persistent deficit may benefit both, on the other hand, if this is the result of international lending. If, in a mature economy, capital is so plentiful in relation to investment opportunities that the real net rate of return on marginal projects is, say, 5 per cent, whereas in a 'newer' country, with unused land and mineral resources perhaps, the use of additional capital will augment national production by, say, 10 per cent per annum, it will be to the real benefit of both countries if the 'capital-hungry' country borrows from the 'capital-sated' country at any intermediate rate of interest. The former can use the proceeds of the loan to import capital equipment, or to purchase consumer goods while its own resources are used to increase investment instead. The lending country can use its interest receipts to pay for additional imports of goods and services and thus can raise its standard of living by more than if it had used the capital of the loan for domestic investment instead.

It will be observed that the borrowing country can find the foreign currency to pay its annual interest charges, ignoring third countries for the sake of simplicity, only by exporting from its expanded production goods and services to the value of its interest payments. If the creditor country restricts its imports it will make it all the more difficult for the debtor nation to meet its interest charges. Ultimately the creditor country must run a current deficit if the debtor country is to be able to repay the capital of its loan, unless the creditor country is willing to go on extending new loans or to make gifts; otherwise the debtor country will experience chronic balance-of-payments difficulties.

A second reason for pursuing a policy of keeping exports in excess of imports is to make gifts to other countries, in order to accelerate their economic development, to strengthen their military position, or to secure their goodwill. The United States has since the war made very large gifts to many countries, including Britain, for these reasons. Britain in turn has made grants on a smaller scale to speed up the development of Colonial territories.

Thirdly, a country may aim at a persistent current surplus in order to rebuild its gold and foreign exchange holdings to a level sufficient to enable it to use them to meet temporary deficits in the future. It cannot succeed in this, however, unless other countries are willing to experience current deficits corresponding to its own surpluses, or unless some countries are lending or making gifts in excess of their own current surpluses to enable a third group of countries to finance large current deficits, or unless world gold production is rising (or being released from private hoards). Gold-producing countries can use their current gold output to pay for net imports of goods and services that form the counterpart of the net exports of the surplus countries.

Since the war Britain has aimed at a persistent current surplus for all these reasons. We have attempted to rebuild our reserves, repay old debts, extend new loans to other Commonwealth countries, and to make gifts to Colonial territories. Despite the receipt of U.S. aid, these have amounted to a formidable charge on our real resources at a time when domestic demands have been pressing.

## THE DETERMINATION OF EXCHANGE RATES
### Fixed Exchange Rates

The exchange value of a country's currency, in terms of another or of gold, may be fixed by the action of its central bank, if it is prepared to buy or sell its own currency at fixed prices. As a central bank can always create its own currency but not gold or foreign exchange, its ability to support its fixed exchange rate turns in practice on the adequacy of its gold and foreign exchange reserves. In 1949 the United Kingdom was forced to devalue its exchange rate, that is to lower the foreign exchange value of the pound, from a declared 'par' rate of $4.03 to the pound to one of $2.80, because its gold and dollar reserves did not seem capable of meeting the contemporary strains they had to bear. At present the exchange value of the pound is fixed, in accordance with the rules of the International Monetary Fund,* at a par value of $2.80. Under the rules of the Fund the government undertakes to prevent the foreign exchange value of the pound from fluctuating by more than 1 per cent on either side of the par value of $2.80. The authorities therefore have to be prepared to sell dollars and buy sterling to prevent the rate of exchange against the dollar from falling below the lower limit of $2.772 and to sell sterling and buy dollars to prevent the rate from rising above the upper limit of $2.828. In practice, official intervention occurs short of these limits.

### Free Exchange Rates

It was once held that exchange rates, if free from official intervention, would tend towards their so-called 'purchasing power parity' in terms of the goods and services of different countries. If price-levels in Britain and the U.S.A. are such that £1 will buy in this country as much as $3 will buy in the United States, then, according to this theory, the rate of exchange between sterling and the dollar will tend towards $3=£1. Any other rate of exchange would make either American or British goods too dear in world markets.

The theory has a solid core of truth; if a country's money costs of production are too high in relation to those of its competitors at the ruling exchange rate its exports may be too small and its imports too large for it to balance its foreign transactions. But beyond this the directness of the theory is illusory. For which goods and services shall we choose in comparing prices? At one extreme are standardized commodities like rubber that are sold on world markets and have a single *world* price determined by world supply and demand, which, given the rate of exchange, in turn *determines* their domestic price in any one country if world

* See page 587.

trade is free. At the other we have those goods, like immovable property, and those services, such as internal transport, that are not traded internationally at all. The principle of comparative costs implies that those goods and services that embody a relatively high share of the scarcest factor of production will be relatively expensive in terms of their money cost in other countries. Because hairdressing is not an internationally traded service and uses a high proportion of labour as opposed to capital, a man's haircut will cost the equivalent of, say 7s. 6d. in New York but only 2s. 6d. in London if the rate of exchange is $2.80=£1. This does not mean that the pound is worth $8.40; and to choose an average of the prices of a multitude of goods and services raises many problems.

There is no simple alternative to the statement that any rate of exchange is determined by supply and demand in the foreign exchange markets of the world (in which the principal dealers are banks). The principal forces in operation can be briefly enumerated.

### The Current Balance of Payments

A country's currency will be offered and foreign exchange demanded in order to pay for its imports, whereas, in exporting, a country creates a demand for its own currency. The state of its balance of payments on current account will therefore be an important element in the determination of its rate of exchange. A country's balance on current account will depend on: the strength of demand for goods and services in its domestic market as compared with that in the rest of the world; the relationship between its domestic costs and those abroad, given the rate of exchange; the appeal of its products and the vigour of its sales techniques; and the force of import restrictions which it and other countries may impose. These factors will influence the volume of its imports and exports; and given these quantities its balance of payments will depend on its terms of trade.

As the prices of most manufactured goods remain relatively steady from month to month, sharp changes in the terms of trade are due usually to fluctuations in the prices of foodstuffs and raw materials, of which a country may be a net importer or exporter. But the volume of international trade and the terms of trade between manufacturing countries and those exporting primary products is closely interrelated, for the volume of manufactured goods that the latter can import depends ultimately on their export income (apart from their receipts of gifts and loans). As world demand for many foodstuffs and raw materials is not very elastic, the export income of the countries producing these goods will to a great extent reflect changes in the prices of their exports. If primary product prices fall, therefore, the terms of Britain's visible trade tend to improve, but it may become more difficult for her to sell her exports of manufactures in the primary producing countries; the net effect on Britain's current balance will also depend on the course of her income from overseas property, much of which is situated in food- and raw-material-producing countries like Australia and Canada. If the volume of trade were to fall, Britain's earnings from shipping would decline, unless the freights of liner shipping, of which Britain is a substantial exporter, fell less than those of tramp shipping, in which this country tends to be an importer. The upshot of these different factors is not easily predicted.

A country's balance of payments will also suffer if the pattern of its output is unfavourable. If its productive capacity is concentrated on goods for which overseas demand is low and inelastic, it will be difficult for it to achieve full employment and a balance in its overseas payments. It may be impossible to sell its excess of output over home requirements at prices high enough to pay for its imports, in the absence of import controls, whereas devaluation, which would have the effect of lowering its export prices in terms of foreign currency, might achieve little if overseas demand for its goods were inelastic. The dislocation caused by natural catastrophe or by war may be important causes of what is sometimes described as 'structural maladjustment' in a country's pattern of production.

### International Capital Movements

With fixed exchange rates, if a country is politically stable and has a reputation for creditworthiness, it will tend to attract long-term capital from overseas if it offers higher rates of interest on long-term securities than those elsewhere or a prospect of high rates of return from investment in real assets. Low interest rates in a country with a developed capital market, on the other hand, will attract overseas borrowers in the absence of restrictions on international lending. The movement of long-term capital will therefore tend to augment the demand for the currency of high interest-rate countries and swell the supply of the currency of those with relatively low interest rates.

Short-term interest rates may be an even more important influence. Short-term funds are held in another country as international working balances by banks and commercial concerns and as mobile 'speculative' balances, sometimes described as 'hot' money. The latter are held for fear of political instability, of exchange control, or a fall in the exchange rate of the currency in the country in which their owners are resident, or in the hope of a rise in the exchange rate of the currency in which they have been invested.

When the stability of exchange rates seems assured, the movement of short-term funds will reflect the relative level of money-market rates of interest in different financial centres. When exchange rates are thought to be unstable, international differences in short-term rates of interest will usually be small compared with the magnitude of the loss or gain that may be experienced through an alteration in exchange rates. Expectations of changes in exchange rates may therefore cause violent movements in international funds from one centre to another, strengthening the demand for a strong currency and weakening still further the position of a currency that is thought to be weak. When expectations of a change in exchange rates are firmly held, even working balances may be transferred to the strong financial centre, and interest rates there will tend to fall while those in the weak centre will rise, unless the authorities intervene.

When the exchange rate of a country's currency is expected to fall, its foreign exchange position is also likely to be adversely affected by the emergence of the 'leads and lags' in its payments and receipts mentioned on page 489.

## Gold Transactions

A currency may be offered for the purchase of gold abroad if it is available there on relatively favourable terms, and there will be a foreign demand for a country's currency if gold is bought by foreigners from its bullion dealers.

## Official Intervention

As already stated, the authorities may intervene in the foreign exchange market, offering its own currency, gold, or foreign currency in order to influence the rate of exchange. The authorities may operate so as to 'peg' the rate at a certain level, to prevent it from exceeding certain limits of fluctuation, or merely to smooth out day-to-day movements while not resisting the force of a longer-term trend.

### THE OPERATION OF THE GOLD STANDARD

A country's currency is on the gold standard when the value of its monetary unit is fixed in terms of a given weight of gold and when gold can be freely held, imported or exported. To support this value the country's central bank must be prepared to buy and sell gold at stated prices. Before 1914 gold coins actually circulated in the gold standard then in operation; the weight of gold of which the pound sovereign had to consist was prescribed by statute, and Bank of England notes were freely convertible into gold. The result was to fix the gold value of the pound and the sterling value of gold. After its suspension between 1914 and 1925 the gold standard was restored in this country in a modified *gold bullion* form; no gold coins were minted, and the Bank of England would buy and sell gold only in minimum quantities of 400-ounce bars, thus economizing in the use of gold. This system lasted until the United Kingdom was forced to leave the gold standard in 1931 and to adopt a policy of flexible exchange rates at a lower gold value.

Whether a country is on the classic or the bullion form of the gold standard, the essence of its operation is that the rate of exchange of its currency is fixed in terms of any other currency that is linked to gold. The gold content of the pound was equivalent to a par rate of exchange with the U.S. dollar of $4.867=£1. The market rate of exchange between the pound and the dollar could fluctuate only by a very narrow margin round this level. If the sterling price of dollars rose sufficiently above this—that is, if the dollar exchange value of the pound fell—it would pay dealers wanting dollars to buy gold from the Bank of England at its fixed selling price and ship it to the United States for exchange into dollars there. The point at which this operation became profitable—the so-called *gold export point* of the exchange—would depend on the cost of shipping and insurance. Before 1931 the gold export point was at about $4.848. Corresponding to this was the *gold import point* of the pound, at a rate of about $4.892, at which it became profitable for foreign dealers wanting pounds to sell dollars to their own central bank for gold, ship it to London and there turn it into pounds. Thus the rate of exchange between the pound and the dollar could not move beyond the gold import and export points.

When a country on the gold standard experienced a balance-of-payments deficit and its rate of exchange thus fell to its gold export point, it would experience a loss of gold, which would cause a corresponding fall in the cash reserves of the commercial banks if no counter-action were taken by the central bank. For, as dealers paid for their foreign exchange by buying gold from the central bank and exporting it, their payments to the central bank would involve a reduction in their deposits with the commercial banks and in the latters' balance with the central bank. The fall in the cash reserves of the commercial banks, if they maintained a fixed cash ratio, would cause a multiple contraction in deposits and a rise in interest rates.

Secondly, if a central bank experienced a persistent loss of gold it would take steps to check the outflow. The classic instrument of central bank policy is its rediscount rate, the Bank rate of the British system. Before 1914, when the gold reserve of the Bank of England was remarkably small, the Bank of England would raise Bank rate when its gold reserves declined, thus reinforcing the increase in money-market rates of interest and exerting a restrictive influence on the provision of credit, especially through the medium of the commercial bill.

The country experiencing the inflow of gold, if it followed the 'rules' of the gold standard, would allow a multiple expansion of its quantity of money, accompanied by a reduction in the level of its short-term rates in general and the central bank's rediscount rate in particular.

In the years before 1914 the gold standard worked with considerable efficacy in stabilizing the Bank of England's gold reserve. It was thought to work, according to the classic exposition offered by the Cunliffe Committee in 1919, in two ways. First, the rise in short-term interest rates in the country losing gold and the fall in interest rates in the country gaining gold would lead to a movement of short-term capital to the former, restoring part, at least, of its gold holdings, a movement that rested on the assurance of the fixity of exchange rates.

This process afforded quick but superficial relief to the deficit country's capital account. A current account deficit would take longer to remedy, and the second method of operation of the gold standard was regarded as fundamental. This was the effect thought to be exerted by the rise in interest rates and the fall in the quantity of money on the level of business activity. These forces, operating through a reduction in credit, were held to cause a decline not so much in output and employment as in costs and prices, which in turn would stimulate the deficit country's exports and reduce its imports until its current account was once more in balance, whereupon Bank rate could be reduced to a less onerous level. Correspondingly, the surplus country was presumably expected—although this was less clear—to experience a rise in costs and prices until its current surplus disappeared.

This explanation, which has been greatly simplified here, is too clear a description of how the system did work. In the first place, the 'rules' of the gold standard were frequently not followed. Central banks, including the Bank of England, did not always react in this way to the flow of gold, especially if it was expected to be temporary, both before 1914 and during the nineteen-twenties. Central banks tended to neutralize the effect on their monetary system of an inflow of gold but were more inclined to restrict credit when there was an outflow, so that the gold standard tended to have a restrictive bias in the world as a whole, but one that was probably not serious when world gold production was rising strongly. Secondly, the gold standard worked too smoothly for this analysis as far as Britain was concerned in the period before 1914; the correspondence between price movements and gold-flows is far from clear. For this there were broadly two reasons.

First, a rise in short-term rates of interest in London was remarkably successful in attracting short-term funds to this country because of London's special place as the predominant international creditor. A rise in money rates in London cut down new borrowing by foreigners there and caused a repatriation of funds accruing on maturing short-term loans made by London banks and discount houses, notably in the form of bills discounted.

Secondly, the explanation offered regarding the way in which a balance-of-payments surplus or deficit might be self-correcting was inadequate. By concentrating on changes in price-levels it ignored the direct effect of an alteration of a country's balance on current account on the level of domestic income and activity.

## NATIONAL INCOME AND THE BALANCE OF PAYMENTS WITH FIXED EXCHANGE RATES

If a country on a fixed exchange rate develops a deficit in its current account, and its price- and wage-levels remain relatively stable, the effect is to cause a multiple reduction in its domestic income and activity, in the absence of government action. This applies whether the fixed exchange rate is maintained in the form of the gold standard or by the intervention of the authorities in the foreign exchange market as at present. A fall in exports, for example, reduces the incomes of those employed in the export industries, causing them to cut their own consumption, which in turn reduces incomes in the consumer goods industries, and so on. A fall in domestic activity and incomes in relation to those of other countries will automatically cause the deficit country's imports to decline and thus improve the state of its balance on current account. If the deficit were caused by a shift of home demand in favour of imports, the incomes of industries producing for the home market would be affected directly.

In this sequence there are therefore two 'multiplier' effects: the 'domestic' multiplier, reflecting the marginal propensity to consume, and the 'foreign' multiplier, varying with the marginal propensity to import. The latter expression refers to a change in imports due to a change in a country's real national income. If the marginal propensity to import is, say, one quarter, a fall in domestic incomes of 100 will cause a reduction in imports of 25, giving some relief to the balance of payments and checking the decline in domestic incomes. Given the domestic multiplier, therefore, the process of contraction will be shorter the greater is the marginal propensity to import.

In the same way the country whose national income has been increased as a result of the development of an export surplus will spend part of the rise in its income on imports, reflecting its own marginal propensity to import, which may be high if it is already in a state of full employment. The increase in the imports of the surplus country provides relief for the balance of payments of the deficit country and helps to check still further the decline in the latter's national income.

As a result of these 'income-effects', the development of balance-of-payments disequilibria goes some way towards self-correction under a system of fixed exchange rates, but the process is unlikely to be completely self-adjusting. In a world of inflexible or at least 'sticky' prices, the deficit country is likely to be left with a lower level of domestic activity and incomes as well as some deficit on current account. If a decline in exports and in home consumption causes domestic investment to fall, or if the process of contraction is hastened by a central bank's obedience to the rules of the gold standard, the reduction in income, output and employment may be severe, although a current balance may be restored if the government is willing to deflate far enough.

If a country is experiencing inflation, on the other hand, so that there is an excess of aggregate demand in its home market, these corrective forces are likely to be weak. If exports fall because of a reduction in overseas demand or a rise in domestic prices, there may be no reduction in real incomes and therefore no decline in imports, for the goods that were formerly exported may be merely sold at home.

### FIXED EXCHANGE RATES WITHOUT THE GOLD STANDARD

Since the war a system of fixed exchange rates has been operated without the application of gold standard. It differs from the classic operation of the gold standard in several respects. Central banks usually take action so as to prevent a change in their reserves of gold and foreign currency from causing the multiple alteration in bank deposits called for under the 'rules' of the gold standard, so that changes in the availability of credit and in the level of interest rates are much less vigorous.

This country's reserves of gold and foreign exchange are now held by the Exchange Equalization Account; this is operated by the Bank of England as agent for the Treasury and was set up in 1932 to smooth out day-to-day fluctuations in the rate of exchange. It now acts so as to hold the rate of exchange within the narrow limits prescribed by the rules of the International Monetary Fund.

The Account is supplied with Treasury bills, which it can liquidate in order to provide itself with sterling, which it will have to pay out when it is accumulating gold and foreign exchange. In the simplest case the Account can obtain sterling to finance its purchases of foreign exchange by allowing its 'tap' bills to run off; the Exchequer has then to find an equivalent amount of finance from other sources, e.g. by selling tender bills to the banking system. The precise incidence of the operations of the Account on the banking system will depend on whether the authorities take steps to offset a rise or fall in the level of deposits and the liquid assets of the banks which is the usual consequence of an accumulation or loss of gold and foreign exchange.

International deficits are still settled partly by gold movements between central banks, but legal restrictions are applied to private transactions in gold. There is also a distinct psychological difference between the system of the gold standard, in which the fixity of exchange rates is taken more or less for granted, and that in which the fixity of exchange rates is an important objective of government policy but one that may not override all others, including the maintenance of full employment, so that the possibility of periodical adjustments in rates of exchange has to be reckoned with. In a system of stable but not invariable exchange rates, or under a gold standard whose maintenance can no longer be taken for granted, capital movements are much less responsive to international differences in interest rates and are much more likely to reflect hopes and fears regarding changes in exchange rates.

### VARIATIONS IN EXCHANGE RATES

The effect of a change in the rate of exchange on a country's balance of payments can be considered first in relation to its balance of trade. Let us consider only two currencies, the pound and the dollar, and let us suppose that the exchange rate for the pound is reduced from $3=£1 to $2·5=£1. If the domestic price-levels in each country do not change, this means that goods produced in Britain can, if necessary, now be sold at a lower dollar price, while goods produced in the U.S.A., if their dollar price does not change, will cost more in terms of pounds, so that both the supply of and the demand for goods and services sold by the one country to the other may be affected.

## Possible Effects on Exports

If British exports, which we can call 'bicycles', have a home cost, including profit, of £10 and were previously sold in the American market for $30, British exporters will now be faced with a different market situation. If they maintain their dollar selling price at $30 they will now make larger sterling profits per bicycle, for $30 will now be worth £12 compared with £10 previously. This consideration alone would ordinarily induce them to sell more bicycles in the U.S.A. and fewer at home and to raise their total output. On the other hand, as British bicycle exporters increase their bicycle shipments to the U.S.A. the American market may not be able to absorb an increase in the number of British bicycles sold without some fall in their *dollar* price.

Whether it will pay British bicycle exporters to sell a relatively small number of bicycles in the American market at a relatively high dollar price or a larger number at a lower dollar price will depend on the conditions of the market. If there is excess capacity in the British bicycle industry, so that the supply of bicycle exports is relatively elastic, a relatively large increase in bicycle shipments to the U.S.A. may follow a fall in the sterling rate of exchange. Given an enlarged supply in the American market, the effect on the *dollar* price of bicycles will depend on how elastic is the American demand for bicycles. If the conditions of supply and demand were such that the outcome was an expansion of bicycle exports from 1 million to 1,100,000 and a fall in the dollar price from $30 to $25 each, the receipts in *sterling* earned from bicycle exports would have increased from £10 million to £11 million, but their total *dollar* value would have fallen from $30 million to $27,500,000. The increase in the *sterling* value of exports would help in alleviating any home unemployment that might have existed, but the fall in the *foreign currency* value of export receipts would in itself aggravate the problem of the balance of payments.

The fall in dollar earnings in this illustration is the result of the impact of an elastic supply of exports on a relatively inelastic demand. The sterling price of bicycles has remained at £10 because of the desire of British manufacturers to increase output and because of their ability to do so without a rise in unit costs, but in face of a reduction in the American price of one-sixth the number of bicycles sold has risen only by one-tenth. Assuming that the devaluation of sterling leads to *some* enlargement of the supply of British bicycles in the American market, their dollar proceeds would be increased only if the elasticity of the American demand were greater than unity. At a new dollar price of $25, at least 1·2 million bicycles would have to be exported for dollar receipts not to be lower in the new situation.

## Possible Effects on Imports

Whereas the dollar value of Britain's exports might actually be reduced by the depreciation of the exchange rate, its effect on the dollar value of imports could not be unhelpful to the balance of payments measured in terms of dollars. If Britain had been importing, say, 12,000 American cars at a dollar cost of $3,000 each and a sterling price of £1,000, the total dollar value of these imports would have been $36 million. If, on a fall in the exchange rate from $3 to $2·5 to the pound, their dollar export price remained unchanged and British demand for these goods at their new sterling price of £1,200 each were to fall to 11,000, the total dollar cost of these imports would be reduced from $36 million to $33 million. If Britain's demand for American cars were more elastic, a rise in their sterling price would produce a greater reduction in the number sold and thus a greater reduction in their total cost in dollars.

## Possible Effects on Supply Price

In this illustration neither the dollar price of American exports nor the sterling price of Britain's exports has changed. American exporters are assumed not to have reacted to a fall in their sales in the British market by reducing their dollar price, and British exporters are assumed to have been in a position in which they could and would raise the quantity exported at a constant sterling price. Both conditions are unlikely to apply in practice; there would probably be some increase in the sterling price of Britain's exports except in the event of severe excess capacity, so that their dollar price would not fall by as much as the change in the exchange rate. This would have the effect of reducing any *loss* of dollars from our exports to the U.S.A. if demand there were inelastic, but of reducing the *gain* if American demand were elastic. If Britain were an important customer for American

20

goods, there would also, it is probable, be a reduction in the dollar price of some American exports, so that their sterling price would not rise by as much as the full change in the exchange rate.

## A Summary

The upshot of this rather complex array of possibilities is that, generally speaking, a country will improve its balance of trade in terms of foreign currency if its demand for imports or the overseas demand for its exports is sufficiently elastic. If foreign demand for its goods were highly inelastic, it is conceivable that the devaluation of a country's currency would react adversely on its balance of trade; and it would actually require the appreciation of the exchange rate for an improvement in the balance of trade to be secured. However, whereas world demand for certain products, especially raw materials with no close substitutes, may not be elastic, the demand for the exports of any one country sold in competition with those of others is likely to be much more sensitive in the long run. Exchange depreciation is also likely to increase the *range* of goods exported by the depreciating country. In practice the situation in which a reduction in the exchange rate of a single country will not cause the balance of trade to improve is a rare one.

Three qualifications to this conclusion have to be noted. First, the conditions of supply and demand may be such that a large degree of depreciation may be needed to achieve a small improvement in the balance of payments. The depreciating country's export prices may fall heavily in terms of foreign currencies if its supply of exports is elastic but if overseas demand is inelastic, causing its terms of trade to deteriorate sharply. This would involve a loss of real national income if the economy were already in a state of full employment. Secondly, exchange depreciation by any one country may be neutralized by retaliatory import restrictions in its main markets or by exchange depreciation on the part of its competitors. Thirdly, an improvement in the balance of trade adds to domestic money incomes and expenditure. If the depreciating country is suffering from inflation, the increase in the profits of exporting industries and the rise in import prices in terms of domestic currency are likely to cause further wage increases. Eventually the balance of payments may deteriorate once more. Exchange depreciation may therefore be a dangerous as well as an ineffective policy for curing the adverse balance of trade of an economy in an inflationary condition; for it to succeed, the government must take steps to check home demand.

## The Exchange Rate and Capital Movements

Exchange depreciation, if it is not regarded merely as the forerunner of a further decline in the exchange rate, may augment a country's foreign exchange reserves by checking a speculative outflow of short-term funds or by attracting a speculative inflow, if it is believed that the new exchange rate is secure or is even likely to be raised before long. An inflow of long-term capital may also be stimulated by exchange depreciation, in that the fear of a fall in the exchange rate might previously have deterred foreign investors from acquiring assets in a country with a weak balance of payments.

### FORWARD EXCHANGE

'Futures' markets exist in foreign currencies as well as in goods, allowing forward commitments to be covered. A British importer who is committed to paying a certain sum in dollars in, say, three months can protect himself against the risk of a rise in the cost of dollars in terms of sterling by purchasing dollars three months forward. In three months' time, that is to say, he will have to pay sterling for dollars at a rate of exchange that is decided at the time he enters into the forward contract. A British exporter who is due to receive dollars in three months can assure himself of a certain payment in sterling by entering into a contract to buy sterling three months forward; in three months' time he will hand over his dollar earnings and receive sterling in return, having protected himself against a rise in the 'spot' price of sterling in terms of dollars during the period.

These contracts will be made with banks acting as foreign exchange dealers. When a bank agrees to provide a currency at a specified rate of exchange at some point of time in the future, it too is entering into a commitment that exposes it to the risk of an adverse movement in exchange rates; and it will normally cover its commitment in one way or another. It may be able to 'marry' forward transactions made in opposite directions, setting off a contract to supply dollars forward against another to purchase dollars forward, so that only its net position exposes it to risk.

In the case of large transactions, however, or when it is evident that the effect of a series of small transactions will be to leave it a net buyer or seller of forward exchange, the bank will take deliberate action to 'hedge'.

It will do this in the first place by matching a forward commitment by buying or selling for immediate delivery, that is by buying or selling 'spot'. If, for example, a bank has undertaken to sell dollars forward, it will immediately buy an equivalent amount 'spot' in order to cover itself against the risk of a rise in the 'spot' price of dollars. Later it will buy the same amount of dollars forward from another dealer and, as it will no longer need its spot dollars, it will sell dollars 'spot'.

Spot and forward rates in a free market will be determined by supply and demand, reflecting four types of transactions. First, there are the commercial transactions of traders and others who will be seeking cover for operations entered into in the normal course of trade. Secondly, there are the transactions of speculators. Thirdly, there are those entered into by financial institutions seeking a high rate of return on short-term funds. Finally, the authorities may intervene in one market or the other.

Given the impact of commercial transactions and any official intervention, speculation and the level of money-market interest rates in different financial centres will determine the margin between spot and forward rates. A speculator who believes that the exchange rate for a currency will fall may sell that currency forward, hoping to complete the transaction by purchasing the currency spot at a lower rate in the future. His action will tend to depress the forward rate in terms of the spot rate. Speculation in favour of a currency will tend to raise the forward rate in terms of the spot rate. Of course, the spot rate, too, may be affected by speculative transactions.

If interest rates are higher in London than in, say, New York, there will be some tendency for banking funds to be attracted to London. But unless their holders are prepared to accept the risk of a fall in the exchange rate for sterling, they will cover themselves by a forward sale of sterling, renewing the transaction if desired when the initial contract matures. Thus the existence of relatively high money-market rates of interest in London will tend to depress the forward rate for sterling in terms of the spot rate.

In the absence of any pressure of speculation in one direction or another, therefore, a currency will tend to stand at a forward discount if its interest rates are relatively high. That is to say, the price of forward pounds will be lower than the price of spot pounds in terms of dollars if British interest rates are higher than those in New York. The size of the forward discount or premium will tend to be related to the difference in interest rates. For example, if the Treasury bill rate in London is 6 per cent per annum when that in New York is 4 per cent, it will not pay a bank with surplus funds to transfer them from New York to London if the forward discount on sterling is greater than 2 per cent of the spot rate, when calculated on an annual basis (ignoring the question of expenses). If the spot rate for sterling were $2.80, for example, the transfer of 'covered' funds would be unprofitable if three-month sterling stood below $2.786. It thus follows that speculation against a currency, by depressing the forward rate, may make it unprofitable to hold funds in a weak financial centre even though its interest rates may be higher than elsewhere.

### FIXED VERSUS FLEXIBLE EXCHANGE RATES

The question of whether fixed exchange rates are preferable to flexible rates is a continuing and complex one that embraces many-sided problems concerning the structure of the world economy and the political wisdom of governments. Traditionally the case for fixed exchange rates is that they provide a necessary element of certainty in financial calculations and thus encourage both international trade and international lending. It is true that the operation of forward exchange markets enables future commitments to be covered, but the cost of forward cover may be prohibitive when it is most needed. Fixed exchange rates have traditionally also received the favour of those to whom the prospect of intervention by governments in the field of exchange manipulation is not an attractive one, partly because of the danger of competitive and therefore continual exchange depreciation, and partly because of the fear that governments will resort to recurrent exchange depreciation in order to reconcile inflation with a balance of foreign payments and so put off the task of preventing inflation itself.

One important argument against fixed exchange rates is that strain in the system of world trade may cause the whole framework to crack where a system of flexible exchange rates would allow it to bend. Before 1914 the special conditions of world trade and finance, the role of Britain, and the seeming assurance of political stability allowed the gold standard to function with success. In the decade following the war, however, the American crash, the growth of protection, and the instability of capital movements imposed too great a strain on fixed exchange rates. For whereas flexible exchange rates may allow disequilibrium between the supply of and demand for a country's currency to be removed by a spontaneous change or series of small changes in the rate of exchange, in a system of fixed exchange rates any disequilibrium that cannot be sustained by transfers of foreign exchange reserves or removed by a change in interest rates will shift the burden of adjustment to a country's domestic level of incomes and prices, and, if its prices and wage-rates are 'sticky', to its level of output.

Through the medium of fixed exchange rates inflation or deflation in one important trading country may spread to another; a country has less freedom of command over its domestic economic conditions if it cannot avoid importing inflation or deflation by allowing its exchange rate to rise or fall. Any distortions of the pattern of world trade owing to import controls and tariffs, or to the failure of creditor countries to import sufficiently to allow debtor countries to discharge their obligations, sets up similar pressures, which may be extended if, as has often been the case, the creditor countries have taken steps to prevent an accumulation of gold under a fixed exchange rate system from leading to an expansion of domestic credit and a sufficient fall in their interest rates.

The argument that through spontaneous and perhaps small variations in exchange rates the supply of and demand for foreign currencies can be kept in continual balance may therefore seem an advantage, especially when the alternative is the prospect of a very large change in exchange rates from time to time. But the matter is not easily decided. For much will depend on just how large these spontaneous variations have to be to keep the foreign exchange market in balance. If a country's economic structure is not in harmony with the course of world trade, or if the latter itself is subject to continuing strains owing to economic and political instability, technical change, or government policy, large fluctuations in exchange rates may conceivably be required to maintain equilibrium even in a system of flexible exchange rates, implying a marked deterioration in the terms of trade and therefore a loss of real national income of the depreciating country. The same might be true if the overseas demand for the exports of a country in balance of payments deficit was relatively inelastic. A spontaneous fall in the exchange rate of a country suffering from inflation may be both ineffective and dangerous; however, it is also true that for a country suffering from persistent inflation, a series of small reductions in the exchange rate may aggravate the pressure of inflation less than do frequent but much larger reductions, for the latter will almost certainly intensify the demand for higher wages, whereas the former may not if wage-rates are in any case tending to move upwards under the force of excess demand.

The size of the variations in exchange rates needed to maintain a balance in the market for foreign currency will also depend on the flow of speculative capital. If a country's exchange rate depreciates owing to the deterioration of its current balance of payments, the movement will be checked if its currency is bought by speculators who expect the depreciation to be temporary. But a country is capable of absorbing a deficit, with fixed exchange rates, if it has sufficient exchange reserves. The critics of fixed exchange rates since the war, however, have usually maintained that the exchange reserves of the United Kingdom, in particular, as a financial centre have been too low to support a fixed exchange rate and that speculation has tended to work against the system rather than with it. For speculation against a financial centre like London may tend to recur just because its reserves are known to be low and, by drawing down its reserves still further, make the prospect of devaluation seem even more likely.

A fixed rate offers a 'one-way option' to the 'bear' speculator, who loses little if the supposedly weak currency is not devalued. With flexible exchange rates, on the other hand, the 'bear' runs the risk of having to 'cover' at a higher exchange rate if his view proves wrong, and the risk may be great if the weak currency is supported by official intervention, and very great indeed if such intervention induces other 'bears' to cover before he can. However, the choice may really be between periodic but intense bouts of speculation and perhaps lighter but probably more widespread and frequent speculation. If large fluctuations in exchange rates were needed to maintain international trade in balance, the risk that speculation would aggravate rather than cushion such fluctuations might be high, for a fall in a weak country's exchange rate might be interpreted as proof of weakness that had previously been only suspected, leading to speculation against, and not in support of, its currency.

For the traditional reasons, therefore, a system of stable exchange rates has been maintained since the war; attempts have been made to augment the reserves of countries in temporary balance-of-payments difficulties, and the use of direct controls over foreign payments has been internationally acceptable in certain circumstances. Under the system periodic adjustments in exchange parties, as in 1949, are not ruled out.

### DIRECT CONTROLS AND THE BALANCE OF PAYMENTS

#### Control over Capital Movements

The disruptive effect of speculative capital movements may lead to the imposition of official restrictions on capital transactions. Exchange controls may be used to support an exchange rate that would otherwise be under pressure or to enable an independent monetary policy to be pursued by a country with a fixed exchange rate; they may be aimed at preventing either an outflow or an inflow of speculative capital or used to prevent an outflow of long-term capital due to a lack of sympathy with a government's political or economic policy towards owners of property. Capital movements in the form of 'leads' and 'lags' are hardly controllable, except in so far as restrictions on bank loans to non-residents may prevent overseas importers from borrowing a country's currency in order to delay having to part with their own in order to settle their debts. Controls over capital transactions cannot be taken far by any country, such as Britain, that seeks to maintain its position as an international banker.

#### Controls over Exports and Imports

Export subsidies may seem an attractive alternative to devaluation to a government faced with balance-of-payments difficulties, if the foreign demand for its products is elastic. But they are effective only if they are not copied by competing exporting countries, and are generally regarded, with justification, as internationally to be deplored. If a country's exports are sold in conditions of inelastic demand, taxes on exports may improve its balance of payments, but, it is probable, so would the appreciation of its exchange rate.

Direct controls over imports for balance-of-payments reasons are more common. In the form of either quotas or tariffs they may appear less unattractive to governments than devaluation, for economic as well as political reasons. Any improvement in the balance of current payments is inflationary when full employment already exists, but import restrictions may be slightly less inflationary than devaluation if, as they may do in certain cases, they avoid the worsening of the terms of trade that devaluation may involve. Import restrictions may also seem attractive to a government that believes that it can choose better than the community acting through the price mechanism as to what are 'essential' and what are 'non-essential' imports. It may hope to influence the distribution of real incomes in this way.

Governments may also be attracted to the belief that a balance-of-payments deficit caused by an excess of home demand should be tackled 'directly' by import controls, while the domestic condition of the economy can be treated separately. This distinction is largely fallacious. Any policy that removes excess demand will improve the balance of payments, whereas a policy that relies on import controls and leaves domestic demand at an inflationary level only aggravates the domestic situation and thereby ultimately defeats itself; if a country's costs are too high import controls are also likely to prove ineffective. Import controls that fall with special force on certain overseas countries may also lead to retaliation, whereas the effect of exchange depreciation on the exports of other countries is usually more widely dispersed.

### Discriminatory Controls

Discrimination consists of applying controls on transactions with another country or group of countries that are not imposed, or not with the same force, on the rest of the world. Discrimination means the substitution of some measure of bilateral for multilateral balancing in international trade. If country B has a deficit with country A, it can use the proceeds of its surplus with C to pay for its deficit with A, if international currencies are freely convertible into each other. But if C will not allow its debt to B to be transferred to A the balance between A and B and between

B and C will have to be adjusted bilaterally; imports and exports will have to be matched for these pairs of countries separately.

This situation may arise if country A tends to have a persistent surplus with both B and C and if C's holdings of A's currency (or gold) are not sufficient for C to use them to finance both her current deficit with A and that with B. C may have a large surplus with a fourth country, D, so that C's trade may be in overall balance, but D may have a deficit with A so that D is unable to pay C in A's currency. In these circumstances, in which A's currency is generally 'scarce', deficit countries may prefer to concentrate on reducing their deficit with A alone by discriminatory measures rather than to adjust their trade with all countries taken together, by cutting their imports from countries which are already in deficit, thus forcing them to reduce *their* imports still further, and so on. Trade between the discriminating countries may instead be held at a relatively high level.

The justification for this discrimination might be that country A was not pursuing an appropriate creditor policy, instead restricting imports in order to protect her own industries. Alternatively, A's persistent surplus might arise from the pressure of demand for her goods owing to chronic inflation elsewhere, or to her greater efficiency, or to the disruption of productive capacity in the rest of the world as a result of war. Some of A's goods might seem so 'essential' that other countries might regard her currency as especially desirable and not to be given up in settlement of deficits with countries other than A. All this, of course, ignores the question of the relative prices of the 'scarce' and other currencies, but discrimination against A might seem a preferable alternative to exchange depreciation by the deficit countries if a very large reduction in their exchange rates would be required to maintain a multilateral balance of payments.

Post-war international trade has borne some resemblance to this situation. The experience of a persistent dollar shortage at the existing level of exchange rates led the United Kingdom and certain other countries to impose discriminatory trade restrictions on 'non-essential' imports from the U.S.A. and other dollar-area countries such as Canada and Cuba, in order to conserve their holdings of dollars. Furthermore, the United Kingdom has restricted the freedom of overseas holders of sterling to exchange it for dollars. This is the problem of the restricted convertibility of sterling. Discrimination may also be a means whereby the impact on international trade of a slump in a major trading country like the U.S.A. can be softened in the rest of the world, but it has not so far been used in this way.

The development of the discriminatory system of Imperial Preference before the war has already been indicated. Imperial Preference was aimed generally at providing a secure market for the produce of other Commonwealth countries in return for preferences on British manufactures, but the growth of industry in the Commonwealth countries anxious to protect themselves from competition from British goods, the desire of certain Commonwealth countries to increase their exports of primary products outside the system, as in the case of Australia and her sales of wool to Japan, and the need of Britain to increase her trade with the rapidly growing markets of Europe, have since tended to weaken the support given to the whole system.

Bilateral agreements may be forced on small and weak countries by larger ones who are their main markets for goods the supply of which cannot easily be diverted elsewhere. The larger countries can require the weaker countries to take specified amounts of their own goods at relatively high prices, as a condition for continuing to purchase the exports of the weaker. Both Germany and Britain practised this policy before the war.

Since January 1948 the General Agreement on Trade and Tariffs has been in operation. G.A.T.T. has been accepted by thirty-five countries and represents an attempt to secure a reduction in tariff rates by round-table bargaining. The key intention of G.A.T.T. is to reduce the welter of discriminatory tariffs by imposing the Most Favoured Nation technique of tariff reduction. Each contracting party is obliged to accord unconditionally to all other parties all new advantages, favours, privileges and immunities which it may in future grant to other countries. There is also a code of 'good behaviour' regarding various aspects of trade, such as customs regulations, quotas, and subsidies. Under G.A.T.T., periodical reductions in tariffs have been negotiated since 1948.

# CHAPTER 40

# BRITAIN AND THE INTERNATIONAL ECONOMIC BACKGROUND 1914–39

The object of this chapter and the next is to sketch in very broad outline some of the main economic changes of the past fifty years that help to throw light on the international economic problems of the world in general, and those of Britain in particular, since the war.

### THE PRE-1914 WORLD—THE HEYDAY OF BRITAIN

Before 1914 the network of international trade and payments was multilateral, with convertible currencies and a large area of free trade. The system was dominated by Britain but was also sustained by her. Britain provided an open, expanding, and relatively stable market for foodstuffs and raw materials. Her imports of primary products, together with her long-term lending, enabled the rest of the world to pay for Britain's exports. The stability of exchange rates and the creditworthiness of governments seemed assured. The gold standard worked, not without strain as far as countries other than Britain were concerned, but smoothly enough in the twenty years or so before the outbreak of war, in which the volume of international trade was growing fairly rapidly and in which the flexible lending facilities provided by London as the world's banker could be drawn on to tide over temporary difficulties.

Even before the disruption caused by the First World War, it can now be seen, the seeds of future economic adversity were being sown for this country. Britain's prosperity depended on her exports, which accounted for about 30 per cent of her national income in 1913, and especially on three groups of products: coal (we exported almost a hundred million tons in 1913), iron manufactures, and cotton textiles. In the years 1911–13 textiles as a whole made up one-half of Britain's exports of manufactured goods.

By 1914 Britain had already lost her industrial if not her financial supremacy. Britain's iron and steel output, which forty years earlier had exceeded the combined total of Germany and the U.S.A., had been surpassed by both. The rate of expansion of Britain's engineering trades was now slower than in France, Germany, and the U.S.A., and, what was of much greater significance, Britain had lagged in the application of the new chemical and steel techniques and in the development of the internal-combustion engine. European and American markets for British cotton textile exports were contracting owing to an increase in the production of these countries, a phenomenon later to be repeated in our markets in Asia.

Britain's industrial expansion in the second half of the nineteenth century was based on a share in world trade of manufactured goods that simply could not be maintained once other countries had developed industrially. In the closing years of the seventies this share was nearly two-fifths; by 1911-13 it had fallen to not much more than a quarter. In general, foreign competition was growing where Britain once had no rivals; and where British exports and British capital had once found rich and undeveloped markets, industrialization was taking place, often behind protective tariffs. Sooner or later our basic exports of iron products and simple consumer goods like textiles were bound to face shrinking markets, or at least markets that were growing less rapidly than our own imports.

In the twenty years before the outbreak of war in 1914, however, the decline of Britain's exports relatively to those of other countries was masked by the growth of world trade in manufactured goods as a whole. The need for adjustment was also postponed by the improvement in our terms of trade in this period and by the growth of our 'invisible' exports; Britain dominated world shipping, insurance, and banking, and a rising income flowed in from our substantial overseas investments.

### 1919-1929—INTERNATIONAL UNEASINESS AND BRITISH STAGNATION

The end of the war was followed by a short but sharp restocking boom, brought to an end by restrictive credit policies and by the arrival in Europe of the materials and foodstuffs which had accumulated in other countries during the war. The trough of the ensuing slump, which was equally sharp, was over by 1923, but in the remainder of this period Britain did not share in the experience of high employment and output recorded by other countries outside central Europe. Britain's production and exports did not regain their pre-war volume, and the lowest proportion of insured people out of work was 8 per cent, the average for 1927. This poor performance, during a period in which world manufacturing production is thought to have averaged one-quarter more than its pre-war level, is attributable to three factors.

First, the authorities pursued a policy with a deflationary bias. It was decided after the war to return to the gold standard, which had been suspended in 1914, at the pre-war parity. In order to bring the exchange rate, which was now a flexible one, back to its pre-war level, the balance of payments had to be kept in surplus; but as during this period the United Kingdom, although lending less than before the war, was tending to lend abroad on long-term more than its surplus on current account, recurrent restrictive monetary pressure had to be applied. Any policy of high interest rates undertaken by the U.S.A., such as that implemented to damp down the American boom after 1923, had to be reproduced here, in order to prevent an outflow of short-term funds. Of even greater importance was the fact that the British price-level, which, not surprisingly, had risen more than the American during the war, had to be reduced in relation to that of the United States, a policy which involved restraining the level of demand in this country in relation to that in the U.S.A. This task was intensified by the fact that American prices did not rise much in the boom of 1924–9 owing to a rapid increase in manufacturing productivity and a fall in American agricultural prices.

Secondly, one important stimulus to recovery in the United States and in continental Europe—a housing boom—did not develop in Britain, partly because of a combination of high building costs and high interest rates.

The third and most important reason was the weakened position of Britain within an international framework that had itself changed to this country's disadvantage.

The return to gold at the pre-war parity in 1925 handicapped our exports. It is now generally accepted that, on the basis of the relative movement in American and British wage-costs since 1914, this parity amounted to an over-valuation of sterling perhaps by about 10 per cent. Its long-term effect was perhaps most unfavourable in discouraging the development of new export industries, but the contemporary burden was heaviest in the staple export trades, above all in coal. The general strike in 1926, like the industrial unrest which preceded it, was in great measure due to the deflationary stresses that accompanied the restoration of the pre-war rate of exchange. Britain's coal output never reached its pre-war level, and her coal exports did so only during the occupation of the Ruhr. Other countries raised their coal output and imported an increasing volume from Germany and Poland. The use of coal abroad was also restricted by the development of fuel oil and by technical economies in the production of gas and electricity.

The history of the cotton trade in this period is also one of decline. By 1925 world consumption of cotton textiles had regained its pre-war level, but world trade in cotton textiles was considerably smaller than in 1913. Lancashire was producing and exporting less than before the war, continuing to lose ground to Japan. Wool textile exports were also adversely affected by the increasing self-sufficiency of our previous markets. Our exports of iron and steel manufactures had suffered from the expansion of domestic production elsewhere, from growing competition by Germany and other countries, and from the succession of the iron by the steel age, in which we were not the leader.

Throughout the twentieth century the need for Britain to adapt herself to three sorts of changes has been a recurrent theme in almost every discussion of our underlying economic problems, namely: the emergence of other and even more powerful industrial nations; the ability of our erstwhile markets to provide for themselves the consumer goods and industrial equipment in which we once excelled; and the technical shift away from the cotton, iron, and steam age. Britain's difficulties in the inter-war years were due partly to her dependence on exports of goods in which international trade was undergoing an absolute or a relative decline. In 1929 textiles still accounted for over two-fifths of our exports of manufactured goods, whereas Germany and the U.S.A. were striding ahead in the production of the newer forms of consumer goods, vehicles, and industrial tools that were enjoying expanding international markets. The failure of Britain to adapt herself to a changing world was as important as the over-valuation of the pound; although it may have been aggravated by it. At the same time, our markets in the Empire were no longer growing rapidly; the increase in world agricultural and mineral capacity caused by the expansion of agriculture outside Europe during the war and its recovery in Europe after 1918 caused commodity prices to fall, thereby restricting the growth of incomes in the primary producing countries, whose purchases of manufactures were also adversely affected by a growing spirit of protection.

Finally, the international monetary scene had altered sufficiently to disrupt the working of the gold standard. The stability of currencies could no longer be taken for granted following the great inflations of Germany and Austria. The obligation to render large payments to international creditors, on balance to the U.S.A. and France, on account of reparations and inter-ally debts, imposed upon Germany and other countries the need to obtain large export surpluses in a period in which almost every other country, with the exception of Britain but including the chief creditor, the United States, was trying to keep down its imports by means of protective tariffs. The 'rules' of the gold standard were not followed by central banks either, for the effect of the inflow of gold on their domestic monetary situation was neutralized by the authorities in both the U.S.A. and France. Gold and foreign exchange reserves thus became concentrated in the hands of the creditor countries. To these sources of instability were added the powerful shocks caused by the rush of 'hot' money from one country to another.

The world had experienced monetary disturbances before, but the financial mechanism whereby shocks had previously been absorbed had undergone an important change. The undisputed dominance of the financial world by London had given way to a system with two centres, London and New York. Before 1914 the flexible short-term and long-term capital facilities of London provided buffers that could be stretched or contracted easily, according to the direction in which gold had to flow to preserve international equilibrium, minimizing the adjustments that had to be made on current account. But now London's gold reserves were too small for them to support the operations of a major centre with comfort, whereas an attempt by Britain to rebuild her reserves by reducing her overseas lending would have been incompatible with the position of world banker to which she still aspired.

The development of a two-centre system meant that one was likely to be under chronic strain from movements in funds to the stronger, setting up pressures from which a one-centre system was relatively free. The burdens of war and the changes in international trade had weakened London as a financial centre, and whereas the old centre was soft, the new was hard. That is to say, London was an abundant lender, whereas psychologically and institutionally New York was less suited to the role that events had thrust upon her. New York, for example, was less likely to match a short-term capital inflow by re-lending on long-term account. Whereas the operation of the London discount and new-issue markets before 1914 had served to keep funds moving in each direction, to and from London, New York was more likely to become a persistent international liquidity 'trap'.

### THE COLLAPSE OF THE GOLD STANDARD

When the speculative boom on Wall Street broke in the autumn of 1929 American financial institutions began hurriedly to call in their loans from other countries as they fell due, in order to maintain their own liquidity. With the collapse of American lending the major debtor countries, Germany and Austria, were placed in financial difficulties that led eventually to a number of bank failures there in 1931. Against a background in which the sharp break in commodity prices and the onset of the American slump had already strained the fabric of international trade, an international liquidity crisis then developed.

To this, London was forced to succumb. Britain had substantial long-term investments, but these could not be easily realized. She was also owed short-term loans, but those in Austria and Germany were frozen by moratoria. The gold reserves of London were not large enough to cope with the outflow of short-term funds, a movement that was hastened by the political crisis in Britain at the time and coincided with a serious deterioration in Britain's current account. Britain was forced to leave the gold standard in September 1931, and the exchange rate was allowed to go free at a lower level. The depreciation of sterling was followed by a number of other countries practically at once. Within a year foreign exchange controls were in operation in more than twenty countries, and a long list of countries, including Britain, felt obliged to adopt or intensify import duties or quotas.

An attempt was made to patch up the broken framework. The burden of war debts was lightened, and a World Economic Conference was summoned to meet in June 1933 to consider the resumption of international lending, the liberalization of trade, and the restoration of the gold standard. Whether or not this attempt at salvage would have succeeded we cannot know, for the conference disbanded following the shock of America's decision to devalue. Her action was taken not so much to protect her own reserves, which were immense, but to assist her internal recovery from the slump and to counter what was considered the 'competitive' devaluation of sterling. In 1936 France, the last of the major countries to adhere to the gold standard at the old parity, was finally forced to devalue.

Following the devaluation of the franc the desire to avoid another cycle of exchange instability led the U.S.A., France and the United Kingdom to agree not to undertake major alterations in their exchange rates without consultation; this tripartite agreement was later joined by Switzerland, Holland and Belgium. To this extent one aspect of the gold standard, the stability (if not the fixity) of exchange rates, was largely restored. In Britain it was no longer possible to buy or sell gold at a fixed price, but by the operation of the foreign exchange market sterling could be freely converted into other currencies at the current rate of exchange; day-to-day disturbances were softened by the operation of the Exchange Equalization Account set up in 1932. The final relationship between the pound, the dollar, and the franc was not very different from what it had been before Britain left the gold standard in 1931.

## THE EMERGENCE OF THE STERLING AREA

The depreciation of sterling in 1931 brought into relief what was soon to be described as the 'sterling bloc' but is now known as the 'sterling area'. Under the pre-war gold standard the major part of world trade had been conducted in sterling, much of it being financed by short-term loans raised in London, especially through the medium of the 'bill on London'. Foreign banks and other institutions had found it convenient to keep their working balances in London, where they could earn interest that gold did not, and where they could at any time be converted into gold at a fixed price if not used, as they so often were, to finance payments to other countries equally willing to hold sterling.

In the post-war decade, a sterling-using group was beginning to emerge on a more formal level, for a number of countries, following the example of India, adhered to a sterling exchange standard, holding their reserves in sterling and linking their exchange rates to the pound, which after 1925 meant being on the gold standard at one remove.

With the depreciation of sterling in 1931 the division of the world into different currency groups became clear. In the Western Hemisphere currencies were closely related to the dollar, while in Europe a number of countries relied on exchange and import controls to maintain, eventually with little success, their nominal attachment to the gold standard. When Britain left the gold standard a number of other countries, chiefly Eire and the other members of the Commonwealth other than Canada, which was half in and half out of the dollar area, pursued a policy of maintaining their exchange rate at a stable level in relation to the pound and of holding a substantial part of their reserves in sterling. They were shortly joined by several other countries, particularly the Scandinavian countries, Argentina, and Japan.

All the countries in the sterling bloc were closely dependent on their trade with Britain, and the Commonwealth members of the group had close banking and other financial ties with the mother country. Several advantages were to be obtained by the members of the group. The pound was still used to finance a large part of the world's trade, so that it was convenient to hold reserves in London, and the fact that the British domestic economy suffered less severely than most from the slump offered some hope of economic stability.

## 1929-39—TRADE DEPRESSION AND PARTIAL REVIVAL

The severity of the international depression was due largely to the force of the slump in the U.S.A. and its effect on international trade. With the cessation of the housing boom and the diminution of the previous stimulus to investment provided by the development of the motor-car and the spread of the railway network and electricity supply system, some recession in the U.S.A. was perhaps inevitable. But the downward spiral was intensified to an unprecedented extent; the crash on Wall Street shattered business confidence and caused a scramble for liquidity at a time when the level of business and farm indebtedness was relatively high. But the main cause of the severity of the slump is regarded by many economists to have been the utter collapse of commodity prices, which caused huge losses in company accounts, depressed business confidence still further and, by causing ruin in the farming areas of the United States, forced many American banks to suspend payment between 1930 and 1932.

The sharp fall in American industrial production of one-half between 1929 and 1932 reduced her imports of raw materials and, because of the weight of the United States in international trade, was transmitted to other countries. The world slump was aggravated still further by the drying up of international lending and the international monetary crisis. Between 1929 and 1932 world production of manufactured goods fell by 30 per cent, but world trade in these products fell by two-fifths, largely because of the collapse in the purchasing power of the agricultural and raw-material-producing countries, which still took the bulk of world exports of manufacturers. Whereas the average price of manufactured goods entering world trade in these three years is thought to have fallen by less than two-fifths, international raw-material and foodstuff prices fell by about one-half.

World revival began in 1932 and continued until 1937. But whereas world production of manufactured goods in 1937 was about one-fifth higher than in 1929, world trade in manufactured goods was still more than one-tenth lower. For the slow recovery of world trade in manufactures the low level of commodity prices, the indebtedness of the primary-producing countries at a time of low international investment, and the spread of import restrictions were responsible. World prices began to move up sharply in 1937 until the outbreak of recession in the U.S.A. late in that year, but on this occasion the effect of the American slump in other countries was checked by rearmament.

The United Kingdom had not shared to any great extent in the boom and suffered less than other manufacturing countries from the world depression; in the three years to 1929 industrial output in Britain fell by about 15 per cent, compared with a drop of one-half in the U.S.A. and Germany. After 1932 recovery got under way in Britain, impelled by the stimulus given to building by the cheap-money policy, a cyclical upswing in the demand for houses, by the enlargement of the public's purchasing power caused by the fall in import prices, by the development of the newer industries, and later by rearmament. But even at the outbreak of war in 1939 full employment had not been experienced for almost twenty years.

BRITAIN AND INTERNATIONAL TRADE 1931–9

Britain's import duties played a minor role in her economic revival, and her position in international trade continued to deteriorate. Sterling was still overvalued in relation to Britain's wage costs. Her textile exports came under intense pressure from Japanese competition, and the share of Britain's exports taking the form of producer goods and the newer consumer goods, although rising, was still insufficient. Britain attempted to support her exports by means of bilateral agreements. Under the Ottawa Agreement of 1932 Britain and the Dominions agreed to grant each other preferential rates of tariff; the Colonies were obliged to grant preferences to the United Kingdom, with severe restrictions on the importation of Japanese textiles. Other small countries, e.g. Scandinavia and the Baltic states, who were especially dependent on the British market, were persuaded to increase the share of their purchases provided by Britain, with special provisions for expanding the sale of British coal.

These measures, which for the most part merely exploited Britain's bargaining and political power, certainly had the result of maintaining her share in the trade of these countries. But whether the net effect was to this country's advantage is doubtful. The countries excluded by these agreements transferred their efforts to other markets, in which Britain was forced to give ground, and bought less from our Commonwealth customers, whose total demand for imports was probably not much increased, if at all, by these discriminatory arrangements. In so far as Lancashire gained, the Colonies that were deprived of cheap Japanese textiles lost.

Despite these measures, which might have provoked retaliation sooner or later, Britain's share of world trade continued to decline. In the twenties the deterioration of this country's position in visible trade had been masked by the increase in her invisible income. Because of the world slump in shipping and the fall in the return on British-owned investments in primary production in the Commonwealth, this, too, declined. In the thirties, however, the improvement in her terms of trade caused by the steep decline in the prices of agricultural products and raw materials came to Britain's assistance, and until the devaluation of the franc there was an inflow of short-term funds. These postponed the need for structural readjustment, but even so Britain's balance of payments on current account was in chronic deficit during the thirties, and on the outbreak of war we were already living on our past accumulation of foreign assets.

# CHAPTER 41

# BRITAIN AND THE INTERNATIONAL ECONOMIC BACKGROUND SINCE THE WAR

## POST-WAR STRUCTURAL PROBLEMS

The Second World War caused a great distortion of world trade that would have given rise to immense economic problems even if appropriate financial policies had been followed in all countries. The magnitude of this strain can now been seen more clearly than in 1945, when the hope of a 'return to normal' obscured the clarity of contemporary economic observation; in considering the brief description of post-war problems that follows, that we have the gift of hindsight must not be forgotten.

Broadly speaking, the war enriched the Western Hemisphere, Australasia and some parts of Africa, but disrupted Europe's productive capacity, forced belligerent countries to run down their exchange reserves and their overseas investments, and left some of them encumbered with debts. This net loss of overseas assets was most important in the case of the United Kingdom.

The pattern of trade had altered greatly to Europe's disadvantage. The terms of trade had shifted sharply against manufacturing countries and in favour of most agricultural and raw-material producers, for the output of foodstuffs and materials was relatively inelastic in the short run, whereas the demand for them had been greatly increased as a result of full employment and inflation in the manufacturing world. The exportable surpluses of the primary-producing countries in Australasia and South America were also diminished by the increase in home demand caused by inflation and by the shift of resources away from agriculture to industry in these areas. In South-East Asia and in Europe the output of agricultural products had been greatly reduced as a result of war, which, together with the existence of full employment, led to a much higher level of demand for imports than before the war. An abnormally high proportion of this demand became concentrated on the U.S.A. and Canada, for it was here that the output of grains, cotton, fats and oils, metals, and hides had expanded.

It was in this urgent demand for dollar food and materials that the post-war 'dollar shortage' first became apparent. With the deterioration in their terms of trade, it imposed upon European countries the necessity for earning a very much higher level of dollars, in real terms, than before the war, either directly from the U.S.A. or from other countries which themselves earned dollar surpluses. In the earlier post-war years, at any rate, the possibility of a great expansion of Europe's exports of manufactured goods to the U.S.A., itself the world's greatest manufacturing country, seemed none too bright. In the immediate post-war alignment of costs and exchange rates there was no wide range of goods in which European producers were in an obviously more favourable position. As for those in which Europe did have the advantage in price or design the American market seemed an uncertain one, prone to internal recession and the imposition of tariff or other restrictions on those imports which managed to surmount a cumbersome Customs procedure and to pay for the cost of setting up expensive sales services. Europe's inflation restricted her exports in general.

The U.S.A.'s imports, although higher than before the war, had not kept pace with her national income, and they were concentrated on goods drawn from those countries where, by and large, European exporters were at a disadvantage. American prosperity provided most benefit to Canada, with its paper and metals, and to South America, with its coffee and oil. Here political ties with the U.S.A. and the predominance of American capital put European countries at a disadvantage, so that it was not easy for them to earn dollars indirectly. As for the rest of the world, dollars could be earned there, but one important change had occurred for the worse: the American policy of maintaining a fixed dollar price for gold, when other commodity prices had increased, reduced the real value of the stock of gold held as international monetary reserves. It also restricted the dollar value of South Africa's gold output; this had played an important part in the triangular route by which Britain and other countries had paid for their dollar imports before the war.

The result of this combination of factors was to present Western

Europe with an unsupportable dollar deficit in its balance of payments if the demand for dollar imports were to go unchecked, and one that would have been formidable enough in the absence of inflation, which heightened it. There were various possible solutions. But deflation to the point of serious unemployment, the remedy of the gold standard, was out of the question, and adjustment merely by exchange depreciation after the war to whatever level of exchange rates would have balanced an unrestricted demand for dollars with their supply would have caused a further serious deterioration in Europe's terms of trade at a time when inflation made devaluation a dangerous expedient. Some reduction in Europe's real income, in the form of an increase in exports and the restriction of imports, was inevitable, but this could be minimized by the use of controls.

That the end of the war would bring problems of reconstruction was clear and that their solution called for international co-operation was accepted. In 1944 an international conference was held at Bretton Woods in the United States to consider the steps required to restore world trade on the return of peace. The desire of the American government to moderate the restriction of imports from the U.S.A. contributed to its preoccupation with hastening the return to a multilateral system; the British approach laid more emphasis on the possibility that a post-war American slump would force the rest of the world to resort to desperate restrictive measures unless an international credit mechanism were established and some measure of discrimination allowed. At Bretton Woods the American view generally prevailed, but neither side appreciated fully the magnitude of what came to be known as the dollar shortage; and that inflation rather than deflation would constitute the chief monetary problem of the post-war world was not foreseen.

The size of the adjustment needed to restore a dollar balance, and the speed with which it had to be done in view of the inadequacy of Europe's foreign exchange reserves, made complete reliance on the free play of supply and demand intolerable. Some measure of control over imports and foreign exchange transactions proved unavoidable, and controls discriminating against dollar payments were retained by most countries outside North America. With the passage of time these restrictions have come to bear less heavily on transactions within the non-dollar world—that is on payments between countries other than the United States, Canada, and some of the Latin-American republics—and gradually their impact on dollar payments has lost part of its force as the worst of the dollar shortage has been overcome.

Even so, American assistance has proved necessary on a scale the generosity of which is without precedent. During the period between the end of the war and the beginning of the 'Marshall Plan' in April 1948, the United States provided the rest of the world with aid to the amount of nearly $16,000 million, of which about three-quarters went to Western and Southern Europe. The American government's appreciation of the grievous state of the European economy in 1947 led to the European Recovery Plan— the 'Marshall Plan'—under which aid totalling $13,600 million was given to Western Europe between 1948 and 1950. Britain received $2,784 million of this total. Within the next five years, in which the Korean war placed fresh defence burdens on European economies, American foreign aid appropriations came to $28,000 million; of this, about one-half represented military equipment. During this period Britain received $986 million.

In all, the U.S.A. made available, through loans or gifts in cash and kind, about $51,000 million net in the ten years following the end of the war, of which Western Europe received $33,000 million and the United Kingdom alone some $8,000 million, $3,750 million of this taking the form of the 1946 loan. The assistance given by the U.S.A. over these ten years represents roughly double the gold and dollar reserves possessed by the main receiving areas at the end of the period.

The supply of dollars has also been raised by American private lending. But the contribution this has made to Europe's dollar reserves has been small, for the bulk of the U.S.A.'s foreign investments are held in Canada and the Latin-American republics, in the form of direct investments in oil, mining, and manufacturing facilities, the products of which can usually be bought only for dollars; they have served, indeed, to reduce the dependence of the U.S.A. on other, non-dollar, sources of supply. Private American investment abroad still plays, and is likely to continue to do so in these days of unsettled political conditions, a much smaller part in promoting world trade than did British investment before the First World War.

INTERNATIONAL MONETARY INSTITUTIONS

The Bretton Woods conference envisaged that, after an initial post-war period of conversion and reconstruction, in which American assistance and some measure of direct control over international payments would be necessary, rapid progress could be made towards a system of liberal and multilateral trade in which currencies would be freely convertible, at least for current if not for capital transactions. The general philosophy expressed at Bretton Woods looked to a return to arrangements not unlike those of the gold standard, in so far as convertibility and the general stability of exchange rates were concerned, but free from the defects and rigidities of that system.

All countries were expected to maintain a high and stable level of employment, avoiding both the extremes of deflation and inflation that, under the gold standard, transferred similar strains to the domestic economy of other countries. In certain circumstances the imposition of controls, including discriminatory controls and those over capital transactions, was foreseen as an alternative to the fluctuations in interest rates, prices, and employment by which adjustments in the balance of payments were secured in the strict operation of the gold standard. As a last resort devaluation was also to be permitted, but only after international consultation. To ease the path of international adjustment by the provision of credit and to supply the rules of this system with some explicit constitutional authority, two international bodies were established, the International Monetary Fund and the International Bank for Reconstruction and Development.

### The International Monetary Fund

About sixty countries belong to the I.M.F., the chief non-members being New Zealand, the U.S.S.R., and the other Communist countries of Eastern Europe. The Fund plays two parts, administering the rules of the new system and pooling credit.

The most important of the rules is that each member must declare a 'par value' for its currency in terms of gold and prevent fluctuations in its exchange rate beyond 1 per cent on either side of that par value; the United Kingdom chose a par value, when the Fund commenced operations in March 1947, equivalent to a rate of exchange of $4.03=£1, reduced to $2.80 in September, 1949. If a country wishes to change its par value by more than 10 per cent it is obliged under the rules to consult the Fund in advance.

In order to protect the system of stable exchange rates against temporary disturbances the Fund incorporates a credit pooling arrangement. The I.M.F. cannot create international credit; it can only lend the gold and currencies that have been deposited with it. Each member has a quota, expressed in U.S. dollars and related to the size of its pre-war trade. Quotas determine the voting power and the subscription of each member and the normal limitations on its use of the Fund's resources.

Each member must pay to the Fund a subscription equal to its quota, not more than 75 per cent being payable in its own currency and the remainder in gold or U.S. dollars. Quotas at 30 April 1958 totalled the equivalent of $9,000 million, of which that of the United States represented $2,750 million and that of the United Kingdom $1,300 million. The Fund's resources are made available essentially on a short-term and revolving basis. Members may purchase from the Fund gold and foreign currency in return for an equivalent amount of their own currency. Generally, a member's purchases of gold and foreign exchange may not exceed the point at which they would cause the Fund's holdings of its currency to increase by more than 25 per cent of its quota during any twelve-month period, nor if the purchase would cause the Fund's total holdings of its currency to exceed twice the amount of its quota. The limit to a member's purchases of gold or foreign currency therefore depends not only on its previous drawings but also on the purchases of its own currency by other countries. In addition, however, 'standby' arrangements can be made to assure the right of a member to the Fund's resources up to specified limits and within an agreed period, without reconsideration of the member's position vis-à-vis the Fund at the actual time of drawing.

Drawings are expected to be repaid, as a general rule, in not more than three to five years, unless reduced by the purchase of the member's currency by another member. Repayments are also expected if a member's monetary reserves increase materially. Interest charges are imposed on purchases from the Fund; these charges are increased the larger the drawings made by a country in relation to its quota and the longer the period during which the Fund holds its currency.

These arrangements are designed to enable member countries to cope with purely temporary balance-of-payments difficulties without the need for exchange depreciation or severe import restrictions. The contingencies envisaged included seasonal strains, capital movements, and crop failures, for example. An alteration in a member's par rate of exchange was envisaged only if the country's balance of payments was in a state of 'fundamental disequilibrium', a condition that was never precisely defined. If one country is in such persistent balance-of-payments surplus that drawings on the Fund's holding of its currency by other members 'seriously threatens the Fund's ability to supply that currency' (Section 3), the Fund is empowered to declare it a 'scarce currency'. In this case the Fund can ration its remaining supply, and the other members can discriminate against the same currency in order to avoid the need for pointless restrictions among themselves. It is not clear whether such a situation would imply a 'fundamental disequilibrium' on the part of the surplus country, calling for an upwards revaluation of its exchange rate; Section 3 was mainly designed to deal with the consequences of an American slump.

The Fund has not been a great success. It provided for a moderate and temporary American recession; its founders did not foresee the emergency of a persistent dollar shortage due to more lasting causes. The cost of the cold war, the inability of member countries to prevent inflation, and a tendency to prefer direct controls rather than other measures have also induced members to disregard the Fund's rules. Speculative movements of short-term funds have been larger and more difficult to handle than had been foreseen. The cumbersome administrative arrangements of the Fund make consultation almost impossible if secrecy regarding exchange-rate adjustments is to be maintained, and the rules of the Fund make no provision for the special circumstances in which a world currency like sterling is used.

Several countries have ignored even the rules concerning stability of exchange rates; some, especially in South America, have operated systems of multiple exchange rates, and France, Canada and certain other members have allowed their exchange rates to fluctuate without declaring a formal par value. In 1949 the pound was devalued by 30 per cent in terms of the dollar, taking many other currencies with it, without real consultation with the Fund.

The scale of post-war economic problems was greatly under-estimated when the Fund was set up. Gross drawings from the Fund up to 30 April 1958 amounted to $3,016 million, a small sum compared with the scale on which U.S. assistance has been pro-vided by loans and grants. In recent years, however, there have been signs that the lending activities of the Fund have at last been coming to life, and $1,800 million of this total of drawings was provided ⁚ ı the period after 1955. In December 1956, for example, in order to meet a sudden lack of confidence in sterling during the Suez crisis, the United Kingdom obtained from the Fund a drawing of $561 million and a standby arrangement for $739 million.

## The World Bank

The International Bank for Reconstruction and Development, often described as the 'World Bank', was set up as a result of the Bretton Woods conference to meet a different need, that of development rather than payments. It was intended partly to fill the gap left by the decline in long-term international lending and also to provide funds for worthwhile projects which, because of their large scale or their very long-term nature, would not ordinarily attract private finance. The Bank lends only on government projects or those that receive a government guarantee; it therefore confines itself to fixed-interest loans.

The capital of the Bank is $10,000 million. One-fifth of its members' subscriptions are paid up, the remainder being callable to meet the Bank's obligations on account of loans it has raised itself. Two per cent of a member's subscription is paid in gold or dollars, the remainder being payable in the member's own currency. At the end of 1957 the Bank's available resources amounted to $3,375 million, of which $1,321 million represented payments of subscriptions and $1,269 million funds raised by the Bank on bonds issued in the U.S.A., the United Kingdom, Canada, Switzerland, and Holland. The remainder consisted largely of repayments of principal, and of loans by the Bank which had been transferred to other lenders. In the eleven years in which the Bank had been functioning by the end of 1957, it had disbursed over $2,500 million, about 80 per cent in dollars, in loans made in more than forty countries. It has also provided valuable technical advice to its customers. The Bank has pursued a cautious policy and, like the Fund, is too small an instrument, if a highly efficient one, to make much of an impact on world payments problems.

### The International Finance Corporation

The exclusion of other than government or government-guaranteed projects from the World Bank's operations was the main cause of the establishment of the International Finance Corporation in 1956. The Corporation aims at investing in commercially productive private undertakings in association with private investors in cases where sufficient private capital is not available on reasonable terms. The Corporation may not hold ordinary or preference shares, but this is the only restriction on the form of its investments. The Corporation is intended to concentrate on investments in industries in underdeveloped countries and seeks to revolve its funds by eventually selling its assets to private investors. The Corporation began life with thirty-one member countries and capital amounting to $100 million; it is also authorized to raise funds in the world's capital markets.

### The European Payments Union

Following the failure of this country to maintain the convertibility of sterling for more than a few weeks in 1947, trade between European countries became entangled in a mass of bilateral agreements. Their general effect was to restrict unnecessarily the level of intra-European trade. In the following year an attempt was made to set up a more satisfactory payments scheme, but this was highly cumbersome and did not withstand the devaluation of sterling in 1949. In 1950, assisted by the general recovery of Western Europe's economy, the European Payments Union was established, and its operation, until its dissolution at the beginning of 1959, was perhaps the most successful of any of the post-war international monetary institutions.

The membership of E.P.U. consisted of those countries in the Organization for European Economic Co-operation, a body set up in 1947 to deal with the receipt of Marshall Aid and to promote European recovery by co-operation. In the O.E.E.C. were all the countries of Europe save the Soviet bloc, Spain, Yugoslavia, and Finland. The associated monetary systems of O.E.E.C. countries, such as the franc area and the sterling area, were also linked to E.P.U.

The Union had three main objects: to liberalize intra-European trade; to prevent the need for discrimination between its members; and to provide an international credit mechanism. Member countries had to refrain from imposing restrictions on a specified percentage of their trade with other member countries, and non-discrimination was secured by the clearing system of the Union.

Every month the central bank of each member country reported its payments to and from each other member to the agent of E.P.U., the Bank for International Settlements, which was set up in 1929 to deal with Germany's war reparations. The B.I.S. cleared these balances, showing each member's final position vis-à-vis E.P.U. *as a whole.* Each country had a quota, measured in dollars, within which its month's balance with the Union was settled partly in gold or dollars and partly by receiving or giving a credit from or to the Union as a whole. As its payments depended on its position with the Union and not with other members as individual countries, there was no need for any country to discriminate against any other member country. Up to July 1954 monthly settlements required gold payments depending on the proportion of its quota that each country had used up in its cumulative debit or credit position. For the following year monthly settlements for a country still within the limits of its quota were half in gold and half in the form of credit, but after July 1955 settlement was 75 per cent in gold and only 25 per cent in credit. A debit country that had exhausted its quota paid entirely in gold, and a credit country whose cumulative credit position with the Union exceeded its quota received its monthly settlement wholly in gold. E.P.U. was wound up at the beginning of 1959, when sterling held by non-residents became fully convertible on current account, for sterling was the main currency used in the international transactions of E.P.U. countries. The Union has been replaced by the European Monetary Agreement.

## European Monetary Agreement

Under the European Monetary Agreement, payments between European countries are now settled 100 per cent in gold or dollars, and the question of credit facilities is separated from that of clearing outstanding balances between member countries. A monthly clearing is operated, which central banks can, however, choose to avoid by allowing balances to be put through the ordinary foreign exchange markets, and the maximum amount of 'interim finance' that central banks are obliged to extend to other central banks between monthly settlements is limited. Because of certain provisions relating to the rates of exchange at which monthly settlements take place, it does not appear that the formal clearing will be very much used. A European Fund, financed partly by the balance of E.P.U. funds, is available for the provision of straightforward credits to member countries; at present (January 1959) the question of further contributions to the Fund by member countries does not yet appear to have been finally settled.

### THE BRITISH EXCHANGE CONTROL SYSTEM

The danger that the facility of converting sterling into other currencies, if freely granted at the existing exchange rate, would involve the United Kingdom in heavy dollar losses, prevented formal convertibility, even for current-account transactions, until the end of 1958, and today sterling held by non-residents that has arisen out of certain capital transactions is still restricted in use. But even before the relaxation of exchange control over sterling held on current account at the end of 1958 sterling was once more fulfilling many of the functions of a convertible currency, because the British regulations had been progressively eased so as to permit the transfer of sterling from one country to another within certain wide limits.

Estimates vary as to the extent sterling is used, but it is thought that about two-fifths of the world's trade has been financed by sterling in recent years. The Bank of England operates the country's exchange control regulations on behalf of the Treasury, but control over imports and exports of merchandise lies with the Board of Trade; control over imports from dollar countries and from Europe has been considerably relaxed in recent years. If the

Board grants an import licence, or if no licence is required for the goods concerned and their country of origin, permission for the acquisition of foreign exchange is automatically granted by the Bank of England, as long as the regulations concerning currency of payment are complied with. Certain specified currencies, e.g. those of Canada and the U.S.A., that are received by U.K. residents from export sales must usually be handed over to an authorized dealer, usually a bank, within six months. Foreign travel and emigration are subject to special regulations.

Exchange control by this country is administered according to the terms of the 1947 Exchange Control Act and its many subsequent modifications made in the direction of greater freedom. The general aim of the British regulations has been to permit as widespread a use of sterling as is compatible with the need to conserve gold and 'hard' or 'scarce' currencies, which until 1959 were mainly United States and Canadian dollars, and to a lesser extent E.P.U.-member currencies.

The following sections outline the general framework of exchange control in the period before the restoration of non-resident convertibility at the end of 1958; an account is of value in presenting a broad survey of the methods used.

Control over the use of sterling is the key to the system of exchange control, for sterling balances, that is bank deposits and government securities held by overseas residents in the United Kingdom, represent short-term claims on this country. Sterling accruing to North American residents through current transactions was fully convertible into dollars even before 1959, and so the flow of sterling in this direction was carefully regulated; the movement of sterling to E.P.U. countries also set up a contingent gold and dollar claim. The problem of exchange control is magnified by the very size of the sterling balances. During the war Britain's outlays in India, Egypt, and many other countries whose goods and services were vital to her war effort were paid for partly by additions to the sterling balances held by these countries. Their local traders were paid in domestic currency, but claims on Britain remained in the hands of their central and commercial banks.

Before the war overseas sterling holdings amounted to about £750 million. By the end of 1947 they had grown to roughly £3,600 million, of which £1,860 million were 'blocked' or restricted as to the speed with which they could be drawn on. The counterpart of these liabilities exists in the exchange reserves of other countries, so that the sterling balances have helped to sustain world trade by augmenting the low level of post-war international liquidity, which by 1958 was again emerging as a serious international problem. But they have been a crucial element in Britain's foreign exchange policy, for although only part of these balances may be true commercial liabilities, in that

TABLE 30. *Overseas Sterling Holdings*[1]

As at 31 December

| Non-sterling countries | 1945 (£m.) | 1947 (£m.) | 1949 (£m.) | 1951 (£m.) | 1955 (£m.) | 1957 (£m.) |
|---|---|---|---|---|---|---|
| Dollar Area* | 36 | 21 | 36 | 38 | 58 | 35 |
| O.E.E.C. countries | 421 | 481 | 439 | 409 | 213 | 258 |
| Other countries | 777 | 807 | 589 | 571 | 426 | 275 |
| Total | 1,234 | 1,309 | 1,064 | 1,018 | 697 | 568 |
| *Sterling Area countries** | | | | | | |
| U.K. colonies | 447 | 502 | 582 | 968 | 844 | 882 |
| Other countries | 2,007 | 1,786 | 1,771 | 1,825 | 2,035 | 1,817 |
| Total | 2,454 | 2,288 | 2,353 | 2,793 | 2,879 | 2,699 |
| ALL COUNTRIES | 3,688 | 3,597 | 3,417 | 3,811 | 3,576 | 3,267 |

[1] Excluding balances held by non-territorial organizations such as the I.M.F. These amounted to £645 million at 31 December 1957.
* See text.
SOURCE: Cmd. 8201, 9119, 122.

other countries need to hold a certain volume of sterling for trading purposes, the sterling balances have posed a continual threat to Britain's external solvency in the form of a run on her relatively small gold and dollar reserve. The knowledge that this reserve is small in relation to Britain's short-term liabilities has tended to intensify the problem of maintaining confidence in sterling.

After the war many bilateral agreements were made with individual countries restricting the transferability of their sterling balances to other countries, but gradually the area of transferability has been enlarged. Between 1954 and the end of 1958 sterling accounts, that is balances with banks in the United Kingdom, were divided into the following categories:

Scheduled Territories
American and Canadian Accounts
Registered Accounts
Transferable Accounts
Blocked Accounts

The *Scheduled Territories* are the countries within the sterling area, comprising the United Kingdom and most other Commonwealth countries except Canada, in addition to Eire, Iraq and Kuwait, to name some of the most important non-Commonwealth members. On the outbreak of war, the enemy and most of the neutral members of the pre-war sterling bloc dropped out.

Whereas the pre-war sterling bloc was a spontaneous and informal grouping, the post-war sterling area has, from the point of view of Britain's exchange control regulations, a legal boundary. Residents of the United Kingdom are allowed by the British regulations to make payments in sterling freely to other sterling area residents for both current and capital transactions. The other members of the sterling area generally allow a similar freedom regarding payments in sterling within the sterling area as far as current transactions are concerned (and as far as their import licensing restrictions permit), but some of them, e.g. South Africa, Australia, and New Zealand, control capital transfers. But by and large there is a wide measure of freedom in the use of sterling within the area.

*American and Canadian Accounts* refer to sterling balances held by residents of the United States, Canada, and a number of South American countries, for example Bolivia, Cuba, Mexico, and Venezuela. Sterling held in these Accounts was freely convertible into dollars or gold (through the London market) and could be transferred between the residents of different countries within the group as a whole.

*Registered Accounts* were those held by residents of countries outside the sterling area other than those of American and Canadian accounts and were sterling balances earned by the sale of gold in the London market or by the sale of dollars to an authorized bank in the U.K. They could also be fed from an American or Canadian account. Sterling held in registered accounts was freely convertible into Canadian and U.S. dollars and could be used to purchase gold in London. From our point of view, therefore, they were indistinguishable from American and Canadian accounts, which for the sake of convenience can all be called American accounts.

*Transferable Accounts* referred to sterling held by residents of all other countries outside the sterling area and the American Account system. Payments could be made from any one transferable account to another, e.g. a trader in Holland could use his balance in London to pay for goods bought from a trader in Belgium.

Finally, there remain the *Blocked Accounts*. These arise through certain transactions of which the sterling proceeds are not placed at the free disposal of non-residents, e.g. through certain security transactions. Transfers between blocked accounts, however, are permitted freely. For the moment they can be ignored.

There were thus three groups of countries in the pre-1959 system: the sterling area, the dollar area, and the transferable account area, within each of which the use of sterling was free from restriction by the British exchange control authorities and wholly or relatively free from interference by the authorities of the other countries concerned. What of their relationship to each other? The general principle was that the Bank of England would permit the free transfer of sterling from a relatively 'hard' area to a relatively 'soft' area.

In other words, sterling from an American account could be paid without restriction into a transferable account or a sterling area account. As far as the British authorities are concerned, sterling could be paid from a transferable account to a sterling area account, but not, without their permission, to an American account. Permission was required for the payment of sterling from a sterling area account to transferable or American accounts; this generally depended on the system of import licensing.

In this way sterling could be used over wide areas as an international currency. It was not fully or formally convertible by non-residents until 1959, as it is on current account now that payments can be freely made from what were transferable accounts to American accounts (as was also the case for a brief period in 1947). But sterling held in transferable accounts and by residents in certain sterling area countries could be transferred into dollars through various channels, and the scope for converting sterling into dollars, at *some* rate of exchange, was much more extensive than these regulations might seem to indicate.

### The Extent of Convertibility

First, sterling accruing to a transferable account could be handed over to the central bank of the country concerned, so that the country established a claim on E.P.U., and the United Kingdom incurred a corresponding debit to be settled either 75 per cent or wholly in gold.

Secondly, the private owner of sterling held in a transferable account could sell his sterling for dollars on one of the free markets existing in transferable account sterling, e.g. in Zurich or New York. The buyer of the transferable account sterling on the market had also to be, nominally at any rate, a resident in a transferable account country, so that as far as Britain was concerned no direct dollar loss was involved. As the buyer of this sterling was restricted in its use to payments to other transferable accounts or to sterling area accounts, this sterling was not as useful as American account sterling. It therefore commanded a dollar price lower than American account sterling on the official London and New York markets. The size of the discount on transferable account sterling depended on the volume of sterling held in these accounts and on the demand for sterling as opposed to the demand for dollars by residents of these countries.

From 1955 the Bank of England also operated so as to support sterling in this market at times when the discount widened to an undesirable extent, mainly in order to prevent 'commodity shunting'. This was a process whereby sterling goods, like wool or rubber, could be bought for sterling from a transferable account, ostensibly for consignment to, say, Holland, but shipped to a dollar country for payment in dollars, which could then be used to recover transferable account sterling at a profit, if the discount on transferable sterling was in excess of the extra handling costs. The result was that sterling area sales that would have otherwise augmented the sterling area's dollar reserves (or reduced the sterling area's liabilities to the dollar world) merely reduced the total of transferable account sterling outstanding.

Thirdly, although private residents of the sterling area do not have an automatic right to convertibility, the sterling balances of sterling area countries have been convertible into dollars as part of the arrangement whereby members of the area have access to its central pool of dollars, restraint in the use of the dollar pool being a matter of informal understanding as far as the self-governing members of the area are concerned. The extent to which residents of the United Kingdom can obtain imports from dollar sources is governed by this country's system of import licensing.

Fourthly, in certain sterling area countries, such as Kuwait and Hong Kong—to which sterling payments are 'screened' by the Bank of England—'free' markets exist in which sterling held by residents of these countries may be sold for dollars. As this sterling is 'resident' sterling, that is restricted to use in the sterling area only, this species of 'free' sterling would usually command a lower dollar price than transferable account sterling.

Fifthly, blocked sterling (which still exists) can also be sold for dollars, at a price, to non-residents wishing to purchase British securities.

Finally, certain commodities produced in dollar countries could even before 1959 be sold through the London market to residents of other countries, other than American account countries, for sterling.

### The Step towards Full Convertibility on Current Account

At the end of 1958, in concert with similar steps taken by other European countries, the British government announced an important measure of relaxation of the system just outlined. The distinction between American, transferable and registered accounts was abolished, and a homogeneous class of 'external account' sterling was created, within which transfers are freely permitted at the official rate of exchange. This move was made possible by the considerable improvement in the strength of sterling in 1958.

It should be noted that capital transactions are still subject to control. Restrictions on capital transactions will probably be more enduring, particularly on those by residents of the sterling area themselves, who are unlikely to be allowed to purchase non-sterling assets freely in the foreseeable future. The risk of an outflow of capital arising through political changes, or through the fear of political changes, is an obvious obstacle to greater freedom in this sphere.

## Blocked Accounts and Security Transactions

Blocked accounts, which still exist, refer to certain sterling balances held by residents of countries outside the sterling area, other than Denmark, Norway, and Sweden. The purpose of these accounts is to hold funds that are not placed at the free disposal of non-residents, funds arising mainly from capital transactions. Non-residents of the sterling area may use foreign exchange to buy British securities in London, for example, but the proceeds of resale are generally placed in a blocked account. Sterling in one blocked account may be transferred to another and may be used to buy a sterling security on a stock exchange in the United Kingdom as long as that security cannot be redeemed within five years, the proceeds on maturity being remittable to the holder's country.

Blocked account sterling is negotiable in 'free' markets abroad. A holder of blocked sterling may sell it for dollars in New York; as the purchaser can only use this sterling to buy sterling securities, this brand of sterling, too, will also generally stand at some discount below the dollar exchange rate for external account sterling. Blocked account sterling has become known as 'security sterling' because of the use to which it may be put. It is also sometimes described as 'switch' sterling.

At the other end of the scale are residents of the United Kingdom, who can buy non-sterling securities only from other U.K. residents or by first purchasing for sterling the foreign currency held by other U.K. residents as a result of their sales of securities. If a U.K. resident sells a non-sterling security abroad he must either reinvest the proceeds within a certain period in another security payable in the same currency, or hand over the foreign currency obtained to the British authorities (or lodge the proceeds to the order of a bank if they are blocked by the regulations of the country concerned). The dollar counterpart of dollar securities held by U.K. residents is often described as 'security dollars', since their use is circumscribed in this way. The price at which security dollars change hands between U.K. residents, given the size of the total pool of security dollars, depends on the desire by U.K. investors for American or Canadian securities rather than British stocks. This desire reflects ordinary investment considerations, including tax concessions on overseas stocks, and the relative preference for assets valued in dollars rather than in sterling. Security dollars have commanded a premium—the so-called 'dollar premium'—which is reflected in the prices of American and Canadian securities quoted on the London Stock Exchange as compared with their prices quoted in the U.S.A. or Canada, converted at the official rate of exchange. The size of the dollar premium may also be influenced by the action of the British authorities, who have periodically sold part of their own holdings of dollar securities requisitioned during the war.

### THE POST-WAR STERLING AREA

The British system of exchange control formally delineates the post-war sterling area, but it remains essentially a group of countries bound by a complex of economic and political ties, rooted in custom but sustained by the awareness of its reciprocal advantages. On the one hand the British authorities permit almost complete freedom in the use of sterling within the area, and on the other the rest of the group, with the main exception of South Africa since 1948, place the greater part of their dollar receipts in the central reserve held by Britain on behalf of the area as a whole. The main foreign exchange reserves of the members of the area outside the United Kingdom, that is to say, are held individually as sterling balances in London.

In acting as banker to the sterling area, Britain, too, has access to the central pool of gold and dollars, and these reserves help to support London's business as a financial centre, which contributes towards Britain's invisible income. Britain also receives a large part of the benefit of whatever discrimination in import restrictions or exchange control is practised by the sterling area against the rest of the world, especially against the dollar area, with the aim of keeping the central reserve intact, so that British exporters receive some measure of protection against outside competition. However, the extent of this discrimination has greatly diminished in recent years.

The other members of the sterling area derive certain advantages from keeping their reserves in sterling, which is an acceptable medium of payment in many countries. Their sterling balances can be converted into dollars in order to meet their own dollar deficits when necessary, by drawing on the central reserve; and pooling economizes the use of reserves. Britain has been playing a growing part in the trade of the Colonies since the war and a somewhat diminishing one in that of the independent members of the group, but even here she remains their largest single trading customer. The pattern of trade with Britain is still basically complementary, if less so than before the war. Britain exports manufactured goods to the rest of the sterling area and takes their agricultural produce and minerals in return, offering an open market that the U.S.A., for example, with its own important meat, dairy, wool, and mining interests, cannot.

Finance has played a great part in the development of the sterling area and in the benefits enjoyed by individual members. The United Kingdom has always been the main source of overseas capital for the Commonwealth members of the area. Access to the London market is a *quid pro quo* for the willingness of other members of the area to pool their dollar reserves and exercise restraint in their use. Since the war there has been a tendency for the Colonies to be net savers and the independent members to be net spenders of the dollar pool, but fundamentally the flow of capital within the area depends on the ability of Britain to save sufficiently to meet the investment needs of the rest of the area in addition to those of her own.

Drawings by the Colonies on the central reserve can, of course, be controlled directly by the British government. Apart from this, the operation of the sterling area is remarkably informal. The United Kingdom's influence is naturally strong, but there is no central control over the area; its members, other than the Colonies, pursue their own economic policies, aligned only by informal contact between Ministers and officials. No legal restrictions are placed by the United Kingdom on resort to the central pool by other sterling area countries. Apart from the Colonies, the latter are bound only by self-restraint, by the size of their sterling balances, on which they have to draw in order to obtain dollars from the pool, by the knowledge of the advantages that these arrangements bring to them, and by the ability of Britain to supply them with both capital and goods on terms as favourable as other countries. The supply of capital from Britain to the rest of the sterling area in the short run enlarges the ability of the receiving countries to draw dollars, it is true, for it adds to their sterling balances. But in the long run the willingness of member countries to place their dollar earnings in the pool, and thus their membership of the sterling area, depends in part on the assurance that British capital will be forthcoming if necessary.

Because of the function of the reserve of gold and dollars held by the United Kingdom as a central reserve for the whole group, the balance of payments of the sterling area as a whole with the rest of the world, particularly with the dollar world, is of more importance than the balance of payments between the members of the area. A special responsibility falls upon Britain as custodian of the reserves. As the financial centre of the sterling area, for example, London feels, in the form of an outflow of funds, the main effects of any weakness in sterling, of any lack of confidence in the exchange rate, and perhaps of any speculation in favour of another major currency. As changes in the balances of payments of the rest of the sterling area will be reflected in the movement of sterling balances, they will also impinge on the state of the London capital market, depending on the form in which the balances are held.

As banker to the area, Britain must usually be the first to correct a serious loss of dollars from the pool until the other members of the area take appropriate measures. By the nature of their economies the primary-producing countries in the sterling area possess less flexibility in the policies they can pursue. Economically the weightiest member of the area, the largest importer of dollar goods, and the focal point of foreign attention, a large part of the responsibility of maintaining the reserve intact falls on Britain. Since the war both banker and customers have contributed to the sterling area's financial difficulties.

## STERLING CRISES 1947–1957

At the end of 1937 the gold and dollar reserve held by the United Kingdom amounted to over $4,000 million, equivalent to more than four-fifths of the annual imports by the whole sterling area from non-sterling countries, or nearly 100 per cent of their imports if the $500 million held by the other sterling countries in gold is taken into account. At the end of 1957 the United Kingdom held $2,273 million in gold and dollars and the rest of the sterling area about $1,000 million, a total that by this time was equal to only one-quarter of the sterling area's imports from the outside world. In 1937 the central reserve was approximately one-third larger than the sterling balances; at the end of 1957 the reserve covered only one-third of the sterling balances outstanding, the deficiency having been even larger before the devaluation of the pound in 1949. This fall in the ratio of reserves to imports and to short-term liabilities summarizes the central problem of the sterling area in the post-war world.

Figure 9 reproduces the fluctuations in the central reserve of gold and American and Canadian dollars held by the Exchange Equalization Account on behalf of the sterling area. In the post-war decade the reserve has been subject to periods of intense strain that justify the description of 'crises', in that the reserve

Fig. 9. United Kingdom gold and dollar reserves 1946–57 (quarterly).

has not been large enough to stand even temporary stresses without the application of corrective but crude expedients to stem the loss. If the purpose of a reserve is to tide over a temporary deficit, it may be said that the sterling area's reserve has hardly been one at all. The explanation is that in the first half of the post-war decade, at any rate, the sterling area was running such a large deficit each year, financed partly by American assistance, that any marked change for the worse threatened to bring the reserve to exhaustion, and throughout the whole period a loss of dollars on current account has tended to be magnified by capital movements. The smaller the reserve, the greater is the tendency of other countries to draw upon it for fear of its exhaustion or to speculate against sterling in anticipation of its devaluation. The central reserve has been too small to allow a long-run economic policy to be pursued without interruption by undesirable short-term safety measures.

There has been no single cause of the 'crises' of 1947, 1949, 1951, 1955 and 1957. With the possible exception of 1949 and

TABLE 31. *Gold and Dollar Transactions of the Sterling Area— the Years of Crisis, 1947–57*

| | 1947 (U.S. $m.) | 1949 (U.S. $m.) | 1951–2 (U.S. $m.) | 1955 (U.S. $m.) | 1957 (U.S. $m.) approx. |
|---|---|---|---|---|---|
| *Transactions with Dollar Area* | | | | | |
| United Kingdom | | | | | |
| Current balance | −2,301 | −1,117 | −1,500 | −700 | −329 |
| Miscellaneous items | −372 | −6 | −267 | +6 | +270 |
| Total | −2,673 | −1,123 | −1,767 | −694 | −59 |
| Rest of Sterling Area (net)[1] | −759 | −132 | −44 | +556 | +753 |
| *Transactions with non-Dollar Area* (net) | −699 | −276 | −626 | −629 | −848 |
| *Total gold and dollar balance* | −4,131 | −1,531 | −2,437 | −767 | −154 |
| Financed by: | | | | | |
| Grants and loans to U.K. government (−)[2] | −3,513 | −1,364 | −255 | −125 | −294 |
| Change in reserves | −618 | −167 | −2,182 | −642 | +140 |

[1] Including sales of gold in the United Kingdom.
[2] Drawings on the I.M.F. and loans and grants received (gross) from the U.S. and Canadian governments, including loans from the U.S. Import-Export Bank and U.S. defence aid. The latter item is usually shown in the current account of the U.K. in the official balance-of-payments White Papers.
SOURCES: U.K. balance-of-payments White Papers.

to some extent that of 1957, serious inflation has certainly played its part, and the dollar problem would have been of a different magnitude if inflation in the United Kingdom and in the rest of the sterling area, especially in Australia and India, had been prevented. But the crises of 1947 and 1949 form part of *the* post-war dollar problem, whereas those of 1951, 1955 and 1957 had more local causes.

The 1947 crisis occurred in July–August when, under the Anglo-U.S. loan agreement, currently accruing sterling held by non-residents was made freely convertible for current transactions. The speed with which this facility was exploited added to the already very large dollar deficit of the sterling area due to the need to restock with dollar goods at a time of rising American prices. Without the fiasco of convertibility, which had to be suspended after five weeks, the dollar deficit could have been met by the American and Canadian credits, of which $3,273 million had to be drawn in 1947. By the end of the year these loans, which had been intended to tide Britain over four years of reconstruction, were practically exhausted.

In 1949 the United Kingdom achieved a small overall surplus, and the dollar deficit of the whole sterling area was not much more than one-third of that in 1947 and even smaller than that of 1948, which was an uneventful year. The total loss of reserves, thanks to Marshall Aid, was only $167 million, compared with $223 million in 1948 and $618 million in 1947. Nevertheless, in 1949 the pound had to be devalued, whereas in the much more unfavourable year of 1947 the exchange rate was maintained.

The immediate reason was a decline in the dollar reserve in the summer of 1949 to its lowest post-war figure, owing to a combination of three factors: a sharp fall in sterling area export receipts resulting from the American recession of that year; a purely seasonal decline in commodity earnings in July–September; and widespread speculation against sterling due to the expectation of a post-war realignment of exchange rates in which the devaluation of the pound, it was not difficult to predict, would play a leading part.

The crisis of 1951–2 was largely a consequence of the Korean war. Following a year in which imports had been restricted by official controls, which had been tightened to deal with the crisis of 1949, Britain and the rest of the sterling area experienced a very sharp increase in the volume of imports needed to rebuild stocks. This occurred at a time when import prices had risen substantially following the great demand for commodities stimulated by world-wide rearmament, but sterling area commodity export receipts were beginning to fall owing to the retreat of commodity prices from their peaks as the almost panic-stricken demand for materials subsided. Britain's exports to dollar countries were restricted by the strong pull of inflation both at home and in other sterling markets. With U.S. aid now at a low level, the central reserve fell with alarming rapidity after the middle of 1951, Britain being joined by Australia, India, Pakistan, and Eire as large drawers on the dollar pool.

In 1955, when world trade was rising rapidly, commodity prices were fairly stable, and external conditions generally favourable, the United Kingdom was mainly responsible for the loss of dollars. A sharp increase in the volume of imports occurred owing to inflation and the need to augment stocks after a year in which their level had not kept pace with national expenditure. The relaxation of controls also played its part. In the second half of 1956 a further fall in reserves took place; a small increase in Britain's dollar imports coincided with a seasonal decline in sterling area commodity receipts, with the emergence of a large deficit in India's balance of payments owing to her ambitious development programme, and with the Suez crisis, which caused a widespread loss of confidence in sterling.

In 1957 the strain in the gold and dollar reserve was concentrated mainly in the third quarter. The usual seasonal deterioration was accentuated by a fall in the export earnings of several sterling area countries other than the United Kingdom, owing to the decline in commodity prices associated with the slackening of the world boom. At the same time a partial devaluation of the French franc set off an intense movement of currency speculation in Europe, centring on the belief that the Deutsche Mark was about to be revalued upwards; the withdrawal of funds from the U.K. by non-residents led to large deficits with the E.P.U. Thirdly, the rise in wages and prices in this country led to growing doubts as to the determination and the ability of the British government to prevent a devaluation of sterling.

In the fourth quarter of the year the loss of gold and dollars was reversed. The sharp increase in Bank rate from $4\frac{1}{2}$ to 7 per cent in September checked the loss of confidence in sterling, and the receipt of a loan of $248 million from the U.S. Export-Import Bank reinforced the change in sentiment. Statements by the German authorities that no change in the value of the Deutsche Mark was contemplated halted the movement of funds into Germany. Taking 1957 as a whole, the position on capital account showed an improvement, in that the rise in the gold and dollar reserves of £50 million was accompanied by a fall in the sterling balances of £178 million.

Over the ten years 1946–56 the central reserve of the sterling area fell by nearly $350 million. But the total dollar deficit of the area was roughly $10,000 million, practically the whole of which was met by grants and loans from the United States, Canada, the World Bank, and the I.M.F. In more ways than one, however, the devaluation of sterling marks a dividing line in this record, for more than three-quarters of the deficit was incurred in the four years 1946–49.

Over the period as a whole there has been a fairly persistent pattern of dollar transactions. The United Kingdom has had a large current deficit with dollar countries and Western Europe, not entirely offset by grants and loans. Since 1949 the rest of the sterling area has had a net gold and dollar surplus, but within this group there has been a division between the Colonies and the independent members of the area. The former have earned a surplus each year with the dollar area; the latter have generally been in deficit, but making up for this by the sale of gold, largely by South Africa, in London. Since 1947 the United Kingdom has had a large current surplus with the rest of the sterling area that has exceeded the contributions of this group to the central gold and dollar pool.

That the sterling balances of the rest of the sterling area, as Table 30 indicates, were larger at the end of 1957 than twelve years earlier is due to the flow of capital to these countries as a whole from the United Kingdom, which has been of the order of the dollar loans and grants received by this country. The main beneficiaries have been South Africa and Australia, but part of the outflow has taken the form of short-term funds, especially in the movement of 'hot' money during the 1947 crisis. The rise in the sterling balances of the Colonies is also in part due to the investment in these countries of United Kingdom funds, including government grants, but it reflects in large measure the fact that the contribution to the dollar pool made by these countries has exceeded Britain's surplus with them. The Colonies have thus been net lenders to the sterling area. The various marketing boards in the Colonies withhold part of their commodity earnings from producers in good years, in order to tide them over bad times; and the operation of the currency systems of the Colonies generally makes it inevitable that foreign exchange reserves are transformed into sterling balances.

### BRITAIN'S POST-WAR BALANCE OF PAYMENTS

Whereas her productive capacity was not as greatly impaired by the war as that of other European belligerents, Britain's position in international trade and finance had been more seriously damaged. The war transformed the United Kingdom from a net creditor into a net debtor on capital account. At the end of 1938 Britain possessed overseas investments with a nominal value of £3,545 million and a gold and dollar reserve of nearly £1,000 million. By the end of 1945, the nominal value of her overseas investments had fallen to £2,329 million and the gold and dollar reserve to £600 million; long-term liabilities to the U.S.A. and

TABLE 32. *Annual Current Balance of Payments of the United Kingdom, 1924-47*

| Annual average (£m.) | Visible balance (£m.) | Invisible balance (£m.) | Current balance (£m.) |
|---|---|---|---|
| 1924–8 | −381 | +448 | +67 |
| 1934–8 | −346 | +325 | −21 |
| 1946–7 | −290 | −80 | −370 |

SOURCE: *Bank for International Settlement: 'The Sterling Area'* (Basle, January 1953).

Canada of £1,200 million had been incurred, and the sterling balances had risen to £3,700 million. In round figures, Britain's net overseas assets of £3,500 million had been turned into net overseas liabilities of roughly £2,000 million by nominal value. In market values the position was less serious, owing to the rise in the prices of Britain's equity investments abroad after the war.

As a counterpart to this deterioration on capital account, net interest earnings were lower at the end of the war than before it, even though the low rate of interest payable on the sterling balances during the period of 'cheap' money helped to soften the loss. The invisible balance as a whole, however, suffered two additional changes for the worse. Britain's merchant fleet at the end of the war was only half its pre-war size, and heavy government payments had still to be incurred on military and other overseas transactions.

2 R

Table 32 shows that if the invisible surplus of the pre-war years had been earned, Britain would have started the post-war era with a small current surplus. The deterioration on her invisible account was even more serious than Table 32 appears to indicate, for while both import and export prices had risen substantially since 1938, Britain's terms of trade had deteriorated; the post-war equivalent of the pre-war visible deficit would have been about £900 million.

Evidence of Britain's post-war recovery in the face of these problems is not hard to find. By 1957 her industrial production was running 50 per cent above that twenty years earlier, and despite the heavy burden of defence the volume of exports in 1957 was 70 per cent above the high pre-war level reached in 1937. The composition of Britain's exports has altered in favour of those manufactured goods, like engineering products, in which the rise in world trade has been relatively fast; many of the structural maladjustments of the inter-war years have at last been righted. However, as import prices had almost quadrupled over these twenty years whereas Britain's export prices had only trebled, this 70 per cent increase in visible exports was needed to pay for a practically unchanged volume of visible imports.

As Table 32 shows, the United Kingdom's current balance of payments has experienced wide fluctuations, associated mainly with swings in the value of visible imports. These have been due to three causes—bursts of inflationary pressure, fluctuations in the level of stockbuilding, and changes in import prices. All three were responsible for the large visible deficits of 1947 and 1951 and the first two for the smaller one of 1955. Conversely, the years in which a current surplus has been earned have been mostly those in which the level of stockbuilding was relatively low and even negative (as in 1950) or in which import prices have fallen (as in 1952–3 and in 1958).

The United Kingdom's invisible balance has improved considerably since the end of the war. In some years the invisible surplus has surpassed the pre-war average, despite the high cost of government expenditure, largely on our military bases overseas. The volume and the value of Britain's visible exports have followed a relatively steady upward curve.

Since the remarkable economic recovery of Western Germany, Britain's exports have had to fight for increasingly competitive markets, as Table 33 indicates, but the rapid rise in world trade

TABLE 33. United Kingdom Current Balance of Payments, 1946–57

| | 1946 (£m.) | 1947 (£m.) | 1948 (£m.) | 1949 (£m.) | 1950 (£m.) | 1951 (£m.) | 1952 (£m.) | 1953 (£m.) | 1954 (£m.) | 1955 (£m.) | 1956 (£m.) | 1957[1] (£m.) |
|---|---|---|---|---|---|---|---|---|---|---|---|---|
| *Visibles* | | | | | | | | | | | | |
| Imports (f.o.b.) | 1,082 | 1,560 | 1,794 | 1,978 | 2,383 | 3,491 | 2,944 | 2,888 | 3,006 | 3,432 | 3,462 | 3,573 |
| Exports (f.o.b.) | 917 | 1,145 | 1,602 | 1,841 | 2,250 | 2,748 | 2,827 | 2,672 | 2,820 | 3,076 | 3,411 | 3,517 |
| Balance | −165 | −415 | −192 | −137 | −133 | −743 | −117 | −216 | −186 | −356 | −51 | −56 |
| *Invisibles* (net) | | | | | | | | | | | | |
| Shipping | +28 | +35 | +77 | +91 | +141 | +132 | +110 | +134 | +149 | +123 | +105 | +110 |
| Interest, profits and dividends | +62 | +93 | +89 | +94 | +154 | +129 | +91 | +74 | +76 | +77 | +114 | +110 |
| Government | −323 | −149 | −76 | −139 | −136 | −154 | −172 | −158 | −174 | −182 | −193 | −164 |
| Other | +100 | −7 | +103 | +122 | +274 | +229 | +214 | +252 | +313 | +219 | +257 | +251 |
| Balance | −133 | −28 | +193 | +168 | +433 | +336 | +243 | +302 | +364 | +237 | +283 | +307 |
| CURRENT BALANCE (excl. defence aid) | −298 | −443 | +1 | +31 | +300 | −407 | +126 | +86 | +178 | −119 | +232 | +251 |
| Defence aid, net | — | — | — | — | — | +4 | +121 | +102 | +50 | +46 | +26 | +21 |
| CURRENT BALANCE (incl. defence aid) | −298 | −443 | +1 | +31 | +300 | −403 | +247 | +188 | +228 | −73 | +258 | +272 |
| Volume of imports | 72 | 79 | 83 | 89 | 89 | 100 | 92 | 99 | 100 | 111 | 111 | 115 |
| Volume of exports | 54 | 61 | 77 | 85 | 101 | 100 | 94 | 96 | 100 | 107 | 114 | 118 |
| Import prices | 57 | 71 | 78 | 79 | 90 | 119 | 116 | 101 | 100 | 103 | 105 | 107 |
| Export prices | 63 | 71 | 78 | 79 | 84 | 99 | 103 | 101 | 100 | 102 | 106 | 111 |

SOURCE: *Balance-of-payments White Papers.*

[1] Provisional figures.

has enabled Britain to increase the volume of her exports despite a fall in her share in overseas markets after 1950. Between 1948 and 1956 the average annual rate of increase in world trade in manufactured goods was nearly 9 per cent, against one of only 2 per cent in the first forty years of this century and one of 4 per cent in the second half of the last. Owing to the liberalization of import policies and the pattern of industrialization, world trade grew even more rapidly than world production of manufactured products in the post-war decade, and it is not difficult to see in this remarkably rapid growth of trade an element of abnormality, the passing of which would result in even keener competition in international trade.

TABLE 34. *Shares in World Exports of Manufactured Goods,*
*1937–57*

|  | 1937 (%) | 1950 (%) | 1957 (%) |
|---|---|---|---|
| United Kingdom | 21·9 | 25·5 | 18·1 |
| Western Germany | 22·8 | 7·3 | 17·5 |
| Other European countries | 23·2 | 30·2 | 27·6 |
| United States | 19·9 | 27·3 | 25·3 |
| Canada | 4·9 | 6·2 | 5·5 |
| Japan | 7·3 | 3·5 | 6·0 |

SOURCE: *Board of Trade Journal.*

Her post-war debts, the role that she plays as centre of the Commonwealth and sterling area, and the heavy cost of armaments place upon Britain's shoulders tasks that many of her competitors do not have to bear. To play the part of a major world power, to act as financier to the sterling area, and to enjoy the fruits of modern technology in the form of a high level of consumption for all, demands a level of productivity in excess of that so far achieved. The government has stated that the United Kingdom requires a current surplus *averaging* £300 million per annum, in order to repay its debts to North America, repay holders of sterling balances, invest in the Commonwealth, and to rebuild the gold and dollar reserve to a level at which the inevitable disturbances that occur from year to year may be more easily withstood. In the absence of a sufficient rise in output this aim requires either a level of saving in excess of the average experienced since the war or the diminution of Britain's ambitions in the field of military power or home investment.

In theory a solution might be sought along any or all of these lines. However, some economists would argue that to curtail home investment would be a self-defeating remedy, detrimental to Britain's productivity. They would prefer to see a higher level of saving, achieved if necessary by the government, even at the cost of increased taxation, or would even advocate the abandonment of Britain's role of international banker, on the grounds that the maintenance of foreign confidence in sterling, which is crucial to the role of London as a financial centre, may require a policy with a deflationary bias. But whether either of these two paths could be followed without yet more serious economic and political disadvantages is doubtful. The experience of recent years is not unpromising; saving has been held at an encouragingly high proportion of the national income, and with the progress of postwar reconstruction in the case of both fixed assets and stocks, the demands of domestic investment have become somewhat less pressing. The most satisfactory solution, however, would be an improvement in Britain's efficiency in relation to that of her competitors, brought about by a more economic use of her existing assets.

# PART VIII

# CHAPTER 42

# GOVERNMENT POLICY AND ECONOMIC STABILITY[16]

That government action and inter-government co-operation are required to prevent the extremes of depression and inflation is now a commonplace. But in the reaction from laissez-faire and fatalism the extent to which governments can control the course of economic activity in order to maintain what is all too loosely described as economic stability stands in danger of being exaggerated. The object of this chapter is to introduce some of the problems regarding the ends and means of economic policy.

### THE RECONCILIATION OF ENDS

In the field of economics the art of government is not so much the art of the possible as that of balancing the incompatible. It is not difficult for an authoritarian government to achieve any one aim if it is prepared to sacrifice others with which this is irreconcilable. In a free society, however, the government's powers of coercion are limited, and its economic policy must conform with certain political ends which may even be conflicting. As a result, for example, the scope of government action is limited by the liberty of the individual to choose his occupation and his place of work and to dispose of his wealth according to his tastes, and by the institution of free or collective wage-bargaining. Political considerations are implicit in most acts of economic policy, if only because most economic measures influence the distribution of real incomes, and on the surface of our political life, at least, this has been a matter of vigorous controversy, often overshadowing the technical aspects of economic policy.

On the technical plane, objectives that seem desirable in themselves may be difficult to reconcile. Is it stability of employment, of prices, or of exchange rates at which economic policy is to aim ? The gold standard, for example, gave priority to the stability of exchange rates, implying a lack of control over employment and prices. Since the Second World War, on the other hand, politicians have promised, and the community has demanded, the best of all worlds, but it is apparent that stability of employment may not be possible without some instability of domestic prices or exchange rates.

Of course, 'if only' consumers, trade-unionists, and business-men would refrain from pursuing paths that they conceive to be in their best interests, policy-making would be that much easier. Greater working effort, voluntary restraint in spending, in demand-ing higher wages, or in seeking high profits, for example, would help the government to prevent inflation. Since the war, govern-ments of both political parties have sought to use exhortation as an economic instrument, partly out of an appeal to a collective self-interest and partly out of the belief that the need for 'restraint' is also a moral one. This may be so, but the task of any government is to succeed in an imperfect world, and exhortation is tantamount to an admission of the limitations of policy-making and perhaps of policy-makers as well.

### How Much Unemployment?

A White Paper of 1944 pledged the Coalition Government to the maintenance of a 'high and stable' level of employment. Since then this objective has been recast in the politically more highly charged term 'full employment', of which no precise definition exists that both commands general assent and serves as a reliable guide to economic policy. In the opinion of some economists, including the author, the choice of technical instru-ments for preventing inflation is secondary to the question of whether inflation can be avoided at all once the level of unemploy-ment falls below a certain level. This fear is not based on the view that heavy unemployment is desirable in order to break the bargaining power of trade unions or, indeed, that trade unions should be held responsible for the existence of inflation. It rests on the observation that the level of aggregate demand which is necessary to depress unemployment below a certain figure is bound, by the very nature of the problem, to be one that is chronically in excess of aggregate supply, resulting in a continual upwards pressure on wage-rates and prices as a result of the competition by employers for scarce labour.

The question is one of deciding at what point the unsatisfied demand for labour exceeds the number of suitable people available for work. Some frictional unemployment is inescapable, for the flexibility needed by a changing economy is incompatible with guaranteeing everyone continuous employment. The less mobile is labour the larger will this frictional unemployment tend to be, especially when unemployment is concentrated in particular areas owing to depression in certain industries. It is also usually accepted that there is also a small element of the working population that is ordinarily unemployable, in the sense that there are some people, usually of above-average age, who are unable to obtain regular work except in times of acute labour shortage. There is therefore some level of unemployment that cannot be reduced *except* in conditions of demand inflation.

There is certainly room for argument as to the measure of this minimum level and its application in practice. The need to allow for geographical differences in the state of the labour market, the degree of mobility of labour, and the extent to which the official statistics of unfilled vacancies are a true representation of work available are examples of factors that complicate the practical application of any general rule. As to the main issue of principle involved, average unemployment over the year has fallen to as little as 1 per cent in the post-war decade, and with this experience the idea of what can be considered a normal level of unemployment in an economy in full employment has generally become more ambitious in political and industrial circles. The experience of the post-war years also indicates, however, that whereas the difference between a level of unemployment of 1 per cent and of, say, 2 or 2½ per cent is quantitatively small, there is likely to be an important qualitative difference in the state of the labour market; and the opinion of the author is that a true level of full employment is one with average unemployment somewhere between 2 and 3 per cent. At this level, the number of unfilled vacancies notified to the employment exchanges might fall short of the number of unemployed; the former would probably underestimate the full extent of available work.

### THE DIFFICULTY OF ENDING INFLATION

It is more difficult to bring inflation to an end than to prevent it from starting. When order-books are substantial, business expectations highly optimistic, and consumers accustomed to the idea of continually rising prices, the ability of government policy to check aggregate expenditure through monetary or fiscal action is greatly weakened. Moreover, to some the cure may seem as bad as the disease. This is because inflation can only be halted if a sufficient part of the population is prevented from reacting to the previous rise in prices by maintaining their real expenditure (or by raising their real expenditure by as much as national output, if the latter is increasing). It is because the reactions of consumers, businessmen, and trade unionists may be entirely defensive, and therefore seem entirely just, that the process of inflation is often protracted in the form of cost inflation, which is not terminated when each round of excess demand is removed. Ultimately it may be impossible to halt inflation without causing a temporary fall in total demand to below its full-employment level, for government policy may fall with particular force on certain sections of the economy, and trade unionists and businessmen may not be convinced that defensive price and wage increases cannot be supported indefinitely unless some degree of recession occurs.

## INFLATION AND ECONOMIC GROWTH

The contention that a satisfactory rate of economic growth is impossible in a free society without some degree of inflation is one that has its supporters; it stems from the opinion that a high level of capital investment will not be achieved in a private-enterprise economy without the stimulus afforded by the high profits and the high wage costs of inflation uninterrupted by even a light and temporary recession. Were this so, the future of private industry might be bleak, for the case for nationalization and the extensive use of direct controls would be greatly strengthened.

The social tension and injustice created by inflation, in which the economically weak are the sufferers, may seem to many to be its chief or even sole disadvantage; but in the opinion of the author inflation has serious economic drawbacks even in an economy free from balance-of-payments difficulties. Easy profits blunt the working of the price mechanism and lead to the misdirection of investment, and shortages of labour and materials diminish the flexibility and the productivity of the economy. The supporters of mild inflation as a prescription for economic expansion underestimate the stimulus to cost-reducing investment provided by business competition, the force of which is weakened by inflation. They also belittle the probability that a 'creeping' inflation would start to gallop once its persistence became evident throughout the community and an increasing number of people took mutually-frustrating steps to protect themselves against it.

## GENERAL PROBLEMS OF TECHNIQUE

A government that seeks the maintenance of economic stability is faced with a number of general problems of technique that exist whatever instruments of policy it applies. They concern knowledge, forecasting, time-lags, and the mobility of resources.

That a successful policy of economic stabilization requires accurate knowledge of what is happening at the time it is implemented may be self-evident, but it is only in recent years that anything like a determined attempt has been made to obtain adequate, accurate, and up-to-date information for the express purpose of economic diagnosis. But statistics take some time to collect, and in many cases speed may be obtainable only at the cost of accuracy.

The presence of blind-spots in the government's view of the current state of the economy would not be important if policy could be based on a limited number of data that were in some sense 'strategic' or representative of the state of the economy as a whole, *and* if the government had at its disposal a powerful yet flexible instrument that could be used to achieve its major objective by its inherent selectivity or its overall force. In the days of the gold standard before 1914, for example, there was one vital indicator, the Bank of England's gold reserve, and one predominant instrument of policy, Bank rate, that seemed to be both omnipotent and flexible.

Since then our economic objectives have become more numerous and more complex, and the consequent need for a wider range of economic information has been enlarged still further by the refinement of economic analysis, with its more recent distrust of statistical aggregates and its lack of faith in any one instrument of policy. Less reliance has come to be placed on general measures affecting 'consumption' or 'investment' in the abstract. While there exist important differences of opinion as to the degree of discrimination at which policy should aim, it is clear that accurate diagnosis and effective prescription call for more detailed knowledge, and it may be that more selective instruments will continue to be required than was once thought to be the case.

Economic policy requires economic forecasts. The government must be able to predict within some range of error the effects of its own actions on the economy. Even if they are not made explicit, quantitative forecasts underlie all acts of economic policy. By how much will an increase in taxation reduce personal consumption? By how much will a fall in interest rates stimulate investment? By how much will exports or imports be affected? If the government's information were up-to-date, *and* if economic policy could be tightened or loosened from day to day, *and* if the effect of its action were fully instantaneous, forecasting need only be limited to the events of the day. An error today could be reduced by a further twist of the screw in one direction or the other tomorrow. But certain types of policy can be altered only periodically—by means of a Finance Act, for example—and the effect of most measures is not fully instantaneous but works itself out only over some period of time. These factors make it impossible to maintain economic stability merely by a mechanical reaction to a set of daily[17] data; time-lags are inherent in policy-making.

Because of the existence of different types of time-lag, economic policy is likely to overshoot the mark, being apt to proceed by jolts, achieving the desired state of affairs through a series of oscillations around the target at which it is aiming. The range and complexity of the forecasts that are required will depend on whether the government acts only to correct instability that is known already to have occurred or is ambitious enough to attempt to anticipate that which seems to lie ahead. The objective of *continuous* full employment requires the government to pursue the latter course, to take action while the current situation is still stable. Such a policy is inherently more difficult; and, furthermore, unless the instruments of policy act quickly and powerfully it may run the risk of causing the very instability it seeks to avoid, by indicating to the public that the government sees a change in the economic climate ahead.

Finally, economic policy must take into account the nature of the resources with which it is dealing. If industries employing women, for example, experience a decline in exports, full employment will not be maintained by a policy that stimulates the demand for the goods of industries employing men. Unemployment that is concentrated in South Wales is not easily removed by an expansion of demand that is geographically diffused. The more specialized are a country's resources and the less willing are men and women to move into different areas or different jobs, the greater will be the difficulty of maintaining full employment and the sharper will be the fluctuations in incomes and prices.

## ECONOMIC STABILITY AND INTERNATIONAL TRADE

The ways in which the government can influence a country's balance of payments have already been introduced. The most difficult problem of maintaining economic stability in the face of pressures arising externally concerns the maintenance of full employment in the event of a slump in overseas markets. The extent of the difficulty will depend in the first instance on how widespread is the fall in overseas demand and on whether exports can be easily transferred from one foreign market to another. The greatest danger of an intractable collapse of demand would occur in the event of an American depression, because the fact that the U.S.A. produces about one-half of the non-Soviet world's output of manufactured goods means that a serious fall in American activity may be felt throughout the world. If, as in the recessions of 1929–32, 1937–8 and 1948–9, the fall in American demand causes a sharp fall in her imports of raw materials owing to the running-down of stocks, raw-material prices may decline severely and with them the purchasing power of primary producing countries.[18]

If countries outside the U.S.A. are forced to protect their own foreign exchange reserves against the world at large in such a situation a multiple decline in world trade will ensue. The critical questions, therefore, are whether the level of foreign exchange reserves possessed by the countries affected are sufficient to enable them to avoid taking restrictive action and, if they cannot, whether they can quickly discriminate against the U.S.A. in order to prevent their individual actions from aggravating the problems of other countries already in difficulties. Discrimination might even have to take the form of a widespread depreciation of non-dollar currencies in the event of a severe American slump. Even so, it is unlikely that the world could escape entirely the deflationary effects of a depression in the U.S.A. of, say, the magnitude of that in 1937–8.

As far as any individual country whose overseas markets have weakened is concerned, two important questions arise. The first relates to the mobility of resources. If the fall in overseas demand is concentrated on industries for whose products home demand is bound to be limited, and if resources cannot easily be transferred to other trades, unemployment will be protracted.

Secondly, unless its exchange reserves are adequate a country may have to take special steps to protect its balance of payments if it pursues a policy of bolstering home demand, for the volume of imports will thereby be increased. If it maintains a fixed exchange rate, action taken to stimulate home demand by reducing interest rates, for example, may have the effect of causing an outflow of foreign funds; and if there were any doubt as to its ability to maintain its exchange rate a financial centre like London might suffer severely. A policy of high interest rates designed to check an outflow of capital would render more difficult the aim of maintaining home demand. A financial centre, especially if its exchange rate does not seem secure, may be especially vulnerable to a serious world recession, unless exchange depreciation or import and exchange controls can be applied. Indeed, no country faced with a serious fall in its exchange reserves owing to a collapse in overseas demand may be able to avoid import restrictions if it attempts to maintain full employment under a regime of fixed exchange rates.

These problems have been sketched here with perhaps too heavy a hand; by 1958 the post-war world had still remained free from an international recession of any severity. This good fortune is attributable to the absence of a cyclical downswing serious enough to be classed with pre-war cycles, and indeed in most countries the level of internal demand has been persistently upwards. The foreign exchange problems of the United Kingdom during a period of American recession, as in 1957–8, have been eased by the improvement in her terms of trade that has been a direct consequence of the slackening in world activity.

In the U.S.A., post-war dips from full employment have been slight. The temptation to declare that the age of the business cycle is over may be strong, but it is worth observing that we can be said to have been living in a capital-hungry 'long wave', in which booms are bound to be vigorous and recessions weak. The cautious student of economic affairs will consider the prediction of everlasting boom in the light of the similar predictions made in the 'golden age' of American business, just before the most severe industrial crash the world has ever known. While there is every reason to hope that a severe depression can be avoided in the industrial world with the aid of government policy, the possibility that difficult problems of structural readjustment may arise through the occurrence of even mild international recession is less remote.

## GOVERNMENT POLICY AND AGGREGATE DEMAND
### Direct Controls

Direct controls may be used to regulate purchases, sales, production, or prices. Controls may be positive, in the sense that they can be used to steer resources into particular channels, but they cannot be positive as far as the total volume of expenditure is concerned, for businesses cannot be obliged to produce at a loss. In the aggregate their use is confined to checking demand.

Individually, direct controls may have narrow objects: to divert resources towards or away from specified uses; to prevent windfall profits from accruing to sellers of a commodity in intense demand but subject to an inelastic supply; or to influence the distribution of real incomes more generally. In so far as all direct controls are adopted in order to secure a pattern of output, usage, and prices other than that which the free operation of the market would produce, their justification depends on whether the choice of the government is superior to that implemented through the market-place and on whether the alternative use of taxes and subsidies, which interfere less with freedom of choice, would not secure the desired pattern with more positive inducements to expand the output of scarce commodities and with fewer shortages. As far as the more general question of preserving economic stability is concerned, the supporters of direct controls are apt to give less weight to these considerations and to stress instead their function of checking aggregate demand and of preventing a spiral of defensive cost and price reactions by holding down the price-level, even at the expense of creating the shortages of a suppressed inflation.

Consumers' expenditure can be checked by statutory rationing, and capital investment can be curtailed by building licences and by control over the supply of basic structural materials such as steel. Licensing systems aimed at restricting capital investment in peacetime are apt to be over-indulgent, if only because so many

2 S

capital projects seem nationally desirable in themselves, so that the volume of 'essential' investment for which permits are granted may exceed the real resources available.

### Controls over Public Expenditure

The government's own capital outlays, together with those of the local authorities and the nationalized industries, present a wide field in which expenditure can be increased if the government so desires, but subject to the technical difficulty of the time-lag before new plans can be implemented. An effective public works policy for checking unemployment must therefore be supported by plans prepared in advance. When the object is to check expenditure, it may be some time before existing programmes of construction can be curtailed. Current expenditure on the social services, on the other hand, is technically more elastic.

Other problems involved in using the central government's control over the public sector to maintain economic stability arise through the force of political considerations and the incompatibility of individually desirable economic objectives. In this country, at any rate, these work more strongly in the direction of increasing public outlay as a whole than of reducing it, but the need for holding down the total of government spending to prevent inflation is likely to mean that public outlays in particular fields may well be inadequate for some years, just because of the directness of official control. Roads and hospitals have been examples of this in the post-war period. Moreover, like any other direct control, government control over public capital projects may even prove too convenient an instrument, so that public expenditure on certain projects may be checked or expanded at intervals with excessive force in order to preserve general economic stability, without adequate consideration of whether retrenchment or expansion in these fields is nationally more desirable than similar action in other areas of the economy.

### Fiscal Policy

A change in government current expenditure on goods and services, with unaltered tax-rates, has a multiplier effect, depending on the marginal propensity to consume and the marginal rate of taxation. Part of a change in expenditure with tax-rates unaltered will be offset by tax receipts out of the new level of income. A change in tax-rates, with government current expenditure un-altered, on the other hand, also has an expansionist or contraction-ist effect, but the final change in national income and expenditure may be less even though the planned change in the surplus or deficit is the same. This is because part of an increase in taxation may be met out of saving and part of a reduction in taxation may be saved, so that the impulse to be 'multiplied' may be smaller than that which results from a change in government expenditure alone. Because a change in government current outlay may have a more powerful effect on national income and expenditure than a corresponding change in tax-rates, a rise in government expendi-ture accompanied by an equivalent increase in tax-rates may be expansionist.

The necessity for seeking Parliamentary approval may reduce the frequency with which general changes in fiscal policy can be made. Fiscal policy is an appropriate instrument for causing vigorous changes in demand, but it is not without its technical limitations. If people and companies can pay taxes by reducing their current saving or by drawing on past savings, fiscal policy is weakened as an anti-inflationary weapon. The effect of high marginal tax-rates on effort and enterprise may be an even greater drawback to the use of high direct taxation to prevent inflation, whereas high indirect taxes may stimulate wage-claims unless concentrated on 'luxuries'.

The limitations on the use of fiscal policy as an expansionist instrument are weaker, as long as the principle of an unbalanced Budget is acceptable to the business community as a legitimate instrument of policy. In the pre-war slump this was not so in the United States.

A Budget deficit[19] may be used to 'prime the pump' of national expenditure in a slump by its operation through both 'multiplier' and 'accelerator', and if successful the deficit will be reduced automatically as incomes and tax receipts increase and total unemployment benefits fall. The success of deficit finance as a pump-primer depends on whether private investment is stimulated sufficiently, and this will turn on the extent to which businessmen believe that the recovery in total demand will outlast the period of Budget deficits.

Fiscal policy can be used to influence private investment more directly than through the operation of the 'accelerator'. Variations in company taxation may influence investment even if there is no accompanying change in monetary policy. The use of changes in depreciation allowances has already been discussed in Chapter 18.

### Monetary and Credit Policy

If hire-purchase regulations are included within the term, monetary and credit policy can be used to affect either consumption or investment. The sale of consumers' durable goods on hire-purchase terms can be influenced by variations in the minimum deposit and maximum period of repayment, and bank advances to hire-purchase finance companies can be controlled directly by official instructions to the banks or by the general influence over the level of advances that can be exerted by the authorities. The restriction of bank advances may force borrowers to reduce their consumption generally in order to repay their overdrafts. The experience of capital gains or losses due to monetary policy may also affect consumption.

A change in monetary conditions may also be required to support a policy aimed at influencing consumption by fiscal means. If the national income is to be expanded by a reduction in taxation, an increase in the quantity of money may be required to finance the demand for higher money balances to enable the 'transactions' and 'contingencies' motives to be satisfied without a rise in interest rates, which might check investment. Budget deficits should be financed by means appropriate to the government's general objective—through the banking system when a vigorous expansionist effect is desired, and through public issues when it is desirable to restrict liquidity.

Hire-purchase restrictions apart, the main weight of monetary policy as a stabilizing instrument, as traditionally understood, is felt on investment, whereas fiscal policy operates mainly on consumption. The choice between the two methods is therefore partly one between varying consumption and varying investment. The efficacy of monetary policy as a method of influencing the level of investment depends in the first instance on the ability of the authorities to achieve the pattern of interest rates and the supply of finance that they wish to create. Even with the assistance of direct intervention, the long-term rate of interest will not be responsive in a downwards direction if investors are afraid that a fall will be shortlived. As for a policy of tight money, open market operations may be difficult to carry out on a large scale once a boom has got under way, so that the bond market is in any case tending to come under pressure because of the excess of planned investment over planned saving, the rising demand for active money balances, and possibly a growing expectation that an official policy of higher interest rates is likely. Open market bond sales in these circumstances may threaten to cause a sharp rise in interest rates.

Control over the banking system presents a number of other problems. A series of Budget deficits, balance-of-payments surpluses, or government debt redemptions may lead to high bank liquidity ratios unless the authorities are able to fund in sufficient volume or resort to some device such as compulsory special deposits. The authorities have also to decide whether economic stability requires control over the volume of advances or deposits in general; since the war the authorities have shown themselves to be more concerned with the former. Even if liquidity ratios are not excessive, advances may escape an official restrictive policy if they can be increased at the expense of selling investments. Official 'requests' for the restriction of advances have not proved entirely successful. Looking at the problem that might arise in a slump, there is the difficulty that, if the outlook for bond prices were uncertain, the banks might prefer to hold excess liquid assets rather than to expand deposits by purchasing bonds, and their caution as to business prospects might make them reluctant to expand their advances with sufficient vigour.

Monetary policy operates through changing the quantity of money or the terms on which business can obtain finance. It is not the case that a business can obtain all the bank finance it requires by offering a high rate of interest, because bank advances are rationed between creditworthy borrowers and not offered to the highest bidders. Outside the capital market, too, there are elements of rationing. Investors do not like to put too many of their eggs in one basket, so that there may be limits on the availability of finance to any one borrower, depending on his status. The Capital Issues Committee is also an instrument of rationing. There is, therefore, some justification for considering the quantity of finance and its terms separately when assessing the effect of monetary policy on business investment.

On the whole, investment has not proved very sensitive to

changes in interest rates. When there is inflation and order books are full, the rate of interest at which planned investment would equal planned saving is well in excess of that ruling in the market. Once a long 'queue' for capital goods has developed, so that business plans to undertake capital investment exceed the capacity of the capital-goods industries, a very sharp fall indeed will have to be secured in intended investment for the level of actual capital expenditure to be reduced. Monetary policy has to be applied with vigour in the early stage of the boom if this situation is to be prevented, but the authorities may be inhibited from acting with sufficient promptness by the fear of checking the pace of real economic expansion.

Of course there is *some* level of interest rates that will equate planned investment and saving even when a boom has reached its most vigorous stage, but the practical question is whether the government will then be prepared to force interest rates to this very high level needed to prevent excess demand. The government may be unwilling to accept a large increase in the cost of the national debt. Secondly, high interest rates reward the current saver in terms of income, but they impose a heavy penalty on past savings in the form of capital losses, and it is doubtful how far very large and frequent swings in interest rates are compatible with the smooth operation of the capital market. Moreover, if interest rates are pushed up to unprecedentedly high levels in a boom, it becomes correspondingly harder to push them down to very low levels in any later slump, for investors do not like to be bitten twice.

The efficacy with which monetary policy can revive investment in a slump depends partly on how low interest rates can be driven, bearing in mind the effect both on home investors and on the owners of foreign funds, who may withdraw them elsewhere in a regime of fixed exchange rates. If businessmen are pessimistic, however, the power of monetary policy is bound to be limited, particularly if the demand for houses and commercial buildings is not easily revived. In the case of both boom and slump, the level of ordinary-share prices may be highly important in regard to the cost of external finance and its effect on business confidence, but the response of investors to a tightening of monetary policy in a boom will be small if the power of the authorities to check the boom is thought to be weak, and conversely in a slump.

Changes in the quantity of money affect interest rates; there is no way of restricting the supply of finance without allowing interest rates to rise. If the authorities are unwilling to accept an increase in interest rates, therefore, their control over the supply of money is to that extent restricted. But certain types of monetary policy act more by checking the supply of finance than by raising interest rates, partly because some rates of interest, e.g. bank overdraft rates, are 'sticky'. A policy that concentrates on the use of Bank rate, for example, is different in emphasis from one that sets out to reduce bank liquidity more directly. One method may be more effective in influencing business expectations than the other, and the response of investors, too, may be different.

Limitations on the availability of finance may be effective barriers against inflation. If finance is short, capital projects *must* be postponed and working capital economized; a previous increase in stocks may be checked or even reversed. In the postwar period the government has sought to contract the supply of bank finance to business and to limit recourse to the new-issue market by requiring the approval of the Capital Issues Committee.

These, however, are only two of several sources of finance. The business sector may itself be highly liquid, so that official restrictions are by-passed. Moreover, firms with excess cash may be willing to finance other businesses to which they supply goods, through the medium of trade credit. Through this channel firms whose activity is regarded as 'non-essential' by the authorities, and therefore placed low in the queue for bank or new-issue finance, may nevertheless obtain part of the funds they require, if indirectly, from those who have been allowed easy access to bank advances or the new-issue market. Local authorities and hire-purchase finance houses, if they are willing to pay sufficiently high interest rates, may be able to replace bank or new-issue finance by offering attractive rates of interest on short-term deposits, thus tempting money out of 'idle' balances. If the economy as a whole is highly liquid, therefore, a policy intended to restrict the supply of finance by blocking one or two of its channels is likely to be ineffective.

It cannot be said that either here or in the U.S.A. the moderate degree of monetary restriction applied since 1951 has been particularly successful in checking inflation, and the British authorities appear to have moved closer in recent years to the view that Bank rate is a more effective instrument for influencing international capital movements than for controlling the domestic economy. If moderate credit restriction has failed to prevent inflation, however, the lesson is not that monetary policy can be dispensed with, but that it may have to play a secondary role to fiscal policy in a boom unless it can be tightened with sufficient vigour at an early stage, or unless interest rates are forced up to very high levels when the boom is well advanced. In any case, monetary policy will be weakened if fiscal policy is pulling in the opposite direction. Finally, in a world in which full, not to say overfull, employment is taken for granted, *any* form of disinflationary policy is bound to be handicapped, and even if the permanence of full employment is not taken for granted the success of any disinflationary policy will depend in large measure on the promptness with which it is applied. The same is probably true of a policy aimed at checking a recession.

# CHAPTER 43

# INTEREST RATES SINCE THE FIRST WORLD WAR

## 1919–1931

The first half of this period is dominated by the post-war boom and ensuing slump and by the restoration of the gold standard. The cost of the floating debt, which had been expanded during the war, made a rise in Bank rate expensive for the Exchequer, and the authorities hoped to restrict the use of Bank rate to check the boom by inducing the banks to hold down advances voluntarily. Nevertheless, the sharp rise in prices and the weakness of the exchange rate which had begun in 1919 obliged the authorities to raise Bank rate to 7 per cent in April 1920, and the long-term rate of interest followed to a level of 5½ per cent in the autumn of that year. Despite the fact that the peak of the boom had been passed some seven or eight months previously, Bank rate was maintained at 7 per cent until April 1921, largely to restore the Bank of England's gold reserve, which was still tending to fall. With the onset of the slump the long-term rate of interest took the lead in falling some months before Bank rate was reduced.

Following this, short-term interest rates were brought down rapidly, the existence of serious unemployment and a recovery in the exchange rate inducing the Bank of England to lower its Bank rate to 3 per cent in July 1922. The rise that began a year later was due entirely to the policy of returning to the gold standard at the pre-war parity. The domestic situation was still one of excessive unemployment, but the increase in the rediscount rate of the American authorities, where a minor boom was developing, was exerting pressure against sterling. In 1924 the Bank of England sought to restrict the supply of sterling on the foreign exchange market by imposing an informal control over new foreign issues, and money-market rates were raised; but this did not suffice to support the exchange rate, and Bank rate was increased. The rise to 5 per cent in 1925 marked the prelude to the restoration of the gold standard. At this time 11 per cent of the insured labour force were still out of work, but the Bank of England seems to have held the view that at 5 per cent Bank rate would do more to attract foreign funds than aggravate domestic deflation.

During certain of these years, it will be seen from Figure 10, the Treasury bill rate stood well below Bank rate, first during the slump, when market rates automatically fell to low levels, and again in 1924. The long-term rate of interest remained at not much less than 4½ per cent despite the low level of money rates between 1922 and 1925. For this a policy of funding was largely

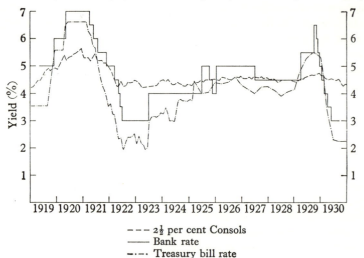

--- 2½ per cent Consols
——— Bank rate
—·—· Treasury bill rate

Fig. 10. Interest rates 1919–30.

responsible. The large volume of Treasury bills outstanding at the end of the war was a source of great concern to the authorities, who feared that it would destroy their control of banking liquidity. During the 1920 boom, for example, the banks had been able to expand advances by running down their Treasury bill portfolios, which forced the Exchequer to borrow from the Bank of England, augmenting bank cash reserves and depressing money rates at a most inappropriate time. Part of the bill issue was also in the hands of overseas holders, who might wish to sell them just when it was necessary to tighten banking conditions in this country. Between 1921 and 1923 a series of conversion operations was carried out that reduced the floating debt by 40 per cent, but only at the expense of causing a wide spread between short-term and long-term rates of interest, a gap that was without precedent.

The remainder of the period until the suspension of the gold standard in 1931 is marked by the task of protecting the gold reserve in the face of rising interest rates in the U.S.A On the other hand, domestic conditions in the United Kingdom did not call for a restrictive monetary policy, for there was still serious unemployment. The policy adopted by the Bank of England was to use open market sales of bills to force market rates close to Bank rate, so that the increase in the former could serve to attract foreign funds without the necessity for a very high Bank rate, which would have resulted in high bank overdraft charges and might have weakened business confidence. In these years the return to the gold standard at the pre-war parity and its effect on unemployment were coming under serious criticism in this country. The Bank of England was concerned to avoid measures that would bring the gold standard into disrepute. Open market operations also led the banks to sell investments rather than contract advances, so adding to the factors making for high long-term rates.

With the international financial crisis of 1929 a high Bank rate became a necessity to protect the gold reserve. The outflow of gold itself acted so as to make market rates rise, that is to make Bank rate 'effective' as under the pre-war gold standard.

After the first shock of the international crisis the rise in Bank rate was sufficient to draw gold out of the weaker centres of Europe, and with the development of the American recession and the decline in interest rates in the U.S.A. from 1930, short-term rates were allowed to fall in this country. Long-term yields, however, remained high, because the uncertainty of the period allowed no assurance that Bank rate could be held down. Indeed, with the renewed balance-of-payments crisis of 1931 another sharp increase in Bank rate was made in a final attempt to save the gold standard. But the cost was too great, unemployment in Great Britain had already reached 20 per cent of the total insured population, and the pound was allowed to depreciate.

## 1931–1939

Following this, interest rates began to fall; the devaluation of an international currency like sterling is bound to provoke the thought that other currencies may follow, and there was an inflow of funds to London. The disgorging of gold by India, where devaluation offered an attractive opportunity to private holders to sell at a profit, also reinforced the recovery in the Bank's reserve. The inflow of funds added to the liquidity of the capital market at a time when the natural effect of trade depression was in any case to produce low interest rates.

In the second half of 1932 the authorities took advantage of the situation to embark upon a cheap-money policy that centred on

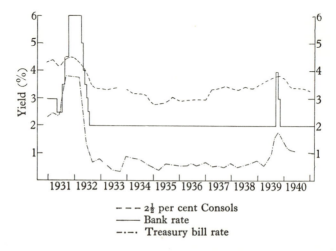

- - - 2½ per cent Consols
——— Bank rate
—·—· Treasury bill rate

Fig. 11. Interest rates 1931–40.

the conversion in December of 5 per cent War Loan 1929/47 into the 3½ per cent War Loan that exists today. Bank rate had already been brought down to 2 per cent and the Treasury bill rate to ¾ per cent; for the next twenty years Bank rate remained ineffective as a determinant of money-market rates. To support the conversion the cash reserves of the banks were swollen by open market operations, departmental funds were used to support the long-term market, foreign issues in London were controlled, and a psychological offensive was undertaken by the authorities with the intention of putting the financial community in a receptive state of mind. The very size of the new stock, £2,000 million, was an advantage, for it was a large-enough tail to wag the whole market dog and bring yields on other stocks down to its level.

The operation was a great success, only £165 million, or 8 per cent, of the old War Loan not being offered for conversion into the 3½ per cent stock. Its success was instrumental both in assisting the recovery from the depression and in reducing the interest charge of the national debt, a factor of some importance to a government that had been elected in 1931 on a programme of economy.

The cheap-money policy, which, of course, was assisted by the depression itself, was maintained in a number of ways. The Bank of England pursued a policy of increasing bank cash reserves by open market purchases of bills and by its gold operations. With the demand for advances restricted by the low level of prices and business activity, the increase in bank cash reserves caused bank investment portfolios almost to double between 1932 and 1937 and enabled long-term rates to be held down despite the gradual recovery in business conditions. Departmental funds were also used to purchase bonds, to underwrite new issues of government securities and to take up maturing stocks. An informal control was maintained over competing issues of foreign issues and trustee securities, including those of the local authorities.

The year 1935 marks a dividing line in the pre-war period. Until then the low level of business activity and the inflow of foreign funds tended to prolong the effect of the conversion operation, and long-term rates of interest fell. After 1935 the recovery in business activity, aided by rearmament, the return of funds to France following the devaluation of the franc, and growing international tension caused long-term interest rates to rise. The Treasury bill rate, on the other hand, remained at not much more than ½ per cent, owing to the shortage of liquid assets available to the banking system that resulted from the operations of the Exchange Equalization Account and the scarcity of commercial bills. The dearth of liquid assets tended to accentuate the rise in long-term yields.

## 1939–1945

The course of interest rates during the Second World War presents a contrast to that in the First. Until 1917 government controls over the use of resources were sketchy and taxation light by the standards of 1939–45, while until the entry of the United States into the war the foreign exchange situation was weak at a time when exchange control was far from complete. The technique of financing a major twentieth-century war had not been developed, and considerable emphasis was placed on raising long-term loans to finance the huge Budget deficit, even on unduly generous terms. The Treasury bill rate was allowed to rise to $5\frac{1}{2}$ per cent in 1916, when especially high yields were regarded as necessary to keep foreign funds in London, and at the beginning of 1917 long-term interest rates climbed to their peak with the issue of 5 per cent War Loan. The yield on $2\frac{1}{2}$ per cent Consols rose to $5\frac{1}{2}$ per cent.

In the Second World War, on the other hand, the Treasury bill rate was kept at 1 per cent, and long-term rates of interest were brought down from $3\frac{3}{4}$ per cent to 3 per cent. This presents one of the rare examples of a successful cheap-money policy at a time of inflation. It was achieved by the rigorous use of direct controls over private consumption and capital expenditure, by the techniques of suppressed inflation, which led to the creation of unspendable purchasing power, by the isolation of the British capital market by means of exchange control, and by the exercise of 'moral suasion' over investors, particularly over institutions such as the insurance companies.

The Budget deficits of the war swelled the cash reserves of the banking system, and although excess cash was mopped up by compulsory Treasury Deposit Receipts and the Treasury bill issue, the banks were enabled by their high liquidity ratios to expand their investments from £600 million on the outbreak of war to £1,126 million in August 1945. Advances were actually reduced from £985 million to £756 million, but total deposits rose from £2,177 million to £4,747 million. As part of this policy the government security holdings of the Bank of England rose from £408 million to £1,610 million.

## 1945–1951

In 1943, and again in the 1944 White Paper on Employment Policy, the coalition government affirmed in broad terms its intention of continuing a policy of low interest rates in the interests of post-war reconstruction. Following its election in 1945, the Labour government embarked on an attempt to reduce the long-term rate of interest to $2\frac{1}{2}$ per cent. Several advantages may have been sought from this, including a reduction in the national-debt charge, a cheaper basis for compensating holders of securities in nationalized industries, and permanently lower industry rates as a means of redistributing the national income. The government probably subscribed to the belief, in which it was not alone, that a post-war slump was not far off and that a low interest rate would be a useful preliminary counter-measure. The government relied on the formidable apparatus of control, inherited from the war, to keep inflation in check.

The technique pursued was to combine a vigorous psychological campaign aimed at convincing investors of the authorities'

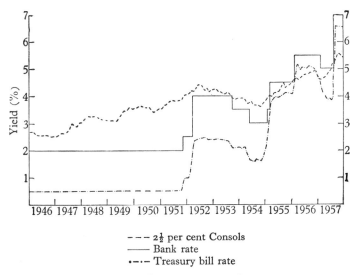

--- 2½ per cent Consols
——— Bank rate
•—•— Treasury bill rate

Fig. 12. Interest rates 1946–57.

determination and ability to reach the 2½ per cent line with an expansion of the money supply and a reduction in money-market rates. The latter came at an early stage; in October 1945 the rate on T.D.R.'s was reduced from 1·125 to 0·625 per cent and the Treasury bill rate from 1 to ½ per cent; the banks were asked to set their deposit rate at a maximum of ½ per cent, 1 per cent previously having been paid on deposits outside London. Departmental funds were used to support the gilt-edged market, causing a rise in bank deposits and in bank liquidity ratios. The tendency for switching 'long' to raise short-term bond yields was countered by calling a number of short-term issues for redemption, and the supply of medium-dated bonds through the 'tap' was also cut off. Both devices tended to magnify the rise in bank liquidity.

The climax of this policy came with the issue of 2½ per cent Treasury stock, redeemable 1975 or after, at par for cash, the proceeds of which were to be used to retire the 3 per cent Local Loan stock. After this the attempt to hold the 2½ per cent line began to grow more difficult. The creation of bank deposits on a large scale made more difficult the prevention of inflation in an economy that was already excessively liquid. With the gradual appreciation of the scale of the country's post-war problems the possibility of the government's being able to *maintain* a rate of interest as low as 2½ per cent, which, after all, had not been achieved either during the war, when controls were practically all-embracing, or during the slump, when capital investment was at a low level, looked increasingly doubtful. Sooner or later an increase in interest rates seemed likely. As the Chancellor's determination to hold the 2½ per cent line became more vocal, the distrust of investors grew.

With the prospect of an increase in the supply of gilt-edged stocks owing to nationalization and the development of the fuel crisis in the winter of 1946/7 the gilt-edged market weakened. With interest rates at such a low level that there was no prospect of any further fall and some risk of a rise, the market became increasingly unsettled. Inevitably the desire to avoid capital losses speeded up the reversal of the previous fall in interest rates, and the authorities were reluctant to support the market yet again at the expense of creating a further increase in bank liquidity. The cheap-money policy associated with Dr. Dalton had been defeated by the distrust of investors even before it was finally destroyed by the convertibility crisis of August 1947.

For the rest of this period until 1951 the Treasury bill rate remained pegged at ½ per cent; the long-term bond market was allowed to go relatively free but without any attempt by the government to pursue a positively disinflationary monetary policy in the orthodox sense. Broadly speaking, the aim of the government was to counter inflation by fiscal policy, by controls, and by wage and dividend restraint, and to support, at a market rate of ½ per cent, whatever level of deposits was required to finance whatever national income arose from its policies. The Bank of England stood ready to provide through its 'back door' all the cash that was required by the banking system to maintain its cash ratio.

The main check to the supply of finance to business and other borrowers took the form of requests to the banks not to lend for 'non-essential' purposes and of the control over new issues. As the business sector was comfortably liquid, neither form of direct control had any marked effect on capital investment. As far as the banking system was concerned, the main potential threat came from the decline in the country's gold and dollar reserves, which provided the authorities with sterling that was used to retire floating debt, but not sufficiently to bring liquid-asset ratios down to their minimum. Only in 1949 was there any reduction in the total of bank deposits and currency in the hands of the public.

This policy meant that, within the framework of controls and fiscal policy, no substantial increase in the rate of interest need arise from any excess of planned investment over planned saving or from any increase in the demand for 'active' cash balances due to a rise in the money value of the national income. As long as the banks possessed surplus liquid assets, they could, *if they wished*, always take up bonds sold by businesses or by individual investors to finance inflation. In this situation the behaviour of long-term rates of interest was determined mainly by the expectations of investors in general and of the banks in particular, and long-term rates of interest tended to be unstable.

In the months before and after the devaluation of sterling interest rates experienced a pronounced rise as a result of the outflow of capital and investors' fears regarding the economic situation. Following the outbreak of the Korean war the balance-of-payments surplus enjoyed by the United Kingdom and the rest of the sterling area exerted a downwards pressure on long-term interest rates, but one that seems to have been restricted by the operations of the authorities, for the liquid-asset ratios of the banks were actually reduced slightly in the face of a large increase in the gold reserve. In 1951 the loss of gold similarly appears to have been prevented from having its full effect on long-term interest rates, but interest rates nevertheless rose because of the pressure of inflation at a time when investors were concerned at the balance-of-payments crisis and aware that a Conservative victory in the general election of that year might mean the return to a more orthodox policy of dear money.

2 T

## 1951–1957

In October 1951 the newly-returned Conservative government took its first steps towards a more orthodox monetary policy. The banks were 'induced' to replace their excess Treasury bills by Serial Funding stocks, and Bank rate was raised to 2½ per cent. Apart from the absorption of the excess liquidity of the commercial banks these measures were largely psychological, the overture to a new policy rather than a new policy itself. The Bank of England continued to provide the discount market freely with cash through the 'back door', and the Treasury bill rate was held a full 1½ per cent below Bank rate with the further assistance of the device whereby the market, if forced 'into the Bank', was allowed seven-day advances on the security of Treasury bills at a rate ½ per cent below bank-rate. The banks' call-money rate was set at a low level with official approval. As investors became aware of the possibility of a real tightening of monetary policy, the continued loss of gold and dollars and the pressure on bank liquidity that this entailed caused the long-term rate to increase. The rise in prices and costs, by increasing the demand for 'active' balances, worked in the same direction. After the turn of the year the rise in the Treasury bill rate anticipated the sharp increase in Bank rate that was to come in March 1952.

The increase in bank-rate of 1½ per cent was of an order calculated to restore foreign confidence in sterling, but the gap between Bank rate and market rates was maintained. Long-term yields rose until the middle of the year, impelled by the continued concern at the loss of foreign exchange and by bank sales of long-term stocks designed to replenish their liquid-asset ratios and shorten the term of their portfolios. In July 1952, however, yields in the long-term market fell as quickly as they had risen, on the sudden realization that the crisis was over and that no further monetary restriction was likely; yields were high enough to appear very attractive to the long-term investor.

For the next two years interest rates declined. The balance of payments was improving and the rise in the gold and dollar reserve strengthened the confidence of investors. In the U.S.A., money rates were brought down in order to 'reflate' the economy after the minor recession of 1953. This factor, together with the strength of the sterling area's current dollar balance—which was enjoying the delayed effect of the import cuts of 1952—led to a marked inflow of overseas funds into London in 1953-4. The authorities allowed money-market rates to fall with this movement, and Bank rate was reduced. Until the middle of 1954 the domestic situation was not particularly inflationary—the restriction of capital investment introduced in 1952 and the fall in import prices held back inflation. The authorities took advantage of the reduction in Bank rate to remove the facility of borrowing at the special rate of ½ per cent below Bank rate.

The fall in money-market rates and in long-term yields came to an end in the second half of 1954 with the resurgence of inflationary pressure and the evidence of some deterioration in the dollar balance. Throughout 1955 the force of demand inflation, the two increases in Bank rate, the restriction of bank advances, and finally the diversion of local authority borrowing to the open market drove up long-term yields. The loss of gold and dollars caused disquiet in the financial world.

The Treasury bill rate was forced closer to Bank rate by the denial of assistance to the discount market through the 'back door', and this opened a gap between the deposit rate of the banks— which moved with Bank rate—and the Treasury bill rate. Commercial and financial concerns were thereby induced to transfer idle balances from deposits held with the banks to purchase Treasury bills, and the resultant pressure on bank liquidity ratios obliged the banks to sell investments in the first half of 1955, thus strengthening the rise in long-term yields. The banks were asked by the authorities not to allow their liquidity ratios to fall below 30 per cent.

In 1956 the pressure of demand inflation began to subside, but the rise in costs and prices continued to increase the demand for 'active' balances. In February, Bank rate was increased by a further 1 per cent, partly to check the inflation but mainly to restore foreign confidence in sterling, which had weakened once more. Long-term yields continued to increase as the gilt-edged market reacted to the Suez crisis.

With the cessation of hostilities yields in the long-term market followed the sharp fall in the Treasury bill rate which got under way towards the end of 1956. The loss of gold and dollars had enabled the authorities to reduce the supply of Treasury bills and there was apparently a brisk demand for bills from sources outside the clearing banks, as in 1955. The seasonal Exchequer surplus made possible a further reduction in the bill issue.

At the same time the authorities pursued a funding policy, selling bonds in order to reduce the floating debt and bring bank liquidity under control. Normally this would have the effect of raising long-term rates of interest, but on this occasion the fall in the Treasury bill rate led to the expectation of a reduction in Bank rate, and in these circumstances investors felt they could look ahead to lower, not higher, long-term yields. The general assumption appeared to have been that open market sales could only be made on a market in which security prices were rising. For the time being, at any rate, the banks were in a position to stand some loss of liquid assets, and the closure of the Suez canal had brought some relief from excess demand in certain sectors of the economy, notably in vehicles.

Bank rate was reduced at the end of January following the fall in market rates. While money rates continued to fall, long-term rates of interest reversed direction almost immediately. The issue of a new stock obviously designed to show the market that the authorities were prepared to hold down gilt-edged prices, the weight of the funding sales, and the development of an apparently uncontrollable cost inflation combined to force the long-term rate of interest up to the highest level reached since 1920.

In September 1957, in response to the danger of inflation and the outflow of foreign funds set off by the prospect of the revaluation of the German mark, Bank rate was increased by 2 per cent to 7 per cent, and the Treasury bill rate was held close to this by keeping money-market conditions tight. The rise in long-term rates, however, was comparatively small, so that the downward yield curve of a temporary 'crisis' was established. Before long the evident determination of the government to halt inflation at last and the realization that the German mark was not going to be revalued reinforced the natural attraction of high money rates and reversed the outflow of funds from the country. With the recovery in the gold and dollar reserve the Treasury bill rate began to fall in anticipation of a reduction in Bank rate. The tailing-off in the capital investment boom and the steady, if slow, rise in unemployment pointed to some danger of an internal recession. With money rates in the U.S.A. at low levels, Bank rate was brought down to 5 per cent by the summer of 1958, the fall in the Treasury bill rate to 4 per cent at the beginning of August indicating that some further reduction was expected. Long-term yields also declined, but by comparatively little, for the official policy of selling long-term stocks to the public was still applied in the first half of 1958, and there were signs of a large potential demand for long-term funds on the part of local authority and overseas borrowers. The view that, overall, the pressing demand for capital would render appropriate the maintenance of a relatively high long-term rate of interest seemed to have become accepted by investors as well as by the authorities.

# APPENDIX OF LATE NOTES

155    [1] The Prevention of Frauds (Investment) Act, 1939, consolidated with other legislation in an Act of a similar name in 1958.

183    [2] However, insurance policies can be taken out against the insolvency or protracted default of trade debtors.

255    [3] Certain sections of these Acts were consolidated in the Prevention of Frauds (Investment) Act of 1958.

259    [4] In February 1959, under a general consent order, the Treasury suspended all previous requirements whereby application had to be made to the C.I.C., except for transactions effected by residents outside the U.K. This relaxation was intended to stimulate capital investment.

280    [5] It is true that many applications may have been withdrawn during negotiations; on the other hand many 'enquiries' regarding the possibility of a loan do not reach the stage of a formal 'application'.

284    [6] The main business of this company is the insurance of trade debts in this country.

301    [7] This does not mean that in other countries there is no such division of functions in practice; the distinction is that in London each Stock Exchange *firm* must declare itself to be either a stock-broking or a jobbing firm.

303    [8] Whether this has been the result of a shortage of capital on the part of jobbers is open to controversy; jobbers can usually reinforce their own resources by borrowing from the banks.

304    [9] The fortnightly account system gives the jobber more elbow room than would settlement for 'cash'; it thus helps him to act more as a shock absorber. The gilt-edged market does not have to bear the same strains.

348    [10] This intention was implemented in 1959.

367  [11] Under the overdraft system a bank's customer is allowed to draw cheques beyond his credit balance, up to an agreed limit. Interest is charged only on the debit balance outstanding; thus the cost of borrowing is minimised.

369  [12] Including the merchant banks or acceptance houses.

388  [13] This is an artificial example, in that the banks would not sell bills if their liquid asset ratios were already at a minimum.

391  [14] In this somewhat artificial example the banks in Stage IV are shown as replenishing their money market assets out of surplus cash, e.g. by purchasing bills sold by the Bank of England. In practice the whole process would be compressed.

529  [15] Some economists would accord to inventories a leading role in the turning point of a 'normal' business or trade cycle.

617  [16] This book went to press too early to incorporate the authoritative discussion of these and related problems presented in the Report of the Committee on the Working of the Monetary System (Cmd. 827, H.M.S.O., London, 1959).

622  [17] The word 'daily' should not, of course, be taken literally; but the argument applies even to quarterly data.

623  [18] The experience of the American recessions of 1953–4 and 1957–8 was less discouraging. In the former commodity prices were sustained by the growing demand of Western Europe; in the latter high cost domestic producers in the U.S.A. suffered more than overseas producers of commodities, except for the impact of American quotas imposed on imports.

627  [19] The U.K. has usually had a large Budget surplus on *current* account since the war. Expansionist policies have operated through a reduction in this surplus without going so far as to aim at a current deficit.

# SUGGESTED READING

## GENERAL

There are several authoritative standard text-books covering the broad field of modern economic analysis, e.g.:

P. A. Samuelson, *Economics—An Introductory Analysis* (4th ed., McGraw-Hill, London, 1958)

F. C. C. Benham, *Economics* (5th ed., Pitman, London, 1955)
The former has a rather wider range and is written against an American background.

## PROBLEMS OF ECONOMIC GROWTH AND DEVELOPMENT

C. P. Kindleberger, *Economic Development* (McGraw-Hill, London, 1958)

G. M. Meier and R. E. Baldwin, *Economic Development* (John Wiley, New York, 1957)

## THE MARKET ECONOMY AND BUSINESS BEHAVIOUR

R. S. Edwards and H. Townsend, *Business Enterprise* (Macmillan, London, 1958)

G. C. Allen, *British Industries and Their Organisation* (3rd ed., Longmans, London, 1958)

National Bureau of Economic Research, *Business Concentration and Price Policy* (Princeton University Press, 1955)

E. A. G. Robinson, *Monopoly* (Cambridge University Press, London, 1941)

E. H. Chamberlin (ed.), *Monopoly, Competition and Their Regulation* (Macmillan, London, 1954)

American Economic Association, *Readings in The Social Control of Industry* (Blakiston, Philadelphia, 1949)

B. Yamey, *Resale Price Maintenance* (Pitman, London, 1954)

*Reports of the Monopolies Commission* (H.M.S.O., London)

## LABOUR AND TRADE UNIONS

P. Sargent Florence, *Labour* (Hutchinson, London, 1949)

J. T. Dunlop (ed.), *The Theory of Wage Determination* (Macmillan, London, 1957)

2 U

A. Flanders and H. A. Clegg (eds.), *The System of Industrial Relations in Great Britain* (Blackwell, Oxford, 1954)

B. C. Roberts, *National Wages Policy in War and Peace* (Allen & Unwin, London, 1958)

B. Wootton, *Social Foundations of Wage Policy* (Allen & Unwin, London, 1955)

### COMPANY FINANCE

F. W. Paish, *Business Finance* (Pitman, London, 1957)

L. G. Whyte, *Principles of Finance and Investment*, Volume II (Cambridge University Press, London, 1949)

National Bureau of Economic Research, *Conference on Research in Business Finance* (N.B.E.R., New York, 1952)

L. C. B. Gower, *The Principles of Modern Company Law* (2nd ed., Stevens, London, 1957)

### COMPANY ACCOUNTS AND THEIR INTERPRETATION

S. W. Rowland and B. Magee, *Accounting* (Gee & Company, London, 1949)

W. T. Baxter (ed.), *Studies in Accounting* (Sweet & Maxwell, London, 1950)

Harold G. Edey, *Business Budgets and Accounts* (Hutchinson, London, 1959)

R. A. Foulke, *Practical Financial Analysis* (McGraw-Hill, London, 1953)

*Royal Committee on the Taxation of Trading Profits* (Cmd. 8189, H.M.S.O., London, 1951)

### INSTITUTIONS OF THE CAPITAL MARKET

Sir Oscar R. Hobson, *How the City Works* (News Chronicle Book Department, London, 1955)

N. Macrae, *The London Capital Market* (Staples Press, London, 1955)

R. F. Henderson, *The New Issue Market and the Finance of Industry* (Bowes & Bowes, Cambridge, 1951)

Various Authors, *The Stock Exchanges* (The Institute of Bankers, London, 1954)

F. E. Armstrong, *The Book of the Stock Exchange* (5th ed., Pitman, London, 1957)

Investors' Chronicle, *Beginners Please* (Eyre & Spottiswoode, London, 1955)

M. S. Rix, *Stock Market Economics* (Pitman, London, 1954)
M. S. Rix, *Investment Arithmetic* (Pitman, London, 1956)

### THE BANKING SYSTEM AND MONETARY POLICY

R. S. Sayers, *Modern Banking* (4th ed., Oxford University Press, 1950)
W. Manning Dacey, *The Banking Mechanism* (2nd ed., Hutchinson, London, 1958)
R. S. Sayers, *Central Banking After Bagehot* (Oxford University Press, 1957)
E. Nevin, *The Mechanism of Cheap Money* (University of Wales Press, Cardiff, 1955)

### PUBLIC FINANCE

U. K. Hicks, *Public Finance* (2nd ed., Nisbet, London, 1955)
American Economic Association, *Readings in Fiscal Policy* (Allen & Unwin, London, 1955)
W. J. Blum and H. Kalven, *The Uneasy Case for Progressive Taxation* (University of Chicago Press, 1953)
J. M. Buchanan, *Public Principles of Public Debt* (Richard D. Irwin, Illinois, 1958)
*Final Report of the Royal Commission on the Taxation of Profits and Income* (Cmd. 9474, H.M.S.O., London, 1955)

### NATIONAL INCOME STATISTICS

H. C. Edey and A. T. Peacock, *National Income and Social Accounting* (Hutchinson, London, 1954)
R. Marris, *Economic Arithmetic* (Macmillan, London, 1958)
Central Statistical Office, *National Income Statistics: Sources and Methods* (H.M.S.O., London, 1956)

### THE DETERMINATION OF THE NATIONAL INCOME AND SECURITY PRICES

A. C. Day, *Outline of Monetary Economics* (Oxford University Press, 1957)
A. H. Hansen, *A Guide to Keynes* (McGraw-Hill, New York, 1953)
J. M. Keynes, *The General Theory of Employment, Interest and Money* (Macmillan, London, 1936)

American Economic Association, *Readings in the Theory of Income Distribution* (Blakiston, Philadelphia, 1946)

F. A. Lutz, 'The Pattern of Interest Rates' (*Quarterly Journal of Economics* (U.S.A.), Volume LV, 1940–41), reprinted in American Economic Association, *Readings in The Theory of Income Distribution*

G. Harberler, *Prosperity and Depression* (4th ed., Allen & Unwin, London, 1958)

American Economic Association, *Readings in Business Cycle Theory* (Allen & Unwin, London, 1950)

R. A. Gordon, *Business Fluctuations* (Harper, New York, 1952)

J. S. Dusenberry, *Business Cycles and Economic Growth* (McGraw-Hill, London, 1958)

E. Lundberg (ed.), *The Business Cycle in the Postwar World* (Macmillan, London, 1955)

A. J. Brown, *The Great Inflation* (Oxford University Press, London, 1955)

C. Bresciani-Turroni, *Inflation* (Halley Stewart Publications, London, 1937)

*Reports of Council on Prices, Productivity and Incomes* (H.M.S.O., London)

Hargreaves Parkinson, *Ordinary Shares* (Eyre & Spottiswoode, London, 1944)

A. G. Ellinger, *The Art of Investment* (Bowes & Bowes, London, 1955)

## INTERNATIONAL TRADE AND PAYMENTS

P. T. Ellesworth, *The International Economy* (Macmillan, New York. Revised ed.)

J. Viner, *International Trade and Development* (Oxford University Press, 1957)

L. A. Metzler, 'The Theory of International Trade', in H. S. Ellis (ed.), *A Survey of Contemporary Economics* (Irwin, London. Reprint 1957)

R. F. Harrod, *International Economics* (Nisbet, London, 1957)

J. E. Meade, *The Balance of Payments*, Volume I (Oxford University Press, London, 1951)

American Economic Association, *Readings in the Theory of International Trade* (Allen & Unwin, London, 1953)

## PROBLEMS OF GOVERNMENT POLICY AND ECONOMIC STABILITY

L. C. Robbins, *The Economic Problem in Peace and War* (Macmillan, London, 1947)

K. E. Boulding, *Principles of Economic Policy* (Prentice-Hall, New Jersey, 1955)

W. A. Lewis, *The Principles of Economic Planning* (Dobson, London, 1948)

I. M. D. Little, *The Price of Fuel* (Oxford University Press, 1953)

Ben W. Lewis, *British Planning and Nationalization* (Twentieth Century Trend, New York, 1952)

E. Lundberg, *Business Cycles and Economic Policy* (Allen & Unwin, London, 1957)

J. Tinbergen, *Economic Policy: Principles and Design* (North-Holland Publishing Co., Amsterdam, 1956)

J. E. Meade, *The Control of Inflation* (Cambridge University Press, London, 1958)

## BRITAIN AND THE INTERNATIONAL ECONOMY 1919–58

W. A. Lewis, *Economic Survey 1919–39* (Allen & Unwin, London, 1949)

H. W. Arndt, *The Economic Lessons of the Nineteen-Twenties* (Oxford University Press, London, 1944)

League of Nations, *International Currency Experience* (Reprinted by United Nations, 1949)

Sir Dennis Robertson, *Britain and the World Economy* (Allen & Unwin, London, 1954)

C. P. Kindleberger, *The Dollar Shortage* (Massachusetts, Institute of Technology, 1950)

Judd Polk, *Sterling: Its Meaning in World Finance* (Harper Bros., New York, 1956)

B. Tew, *International Monetary Cooperation 1945–56* (Hutchinson, London, 1956)

W. M. Scammell, *International Monetary Policy* (Macmillan, London, 1957)

H. Johnson, *The Overloaded Economy* (University of Toronto Press, Toronto, 1952)

Economic Commission for Europe, *Annual Surveys*; in particular *Economic Survey of Europe Since the War* (1953)

*Economic Survey* (H.M.S.O., London. Annually since 1947)

A. R. Conan, *The Sterling Area* (Macmillan, London, 1952)

A. C. Day, *The Future of Sterling* (Oxford University Press, London, 1957)

G. D. N. Worswick and P. H. Adey (eds.), *The British Economy 1945–50* (Oxford University Press, 1952)

### INTEREST RATES 1919–58

E. V. Morgan, *Studies in British Financial Policy 1914–25* (Macmillan, London, 1952)

Burton C. Hallowell, *A Study of British Interest Rates 1929–50* (Connecticut General Life Insurance Company, Connecticut, 1950)

In addition to the above bibliography, the Report of the Committee on the Working of the Monetary System (Cmd. 827, H.M.S.O., London, 1959) will be found of great value with regard to the study of financial institutions and of the problems of monetary policy in particular.

# INDEX